Spencer, S.

A volume of a series in religion, edited by
LUTHER A. WEIGLE, DEAN EMERITUS OF
THE YALE UNIVERSITY DIVINITY SCHOOL, *and*
CLARENCE P. SHEDD, STEPHEN MERRELL
CLEMENT PROFESSOR OF CHRISTIAN METHODS,
YALE UNIVERSITY DIVINITY SCHOOL

ESSENTIALS OF
BIBLE HISTORY

ELMER W. K. MOULD

THE LATE ALEXANDER CAMERON MACKENZIE PROFESSOR
OF BIBLICAL HISTORY AND LITERATURE
ELMIRA COLLEGE

REVISED EDITION

THE RONALD PRESS COMPANY

6

Library of Congress Catalog Card Number: 51-10708
PRINTED IN THE UNITED STATES OF AMERICA

I WOULD HONOR
THOSE WHO TAUGHT ME
AND
THOSE WHOM I HAVE TAUGHT
THESE THINGS

FOREWORD TO REVISED EDITION

The remarkable success of this textbook of Bible history, since its publication twelve years ago, led the publishers to request Professor Mould to prepare a revised edition. Much new light upon the Bible has come from research in Biblical archaeology during these years. The purpose of the revised edition is to put the student fully abreast of the new insights and corrected interpretations which have resulted from these investigations. Further, the revision presents, in various places, an improved organization of material, the outcome of suggestions from teachers and students who have used the book in college courses.

Before his death on November 15, 1950, Dr. Mould had brought to completion the work of revision. In this arduous undertaking he enjoyed the advice and assistance of his wife, Mrs. Gertrude Tyndall Mould, who had shared with the writer in the solution of the many vexing problems of authorship and had been an eminently able and encouraging helpmeet in every sense of the word.

In a brief Foreword which he had prepared, the author expressed his indebtedness to his secretary, Mrs. Marjorie Wilder Ross, for painstaking and skillful help in preparing the manuscript of the revision.

The author accomplished this revision with the same scholarly competence and good judgment that characterized the original work. As a compact, comprehensive, one-volume textbook of Bible history, for the use of college and seminary students, for ministers and for laymen who take the Bible seriously, and for the general reader who is concerned to understand the place of the Bible in literature and history and religion, this book is not excelled by any other. Professor Mould was an accurate scholar and a gifted teacher, and he will continue to teach for many years through the wide reading and use of this book.

LUTHER A. WEIGLE

Yale University
March 1, 1951

PREFACE TO FIRST EDITION

The Bible itself is not a textbook. It is a source book. What the student needs is a textbook to guide his study of the Bible. Such is the purpose of this book. Throughout the body of the text are numerous citations of Bible passages by chapter and verse numbers. When the student comes upon such citations he should immediately read the Bible passages specified. If he fails to do so, much of the textbook material will be unintelligible to him. Some of these Bible passages are starred because they are basically most important. Such starred passages must by all means be read. The grand total of the starred passages will give the student a good basic understanding of what the Bible is about. The reading of the starred passages represents the minimum for the average student. The more thorough student will read the other passages cited in the text, though not starred. The footnotes contain numerous references, which it is not necessary for the student to look up; they are given to show the basis of the views expressed in the text.

This text aims to bring into view many lines of interest—geography, ethnology, archaeology, anthropology, sociology, history, literature, ethics, religion—in their bearing upon the Bible. The text is designed for the student for whom it is his first course in technical Bible study. His interest being stimulated, a student will wish to read more widely than the textbook itself. What he then needs to know is where to turn next to carry forward his interest. A bookshelf is therefore given, containing a few titles to which the student may profitably turn first for wider reading. No attempt is made to give an extended bibliography. Bibliographies are to be found in the supplemental books, and moreover, the student sufficiently interested to read beyond the bookshelf will seek guidance from his teacher.

The aim of this basic Bible course is to furnish the student a foundation for intelligent appreciation of the Bible in the English language through an understanding of the life which produced and is reflected in the Bible. No person may justly claim to be liberally educated who is ignorant of the most important book in the English language, and the Bible is universally acknowledged to be that book. The Bible therefore has a vital place in the curriculum of the liberal arts college, and it is for the liberal arts student that this textbook is intended.

This basic Bible course starts on the human-interest level with a study of Biblical lands and peoples, and their manners and customs of daily life. The study of the development of Biblical history is closely integrated with ancient history in general. The point of view of this textbook is historical, and it aims to guide the student to correct historical understanding and interpretation and constructive historical appreciation of the Bible. Principal attention is given to the development of culture among the ancient Hebrew people, stressing both the sources which contributed to that culture and the creative cultural achievements of the Hebrews in literature and religion. The study of the origin and development of the Hebrew religion, and the rise of Christianity within Judaism and its expansion into a universal religion, not only affords the student an excellent introductory acquaintance with the technical study of religion but stimulates him to evaluate the ethics and religion of the Bible and thus to appreciate the source of one of the major elements in our modern Western civilization.

Except where other versions are specifically cited, the Bible text used is that of the American Standard Edition of the Revised Bible, copyright 1901 and 1929 by the International Council of Religious Education and used by permission of the Council, and of the publishers, Thomas Nelson and Sons. Other acknowledgments are made in footnotes.

In the field of Biblical scholarship many have labored and I have entered into the fruits of their labors. To all such I owe a great debt. I would express my special gratitude to Dr. Frederick Lent, former president of Elmira College, for generous encouragement to undertake and continue the preparation of this text; also to Dr. Harry C. York, for several years my colleague, who offered innumerable suggestions and criticisms of great value, and cooperated cordially in using much of this material in preliminary mimeographed form in classes at Elmira College. I am under obligation also to Mrs. Claire Richardson Dalton and Miss Alberta Dytman for generous and painstaking secretarial assistance in preparing the manuscript.

ELMER W. K. MOULD

May 1, 1939

CONTENTS

CHAPTER 1

CHAPTER 2

ix

CONTENTS

CHAPTER 6

CHAPTER 7

CHAPTER 8

CHAPTER 9

CHAPTER 10

CULTURE IN CANAAN IN THE ERA OF HEBREW SETTLE-
MENT 165

CHAPTER 14

CHAPTER 16

CHAPTER 17

CHAPTER 18

CONTENTS

CHAPTER 19

CHAPTER 20

CHAPTER 21

CHAPTER 22

CHAPTER 23

CONTENTS

CHAPTER 24

CHAPTER 25

CHAPTER 26

CHAPTER 27

CONTENTS

ILLUSTRATIONS

MAPS AND DIAGRAMS

ABBREVIATIONS

a.	The first half of the verse indicated.	*infra.*	Below, the following.
Ab.	Aboth, Sayings of the Jewish Fathers.	*in loc.*	*In loco,* in (at) the place in question.
Am.	Amos.	Isa.	Isaiah.
A.U.C.	*Ab Urbe Condita,* From the founding of Rome.	Jas.	James.
		Jer.	Jeremiah.
		Jgs.	Judges.
b.	The second half of the verse indicated.	Jn.	John.
		Jon.	Jonah.
Bar.	Baruch.	Josh.	Joshua.
Ca.	*Circa,* about, approximately.	Jub.	Jubilees.
Cant.	Canticles, the Song of Songs.	Jud.	Judith.
Cap(s).	Capital letter(s).	Kgs.	Kings.
Cf.	Compare.	Lam.	Lamentations.
Chap(s).	Chapter(s).	Lev.	Leviticus.
Chr.	Chronicles.	lit.	Literally.
Col.	Colossians.	Lk.	Luke.
Cor.	Corinthians.	*loc. cit.*	*Locus citatus,* the place which has been cited.
d.	Died.		
Dan.	Daniel.	Macc.	Maccabees.
Deut.	Deuteronomy.	Mal.	Malachi.
Eccl.	Ecclesiastes.	Marg.	Margin.
Ed.	Editor; edition.	Matt.	Matthew.
E.g.	*Exempli gratia,* for example.	Mic.	Micah.
En.	Enoch.	Mk.	Mark.
Eph.	Ephesians.	Nah.	Nahum.
Est.	Esther.	Neh.	Nehemiah.
Ezk.	Ezekiel.	N.T.	New Testament.
Ezr.	Ezra.	No.	Number.
Ex.	Exodus.	Num.	Numbers.
Ext.	Extra.	Ob.	Obadiah.
f.	Following; the next verse, chapter, or page following the one numbered.	O.T.	Old Testament.
		op. cit.	*Opus citatum,* the work which has been cited.
ff.	Following; the two verses, chapters, or pages following the one numbered.	p.(pp).	Page (s).
		passim	In scattered places.
		Pet.	Peter.
fn.	Footnote.	Phil.	Philippians.
Gal.	Galatians.	Philem.	Philemon.
Gen.	Genesis.	pl.	Plural.
Gk.	Greek.	Prov.	Proverbs.
Hab.	Habakkuk.	Ps(s).	Psalm(s).
Hag.	Haggai.	pub.	Published, publisher.
Heb.	Hebrew(s).	q.v.	*Quod vide,* which see; look up.
Hos.	Hosea.		
ibid.	*Ibidem,* the same.	Rev.	Revelation.
i.e.	*Id est,* that is.	rev.	revised.

Rom.	Romans.	Tob.	Tobit.
RV.	Revised Version.	Vers.	Version.
Sam.	Samuel.	*Vid.*	*Vide,* see.
Sib.	Sibylline Oracles.	viz.	Namely.
Sir.	Sira(ch), Ecclesiasticus.	vol(s).	Volume(s).
Sol.	Solomon.	vs(s).	Verse(s).
supra	Above; the foregoing.	Wisd.	Wisdom.
St.	Saint.	Zad.	Fragments of a Zadokite Work.
T.	Testament.		
Thess.	Thessalonians.	Zech.	Zechariah.
Tim.	Timothy.	Zeph.	Zephaniah.
Tit.	Titus.		

ESSENTIALS OF
BIBLE HISTORY

Chapter 1

THE BIBLICAL WORLD

The study of geography is basic to the study of the history and culture of any nation. Man's mode of life and thought is responsive to physical environment, and the destiny of any people is in part shaped by the physical features of the land in which they live. The physical geography of Palestine helps to explain its eventful history. Certainly the political career of the Hebrew people was due to Palestine's location with reference to other countries. It was the bridge between the Fertile Crescent and Egypt and the meeting ground of their respective civilizations. Through Palestine necessarily passed the caravans of commerce and the armies from the east and from Egypt. Throughout Old Testament history, Palestine was ground between these upper and nether millstones. When mighty empires arose and ventured forth to world conquest, Palestine was first to feel the effect. Judea's elevation and isolation made the people of Judah what they were, and in contrast Samaria's openness contributed to a different career for its inhabitants. In the north, Mount Lebanon fairly shoved the Phoenicians into the sea and forced them to become the maritime nomads of antiquity. Not so the south of Palestine, and the Hebrews never became a seafaring people. This physical nature of the land made some difference also with the development of culture among the Hebrews. There was nothing about the land that would stimulate its inhabitants to art, but the nature of the country did awaken a sense of religious dependence and influenced their religious conceptions.[1] Moreover, Palestine was by reason of its location a frontier between nomadic and settled civilizations. The Hebrews entered this "gate of the peoples," [2] and in the end they departed through it to dwell in dispersion among the nations. That is to say, Palestine's geographical position is a basic reason for the Jewish Diaspora. Some knowledge of Biblical geography, therefore, is essential to an understanding of the Bible, and with Biblical geography our course of study properly begins.

---

[1] Cf. C. C. McCown, "The Geographical Conditioning of Religious Experience in Palestine," in H. R. Willoughby, *The Study of the Bible Today and Tomorrow* (Chicago: 1947), pp. 231–246.
[2] Cf. Ezk. 26:2.

The Extent of the Biblical World

The Biblical world extended from Spain on the west to the Persian Gulf on the east, and from the Black and Caspian seas on the north to Nubia and the Gulf of Aden on the south. The principal theater of events in Biblical history was the lands at the eastern extremity of the Mediterranean Sea, viz., Palestine and adjacent countries. This Biblical world may best be studied under four heads: (1) the Fertile Crescent; (2) Egypt and the Sinai Peninsula; (3) Palestine, which is within the Fertile Crescent, to be sure, but separately studied because of its importance; (4) the North Mediterranean World.

The Fertile Crescent

The "Fertile Crescent" is a name felicitously applied by Professor J. H. Breasted [3] to the crescent-shaped strip of land which begins with Palestine at the southeastern corner of the Mediterranean Sea, then stretches northward along the Mediterranean coast through Syria, thence northeastward to the upper waters of the Euphrates and Tigris rivers, and from there southeastward along the course of those streams to the head of the Persian Gulf, which is the eastern terminus of the Crescent. The Fertile Crescent thus forms a kind of amphi-theater, backed by the Zagros Mountains on the east, the Taurus Mountains on the north, and the Mediterranean Sea on the west. South of the Fertile Crescent and enfolded by it is the Arabian Desert, about 500 miles across from Palestine in the west to Babylonia in the east. Professor Breasted likens the Fertile Crescent to the shore of a bay, the bay itself being a desert.

Along the northern border of this desert is a fringe of grasslands,

> the strip of herbage strown
> That just divides the desert from the sown.

The grass is scanty, to be sure, for the winter rains are meager, and when these rains fail the grasslands furnish no pasturage for the flocks of the desert nomads. These nomads then push into the Fertile Crescent and come into conflict with others of their kind who have gone there before them. Throughout the centuries nomads have been thus drifting in from the sandy desert to the fertile lands. In the course of time they become established and give up the wandering life of the nomad for the settled life of the agriculturist. This drifting of nomads into the Crescent is, as a rule, gradual, but at times it be-comes a wholesale migration. The history of the Fertile Crescent is

[3] James Henry Breasted, *Ancient Times* (New York: 1916), p. 100.

the story of such migrations and the ensuing struggles for possession
of the fertile lands, followed by the transformation of the nomads into
settled agriculturists. This is precisely what we encounter in Old
Testament history, which recounts the migrations of a Semitic nomad
people called the Hebrews through the Fertile Crescent until they
finally settle in Palestine, are there transformed into agriculturists
and develop a culture of their own. The Hebrews were not, however,
the first people to drift into Palestine. Indeed, as early as the third
millennium B.C. Semites were drifting into that land. When, therefore,
the Hebrews crowded into Palestine, they came into conflict with their
Semitic predecessors there.

The chief feature of the Fertile Crescent is the Tigris-Euphrates
river system. These rivers rise in the central mountains of Asia
Minor,[4] on either side of Lake Van, and both empty into the Persian
Gulf. They follow, however, widely divergent courses. The Tigris
flows almost directly southeastward.[5] The Euphrates, on the contrary,
first flows toward the Mediterranean, then bends southeastward and
flows through the desert to the Persian Gulf.[6] The Tigris, keeping
near the Persian Mountains, is fed by many swift streams from the
Armenian Plateau. The Euphrates depends on the snows of its mountain sources and receives no great tributaries. It therefore gradually
dwindles as it flows through the hot desert. It joins the more volumi-
nous Tigris about seventy miles from the head of the Persian Gulf,
but in ancient times the two streams flowed separately into the gulf.
These two rivers together bring down such enormous quantities of silt
that at their common delta mouth the land is building up southeastward at the rate of a mile and a half in a century. The ancient city,
"Ur of the Chaldees," now some seventy miles inland, may once have
been a seaport town.

These two rivers flow through a plain between the desert and the
Persian Hills,[7] stretching from the highlands of Armenia in the north [8]
to the Persian Gulf.[9] It was anciently known as the "Land of the Twin
Rivers." The northern section was called "Aram Naharaim," i.e.,
"Syria of the Two Rivers." At a later time the Greeks called it Mesopotamia, a term meaning "between the rivers." Today it is commonly
spoken of as Upper Mesopotamia. Here the great Assyrian kingdom
developed. Lower Mesopotamia was the Biblical Shinar, or Chaldea.
Here the kingdom of Babylonia developed.

Mesopotamia is semitropical in climate. For moisture to grow crops,
the whole country is dependent upon the two rivers because there is
scant rainfall in winter and practically none in summer. The melting

---

[4] 150 miles apart.
[6] It is 1,800 miles long.
[8] 7,000 feet above sea level.

[5] It is 1,100 miles long.
[7] The plain is 300 miles broad.
[9] The plain is 700 miles long.

snows on the distant mountains of Asia Minor flood the rivers in April and May. To drain the rivers in floodtime, and to irrigate the country in the dry season, an extensive system of canals and reservoirs was built in ancient times. This fertile land between the two rivers in their lower courses was naturally fitted to become the home of one of the earliest advanced civilizations.

Lower Mesopotamia, or Babylonia, is a broad, low plain extending from near ancient Babylon to the Persian Gulf,[10] approximately the size of the state of West Virginia. In very ancient times it was famed for its productivity. Herodotus, an early Greek historian, asserts that it averaged two hundredfold.[11] The general truth of this statement is attested by the ruins of such ancient cities as Babel, Calneh, Erech, Akkad, and Ur, which archaeologists have unearthed in recent decades.

Upper Mesopotamia, or Aram Naharaim, comprised the higher land drained by the Tigris-Euphrates river system as far north as the borders of modern Armenia. Its area was several times that of Babylonia but its fertility much less, most of it being better suited to grazing than to agriculture. Being higher as well as more northerly, its climate was cooler and more bracing, more subject to contrasts. On its eastern half rose the kingdom of Assyria, in size only a trifle smaller than the state of Nebraska, with its capital at Nineveh on the Tigris, a kingdom that played an important and disastrous part in the fortunes of the Hebrew nation.

Syria (Aram) was the region lying between northern Palestine and the upper Euphrates. Its fortunes were intimately connected with those of Palestine throughout the course of Biblical history. Near its southern limit was the flourishing city of Damascus, ever the seat of powerful kings and today known as the oldest city in the world. The principal river of Syria is the Orontes which rises west of Damascus in the trough between Lebanon and Anti-Lebanon and flows north to Antioch where it turns west and empties into the Mediterranean.[12] One of the most important places along the Orontes in Old Testament times was Riblah, which served as a military base for the armies of the great nations.

All the lands of the Fertile Crescent figured prominently in the history of the Hebrews. When we first meet the Hebrews in the Old Testament they are a nomadic people wandering from Ur of the Chaldees northward and westward, settling for a time at Haran in Upper Mesopotamia on one of the tributaries of the Euphrates,[13] and then drifting down the western horn of the Crescent to the land of Canaan, or Palestine, as we now call it. Throughout the Old Testament period

---

[10] Approximately 200 miles.   [11] Book I, § 193.
[12] It is 246 miles long.   [13] The Balikh.

the Hebrews were in constant contact with the kingdoms and peoples of Mesopotamia. Ultimately the Hebrews were carried into captivity to Babylon.

Egypt and the Sinai Peninsula

The Nile River makes Egypt. It is formed by two great tributaries, the White Nile and the Blue Nile. From the remotest source of the White Nile, three degrees south of the equator, to the Mediterranean, the total length of the stream is 3,500 miles.[14] The Blue Nile rises in the mountains of Abyssinia and unites with the White Nile at Khartum, some 1,350 miles from the Mediterranean. From this junction the Nile flows due northward, carving a fertile valley ten to thirty-one miles broad along the eastern margin of the Sahara Desert. It enters the Mediterranean through a vast delta of fine, deep silt. Except at the first, second, and fourth cataracts, the Nile is navigable throughout its entire course.

There have always been two Egypts, northern and southern. Lower (northern) Egypt is the Nile Delta. Upper (southern) Egypt is only a narrow ribbon of verdure, two to ten miles wide, along the river margin. In ancient times the southern boundary of Egypt proper was the first cataract of the Nile, at Assuan, some 500 miles from the mouth of the river. In the river at Assuan was the island of Elephantine where an important Jewish colony existed in the sixth and fifth centuries B.C.

Practically no rain falls in Egypt. The winds are dry and hot. The land is therefore utterly dependent on the river, whose abundant waters never fail. The copious waters of Lake Victoria Nyanza [15] and the melting snows of Mount Ruwenzori feed the White Nile, and heavy summer rains flow down from the Abyssinian mountains into the Blue Nile, which swell the stream so greatly that it floods its Egyptian valley between August and November and annually deposits a thin layer of mud in which Egypt's crops are raised. Without the Nile, Egypt simply would not be.

Just southeast of the Nile Delta lay Goshen, a triangular area of fertile land comprising less than a hundred square miles. This is the part of Egypt which most concerns Old Testament history, for here the Hebrews dwelt for many years as slaves. Running eastward through Goshen to the Bitter Lakes (which are now part of the Suez Canal but which anciently, in all probability, formed a part of the Gulf of Suez) is the Wadi Tumilat, now usually a dry stream bed but

[14] The total length of the Missouri-Mississippi river system is 4,200 miles.
[15] Next to Lake Superior in the United States (31,200 square miles), Victoria Nyanza (26,000 square miles) is the largest lake on the globe.

in ancient times the site of a large canal and busy cities. This was the scene of the Hebrew exodus under Moses.

Located on the Mediterranean coast at the northwest extremity of the Nile Delta was the city of Alexandria, founded by Alexander the Great in 332 B.C., which in New Testament times was one of the three most important centers of Judaism (the other two being Jerusalem and Babylon) as well as one of the most important centers of early Christianity.

East of Egypt and the Gulf of Suez lies the triangular-shaped peninsula of Sinai, linking Asia and Africa. On its northwest is the Mediterranean Sea, to its southwest is the Gulf of Suez, and to its southeast the Gulf of Akabah, two arms of the Red Sea. This peninsula is a desert, an arid plateau in the north and in the south a mass of mountains, some more than 8,500 feet high. Northward toward the Mediterranean lies the Wilderness of Shur, a plain of white sand. South of that is the Wilderness of Paran, a barren tableland of limestone, scene of the famous wilderness wandering of the Hebrews. The southernmost part of the peninsula, where mountains rise peak on peak, is the Wilderness of Sinai, so called because an early tradition (not earlier than the Christian era, however) located Mount Sinai at one of these peaks, Jebel Musa. This identification has been generally abandoned in recent years as a result of archaeological and historical researches which have established the probability that the route of the Hebrew exodus lay almost due east from Goshen across the Wilderness of Paran to the foot of the Mount Seir Range, north of the Gulf of Akabah, where in all probability Mount Sinai was located.

Palestine

Northeast of the Sinai Peninsula lies the land of Palestine, the western horn of the Fertile Crescent. The name Palestine is derived from the Philistines who entered the land about the same time as the Hebrews and contended with them for its possession.[16] Prior to that time it (more specifically the part between the Mediterranean and the Jordan River) was known as the Land of Canaan because inhabited by the Canaanites. Certain ancient Assyrian inscriptions refer to it as the Land of the Amorites who preceded the Canaanites. An interesting ancient Egyptian inscription of the twenty-sixth century B.C. calls it the "Land of the Gazelle's Nose," probably because of the contour of Mount Carmel on the coast. Today it is often spoken of as the Holy Land. It is striking that the Hebrews, whose occupancy of the land

---

[16] In the King James Version of the Bible, the name Palestina occurs in Ex. 15:14; Isa. 14:29, 31; "whole Palestina" of this version = "Philistia, all of thee" of the Revised Version, and means the entire land and not only the coastal plain.

made it forever famous, never fastened their name upon the country.[17]

Palestine is about as large as the state of New Hampshire.[18] At most it comprises scarcely 12,000 square miles of land, stretching from north to south about 150 miles and from east to west about 80 miles. It lies between 31° and 34° north latitude, approximately the same as most of the state of Georgia. Though small, it is a land of astonishing contrasts. High mountains and deep valleys cut it north and south, east and west. Because of its broken configuration, almost every variety of climate is represented; in the lower Jordan depression it is almost equatorial; in the mountainous areas it is subtemperate.

Palestine has an unusually broken terrain. Geologists tell us that once the entire region lay beneath the ocean; that titanic forces pushed the earth's crust upward, then crumpled it here in a huge fold known as the Great Rift, which runs nearly north and south and is even traceable well down in middle Africa at Lake Tanganyika. This rift is the long, deep trough of the Jordan Valley and Dead Sea Basin, cleaving Palestine to a depth of a quarter of a mile below sea level.

This land of Palestine was indeed an awe-inspiring spectacle when Moses looked upon it from the heights of Pisgah (Deut. *34:1–4), where indeed the entire terrain can be viewed when the atmospheric condition nowadays termed unlimited visibility prevails. But today one may gain an even more awe-inspiring view of Palestine from the air.

Let us imagine an airplane survey trip along the line of this Great Rift. We take off at Antioch in Syria and fly southward along the course of the Orontes River, the most northerly trace of the Great Rift. As we approach the source of the Orontes, then of the Leontes,[19] also called the Litani, the formation of the groove is more evident, for on the west is Mount Lebanon and on the east is Anti-Lebanon, and in the trough between them is the land known in Bible times as Hollow Syria (Coele-Syria).[20] We follow on southward along the course of the Leontes until that stream makes a right-angled turn to the west toward the Mediterranean. Right here begins Palestine proper.

* Starred passages are basically most important and therefore should be read.

[17] Cf. G. E. Wright and F. V. Filson, *The Westminster Historical Atlas to the Bible* (Philadelphia: 1945), pp. 17–22, 53–66.

[18] It is interesting to compare a map of Palestine with one of New Hampshire and note how the course of the Connecticut River roughly resembles the Mediterranean coast of Palestine.

[19] The watershed in this depression lies a little to the west of ancient Baalbek. Here the Orontes and Leontes rise, about a mile apart. The Orontes is 246 miles long, flows north, and empties into the Mediterranean. The Leontes is about 80 miles long, flows south, and empties into the Mediterranean.

[20] The highest peak in the Lebanon range is 11,024 feet, near Tripolis. The highest in the Anti-Lebanon ridge is 8,755 feet. Anti-Lebanon and Mount Hermon form practically one system. The ancient name of Anti-Lebanon was Amana (Cant. 4:8).

Upon our left (east), and standing sentinel over the land of Palestine, is snow-capped Hermon, towering nearly two miles into the air.[21] At the base of Hermon are the sources of the Jordan. We follow the course of the Jordan through the Ghor, as this Palestinian part of the Great Rift is called.

To the west of the upper Jordan, Lebanon "casts forth its roots" [22] to form the high, rolling hills of Galilee. Directly across the Jordan (east) are the rich grainfields of Bashan. Between Galilee and Bashan, the Jordan forms the marsh of Lake Huleh, and then, fifteen miles south of that, widens out into Lake Galilee.

Directly south of Galilee is a sudden break in the mountainous western ridge where the broad Plain of Esdraelon connects the Mediterranean coast with the Jordan Valley. South of this gap the mountainous ridge rises once more to form central Palestine, commonly called Samaria. East of the Ghor, opposite Samaria, is the not greatly dissimilar country of Gilead.

The Ghor widens and deepens in the lower course of the Jordan until this stream finally loses itself in the Dead Sea.[23] As we fly southward over this body of water we realize that directly beneath us is the lowest known place on the earth's surface, 1,286 feet below sea level. Over and about the Dead Sea is the very appearance of death. Once a fresh-water lake many times its present size, its now ponderous, salty bulk spreads death and desolation about its shores. The gaunt naked cliffs and eroded bluffs that hold it in embrace stand out through a vaporous haze that rises continuously from its surface. It is a marvelous spectacle but depressing.

Just west of here the highlands of Judea fairly overhang the Ghor, the edge deeply scored by gorges which are impassable save at four or five points, while directly overlooking the Dead Sea is a wild, desolate region, the notorious Wilderness of Judea. East of the Dead Sea rise the heights of Moab, edge of that vast plateau which is the Arabian Desert. From our plane the deeply gouged sides of this upland are clearly visible, the work of eroding streams that have made the margin of the plateau a succession of flutings and irregular scallops.

Southward beyond the forty-seven mile stretch of the Dead Sea we fly, still over the Great Rift, in this part known as the Arabah. To our left (east) is the Mount Seir Range, and the land of Edom, and the interminable reaches of the desert. On our right (west) is the

---

[21] 9,200 feet. "Which Hermon the Sidonians call Sirion, and the Amorites call it Senir." (Deut. 3:9.)

[22] Hos. 14:5.

[23] For excellent views of the Jordan in its course through the Ghor, some of them taken from the air, cf. Nelson Glueck, *The River Jordan* (Philadelphia: 1946), frontispiece and Plates 1, 2, 3, 4, 34, 35, 39, 40, 113.

wilderness known as the Negeb (the South Country). The floor of
the Great Rift rises again to ocean level, then above,[24] and then it
declines to the Gulf of Akabah, 110 miles south of the Dead Sea. This
gulf is itself part of the Great Rift.

At the head of the Gulf of Akabah we leave the Rift and nose our
plane northwestward toward the Mediterranean. A flight of 125 miles
takes us across the Wilderness of Paran, past the southern edge of
the Negeb, and along the course of the "River of Egypt," [25] to the
Mediterranean. Here we turn to follow the coast northward.

Presently we come to the Plain of Philistia, broadest in the south,[26]
gradually narrowing toward the north. Its entire length covers thirty-
five miles. East of this plain lie the rolling hills of the Shephelah or
lowland district between Philistia and the plateau of Judea.

From Joppa northward for fifty-five miles the coastal plain is called
the Plain of Sharon, a very fertile strip about eight miles wide,
terminating abruptly at Mount Carmel.

All along the Mediterranean we have observed how very regular
the seacoast is. Nowhere is there a real harbor. The only irregularity
on the coast is where Mount Carmel juts into the sea. Immediately
north of Carmel is Haifa, the nearest approach to a harbor anywhere
in Palestine. Haifa is the northwestern terminus of the transverse
Plain of Esdraelon. This plain is often called the "Key of Palestine."
It is a fitting place to end our airplane journey.

Our imaginary trip has called attention to every one of the eight
major features of the physical geography of Palestine, viz., (1) the
Jordan depression; (2) the coastal plains; (3) the transverse Plain
of Esdraelon; (4) the mountainous backbone between the coast and
the Great Rift; (5) the Shephelah; (6) the Wilderness of Judea;
(7) the Negeb; and (8) Eastjordania. We may now pay closer attention to important details in each of these.

The Jordan Depression. The paragraphs below explain the chief
topographic features of the famous Jordan Depression.

1. The Jordan is "Earth's Most Storied River." It rises at Mount
Hermon in three sources, the remotest and highest being at Hasbeiya,
1,700 feet above sea level. The name Jordan, which means "the de-
scender," well describes the character of the stream. Within forty miles
from Hasbeiya it descends to Lake Huleh, 230 feet above sea level.
The descent of another branch from its source at Banias to Lake
Huleh, a distance of only twelve miles, is over 1,000 feet. In the ten
miles from Lake Huleh to Lake Galilee, the stream drops to 696 feet

---

[24] 723 feet at the highest point.
[25] *Wadi el Arish,* in antiquity often regarded as the border between Egypt and
Canaan.
[26] Expanding twelve miles or more from the coast.

below sea level. In the seventy-nine miles from Lake Galilee to the Dead Sea, the drop is to 1,286 feet below sea level. In direct distance, therefore, the Jordan is about 135 miles long, and in this distance it falls over 3,000 feet, an average of twenty-two feet per mile. In its lower reaches it varies from 80 to 180 feet in width and is from five to twelve feet deep.[27]

2. Lake Huleh[28] is a triangular body of water three miles across. It is situated in an enormous swamp, some five miles broad, impassable because of the dense growth of reeds and papyrus. The marsh abounds in waterfowl. Northward beyond the swamp is a rich farming region extending to the foot of the mountains.

3. Lake Galilee, in Old Testament times called the Sea of Chinnereth, a term which means "harp-shaped,"[29] is fourteen miles long and nine miles wide. On the west shore of the lake is the Plain of Gennesaret, a mile wide and four miles long. The soil here is still rich and the productive gardens of this plain once supported a large population. In New Testament times this little plain was a garden spot. Numerous tiny streams flowed through it, and abundant harvests were gathered for ten months each year from its orchards, vineyards, and fields.

4. The Ghor. Soon after it leaves Lake Galilee, the Jordan is joined by the turbulent Yarmuk from the east, which doubles its volume and muddies the stream for the rest of its course in the Ghor. The Jordan Valley is on two levels. The upper level is the Ghor (depression); the lower level is the Zor (thicket). In places the difference in height between them amounts to 150 feet.[30] The valley is broadest at the Plain of Jericho, which is fourteen miles wide. In Biblical times this plain was very fruitful. In such a ditch, so far below sea level, the heat is intense. On both sides of the Ghor highlands rise from two to three thousand feet. The winds sweep over these heights in such a way that the valley beneath is a veritable hotbed and vegetation grows rank. Here the date palm flourishes because of the practically tropical climate.

5. It is estimated that six and one-half million tons of water enter the Dead Sea daily from the Jordan and the Arnon rivers, and an equal volume of water is evaporated daily from the Dead Sea. The residue of salts left behind after such evaporation has through the centuries grown so great that the Dead Sea is now five times as salty as the ocean. It contains 25 per cent of mineral salts, about the

---

[27] Cf. Glueck, op. cit.
[28] Its ancient name is not known. Some identify it as the Waters of Merom (Josh. 11:5, 7). Its modern name, Bahrat el-Hûleh, means Lakelet of Huleh.
[29] The derivation of this name from the Hebrew word for harp is disputed by some scholars.
[30] Cf. Glueck, op. cit., pp. 63, 71.

same as the Great Salt Lake of Utah. Of this, 7 per cent is common salt. The nauseous, bitter taste of the water is due to chloride of magnesium, while chloride of calcium makes it smooth and oily to the touch. The minerals contained in this body of water are estimated to be worth fabulous sums. These valuable mineral salts are now being extracted in the factories of Palestine Potash, Ltd., located near the mouth of the Jordan. The Arabs today call the Dead Sea the "Sea of Lot."

6. The Arabah, south of the Dead Sea, is for the most part an uninhabitable land of sand and stones.

The Coastal Plains. The Hebrews never became a seafaring people for there were no harbors on the Mediterranean to encourage shipping. Jaffa and Haifa have done service as seaports. When the ancient Hebrews ventured to operate a merchant marine, they made their naval base at the head of the Gulf of Akabah. In New Testament times Caesarea, built by the Romans, served as a seaport on the Mediterranean.

1. The Plain of Philistia, in southwest Palestine, was the home of the Philistines, inveterate foes of the ancient Hebrews. It is a land of grain and cattle. The most important cities were Gaza, Ashkelon, Ashdod, Ekron, and Gath. To the east of this plain lie the rolling hills of the Shephelah or lowland.

2. The Plain of Sharon, north of Philistia, is crossed by a few small streams. In its rich loam excellent grain is raised. Its eastern part becomes an undulating plateau and rises to the hills of Samaria. Here the hillsides provide pasture for sheep but are not fit for crops because they are robbed of their soil by the swift streams which carry it down the plain. The Greek name for Sharon was "The Forest" because it was once covered by a dense oak forest. The trees have now disappeared, however, except for a very small remnant. This plain was famed in ancient times for its luxuriant fertility and pastures. The most important cities in this plain were Joppa and, in New Testament times, Caesarea. Here is located the modern all-Jewish city of Tel Aviv.

3. The Plain of Acre and Phoenicia. The coastal plain is interrupted by Mount Carmel. North of this mountain lies the Plain of Acre, narrowing down to the north until it becomes a mere ribbon of land along the coast. This was the home of the Phoenicians. The Phoenicians were a maritime people whose ports were Tyre and Sidon. Beirut, in Syria, is the most useful harbor along the entire coast today.

The Plain of Esdraelon. The great transverse Plain of Esdraelon begins at the Mediterranean coast just north of Carmel and stretches southeastward to join the plain of the Jordan. It is a huge, level, treeless expanse whose valleys connect in every direction with all parts of the land. It is extremely fertile. Its very name bears tribute to its fertility, for Esdraelon is the Greek word for "Jezreel," which means "God's sowing." Where the southeastern end of Mount Carmel [31] eases off into low hills, the valley of Dothan, likewise renowned for fertility, is located. This valley connects Esdraelon with the coastal plain of Sharon. The Plain of Esdraelon, the highest point of which is only 200 feet above sea level, slopes toward the Mediterranean and is drained by the river Kishon. The eastern extension of the Plain of Esdraelon is the valley of Jezreel which drains toward the Jordan. Three mountains rise above the margins of Esdraelon. Mount Tabor, more than 1,800 feet high, near the foot of Lake Galilee, is on the northern side of the plain. Opposite it, on the south side of the valley, is Little Hermon, or the Hill of Moreh, 1,690 feet high. Still farther south is Mount Gilboa, a range or ridge ten miles long and 1,700 feet high. On a spur at the northwest end of Gilboa is Jezreel, and at its eastern end is the historic Bethshean at the very throat of the valley of Jezreel. Megiddo lay at about the middle of the lower border of the plain and a few miles southeast of it was Taanach, both of which were important strongholds controlling the plain. The Plain of Esdraelon has been the battleground of the ages.

The Mountainous Backbone. Between the coastal plains and the Jordan Valley is the mountainous backbone of the country, broken decisively, as noted, by the intersecting Plain of Esdraelon.

1. *Galilee.* North of the transverse plain lies mountainous Galilee. A well-defined geological fault marks off Lower Galilee from Upper Galilee, which is a lofty plateau much over a thousand feet above sea level whose hills are an outlying part of the lofty Lebanon. There are broad plateaus broken by wide, deep valleys, well watered by numerous streams. The Leontes (Litani) River in its east to west course is generally considered as marking the northern boundary of Palestine proper and the southern boundary of Syria. The highest point in Galilee is Jebel Jermuk,[32] northwest of the Sea of Galilee. West of the middle of Lake Galilee is a mountain called Horns of Hattin,[33] and southwest of the lake is Mount Tabor, already mentioned. In New Testament times the most important city of Galilee was Sepphoris, located in Lower Galilee about four miles northwest of Nazareth, a village famous forever as the home of Jesus Christ. About two miles south of Nazareth lay the important village of Japhia. Some of the Galilean hills, like those about Nazareth, are bare and white, but

---

[31] Carmel is a hog-backed ridge 12 miles long, extending southeastward from Haifa. Its highest point is 1,810 feet above sea level.
[32] 4,000 feet high.   [33] 1,200 feet high.

elsewhere are woods and thick bushes with vineyards, olive groves, grainfields, and gardens.

2. *Samaria.* South of the Plain of Esdraelon lies Samaria, a region of fruitful valleys, wooded hills, and copious springs. Here is the haven of the Palestinian farmer. The limestone of the mountains corrodes under sun and rain, and the silt enriches the soil on the hillsides and in the valleys. It is such disintegration of the limestone rock which throughout the ages has fertilized the soil, for no other fertilizer has ever been added. It was doubtless such regions as Samaria, Sharon, and Esdraelon which made Palestine seem to the nomad Hebrews, emerging from the desert, "a good land, a land of brooks of water, of fountains and springs, flowing forth in valleys and hills; a land of wheat and barley, and vines and fig trees and pomegranates; a land of olive trees and honey." [34]

Samaria of the New Testament was called Mount Ephraim in Old Testament times. Within its borders occurred many of the greatest events of Biblical history. It was only about twenty-five miles in length from the edge of Esdraelon on the north to the rugged Land of Benjamin on the south. [35] From east to west, Samaria stretched from the Jordan to the Plain of Sharon.

The general elevation of Samaria is about 2,000 feet above sea level. It is a series of ridges with plains and valleys between. It can be easily crossed in almost any direction, a fact conducive to foreign influence. The land slopes gradually to the west to the coastal plain, but to the east it drops rather precipitously to the Jordan Valley.

In the heart of Samaria are two of Palestine's most famous mountains, Ebal, [36] the "mount of cursing," and Gerizim, [37] the "mount of blessing" (Deut. 11:29; 27:12 f.). Between Ebal and Gerizim lie the valley and city of Shechem, the latter one of the most ancient and important cities of all Palestine. Six miles northwest of Shechem is the hill of Samaria, site of the ancient city of Samaria, once capital of the northern Hebrew kingdom. Shiloh and Gilgal were important communities of southern Samaria.

3. *Judea.* South of Samaria is Judea, a broken tableland two to three thousand feet high, enclosed by tangled mountains slashed by narrow winding gorges. Judea is rocky, barren, and rugged, a stony region of scrub and thin pasture, a land of the shepherd rather than the farmer. On every hand are mountains and wilderness. It is only fifty-five miles in length from north to south, and thirty miles wide, approximately as large as the state of Rhode Island. Throughout its length and breadth there are not more than six or seven streams that have water throughout the year. Only near Bethlehem

[34] Deut. 8:7 f.
[36] 3,076 feet high.

[35] Just south of Bethel.
[37] 2,484 feet high.

and southeast of Hebron are there fertile spots to justify the Biblical references to Judea as a land of grain and wine and oil. Its southern end is wild and desolate, merging into desert. The tribe of Judah had indeed a poor heritage. Hemmed in by wilderness and desert, dwelling in mountains, separated from the other tribes, isolated from progress, conquest, or commerce, the people of Judah developed hardihood and courage, high principles and morals, a separateness that enabled them to outlast all the other Hebrew groups.

Judea had the greatest city in all the land, Jerusalem, "the Holy City." It stands on a mountain tableland, 2,593 feet above sea level, thirty miles from the Mediterranean, eighteen miles from the head of the Dead Sea. On its east is the Valley of the Kidron separating it from the Mount of Olives. West and south of the city is the Valley of Hinnom. Northward, the city wall is its sole defense. North of Jerusalem the important communities were Bethel, Ramah, and Mizpah. South of it the important cities were Bethlehem, Hebron, and Beersheba.

The southern boundary of Palestine proper is the Wadi Ghuzzeh, which rises near the Dead Sea, makes a wide bend southward, passes by Beersheba, then bends northward to reach the Mediterranean just south of Gaza. "From Dan to Beersheba" [38] connoted the total length of the country.

The Shephelah.   Between Judea and the Philistine plain on the west is an open, rolling region, about 500 feet in elevation, known as the Shephelah (a word meaning "Lowland"). It is a region of bare and irregular hills, lying in a curve from Jaffa to Gaza. The Shephelah is crossed by wide valleys containing streams and grain-fields, which continue as narrow gorges into the Judean Mountains. The most important of these valleys are, in order, from north to south, the Valley of Aijalon, the Valley of Sorek, the Valley of Elah, and the Brook Besor, the last marking the southern limit of the Shephelah.

The Wilderness of Judea.   Throughout most of its length Judea is bordered on the east by a rough, uninhabited area, forty miles long and twelve miles wide, overlooking the Dead Sea, waterless, treeless, cut by gorges a thousand feet deep. This is the Wilderness of Judea, fittingly named Jeshimon, i.e., "Desolation." Halfway down the wilderness, on the edge of the Dead Sea, is the fertile oasis of En-gedi, "Spring of the Kid," reached from the rugged plateau by a precipitous pass. About halfway between En-gedi and the southern end of the Dead Sea is Mount Masada, 1,300 feet high.

[38] 1 Sam. 3:20.

The Negeb. Southward of Beersheba, on the southern border of Judah, is the Negeb, i.e., the "South," or "South Country," which merges into the Wilderness of Zin (to be distinguished from the Wilderness of Sin, which is Sinai).[39] The Negeb is the "dry" or "parched land," a region of limestone hills strewn with flints. Vegetation is of the sparsest. There is only one stream of running water in the whole region, Ain el-Guderat (near Kadesh), which irrigates the fields for some two or three miles, where grain and trees are found. In this wilderness was the oasis of Kadesh, about fifty miles south of Beersheba, the central rendezvous of the Israelites during the period of wilderness wandering.

Eastjordania (Transjordan). In the extreme north, at the foot of Mount Hermon eastward, lies a fruitful plain in the midst of which is the city of Damascus. This plain is watered by the beautiful Abana River which divides into several smaller streams whose surplus waters gather and are lost in a lake at the eastern edge of the plain on the border of the desert.

South of the Damascus plain and east of the great depression of the Jordan lies a highland country, the average elevation of which is 2,000 feet. To the east is the Arabian Desert. On the fringe of the desert is the highway from Damascus to Mecca. This is the eastern boundary of Palestine. Eastjordania is divided into three principal districts, corresponding roughly to the districts west of Jordan: thus, opposite Galilee lies Bashan, opposite Samaria lies Gilead, and opposite Judea lies Moab overlooking the Dead Sea.

1. Bashan extends from Mount Hermon southward about thirty-five miles to the Yarmuk River, a stream fed by several branches and nearly as large as the Jordan when it empties into that stream five miles south of Lake Galilee. It is here at the junction of these two rivers that the Rutenberg hydroelectric plant is now situated. Just north of the Yarmuk lies the great Hauran plain, a level, treeless area, fifty miles long and from fifteen to twenty miles wide, of loose volcanic soil over limestone, very fertile and largely tilled. This is the granary of all Palestine; it is a land of wheat and cattle and sheep. The "bulls of Bashan" are proverbial.

Between the Plain of Hauran and the desert on the east lies the Lejah, or "Refuge," called by the Greeks Trachonitis, i.e., "rough, rocky ground." It is a vast mass of congealed lava some 350 square miles in area. Here was the ancient "Kingdom of Og."

2. The district of Gilead lies south of the Yarmuk River. Gilead has always been a land of noble forests and of orchards and spice gardens, one of the prettiest parts of Palestine. The elevation is some-

[39] Cf. *supra,* p. 8.

what greater than that of Bashan but there is less volcanic deposit and more limestone. The "balm of Gilead" was a famous ancient product. It has long been sought for among the trees of the district but without success.

Jebel Osha is the highest peak,[40] the most sightly place in the east Jordan country. From it one may look west and view "the Promised Land." The Jabbok River divides the district into northern and southern Gilead. The southern limit is at the head of the Dead Sea.

3. Moab lies directly east of the Dead Sea. It is a treeless plateau, about thirty miles wide, 4,300 feet higher than the Dead Sea and 3,000 feet higher than the Mediterranean. Its central portion is level and rolling, and even the easternmost strip bordering the desert is well watered and productive, suitable for pasture land in good rainy seasons. Moab has ever been a land of sheep and wheat. Because it lies open to the desert on the east and south, it has always been a rich prey for marauding Arabs. The Arnon (Mojib) River, which flows through a precipitous ravine, 2,130 feet deep, into the Dead Sea at a point near the middle of its eastern shore, is sometimes considered the southern boundary of Moab. More generally, however, Moab is regarded as extending to the Brook Zered at the southern end of the Dead Sea.

4. Edom lies south of Moab. Ancient Edom was a hundred miles long, from Moab to the Wilderness of Paran, and twenty miles wide from the Arabah and the Wilderness of Zin on the west to the Arabian Desert on the east. It was not a particularly desirable region but managed to support a sparse and hardy population.

This entire territory of Eastjordania and as far south as the Gulf of Akabah is in the domain of the (since 1946) independent Arab state whose official name is Memlekiyeh Hashmiyeh Ordaniyeh, that is, the Hashemite Jordan Kingdom.

The Climate of Palestine.   Palestine lies in the subtropical zone along the southern edge of a belt of prevailing westerly winds. West winds in Palestine are always cool and moisture bearing. In spring and autumn east and southeast winds bring enervating high temperature and low humidity, but in winter clear skies and invigoration.

Only west of the central watershed is the rainfall abundant; elsewhere rains are uncertain, which is the principal hindrance to the economic development of the country. The duration of the rainy season is about 190 days. This does not at all mean that it rains for that length of time. Indeed, the uncertainty of rainfall and the devastating effects of years of drought were noteworthy throughout Biblical times as well as today.

---

[40] 3,595 feet in elevation.

There is a great variation of climate in Palestine In the central districts and also east of the Jordan it is very healthful. The Romans spoke of Eastjordania as "Palestina Salutaris." Along the Mediterranean coast it is, of course, very wet in winter, but it never snows or freezes there and in summer it is very hot. Up in the Lebanon Mountains is the most delightfully healthful region of all, the summers being temperate. Snow lies on the top of Mount Hermon the whole year round. But in the deep Jordan Valley, far below sea level and unreached by the cooling and moisture-bearing sea breezes, the climate is extremely hot and enervating.

On the basis of the foregoing we can appreciate the "Thunderstorm Psalm" (Ps. *29), one of the most exquisite nature poems in the Bible.[41] The storm gathers over the waters of the Mediterranean and it is there that the thunder, "the voice of the Lord," is first heard. The repetition of this phrase seven times skillfully imitates the successive peals of the terrifying thunder as the destructive storm breaks over the land. The first area of its destructive spread is Mount Lebanon where it tears the mighty cedars and tosses them about as though the forest were alive. The storm sweeps down the mountain side and across the face of the country to the desert. Suddenly the noises are hushed and all is well, for "Heaven cries Glory and earth echoes Peace."

The North Mediterranean World

This included Asia Minor, Macedonia, and Greece, the islands in the Aegean and Mediterranean, and Italy. This part of the Biblical world is of chief importance in New Testament study, especially in connection with the missionary journeys of St. Paul.[42] Just a glimpse at the main highways that affected Palestine will be given here.

The great highways from the Euphrates and from Palestine and Syria met at Antioch on the Orontes, which made this city an important commercial center. It was also an important religious center for the ancient world. It was the home base of St. Paul's missionary travels.

An important feature of Asia Minor is the Taurus Mountains, a range that extends from the Euphrates to the Aegean Sea through the southern part of Asia Minor and forms the southern boundary of the Anatolian Plateau. This range separated Orient from Occident; it was the boundary and barrier between Semitic and Hellenic culture. In southeastern Asia Minor (near the northeastern corner of the

---

[41] A study of the technical makeup of Hebrew poetry is given in subsequent chapters. Cf. pp. 112 ff., 299 ff.

[42] Cf. Wright and Filson, *op. cit.,* pp. 87–91.

Mediterranean) is the famous pass known as the Cilician Gates through which ran the main highway from Antioch in Syria to Ephesus on the Aegean. Just south of the Cilician Gates lay the ancient city of Tarsus, birthplace of St. Paul and important center of civilization in New Testament times. Other important cities in the interior of Asia Minor, all connected with the life of St. Paul, were Derbe, Lystra, Iconium, and Antioch. On the coast of the Aegean the most important city was Ephesus, where the highways from the east and from the north converged to form the main overland route to Rome. In New Testament times Ephesus was the most important religious center in all Asia Minor.

In these later centuries numerous highways, mostly built by the Romans, spread like a network over all the northern Mediterranean countries. They exerted immense influence economically, politically, and religiously, for they bound the Roman world into a unity. In our New Testament study we shall appreciate their importance in the westward spread of Christianity from Palestine to Rome.

Little need be said here about Greece and Italy, for the student is likely to be more familiar with them from previous study of geography. In Macedonia and Greece the important cities connected with the life of St. Paul were Philippi, Thessalonica, Beroea, Athens, and Corinth. The last-named was of such strategic importance that the ancients called it the "Bridge of the Sea." It lay on the narrow neck of land which connects the Peloponnesus with northern Greece and separates the Corinthian Gulf from the Saronic Gulf, key to one of the three great highways from west to east, for across this isthmus all cargoes had to be transshipped.

All routes led to Rome. Caravans on the highways and ships on the Mediterranean made their way back and forth. Government, business, and religion were promoted by land and sea. St. Paul used both. The climax of his career was his sea voyage to Rome. He entertained the hope of visiting Spain but there is no evidence that he ever did so.

Chapter 2

THE PEOPLES OF THE BIBLE

In Biblical times, who lived in that world with which we became acquainted in Chapter 1? The principal people of the Old Testament are the Hebrews, a people belonging to the Aramaean branch of the Semitic family. By Semitic is meant that part of the human race of which the Arabs are today the purest representatives, and by Aramaean is meant that minor division which, as far back as historical records go, was already long settled in Syria and Mesopotamia. Sometimes the Hebrews are called "the people of Israel," or Israelites, because of their descent from Israel, a name which was first given to Jacob and which means "the one who strove with God." [1] Israel was therefore a sort of religious term. In later centuries they were called Jews, especially from the Babylonian exile in the sixth century B.C. onward. This was because their home was in Judah. The new Jewish national state established in Palestine in 1948 is known as Israel, and its citizens are known as Israeli. Both the Fertile Crescent and Palestine were inhabited by peoples of advanced culture before the Hebrews appeared upon the stage of history, and throughout the Old Testament period the Hebrews had as neighbors many nations which constituted an environment that, for good or for ill, profoundly influenced them.

Semitic Beliefs about the Origins of Races

How did the human race originate and how did it become divided into so many branches with such diverse languages and social institutions? Speculation upon this question has ever been one of the primary interests of the human mind, and peoples the world over have developed legends about the causes for the differences which mark off the several nations of the earth.

The Old Testament Hebrews developed their legends about the origins of mankind and human institutions and especially about the beginnings of their own race. These legends have come down to us in a Hebrew book of origins known as *Genesis*. The story of man's origin in Gen. *2 asserts that all sprang from a common ancestor,

[1] Gen. 32:28.

21

Adam. The story of Adam's temptation and sin, in Gen. *3, is intended to account for the beginning of moral evil in the human race, and this is carried further in Gen. *4:1–16 which depicts how the jealous murder of his brother Abel forced Cain and his descendants into less hospitable and productive regions of the earth. Thus is suggested the spread of the human race from an original central habitat. The increase of moral evil in the world led to vast flood disasters (Gen. *6–8) by which the human race was all but obliterated. The motif of the flood story is ethical, to affirm the principle of the destruction of evil and the survival of the morally fit, for it was "righteous" Noah [2] who became the new progenitor of mankind (Gen. *9:1–19). From Noah's three sons, Shem, Ham, and Japheth, all peoples were descended. Thus did primitive Hebrew speculation account for the origin of nations (Gen. 10–11).

All ancient peoples seem to have thought of the world as roughly disc-shaped, with a ring of water (the ocean) encircling it. Two early maps, one by Hecataeus of Miletus (517 B.C.) and the other by Herodotus (circa 450 B.C.), show this clearly. Both supposed Asia and Africa to extend over only a fraction of their true area. The map of Eratosthenes of Alexandria shows that by 200 B.C. doubt had been cast on the idea of a perfect disc-shape for the land areas, but even he held to a grotesquely contracted Africa and a scarcely less constricted Asia.

Numerous Old Testament allusions imply that the early Hebrews shared the prevailing view of world geography. What difference there was in their mental picture was probably due to the universal human tendency to conceive of oneself as standing at the center of things. This would be the more natural in the case of the Hebrews because of their belief that Eden, Ararat, and Babel were all near the center of human beginnings. They probably thought that the Fertile Crescent was the largest fertile tract on the whole earth and that the farther one went away from the Fertile Crescent the more barren and inhospitable the earth became. They no doubt supposed Arabia, destined home for Shem and his descendants, to be about as large and desirable as Ham's Africa and Japheth's Eurasia.

Gen. 11:1 asserts the original unity of the whole human race. Gen. *11:2–9 accounts for the different languages, and so for the different races, as a penalty for building the Tower of Babel. Gen. 10:2–5 accounts for the northern peoples as sons of Japheth. Eastern peoples (10:6–12), southern peoples (10:13 f.), and Palestinian peoples (10:15, 18b–19) are all grouped together as descendants of Ham. According to Gen. 10:21, Shem was "the father of all the children of Eber," i.e., the Hebrews. The word 'eber means "the other

² Gen. 6:9; 7:1.

side," and the Hebrew word *'ibri* is explained as denoting those who came from the other side of the river, i.e., the Jordan or the Euphrates, for they came from Haran in upper Mesopotamia.[3] Gen. 10:21, 22, 24–30 lists the remote Arabian ancestors and kinsmen of the Hebrews.

The world according to Hecataeus of Miletus, a geographer of the late sixth century B.C.

The world according to the Greek historian and traveler, Herodotus, fifth century B.C.

The world as pictured by the Hebrews of Old Testament times. (*Conjectural*)

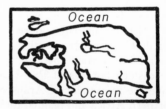

The world according to the Alexandrian mathematician and geographer Eratosthenes, *circa* 200 B.C.

Their more immediate ancestors are given in 11:18, 20, 22, 24, 27b. It is evident that the basis of classification in these chapters is geographical rather than ethnographical. Thus did Hebrew thought account for the origin of the different races and allocate the Hebrews as one small branch in that family of nations known as the Semitic, i.e., Shem-ites or descendants of Shem.

At the dawn of history the Semites were in North Arabia, wherever they may have originated. From the rather barren tablelands of Arabia, Semites have for untold centuries spread fanwise into the Fertile Crescent.

[3] Gen. 12:5; 24:4, 7, 10. Philo Judaeus* (*vid. infra*, p. 463) explains "Hebrew" as meaning "migrant"; *On the Migration of Abraham*, §20, Loeb Classical Library, *Philo*, vol. IV, p. 143.

The Succession of Migrations into Palestine

The Semitic peoples were nomads, which means that they were ceaselessly shifting about in search of water and pasture for their flocks and herds. The scant supplies of the desert were ever urging them to move toward the northern grasslands and thence into the attractive valleys of the Fertile Crescent. At times such migrations became great inrushes of hordes from the desert, overwhelming the towns of the Fertile Crescent and subjugating the more highly civilized agricultural settlers already established there. This objective gained, the invaders in turn soon exchanged the wandering life of the nomad for the settled life of the agriculturist. Great migrations of Semitic nomads from Arabia seem to have occurred about once every thousand years. Around 3500 B.C. such nomads migrated into Assyria and Babylonia, probably via Palestine, Syria, and the Euphrates. This migration possibly reached Egypt, introducing a Semitic element into the stock of the predynastic Egyptians. About 2500 B.C. there was a similar invasion along the same route to the very same countries, marked by the settlement of Palestine and Syria en route and by an invasion of Egypt. Included in this movement were the tribes which founded the maritime power of the Phoenicians. Again, about 1500 B.C., Semitic nomads poured simultaneously into all parts of the Fertile Crescent. It was this movement which brought the Hebrews to Palestine. Around 500 B.C. another desert nomad migration reached the eastern borders of Palestine and Syria.[4] Finally, about A.D. 500, came the movement of Arabs which swept through Asia Minor and northern Africa and planted their language and religion in those lands.

The Earliest [pre-Amoritic] Settlers in Palestine. As long as there have been human beings anywhere on earth, they have been in Palestine. The soil of Palestine has yielded skeletal remains of the very earliest type of man known to anthropology. In 1925 there was found in a cave in Galilee [5] part of a Neanderthal skull. This Galilee skull is 40,000, perhaps even 100,000 years old. In 1932 skeletons of a similar type were found in caves at the foot of the western slope of Mount Carmel.[6] For this type of fossil man scholars have proposed the name *Palaeanthropus Palestinensis.* Twelve more or less complete Neanderthal or Neanderthaloid skeletons have been found. Later in 1932 there were found on the walls of caves southeast of Jerusalem [7] carvings which represent the realistic art of prehistoric Palestinians.

---

[4] *Vid. infra,* p. 346.
[5] In Wadi el Amud. Cf. C. C. McCown, *The Ladder of Progress in Palestine* (New York: 1943), pp. 19 ff.
[6] Wadi el Mughara. Cf. *ibid.,* pp. 23–30.
[7] In a cave called Umm Qatafa, in the Wadi Khareitum, near the site of ancient Herodium, about five miles east of Bethlehem.

All these belong to the Palaeolithic (Old Stone) Age, i.e., prior to 12,000 B.C. Other types also existed in the land in the remote past. Skeletal remains of more than one hundred individuals of the Middle Stone Age (12,000–8000 B.C.) have been found. One of the best known types is the Gezer man, for the reason that Gezer, on the coastal plain, has been subjected to as thoroughgoing excavation as any other site in Palestine.[8] Gezer furnished evidence of the existence of a race of small stature, muscular, with elongated skulls and thick, heavy skull bones. They were cave dwellers of the Neolithic Age, i.e., from 8000 to 4500 B.C. They had domesticated animals and fashioned implements of bone. Other prehistoric cave dwellers of a larger stature and of a different stock lived not only at Gezer but also in Galilee, in the Negeb, and east of Jordan. Competent scientific opinion holds that by 8000–6000 B.C. a fully developed *Homo sapiens* of the white race inhabited Palestine.[9]

Does the Old Testament contain any reflections of such prehistoric settlers of Palestine? Possibly so in the "Canaan, son of Ham" of Gen. 9:22, 25 ff. The prehistoric race which occupied the land was non-Semitic, whereas the historic Canaanites were Semites. Possibly also authentic names of aboriginal settlers are really preserved in the legendary Anakim, Avvim, Rephaim, Emim, and Zamzummim which are referred to several times.[10] These legendary peoples preceded the Amorites in Palestine, but afterwards, through the blur of tradition, they came to be (mistakenly) regarded as Amorite subdivisions. So far as can be learned from the records, the Emim ("dreadful ones") lived in the area of Moab; the Zamzummim ("murmurers" or "stammerers," i.e., speakers of a barbarous tongue) [11] or Uzim, in the area of Ammon, east of Jordan. There were Horites in the Mount Seir region before the Edomites displaced them. It has been conventional to regard the Horites as a legendary race of cave dwellers. More recent scholarship identifies them as an offshoot of the Hurrites, or Hurriaṇs, one of the important peoples of western Asia in the third and second millennia B.C.[12] In southern and southwestern Palestine were the Anakim, centering around Hebron, and the Avvim, near Gaza. Rephaim (giants) was perhaps a collective name for all these aborigines. There was also believed to have been a people called Nephilim ("meteors").[13]

[8] It was done by R. A. S. Macalister, who reports the work in his *The Excavation of Gezer* (1912).
[9] For an authentic account of the search for the earliest inhabitants and of man's slow ascent in Palestine, cf. McCown, *op. cit.*, pp. 31–53.
[10] Deut. 2:11, 20, 23; 3:11, 13; Josh. 13:3 f.
[11] So Macalister.
[12] Gen. 14:6; Deut. 2:12, 22. Cf. W. F. Albright, "The Horites in Palestine," in *From the Pyramids to Paul*, ed. by L. G. Leary (New York: 1935), pp. 9–26.
[13] Num. 13:33; cf. Gen. 6:1–4. Cf. W. F. Albright, *From the Stone Age to Christianity* (Baltimore: 1940), p. 226.

Such names as Nephilim, Rephaim, and Anakim, whatever they may mean, point to the existence in Palestine of a tall race which was non-Semitic and which was still there when the Hebrews invaded the land. East of Jordan, in Bashan, Og, king of Bashan, and his people constituted a remnant of the Rephaim.[14] Somewhere in central Canaan, west of Jordan, there was a land of the Rephaim.[15] Near Jerusalem there was a Valley of the Rephaim.[16] Even to the present day one of the chief towns of the region southwest of Jerusalem is called Beit Jibrin, the "House of the Giants." In the area of Beit Jibrin are labyrinths of caves of varying size and complexity, the homes of these ancient "Giants." One such cave is four hundred feet long and eighty feet high; another has as many as sixty chambers. Pick marks on the walls evidence the use of metal tools in excavating the chambers, which fact places the Rephaim in the overlap of the Stone Age and the Bronze Age, i.e., the Chalcolithic Age.

Such were the inhabitants of Palestine when the first Semites intruded upon them. The newcomers apparently were no match for the tall race that was established in the south, for the Rephaim and the Anakim were still there when the Hebrews arrived in a much later century. But the first intruding Semites did completely submerge the Gezerite cave dwellers and their kind. These first Semites were culturally little above the troglodytes whom they dispossessed. They knew and used bronze and a simple form of potter's wheel. They lived in the caves of their predecessors until they began to construct houses, which were of the type in vogue in the land down to the present.[17]

The Amorites. The Amorites represent the earliest wave of Semites, those who entered the Fertile Crescent about 3500 B.C. On the monuments they are represented as having beards, but with the upper lip shaved. They settled in Mesopotamia, Syria, and Palestine, with the center of their political organization in the middle Euphrates region. In Palestine their chief strongholds developed in the Lebanon and Anti-Lebanon district. That the entire district of northern and southern Palestine was called the "Land of the Amorites" by Babylonian and Assyrian chroniclers attests Amorite pre-eminence at an early date. Amos, writing in the eighth century B.C., shows that Hebrews used the same expression.[18]

In Palestine the Amorites were the highlanders. There is mention of Amorites living southwest of the Dead Sea,[19] and of Amorite kings in ancient Jerusalem, Hebron, Jarmuth, Lachish, and Eglon.[20] At the

---

[14] Deut. 3:3–11; Josh. 12:4; 13:12, 30, 31.
[15] Josh. 17:15.
[16] Josh. 15:8; 18:16; 2 Sam. 5:18; 23:13; 1 Chr. 11:15; 14:9; Isa. 17:5.
[17] Cf. *infra*, pp. 145 ff.   [18] Am. 2:10.
[19] Gen. 14:7, Deut. 1:7, 44.   [20] Josh. 10:5.

AMORITES [21]

beginning of the twelfth century B.C. the two chief Amorite kingdoms were those of Sihon and Og, east of Jordan, doubtless the last remnants of the great Amorite power. These petty kingdoms were conquered by the Hebrews under Moses. That the language of the

[21] Relief on portion of wall in temple of Ramses III, Medinet Habu, Egypt. The hieroglyphic inscription in the oblongs describes the scene as an Amorite chief and his troops defending their walled city. Courtesy of The Oriental Institute, University of Chicago.

Amorites represents simply an earlier stage of the Hebrew language
is strong indication of close blood relationship between the two
peoples.

Canaanites and Phoenicians. The Canaanites and Phoenicians
represent a subdivision of the Aramaean branch of Semites that
moved up the Euphrates toward the Mediterranean coastlands between 3000 and 2000 B.C. Some of them (the Phoenicians) settled
along the coast and others (the Canaanites) located inland. It was
the latter who gave their name to the entire land, viz., "the land of
Canaan." [22] Specifically the land of Canaan means the territory west
of the Jordan River and the Dead Sea.

The tribal subdivisions of the Canaanites have not yet been
definitely established. Hivites, Perizzites, and Jebusites were kindred
groups and were of either Canaanite or Amorite origin.[23] Hivites
(northern Palestine) and Perizzites (southern Palestine) were simply villagers as opposed to townspeople. The Jebusites centered at
Jerusalem.[24] It is possible that the Canaanites were originally just
a branch of the Amorites, the Canaanites being those who at first
gravitated to the seacoast, while the Amorites went to the Anti-
Lebanon and east Jordan districts. At least it is evident that originally
the Canaanites were the lowlanders, inhabitants of the coastal plain
and the Jordan Valley, just as the Amorites were the highlanders.

The Phoenicians are classed with the Canaanites as far back as
records mention them, viz., to about 1600 B.C.[25] Both are supposed
to have formed part of one general movement of Aramaean groups
from Arabia. They became differentiated from other Semitic groups
after settling on the coast, from which they may have dispossessed
an earlier seafaring population. In the Bible they are usually called
Sidonians because their chief city was Sidon.[26] Their language was a
dialect of the Semitic and differed only slightly from the Hebrew of
the Old Testament.

The Hebrews. The Tell el 'Amarna letters mention the Habiri
(Khabiru) as nomadic plunderers who raided Canaan in the first half
of the fourteenth century B.C. Thus Abd-Khiba, local ruler of Jerusalem, writes to the Pharaoh of Egypt, who is sovereign over the land
of Canaan, that the Habiri are plundering all the lands of the king.
He says that certain princes of Canaan have given the king's land to
the Habiri. Abd-Khiba complains that Gazri (Gezer, in the center of

[22] Gen. 12 :5. This title appears *circa* 1800 B.C. in Egyptian inscriptions, and again
in the Amarna letters of 1400 B.C., discussed *infra*, pp. 48–49.
[23] It would be dogmatic to assert which.
[24] Josh. 15 :63; 2 Sam. 5 :6.
[25] Cf. W. F. Albright, *Archaeology and the Religion of Israel* (Baltimore: 1942),
pp. 68 f.
[26] Josh. 13 :4; 6; Jgs. 3 :3.

SEMITES [27]

Canaan), Ashkaluna, and Lakis (Ashkelon and Lachish, in the south) have given provisions to the Habiri and that "the land Shakmi (Shechem, in the north) has given everything to the Habiri." This shows how completely Canaan was overrun by the Habiri.

The word Habiri is an old Babylonian term which means a nomad, bandit, or mercenary. Its Hebrew equivalent is 'ibri, which comes

[27] Relief on north wall of first court of the temple of Ramses III, Medinet Habu, Egypt, portraying Semite prisoners captured in the Syrian wars. Courtesy of The Oriental Institute, University of Chicago.

from a verb, *'abar,* meaning "to cross over." The Habiri were crossers-over, or boundary-crossers; i.e., they were nomadic raiders or plunderers who came from their desert haunts to pillage this or that country in the Fertile Crescent. People styled Habiri were found among the Babylonians and Assyrians as far back as the twenty-first century B.C.; also among the Hittites; and in the fifteenth and fourteenth centuries B.C. in Syria, Phoenicia, and Canaan. Among the last-mentioned, one group which raided and stayed in Canaan was characterized as Habiri, to which group the name has stuck throughout history. They are the people we call the Hebrews. The Tell el 'Amarna picture of the plundering Habiri invaders crowding into Canaan from the desert is certainly true historically of the Hebrews. The story of tribal lawlessness narrated in Gen. *34 reads so like Abd-Khiba's remarks about Shechem and the Habiri as to intimate that the Genesis narrative may be a popular Hebrew version of that historical incident. It tells how two tribes, Simeon and Levi, attacked Shechem and massacred the inhabitants, but lost out in the end, for Simeon was forced back to the desert and disappeared from history and Levi lost its tribal identity.[28]

Hebrew traditions uniformly stress direct descent of twelve tribes from twelve sons of Jacob. Close inspection of the Bible records shows how artificial this simple scheme was, since there never were exactly twelve tribes at any given time, while at different periods the list of tribes in the Hebrew confederation varied. This confusion about the tribes implies the confusion and contentions of the various Habiri of different periods, which Hebrew literary device fashioned into stories of family quarrels among the children of the several wives and concubines of the patriarchs, especially of Jacob.[29] Among the enumerated tribes there is a basic distinction between the southern tribes (Judah) and the northern tribes (Israel).[30] Judah came from the wilderness south of Canaan.[31] Israel came from Aram to the northeast of Palestine.[32]

There are strong hints, moreover, that Israel and Jacob were really separate individuals, inasmuch as certain stories associate their names with widely separate localities, for the most part. It seems certain, for one thing, that there was an Israelite tribe in Canaan at the same time that the Jacob clans were in Egypt. For the Pharaoh Merneptah

---

[28] A later age identified Levi with the priesthood.
[29] See further, *infra,* pp. 92–93.
[30] *Ibid.*
[31] For example, the narratives which link Abraham with the south, with Beersheba (Gen. 21) and Hebron (Gen. 23), and with a journey to Egypt (Gen. 12:10–20) imply this.
[32] The Genesis narratives associate Jacob with Bethel (Gen. 28), Shechem (Gen. 34), Gilead, east of Jordan (Gen. 31), and with Aram (Gen. 28, 29). Deut. 26:5 speaks of Jacob as a "nomad Aramaean."

(1225–1215 B.C.), celebrating a triumphant march through Palestine, chanted this "Hymn of Victory":

> Canaan is seized with every evil;
> Ashkelon is carried away;
> Gezer is taken;
> Yenoam is annihilated;
> Ysiraal (Israel) is desolated, its seed is not.

The later historical union of these Jacob and Israel tribes gave rise to the tradition of the change of names in Gen. 32:27 ff. Even this, however, represents a simpler family tree than the facts warrant. Into Hebrew blood from earliest times there was injected an uncounted number of infusions from non-Semitic as well as Semitic peoples. To name but three illustrative cases: Joseph's sons, Ephraim and Manasseh, were the offspring of the Egyptian Asenath;[34] Moses' wives were Zipporah, a Midianite,[35] and an unnamed Cushite;[36] while in one instance at least an entire clan, the Kenites, joined Judah in its invasion of southern Canaan[37] and was later counted among the prominent Hebrew families.[38] All this is evidence that the Hebrews were a mixed race.

The Hebrews represent a movement of Semites from the Euphrates Valley toward western lands long after the Canaanites entered Palestine, perhaps *circa* 1500 B.C. For centuries they contested the possession of Canaan with the Canaanites. They finally won, but in the process absorbed many elements of Canaanite culture.[39] This conquest of Canaan constitutes one of the most important chapters in Hebrew history, for it marks the first profound social transformation of that people.

The Semitic Neighbors of the Hebrews

Most of the peoples who were neighbors to the Hebrews were Semites like themselves. This was true of most of the dwellers in the Fertile Crescent and of those who lived in the desert to the east and south. Only the Egyptians and Philistines on the southwest, and the peoples bordering the Fertile Crescent on the northwest, north, and northeast, were distinctly non-Semitic.

Semitic Peoples West of Jordan. In Canaan lived certain neighboring peoples with whom the Hebrews ultimately fused. The best known were the Canaanites and the "Amorites of the Hill Country."

[34] Gen. 41:50–52.
[35] Num. 12:1.
1 Chr. 2:55.

[35] Ex. 18:1–7.
[37] Jgs. 1:16; 4:11.
[39] *Vid. infra*, pp. 254–259.

A CANAANITE GIRL [33]

[33] Restoration drawing of fragmentary ivory open-w
probably a furniture inlay, found with an ivory hoar
prince of Megiddo, now in the Oriental Institute Mu
Institute, University of Chicago.

1. *The Canaanites.* As was pointed out in the foregoing, the Canaanites were the inhabitants of the lowlands of the west Jordan country when the Hebrews entered that region. These Canaanites had no central political organization but lived in independent cities under petty kings. They were subject to Egypt from about 1500 B.C. to about 1200 B.C., i.e., for three centuries prior to the definitive Hebrew conquest.

Long before the Hebrews entered Canaan the Canaanites had become acquainted with Babylonian culture, and as a result the Canaanite culture was much superior to that of the Hebrews. In the course of time the Canaanites disappeared because they were absorbed into the Hebrew nation and their culture with them. It was from them that the Hebrews learned agriculture, their religion profoundly affected that of the Hebrews, and it was their language that became the Hebrew of the Old Testament.

2. *"Amorites of the Hill Country."* These were the peoples who inhabited the mountainous and less accessible parts of Palestine when the Hebrews first entered Canaan and for some time thereafter. The more or less related groups referred to in the Bible by their local or clan names, viz., Hivites, Perizzites, Girgashites, Jebusites, and others, may be the ones meant by the collective designation, "Amorites of the Hill Country." [40] Many, possibly all, of these clans or tribes intermarried with the Hebrews and so were in time absorbed by them.[41] They disappeared from history with the rise of the Hebrew monarchy, *circa* 1000 B.C.

Semitic Peoples East of Jordan and the Dead Sea. Several Semitic peoples closely akin to the Hebrews but fusing with them only slightly lived east and south of Jordan and the Dead Sea.

1. *Moabites and Ammonites.* Moab and Ammon were two closely related tribes or nations just east of the lower Jordan and Dead Sea region, the Ammonites dwelling north of the Moabites. Gen. 19:36 ff. represents the two peoples as descended from Lot, nephew of Abraham, through two sons named Ben-ammi and Moab. This is proof that the Hebrews regarded them as rather close kinsmen. Indeed, all three peoples, Moabites, Ammonites, and Hebrews, belonged originally to one group. Their languages were almost identical. The interesting story in Gen. *13 throws light on the causes which led to the separation of this original group of nomads into subdivisions, one of which (Lot) still further divided to form the Moabites and the Ammonites. The principal cause, it is clear, was economic, viz., the desire of all nomads for more and better pasture lands. Throughout Hebrew history the Ammonites frequently clashed with the

---

[40] Cf. *supra,* p. 26 ff.   [41] Jgs. 3:5 f.; Ezk. 16:3.

Hebrews. The Moabites, on the contrary, were almost uniformly friendly. Ruth, an ancestor of David, greatest king the Hebrews ever had, was a Moabite.

2. *Edomites*. These, according to Gen. 25 :23, 25, 30, were a people descended from Esau, just as the Hebrews were descended from Esau's brother Jacob. The Jacob-Esau stories (Gen. 25–27, 33) show that the Hebrews regarded the Edomites as about the closest of their kinsmen. Notwithstanding this fact, intense rivalry existed between the two peoples and through much of their history there were bitter struggles between them, just as there had been between their twin ancestors. At the height of the Hebrew power the Edomites were for a time their subjects, but in later centuries the relationship was almost exactly reversed. Throughout most of the Old Testament period the Edomites occupied the strip of habitable land between the Mount Seir Range and the Arabian Desert.

Semitic Peoples South of Canaan. 1. The Amalekites were a branch of the Edomites [42] which early severed connection with the parent group. They are generally referred to as living in the Sinai Peninsula, but evidently they were a restless, roving, and occasionally marauding group that had no fixed boundaries. They apparently were to be found in greatest strength in the Negeb.

2. The Kenites were localized south of the mountains of the Negeb. They were closely related to the Amalekites, being probably a branch of them. In David's time, *circa* 1000 B.C., they lived south of Judah.[43] Ultimately they were absorbed into Judah.

3. The Midianites were localized near Mount Sinai.[44] They were relatively inoffensive and unwarlike Bedouins, once referred to as allied with the Amalekites in marauding.[45]

4. Various North Arabian groups are mentioned in the Bible [46] as descendants of Ishmael (Abraham's son by a handmaiden) and Keturah (Abraham's concubine).

Fertile Crescent Neighbors. Most of the Fertile Crescent peoples were Semites, but less closely akin to the Hebrews than the nations and tribes discussed in the foregoing.

1. *Phoenicians*. The ancestry of the Phoenicians has already been noted.[47] At first they had no central government but were organized in a loose federation of city-states which gradually came under the authority of Tyre. Their most flourishing period lasted nearly three centuries, from 1100 B.C. until their conquest by Assyria in 876 B.C. Relations between Phoenicians and Hebrews were uniformly friendly in Old Testament times.

42 Gen. 36 :12.
44 Ex. 2 :15–17.
46 Gen. 25 ; 1 Chr. 1 :29–33.
43 1 Sam. 27 :10 ; 30 :29.
45 Jgs. 6 :3.
47 *Supra*, p. 28.

2. *Aramaeans of Syria and Upper Mesopotamia (Aram-Na-haraim)*. These people are usually called Syrians in the Old Testament. They were kindred groups of Semites and had since very early times occupied the long middle sector of the Fertile Crescent from the

ARAMAEANS[48]

northern border of Palestine almost to the western edge of Babylonia. They spoke a language which, with its dialects, is known as Aramaic. They became the overland traders of the ancient world, largely because they lived right between Babylonia on the one side and Palestine and Egypt on the other.

3. *Babylonians and Assyrians*. The Babylonians were the dwellers in the Babylonian Plain between the Euphrates and Tigris rivers

[48] Relief of Aramaean King Barrekub and scribe, with Aramaic inscription above their heads, from the king's palace, Senjirli, Anatolia, *circa* 8th century B.C., in the Berlin Museum. From *Orient-Kommittee, Berlin, Ausgrabungen in Sendschirli*, IV, p. 346.

in their most southerly course. The Assyrians occupied the Tigris Valley northwestward from Babylonia. They were peoples of more or less mixed racial character, partly Semitic and partly of other

BABYLONIAN KING HAMMURABI [49]

stocks from beyond the mountains to the east and north. The Babylonians had already reached a high stage of culture as early as 3500 B.C. The Assyrians became a power much later, *circa* 2200 B.C.

[49] Relief from Iraq depicting the king wearing a long beard, turban, necklace and bracelets. From H. R. Hall, *Babylonian and Assyrian Sculpture in the British Museum*, Pl. IX. Courtesy of the British Museum.

ASSYRIANS [50]

[50] Relief of King Sargon II (722–705 B.C.) and his Vizier, from Nineveh. From Botta and Flandin, *Monuments de Ninive*, Paris, 1849, I, Pl. R.

The Babylonians were more closely related to the Hebrews than were the Assyrians. The Hebrews traced a remote ancestry to them,[51] and throughout Hebrew history contacts with Babylonia were fairly frequent. Especially was this true of later centuries when Palestine was ruled by either Assyria or Babylonia. After the exile in the sixth century B.C., when thousands of the leading Hebrew families were deported to Babylonia, some of the most important transformations in Old Testament religion, life, and culture took place.

Non-Semitic Neighbors of the Hebrews

The Philistines. From about 1200 B.C. on, a vigorous people known as the Philistines seized and held the plain along the Mediterranean coast in southwestern Palestine. They came from Crete, which, in the Bible, is called Caphtor.[52] Their original home had been in Lycia in Asia Minor.[53] They migrated at an early date to Crete, passed some time there, and were driven out by invading barbarians from the north. The Philistines were part of a confederation of groups from the Levant, Asia Minor, and North Syria which made a bold attempt to invade Egypt but were foiled by Ramses III at Pelusium, near the old mouth of the Nile (1196 B.C.). Thereupon the Philistines turned back and settled the almost equally desirable plain to the northeast. Thus at just about the time when the Hebrews were beginning the conquest of the hill country of Judea to the east, the Philistines were forcing their way into the Canaanite strongholds and obtaining supremacy of the coastal plain and the Shephelah.

For two centuries the Hebrews and Philistines waged an intermittent struggle for supremacy. The advantage was at first decidedly with the Philistines. In fact, for possibly a century or more the Philistines were partial or complete masters of the hill region where many of the Hebrews lived. One of the dominant causes which led to the formation of the Hebrew monarchy was the necessity for united and aggressive action on the part of the Hebrews, under competent and energetic leadership, to cope with the Philistine menace. One thing which gave the Philistines their advantage was the fact that they were equipped with iron weapons and the Hebrews were not. This is illustrated in the story of Goliath, with his powerful armor and weapons, and in the mountain warfare recounted in 1 Sam. *14

---

[51] Gen. 11:31.
[52] Am. 9:7; Deut. 2:23; Jer. 47:4.
[53] Their style of dress and armor ally them with the Lycians and Carians. So do Egyptian accounts of them. On the other hand, their pottery and some features of their architecture link them with Crete. More light on the early Cretan connections of the Philistines is anticipated from the archaeological excavations now going on in Crete.

FOREIGN PRISONERS IN EGYPT [54]

and 17. The Hebrew king David put an end to Philistine aggression [55] but enmity between the Hebrews and the Philistines continued until both peoples were overcome by the Assyrians. So deeply did the Philistines impress themselves upon later ages that the name of the whole region finally changed from Canaan to Palestine.

Egyptians. Although a small Semitic infusion is discernible among the Nile dwellers, they were predominantly non-Semitic, with Libyan blood strongly in evidence. For some two thousand years Egypt exerted almost continuous influence upon the Hebrews. Beginning with the entrance of certain Hebrew clans into Goshen in the days of Joseph, and continuing to New Testament times, Egypt was intermittently hospitable and oppressive, with hospitality the rule rather than the exception. The story of Joseph [56] is a picture of Egypt in her more generous mood. The galling servitude under the Pharaoh "who knew not Joseph" [57] and the seemingly inexcusable execution of King Josiah [58] are examples of Egypt at her worst.

Other Non-Semites in Occasional Contact with the Hebrews. Of the peoples with whom the Hebrews rubbed elbows for briefer

[54] Relief from Ramses III's temple, Medinet Habu, Egypt, portraying prisoners of war from Ramses III's foreign conquests. Reading from the left: Libyan, Semite, Hittite, Philistine (Sea Peoples), Semite. Courtesy of The Oriental Institute, University of Chicago.

[55] Cf. *infra*, pp. 158–164.   [56] Gen. 41–47.
[57] Ex. 1 :8–14.   [58] 2 Kgs. 23 :29.

EGYPTIAN PHARAOH RAMSES II [59]

periods, the following are notable: 1. The Hittites of Asia, at the
height of their power in the fourteenth century B.C., included northern
Syria in their kingdom.[60] Their power was broken early in the twelfth
century B.C., but they continued for some time thereafter to influence

[59] Colossal figure of Ramses II at Abu Simbel in Egyptian Nubia. Two such
statues, 75 feet high and hewn from the sandstone cliffs, stand on either side of the
cliff temple. Courtesy of The Oriental Institute, University of Chicago.

[60] The Hittite kingdom was essentially a feudal aristocracy. It later became a
hereditary monarchy.

world politics. Whether the Hittites ever penetrated Palestine in any large numbers is uncertain. Abraham bought the cave of Machpelah from the "children of Heth"; [61] Esau married Hittite women; [62] Uriah the Hittite figures conspicuously in the career of King David.[63] It is

PERSIAN KING CYRUS [64]

possible that the term Hittites is used in these passages as a general and indefinite label for persons whom the Hebrews recognized as of an alien race, i.e., non-Semites. 2. The Scythians in the latter half

[61] Gen. 23:3.   [62] Gen. 26:34.   [63] 2 Sam. 11.
[64] Relief of four-winged genius from the palace of Cyrus at Pasargadae, Iran.

of the seventh century B.C. came down the Mediterranean coast out of Asia Minor or beyond, devastating all in their path, and played a decisive part in the downfall of mighty Assyria. 3. The Persians from 539 to 333 B.C. were the masters of all Western Asia, and therefore Jews everywhere were under their rule. They permitted the Jews to return from exile and reconstruct their homeland in Palestine. 4. The Greeks in 332 B.C. conquered the whole eastern world and for nearly two centuries impressed their culture upon the Jewish people. 5. The Romans in 63 B.C. engulfed Palestine. The New Testament records the story of Jews and Christians going about their daily life under the vigilant eye of Roman officialdom.

Chapter 3

DIGGING IN BIBLE LANDS

Articles describing the dramatic discoveries made by archaeologists in the years since the close of World War I, and the amazing treasures which have been unearthed, are numerous. Daily papers carry columns about such finds; the Sunday supplements describe and illustrate them; popular magazines carry more extensive stories. Such articles rarely fail to play up the relationship which these discoveries have to the Bible. This has at least the merit of making it clear that the study of the Bible involves more than the book itself; it involves the study of everything that throws light on the book's meaning. For reconstructing the history of the Hebrews and the Christians of Biblical times we employ as source materials not alone the Bible but also the evidence furnished by the discoveries of archaeologists and all else that can be learned from other non-Biblical sources of information about the ancient Near East. In subsequent chapters of this book there will be frequent references to, and citations from, such archaeological sources of information. The present chapter aims merely to introduce the reader to the importance as well as the romance and riches of Biblical archaeology and to acquaint him with a few of the best-known monuments of the Old Testament and with the importance of archaeology for Bible study.[1]

Beginnings of Biblical Archaeology

In the twelfth century A.D. a Jewish traveler, Rabbi Benjamin of Tudela, identified the sites of Babylon and Nineveh and noted the high temple *ziggurats*[2] which are now regarded as similar to the Biblical Tower of Babel described in Gen. 11 :1–9. In the sixteenth, seventeenth, and eighteenth centuries other travelers to the region remarked upon other outcrops of ruins which subsequent investigations proved to be the remains of civilizations of a long-forgotten past. Such visitors to Mesopotamia were contented with the identification of sites

---

[1] Cf. W. F. Albright, *From the Stone Age to Christianity* (Baltimore: 1940), pp. 1–6, 20–27; Jack Finegan, *Light From the Ancient Past* (Princeton: 1946), pp. 3–8.
[2] Literally, "mountain peaks"; Mesopotamian ramped temple towers. Cf. W. F. Albright, *Archaeology and the Religion of Israel* (Baltimore: 1942), p. 152.

and the collection of such relics as lay exposed or near the surface. No methodical excavating was undertaken.

Early in the nineteenth century, Claudius James Rich of the British East India Company excited Western scholars by his surveys in the mounds that dotted the Tigris Valley. Yielding to the pick and shovel of the excavator, these mounds revealed to a wondering world palaces, sculpture, and libraries antedating those of Greece and Rome, and an unknown language, written in strange characters (cuneiform) [3] that seemed to defy every effort to decipher their meaning. So it was almost the middle of the nineteenth century when the really vital secrets of the past began to be unlocked. By that time Sargon's palace at Nineveh, more than forty centuries old, had been uncovered, the splendid sculptures of which now grace the Louvre at Paris; while at Nimrud, only fifteen miles from Nineveh, three other royal palaces had been found, together with a state inscription naming Jehu of Israel. This was bringing Babylonia and the Bible close together indeed!

In 1837 Sir Henry Rawlinson gained undying fame by translating the first complete cuneiform sentence, this being the name, titles, and genealogy of the Median king, Darius. The Western world was thrilled anew. What new and undreamed of light might not these characters shed upon the ancient past! As a result of Rawlinson's work in unlocking the door to the ancient Babylonian language, and the work of scholars since his time, the inscribed stones and clay bricks that have been dug up by thousands can be read and translated almost with the ease and certainty of classical Greek or Latin.

In 1872 George Smith gave the scholarly world a fresh shock by his epochal translation of a fragment of a Babylonian flood story which had been brought to the British Museum. Incomplete as it was, its likenesses to the story of the great flood in Gen. 6–8 were too striking and too numerous to be dismissed as coincidences. This find was literally astounding. What did it portend for Biblical interpretation? [4]

In the seventeenth and eighteenth centuries European travelers in Egypt brought away various antiquities and wrote descriptions of the ruins which so conspicuously dot the land. Systematic examination of Egyptian antiquities began with Napoleon's invasion of Egypt in 1798. The greatest advances were made after Egypt came under English control, and especially since World War I. [5]

---

[3] Cuneiform is the name given to the archaic Babylonian characters. It comes from the Latin word *cuneus*, a "wedge," the tool used for impressing the characters on soft clay, which was then baked.

[4] A résumé of the history of archaeological research in Babylonia and Assyria can be found in G. A. Barton, *Archaeology and the Bible* (7th ed.; 1937), pp. 33–53.

[5] For an account of the beginnings of archaeological research in Egypt see Barton, *op. cit.,* pp. 5–11.

The first scientific investigation of localities and antiquities in Palestine was made by Professor Edward Robinson of New York City in 1838. Since that time exploration has been promoted by numerous institutions, American and foreign. Down to the time of World War I such work was greatly hampered by Moslem fanaticism and Turkish official greed. After Palestine came under English control, archaeological exploration there made amazing progress.[6]

For a really adequate appreciation of this vast archaeological work, which is under way in every corner of the ancient Biblical world, one has only to turn to the histories of these ancient civilizations that are continually appearing and to visit our great museums which treasure the specimens of Babylonian, Assyrian, Egyptian, and Palestinian archaeology. Sumerians, Hittites, and Philistines are no longer dim shadowy peoples; Shishak, Mesha, and Sargon are no longer mere names of three of Israel's foes. They and others now live before us. New discoveries follow every year, and from the light thus thrown upon the past there emerges a steadily deepening understanding of the Bible and the peoples who move across its pages. Much that used to be mere speculation and conjecture has now given way to certainty, bafflement to understanding and appreciation, and the origin of the Jewish and Christian religions becomes more clearly understood.

Some Finds in Babylonia

Parallels to the Early Chapters of Genesis. The fragments of the Babylonian flood story translated by George Smith in 1872 were pieced out by other tablets subsequently unearthed and now make up an epic poem of about three hundred lines, over two hundred of which are about the flood proper. These supplemental discoveries quite confirmed the original inference that a close literary connection existed between the Biblical flood story and the Babylonian poem.[7]

Equally fascinating and much more extensive are the Babylonian stories about creation.[8] Other interesting discoveries are Babylonian parallels to the Bible stories of man's temptation and fall (Gen. 3).[9] These are, however, unlike the Biblical accounts, about the only resemblance being that both narratives tell how mortal man just missed immortality here on earth because he did not eat food that would have conferred eternal life. Strangely enough, a copy of this poem found

---

[6] For an account of exploration in Palestine see Barton, *op. cit.*, pp. 94–141; W. F. Albright, *The Archaeology of Palestine and the Bible* (New York: 1933), pp. 13–62.

[7] For a translation of the Babylonian flood narrative see Barton, *op. cit.*, pp. 327–331; I. M. Price, *The Monuments and the Old Testament* (Philadelphia: 1925), pp. 121–127; Laura H. Wild, *A Literary Guide to the Bible* (New York: 1922), pp. 78–80.

[8] Cf. Barton, *op. cit.*, pp. 279–308.   [9] Cf. Barton, *op. cit.*, pp. 311–316.

its way into Egypt not later than the early part of the fourteenth century B.C. and was recovered with the Tell el 'Amarna tablets. If Egypt was acquainted with the Babylonian story a century before Moses' day, it is natural to suppose that it was known pretty generally in the centuries following and would have been known to the Hebrews.

FRAGMENT OF CREATION TABLET [10]

Another interesting and arresting parallel is the Babylonian list of extraordinarily long-lived individuals, reminding one of Methuselah and his nine companions in Gen. 5. In one such early list, which gives only the length of the reigns of the kings, not their full age at death, we find the Biblical figures outdone by such statements as these: "Arpi . . . ruled 720 years; . . . Melam-kish ruled 900 years; Barsalnunna ruled 1,200 years." One king ruled 21,000 years, two others 36,000 years each, and Enmenluanna ruled for 43,200 years.[11] The most extravagant of all was one king's reign of 72,000 years! [12] Compared with these, Methuselah at 969 died in infancy.

[10] Lower portion of a cuneiform tablet containing an account of creation, founding of principal cities of Babylonia, and deluge. From Nippur. Courtesy of The University Museum, University of Pennsylvania, Philadelphia.

[11] Cf. Barton, op. cit., pp. 317–326.

[12] Cf. Edward Chiera, They Wrote on Clay (Chicago: 1938), pp. 102 ff. Chiera accounts for the exaggerated longevity of the antediluvian worthies by the theory that both Babylonian and Hebrew writers divided up the time they supposed had elapsed prior to the flood among the few names that tradition had furnished them.

The Code of Hammurabi. On the site of ancient Susa (Shushan), 250 miles east of Babylon, there was discovered in 1901–1902 an inscribed monument nearly eight feet high by two and one-half feet thick. It was found by chance by the French archaeologist, M. J. de Morgan. It is the Code of Hammurabi, king of Babylonia at about

THE HAMMURABI CODE [13]

the time of Abraham, possibly the same person as the Amraphel of Gen. 14:1. The monument is now in the Louvre in Paris. The upper third of the monument consists of a bas-relief representing the sun god Shamash conferring upon King Hammurabi some sort of divine authority or approval. Below are 3,600 lines of cuneiform writing that

[13] Oriental Institute cast of the famous stela found at Susa, Iran, dated to about 1780 B.C. The original is in the Louvre. Courtesy of The Oriental Institute, University of Chicago.

sets forth in full the basic laws of the realm. The stone was originally set up in the temple of the patron god Marduk at Babylon, but was later carried by victorious Elamite armies to their capital city Susa, there to remain through centuries of oblivion. This complete and extensive code, affording minute insight into the social and ethical standards upon which the legislation of old Babylonia rested, gave a basis for comparison with the Old Testament laws. It was a great surprise to learn how very advanced were the Babylonians of 2000 B.C. and earlier, not alone in their fine sense of justice but also in the practical good sense they showed in adapting penalties to meet the merits of the various cases which arose for adjudication. How far the influence of this fine set of laws may have spread over the eastern Mediterranean world can only be surmised.[14]

Some Finds in Egypt

The Tell el 'Amarna Letters. One of the most valuable of all documents for a knowledge of Palestinian history before the Hebrew conquest is the so-called Tell el 'Amarna tablets found in Egypt in 1887–1888 and now located in various museums. They were letters, written in Babylonian cuneiform on some four hundred clay tablets, from governors and lesser officials in Palestine and other northern countries between 1400 and 1350 B.C. to the Egyptian Pharaohs of that period, Amenhotep III and Amenhotep IV (Ikhnaton). These letters show that by 1400 B.C. Palestine was inhabited by agriculturists and city dwellers who were highly civilized and possessed of much wealth, and that much trade was carried on between Egypt and the east Mediterranean ports. They also show that less than fifty years later Palestine was in the throes of revolt against Egyptian overlordship, in which certain Hebrew clans, the Habiri already referred to,[15] were taking a leading part. Some of these letters were, in fact, urgent appeals from still loyal officials to the Pharaoh for military aid to prevent complete capture of Palestine by the Habiri and their allies. Thus the governor of Uru-salim (Jerusalem) begged for reinforcements to be sent immediately:

> The Habiri plunder all the countries of the king, my lord. . . . The district of the city Gezer, the district of the city Askelon, and the city Lachish have given them food. . . . Caravans of the king were actually captured in the fields adjacent to the city Aijalon. . . . Lost is the land of the king. All of it is taken from me. . . . Lo, the Habiri take the cities of the king! . . . May the king send fifty men as guards to protect the land.

[14] For a complete translation of this code see Barton. *op. cit.*, pp. 378–406; Price, *op. cit.*, pp. 196–232; Hastings, *Dictionary of the Bible*, ext. vol., pp. 599–608; J. M. P. Smith, *The Origin and History of Hebrew Law* (Chicago: 1931), pp. 181–222.   [15] *Supra*, p. 28 ff.

A later letter wails:

> They have won over the soldiers of Gezer, the soldiers of Gath,
> and the soldiers of Keilah. They have seized the country and the
> city of Rubute. The country of the king is fallen away to the
> Habiri. And right now a city of the district of Uru-salim even,
> Bethninib (Beth-shemesh), a city of the king, has gone over to
> the men of Keilah!

As recently as the winter of 1933–1934, eight new cuneiform tablets
were found at Tell el 'Amarna.[16]
What has been gleaned from the 'Amarna correspondence and
from the mounds of Palestine has led to a complete revision of the
previously prevailing assumption that the Canaanites dispossessed by
the Hebrews were only crude and barbarous peoples. On the contrary,
they were more advanced in culture than were their Hebrew conquerors.[17] Two of the 'Amarna letters were written to a Semite
named Dûdu (David), who held an official position in Egypt similar
to that of the Biblical Joseph.[18]

The Assuan Papyri. The 'Amarna letters were written on clay
tablets in cuneiform characters. This cuneiform writing originated in
ancient Babylonia and its employment outside that region did not
long continue. In countries to the west and south, different techniques
superseded the cumbrous clay-tablet process. Thus in ancient Egypt
a different kind of material was used, viz., papyrus. This was made
by peeling the papyrus plant into strips and laying them side by side
to the desired width; on top of this a second spread was laid trans-
versely. These two thicknesses were subjected to pressure and heat,
and the product was a sheet of writing material on which the characters were written with a kind of ink. A famous specimen of this is
the so-called Assuan papyri, dated in the fifth century B.C., and
written in Aramaic, at that time the international language. These
letters were dated exactly, in both Egyptian and Aramaic months,
and in some instances even the days were given, all of which makes
them of very great historical value.
The papyri were found on the island of Elephantine, just opposite
the city of Assuan, at the foot of the first cataract of the Nile. The
Egyptians called this island Jeb (elephant) because they are said to
have seen the first African elephant here. On this island there was a
very important Jewish colony during the period when the Persian
Empire dominated the ancient world. The letters throw a vivid light

---

[16] Cf. C. H. Gordon, *The Living Past* (New York: 1941), pp. 133 f.
[17] For a translation of some of the Tell el 'Amarna letters, cf. Barton, *op. cit.*,
pp. 441–448.
[18] Cf. Barton, *op. cit.*, pp. 368–370.

on the economic and social status of the Jewish people of this colony.[19] The papyri are now in various museums in Cairo, Berlin, London, and Oxford.

The most astonishing and interesting of these Assuan papyri is a letter written in the year 407 B.C. by representatives of this Jewish group at Jeb to Bagoas, the Persian governor of Jerusalem. These Jews complain that the Persian governor at Jeb had destroyed the temple of Yahu, their God, three years previously.

> They went up into this temple, they leveled it to the ground, and the stone pillars they broke in pieces. And they destroyed the five stone entrances (!) made of cut stone, which were in the temple, and the swinging doors and the bronze hinges of each. And the roof of cedarwood, all of it . . . and the other things there, all of them they burnt with fire. And the vessels of gold and silver, and other like things in this temple, they took and appropriated for themselves.

AN ELEPHANTINE LETTER [20]

[19] Vid. infra, p. 357.
[20] From James H. Breasted, Ancient Times, New York and Boston, 1916, p. 215. Reproduced by permission of Mr. Charles Breasted and of Ginn and Company, publishers.

The letter then recites that this temple had existed there since before Cambyses came to Egypt (which was in 525 B.C.), and had never previously been disturbed. Moreover they complain that they are not permitted to rebuild. They therefore ask Bagoas to authorize such reconstruction.

> Let a letter from thee be sent to them concerning the temple of Yahu, to build it in Jeb the fortress, as it was formerly built; that meat offerings, incense, and burnt offerings may be offered in thy name on the altar of Yahu.

Among the papyri was also found the answer that came from Bagoas authorizing the rebuilding of the temple.[21]

Thus out of Egypt, thanks to the archaeologists, have come these two great contributions to a larger understanding of the Old Testament: one, the 'Amarna letters, illuminating the historical situation in Canaan in the fifteenth century B.C., before ever the Hebrews conquered that land; the other, the Assuan papyri, throwing a flood of light upon a period in Jewish history about which the Bible itself is silent,[22] the period after the Hebrew kingdom was destroyed and Jerusalem with its great temple of Yahweh had been razed.[23]

Some Finds in Palestine

The Moabite Stone.   Palestine has furnished very little inscriptional material, but there are two discoveries of exceptional interest.[24] One is a tablet erected not by a Hebrew ruler but by a king of a supposedly inferior people, by Mesha of Moab, and recovered about three quarters of a century ago. Credit for the discovery must be divided between two persons, a German missionary and a French official. In 1868 the missionary, the Reverend F. A. Klein, found at modern Dibon, a village just north of the Arnon River east of the Dead Sea, an inscribed stone measuring about 3½ x 1 x 2 feet. Though not dreaming of the great historical value of his find, Mr. Klein was sufficiently impressed to copy a few words in the strange archaic characters and to negotiate for the purchase of the stone for the Berlin museum. Sale was agreed upon for about four hundred dollars. But it seems that M. Clermont-Ganneau, attaché of the French consulate in Jerusalem, already knew of the existence of the stone

---

[21] For a translation of some of the Assuan papyri, cf. Barton, *op. cit.*, pp. 486–490.

[22] The only Old Testament hint about the Elephantine temple is in Isa. 19:19–22.

[23] "Yahu" is a variant form of "Yahweh," the name of the Hebrew national deity. Cf. *infra*, p. 131.

[24] A good summary of recent excavations and discoveries in Palestine is in Jack Finegan, *Light From the Ancient Past* (Princeton: 1946), pp. 133–168; cf. also G. E. Wright and F. V. Filson, *The Westminster Historical Atlas to the Bible* (Philadelphia: 1945), pp. 103–106.

THE MOABITE STONE [25]

[25] Oriental Institute cast of the Moabite Stone. The original is in the Louvre. Courtesy of The Oriental Institute, University of Chicago.

and had even had a few lines copied. Learning of the German negotia-
tions he dispatched an agent to get possession of the find, making an
indiscreetly high offer of nearly five times the price already agreed
upon between the Arabs and the German. The offer of so huge an
amount for a mere stone bearing unintelligible characters aroused the
cupidity and suspicions of its ignorant owners who fancied that it must
be a talisman of incalculable magic power. The further attempt by
an agent of M. Clermont-Ganneau to secure a squeeze (i.e., a pulp-
paper impression) of the inscription intensified such superstitious
convictions of the owners. Before either purchaser got possession of
the stone, the Arabs built a fire under it, then deluged it with water,
which broke it into hundreds of fragments. Fortunately most of these
fragments were later recovered and pieced together by the aid of the
squeeze. Although the latter was poorly made, it was sufficiently
legible in most places to make certain the restoration of the larger part
of the inscription. The restored stone is now in the Louvre at Paris.

From information furnished by the stone itself, supplemented by
what can be culled from the Bible, we know that this tablet was
erected by King Mesha of Moab about 850 B.C. in commemoration of
his successful revolt from Israel.[26] The corresponding Biblical account
is in 2 Kgs. 3. It is far more interesting as a sample of writing in the
Old Semitic script [27] and for the light it sheds on the close similarity
in religious ideas then existing between the Hebrews and the
Moabites. For example, Mesha declares that Moab had been "oppressed" by Israel, thus exhibiting the same feelings that the Hebrew
writers had about similar oppression by their foes.[28]

We also learn that the Moabites reasoned exactly as did the
Hebrews, for Mesha asserts that the oppression was "because Chemosh
(their god) was angry with his land." [29] Moreover, when Mesha captured a Hebrew city, he exultantly massacred all its inhabitants—
men, women, and children, "a pleasing sight to Chemosh," he tells us,
"for to Ashtarchemosh I had devoted it." [30] But though Mesha, like
his Hebrew contemporaries, gloried in the butchery of his nation's
foes, toward his own people he showed himself a benevolent monarch,
building reservoirs and cisterns, fortifications and roads, and pro-
moting industries.[31]

The Siloam Inscription. A second Palestinian find of peculiar
interest is the famous Siloam inscription, likewise written in the Old
Semitic script, describing the actual cutting of the Hezekiah aqueduct,
one third of a mile long, through solid rock beneath Jerusalem, some-

[26] *Vid. infra,* p. 229.   [27] Cf. *infra,* pp. 203 ff.
[28] Cf. Jgs. 2:18; 4:3; 10:12.   [29] Cf. Jgs. 2:20; 3:8; 10:7.
[30] Cf. Josh. 6:17, 21; 8:2, 26.
[31] A complete translation of the monument is in Barton, *op. cit.,* pp. 460 f.; Price,
op. cit., pp. 278 ff.; Hastings, *Dictionary of the Bible,* iii, p. 407.

time prior to 700 B.C., in order to provide the city with a constant supply of water in the event of a siege.[32] It seems that in 1880 a small boy, playing in the water that flows into the Pool of Siloam near the southeastern corner of the city, slipped and fell, and from where he lay he noticed some crudely scratched letters on the side of the tunnel.

THE SILOAM INSCRIPTION [33]
(From a Photograph of an Impression traced in 1881, showing Hebrew characters of about 700 B.C.)

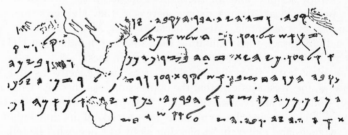

FACSIMILE OF WRITING OF THE SILOAM INSCRIPTION

This came to the attention of some archaeologists in Jerusalem who made investigation and found the scratches to be a record by the very workmen who cut the tunnel. It is so brief, and at the same time so characteristic, that it is here quoted in full.

> The piercing-through: Now this is the way the cutting through happened. While yet the masons were wielding the pick, each toward his fellow; and while there was yet three cubits to be cut through, there was heard the voice of someone calling to another;

[32] Cf. 2 Kgs. 20:20.
[33] *Vid. infra,* p. 256. From C. S. Knopf, *The Old Testament Speaks* (New York: 1933), p. 232.

for there was a fissure in the rock on the right hand. Then, on
the day that the cutting-through was completed, the stonecutters
struck, each to meet his fellow, pick against pick. So the water
flowed from the source to the pool, 1,200 cubits. And 100 cubits
was the height of the rock above the heads of the diggers.

The entire conduit, which was cleaned out in 1909–1911, proved to
be about six feet high throughout its somewhat tortuous length to the
so-called Virgin's Spring that pours forth from the base of the hill
east of the city. Thus by a remarkable engineering feat King Hezekiah
not only insured Jerusalem against the worst possible horror that
could accompany a siege, but at the same time deprived the foe of a
convenient water supply, for every drop of water was thus conducted
from the abundant spring, and its very existence was artfully concealed from any enemy. The monument is now in a museum at
Istanbul.

Digging Up a Biblical Town

How archaeologists go to work to uncover a Biblical town and
recover and interpret its treasures can best be learned from the archaeologists themselves. A scientific account of such procedure is given by
Professor W. F. Albright, of Johns Hopkins University, in his *The
Archaeology of Palestine and the Bible,* in chapter 2, "Unearthing a
Biblical City." [34] Professor Albright describes his own work in un-
covering Tell Beit Mirsim, which was ancient Kiriath-sepher, renamed Debir by the Hebrews, in southern Palestine. Professor C. C.
McCown in *The Ladder of Progress in Palestine,* discusses, in chapter 1, "The Magic of Method," [35] and gives good accounts of the most
important recent excavations in Palestine at Tell Beit Mirsim,[36] at
Bethshean,[37] at Megiddo,[38] and at Gerasa.[39]

One of the earliest pieces of thorough excavation in Palestine was
made at Gezer by R. A. S. Macalister. In his little book, *A History of
Civilization in Palestine,* he gives a realistic picture of ancient Gezer
as revealed by archaeology.[40] A full account is in his *The Excavation
of Gezer.*[41]

Professor Nelson Glueck in *The Other Side of the Jordan* describes
the technique of archaeological exploration as he conducted it in his
total survey of Transjordan.[42] Professor Cyrus H. Gordon in *The*

[34] (New York: 1933), pp. 63–126.   [35] (New York: 1943), pp. 1–17.
[36] Pp. 85–99.
[37] Pp. 151–170. Cf. Alan Rowe, *The Topography and History of Beth-shan*
(Philadelphia: 1930).
[38] Pp. 171–191.   [39] Pp. 309–325.
[40] (London: 1921), pp. 33–48.   [41] (3 vols., London: 1912.)
[42] (New Haven: 1940), pp. 1–32.

THE TELL EJ–JUDEIDEH

43 A step-trench dug into the mound of Tell ej-Judeideh in North Syria to determine its occupation strata. Courtesy of the Oriental Institute, University of Chicago.

BYZANTINE PERIOD. *Ca.* A.D. 6th century. Remains of a Christian Monastery.

ROMAN PERIOD *Ca.* 1st century B.C.–A.D. 4th century. Mound evidently unoccupied except by farmers who dug numerous storage pits. Material culture similar to that of Roman Antioch.

PERSIAN AND HELLENISTIC PERIODS. *Ca.* 5th–1st centuries B.C. The last village to be inhabited on the top of the mound, extending from the time of the Persian empire to the Roman conquest of Syria.

THE SYRO–HITTITE PERIOD. *Ca.* 10th–6th centuries B.C. A rich period with many importations from Greece, Cyprus, Mesopotamia and Egypt. The signs here shown are Hittite hieroglyphs selected by an artist to designate the period.

THE SUB–MYCENAEAN PERIOD OF THE 1ST IRON AGE. *Ca.* 12th–11th centuries B.C. Distinguished by a pottery, perhaps originating in Cyprus, of which this jug is a fine example. Contemporary with Philistine pottery and the period of the Judges in Palestine.

THE LATE BRONZE AGE. *Ca.* 15th–13th centuries B.C. Typical remains of the period, characterized by intensive, international commerce. The vessels shown were imported from Cyprus, and both Syria and Palestine were flooded with them. City probably destroyed about 1200 B.C. by the "Sea Peoples," one group of which was known as the Philistines in Palestine.

THE MIDDLE BRONZE AGE III. *Ca.* 17th–16th centuries B.C. The time just before and after the Egyptians threw out the foreign Hyksos and began the reconquest of Palestine-Syria. Figurines of the type here shown became popular. Representing the fertility or mother goddess, they were a magical aid in insuring the fertility of nature and man.

THE MIDDLE BRONZE AGE II. *Ca.* 20th–17th centuries B.C. The "Amorite" Age of northern Syria and Mesopotamia, during which Hammurabi came to power in Babylon, the Hyksos conquered Egypt, and the Hebrew patriarchs lived in Palestine.

THE MIDDLE BRONZE AGE I. *Ca.* 22nd–20th centuries B.C. The transitional period from Early to Middle Bronze. Characteristic pottery a fine series of cups and goblets. Some fine copper tools and weapons, of which the small bronze axehead here shown is an example.

THE EARLY BRONZE AGE IV. *Ca.* 24th–22nd centuries B.C. Beginning of the goblet ware in a time of great disturbance throughout the Near East. In Palestine it is a dark age when many great cities were abandoned, perhaps destroyed, and people reverted to a largely nomadic existence.

THE EARLY BRONZE AGE III. *Ca.* 27th–25th centuries B.C. Beginning of brittle red-cored pottery and of indigenous painted wares. Characteristic is the highly burnished red or polished red and black ware (called Khirbet Kerak ware in Palestine). Early Dynastic cylinder seals (example shown) imported from Mesopotamia. The Old Kingdom or Pyramid Age in Egypt.

THE EARLY BRONZE AGE II. *Ca.* 30th–27th centuries B.C. First appearance of pottery similar to that imported from Palestine and Syria into Dynasties I–II in Egypt. Cylinder seals of Proto-literate period from Mesopotamia. Group of three male and three female copper figurines found. Male shown is circumcised and wears a silver hat.

THE EARLY BRONZE AGE I. *Ca.* 32nd–30th centuries B.C. First appearance of metal at this site, a copper dagger, pin, arrowhead, chisel and drills. First appearance of "Cananean" type flint sickle blades. Great variety of pottery forms, some excellently made and decorated comparable to similar wares in the Early Bronze I of Palestine. Period of rapidly developing culture and population density.

LATE NEOLITHIC TO CHALCOLITHIC PERIODS. *Ca.* 45th–38th centuries (?), B.C. First village established at the site *ca.* 4500 B.C. Many flint and bone implements. Stamp seals. Bones of pigs and oxen. Some stone bowls beautifully made. Pottery mostly crude but some excellently fired and decorated. A few worn pieces of the beautiful "Halaf" painted ware, imported from northern Mesopotamia. Site evidently unoccupied between early Chalcolithic and Early Bronze I.

STEP-TRENCH [43]

The author is indebted to Professor George Ernest Wright, of McCormick Theological Seminary, Chicago, Editor of *The Biblical Archaeologist,* for the interpretation of the explanatory symbols.

Living Past explains the techniques of archaeological exploration and of stratigraphic excavation.[44]

The accompanying diagram illustrates stratigraphic dating and helps us to realize the cultural significance of thoroughly scientific excavation.

A unique feature of the University of Chicago Oriental Institute's excavation at Megiddo, which dominates the Plain of Esdraelon, was the purchase of the entire site, thereby insuring no hindrances to the work, which has been as completely thorough and scientific as any ever undertaken. Accounts of this project are given by Clarence S. Fisher, *The Excavation of Armageddon*,[45] and P. L. O. Guy, *New Light from Armageddon*.[46]

Other excavations of considerable interest and importance that have been made in Palestine since the close of World War I have been those conducted by the British archaeologist, John Garstang, at Jericho; [47] by Professor W. F. Badè of the Pacific School of Religion, at Tell en-Nasbeh, in central Palestine, which site he thinks is ancient Mizpah; [48] by Professor Elihu Grant of Haverford College, at Beth-shemesh, west of Jerusalem; [49] and at Gerasa, in Eastjordania, by Yale University with the British School of Archaeology in Jerusalem (1928–1930) and the American School of Oriental Research in Jerusalem (1930–1931, 1933–1934).[50]

An essential tool for every serious student of the Bible is a handbook which describes, illustrates, and interprets the discoveries of archaeology throughout the Biblical world. Excellent books are the late Professor George A. Barton's *Archaeology and the Bible*,[51] Professor Millar Burrows' *What Mean These Stones?* [52] and Professor Jack Finegan's *Light From the Ancient Past*.[53] The student who would keep continuously abreast of developments in Biblical archaeology should consult the *Biblical Archaeologist*, whose articles are designed for nontechnical readers and are written by scholars competent in archaeology.[54]

[44] (New York: 1941), pp. 15–41, 60–91. Cf. especially p. 62, on stratigraphic dating.
[45] (Chicago: 1929.)
[46] (Chicago: 1931.)
[47] A brief account of its results may be found in his *The Foundations of Bible History* (New York: 1931), especially pp. 130–134, 386–388.
[48] Cf. W. F. Badè, *Excavations at Tell en-Nasbeh 1926 and 1927* (Berkeley: 1928).
[49] Cf. Elihu Grant, *Beth-shemesh* (Haverford: 1929).
[50] Cf. C. H. Kraeling (ed.), *Gerasa, City of the Decapolis* (New Haven: 1938).
[51] Published by the American Sunday School Union (Judson Press, Philadelphia: 1937, 7th and final edition).
[52] Published by the American Schools of Oriental Research (New Haven: 1941).
[53] Published by the Princeton University Press (1946).
[54] Published quarterly by the American Schools of Oriental Research, New Haven.

Chapter 4

THE CULTURE OF THE ANCIENT BIBLICAL WORLD

For a proper appreciation of the Hebrews of Biblical times one needs to compare their life and culture with that of the other peoples who figure prominently in their history. The two great civilizations that arose in the Nile Valley and along the Tigris and Euphrates rivers met in Palestine and determined the civilization of the peoples who lived along the eastern shore of the Mediterranean. Against this background we can appraise the culture of the Hebrews.

Recent archaeological research has vastly enlarged our understanding of the prehistory of the Biblical world and especially of Palestine. By prehistory is meant the ages prior to written records, i.e., before *circa* 3000 B.C., ages which we can interpret only through the artifacts which have been recovered in excavations. Prehistory comprises (1) the Stone Age, which began 200,000, some would say even 500,000, years ago, and which is subdivided into (a) the Paleolithic, or Old Stone Age, from the beginning to *circa* 12,000 B.C.; (b) the Mesolithic, or Middle Stone Age, *circa* 12,000–8000 B.C.; (c) the Neolithic, or Late Stone Age, *circa* 8000–4500 B.C.; and (2) the Chalcolithic Age (the overlap of the Stone Age and the Bronze Age), *circa* 4500–3000 B.C.

The first historical period is the Early Bronze Age, *circa* 3000–2000 B.C. Then the first great states arose in Egypt and in Mesopotamia. The Middle Bronze Age extended from *circa* 2000 to 1500 B.C. Then the Hebrew people emerged into history, and the Bible narrative commences with the migrations of the patriarchs. The Late Bronze Age extended from *circa* 1500 to 1200 B.C. Then the Israelites were slaves in and escaped from Egypt. The beginning of the Iron Age, *circa* 1200 B.C., was the beginning of the period of the "judges," i.e., of the definitive conquest and settlement of Palestine by the Hebrews. At that time human culture was elsewhere far advanced; the Hebrews were crude indeed.[1]

[1] Cf. G. E. Wright and F. V. Filson, *The Westminster Atlas to the Bible* (Philadelphia: 1945), p. 15. For an integrated survey of the culture of the early ages throughout the Biblical world, cf. W. F. Albright, *From the Stone Age to Christianity* (Baltimore: 1940), pp. 88–179.

The Culture of Ancient Egypt

The spectacular evidences of Egypt's ancient culture are well known. The pyramids date back to nearly 3000 B.C. A calendar of 365 days was in use as early as 4236 B.C.[2] The art of writing had reached a stage of notable development and use in this same early period. A civilization of such attainment must have started many centuries earlier, probably even millennia earlier.

The story of Egyptian civilization covers one of the longest spans of continuous history any one land has known. In earliest (predynastic) times Egypt was divided into forty-two nomes (districts) which, after conquests of one by another, consolidated into two kingdoms known as the kingdom of Lower Egypt, comprising twenty nomes in the delta, and the kingdom of Upper Egypt, formed by the other nomes along the Nile from Cairo south to the first cataract. Egypt was always two Egypts; this is reflected in the Old Testament name for Egypt, Mizraim (pl.). The kings of Egypt were always styled the "King of Upper Egypt and Lower Egypt." This consolidation into two kingdoms occurred circa 4200 B.C. The First Union of these two into a single nation occurred circa 4000 B.C.[3] The numbered dynasties commence with the Second Union, which began with Menes, circa 3400 B.C. Within five centuries after Menes, Egypt was embarked upon an astounding program of pyramid building. These pyramids are the mighty masses whose tops still pierce the sky line of the Nile Valley just south of Cairo, tombs of imperious monarchs who thought to attain immortality by preserving their bodies from decay and their resting places from desecration.

Fortunately, some of these monarchs adorned their tombs with inscriptions which are technically called the "Pyramid Texts," and beautiful painted wall reliefs decorate the chapel chambers connected with their tombs. These texts and pictures reveal what daily life was like in the Pyramid Age, and especially what family life was like. Significant as they are for what they reveal of ancient Egyptian art and industry, they are infinitely more significant for what they reveal of ancient Egyptian ideas, for they disclose the historical beginnings of social ethics, with emphasis upon the ideas of justice and righteousness.[4] From this ancient Pyramid Age has come a written

[2] The date favored by Professor J. H. Breasted. Other scholars dispute this early date. At the Buhl Planetarium of the University of Pittsburgh, the machine was run back to June 18, 3251 B.C. to establish the fact that Sirius, the Dog Star, appeared over the eastern horizon just before the sun came up, which phenomenon, some scholars think, was what marked the beginning of the first Sothic cycle when the calendar was invented.

[3] So J. H. Breasted, *The Dawn of Conscience* (New York: 1933), p. 10.

[4] Cf. Breasted, *op. cit.*, pp. 115–128.

document which is of profound interest to the Bible student, the *Maxims of Ptahhotep,* a collection of ethical precepts made by the grand vizier of the Pharaoh Isesi of the fifth dynasty in 2700 B.C. Among these maxims the golden gem is:

> Established is the man whose standard is righteousness, who walks in its way.[5]

Not long after 2500 B.C. the Second Union, also called the Old Kingdom, collapsed and was followed by what is called the Feudal Age, which was at its high noon *circa* 2000 B.C. A powerful, aristocratic, feudal nobility, living in near-regal splendor, sponsored a flood of productivity in the fields of art, literature, and religion which entitles these centuries to be called Egypt's classic period. The writings of this period include fascinating stories of adventure and travel as well as imaginative tales which were told for sheer entertainment, being the earliest known literature of the kind.

Of peculiar interest to the Bible student are the writings which disclose the ethical thinking of this age. *Circa* 2300 B.C. a certain ruler wrote out for the guidance of his son the *Instruction Addressed to Prince Merikere.* It contains this gem of ethicoreligious thought:

> More acceptable is the virtue of the upright man than the ox of him that doeth iniquity.[6]

The same century produced one of the most remarkable writings of all, the tale of *The Eloquent Peasant.* A poor man of the land, unjustly treated by a corrupt official, pleads his cause, even before the Pharaoh himself. It is the earliest known plea for social justice.

> For justice is for eternity. It descends with him that does it into the grave. . . . His name is not effaced on earth, but he is remembered because of right.[7]

The same Feudal Age produced another writing called the *Admonitions of Ipuwer, circa* 2000 B.C., remarkable for its messianism, i.e., the idea that there would come a perfectly righteous ruler, "the shepherd of mankind," who would remedy iniquitous social conditions and in his reign, comfort, happiness, and contentment would be the lot of all.[8] Another document of the time, by a prophet named Neferrohu, *circa* 2000 B.C., expresses this same messianic idealism thus:

---

[5] These maxims may be read in G. A. Barton, *Archaeology and the Bible* (7th ed.; 1937), pp. 508 ff. Cf. Breasted, *op. cit.,* pp. 129–139.
[6] Cf. Breasted, *op. cit.,* pp. 154–158.
[7] *Ibid.,* pp. 183–193; Barton, *op. cit.,* pp. 525–528.
[8] Cf. Breasted, *op. cit.,* pp. 193–199; Barton, *op. cit.,* pp. 529 f.

The people of his time shall rejoice, the son of man shall make his name forever and ever. . . . Righteousness shall return to its place, unrighteousness shall be cast out.[9]

Egyptian culture suffered a serious blow *circa* 1680 B.C. from the Hyksos invaders. The Hyksos were driven out early in the next century, and under the eighteenth dynasty Egypt became the first world empire in history, extending from Mesopotamia to Nubia. This empire lasted from the reign of Thutmose III (1501–1447 B.C.) to the reign of Ramses III of the twentieth dynasty (1198–1167 B.C.). At this time the Hebrews were just emerging from the desert. In this period of the empire Egyptian art emphasized massiveness and display rather than artistic refinement. It centered mainly upon temple construction, of which Karnak and Luxor are the most famous examples. Some conception of this work is gained if one recalls that the Great Hall of Karnak, a single room 338 feet long by 170 feet wide, contains more than 136 stone columns. Of these, the two middle rows of columns are 69 feet high, each column surmounted by a capital on which a hundred men can stand at one time.

Along with the temple building of this period went an increase in priestcraft and ritual and a lessening of ethical sense. In the *Book of the Dead,* which in previous centuries had been a real stimulus to ethical conduct, revisers now suggested clever answers by which a departed soul might meet the Great Examiner at the last judgment when the latter's questions are uncomfortably embarrassing. According to Egyptian belief, the soul at death had to be able to plead "not guilty" to each of forty-two specified sins. Some of these were mere ritual offenses, others were acts which the modern conscience usually condemns also. They included murder, theft, embezzlement (especially of funds held in trust for a minor), false witness, slander, adultery, lying, deceit, and even eavesdropping. How paradoxical that a book which recognized deceit and lying as cardinal sins should have lent itself to the increase of the very spirit of deception![10]

It is a relief to turn from this composite writing to the work of the youthful Amenhotep IV, better known as Ikhnaton,[11] who between 1375 and 1358 B.C. tried his best to lift Egyptian religion from the moral decay then attacking it. His was a beautiful but short-lived effort to establish a genuine monotheism. To his mind God was a

---

[9] Cf. Breasted, *op. cit.,* pp. 201–204. Compare the similar hope expressed in Isa. 11:1–9.

[10] For extracts from *The Book of the Dead,* see *Library of the World's Best Literature,* ix, 5320 ff., and *Columbia University Course in Literature* (New York: 1928), i, 56–59.

[11] The name *Amenhotep* meant "Amen is established"; his new name, *Ikhnaton,* meant "Aton (god of the sun disk) is satisfied."

being to be loved rather than feared.[12] On the tombs and temples of his reign Ikhnaton permitted only the bright, the cheerful, and the wholesomely uplifting to be pictured, in contrast to much that is repulsive in the work of earlier centuries. Moreover, Ikhnaton was a poet of no mean ability and some of his compositions are truly exquisite, notably his "Hymn to Aton." He regards the god Aton as the beneficent father of all mankind, and praises him in these words:

> How manifold are all thy works!
> They are hidden from before us,
> O thou sole god, whose powers no other possesseth.
> Thou didst create the earth according to thy desire.[13]

Psalm 104 of the Bible is remarkably similar to this hymn, the likeness between verse 24 and the quotation just given being most impressive. Ikhnaton was almost a thousand years ahead of his age, and at his death everything he had tried to do seemed to go for naught. Ikhnaton established a new capital in middle Egypt at a place now known as El 'Amarna, where the famous Tell el 'Amarna tablets were found.[14]

Toward the very end of the brilliant period of the empire lived the Pharaoh whose name is, by reason of the publicity given to the discovery of his tomb in 1922, the best known of all Pharaohs, though in reality he was of small account historically, viz., Tutankhamen. The dazzling brilliance and fabulous value of the articles found in his tomb reflect the quality of Egyptian art in the period. Religiously, he was a reactionary. Articles in his tomb revealed that his name had been Tutankhaton, but he repudiated the monotheism of Ikhnaton and reverted to the Amen cult, and changed his name. He abandoned El 'Amarna as capital and moved back to Thebes.

Despite the decadent trend in the quality of the architecture and sculpture of this period, some fine specimens were produced, including such gems as the Abu Simbel temple in Nubia, the mortuary temple of Ramses II at Thebes (the Rameseum), and the statue of Ramses II as a young man, which is now in the Turin Museum.

Other impressive accomplishments or inventions of the period include the shadow clock, which antedated the sundial of the Greeks by nearly ten centuries; sculptured portraiture whose remarkable lifelikeness is proved by comparison with mummies identified as the very subjects of the portraits; and the amazing engineering feat of

---

[12] For a discussion of speculative thought in ancient Egypt, cf. John A. Wilson in *The Intellectual Adventure of Ancient Man* (Chicago: 1946), pp. 31–119.
[13] The entire poem may be found in Barton, *op. cit.,* pp. 502–505.
[14] Cf. *supra,* p. 48 f.

transporting thousand-ton blocks of stone for miles over both land and water.

The most ancient style of writing employed in Egypt was picture writing, now known as hieroglyphics. Such characters are abundantly found on obelisks and on the walls and columns of ruined temples.

ROSETTA STONE [15]

Their meaning was a baffling mystery until the discovery and decipherment of the Rosetta Stone. This black granite slab, 3 feet 9 inches high by 2 feet 4½ inches wide and 11 inches thick, was dug out of the mud at Saint-Julien, near Rosetta, at the mouth of the western arm of the Nile River, in 1799, by the French, in connection with Napoleon's invasion of Egypt. On it are three registers of writing. The top register in hieroglyphics is broken, so that only fourteen lines remain for the most part intact. The middle register

[15] Courtesy of the British Museum, London.

has thirty-two lines in the hieratic, or demotic, i.e., the common or popular native Egyptian script. The bottom register is in Greek capital letters, fifty-four lines, of which twenty-eight are complete. The Greek could be read easily; it recites that the monument was prepared in 195 B.C. by Egyptian priests to honor the Pharaoh Ptolemy Epiphanes. The monument became the possession of the British through their defeat of the French in Egypt, and ever since it has been one of the great treasures of the British Museum in London. Assuming (correctly) that the upper registers tell the same story as the Greek, scholars labored to decipher the hieroglyphics. To the French scholar, Jean François Champollion, goes the credit for successfully solving the mystery. He published his discovery in 1822. It proved to be the key that opened the door to a knowledge of ancient Egyptian history.[16]

All this splendid culture had been achieved long before the Hebrews emerged in the family of nations. To this Egyptian culture the Hebrews owed much. Some of them lived for a time in Egypt, or at least on its border, in Goshen. We have already noted the Egyptian antecedents of the Hebrew tribes Ephraim and Manasseh.[17] The Hebrew tribe of Benjamin was anciently known also as Ben-oni.[18] The word On was the ancient name of the Egyptian city of the sun god, which city was later (by the Greeks) called Heliopolis. That the Hebrew tribe of Benjamin may have had some connection with the cult of On is hinted in the Hebrew prophet Hosea's sarcastic remark about "Beth-aven" ("house of idolatry") instead of "Beth-On," when referring to Benjamin.[19] A few individuals, Joseph and Moses for example, are said to have known Egyptian life very intimately.[20] Some scholars hold that Moses was reared by the priests of On at the behest of the Pharaoh's daughter. Some historians of religion find that a ritual pattern which originated in Egyptian religion spread to Palestine and influenced not only Canaanite religion but Hebrew religion as well.[21] The Hebrew kings Solomon and Jeroboam (tenth century B.C.) maintained close connections with the court of the Pharaohs. Two centuries later, in King Hezekiah's time, there was a pro-Egyptian faction in Judah which was no doubt well acquainted with Egyptian things cultural as well as political. Egyptian literary influence is distinctly to be seen in Prov. 22:17–24:22, which is copied from *The Wisdom of Amenemopet*, dating approximately 1000 B.C.

---

16 Cf. Jack Finegan, *Light from the Ancient Past* (Princeton: 1946), pp. 115 f.; Barton, *op. cit.*, p. 10; Price, *op. cit.*, pp. 15 ff.
17 *Supra*, p. 32.
18 Gen. 35:18.
19 Hos. 5:7 ff. The consonants in the Hebrew words *aven* and *on* are identical.
20 Cf. Acts 7:22.
21 Cf. S. H. Hooke (ed.), *Myth and Ritual* (London: 1933), pp. 68–146.

(i.e., before the era of the Hebrew king Solomon).[22] For example, Amenemopet urges:

> Give thine ear, and hear what I say,
> And apply thine heart to apprehend.
> It is good to place them in thine heart,
> —Woe to him who refuseth them—
> Let them rest in the casket of thy belly,
> That they may be a threshold in thine heart;
> That if a hurricane of words arise,
> They may act as a peg upon thy tongue.

and Prov. 22:17 f. thus:

> Incline thine ear, and hear my words,
> And apply thine heart to apprehend (them);
> For it is pleasant if thou keep them in thy belly,
> That they may be fixed like a peg upon thy lips.

Again, Prov. 23:4 f. reads:

> Toil not to become rich,
> And cease from thy dishonest gain;
> For wealth maketh to itself wings,
> Like an eagle that flieth heavenwards.

And Amenemopet thus:

> Toil not after riches,
> When thy needs are made sure to thee.
> If stolen goods are brought to thee,
> They remain not over the night with thee;
> At daybreak they are no more in thy house.
> They have made for themselves wings like geese,
> And have flown into the heavens.[23]

An Egyptian *Tale of the Two Brothers*,[24] written for Seti II (1209–1205 B.C.), furnishes a most striking parallel to the Biblical story of Joseph. The *Adventure* of *Wenamon, circa* 1100 B.C., illustrates relations between Egypt and Palestine, especially Phoenicia, at the time of the Hebrew "judges".

The Culture of Babylonia and Assyria

The civilization of lower Mesopotamia trails off into the mists of the past. The oldest communities which have been uncovered by

[22] So M. H. Dunsmore, "An Egyptian Contribution to the Book of Proverbs," *Journal of Religion* (1925), pp. 300–308.
[23] These are only sample quotations. For extended quotations and a full discussion of the subject, cf. Barton, *op. cit.,* pp. 511–515; Breasted, *op. cit.,* pp. 321–330, 371–381; W. O. E. Oesterley, *The Book of Proverbs* (New York: 1929), pp. xlvi–l and 188–214, and cf. his *The Wisdom of Egypt and the Old Testament* (London: 1927).
[24] Cf. Barton, *op. cit.,* pp. 365–368.

archaeologists belong to the Neolithic Age.[25] The Lower Babylonian Plain, called Shinar in the older Biblical records,[26] was known as Sumer. The Sumerians were a non-Semitic people who controlled the area during the so-called Early Dynastic Period, *circa* 2800–*circa* 2400 B.C. Toward the end of this period, under the First Dynasty of Ur, Sumerian culture reached a high level as was disclosed in the discovery and excavation of the royal cemetery at Ur.[27] This Sumerian hegemony in lower Mesopotamia yielded to a dynasty of Semitic kings, founded by Sargon I, *circa* 2360 B.C. In the narrow northern plain of Babylonia, where the Tigris and Euphrates rivers are closest together, he founded the city of Agade, which gave to that area the name of Akkad; hence its Semitic peoples are called Akkadians. This First Semitic (or Akkad) Dynasty lasted for about two hundred years [28] and was followed by a Sumerian renascence. The neo-Sumerian period likewise endured for about two hundred years, i.e., until *circa* 2000 B.C. Sumerian culture rose to splendor under the Third Dynasty of Ur.[29] This neo-Sumerian hegemony was liquidated by invasions of Elamites from the hills. Amorite invasions led to the establishment of Amorite dynasties in city-states throughout Meso-potamia. Conflict among these city-states culminated *circa* 1830 B.C. in the triumph of Babylon and the founding of the First Dynasty of Babylon. Among the kings of this first dynasty the great name is that of the sixth, Hammurabi.[30]

The third millennium B.C., i.e., the Early Bronze Age, saw notable achievements in civilization in lower Babylonia. There were city-states of considerable importance; orderly government was main-tained; a system of cuneiform writing was in process of development; the banking and legal professions were recognized; the solar year had been rather accurately calculated; irrigation of the soil was carried on by an elaborate system of canals; and a high degree of skill had been attained in sculpture, metal-casting, gem cutting,[31] and the

---

[25] Summarized by Finegan, *op. cit.,* pp. 13–30.

[26] Gen. 10 :10, 11 :2, 14 :1.

[27] By the British archaeologist, C. Leonard Woolley. Cf. his *Ur Excavations* (2 vols ; Philadelphia : 1927–1934). Summarized by Finegan, *op. cit.,* pp. 33–36 and Figs. 12–16.

[28] Summarized by Finegan, *op. cit.,* pp. 38 ff.

[29] Cf. Woolley, *op. cit.* Summarized by Finegan, *op. cit.,* pp. 41–44.

[30] The variation in the dating of Hammurabi by different scholars seems perplex-ing. Once he was assigned to the twenty-fourth century (*circa* 2342–2288 B.C.). Then the dating was lowered to the twenty-first century (2104–2061) ; (this date was given in the first edition of this book). On the basis of historical records (cuneiform tablets) dug up at Mari on the Euphrates, the date of Hammurabi has been brought down to the late eighteenth and early seventeenth centuries B.C. Professor W. F. Al-bright has repeatedly revised this dating as fresh archaeological evidence required such correction. He gives the date of Hammurabi as 1728–1686 B.C., and of the Code of Hammurabi as *circa* 1690 B.C., in *Bulletin of the American Schools of Oriental Research,* 88 (December, 1942), pp. 28–33.

[31] On the glyptic art of Mesopotamia, cf. C. H. Gordon, *The Living Past* (New York : 1941), pp. 113–132, with its 32 illustrations.

inlaying of metal and stone. Babylonia was also famous for its textiles, especially woolen, as reflected in the "goodly Babylonish mantle" found among the spoils of Jericho.[32]

The inhabitants of this region lacked such stone quarries as were available to the Nile dwellers, so they turned to the excellent clays which abounded and developed a brick style of architecture which is quite correctly described in Gen. 11:3. Brick does not last like blocks of quarried stone, and the five- or six-thousand-year-old ruins of Babylonia have disintegrated much more than Egyptian ruins of equal age. Moreover, a brick construction does not lend itself to the same architectural possibilities as stone, and so there never were such massive and enduring structures in Babylonia as in Egypt.

Enough has come to light from the ancient mounds of the Tigris and Euphrates valleys to prove that this early culture was by no means inferior to that of Egypt. In Babylonia originated, for example, the 60-unit system of notation that has survived even to modern times in our sixty seconds to the minute, sixty minutes to the hour, as well as in the 360 (6 x 60) degrees of the circle. The Babylonians laid the foundation for astronomy through their study of the stars, even though that study was pursued in the interest of astrology. It was, moreover, their system of writing, the cuneiform, that won out against the Egyptian and was for several centuries the common medium of international correspondence. It is also in Babylonia that the most remarkable legal system of ancient times has come to light, viz., the famous Code of Hammurabi, *circa* 2100 B.C. Made up of nearly three hundred [33] separately itemized statutes, it is a most illuminating treatise on justice and penology. We learn, for example, that three distinct social classes were legally recognized, and that rights and penalties varied with the class. The highest class consisted of men of gentle blood, together with certain artisans. The lowest level was the slave group. In between was the middle group of commoners. This legal grouping stood out sharply in all laws which specified fixed penalties, fees, and the like. For example:

> If a man has stolen from a temple or a palace, he shall repay thirtyfold; but if from a poor man (i.e., a commoner), he shall repay tenfold. (§8)

[32] Josh. 7:21.

[33] The number of items on the stele as found is 247. It is estimated that 35 sections of the code were effaced by the Elamite conqueror who carried the monument to Susa. He erased five columns of writing, presumably to make space for his own name, which never got inserted. Cf. *supra*, pp. 47 f. On the creative cultural achievements of ancient Babylonia, cf. W. F. Albright, *Archaeology and the Religion of Israel* (Baltimore: 1942), pp. 31 f. On the philological importance of cuneiform, cf. Albright, *From the Stone Age to Christianity* (Baltimore: 1940), pp. 9 f. On speculative thought in ancient Mesopotamia, cf. Thorkild Jacobsen in *The Intellectual Adventure of Ancient Man* (Chicago: 1946), pp. 125–218.

Similarly, in connection with an elaborate tariff of graduated fees which artisans and professional men were permitted to charge, we find the following regulations governing surgeons:

> If a physician has cured the fractured limb of a gentleman, the patient shall pay five shekels of silver; if he is of the poor-man class, he shall pay three shekels; if it be a gentleman's slave, the owner shall pay two shekels. (§§221–223)

On the other hand, if a surgical operation was followed by the death of the patient, the physician was severely penalized. If his patient was merely a slave, the physician got off by giving the owner another slave of equal value (§219); but if the patient was of the gentleman class, the unlucky physician had his hand cut off' (§218). Thus was the high standard of the medical profession effectively safeguarded in one ancient state. But along with this strict though severely crude justice are also found some commendable touches of consideration and mercy. A man might not squirm out of the consequences of his own indolence.

> If a man has rented a field for cultivation (i.e., evidently, on shares), and then has not cultivated it, he shall give to the owner as much grain as is grown in adjacent plots. (§42)

On the other hand, if a crop fails after the renter has done his part, the contract becomes null and void.

> If a debtor rents a field and a thunderstorm destroys the crop, or if it fails on account of drought, in that year he shall not make a return of grain to his creditor; his contract he shall change, and the interest of that year he shall not pay. (§48)

The code reveals that women could own and sell property and engage in trade. (§§108–111, 150–152, 176–184)

Hammurabi was a great conqueror; he extended his sway westward to the Mediterranean. He was no less great as a ruler, as attested by his famous code. Under Hammurabi, Babylon became the commercial and cultural capital of all western Asia and such she remained until Greece and Rome supplanted her. The Babylonian language and script predominated in Egypt even in the time of Egypt's greatest glory under the eighteenth dynasty. Even Hittite and Mitannian kings used Babylonian writing to correspond with their Egyptian overlords. Spread of the language certainly facilitated the diffusion of culture. As commercial mistress of the ancient world, Babylon was in a position to impress the ideals of business and social ethics reflected in the Code of Hammurabi upon that world through her traders as well as her prestige.

From the time of Hammurabi until the empire of Babylonia fell to the barbarian Kassites from east of the Tigris, *circa* 1500 B.C., Canaan was a small province on the western fringe of the empire. Babylonian civilization was indelibly stamped upon the land, and this civilization the Canaanites transmitted to the Hebrews. Many centuries later (in the sixth century B.C.), the Jewish people were exiled to Babylon. Though many remained there permanently, they maintained some connection with Judea through correspondence, and thus was started another great era of direct Babylonian cultural influence upon the Jewish people.

As yet the Tigris-Euphrates region has released no such stores of rich art treasure as were kept secure in the deep, strong vaults of Egypt's royal tombs. Nevertheless enough has been found in the hard-packed debris of cities like Ur, Nineveh, and Babylon to show that the art of the sculptor and engraver reached a high level, judged even by modern standards. Thus an exquisitely chased vase bearing the arms of the city-state of Lagash, *circa* 3000 B.C., finds its spiritual successors in the marvelous bas-reliefs that adorn the palaces of Ashurbanipal of Nineveh and Nebuchadrezzar of Babylon, nearly twenty-five centuries later. Some of these, such as the wounded and dying lioness of Ashurbanipal's palace and the glazed brick lion of Nebuchadrezzar's, are universally acknowledged to be masterpieces in their respective fields.

Of all the treasures which have come from the mounds of ancient Babylonia and Assyria, nothing matches in importance for Bible study the literary remains which are in the form both of monumental inscriptions and of inscribed baked-clay tablets. The art of cuneiform writing was invented by the Sumerians. The modern decipherment of it was the creative accomplishment of Henry C. Rawlinson, an English officer in the Persian army, who in 1835 discovered the Behistun inscription. On the road from Babylon to the highland of Persia, in the Zagros Mountains, is a peak some 3,800 feet high, one side of which is nearly perpendicular. On this mountain face, *circa* 350 feet above its base and *circa* 500 feet above the level of the highway, is a bas-relief representing King Darius the First's triumphal reception of defeated conspirators, with panels of cuneiform inscriptions in three languages, Old Persian, Elamite (Median or Susian), and Akkadian (Babylonian). To copy the 1,200 lines of the inscriptions was a perilous feat, but Rawlinson did it. It was done again in 1948 by Professor G. G. Cameron of the University of Michigan while serving as annual professor at the American School of Oriental Research at Baghdad. Because Rawlinson understood modern Persian, he first attacked the decipherment of the *circa* 400 lines of Old Persian and published his translation in 1847. Others collaborated in the

THE BEHISTUN ROCK [34]

[34] To the left of the sculpture is a broad single column in Babylonian cuneiform. Beneath that are three columns in the Susian cuneiform. Beneath the relief and to the right are 4½ columns in the Old Persian alphabet. George G. Cameron photograph., reproduced by permission of The Oriental Institute, University of Chicago. On the Behistun inscription, cf. I. M. Price, *The Monuments and the Old Testament* (Philadelphia: 1925), pp. 43–47; Finegan, *op. cit.*, pp. 196 f. Cf. Chiera, *op. cit.* (Chicago: 1938).

decipherment of the other two inscriptions on the (correct) assumption that they told the same story. Ultimately Rawlinson and three other scholars, working independently, produced substantially identical translations of a long historical inscription (about Tiglath-pileser I *circa* 1120–1100 B.C.) that was in the British Museum. They published their results in 1857. That was as great an achievement in the sphere of philology as the invention of radio in the realm of communication. It unlocked the door to a knowledge of the history and culture of all Mesopotamia. To appreciate the art of cuneiform writing one should read the late Professor Edward Chiera's fascinating *They Wrote On Clay*. Its wealth of illustration is most valuable.

Without doubt the most important of all discoveries was the library of Ashurbanipal, found by the archaeologist Hormuzd Rassam in 1854. Ashurbanipal was ruler of Assyria from 668 to 626 B.C.[35] In his palace at Nineveh he gathered together a great library which contained copies of the epics, hymns, and ritual incantations from all the ancient temples of Babylonia, medical treatises, chronicles of the rulers, dictionaries, and treatises on grammar, in fact, every sort of Babylonian and Assyrian literature, in all some 22,000 clay tablets. This astonishing find is the basis for all modern knowledge of ancient Babylonian and Assyrian history and literature. A comparison of this literature with the Biblical literature discloses the sources of many of the thought patterns of the Biblical Hebrews. In the subsequent chapters of our study we shall make numerous references to the ancient Babylonian and Assyrian monuments. Some conception of the importance of this material for Bible study may be gained by noting the amount of space devoted to the subject in such a work as Barton's *Archaeology and the Bible*.[36]

Phoenician Culture

The term Canaan (Canaanites) may be understood in both a broad and a limited sense. In the broad sense it designates the people who controlled Syria and Palestine from Hamath on the Orontes, in the north, to Gaza, on the coast in the south, as early as the third millennium B.C.[37] In this broad sense of the term, Canaanites and Phoenicians were one people, viz., Canaanites; certainly they were one in language and culture. Disaster befell them in the thirteenth and twelfth centuries B.C. when they lost nine tenths of their territory to invaders, to Aramaeans in Syria, to Hebrews and Philistines in Palestine. A remnant survived in Phoenicia under the dominance of Tyre and

[35] Cf. *infra*, pp. 260–261.
[36] In part II, eleven chapters, totaling 110 pages, besides numerous references and citations in other chapters.
[37] Cf. Gen. 10:15–19.

Sidon.[38] We meet this group in the Old Testament and we shall call them Phoenicians in order to distinguish them from those Canaanites (in the limited sense) whom the Hebrews dispossessed and assimilated in Palestine west of Jordan.[39]

The Phoenicians were noted far and wide as a shipbuilding and seafaring people, as well as for fine workmanship in the industrial arts. They were the middlemen who exchanged the products of Babylonia, Arabia, Egypt, and indeed of all the Mediterranean coast countries. Precious stones, metal craftsmanship, glassware, costly textiles, and purple dyes were among the most prized of their articles of commerce.[40] They were also the founders of numerous colonies about the Mediterranean, Carthage being the largest and most famed. Another important Phoenician colony is called Tarshish in the Bible,[41] generally identified as Tartessus in the south of Spain, although there was another Phoenician Tarshish in Sardinia.

Because they were a commercial people, the Phoenicians borrowed from the entire Mediterranean littoral along which their ships coasted in search of trade. Ezekiel *27 is a poem in which the whole city-state of Tyre is pictured as a gorgeously opulent merchant ship that has drawn its wealth from every country far and near. The vivid metaphors imply that Tyre could not help prospering, since nation after nation clamored to trade with it. Isaiah *23 affords a similar picture of the far-flung commercial activity of Tyre. There must have been much truth in this picture. Certainly Phoenician wares were known favorably over the whole ancient world, and the Phoenicians themselves were held in marked respect not alone for their enterprise as traders but also for their originality and cleverness in textiles, woodworking, and other industrial crafts. It was to the Phoenician merchants that the Greeks, and afterward the Romans, owed their alphabets. Greek indebtedness to the Phoenicians for writing materials and the art of writing is immortalized in the Greek word for book, viz., *biblion* (*pl.*) *biblia,* named for the city of Byblos (on the coast of Syria north of Sidon). Thence also came our word *Bible.* The Phoenicians also transmitted to other nations the knowledge of Babylonian art and religion, of mathematics, and of weights and measures.

There were two periods when Phoenician culture directly influenced that of the Hebrews: the first, when King Solomon employed Tyrian architects and artisans to help him in the building of his famous temple and palace; the second, when Jezebel, Tyrian wife of the Israelite

---

[38] Cf. W. F. Albright, *Archaeology and the Religion of Israel* (Baltimore: 1942), pp. 68 f.

[39] On Canaanite-Phoenician civilization in Palestine prior to the Hebrew conquest, cf. G. E. Wright and F. V. Filson, *op. cit.,* pp. 33–36.

[40] Especially purple dyes. That is what gave rise to the name "Phoenicia," from the Greek word meaning *purple.*

[41] 2 Chr. 9:21; Jon. 1:3.

king Ahab, tried to saturate Samaria with Phoenician Baalistic religion. It seems certain that on both occasions the Phoenician influence made a permanent impress. The politic friendliness of the Phoenicians toward other peoples paved the way for a widespread acceptance of Phoenician culture.

Canaanite Culture

Our appreciation of the civilization and culture of Palestine prior to the fifteenth century B.C. is gained from lists of plunder and tribute exacted by Egyptian monarchs and from the Ras Shamra tablets. There was considerable wealth in the region, much of it in the form of gold and silver ornaments and vessels. Cities were strong fortresses,[42] and their defenders were particularly versed in the art of warfare. Egyptian armies found the Canaanite cities well nigh impregnable, and reduced their defenders to submission only through siege and starvation. Small wonder that to the Hebrews, fresh from the desert, Canaanite cities seemed "great and fortified up to heaven!"[43] With their hundreds of war chariots, their bronze scale armor, bronze swords, shields, and spearheads they were a truly formidable people for whom the early Hebrew conquerors of the hills entertained a wholesome respect.

Politically, Canaan was characterized by disunity. Numerous petty princes ruled, each in his own little city. There was no one king over the land, every prince did what was right in his own eyes, and every prince's hand was against every other prince. Co-operation among them, even for public safety, was unknown. Thus the land was in constant turmoil and warfare was the Canaanites' stock in trade.

The Canaanites were skilled craftsmen but hardly great artists. The finest specimen of native Canaanite art which has come to light is a panel found in the temple of Mekal, the great god of Bethshean. The panel, in two registers, depicts the lion-shaped pest god Nergal, driven off by the divine dog who is guardian of the city.

Canaanite smiths wrought cleverly in bronze; the jewelers in gold, silver, ivory, and alabaster; and the weavers, potters, and builders in their trades. Descendants of the Canaanites were traders,[44] what we would call pack peddlers, with a reputation for dishonesty.[45] Hebrew craftsmen imitated Canaanite patterns in jewelry, dishes, cooking pots, jars, and the like.

The Canaanites had an aptitude for music. Egyptians borrowed lyres and other instruments from them and imported Canaanite musicians. In the time of King David (tenth century B.C.) there were

42 Cf. Deut. 3:5.   43 Deut. 1:28.
44 Prov. 31:24. (RV marg.).   45 Hos. 12:7. (RV marg.).

musical families with Canaanite names which were the forebears of the Hebrew musical guilds of later centuries. Hebrews imitated the patterns of Canaanite musical instruments.[46]

Appreciation of Canaanite culture is being steadily increased by archaeological research in Palestine proper and in recent years has been richly augmented by the translation and interpretation of the Ras Shamra tablets. Ras Shamra (Fennel Head) is on the coast of Syria, about twenty miles south of the mouth of the Orontes River. In the second millennium B.C. this city was known as Ugarit. It ceased to exist after the twelfth century B.C. and remained completely buried until it was discovered by chance in 1928.[47]

Two temples were in ancient Ugarit, one to the god Baal and one to the god Dagon. Between the temples was a library. There, hundreds of clay tablets were found which scholars assign to the fifteenth and fourteenth centuries B.C. They are in alphabetic cuneiform and their language is Semitic. This language, wholly unknown just a few years ago, is called Ugaritic.[48]

The literature embodied in these tablets consists of epic poems about Canaanite gods and heroes. The rhetorical structure of this poetry exhibits identically the characteristic parallelism as that which we observe in early Hebrew folklore.[49] An illustrative couplet of synonymous parallelism, in 3 + 3 beat rhythm, the usual cadence of lyric poetry, is shown below.

> For Aliyn Baal is dead,
> For the Prince, Lord of Earth, has perished.[50]

Another smooth couplet in the 3 + 3 rhythm is as follows:

> The mountains will bring thee much silver,
> The hills, the choicest of gold.[51]

Couplets are combined in strophes and at times there are refrains. A strophe illustrative of synthetic parallelism is set out below.

> She seizes the god Mot,
> With a sword she cleaves him,
> With a pitchfork she winnows him,
> With fire she burns him,
> In the millstones she grinds him,
> In the fields she plants him.[52]

---

[46] Cf. W. F. Albright, *Archaeology and the Religion of Israel* (Baltimore: 1942), pp. 14, 126 f.

[47] Cf. Finegan, *op. cit.*, pp. 146–149.

[48] There is now even an Ugaritic Grammar by C. H. Gordon (Rome: 1940).

[49] *Vid. infra*, pp. 112–113.

[50] Cf. C. H. Gordon, *The Loves and Wars of Baal and Anat and Other Poems from Ugarit* (Princeton: 1943), pp. ix–xiii.

[51] *Ibid.*, p. 16.   [52] *Ibid.*, p. 9.

An illustration of 2 + 2 meter is the following:

> Sea collapses
> Falls to earth;
> His face falls
> And his countenance wilts.
> Baal conquers
> And vanquishes Sea,
> He destroys Judge River.[53]

These Ugaritic epics embody legends about kings and myths about gods. Titles by which they are now called are "The Birth of the Beautiful and Gracious Gods," "Building the Palace of Baal," "The Loves and Wars of Baal and Anat," "The Nuptials of Nikkal and the Moon," "King Keret and Princess Haraya," "The Epic of Aqhat," "The Legend of Daniel." [54] Professor Gordon considers that these Ugaritic epics are the most important contribution to ancient literature since Egyptian hieroglyphic and Mesopotamian cuneiform were first deciphered in the nineteenth century.[55]

Competent scholars hold that this Canaanite literature not only indirectly influenced Hebrew poetic style in earliest times, as evidenced in the Ode of Deborah (Jgs. 5),[56] but that it also directly influenced Hebrew literature between the seventh and the third centuries B.C., as attested in Job, Proverbs, Second Isaiah, Ezekiel, Habakkuk, Song of Songs, Ecclesiastes, Jubilees, and parts of Daniel. This points to a Canaanite literary renascence in the seventh century B.C.[57] Parallels between Ugaritic and Biblical literature now number hundreds. As a sample of such parallels, in a manual on the treatment of sick and decrepit horses, one treatment prescribed is the application of a fig poultice, like that applied to King Hezekiah's boil.[58] The "Thunderstorm Psalm" (Ps. 29) reflects a geographical standpoint in Phoenicia, not Palestine, and it is otherwise full of echoes of Canaanite poetry.[59]

Canaanite pictorial art is exhibited in stelae found at Ras Shamra. One stela shows the king of Ugarit presenting an offering to the god

[53] *Ibid.*, p. 21. An appreciation of the poems of Ugarit can be gained from Gordon's book and also from G. A. Barton, *Archaeology and the Bible* (Philadelphia: 1937), pp. 534–543. The contents of the poems are summarized in Gordon's *The Living Past* (New York: 1941), pp. 133–155.
[54] Cf. Umberto Cassuto, "The Palace of Baal," *Journal of Biblical Literature*, LXI, i (March, 1942), pp. 51–56; Albrecht Goetze, "The Nikkal Poem from Ras Shamra," *Journal of Biblical Literature*, LX, iv (December, 1941), pp. 353–374; Finegan, *op. cit.*, Fig. 62; Barton, *op. cit.*, pp. 540–543; Julian Obermann, *Ugaritic Mythology* (New Haven: 1947).
[55] *The Living Past*, p. 155.   [56] *Vid. infra*, pp. 156, 166–169.
[57] Cf. W. F. Albright, *Archaeology and the Religion of Israel* (Baltimore: 1942), p. 243.
[58] 2 Kgs. 20:1–7. Cf. Claude F. A. Schaeffer, *The Cuneiform Texts of Ras Shamra—Ugarit* (London: 1939), pp. 40 f.
[59] *Vid. supra*, p. 19. Cf. H. L. Ginsberg, "Ugaritic Studies and the Bible," *Biblical Archaeologist*, VIII, 2 (May, 1945), pp. 41–58, especially p. 53.

El, who is seated on a throne. Another shows the god Baal holding in his left hand a thunderbolt which ends in a spearhead and in his right hand a mace.[60] There is a statuette of Baal, with the body of bronze, originally clothed in gold leaf, with a helmet of polished stone with horns of electrum. A gold bowl is of exquisite design. A one-mina weight is in the form of a bull.[61] A Canaanite cult table of the twelfth century B.C. depicts a nude goddess holding two doves, and below her are two struggling gods with a serpent and a lion moving toward them.[62]

The status of woman is always a clue to the social culture of any age or people. A document dealing with inheritance makes clear that women, especially the mother of a family, had a high social status at Ugarit.[63] Canaanite social justice is seen in Gaygan's injunction to Keret's son, Yassib, to reprimand his royal father for unsocial conduct:

> Hearken, I pray thee, O Keret the noble! Listen, and let thine ear be attentive. . . . Thou shouldst judge the cause of the widow, adjudicate the case of him that is in anguish of spirit. Thou shouldst deliver the poor man from his oppressors, shouldst feed the fatherless before thee and the widow behind thy back. How long has thou been a brother of the bed of sickness, a friend of the lofty couch? Descend from the king's throne! Let me be king. Upon the seat of thy dominion let me sit.

Very likely this is hypocrisy on Yassib's part, who is up to political chicanery, but not so the upright Daniel:

> He pleads the cause of the widow,
> He judges the right of the orphan.[64]

The epics furnish the names of several deities in the Canaanite pantheon. *El* was the supreme god. His principal wife was *Asherah,* by whom he had seventy offspring. He had another wife, *Rhiny.* These two wives bore him Dawn and Dusk. *Baal (Baal Aliyn)* was the storm god *Hadad* and was king of the gods. He was the son of El and Asherah and was the god of life and fertility. In late April when the latter rains ceased, he was slain by *Mot,* the god of death. The early rains in September meant the resurrection of Baal. His death was avenged by his sister and consort, *Anat,* goddess of love and war, who killed Mot. Baal is also called "the son of Dagon." *Dagon,* a

---

[60] Cf. Finegan, *op. cit.,* Figs. 60–61.
[61] Cf. J. Philip Hyatt, "Canaanite Ugarit—Modern Ras Shamra," *Biblical Archaeologist,* 11, 1, (February, 1939), pp. 1–8 and Figs. 1, 4, 7.
[62] Cf. W. F. Albright, *From the Stone Age to Christianity* (Baltimore: 1940), p. 178.
[63] Cf. Schaeffer, *op. cit.,* p. 42.
[64] Cf. Ginsberg, *loc. cit.,* p. 50.

vegetation god, was one of the oldest Akkadian deities, and was worshiped throughout the Euphrates Valley as early as the twenty-fifth
century B.C. Other deities were *Kathar-wa-Hasis* ("The Fit and
Understanding One"), a sort of Vulcan, the architect of Baal's
palace and the craftsman who fashioned the clubs with which Baal
conquered the sea dragon *Yamm*. *Athtar* the Terrible became Lord
of the Earth after the death of Baal. *Yarih* was moon god.[65] *Shalem*
was god of peace. *El Hokmot* was god of wisdom. *Qadesh-Amrar*
was a donkey-boy sort of god. *Yatpan* was a gangster god, a murderer.
The goddess *Nikkal* was wed to the Moon. *Keret* and *Danel* were
demigods. The tablets attest child sacrifice, sacred prostitution, and
snake worship as features of this early Canaanite polytheism.[66]

The Culture of the Philistines

The Philistines had lived in Crete [67] where they had known one of
the finest civilizations of the ancient world, and they were the most
cultured people in Palestine at any time prior to Alexander's conquest.[68] Arriving on the shores of Palestine after their unsuccessful
attempt to settle in Egypt, they promptly set about the task of building
a modified Cretan state in their new home. They built theaters in
which to hold the "spectacles" or shows which had been the delight
of Cretan life. An interesting episode connected with such an exhibi-
tion is the tale of Samson in the theater of Gaza.[69]

We are utterly ignorant of the language and family life of the
Philistines. Politically they established a strong, orderly government organized under five "lords," [70] one in each of their chief cities.
They had a well-organized army; 1 Sam. 13:5 mentions 30,000
chariots and 6,000 horsemen. Economically they were prosperous.
The fertile plain along the coast yielded abundant produce, even
when other parts of Palestine were suffering famine. The great overland trade route from Egypt to Babylon passed right through the
heart of their country, and Gaza, one of their chief cities, was the
emporium for the trade of North Arabia. The Philistines carried on a
lucrative slave trade.[71] In religion they adopted Semitic deities —
Dagon, of Gaza and Ashdod; Derceto or Atargatis, of Ashkelon;
Ashtart, of Bethshean; Baal-zebub, of Ekron; Baal, of Gaza. Of these,
Dagon came nearest being their universal deity. The Philistine lords
offered sacrifices at the religious festivals in Dagon's temple,[72] and

---

[65] This name possibly survives in Jericho.
[66] For a discussion of the religion of the Canaanites in the light of archaeology,
cf. W. F. Albright, *Archaeology and the Religion of Israel* (Baltimore: 1942), pp.
68–94; G. E. Wright and F. V. Filson, *op. cit.*, p. 36.
[67] Cf. *supra*, pp. 38 f.   [68] 332 B.C.
[69] Jgs. 16:23–31.   [70] Jgs. 3:3.
[71] Cf. Amos's denunciation of it, Am. 1:6.   [72] Jgs. 16:23.

one of the most interesting episodes of Hebrew history has to do with this Philistine god Dagon and his temple (1 Sam. 5 f.). This temple was still in existence in the second century B.C.[73]

To the simple Hebrews of the twelfth and eleventh centuries B.C. (the period of the "judges" and beginnings of kingship), the Philistines inevitably appeared in the guise of arrogant, overbearing foreigners to be feared, despised, and hated. The Samson stories reflect all these animosities in varying degrees. Yet in the intervals between open hostilities, exchange of products went on apace. Pottery made by the Philistines appeared in the hill towns of central Palestine early in the twelfth century, as also sickles and plowshares of iron.

One of the most interesting passages that throws light on the relative cultural status of the Philistines and the Hebrews is 1 Sam. *13:19–22, which should be read preferably in the Chicago Version.[74] The Hebrews bought their axes, sickles, and like instruments from the Philistines, and had to take them back to Philistine smiths for sharpening.[75] The implication is that the Hebrews were ignorant of the art of ironworking. They were still in the Bronze Age. The explanatory remark that the Philistine masters forbade the Hebrews to practice the art of ironworking "lest they make themselves swords or spears" may be quite accurate too, but such a prohibition would have been hard to enforce had the Hebrews known the art already. It sounds as though the Philistines simply refused to teach the new art to their Hebrew vassals. The Philistines are often credited with introducing Canaan to the Iron Age. There is archaeological evidence that the Canaanites knew iron before the arrival of the Philistines.[76] At any rate the Hebrews did not, and that is what placed them, at the outset, at such a disadvantage before the Philistines with their mighty allies, iron and the horse.

Life and Culture of the Hebrews

With the foregoing as a background, we are in a position to study Hebrew culture as it developed from early times and to appraise it with some fairness.

[73] 1 Macc. 10:83 f.; 11:4.

[74] First published under the title *The Old Testament, An American Translation*, edited by J. M. P. Smith; later (when combined with the Goodspeed New Testament) under the title *The Bible, An American Translation* (Chicago: University of Chicago Press).

[75] The marginal note for 1 Sam. 13:21 in the American Revised Version says "the Hebrew text is obscure." The obscurity has been cleared up by the discovery of a little weight marked *payim* (the word mistranslated "file"). A *payim* for the mattocks, etc., means "the price." See illustration in Barton, *op. cit.*, Plate 63.

[76] Cf. Elihu Grant, *Beth-shemesh* (Haverford: 1929), pp. 42 f. In his excavating at Gerar, W. M. Flinders Petrie found two knives which go back to *circa* 1350 B.C., the earliest known manufactured iron that can be dated.

When the Hebrews first entered Palestine they were little removed from the crude level of the Arabian desert tribes. Inured to life under the open sky with no covering but a tent, only slowly did they adapt themselves to town life and city ways, and all this they learned from the Canaanites. They did not exterminate the Canaanites. They first lived among them, then traded and intermarried with them, and finally completely absorbed them and their civilization. At first this new culture was something of a veneer, a borrowed thing which fitted them at times uncomfortably. For some time also the arts and crafts remained in the hands of the non-Hebrew element in the population. After a while the borrowing habit got so strong as to alarm one part of the Hebrews. Some of the prophets were in this group. They sensed that the borrowing was indiscriminate, that bad customs were taken over along with good, debasing forms of worship along with fine art and a sense of beauty.[77]

Unquestionably this avidity to absorb culture had much to do with the rapid social development of the Hebrews throughout the course of Old Testament history. The Hebrews did not usually borrow without change, but placed their stamp indelibly on much that they adopted. Particularly is this true in the higher realm of thought and feeling, in literature, in ethics, and in religion. Here they achieved their greatest triumph. Their capacity for spiritual idealism still challenges the admiration of the world.

[77] Cf. W. F. Albright, *Archaeology and the Religion of Israel* (Baltimore: 1942), pp. 13 f.

Chapter 5

THE EMERGENCE OF THE HEBREW TRIBES

Old Testament history falls naturally into distinct periods, each marked off by some event which proved to be a watershed giving new direction or fresh impetus to the currents of Hebrew life. The first period is commonly designated the Patriarchal Period. It is so called because the type of social organization and control in effect at the time was that of an autocratic family or clan ruled by its "father," i.e., the oldest living male head of the group. The source book for our knowledge of this period is the Biblical book of Genesis. This period covers nearly eight centuries, from about 2000 to 1200 B.C. Throughout these centuries the Hebrews remained nomads or seminomads, continually shifting about the Fertile Crescent in search of a suitable permanent habitat. Their migrations took them through the entire stretch of the Crescent, from Ur of the Chaldees in the east [1] to Canaan in the west, back and forth, and more than once to Egypt and return.

The Daily Life of the Hebrew Nomads

The present-day nomads of the Syrian and Arabian deserts preserve unchanged the manners and customs of the Semites of antiquity. It is, therefore, possible for us to gain a living touch with the Hebrews of whom we read in the Bible, to appreciate what manner of human beings they were and what their daily life was like.

Personal Appearance and Dress. The Hebrews as a race were lean, wiry, and not very tall. Desert life for many centuries inured them to hardy physical endurance. Their dress, like everything else originating in the desert and in nomadism, was characterized by simplicity and utility, blended with love of color.[2]

In very earliest times a loincloth was sufficient for all needs. This was nothing but a strip of skin or cloth wrapped around the hips and secured by a knot. A survival of this type of dress lasted through

[1] Gen. 11:31. On the world of the patriarchs, cf. G. E. Wright and F. V. Filson, *The Westminster Historical Atlas to the Bible* (Philadelphia: 1945), pp. 23–26.
[2] Cf. M. S. and J. L. Miller, *Encyclopedia of Bible Life* (New York: 1944), pp. 48–62.

Old Testament times in the practice of girding one's self, in times of mourning, with sackcloth, a fabric woven of goat's hair. The loincloth also survived in the simple style of dress adopted by certain of the Old Testament prophets, e.g., by Elijah,[3] by Jeremiah,[4] and by Isaiah.[5] Another survival of this type of dress was the *ephod,* a loincloth of linen, probably like a kilt, worn by the priests.[6]

With the increase of affluence the mere strip of cloth became broader and longer, and developed into the coat or tunic. This was like a long loose shirt with long flowing sleeves, reaching to the knees or below. The front and back were each made of one width of woolen or linen cloth, sewed together along the sides and top. Sometimes the coat was so woven that it could be put together without cutting, and sometimes it was woven on a special loom "without seam," e.g., the coat of Jesus.[7] The tunic was usually made of striped and bright-colored cloth. Throughout Old Testament times such a coat was the principal garment worn by people of all classes of society, save possibly slaves and religious ascetics.

Obviously such a long, robelike garment was not well adapted to labor or travel. To overcome this difficulty a girdle was worn. This was sometimes a simple rope, but usually it was a long strip of cloth folded over and over several times and wound about the waist, occasionally with the ends hanging down. The skirt of the tunic was often bloused at the waist. This made a convenient pocket in which to carry tools or bread for a journey. Tying up the tunic out of the way by means of the girdle, to facilitate travel or work, was known as "girding the loins," an expression which became idiomatic for energetic action.

The coat described in the foregoing is to be distinguished carefully from the cloak, which is the outer garment. The ordinary kind of cloak was made from a rectangle of cloth, seven feet wide by four and one-half feet long, folded in about a foot and a half on each side and sewed along the top, with a slit in each upper corner for the hand and forearm to pass through. Sometimes the cloak was made of two pieces of cloth, but the better quality was of one piece. Usually the cloak was made of goat's hair, which sheds water very well; sometimes of sheep's wool or of camel's hair. Often it was woven in broad stripes of alternating dark and light colors. Frequently the outer garment of the shepherds on the hills was made of sheepskins with the fleece left on. Shepherds often wore such a sheepskin garment like a vest, with the ordinary type of cloak over it. In later than nomadic times, following the settlement in Canaan and the increase of wealth,

---

[3] 2 Kgs. 1:8.
[5] Isa. 20:2.
[7] Jn. 19:23.

[4] Jer. 13:1.
[6] 1 Sam. 2:18; 2 Sam. 6:14.

an additional type of outer cloak developed, a long loose robe with very wide sleeves worn over a belted coat and shirt. This, the dress of culture and dignity, characterized the priestly, educated, wealthy, and official classes. It was always indicative of social position and high rank. In time, persons of especially high position came to have their coats made of very fine materials and ornamented with cords and tassels.

In early pastoral times the headdress was simply a piece of cloth, perhaps colored, about a yard square. This was folded diagonally and laid on the head so as to shade the eyes and protect the cheek bones and the back of the neck. Such protection is very essential under the Palestinian sun. It was held in place by a cord, usually of soft, elastic wool, coiled around the head in several rings. This headband could on occasion be drawn down over the eyes and wrapped about the mouth so as to conceal the features.[8]

The use of sandals developed early. They were simply flat soles of leather, wood, or plaited fiber, with loops through which to slip the toes or feet. A leather thong, known as the shoe latchet,[9] was passed through the loops and strapped to the foot.

Women's dress differed little from men's. Interchange was possible, but in time it came to be prohibited.[10] The chief articles of distinctly feminine dress were the veils and mantles. In nomadic times the veils were no doubt made of tough cloth and worn over the head so as to fall down the back. They were used by the women for carrying grass, food, or bundles.[11] The prophet Isaiah scornfully derides the over-dressed women of his day (Isa. *3:18–23), and the prophet Ezekiel, speaking allegorically of Jerusalem, gives a matchless description of the dress of the women of his time (Ezk. *16:10–13). Both these writers, however, describe periods that were much later than the patriarchal era.

It denoted dignity in men and decency in women to be properly and adequately dressed. Bright colors predominated with both sexes, stripes of color being much favored. In times of grief, however, people put on black, while "sackcloth and ashes" became the synonym for intense sorrow.

Dwellings and Home Life.   The tent was the only type of home when the Hebrews were nomads. After the settlement in Canaan the herdsmen continued to dwell in tents, east of Jordan, for example. When this dwelling in tents had become a thing of the past, they still spoke of going home as "going to their tents." [12]

---

[8] 1 Kgs. 20:38, 41.   [9] Gen. 14:23.
[10] Deut. 22:5.   [11] Cf. Ruth 3:15.
[12] Josh. 22:4; Jgs. 19:9; 2 Sam. 20:1; 1 Kgs. 12:16. Cf. M. S. and J. L. Miller, *op. cit.*, pp. 233–240.

Such tents were undoubtedly much like the Bedouin tents of today. Long, narrow strips of dark and sturdy goat's-hair cloth are sewed together to the desired breadth and spread upon nine poles, about six or seven feet high, arranged in three rows of three each, the middle row being slightly higher than the others to give the roof a slope toward front and back. After once wet and shrunk, this material makes a thoroughly waterproof covering. Tent cords are fastened to it and tied to stakes or tent pins driven into the ground with a mallet. Curtains of the same kind of goat's-hair cloth are hung around the exposed sides for protection against sun and wind. A similar curtain, hung on the three middle tent poles, divides the tent into two compartments, one the women's and the other the men's. Guests are received in the men's compartment.

The furniture of the tent is crude and meager. Coarse straw mats serve for chairs and table in the daytime and for beds at night. There is a lamp of clay, a flat or convex metal plate for baking, some pots or pans for cooking, possibly a hand mill or a mortar and pestle. Half-tanned goatskins, hair outward, are made into bags for holding grain, water, buttermilk, or other liquids. Such a bag is swung on a tripod or rocked over the knee to churn butter.

At meals the Hebrews, in nomadic times, sat or squatted on the ground [13] around a large wooden bowl placed on a mat of leather or plaited grass. This mat was usually circular, about two feet in diameter, and was so made that it could be gathered into a bag by a leather thong that passed through holes around the edge.

Food and Its Preparation.   Bread was ever the staff of life, and the term "bread" was used for food in general. Wheat and barley were the chief ingredients, though other cereals were often mixed in. The grain was sifted and cleaned, and then made into flour by rubbing between two stones, or pounding in a mortar, or grinding in a mill. The mortar was a heavy stone, a foot or more wide, hollowed out; the pestle was cylindrical with a convex base. The mill consisted of two stones, "the nether millstone" being larger than the "upper millstone." The upper stone revolved on a spindle fitted into the lower stone, and near the outer edge of the upper stone an upright peg was fitted so as to form a handle by which it was turned. The grinding was usually done by two women who sat facing each other, each alternately grasping the peg and giving the stone a half turn. Through a hole in the center of the upper millstone the grain was fed into the mill. Flour was of three grades: (1) coarse, "bruised grain," [14] pounded in the

---

[13] Gen. 37:25. Cf. C. H. Gordon, *The Living Past* (New York: 1941), pp. 33 f.
[14] Lev. 2:14, 16.

mortar; (2) ordinary "meal"; [15] (3) "fine meal" [16] for honored guests, or "fine flour" [17] for kings and for ceremonial offerings.[18]

A daily baking of meal for a good-sized family amounted to an *ephah* or three measures (*seahs*) of meal, which equals about four and one-half pecks.[19] It was mixed with water, salt was added, and then it was kneaded in the "kneading trough," [20] which was a wooden bowl. This made "unleavened bread." For "leavened bread" a small lump of leavened dough from the previous baking was added. The dough was shaped into flat cakes for baking.

Sometimes the bread was baked on hot stones. In this case a fire was built over the stones and when they were hot the embers were raked aside and the cakes laid on the stones and covered with embers and ashes. This process was repeated when the cakes were turned. Another method of baking was on the "baking pan," a flat plate, probably a convex iron plate, laid over a fire pit with the bulge upward. In later than nomadic times ovens came into use.

Wheat and barley were sometimes eaten raw, the husk being removed by rubbing in the hands. "Parched grain" was ears of wheat or barley roasted on an iron plate or otherwise.[21] "Pottage" [22] was made by stewing the seeds of leguminous plants.

Meat was used very sparingly indeed. Since it was vital to keep the size of the flocks and herds unimpaired, domestic animals were slaughtered very infrequently. Only those animals regarded as "clean" could be eaten. Gen. 7:2 distinguishes (for the time of the flood) clean and unclean beasts, a distinction which can be traced back to a remote period in human history.[23] The lamb was the commonest meat for feasts. It was often killed for a guest, but since it was valued for its fleece as well as for meat, it was rarely eaten by the poorer classes. They used the kid for a small feast. Goat flesh was much relished. Of cattle for food, the calf was esteemed the daintiest.[24]

Animals were killed immediately before being cooked.[25] The throat was cut and the blood poured out to comply with religious ceremonial. The carcass was then flayed, and in the case of larger animals cut up into chunks. Lambs, however, were cooked whole. The meat was stewed in the cooking pot, and when seasoning and vegetables were added it made "savory food." [26] When roasted, meat was simply laid

[15] Jgs. 6:19; 1 Sam. 1:24.
[16] Gen. 18:6.
[17] 1 Kgs. 4:22.
[18] Ex. 29:40 f.
[19] Gen. 18:6; Jgs. 6:19; 1 Sam. 1:24.
[20] Ex. 8:3; 12:34.
[21] Ruth 2:14.
[22] Gen. 25:29.
[23] Lev. 11 and Deut. 14 list the unclean beasts and birds, as the Hebrews ultimately came to regard them.
[24] Gen. 18:7.
[25] Gen. 18:7.
[26] Gen. 27:9.

upon the hot stones, after the embers had been pushed aside, as in the case of bread. Fish do not exist in the desert, of course, but nomads would not eat them even if they came upon a stream where fish were abundant and easy to catch. That just isn't done by nomads because their desert forebears didn't do it.[27]

Milk and its derivatives made up a very substantial part of the daily fare. Goat's milk was thought best,[28] and next, the milk of sheep.[29] Camel's milk was probably used by the patriarchs.[30] Butter was usually made from goat's milk. It was churned by rocking a skin of milk upon the knees, or by suspending the skin from a tripod and beating it with a stick or jerking it to and fro.

Not only was the food of the nomadic Hebrews limited in variety, it was also limited in quantity. It is probable that the masses of the people rarely knew what it was not to feel hungry.

Shepherd Life.   There are two types of nomad. The true Bedouin is the camel-nomad. The camel supplies him with food, drink, clothing, housing, and transportation. With the camel he can exist in arid parts of the desert where shepherds and their flocks could not possibly survive. The ass-nomad dares not venture more than a day's journey from his water supply, and he is dependent on animals other than the ass for his food and clothing. Sheep and goats are still more dependent than asses on water and green pasturage.

In the nomadic period the chief occupations of the Hebrews were cattle breeding, sheep raising, and the activities of pastoral life. Even after their transformation to settled agriculturists, pastoral pursuits retained a vital place in their life.

In nomadic days wealth was reckoned almost exclusively in terms of flocks and herds.[31] Camels, goats, sheep, and cattle were standard media of exchange. Since the main family interest was in the increase of these flocks and herds, the nomads shifted about continually in search of pasturage and wells [32] and there was often bitter strife over these.[33]

Sheep and goats were pastured together unless the land was too rocky and barren for sheep. The shepherd led his flock,[34] but on a journey, one shepherd would drive them while another led.[35] At night the sheep were enclosed in a cave or within a sheepfold, a roughly built enclosure made of field stones, preferably near a well [36] and often having a tower for protection.[37] The flocks of several shepherds mingled together at night in one fold in charge of a porter. If flocks

---

[27] Cf. Gordon, *op. cit.*, p. 28.
[28] Prov. 27:27.
[29] Deut. 32:14.
[30] Gen. 32:15.
[31] Gen. 24:35; 32:5.
[32] Gen. 37:14–17.
[33] Gen. 13:7.
[34] Ps. 23:2.
[35] Gen. 33:13 f.
[36] Ex. 2:16 f., Ps. 23:2.
[37] Gen. 35:21. Eder means a muster of animals, hence a flock or herd.

were left in the field, the shepherds arranged shifts for keeping watch, to guard against thieves or beasts of prey, the shepherd protecting them even at the risk of his life. Shepherds wore an outer garment of sheepskin with the wool left on which served as a covering at night and for protection against exposure.

Sheep know the voice of their own shepherd. They follow him, but will not follow a stranger. They are so well acquainted with other members of their own flock that at daybreak each flock assembles itself and starts after its own shepherd. They are carefully counted as they pass in and out of the fold, and often the shepherd, calling his sheep by name, makes them pass under his rod in order to count them. The shepherd carries a club for the defense of his flock, and when any beast of prey approaches, the sheep rush to the shepherd, perhaps at his call or hiss, realizing the safety that his rod assures. "Thy rod and thy staff, they comfort me" [38] derives its meaning from such experience. The shepherd often carries the little lambs in his bosom or under his arm.

The shepherds had dogs to help them.[39] Every shepherd was skilled in the use of the sling, which he fashioned himself. It was a weapon of defense against beasts of prey and of assistance in caring for the flock, for with it he could drop a stone near a wandering sheep or goat so that it would return to the rest of the flock. Shepherds could sling to a great distance, some of them with remarkable precision.[40] The story of David illustrates this.[41]

If the owner of a flock had no son to tend it, he hired a shepherd. Such a hireling received pay in kind, and often in this way he gradually accumulated flocks of his own.[42] Sometimes, as wages, the hireling received one of the man's daughters as a wife, the term of service in this case being from five to seven years.[43] Gen. *31:38–41 is a fine description of the responsibilities and hard lot of a shepherd.

Pastoral life made a permanent impress upon the thought and language of the Hebrews. The nation was spoken of as a "flock" or as "sheep." The leaders of the nation were called "shepherds." In the Shepherd Psalm (*23) Yahweh himself is called the Shepherd of the people. Much later Jesus is portrayed as the Good Shepherd.[44] In fact, the imagery of shepherd life everywhere permeates Biblical literature. Especially choice passages are the Shepherd Psalm just mentioned; Ezk. *34, "Against the Shepherds of Israel"; Jer. *23:1–4, "Woe to the Shepherds"; Prov. *27:23–27, "In Praise of Pastoral Life"; Matt. *18:12 f., the "Parable of the Lost Sheep"; and Jn. *10:1–16, the "Parable of the Good Shepherd."

[38] Ps. 23:4.
[39] Job 30:1.
[40] Jgs. 20:16.
[41] 1 Sam. 17:40, 49.
[42] Gen. 30:28–35.
[43] Gen. 29:15–29.
[44] Jn. 10:14.

Personal Traits of the Nomad

The physically weak could not survive the hardships and monotony of desert life. It called for physical stamina, for large capacity to endure suffering, for courage and tenacity, and for patience. The need for meeting and overcoming sudden danger, danger due not only to people and things of the earth but also to the hostile supernatural beings which the nomad believed were all about him, made him a person of quick decision.[45]

The nomad was strongly emotional. Embraces and kisses characterized all salutations between familiars. They were easily moved to tears and to wailing aloud.[46] Being impulsive, when uncontrolled they were quite capable of violence and rapine.[47] Yet when controlled by reason the nomad might be a peacemaking individual like Abraham,[48] though even he manifested characteristic Oriental guile.[49] The nomad was by nature vengeful, yet by a praiseworthy forbearance he might forego his opportunity for vengeance, as did Joseph.[50]

The nomad was profoundly respectful of other persons, as manifested in his (sometimes even elaborate) courtesy of address.[51] He was deeply loyal to the other members of his group.

Above all, the nomad's attitude towards the world about him was religious. This will be discussed in Chapter 8.

Social Organization

The Biblical Hebrews were interested in the question of the origins of their social institutions and customs which they had inherited from the remote past. The Hebrew mind always thought in terms of persons, and their thinking about their social organization and customs was personalized, i.e., described in terms of the experience of concrete individuals. The origin of any social institution or custom was explained by saying that so and so was the father thereof. For example, how did there ever come to be nomads? "Jabal was the father of such as dwell in tents and have cattle." [52] This genetic formula is employed in the interesting passage, Gen. *4:16–26, to explain the origin of city life (vss. 16 f.) ; of polygamy (vss. 18 f.) ; of nomadism (vs. 20) ; of the arts of music (vs. 21) and metalworking (vs. 22) ; of the social practice of blood revenge (vss. 23 f.) ; of family life (vs. 25) ; and of religious worship (vs. 26).

45 Ex. 4:24 ff.
46 Gen. 33:4; 1 Sam. 20:41.
47 Gen. 34; 49:5, 7.
48 Gen. 13; 21:22–33.
49 Gen. 20.
50 Gen. 45:1a, 4a, 5a; 50:15–21.
51 Gen. 18:1–5; Ex. 18:7; 1 Sam. 25:23–31.
52 Gen. 4:20.

The Family. The family was the constituent unit of Hebrew society. The term "family" not only referred to the individual household, but in its wider sense it meant the clan or tribe, embracing all who traced their descent to a common ancestor and were bound together by common blood.[53] Strangers were admitted into a family or tribe only by adoption and by taking part in a blood ritual. Such a thing as a homeless or unattached individual was unknown. This nomad tribal system profoundly affected the whole social and political life of the Hebrews.

The father was the supreme head of his family, which included his mother, his wives, his concubines, his children, his daughters-in-law, his sons-in-law, relatives, slaves, and any friends within his gates. Gen. 15:2 has interesting implications about the practice of adoption. Abraham complains that if he has no son, his property will be inherited by Eliezer of Damascus. Was Abraham in debt to Eliezer or vice versa? Had Abraham adopted Eliezer to insure clan solidarity and to prevent his property from passing out of the control of his clan? In antiquity the practice was known of a debtor's adopting a creditor in order to keep the property in the family.[54]

At one time the father had the power of life and death over his children.[55] He arranged the marriage of his sons [56] and had the right to sell his daughters in marriage.[57] Children were under obligation to respect and obey their parents, absolutely. Boys were always preferred to girls and were the guardians of their sisters. The children of concubines had the same standing as those of the wives, except that they did not inherit as much of the property.[58] The son remained in his father's family after marriage and his wife automatically became one of the family. The husband had supreme authority over his wife, and in Old Testament times was permitted to divorce her with apparently little cause.[59] Although woman was a chattel, real and deep affection did sometimes exist, as for example between Jacob and Rachel.[60] Num. 12:14 reflects a custom which shows the low estimate that was placed upon women.

Hebrew women were not shut up in a harem, but mingled freely with men in the performance of social duties. When moving, the work of pitching and striking the tents, packing and unpacking the household goods was the task of the women. They tended the flocks,[61]

---

[53] Cf. Josh. 7:14; 1 Sam. 10:21.
[54] This is disclosed in Hurrian documents found at Nuzi. Cf. Cyrus H. Gordon, *The Living Past* (New York: 1941), pp. 156–178, on "Private and Public Life at Nuzi."

[55] Jgs. 11:39.
[57] Ex. 21:7.
[59] Deut. 24:1.
[61] Gen. 29:6.

[56] Gen. 24:48; 28:2.
[58] Gen. 21:10.
[60] Gen. 29, 30.

prepared the meals,[62] invited guests,[63] and with perfect propriety conversed with strangers in public places.[64]

Family ties were strongly felt. Many laws provided for the protection and avenging of the injured and defenseless by their next of kin. Indeed, blood revenge was the supreme social obligation that rested upon the member of any family. "At the hand of every man's brother will I require the life of man. Whoso sheddeth man's blood, by man shall his blood be shed." [65] Tribes were, therefore, homogeneous, and there was the closest community of feeling among the members of any given tribe. It followed that property was practically held in common.

Intertribal relations went on the assumption that tribes were either acknowledged friends or open enemies. For example, Ishmael, the first-born of Abraham, was "a wild ass of a man, with his hand against everyone and everyone's hand against him." [66] The solitary individual, out of relation to any tribe, was devoid of all protection. An interesting example of this is Cain, upon whom Yahweh graciously put a mark to protect him because, as Cain said, "whoever finds me will kill me." [67] The Semite, therefore, invariably thought of himself not as an individual but as a member of some definite group within which all members were on a basis of equality, sharing in responsibilities, tasks, privileges, and esteem. This fact is basic to any understanding of Hebrew social thinking. Thus the family stood for unity, order, and obedience.

One of the most noteworthy features of nomadic life was the practice of hospitality. Gen. *18:1–16 affords a charming picture of Abraham's gracious hospitality toward the strangers, and their appreciation. Gen. *19:1–11 is a repulsive picture of the lack of hospitality in Sodom. Further light on this practice of hospitality is furnished by the distressing story in Jgs. *19:14–27. With gripping emotional climax this story ends with the outraged woman dead "at the door of the house, with her hands upon the threshold," in pathetic appeal to the law of hospitality which had been denied her for no other reason than that she was a woman.

In early times the family was also the center of all religious observances. As head of the family the father erected altars and offered the sacrifices considered essential for the whole group.

The Nature of Patriarchal Government. Under the patriarchal form of government, the will of the tribe was law, and custom was

---

[62] Gen. 18:6. [63] Jgs. 4:18.
[64] Gen. 24:15–25; 29:9 f. On the status of woman, see Millar Burrows, *What Mean These Stones?* (New Haven: 1941), pp. 247 f.
[65] Gen. 9:5b, 6a. 2 Sam. 14:1–17 gives an instance of the principle of blood vengeance. Also Jgs. 8:18–21; 2 Sam. 2:23; 3:27.
[66] Gen. 16:12. [67] Gen. 4:14 f.

the sole authority. In the tribal group there were as many votes as there were separate families, but the word "family" signified a much larger group than it does today, running often to hundreds of members and being more nearly a small clan. The head of the tribe was variously called patriarch, elder, or sheikh. He was chosen by his fellows because of personal prowess, the size of his family, or his wealth. Virtually, he was a king of a small kingdom whose territory extended wherever the members of his family happened to be, and insubordination, even by a son, might be punished with death. He judged the cases of disputants and offenders, and the clan as a whole enforced his decisions.

It is probable that extreme measures were rarely resorted to and that resentment was seldom felt. The ties of blood and affection would usually triumph over every other motive, and the chances are that a culprit, provided that what he had done did not actually menace the peace and security of the group, was oftener excused than punished. Indeed, we actually find laws, enacted in later times when families joined families in community life and the discipline in one family affected the discipline in all others, compelling the over-compassionate father to punish and not spare.[68]

With the rise of the monarchy the patriarchal form of society was somewhat modified but it was never wholly set aside. It is necessary to bear this in mind in order to appreciate much that happened in Hebrew history.

Nomadic society was indeed simple and barren. Anything like comfort was unknown. There were long but not unbroken periods of arduous toil and severe exposure. At times life was exciting, but for the most part it was merely a matter of routine. Rewards were meager, even for the most strenuous effort. Want and privation were frequent visitors. Although there was little to stimulate individual initiative, yet now and then an exceptional individual did advance beyond his fellows.

The Migration of Abraham

Gen. *11:31–12:10, *13:1–18 portrays the wanderings of the patriarch Abraham through the Fertile Crescent in search of a better home. The causes which led to the migration were religious [69] and economic. Ur of the Chaldees and the Aramaean city, Haran, were both famous for the worship of the moon god Sin. Late Jewish tradition, in the Apocryphal book Judith,[70] states that the Hebrews left Chaldea because they would not worship the gods of the country

---

[68] Deut. 13:6–11. Cf. Deut. 19:11 f., 16–21.
[69] Gen. 12:1.   [70] 5:6–9.

and Jewish and Moslem legends represent Abraham as a religious reformer.

The economic cause was the age-old search of the nomad for better pasturage. Abraham and Lot are represented as possessing large flocks and herds. It was the pressure of famine which drove them to Egypt.[71] After their return to Palestine, their readjustment of territory was motivated by overcrowding, with its accompanying insufficiency of food supply, the cause which accounts for the shifting about of all nomads. Abraham and Lot separated because their herdsmen quarreled,[72] and Lot chose what appeared to be the more desirable pasture land.[73]

The ancients regularly ascribed their prosperity or adversity to divine intervention; therefore, overcrowding, famines, ousting by invaders, and the like, which forced them to seek new homes, were naturally looked upon as means by which God accomplished his purposes with men. Such factors doubtless lay behind the religious motivation of Abraham's migration from Ur and from Haran.[74]

Abraham, Isaac, and Jacob are eponymous heroes, i.e., individuals who in their experiences personify the fortunes of whole tribes or families.[75] The story of Abraham can therefore best be understood as a tribal movement. His company must have made up a large caravan. It was evidently a whole clan, perhaps even a tribe, which migrated. Gen. 14 pictures Abraham as able to muster a powerful fighting force, and despite the suspicion that this particular story has not suffered in the telling, other narratives, like that of the quarrels with Lot's herdsmen [76] and with the herdsmen of Abimelech,[77] show that even in those early days the family of Abraham was really as large as a sizable clan.

The Jacob Stories as Tribal History

The stories of Isaac and Jacob reveal the manner of life of nomadic tribes and their continual shifting about the western part of the Fertile Crescent. The Old Testament narrator, as was customary with early storytellers, traces the fortunes of the Abrahamic family through just a few individuals, Isaac and Jacob holding the center of attention and interest. Although there is little history, in the modern sense of the term, in these stories about Abraham or Isaac or Jacob, nevertheless they are rich in material that is descriptive of the early life and customs of the Hebrew people, something which is

[71] Gen. 12 :10.   [72] Gen. 13 :6–9.
[73] Gen. 13 :10 f.   [74] Gen. 12 :1.
[75] Cf. O. J. Baab, *The Theology of the Old Testament* (Nashville: 1949), p. 56.
[76] Gen. 13 :7.   [77] Gen. 21 :25.

even more valuable for a genuine understanding of them than mere bald facts of history would ever have been.

The stories of the rivalry between Esau and Jacob (Gen. *25: 20–34 and Gen. *27) accurately reflect the antipathy between the Edomites and the Israelites. It was always such antipathy that led to the separation and migration of families and tribes. Jacob went to Haran in Mesopotamia and prospered, but at the cost of family friendship (Gen. 29 ff.). From there he returned to Palestine and settled. The account of his migrations and of the doings of his sons is graphically related in Gen. *32–35, *37 f. The purport of these stories is to set forth Jacob as the immediate ancestor of the Hebrew nation, and his twelve sons as the progenitors of the traditional twelve tribes of Israel. "A nomad Aramaean was my father" [78] was the solemn declaration of later Israelites.

Attention was called on page 30 to the two major tribal subdivisions of the Hebrews, viz., the southern tribes (Judah) and the northern tribes (Israel). Another way of expressing this same distinction among the tribes is to classify them as the offspring of Jacob's wives and concubines (Gen. *35:23–26). Under this scheme, the Leah tribes are understood to be those which came from Aram, and the Rachel tribes those which entered Canaan from the south at the time of the general migration in the fifteenth century B.C. The Rachel tribes are those which went down into Egypt under the leadership of Joseph. The offspring of Jacob's concubines, Bilhah and Zilpah, were the least esteemed of the tribes, doubtless because they were regarded as having the most foreign blood. Another scheme of interpretation distinguishes the Jacob tribes who went down to Egypt from the Israel tribes who remained in Canaan, the ultimate union of the two being symbolized by the identification of Jacob with Israel.

The Migration to Egypt

The descendants of Abraham lived for some time, variously estimated as from three to six centuries, in or near the semiarid Negeb. Then, driven desperate by a succession of famine years, they moved to Goshen in the northeastern border of Egypt.[79] Into these bald facts of history the writer of Genesis has woven the charming Joseph stories. These stories prepare the way for the migration to Egypt by relating (Gen. *37–41) how Joseph, the favorite son of Jacob, was sold by his brothers into slavery in Egypt, and how, through his

[78] Deut. 26:5.
[79] An inscription of the Pharaoh Merneptah (1225–1215 B.C.) mentions the giving of permission to some Edomite Bedouins to pasture their flocks near Succoth, in Goshen. While probably not referring to Hebrew clans, it does establish the credibility of the Jacob migration.

ability and fidelity, he rose to the position of governor [80] of that realm.

To date the Jacob migration with accuracy is not possible and the estimates made by scholars vary. In the main, the preferences expressed are for one or the other of two periods. (1) Some argue for the age of the Hyksos conquerors of Egypt. The Hyksos were powerful foreign invaders who seized control of Egypt and ruled the land for a century, 1680–1580 B.C.[81] The term "Hyksos" has conventionally been held to mean "Shepherd Kings," but Breasted interprets the word to mean "Ruler of Countries." Just who the Hyksos were is problematic. They have generally been thought to be Semites, especially because of the Semitic names connected with them. More recent opinion is that they were of Hittite origin, and that in their invasion of Egypt they were followed by a lot of Semites who mixed in with them. Among such Semites, Joseph and Jacob would be included on this line of interpretation. The statement, "So Joseph bought all the land of Egypt for Pharaoh . . . and the land became Pharaoh's," [82] would seem to imply that the Pharaoh himself represented a foreign power dominating Egypt and that during a famine Joseph assisted him to get complete economic control of the country. (2) Many scholars prefer to date the migration to Egypt in the eighteenth dynasty, 1580–1350 B.C., and, more exactly, either in the reign of the genial Ikhnaton, 1375–1358 B.C., or of Tutankhamen, 1358–1350 B.C.[83]

As for the number involved in the migration, Gen. 46 lists seventy, apparently counting only heads of families. The historical nucleus of this story appears to have been the descent into Egypt of a relatively small band. Records prove that not all Hebrews entered Egypt.

In Egypt, these Hebrew shepherds were settled in a district between the Nile Delta and the Asiatic frontier. It was a triangle about ten miles on a side, much more suited to grazing than to farming, and evidently not attractive to Egyptians. Here the Hebrews lived for several generations, but as to what happened there, tradition has not one word to say.

*   *   *

Do the stories in Genesis tell all that was remembered of early days? If not, why were these particular stories or incidents recorded,

---

[80] Gen. 42:6.

[81] They constitute the fifteenth and sixteenth dynasties of Manetho's sequence of Egyptian rulers.

[82] Gen. 47:20. On the Hyksos, cf. Millar Burrows, *What Mean These Stones?* (New Haven: 1941), p. 89; Jack Finegan, *Light From the Ancient Past* (Princeton: 1946), pp. 84–86; G. E. Wright and F. V. Filson, *The Westminster Historical Atlas to the Bible* (Philadelphia: 1945), p. 28; W. F. Albright, *From the Stone Age to Christianity* (Baltimore: 1940), pp. 151 f., 184.

[83] Cf. further, *infra*, p. 98.

and not others? Is there any discoverable basis of selection which gives unity and coherence to the whole?

The author of Genesis, who lived and wrote many centuries after the events he describes, wishes to make clear how, through the centuries, Yahweh's hand had been in unmistakable evidence in the Hebrews' early development. He does not attempt to write history in any real sense of the word, nor yet biography, nor science, nor even a code of ethics or religion. He just points to a series of events or occasions when Yahweh himself had been clearly in the picture, saving the future people from some threat of extinction from outside foe or inner mistake of judgment and directing them to take advantage of an opportunity which would place them far ahead of their rivals. In this basic purpose is to be found the point of every chapter and incident in Genesis. All else was omitted by the author as irrelevant. The author of Genesis intends his readers to understand that from the very beginning the culture of the ancient Hebrews was a God-centered culture. God's purpose in history, as the author of Genesis conceived it, is given in Gen. *45:5–8.

Chapter 6

THE BIRTH OF THE HEBREW NATION

The period to be surveyed in this chapter is commonly called the Period of the Exodus and the Wilderness Wandering. It extends from about 1220 to 1180 B.C. The Exodus is the first watershed in Hebrew history. By a watershed in history is meant an event or sequence of events which gives new direction to or releases fresh forces or influences in the career of a nation. Following the Exodus, Hebrew development moved toward national organization under the urge of forces economic, social, and religious. Not least among the influences which shaped Hebrew development in this period was the creative leadership of Moses, founder of the Hebrew nation and religion.

The materials for a history of this period are the books of Exodus and Numbers, supplemented by Deuteronomy and by the contributions of archaeology. The books of Exodus and Numbers contain the same basic documentary sources as Genesis. What was said about Genesis in the concluding paragraph of Chapter 5 therefore applies equally to Exodus and Numbers.

The Enslavement of the Hebrews in Egypt

The Hebrews who went down to Egypt settled there as guests of the Pharaoh. The time came when this favorable status changed. Ex. *1 graphically portrays the change which followed upon the death of their powerful advocate, Joseph. "Now there arose a new king over Egypt, who knew not Joseph." [1] This implies a change of dynasty and the rise of a monarch who owed no debt to Joseph. If Joseph's service was done for the benefit of one of the Hyksos kings, then it surely would have been forgotten after the Hyksos control of Egypt was broken. They were driven out of the country in 1580 B.C. If Joseph served one of the kings of the eighteenth dynasty in Egypt, such service would cease to be remembered as of importance after that dynasty weakened and gave place to the nineteenth in 1350 B.C. The Pharaoh who reduced the Hebrews to slavery most probably was

---

[1] Ex. 1:8.

Ramses II, mightiest sovereign of the nineteenth dynasty and ruler of Egypt for sixty-seven years, 1292–1225 B.C.

Ramses II enslaved vast numbers of people in order to carry through the ambitious building enterprises by which he sought to enhance his personal glory. A mighty warrior, he sought to recover for Egypt the political control of Palestine and Syria which had been both won and lost by his predecessors of the eighteenth dynasty. He waged a disastrous warfare with the Hittites, who controlled Syria, and thereby damaged his reputation so severely that all Syria and Palestine revolted against him, the revolt spreading even to the frontier forts in the northeastern delta in Egypt itself. Located on this northeastern frontier were these unassimilated foreigners, the Hebrews. Ramses feared that in case of war these Hebrews would side with the enemy.[2] Therefore, to employ them in strengthening the defenses of that border seemed a clever and sensible plan. So they were put to work on the construction of the nearby supply depots, Pithom and Raamses.[3]

Ramses II was at this time engaged in a stupendous building program all up and down the Nile in a desperate effort to restore Egyptian prestige and doubtless to enhance his own as well. He completed the Great Hall of Karnak. Obelisks and colossal statues, especially of himself, were erected in many cities. Two of these (at Tanis and Ramesseum) were originally single blocks of stone weighing nearly a thousand tons apiece. That the Hebrews should have been impressed into these building operations is neither surprising nor unusual. Such forced levies, particularly of foreign residents, were quite the order of the day. The Hebrews did the same thing themselves in later centuries after they had gained the mastery of Canaan.[4] But usual or unusual, such taskwork proved most galling to the liberty-loving Hebrews, especially after the generations of special exemptions they had apparently enjoyed as the kinsmen of Joseph. So they chafed, then rebelled, and finally made their way back through the desert to their former home in the Negeb.

Duration of the Stay in Egypt and Its Effect on the Hebrews

The length of the Egyptian period is uncertain, estimates ranging from about one to more than four centuries. Ex. 12:40 says 430 years.

[2] Ex. 1:10. For such fear Ramses had very good ground. When, in the time of Ikhnaton, Egypt's hold on Palestine and Syria had relaxed, native princes in Canaan did assert their independence of the Pharaoh by uniting with the invading Habiri. Cf. *supra*, pp. 48 f.
[3] Ex. 1:11. On the identification of Pithom and Raamses, cf. G. E. Wright and F. V. Filson, *The Westminster Historical Atlas to the Bible* (Philadelphia: 1945), p. 37.   [4] Jgs. 1:28, 30b, 33b.

The Septuagint, the Samaritan Pentateuch, and Josephus say 215 years.[5] Gen. 15:13 (really written a long time after the event) records a prediction of 400 years. Gen. 15:16 explains this to be "four generations," which Ex. 6:16–20 confirms by naming "Levi . . . Kohath . . . Amram . . . Moses." The longer period is accepted by scholars who reckon the Pharaoh of Joseph as one of the Hyksos, while those who reckon that ruler to be one of the eighteenth dynasty find the shorter period adequate.[6] It is exceedingly difficult to estimate the cultural effect of the sojourn in Egypt upon the Hebrews. On the negative side we know that they went into Egypt as nomads and that they came out nomads. Located in Goshen, a grazing rather than a farming land, they were practically isolated from the Egyptians and consequently almost untouched by Egyptian civilization. To the Egyptian, every shepherd was an abomination or virtual outcast so that it is fair to infer that the Hebrews in Goshen had little direct contact with the native people. Yet they seem to have learned some rudimentary agriculture, reminiscences of which are commented upon in Num. 11:5 and Deut. 11:10. There are hints that Egyptian forms of worship did make some impress upon them. Their later enslavement, coupled with the inhumanity to which they were subjected, doubtless antagonized them in the end against things Egyptian. It may well be that here and there an exceptional Hebrew had opportunity to become acquainted with the Egyptian culture, such as Moses, who was reared at the court of the Pharaoh [7] and whom Acts 7:22 represents as "instructed in all the wisdom of the Egyptians." Tradition has it that Moses was educated by the priests of On, in the very same temple where Ikhnaton had earlier been educated. Also there were two Israelite clans, Ephraim and Manasseh, which bore a deep impress of Egypt. Ephraim and Manasseh were sons of Joseph, half Egyptian by birth [8] and apparently even more Egyptian by upbringing. In reverting to nomadic life, as Jacob's descendants did after the Exodus, much if not most of the borrowed culture was inevitably lost. Yet the Hebrews could not have been quite the people they became had they never lived in Egypt.

The Leadership of Moses

One measure which the Pharaoh of the oppression adopted for curbing the growing Hebrew power was the killing of male infants.

[5] *Antiquities*, Book II, 15:2.

[6] It is customary to reckon three generations to a century. Four generations would, therefore, imply a period of 133 years or at most 150 years. If the exodus occurred in 1220 B.C. (cf. *infra*, p. 101), an estimate of 133 years brings us back to the reign of Tutankhamen and an estimate of 150 years brings us back to the reign of Ikhnaton as the date of the migration of Joseph and Jacob to Egypt. Again, the estimate of either 400 or 430 years brings us back to the period of the Hyksos domination of Egypt.   [7] Ex. 2:10.   [8] Gen. 41:50.

Ex. *2 tells how Moses was saved from the effect of that edict, and how he was reared at the royal court. The chapter further describes his violent inner revolt at the indignities to which his fellow Hebrews were being subjected, until one day he murdered an Egyptian slave driver and had to flee the country. Somehow evading the guards who patroled the eastern border, he fled across the Sinai Peninsula. Then he "dwelt in the land of Midian." [9] Thither he carried with him the problem of the suffering of his people.

Midian lay near the north end of the Gulf of Akabah. The Midianites were a people whose religious heritage was akin to that of Moses' own people. Moses' life in the new environment is described in Ex. *3 f. Chapter 3 describes the profound religious experience which Moses had in Midian. Under the impulse of that experience he returned to Egypt to deliver his people from oppression. With a well-thought-out plan of action, the result of years of deliberation, he returned at a most favorable time, for the statement in Ex. 2:23 implies the death of Ramses II. That monarch died in 1225 B.C., being more than ninety years of age. During the latter years of this monarch his vigorous rule relaxed and the empire weakened internally. His son Merneptah was himself an old man when he succeeded to the throne. His reign (1225–1215 B.C.) was marked by ominous uprisings and even invasions of lower Egypt. Syria and Palestine revolted, though they were not as yet strong enough to maintain their independence. The Egyptian Delta was invaded by Libyans and northern Mediterranean peoples and was saved from capture only after a stubborn struggle. Egypt was on the defensive and for sixty years the Pharaohs struggled merely to preserve the empire. It was an opportune time for the Hebrews to strike for freedom.[10] It was Moses, aided by his brother Aaron, who fired them to the attempt.

Moses' Demand for the People's Release

Moses' initial move was a courteous but insistent request that the Hebrews be allowed to go beyond the borders of Egypt for a three-day celebration of an ancient religious festival. Such a request would be readily understood, for in that day each nation had its particular god and it was not supposed that a god could be worshiped beyond the borders of his own land. The demand of Moses appeared to be, therefore, merely that the Hebrews be allowed to go only far enough to get within the bounds of their own deity's land so that they could worship him acceptably by sacrifice. But the demand was that they be

---

[9] Ex. 2:15.
[10] On the date of the Exodus, cf. G. E. Wright, "The Present State of Biblical Archeology," in H. R. Willoughby, *The Study of the Bible Today and Tomorrow* (Chicago: 1947), pp. 83 ff.

allowed to go as a people.[11] For the Pharaoh to grant the request as made would have been tantamount to acknowledging the integrity of the Hebrews as a people. Back in the days of Joseph they had been regarded by the Pharaoh as a guest nation residing within Egypt's borders, but now they were not regarded as having any political integrity or rights for they were merely slaves of the Egyptians. By this insistence Moses was trying to eliminate slave-mindedness from the Hebrews themselves and to replace it by a sense of group solidarity. He was preparing for the birth of a nation. Ex. *5:1–6:1; *7:8–12:36 describes a series of disasters which befell the Egyptians, reinforcing this demand and ultimately leading to its granting.

The Deliverance at the Red Sea

To go from Egypt to Palestine the Israelites had a choice of three possible routes. "The way of the Philistines" [12] was much the shortest, provided that one wished to go directly to Canaan, for it followed right along the coast. It was, however, a heavily guarded route because this was the military highway always taken by the armies of Egypt and Egypt's enemies. Therefore the Hebrews avoided it.[13] A second route led directly to the head of the Gulf of Suez. Some scholars, following the suggestion of the Jewish historian Josephus of the first century after Christ,[14] identify this as the scene of the crossing. For with a mountain (the modern Jebel Atakah) at their right and the sandy marshes in front, they would be "entangled in the land" and "shut in by the wilderness." [15] The third alternative, and the route that probably was taken, was "the way of the wilderness," [16] a caravan route which led directly eastward through the wilderness of Paran to the port of Elath at the head of the Gulf of Akabah. Moses, it is to be recalled, had just returned after spending "forty years" with the Midianites, which people, it is now generally believed, lived not far from the Mount Seir Range in the vicinity of the Gulf of Akabah.

Ex. *14 dramatically tells how the troops of the Pharaoh pursued the Hebrews until the latter seemed to be caught in a trap. However, at the *Yâm-Sûph* (literally, the "Sea of Reeds," translated "Red Sea" in most versions) the Hebrews were surprisingly delivered, while their Egyptian pursuers perished by hundreds. The precise site of the crossing of the *Yâm-Sûph* is problematic. Certainly it was not the Red Sea as that term is used today. It is not likely that it was

---

11 Ex. 5:11 ff., 7:16; 8:1, 8, 20; 9:1, 13; 10:3.
12 Ex. 13:17.   13 Ex. 13:17.
14 *Antiquities*, Book II, 15:1.   15 Ex. 14:3.
16 Ex. 13:18. Cf. G. E. Wright and F. V. Filson, *The Westminster Historical Atlas to the Bible* (Philadelphia: 1945), pp. 37–42.

any part of the present Gulf of Suez. It may have been one of the chain of shallow pools farther north known as the "Bitter Lakes." However, 1 Kgs. 9:26 clearly identifies the *Yâm-Sûph* as the Gulf of Akabah. This is supported by Num. 21:4; Deut. 2:1; and Jer. 49:21 which indicate that the *Yâm-Sûph* lay in Edomite territory.[17] W. O. E. Oesterley locates the "Red Sea crossing" here at the Gulf of Akabah. Mount Sinai, located nearby (in the Mount Seir Range), was a volcano.[18] Oesterley's view is that an eruption of this volcano was attended by an earthquake and temporary upheaval of the sea floor.[19] This was the occasion of the Hebrews' escape and the Egyptian disaster. Into this narrative of Ex. 14 are woven three strands of documents, the simplest and most straightforward stating that "Yahweh caused the sea to go back by a strong east wind all the night, and made the sea dry land." [20] On this bared strip the Hebrews crossed, whereas the chariots of the Egyptians who attempted to follow somewhat later were hopelessly mired as "the sea returned to its wonted flow when the morning appeared." [21] The expression, "the waters were a wall unto them, etc." is simply a Hebrew poetic way of saying they were safe from any flanking movement.[22] This deliverance at the *Yâm-Sûph* was always looked back upon as the birthnight of the nation. "The Song of Moses" (Ex. *15:1–18) is a national ode commemorating this great event.

The Wilderness Wandering

If, as seems probable, Merneptah was the Pharaoh of the exodus, the date of these events would be *circa* 1220 B.C. The number of Hebrews leaving Egypt at this time is a puzzle. Ex. 1:15 implies that they were so few that two midwives sufficed for all of them. Ex. 6:16–20 implies a relatively small group. Ex. 12:37 states 600,000 men,[23] which would make a total of some two million individuals when women and children are included. The Hebrew word translated "thousand" in Ex. 12:37, etc., also means "a family group," i.e., six hundred families rather than six hundred thousand. Jgs. 5:8 estimates their number a whole century later at forty thousand. The smaller number is to be preferred in view of what is known of the limited area and productivity of Goshen. It comprises less than one hundred square miles and could hardly sustain over four thousand population.

---

[17] Moffatt translates *Yâm Sûph* as "Gulf of Akâbah" in Num. 14:25; 21:4; Deut. 1:40; 2:1; and everywhere else as "Reed Sea."
[18] Ex. 19:18; Deut. 4:11 f.; Jgs. 5:4 f.; Ps. 68:7 f.
[19] Cf. Oesterley and Robinson, *Hebrew Religion* (New York: 1937), pp. 141–146.
[20] Ex. 14:21b.   [22] Cf. 1 Sam. 25:16; Zech. 2:5.
[21] Ex. 14:27b.   [23] Cf. Num. 1:46; 26:51.

The Route to Mount Sinai (Horeb). It is impossible, and fortunately not important, to identify all the places mentioned in the desert itinerary from Egypt to Mount Sinai (Ex. 15:22–17:16; 19:1; Num. 33:1–15). Even the location of Sinai itself is not a settled matter. Since the sixth century after Christ it has been traditional to identify Sinai with Jebel Serbal or Jebel Musa, mountain peaks at the south end of the Peninsula of Sinai. If this be correct, then the route taken by the Hebrews was probably along the east shore of the Gulf of Suez. This would have taken them past Egyptian mines guarded by troops of the Pharaoh and would have brought them into fresh perils. There is no hint of their having encountered any Egyptian forces after the passage of the sea, and this identification of Sinai is very dubious. It seems preferable to identify Sinai as one of the peaks in the Mount Seir Range in Midian.[24] The Hebrew line of march doubtless was directly eastward across Paran (presumably the route which Moses himself traversed when he fled from Egypt to Midian, and again when he returned) and thence northward along the western foothills of Mount Seir.

Nature of the Journey. As we picture this group journeying through the wilderness, we must keep in mind that they were shepherds and herders wandering about in search of water and pasture.[25] Their diet was mainly milk, butter, and meat from their flocks, supplemented by manna[26] and quails. They were an unorganized band being slowly shaped into a nation by their leader, Moses.

The Covenant at Sinai. The story of the sacred covenant entered into at Mount Sinai (Ex. *19, *24:1–8, *34:10–28) gives the essence of the early Mosaic religion as recalled in later centuries. Its religious significance will be studied in Chapter 8. This covenant was essentially the consciousness of national security under the pledged protection of Yahweh, the deity in whose power and dependability they had come to repose absolute confidence. The people covenanted to worship only Yahweh,[27] and Yahweh covenanted to bring the people into possession of the land of Canaan.[28] How greatly needed was such a solemn pledge is shown by the golden calf incident that took place even while Moses was on the sacred mountain getting the "tables of the law" (Ex. *32). It reveals plainly the spell which the Egyptian

---

[24] Cf. Ex. 3:1; Jgs. 5:4 f., and Deut. 33:2, which should read "Meribath-Kadesh" instead of "the ten thousands of holy ones." Hab. 3:3.
[25] Cf. Ex. 12:32, 38.
[26] Manna is by many interpreters understood to be the exudation of the tamarisk tree. Langdon thinks the word may be derived from the ancient Sumerian word *ma-nu*, a tree sacred to the deity Anu, and usually associated with the tamarisk and date palm in the ancient texts. Stephen Herbert Langdon, *Semitic Mythology* (Boston: 1931), pp. 97 f.
[27] Ex. 34:14.
[28] Ex. 34:11.

Apis [29] cult had woven over many of the Hebrews, as well as their little confidence at the time in the God of Moses.

The testimony of this covenant was the Ethical Decalogue of Ex. *20:1–17 (cf. also Deut. *5:6–21). Thus were the foundations of Israel's social and religious institutions laid at Sinai. What they were we can learn from Ex. 20:22–23:33, "the Book of the Covenant," [30] now regarded by many scholars as the oldest codification of Hebrew law in existence.

Social Progress During the Wilderness Period.   Reference has already been made to the vast improvement in morale observable within the four decades of wilderness life. Whether or not there was appreciable increase in numbers is problematic. The clans did gain valuable experience in the art of organization and co-operation, and in a measure they improved their aptitude for self-government. For this, generous credit is given Moses' father-in-law for valuable suggestions. Ex. *18:13–27 clearly indicates Moses' indebtedness to the Midianites (through his father-in-law) for the scheme of social administration which he set up for the Hebrews at Kadesh. This same pattern of subdividing the social group under rulers of thousands, of hundreds, fifties, and tens was known among the Edomites, among the desert Arabs, and among the Philistines. It was effective for warfare as well as for social control.

There was, of course, plenty of wrangling and friction, and threatened dissolution, instanced in Num. 11, 12, 16, but each case of disaffection and revolt seemed to end in a more closely knit unity and firmer organization. Num. *16, which is a dramatic account of a rebellion against Moses' leadership, shows the kind of human stuff with which he had to work.

There was a growing respect for law and its orderly processes, in contradistinction to the nomadic emphasis upon a clan's complete freedom from external restraint and upon the single law of blood vengeance. Moses adjudicated interclan complaints and his decisions constituted the precedents on which was built up a code of recognized law (cf. Ex. 18:13–26). This is doubtless the basis of the later Hebrew tradition ascribing to Moses the making of their entire legislative code. He did, indeed, establish a basic principle of justice which was capable of extension to all the Hebrews' needs as those developed from generation to generation.

Deep and lasting changes in religion and worship also occurred in this period. The Old Testament writers are silent as to what went on religiously in the Egyptian period, but circumstantial evidence

---

[29] Apis was the sacred bull of Egyptian worship.
[30] Ex. 24:7. Cf. *infra*, pp. 284–287.

intimates that many Hebrews came to esteem the deities of the rich and powerful Egyptians. That they so quickly turned their backs upon all this and learned to cling with passionate, whole-souled devotion to Yahweh, the deity whose very name had only so recently been strange to them, is significant of the great transformation that came over them. By the time they launched their final advance into Canaan it was in the supreme confidence that defeat was unthinkable, since Yahweh marched in the van. Through constant daily association with Moses, the "man of faith," in his simple "Tent of Meeting" where he "talked with God face to face" (Ex. *33:7–11), and by looking at the "Ark of the Covenant" which symbolized the very presence of the deity (Num. *10:35 f.), the Sinai Covenant at last became a living reality to the Hebrews.

During this wilderness period Kadesh was their central rendezvous.[31] There is a Kadesh-barnea, some fifty miles south of Beersheba, which has the most abundant water supply of any place on the Sinai Peninsula, and many think this to be the Kadesh referred to. It was not only an oasis but also a sanctuary that was resorted to by tribes that were either kindred or at least friendly to the Hebrews. About this place the Hebrews lived for a generation, still in a seminomadic state and happy to possess grasslands and water. Their numbers increased and the time came when Kadesh no longer was ample for them. They therefore turned their eyes once more toward Canaan where generations earlier their fathers had pitched their tents.

The wilderness period is always spoken of as lasting "forty years," obviously a round number. It was long enough for the generation which had grown up in serfdom to pass away and for a new generation of hardy, desert-bred warriors to grow up. Those who, at the close of the wilderness period, successfully stormed the Judean cities were a quite different lot from the horde which fled from Egypt four decades earlier. Without a dissenting voice the Hebrews of later centuries gave credit for this change to Moses. Unquestionably he was a remarkable man, one of the great figures of Hebrew history. By his personality he held the people together when discouragements and jealousies threatened to scatter them in roaming fragments.

The Approach to Canaan

The Failure to Enter from the South. An advance of less than 100 miles northward from Kadesh-barnea would have brought the Hebrews into the very heart of Canaan. They considered the possibility of proceeding that way, but scouts sent out in advance

[31] Num. 33:16–36 gives their itinerary from Sinai to Kadesh, and Deut. 1:2 states that it was eleven days' journey.

stressed the difficulties of such an attempt. Southern Canaan was well defended against invasion from the south by the rugged nature of the country. Its inhabitants were already seasoned fighters, in sharp contrast to the Hebrews. Such daring spirits as Joshua and Caleb were ready to make the venture,[32] but the people as a whole were timid and afraid. When, after much vacillating indecision, they finally did make a tardy, halfhearted attempt, they were promptly and decisively repulsed (Num. *13:17–14:45).

The Route to the Jordan. Having failed in the attempt to enter the land from the south, there was but one alternative, viz., to try from the east. This involved a long, hard march through the country east of the Dead Sea to a point north of that body of water, from which they could cross the Jordan.

To get east of the Dead Sea, they first sought to go by the shortest way, directly northeast through the territory of Edom. But the king of Edom refused them passage and fought them off.[33] They were therefore obliged to make a long detour southward toward the head of the Gulf of Akabah, and thence northward on the east side of the Mount Seir Ridge into the land of Moab.[34] The Moabite Plateau, along its eastern edge,[35] proved easier going, but to reach their next objective, the slopes overlooking the Jordan just north of the Dead Sea, they had to fight their way through. In a series of sharp conflicts, King Sihon of the Amorites and King Og of Bashan were vanquished.[36] Thereupon the Hebrews "encamped in the plains of Moab beyond the Jordan at Jericho" [37] where their presence was of such intense concern to King Balak of Moab that he tried to get a soothsayer named Balaam to pronounce a curse upon the intruders in the superstitious hope that their power might be weakened by magic. Num. *22:5–24:25 is a humorous account of the incident.

The Passing of Moses

The pre-eminent interest in the study of history is in persons. Movements are important, but men are more so. What happens to mankind in the mass is due to the interplay of forces, personal as well as impersonal. Man in the mass has never conceived any great idea, fashioned any noble ideal, or initiated any cultural movement. Such things come from creative personalities. The charm of Biblical history lies in the persons whom we meet in the pages of the Bible. In Moses

---

[32] The clan of Caleb did finally conquer the area about Hebron (Josh. 14:6–15; 15:13 f.; Jgs. 1:20). 1 Sam. 25 is a delightful story about a Calebite.
[33] Num 20:14–21.   [34] Num. 20:22–21:20.
[35] Num. 21:11.   [36] Num. 21:21–22:1.
[37] Num. 22:1. On The Route to the Jordan, cf. Nelson Glueck, *The Other Side of the Jordan* (New Haven: 1940), pp. 128–150.

we meet the first of the truly great ones of Israel. Of all the forces—economic, political, and social—which helped to shape the history of the Hebrews in this period, the greatest was the genius of Moses. He was the real creator of the Hebrew nation and the founder of the Hebrew faith. He has through the ages been revered as the lawgiver of Israel and the first of the prophets. He was "the man of God" [38] and the statement "there hath not arisen a prophet since in Israel like unto Moses, whom Yahweh knew face to face" [39] accurately represents Hebrew sentiment in later centuries. The nation mourned his death for thirty days, after which the leadership of Israel passed to a man of a younger generation, to one whom Moses had long been training to succeed him, Joshua the son of Nun. Num. *27:18–23 tells of the solemn commissioning of Joshua, and Deut. *34 of the death of Moses and how he was mourned by Israel.

* * *

We stand now at the second watershed in Hebrew history. All that has transpired up to now falls within the nomadic era. Just beyond lies the social and cultural transition to established life in the land of Canaan attendant upon the definitive conquest of the land by the Hebrews.

[38] Deut. 33:1; Josh. 14:6; Ezr. 3:2, Ps. 90, title. Moses is an Egyptian name, *Mes, Mesu,* which means "son of"—usually of some god, as in *Ramses* = "Son of Ra" or Thutmose = "Son of Thath." Professor Knopf suggests delightfully that "an Egyptian princess, unacquainted with the Hebrew language, called her little foundling 'sonny.'" [*The Old Testament Speaks* (New York: 1933), p. 82.]
[39] Deut. 34:10.

Chapter 7

THE ANTECEDENTS OF HEBREW LITERATURE

In Chapter 4, attention was directed to the highly developed culture that existed in the ancient Biblical world when the Hebrew clans first emerged from the desert. In chapters to follow, we shall see these Hebrews steadily absorbing and adapting this culture and ultimately developing one of their own, of which two major features have proved to be permanent contributions to the world's civilization, viz., literature and religion. We now inquire what seeds of this later creative development are discernible in the nomadic era. In the present Chapter we shall consider the antecedents of Hebrew literature, and in the next, the beginnings of Hebrew religion.

Storytelling as a Social Institution Among the Early Hebrews

Picture such nomads in their times of relaxation, a clan group gathered about their campfire in the evening in front of some tent, or a half dozen shepherds huddled together, their flocks safe in the sheepfold over which they will later arrange to keep watch in shifts throughout the night. Some one of the group tells a story. It may be about an incident of the day's experience which stood out above the usual uneventful routine. Or it may be about some memorable incident that occurred long before in that corner of the countryside where their tents are pitched for the night. Or perhaps some wandering storyteller has come by, and for food and shelter entertains the group with his repertoire. Such campfire storytelling may continue into the night.

This social custom characterized not only the roving clan but also the village group after the Hebrews took up a more settled life in Canaan. Storyteller and listeners gathered at the community well or cistern, or in the broad places before the village gate, or at the local sanctuary on occasions of community religious feasts. Just such groups may be seen among the Arabs today, both out-of-doors among tent dwellers and villagers and even in the homes of the well to do where one may meet the professional storyteller seated on a divan with a group of listeners arranged about him on the floor. Just as there are such professional reciters among the Arabs today, so there were among the ancient Hebrews.

What stories went the rounds of such groups far back in nomadic days? Just such tales as we find in Genesis and Exodus and in parts of Numbers. Indeed it was by just such oral tradition that those tales were handed down generation after generation until finally (but not before the ninth century B.C.) they were reduced to writing. We can well imagine that after each trek by a clan the stories of Abraham's migrations would be rehearsed (Gen. *12 f.). The occasion of a wedding, either among tent dwellers or among villagers, would certainly call for a recital of the story of Isaac and Rebekah (Gen. *24). Women working at their domestic tasks in the home doubtless took delight in this charming idyll, and its leisurely recital no doubt dispelled the monotony of their drab routine. Shepherds at all times would relish the tales about the wily shepherd Jacob, particularly if the day happened to have something analogous to Jacob's experience (Gen. *27–33). The stories about Joseph would furnish themes for a variety of occasions and give a narrator wide scope for exercising his art (Gen. *37, *39–48). And we can believe that for those who went through it, the Exodus from Egypt was an exciting topic for a long time (Ex. *1–14). Was the day marked by some sort of quarrel? Perhaps it was over the water supply. The story of the quarrel of Isaac's and Abimelech's herdsmen would suit their mood (Gen. *26:18–22). Did the group perpetrate or repel a raid? If so, there would be call for the story of Abraham's separation from Lot (Gen. *13), of Abraham's rescue of Lot (Gen. *14), of the rebellion of Korah (Num. *16), of the battle with the Amalekites (Ex. *17:8–16), and the like. Had there been a jealous quarrel among the women? Then the story of the expulsion of Hagar (Gen. *16, *21) or of Jacob's wives (Gen. *30:1–24) would be recalled. Or were the members of the group in a religious mood because it was new moon festival, or Passover, or other feast? Then the story of Jacob's religious experience at Bethel (Gen. *28:10–22) or of Moses' religious experience in Midian (Ex. *3) would be recalled. The Passover feast would call up the story of the departure from Egypt. An occasion of sacrifice would bring out again the story of Abraham's attempted sacrifice of Isaac (Gen. *22). And as their minds got to pondering about God and the world, the stories about creation (Gen. *2) and the Garden of Eden (Gen. *3) and the flood (Gen. *6–8) and the destruction of Sodom and Gomorrah (Gen. *19:1–29) would be rehearsed.

The Characteristics of Early Hebrew Stories

Early Hebrew stories were short stories. The Joseph stories are fairly long but they are really a series of short tales. The storyteller worked out a genuine plot interest by a swiftly moving succession of incidents, and he did not waste words. He made the action vivid, even dramatic. He told his tale with an emphasis on some turn of events or on some trait in an individual in order to make clear his point, for he always told his story with a purpose. Such emphasis would vary both with occasions and with groups. Such differences of emphasis found their way into the written stories when they were finally compiled, for example in Genesis.

Perhaps the most significant element of such storytelling was the depicting of human character. A dominant trait in one individual is offset by a contrasting trait in another, e.g., Esau and Jacob. This is why the Genesis stories mirror so clearly the personal traits of the nomad.[1] The characters in the stories are, moreover, highly individualized. The primitive Semitic mind did not think abstractly or impersonally. The social experiences of the clan were told with delightful invention as the experiences of one individual. It is for this reason that the Abraham, Jacob, and Joseph stories are construed by the historian of today as tribal history.

The storyteller ended his tale abruptly. That was both part of his art and an expression of his own psychological nature, for the nomad is characteristically abrupt.

We can picture the narrator speaking with animation and appropriate gesture, making characters and events realistic to listeners who gave free play to their imagination to follow the tale. Even in their written form the stories have all the vividness and vitality of real life.

Once invented, these popular tales spread quickly from clan to clan. The same repertoire would be repeated in different clans, but with variations in tone and quality and emphasis. Just such variations can be detected in the Genesis stories which were gathered out of different clans by the compiler of the Book of Genesis. An excellent illustration is the story about Hagar; in Gen. 16 there is an emphasis and a social background quite different from those of Gen. 21. In Chapter 17 we shall study in detail the characteristics of the different sources that make up the Book of Genesis. To enter into that subject here would be misleading, for none of these tales existed in written form at the point of time we have reached, viz., 1185 B.C.

Hebrew Folklore

Much of what we have in the early chapters of Genesis is folklore. To call it folklore is not to cast upon it any aspersion, for folklore

[1] Cf. *supra*, p. 88.

means simply folk learning. Many persons think of folklore as a mass of superstitious myths and legends about improbable and exaggerated exploits which are entertaining but unedifying. Such ideas of folklore have been based upon Greek, Roman, Norse, and similar myths. It is of course inevitable that folklore should contain elements of belief no longer accepted literally, for modern science and discovery have enlightened us about many things not understood in ancient times, and folklore is simply the learning of peoples in primitive epochs. Inevitably it reflects primitive ways and primitive standards, for it was a channel by which customs and conventions from the remote past were preserved and passed down from generation to generation unchanged, so far as that was humanly possible. That is why it goes by the name of "lore," i.e., "learning"; each new generation was expected to become letter-perfect in it. Indeed, no nation can faithfully depict its early religious and cultural history otherwise.[2]

There is something refreshing in the thought that the Bible preserves specimens of such folklore, since it proves the Hebrews to have been less ponderously solemn and more vivaciously human than we would otherwise picture them. It is a real relief to find that with them, as with other branches of the human race, religion did not sap spontaneity and joy in living but rather enhanced those qualities.

Folklore in the Bible is to be recognized by certain characteristics. (1) There is in folklore a certain naïveté, a freshness and a seeming unconsciousness of any moralizing or didactic motive. This absence of the didactic is the more remarkable when we recall that folklore was looked upon as learning. In contrast to the didactic style, the Biblical folklore gives full play to the emotions so that a spontaneous frankness and directness results. (2) Folklore is communal in character; i.e., it is a form of expression in which all members of the community are able to share with equal enjoyment, for it deals invariably with themes which treat of human experiences that are the common possession of all. (3) Since it begins in oral form, folklore tends on the one hand to conciseness and on the other to rhythmic and often poetic structure. (4) Folklore is conspicuously objective; i.e., it depicts feelings concretely through the speech and action of the characters, but it never examines or speculates upon those feelings themselves. The reader of folklore is therefore borne along upon the full tide of the emotional experiences depicted in the tale, identifies himself with the characters who take part in it, and feels with them. All of this is better comprehended if we take some specific examples by which to illustrate.

[2] Cf. W. F. Albright, *From the Stone Age to Christianity* (Baltimore: 1940), pp. 33–38.

One of the earliest bits of folklore is the "Song of Lamech," also called the "Song of the Sword" (Gen. *4:23 f.). In its present setting it ostensibly preserves verbatim the fierce exultant chant of a certain Lamech of antiquity on the day when he boasted that he was a person who avenged "seventy and sevenfold." But why mention a matter like that? Why choose to preserve so brutal and blatant a speech as the one utterance by which the name of Lamech should pass into history? The reason is that this was the conventional chant of the blood avenger, the chant by which he lashed his own feelings and resolution to fever heat and steeled himself to risk life and limb to avenge the family honor in accordance with the code of his age. For in the hour of insult each avenger sought to become a Lamech and thus to hold the respect and admiration of his group.

Far more pleasant is the charming little "Song of the Well" which, in Num. *21:17 f., is said to have been sung in a burst of ecstatic release from stark fear when, facing death from thirst in the parched desert through which they were traveling under the leadership of Moses, they succeeded in finding water by digging. But why write out the full text of this song? Why not be content with saying that in this region they would have perished of thirst had they not been fortunate enough to strike water upon digging? Because here was an excellent opportunity to bring in *the* folk song which was always sung as a feature of the ceremony of well dedication. Today the Arabs of certain districts sing a strikingly similar song at the dedication of their wells. It runs thus:

> Spring up, O well,
> Flow copiously.
> Drink and disdain not,
> With a staff have we dug it.

Much of Gen. 1–11 is folklore, i.e., it is early Hebrew learning taught through the medium of stories and gnomic poems, the sources of which lie far back in the dim ages of fantasy and myth. Our enlarging knowledge of other ancient literatures, particularly Babylonian, makes it abundantly clear that the stories about creation, about the origin of suffering and sorrows in the world, and about how there came to be different races and different languages represent what was generally believed by mankind in the dim past. Thus the Babylonian story of a great flood closely parallels the Bible flood story, even in numerous minute details. How did they come to be so much alike? It was pointed out in a previous chapter that the ancient Babylonian culture overspread the entire Fertile Crescent from Hammurabi's time onward, and was absorbed by the Semitic populations all along the Crescent.[3] These Babylonian creation and flood stories were carried along, of course, by oral telling, on the tide of such spreading Babylonian culture. That is how they reached the Hebrews. The Hebrews then absorbed and passed on this Semitic lore. Of course the Hebrews retold such stories in their own way. By inventing and repeating such lore they were giving expression to that basic urge in the human mind which among mature people gives rise to science and philosophy.

The Beginnings of Hebrew Poetry

In the first section of this chapter we tried to visualize a group of nomads gathered before some tent, listening to one of their number. Emotion registered high on such occasions, and under this stress of feeling, thought found expression in rhythmic form, i.e., in brief poem or song, like the "Song of Lamech" and the "Song of the Well," both of which evidence all the characteristic features of folklore.

The distinguishing feature of Hebrew poetry is parallelism, i.e., balance of thought. Hebrew poetry does not depend on words that rhyme, though there are instances of rhyme; nor does it depend on meter, i.e., upon the number, quantity, and accent of syllables, though there is a kind of rhythm produced by the stresses of accent in speaking the words. Its poetic character depends not at all upon words but upon ideas, and its rhythm is a rhythm of thought. This feature of parallelism, found regularly in all poems of the Bible, characterized the Hebrew folk songs long before any of them were reduced to writing. The snatches of folk poems that we find in Genesis, Exodus, and Numbers evidence the three major kinds of parallelism which characterize all Hebrew poetry found in the Bible.[4]

Synonymous Parallelism. The unit of parallelism is the couplet of two lines in which the thought of the second line bears a certain relationship to the thought of the first. When the second line simply repeats the thought of the first, it is technically called "synonymous parallelism."

An example of this is the "Song of Lamech" (Gen. 4:23 f.) which consists of three couplets. In the first couplet, "Adah and Zillah" in the first line are referred to again in the second line as the "wives of Lamech." The synonymous character of "hear my voice" and "hearken unto my speech" is obvious. The second couplet,

> For a mán have I slaín for my woúnd,
> And a yoúng man for the sáke of my bruíse

---

[3] *Vid. supra,* pp. 67–72.
[4] On the poems in the Pentateuch, cf. R. H. Pfeiffer, *Introduction to the Old Testament* (New York: 1941), pp. 271–281.

does not mean that there were two instances of revenge. The assertion in the first line that a man had been killed is explained in the second line by the additional information that he was a young man, while the wound mentioned in the first line is explained in the second as having consisted of bruises.

Synthetic Parallelism.   The second line of a couplet may add an increment to the thought of the first line, either to explain what is meant by the first line or to round out to completion the thought begun in it. This is variously called "synthetic parallelism," or "supplemental," or "incremental," or "complementary," or "constructive parallelism." An illustration of this is found in "The Song of Miriam" in Ex. *15:1.

> I will síng unto Yahwéh, for he hath tríumphed glóriously:
> The hórse and his ríder hath he thrówn into the séa.

This couplet is a striking illustration of a folk song. That it was originally the spontaneous expression of the joyous emotion of a group is only too evident when one tries to feel for oneself the release felt by the Israelites upon the occasion of their escape from the Egyptians. Fancy someone in the crowd calling out this couplet. He has voiced what everybody was feeling. Instantly the crowd catches up the couplet and sings it back antiphonally.[5] The rhythm of the song leads to the rhythm of a dance. "And Miriam the prophetess, the sister of Aaron, took a timbrel in her hand; and all the women went out after her with timbrels and with dances."[6] Thus we have a poem which was the product of direct experience at the very moment of the experience itself. It furnished a choice theme for a much later, more reflective, poet who expanded the brief original into the long poem which the compiler of Exodus included in vss. 2–20 of the chapter, but this belongs with written literature and not with folklore.

Antithetic Parallelism.   There is a third type of parallelism in which the second line of a couplet states the antithesis of the first line. In the "Blessing of Isaac" (Gen. *27:27 ff.), which breathes the very spirit of primitive tribal superiority consciousness, we find an example of "antithetic parallelism" in the third couplet of the final verse (29):

> Cúrsed be thóse that cúrse thee,
> And bléssed thóse that bléss thee.

Meter.   The primitive folk songs from which the foregoing couplets are quoted belong to prewritten Hebrew literature. They were for the

[5] Ex. 15:21.   [6] Vss. 20 f.

ear, not for the eye, i.e., they were recited or sung, not read. In the very reciting of them there are stresses or pulsations of the voice as the words are pronounced. This is what constitutes meter in Hebrew poetry. Meter is not a matter of measured syllables or lines, but is a matter of beats or accents as the words are spoken. Its presence in these very earliest bits of poetry is evidence that it was the spontaneous and inevitable expression of the nomad's mentality. They delighted in such lyrics.

Happily for the person who knows no Hebrew, this kind of rhythm can be brought out in English translation, which makes it possible to appreciate the full beauty of the Biblical poetry. There may be two or three or four beats to a line, or even a swell-line of five beats. The prevailing cadence of lyric poetry is either the three-beat or the four-beat line, designated by the formula $3 + 3$ or $4 + 4$. Both of these are illustrated in the foregoing couplets where accent marks have been inserted to indicate the stresses.[7]

Early Folk Songs

It is surprising how many early folk songs are preserved in the Old Testament, besides those already mentioned. There may have been poetic versions of the Genesis stories that were older than the prose narratives. A hint of this is in two fragments of a poetic version of the Jacob story embedded in the Book of Hosea (*12:3 ff., 12 f.). A ritual incantation associated with the Ark of the Covenant is preserved in Num. * 10:35 f. This chant was sung when the Ark was taken into battle[8] and no doubt also when setting out at other times upon a trek. The "Song of the Arnon" (Num. *21:14 f.) may be part of an early poetic version of the wilderness wandering, the theme of the "Book of the Wars of Yahweh." Ex. *17:16 is an ancient war chant, "Eternal Warfare against Amalek." Another and longer war chant is the "Taunt Song" in Num. *21:27–30 relating to Israel's enemies in Eastjordania and their defeat. This no doubt was sung in succeeding ages as a war chant of Israel, quite regardless of its historical connection, just as some Americans today sing the "Star Spangled Banner" who are quite ignorant of its historical allusions. The poems put into the mouth of Balaam in Num. *24 may be such early folk songs, vs. 24 being regarded by some scholars as an especially ancient fragment.

Such early folk songs bring us very close to the feelings and experiences of the primitive Hebrews. There were certain persons

---

[7] For explanation and illustration of the other types of meter, vid. infra, p. 301. There is a fourth type of parallelism known as "climactic," vid. infra, p. 169.

[8] Cf. infra, pp. 158–159.

especially interested in transmitting these songs, such as the bards or ballad singers referred to in Num. 21:27 ("they that speak in proverbs"). They were perhaps like the troubadours or minne-singers of medieval Europe. These early folk songs were in the mouths of the people centuries before they were ever put into writing.

*   *   *

In this chapter we have been looking at Hebrew folklore, poetry, and tribal stories in the making and their preservation in the oral traditions. Here, then, in the social experience of the people of nomadic days lie the antecedents of Hebrew literature. The only art which characterized the Hebrews in that remote period was the art of poetry and storytelling. It was in the very psychology of the race.

Chapter 8

THE BEGINNINGS OF HEBREW RELIGION

It was in religion that the ancient Hebrew people made their chief contribution to humanity. Religion is not something separate from culture. It is an integral and important part of it. Their religion, therefore, defines the level of culture which the Hebrews attained. Moreover, in the Old Testament religion, which is also technically called the religion of Israel, are to be found the genetic connections of three of the world's now living religions, viz., Judaism, Christianity, and Islam.

Religion as a Form of Culture

To attempt to define religion would confuse, for definitions of religion are legion. We can, however, recognize seven aspects of religion, viz., mystical (or numinous) religious experience, ritual, ecclesiastical organization, doctrine, ethics, social action, and literature. These items constitute a simple pattern for examining and appraising religion objectively. They give us categories into which we can fit the varieties of religious forms as we come upon them in the progress of our study. One of these aspects appeals as paramount to one form of temperament, another to another. This accounts for the prevailing emphases of various sects and denominations at the present time. By employing this whole pattern we are able to study Biblical religion objectively and without sectarian bias.

The nature of mystical religious experience can best be grasped from specific instances of it. The period embraced within this chapter affords some excellent examples: Abraham's experience in Gen. *15; the experience of Jacob at Bethel (Gen. *28:10–22); and the experience of Moses at Sinai (Ex. *3). Each of these experiences, it is to be noted, occurs at a sacred place. The individual believes himself to be in immediate personal contact with the deity, who is seen (often in the form of fire) and heard; this is technically called a "theophany." This awakens a feeling of awe which is compounded of admiration and fear. The experience prompts the individual to a devout act of worship and changes the tenor of his life. Ex. *19:7–25 describes a group experience in which the same components are present as in the foregoing accounts of the experiences of individuals.

In religion, man is primarily concerned with the mysterious phenomena of the universe about him, which mysteries he cannot as yet explain. He may consider these mysterious forces as either friendly or hostile to him. Primitive man certainly regards such forces as personal. If he considers them to be friendly, he will seek to put himself in harmonious adjustment to them and will indulge in such ritual practices as he thinks will secure for him the continued favor of the supernatural beings who control his world and his destiny. This is a form of what we term "worship." If he regards them as hostile to him, then he will indulge in practices which are termed "magic," and which are designed to compel the supernatural powers to favor him. Such ritual matters are the very lifeblood of primitive society and ever tend to become the function of a specialized group in society, viz., priests. Ecclesiastical organization is likely to increase as the technique of ritual is elaborated.

When man reflects upon the nature of the universe about him, and upon the nature and value of his own religious experience, he forms his doctrines about the deity and the deity's demands and purposes. Doctrines grow more elaborate and more diversified as man's religious experience and intellectual capacity advance.

As religion advances, the ceremonial yields priority to the ethical. The deity comes to be considered as a moral being and his demands moral, and so man's duty to God and to man likewise comes to be regarded as moral. This is what happened in the Hebrew religion.

The story of Old Testament religion is the story of a long development. It begins with the primitive religion of the earliest Hebrew nomads and it culminates in the ethical monotheism of the great Hebrew prophets.

As we examine the nature and development of Hebrew religion we shall be particularly interested in four items: (1) the ideas about the deity which prevailed in each epoch studied; (2) the sacred places; (3) the nature of worship; and (4) how religion affected the behavior of the people of the time, especially with respect to ethical standards and ideals.

The Nomadic Religion Before Moses

The religious beliefs and practices of the Hebrews have great antiquity. All Semites were at one time nomads, and the Hebrews shared the beliefs and practices which regularly characterized other Semitic nomads. It is a mistake, however, to suppose that beliefs and practices which are characteristically nomadic are restricted in time to the nomadic era. Their survivals are to be found in much later periods. Religious beliefs and practices have a way of lasting, especially among the average run of people, for popular beliefs and practices in any given age are by no means the same as the beliefs and practices of the religious leaders and creative thinkers of the age. It was so with the Hebrews. There are many ancient religious practices in the Old Testament, the original meaning of which cannot be recovered from the obscurity of antiquity. Examples of holdover customs are: circumcision,[1] the Sabbath,[2] the Feast of Unleavened Bread,[3] the anointing of the stone at Bethel,[4] the prohibition against eating the sinew of the thigh,[5] and the Passover.[6] Such customs are commonly explained by the Bible writers by reference to some historical episode but their original significance can only be conjectured.

Beings Regarded as Divine. The world of the primitive Hebrew was uncomfortably crowded with supernatural beings, benevolent and hostile. To such he had to make very careful adjustment for his own well-being.

1. *Spirits.* Primitive man believed that spirits dwell in trees, springs, wells, streams, the sea, rocks, stones, and mountains, but such spirits had no individuality. To his mind there was a mystery about running water, bubbling springs, and the surging sea. These things seemed really alive. The wind and swaying foliage gave the same impression. The notion that a stone, or rock, or mountain was alive would arise from some unusual or uncanny position or appearance of it. Trees, especially evergreen trees, seemed to him to be the media through which the life-producing energy of the spirits found expression. Deut. 33:16, for example, speaks of Yahweh as "him that dwelt in the bush" (a reference to Ex. 3:2-5). Examples of such sacred trees, springs, and the like will be cited in the division on sacred places.[7]

2. *Teraphim—"Vile Things."* In certain passages where we find the term "teraphim" it seems to mean a household god: Gen. *31:19, 30-35; Jgs. 17:5; I Sam. 19:13, 16. This teraphim belonged to the head of a family, was kept in the house, and was spoken of as a god. Concerning the nature of the teraphim, one can only conjecture. Langdon holds that they were probably figurines of the mother goddess.[8] An interesting light on the story of Rachel's theft of her father Laban's household gods and Laban's anxiety over their disappearance [9] is thrown by certain Hurrian texts which reveal that possession of the household gods made one legitimate heir to the household goods.[10] Evidently Rachel intended to make certain that her husband

[1] Ex. 4:24 ff.   [2] Ex. 20:11.
[3] Ex. 12:17.   [4] Gen. 28:18.
[5] Gen. 32:32.   [6] Ex. 5:3.
[7] *Infra*, pp. 122-125.
[8] Stephen Herbert Langdon, *Semitic Mythology* (Boston: 1931), p. 34. On the mother goddess, cf. *infra*, p. 175.   [9] Gen. 31:19-34.
[10] Cf. Cyrus H. Gordon, *The Living Past* (New York: 1941), p. 178.

would hold a first mortgage on her father's property. Other passages imply that the teraphim was something used in divination.[11] It is possible that it was even used in necromancy. Facts such as the foregoing suggest that the teraphim was a remnant of ancestor worship.

3. *Seraphim—"Burning Ones."* Num. *21:6, 8 describes a case of imitative magic which involved the setting up of a seraph on a pole for persons bitten by fiery, i.e., poisonous, serpents (*seraphim*) to look at for healing. Deut. 8:15 indicates that the seraphim were demons of the wilderness,[12] but Isa. 6:1–6 (esp. vs. 2) indicates that seraphim in certain cases were regarded as of an angelic nature.[13] They are, then, an example of the elevation of supernatural beings from demons to angels. An example of the reverse process, the rating down from gods to demons, is found in the *se'irim.*

4. *Se'irim—"Hairy Ones."* The term se'irim does not appear in English versions of the Bible. Certain versions (incorrectly) translate it as "satyrs."[14] The proper rendering is "he goats." Mount Seir took its name from this goat divinity. 2 Kgs. 23:8 has the meaningless "the high places of the gates," instead of "the high places of the se'irim." According to 2 Chr. 11:15, Jeroboam appointed a priest "for the high places, and for the se'irim, and for the calves which he had made." These passages attest the worship of the se'irim either as gods or as representatives of gods. Later they were rated only as demons. In Isa. 34:14 one feature of the desolation of Edom, which is located in Mount Seir, is to be that "the sa'ir shall cry to his fellow."

5. *Azazel.* In a religious ritual described in Lev. *16:7–28, it is prescribed (vs. 8) that "Aaron shall cast lots upon the two goats: one lot for Yahweh, and the other lot for Azazel." This clearly indicates that Azazel was regarded as a personal being like Yahweh. Originally, Azazel was a god of the flocks. The Azazel ritual was evolved from a primitive ritual offering to a god of the waste who was the leader of the se'irim. Azazel became degraded to a demon and ultimately, as late Jewish literature testifies,[15] Azazel was identified with the author of all evil, i.e., Satan.[16]

---

[11] Jgs. 18:14, 17, 20; 1 Sam. 15:23; 2 Kgs. 23:24; Hos. 3:4; Ezk. 21:21; Zech. 10:2. Cf. *infra*, pp. 127–128.

[12] Cf. also Isa. 14:29; 30:6.   [13] On the serpent cult, cf. *infra*, p. 171.

[14] E.g., Lev. 17:7.   [15] 1 Enoch 6:7; 9:6; 10:4–8.

[16] There were other demonic beings. In Isa. 13:21 f., five different kinds are named. (1) *Ziyyim*, "wild beasts" (wildcats?); in Jer. 50:39 the term is translated "wild beasts of the desert"; it was some animal, supposed to be the incarnation of a demon, and so classed with the *Se'irim*; (2) *'Ochim*, "doleful creatures," which seem to have gathered in groups and by some translators are understood to have been jackals; (3) *Benoth Ya'anah*, "ostriches," literally "daughters of greed," perhaps connected with a belief that demons rode on or assumed the form of ostriches and had voracious appetites; (4) *'Iyyim*, "wolves" or "howling creatures" (the root means "to screech") or "hyenas"; and (5) *Tannim*, "wolves" (rendered "jackals" in the American Standard Version). Isa. 34:14 names a female demon, *Lilith*, "the night monster" or "night hag." Possibly this demon is alluded to in Ps. 91:5, "the night

6. *Elim.* The word *El* means "god." We find it connected with a number of names of places which existed in Canaan before the Hebrews lived there. For example: Jabne*el,* "Let *El* build"; [17] Jezre*el,* "Let *El* sow"; [18] Jiphtach*el,* "Let *El* open"; [19] Migdal*el,* "the tower of *El*"; [20] Beth*el,* "the abode, or sanctuary, of *El*"; [21] Penu*el,* "the face of *El.*" [22] The Egyptian Pharaoh, Thutmose III (1501–1447 B.C.), includes in a list of districts he conquered in Syria Har-*El,* "Mount of God," and Jacob-El and Joseph-El. The preferred Old Testament word for God is *Elôhîm.*

For an understanding of Hebrew religion prior to the time of Moses, one of the most important passages is Ex. 6:2 f.: "And God spake unto Moses, and said unto him, I am *Yahweh;* and I appeared unto Abraham, unto Isaac, and unto Jacob, as El Shaddai; but by my name Yahweh I was not known to them." This means that the pre-Mosaic religion was an *El* religion.

El Shaddai is by some interpreters rendered "God Almighty." However, scholarly opinion now favors the view that this term is derived from Babylonian *shaddu* (mountain), so that El Shaddai means "God of the Mountain(s)." [23] The interesting fact is that the term *El* is in this name found in combination. We find a similar phenomenon elsewhere: Gen. 16:13 f. says, "Thou art *El-roi,*" i.e., a god who sees or can be seen because the deity was said to have visibly appeared at a certain holy well. Gen. 21:33 speaks of *El Olam,* "the Everlasting God" or "the Ancient *El.*" Gen. 35:7 states that Jacob called Bethel by a new name *El-bethel,* "the *El* (God) of Beth*el.*" But Beth*el* means "house of God," which of course implies that an *El* had already been worshiped there before Jacob's time, for it was a very ancient place; unless, of course, the author of Genesis is guilty of an anachronism in projecting the name Bethel so far backward in history. Jgs. 9:46 mentions *El-berîth,* i.e., an *El* who presided over covenants.

Gen. 31:42, 53 is an interesting passage, according to which Jacob, in taking a solemn oath, names "the *El* of Abraham, the *El* of Nahor,

terror." Vss. 5 and 6 of this psalm may refer to four demons in all: (1) night terror; (2) the arrow that flieth by day; (3) the pestilence that stalks in darkness; (4) the destruction that wastes at noonday. [So Oesterley and Robinson, *Hebrew Religion* (New York: 1937), p. 119.] Gen. 14:3 also mentions the "Vale of Siddim," an unknown place understood by some interpreters to be "the demon valley." If this is correct, it means some place which was regarded as the rendezvous of the demons. Deut. 32:17 accuses the Hebrews of sacrificing to the *sedim* (demons) "which are no god," and Ps. 106:37 derides the Hebrews for imitating the practice of the Canaanites in sacrificing their sons and daughters to the *sedim* (demons). Presumably such demons were connected with the terrible god Molech, the god of fire and plague.
17 Josh. 15:11.   18 Josh. 15:56.
19 Josh. 19:14.   20 Josh. 19:38.
21 Gen. 28:18 f.   22 Gen. 32:31.
23 Cf. W. F. Albright, *From the Stone Age to Christianity* (Baltimore: 1940), pp. 184 ff.; G. E. Wright and F. V. Filson, *The Westminster Historical Atlas to the Bible* (Philadelphia: 1945), p. 26.

the *El* of their father (i.e., the gods of their ancestors), and the *Fear* of Isaac." Gen. 49:24 speaks in similar fashion of the "Mighty One of Jacob."

The passages cited in the foregoing abundantly evidence the fact that Hebrew religion before Moses' time was an *El*-religion. Moreover, the Book of Genesis contains not a single personal name which has "Yahweh" in its formation, such as Adoni*jah,* Ahi*jah,* Bena*iah,* Isa*iah,* Jos*iah,* and other -*jahs* so numerous in later centuries, and this fact is strong evidence that the basic patriarchal narratives come from a time when the name Yahweh was unknown to the Hebrews, as Ex. 6:3 explicitly states.

What then shall be done with the equally explicit statement in Gen. 4:26 that it was in the time of Enosh, the grandson of Adam, that "men began to call upon the name of Yahweh"?

A possible explanation of this contradiction between Ex. 6:3 and Gen. 4:26 may be found in the fact stated on p. 30 that the tribes which made up northern Israel were genetically connected with the Aramaeans to the northeast, while the clans that made up Judah were of southern extraction. The latter clans may have known the Yahweh shrines from very ancient times,[24] whereas the Israelites proper only adopted Yahweh worship much later.

7. *The Moon God.* All Semites were once nomads, and the moon was their chief deity. The nomad thought the sun no friend of his. In the daytime he sought refuge from the sun in the shade of some rock in the weary land, for about him was only burning sand. But at night, under the kindly moon and stars, he moved with his flocks and herds. Jgs. 8:21 tells that there were small moons (crescents) around the necks of the camels of the Midianites. In Palestine at the present time such amulets continue to be used on favorite horses. Their use places the animals under the protection of the moon god.[25] Ur of the Chaldees and the Aramaean city of Haran, both of which were connected with Abraham,[26] were centers of moon worship. The name of the moon god was Sin. Sinai no doubt was so called because of its connection with the cult of the moon. Jericho may have been a center of moon worship, in view of the derivation of its name from *jareach,* the word for "moon."

[24] Perhaps the tribe of Levi was one such. As a separate tribe, Levi disappeared before the earliest Old Testament records were produced. Levites localized in the Negeb fought for Yahweh against fellow Hebrews who were devotees of other gods, notably the golden calf (Ex. 32:26 ff.). The name *Judah* (= *Jehudah*), whatever be the exact meaning of this word, certainly comprises *Yahweh* in its formation.

[25] Such pendants are usually blue in color, no doubt in keeping with the superstitious custom of wearing blue glass beads as protection against the evil eye, a kind of sympathetic magic, for it is the glance of a blue eye which the Oriental fears because blue eyes are so rare among them. On sympathetic magic cf. *infra,* pp. 127–128. On the moon god cult, cf. Nelson Glueck, *The River Jordan* (Philadelphia: 1946), pp. 57 f.

[26] *Vid. supra,* pp. **91–92.**

Sacred Places. 1. *Sacred Trees.* The terebinth [27] of Moreh (Gen. 12:6 ff.), where Abraham received a divine manifestation, was at Shechem and was a sacred place long before Abraham was there. The terebinth is an evergreen, and the "terebinth of the teacher (*Moreh*)" indicates that it was a spot where divine "teaching" was given; i.e., it was an oracle tree. In Gen. 35:4 is an interesting narrative of Jacob's burying idols under the Shechem terebinth, the idea prompting such an action presumably being that their power might be nullified by that of the more powerful divinity residing in that tree. Under the same Shechem terebinth Joshua later set up a great stone [28] as a witness lest the people deny God. The Shechem terebinth is mentioned [29] as the place where Abimelech was made king, the purpose being to have the deity witness the coronation. Jgs. 9:6 also mentions a sacred stone pillar beside this sacred tree in Shechem.

The terebinth of Mamre, in Hebron,[30] was a holy place where Abraham built an altar. Gen. 14:13 calls Mamre "the Amorite." Very likely this too was a sacred spot long before Abraham knew it. Abraham also planted a tamarisk tree in Beersheba,[31] where a theophany later occurred,[32] attesting the strongly sacred character it was believed to possess.

Another oracle terebinth is mentioned in Jgs. 4:4 f., where Deborah, the prophetess, sat and gave "judgment" (decision) on matters brought to her. Jgs. 9:37 refers to "the terebinth of Meonenim," i.e., "the soothsayers' (or diviners') terebinth," manifestly another oracle tree. According to 1 Kgs. 13:14, a certain "man of God," sitting under a terebinth tree in Bethel, was lured away by a false prophet. This was probably also an oracle tree and may have been the very tree alluded to in Gen. 35:8. 2 Sam. 5:23 f. is another interesting and instructive passage.[33] David was to understand, when he heard the sound of marching in the tops of the balsam trees, that Yahweh had entered the tree and had "gone out to smite the Philistines."

2. *Sacred Waters.* In the life of the desert nomad water is a vital necessity. He will toil terribly to secure it and fight fearfully to defend his right to it. Therefore springs and wells and streams have for him a religious significance—they are the dwelling place of life-giving deity.

The word *'En* means spring, and place names connected with *'En* are believed to have been originally sacred places. Kadesh was known

---

[27] The terebinth resembles the oak, though unrelated to it. It is related to the so-called turpentine tree. Its wood is sweet-smelling; the nuts which grow on it yield an edible oil.

[28] Josh. 24:26 f.
[30] Gen. 13:18; 18:1.
[32] Gen. 26:23 ff.

[29] Jgs. 9:6.
[31] Gen. 21:33.
[33] Cf. 1 Chr. 14:15.

as *En-mishpat,* i.e., "the spring of decision," signifying that it was an oracle well to which men came for a decision.[34] *En-shemesh,* "the spring of the sun," was probably originally connected with sun worship.[35] Gen. 14:7 mentions Hazazontamar, so called because a sacred palm tree (*tamar*) was there which 2 Chr. 20:2 identifies with *En-gedi,* "the spring of the kid." Near Engedi was *En-eglaim,* "the spring of the two calves," [36] which may have been a sanctuary of the cow divinity Ashtart. For Gen. 14:5 mentions an Ashterothkarnaim, "Ashtart of the two horns," and figurines of Ashtart with two horns have been discovered in Palestinian excavations.

Several sacred wells are mentioned. Num. 21:17 f. quotes the "Song of the Well" [37] in which a well is addressed as though it were a living being (which indeed is a very ancient form of address). At the sacred well in Beersheba, Abraham planted a sacred tree and called there on the name of the Everlasting God.[38] Beer-lahai-roi, as we have seen, was sacred to a local divinity *El-roi,* a "god of seeing," i.e., one who is manifested there.[39] The name Baalath-beer, "the mistress of the well," would indicate that a female spirit was worshiped at this shrine.[40]

An instance of a flowing stream which was a sacred place is the Gihon, to which Solomon was taken to be anointed king.[41] The river Kishon was sacred to a god Kish.[42]

3. *Sacred Mountains, Rocks, and Stones.* Of all the sacred mountains mentioned in the Old Testament, the most important is, of course, Mount Sinai (Horeb) which in Num. 10:33 is called "the mount of Yahweh." [43]

Other notable sacred mountains were Mount Nebo, in Moab, sacred to the deity Nebo, best known through Babylonian worship; Mount Peor, in Moab, sacred to the "Baal of Peor"; [44] Mount Pisgah, in Moab, where Balak, king of Moab, built seven altars and offered sacrifices; [45] Mount Carmel, in northwest Samaria, scene of the famous contest between the prophet Elijah and the Tyrian Baal prophets; [46] and the Mount of Olives, just east of Jerusalem, on which was a sanctuary "where God was worshiped" [47] and where, in the time of Solomon, the gods Chemosh and Molech were also worshiped.[48]

Sanctuaries (i.e., sacred sites) of this early period were commonly marked by a stone pillar (*mazzebah*) such as was erected by Jacob

[34] Gen. 14:7.
[35] Josh. 15:7; 18:17.
[36] Ezk. 47:10.
[37] Cf. *supra,* p. 111.
[38] Gen. 21:33.
[39] Gen. 16:13 f.
[40] Josh. 19:8.
[41] 1 Kgs. 1:33 f.
[42] Cf. Jgs. 5:21.
[43] Detailed consideration is given to this mountain on pp. 132–133.
[44] Num. 25:3.
[45] Num. 23:14.
[46] 1 Kgs. 18.
[47] 2 Sam. 15:30 f.
[48] 1 Kgs. 11:7.

at Bethel, "the house of God." [49] Another such pillar was erected by Jacob to testify that the deity had witnessed to the covenant between him and Laban,[50] although a different source speaks of a "heap," i.e., a cairn, at the spot.[51] Probably at one time both these sacred markers were to be seen there. Joshua set up a great stone (*eben*) under the sacred terebinth in Shechem as a testimony to the laws which he promulgated there.[52] When they crossed the Jordan, Joshua took twelve stones from the river to pile up as "a sign" and "for a memorial." [53] Upon Mount Ebal Joshua erected an altar of "unhewn stones, upon which no man had lifted up any iron," implying, of course, that the indwelling spirit had not been driven out by the hammering.[54] There was an "Ebenezer," i.e., "stone of help," located at Aphek in the northern part of the plain of Sharon,[55] and Samuel, after a successful battle, erected an "Ebenezer" northeast of Jerusalem near Mizpah because "hitherto hath Yahweh helped us." [56] Adonijah "sacrificed sheep and oxen fatlings by the stone of Zoheleth, which is beside En-rogel." [57] This is the unusual instance of a sacred stone by a sacred spring, the "stone of Zoheleth" probably being "the Serpent's stone," and En-rogel probably being "the well of enquiring." [58]

1 Sam. 6:14 states that the cattle which drew the cart containing the sacred Ark halted beside a great stone in the field of Joshua at Beth-shemesh. This passage not only calls attention to another sacred stone, but seems to contain the primitive notion that an animal would voluntarily offer itself to the deity. A similar idea is inherent in the story of the ram caught in the thicket and substituted as a sacrifice in place of Isaac (Gen. 22:13).

4. *Graves*. The sanctity of graves is a belief growing out of a primitive ancestor worship. One notable allusion to a grave regarded as a sacred place is the grave of Sarah (Gen. *23) in the cave of Machpelah, which was, according to Gen. 13:18; 18:1, a sanctuary. So also were the graves of Deborah, Rebekah's nurse;[59] of Joseph at Shechem,[60] which Gen. 12:6 and 35:4 show to have been a sanctuary; and of Miriam at Kadesh.[61] The very name Kadesh (*holy*) proves this spot to have been a sanctuary. But possibly the most instructive instance of all is the grave of Rachel [62] where "Jacob set up a pillar upon her grave" thus making the grave a sanctuary.[63]

[49] Gen. 28:11–22. Cf. C. C. McCown, *The Ladder of Progress in Palestine* (New York: 1943), p. 158.
[50] Gen. 31:44 f.   [51] Gen. 31:46.
[52] Josh. 24:26 f.
[53] Josh. 4:1–14. Especially vss. 6 f.
[54] Josh. 8:30 f., cf. Ex. 20:25 and Deut. 27:5 f.
[55] 1 Sam. 4:1; 5:1.   [56] 1 Sam. 7:12,
[57] 1 Kgs. 1:9.   [58] So Oesterley, *op. cit.*, pp. 37, 46.
[59] Gen. 35:8.   [60] Josh. 24:32.
[61] Num. 20:1.   [62] Gen. 35:20.
[63] Cf. 1 Sam. 10:2.

The fact that there was a cult of the dead is attested by the presence of food offerings found by archaeologists in tombs belonging to the Hebrew as well as the pre-Hebrew periods in Palestine. This accounts for such mourning customs as rending one's garments,[64] slashing one's body and cutting off one's hair,[65] putting on sackcloth,[66] fasting,[67] lamentation and wailing.[68]

Other evidence of the cult of the dead in pre-Hebrew Palestine is to be seen in the dolmens and cromlechs of the land, especially east of Jordan. Dolmens, consisting of upright stone slabs covered by a capstone, marked graves. A cromlech was a circular area formed by standing stones, spaced apart. Inside the circle were dolmens, cairns, and other mounds. Within this area were observed the rites connected with the dead. One such interesting stone circle is on Mt. Nebo, and there is a dolmen on Mt. Pisgah. It is with this locality that Moses' view of the Promised Land is associated, as also his death. More than one place in Palestine was called Gilgal, which means "Stone Circle." Such names attest sacred places of this sort. In some of the cromlechs there are bowl depressions in the floor stones, very likely for drink offerings to the dead.[69] Deut. 26:14 is evidence that the practice of worshiping the dead persisted even to the sixth century B.C.

The Nature of Worship.   The chief items in the worship of the ancient Hebrew nomads were prayer and simple sacrifices. Elaborate sacrificial systems do not characterize nomad religion; they develop in more settled life. Nomads, whenever they arrived at a new camping place, were wont to offer some simple propitiation to the spirits of the place. At the occasional festivals they shared meat with the tribal deity, either in thankfulness or in propitiation, to assure his continued favor. It was a simple worship which later Hebrew prophets commended and to which they urged Israel to revert.[70]

1. *New Moon Festivals.*   The place and significance of the moon god in the life of the primitive nomad has been discussed.[71] Since, in order to avoid the intense heat, the nomad customarily moved his flocks by night, the appearance of the new moon would be an occasion of rejoicing for it would mean that he could now move again. The feast of the new moon was observed by families.[72] Am. 8:4 f. refers to the

[64] Gen. 37:34; 2 Sam. 1:11; 3:31.
[65] Lev. 19:27 f.; 21:1–5; Isa. 15:2; Jer. 16:6; 41:5; 47:5; Ezk. 7:18; Am. 8:10; Mic. 1:16.
[66] 2 Sam. 3:31; Isa. 22:12; Ezk. 27:31.
[67] 1 Sam. 31:13; 2 Sam. 1:12.
[68] Gen. 37:34; 2 Sam. 3:31–34; 1 Kgs. 13:30; Jer. 22:18.
[69] Cf. A. T. Olmstead, *History of Palestine and Syria* (New York: 1931), pp. 24–30, 214.
[70] Am. 5:25; Jer. 7:22.
[71] *Supra*, p. 121.
[72] 1 Sam. 20:5, 24–29.

new moon festival, and Col. 2:16 shows that it continued to be observed clear down to New Testament times. In the Apocryphal book Sira (Ecclesiasticus) is a charming poem celebrating the moon as "the sign of the feast day" (*43:6–10).

2. *Sabbaths.* The origin of the Sabbath is unknown. Some interpreters associate its origin with moon worship, in which festal days were related to the moon's quarters. Thus it was probably a heritage from nomadic life and was in existence long before the Hebrews' entry into Canaan. Originally it was not a day of complete rest from labor but for a change in the week's toil. Thus, 2 Kgs. 4:23 connects the Sabbath with the new moon day as an occasion when one could travel on a beast because the beast was resting from its ordinary labor. Other passages evidence the close connection between new moons and Sabbaths.[73] This character it seems to have kept until the end of the Hebrew kingship.

3. *The Feast of Sheepshearing.* This festival also goes back to nomadic times.[74] It was a joyous festival. 1 Sam. 25:8 calls it a "good day," and vs. 36 of the same chapter says that there was much feasting. The sheepshearing festival persisted longest in Judea, home of shepherds. At such feasts, no doubt, the stories of the clever shepherd Jacob were rehearsed with relish.

4. *Pesach.* The festival of the Passover is of such hoary antiquity that the very meaning of its name, *Pesach,* has not been satisfactorily explained. The term goes back to the primal speech of the desert Semites. From the same root word comes a Hebrew verb meaning "to dance with a limp," which suggests that some form of sacred dance was part of the most primitive Passover ritual. Ex. 3:18; 7:16, etc., represent Moses as requesting the Egyptian Pharaoh to permit the Hebrews to go three days' journey into the wilderness "that we may sacrifice to Yahweh our God." Exactly what the nature of that ancient festival was it is impossible to tell but it seems to have been a nomad's festival involving the offering, in springtime, of the firstlings of the flock. The consuming of a lamb between evening and morning (Ex. *12:8 ff.) is the sort of festival that would characterize wilderness life, for nomads slaughtered only when they sacrificed to a deity. The ceremony was built around the ancient desert conception of the efficacy of blood. The blood of the sacrificial animals was smeared on the tent doors to avert danger from hostile supernatural beings that were abroad in the night. It is significant that the festival which the Hebrew shepherds in Goshen wished to observe involved the sacrifice of animals sacred to the Egyptians.[75]

73 Am. 8:5; Hos. 2:11; Isa. 1:13; 66:23.
74 Gen. 38:12 f.; 1 Sam. 25:2 ff., 36; 2 Sam. 13:23 f.
75 Ex. 8:26.

Religious Practices.   1. *Taboo.* Taboo prohibits contact with holy things, either (a) animals whose flesh may not be eaten because it is "holy" or "unclean," or (b) persons who in any way are peculiarly connected with the deity and his worship, or (c) ground which is dedicated to the deity. The Old Testament term for taboo is *tâmê*, translated "unclean." This "unclean" does not mean impure or loathsome in the sense the word has for moderns, but is simply a ritual term for something that must not be touched or (if an animal) eaten. Lev. 11 and Deut. 14:7–20 list the animals that were not to be eaten by Hebrews. One notes, in Lev. 11, the frequent use of the expressions "have in abomination" and "an abomination." These expressions are applied both to unclean beasts and to the gods of the heathen,[76] but to nothing else. The inference from such juxtaposition is that the creatures regarded as unclean were the divine animals of the heathen. That Israel must scrupulously avoid *those* animals was the dominant idea. This accounts for the Hebrew taboo of the pig. It was the sacred animal of other cults, notably the Ashtart cult.

One of the most interesting stories of taboo is in 2 Sam. *6:6–10 where Uzzah touched the sacred Ark with dire consequences.[77] The primitive conception underlying this is that the supernatural manifested itself in two modes: negatively in taboo and positively in *mana*. The latter will be discussed on page 181.

2. *Refraining from Food.* The idea of refraining from food before or during battle is a primitive belief worth noting. It originated in the notion that the divine strength gained in the rite of sanctifying oneself might, by eating, be lost or neutralized.[78] There are instances of sacrifices offered before a battle or during a campaign, evidently somewhat akin to the foregoing.[79]

3. *The Ban.* The ban was another Semitic institution of hoary antiquity. Whatever was under the ban was withdrawn from common use and thenceforth devoted exclusively to a deity. Whatever was devoted to a deity was devoted to destruction, i.e., total destruction of material wealth, and death for all the conquered. 1 Sam. *15 is a most vivid account of this institution in operation. Josh. *7 is another, with even more gripping and tragic details.

4. *Magic.* The practice of magic is abundantly evidenced from nomadic days to the end of the monarchy in the sixth century, B.C. In Gen. 30:27 Laban says, "I have divined (learned from the omens) that Yahweh hath blessed me for thy sake"; nothing is said about the

---

[76] 1 Kgs. 11:5, 7; 2 Kgs. 23:13.

[77] Cf. the interesting note in C. S. Knopf, *The Old Testament Speaks* (New York: 1933), p. 151.

[78] Josh. 3:5; 1 Sam. 14:24.

[79] Jgs. 6:20, 26; 20:26; 1 Sam. 7:9; 13:10.

process by which he divined. Gen. *44:5, 15 gives an example of hydromancy, i.e., divining by means of a special cup.

Ex. 22:18 commands the death penalty for a sorceress, and Deut. 18:10–14 forbids magical practices. The practice of magic is regarded as harmful in 2 Kgs. 17:17; 21:6 (= 2 Chr. 33:6). The practice of augury is condemned by the prophets [80] but in ways that show the strong grip it had on the people.

Instances of rain-making by magical means are given in 1 Sam. 12:16 ff., 1 Kgs. 17:1. 1 Kgs. *18:42–45 describes a kind of ritual by which Elijah brought rain. It is significant that no mention at all is made of Yahweh in this ritual. Other instances of magical effects upon water are described in Ex. 15:25; 2 Kgs. *2:8, 14, 19–22.

Examples of imitative magic are: the floating axhead imitating the floating wooden stick (2 Kgs. *6:5 f.); the smiting of the ground with arrows by the king of Israel at the command of Elisha, inducing an imitation smiting by the king of his Aramaean foe (2 Kgs. *13:14–19); Elisha's casting of nutritious meal into a kettle to induce the poisonous root to imitate its nutritious nature (2 Kgs. *4:38–41); and Elisha's raising of the dead by a ritual performance to induce the corpse to imitate the living body (2 Kgs. *4:32–35).

We have examples of the magic rod in Ex. *4:2 ff. where Moses' rod turns to a serpent and back again; in Ex. *17:8–11, where, by holding "the rod of God" in his hand, Moses brought victory in battle to the Hebrews; and in Num. *20:8–11 where Moses draws water from a rock by his magic rod.

Music was regarded as having a magical potency to drive away evil spirits or demons (1 Sam. 16:23). 2 Kgs. 6:18–20 depicts Elisha as able to strike blind and restore sight.

5. *Necromancy.* That there was plenty of this going on is shown in Isa. 19:3; 29:4; and 2 Kgs. 21:6. Isa. 8:19 implies that there was trickery about it. A minutely detailed account of the practice is found in 1 Sam. *28:3–25, the story of Saul's resort to the necromancer of Endor. The "Book of the Covenant" (Ex. 20:22–23:33) says nothing about necromancy, but the (later) Deuteronomic code prohibits it emphatically (Deut. *18:10 ff.). Still later codes increase the condemnation, but condemnation of it only testifies to its vogue.

6. *Circumcision.* This rite was not Hebrew in origin and may have come to the Hebrews from the Egyptians. That it was a rite of great antiquity is evidenced by the use of flint knives.[81] Its origin is variously

---

[80] Isa. 2:6; Mic. 5:12; Jer. 27:9.
[81] Josh. 5:2 f.; the place mentioned in vs. 3 may indicate an ancient sanctuary where initiation ceremonies were performed.

assigned to Abraham in Gen. 17:1–14;[82] to Moses in Ex. 4:25 f.;[83] and to Joshua in Josh. 5:3–8.[84] The rite was common to most Semites, the notable exceptions being the Babylonians and Assyrians. It may have been originally a tribal mark to evidence a youth's full membership in his social group and his consecration to the communal god.

7. *Blood Revenge.* Blood revenge characterized the Semites from remotest times and even to the present day it is practiced in Arabia. The basic idea underlying it is the solidarity of the family, clan, or tribe. Any wrong done to one is done to all, and all are bound to avenge it. Examples of this practice are numerous;[85] one of the most dramatic is 2 Sam. *21:1–10. The custom was believed to have divine sanction.[86]

8. *The Blood Covenant.* The blood covenant was a widely practiced desert rite which owed its force to a belief that the living element in an animal was its blood, that blood was in fact life itself.[87] In a blood covenant between two individuals or two groups of persons, the blood of a sacrificial victim was sprinkled or poured over the two parties, this being thought to make them a living unity in that both had been covered by the same blood or "life" (i.e., of a third party).[88] The paramount example of this is Ex. *24:1–8.[89]

Gen. *15:7–18 contains elements of a primitive form of blood covenant. It is implied, though not expressly stated, that Abraham passed between the dismembered parts of the sacrificial animals. Certainly the lambent flame, symbolic of deity, passed between them (vs. 17). The primitive idea was that persons performing this rite entered into and assumed the nature of the animal and thus established a common relationship between them.[90]

The idea underlying this very primitive covenant (*berîth*) ritual is the most important thing we have come upon in the religion of this early epoch.[91] Most of what has been discussed in the foregoing pages belongs in the sphere of animism and magic. The *berîth* concept points the way out of all such superstition. It is the germ of ethical development. That man and the deity could enter into a mutual

---

[82] From the documentary source "P," which originated in the exile. *Vid. infra,* pp. 376 f., and cf. J. A. Bewer, *The Literature of the Old Testament* (New York: 1922), pp. 259–279.

[83] From the documentary source "J". *Vid. infra,* pp. 297 ff.

[84] Or, Joshua restored it after a long lapse.

[85] Cf. 2 Sam. 2:14 ff.; 3:27–30; 14:7, 11; 1 Kgs. 2:5 f.; Deut. 19:12; 21:1–9; Num. 35:24 f., 33.

[86] Gen. 9:6; Num. 35:21; Deut. 19:21.

[87] Gen. 9:4; Deut. 12:23; Lev. 17:12, 14.

[88] Akin to the blood covenant in both form and reasoning was the "blood brotherhood," a rite which consisted in two persons each puncturing a vein or artery and allowing the two blood streams to commingle. The two henceforth felt that they were joined together in the most intimate bond possible.

[89] *Vid. infra,* p. 133.   [90] Cf. Jer. 34:18 f.

[91] On the ethical significance of the covenant idea, cf. G. E. Wright, *The Challenge of Israel's Faith* (Chicago: 1944), pp. 72–74, 77.

relationship in which the deity would act, not upon caprice, but upon reason and in accordance with his pledged word, and that he could be depended upon to keep his covenant, is the starting point of the development of the higher elements in the religion of Israel.

Religion in the Mosaic Age

The Mosaic era falls within the nomadic period of Hebrew life, and what has been said about Hebrew religion thus far applies to it also. There is, however, good reason for treating this era separately for it includes certain experiences which were distinctly new and creative in Hebrew religion. The religious beliefs and practices which we studied in the preceding section persisted long in Hebrew religion as survivals. But what we are now about to study both differentiated Hebrew religion from Semitic nomad religion and started Hebrew religion on the main line of its own peculiar development.

Moses was the creator, not alone of Hebrew nationalism but also of Hebrew religion itself. Ex. *3 describes the personal mystical experience which came to Moses, marking the beginning of the religion technically termed "Yahwism." It was not a monotheism, strictly speaking, but what is known technically as henotheism, i.e., the worship of one particular god to the exclusion of all other deities, though with no thought of denying the reality and existence of such other gods. It is in this latter sense that we must think of the first commandment as being originally understood.[92]

Moses' Experience of God in Midian. This mystical religious experience of Moses, as the record indicates, included the following significant features: it occurred at a sacred mountain; it was in some way connected with a sacred tree; it included a theophany; it evoked in Moses the emotion of awe (a characteristic of mystical experience) and left him convinced that the deity who had visited him was really the same god as the one who had called upon Abraham in Haran and led him to Canaan.

The sacred mountain is Horeb, "the mount of El" (the same as Sinai), situated somewhere near the Wilderness of Midian.[93] The sacred tree is in this case termed a "bush," [94] probably because the word for bush (seneh) sounds so much like Sinai.[95] Warning is given Moses that the spot is sacred by the flame which evidences Yahweh's presence.[96] The theophany overwhelmed Moses with such awe that

---

[92] Ex. 20:3. For the contrary view, that Moses surely was a monotheist, cf. W. F. Albright, From the Stone Age to Christianity (Baltimore: 1940), chap. iv, especially p. 207.
[93] Ex. 3:1.   [94] Ex. 3:2. Cf. Deut. 33:16.
[95] There was a rocky crag by the name of Seneh in Palestine, 1 Sam. 14:4.
[96] Ex. 3:2.

he "hid his face . . . afraid to look upon El." [97] Last of all, the deity formally introduces and identifies himself to Moses as the god of his forebears.[98] From the time he had the religious experience described in Ex. 3, Moses held the following convictions: (1) that the God who had promised Canaan to Abraham, Isaac, and Jacob was now asking henceforth to be addressed as Yahweh; (2) that this Yahweh was offering and promising to deliver the Hebrews from their Egyptian masters; and (3) that he demanded in return their complete loyalty to himself.

Yahweh. It is practically certain that Yahweh was worshiped by others than the Hebrews before he became adopted by them as their national god. He appears to have been either a Midianite deity, one of whose priests was Moses' father-in-law,[99] or else a Kenite god.[100]

Yahweh is depicted in the earlier Old Testament narratives as a god of the mountains.[101] He is a nature deity, manifested in the volcanic activity of the mountain [102] as well as in the storm, earthquake, wind, etc., which raged upon the mountain.[103] It is as a storm god that Yahweh intervenes and discomfits Sisera and his troops in the battle at Mount Tabor, as we shall see.[104] He is also depicted as a storm god in Ps. 29, the "Thunderstorm Psalm," the thunder being Yahweh's voice. He was also conceived as a fire god, not only in the manifestation of the burning bush [105] but also in the "pillar of fire" which guided the wanderers in the wilderness.[106] This last shows that he was also thought of as a wilderness guide.[107] Yahweh was also a war god, helping the nomad Israelites to victory over their wilderness foes (Ex. *17:8–16).[108]

The name Yahweh probably goes back to the aboriginal speech of the desert so that its original meaning cannot now be determined with certainty. Ex. 3:14 explains it as meaning "I AM THAT I AM" or "I AM WHO AM." Some scholars explain its meaning to be, "He causes to be." Moffatt's translation of the Old Testament follows the practice prevalent with French translations and renders the word by "The Eternal." To call God "The Eternal" is probably the best definition of God that can be given, but it is a metaphysical concept much too advanced to be held by a primitive nomadic people.[109]

---

[97] Ex. 3:6.
[98] Ex. 3:6.
[99] Ex. 2:16, 18; 3:1.
[100] Num. 10:29; Jgs. 4:11.
[101] Ex. 3:1; 19:3; 1 Kgs. 20:23.
[102] Ex. 19:16, 18; 24:17; Deut. 4:11 f.
[103] 1 Kgs. 19:11 f.; Deut. 33:2; 2 Sam. 22:7–16.
[104] Jgs. 5:19–23. *Vid. infra*, p. 144.
[105] Ex. 3:2.
[106] Ex. 13:21 f.
[107] Ex. 33:13–16.
[108] There is no known representation of Yahweh in existence.
[109] This proper name of the Hebrew God was written YHWH (or JHWH or JHVH). Hebrew was originally written with consonants only. It is the prevailing opinion of modern Hebrew scholars that this word was pronounced Yahwêh (*Jāhvêh*) (accent on Yáh, *weh* pronounced as *way*). The short form of the name, Yah (Jah), is found in

Sacred Places. The Hebrews of this period were unable to think of God as everywhere present. Certain places were believed to be where he resided, and so were regarded as sacred. Two such places were conspicuous throughout this period.

1. *Mount Sinai* (Horeb). If, as seems probable, the name Sinai is derived from Sin,[110] then this mountain was from remote antiquity a center of moon worship.[111] Rock inscriptions dating from the third millennium B.C. in the Sinaitic Plateau depict the Egyptian moon god Thoth watching the Pharaoh Khufu smashing the skull of a native of the region, which shows that moon worship was associated with this area from hoary antiquity.

That this mountain, variously referred to as Horeb and Sinai, was thought of as the original dwelling place of Yahweh is abundantly clear from Ex. 3 and 19, as also from a very ancient poem in Jgs. 5, the "Song of Deborah" (esp. vss. 4 f.). Even in the ninth century B.C., after the Hebrews had for generations been thinking of Yahweh's dwelling place as the temple at Jerusalem, Elijah the prophet made a long journey to Mount Horeb in order to find Yahweh and converse with him.[112] To men like Elijah, who were sturdy advocates of nomadic ideals, the wilderness mountain rather than the city temple was Yahweh's real home.

Mount Sinai continued to be a spot greatly venerated by Hebrews in all centuries, for it was there, according to their tradition, that a

---

Ex. 15:2 (RVmarg) and Ps. 68:4 (RVmarg). When used as a component of proper names it is *-iah* at the end of such a word and *Jo-* (*Yo-*) or *Jeho-* (*Yeho-*) at the beginning. The ancient Jewish people came in time to hold this name in such reverence that they would not even speak it lest by mispronouncing it they take the name in vain (Ex. 20:7). Whenever, therefore, they came upon YHWH in their Bible, they said instead *Adonai*, which means "Lord." Time came when certain Hebrew scholars (the Massoretes) added vowel markings to the consonants to assist the reader of the Hebrew text to pronounce the words correctly. Under the consonants YHWH they put the vowel markings of the word *Adonai*. The reader would, therefore, look at one word (*Yahweh*) and say another (*Adonai*). Now the consonants of *Yahweh* and the vowels of *Adonai* give the hybrid term *Yehowah* or *Jehovah*. It is thus that one finds it in the American Standard Version of the English Bible. In the King James Version this hybrid term is rendered LORD (all caps.), the word "Lord" (small letters) being used wherever *Adonai* is the word translated. This same practice is followed in the English version of the Jewish *Holy Scriptures* published by the Jewish Publication Society of Philadelphia, and also in *The Old Testament, An American Translation* (= *The Bible, An American Translation*) edited by J. M. P. Smith, published by the University of Chicago Press, and will be followed in the *Revised Standard Version of the Old Testament,* publication of which is anticipated for 1952. Sometimes in the original Hebrew the words *Adonai Yahweh* come together (Gen. 15:8 is an example). Such a combination the English versions just mentioned render as Lord GOD. In these versions, therefore, not only LORD (all caps.), but GOD (all caps.) stands for *Yahweh*, the proper name of the Hebrew deity, while God (initial cap.) is simply the word God (*Elôhîm* in Hebrew) and Lord (initial cap.) is simply the word Lord (*Adonai*).

110 Cf. *supra*, p. 121.

111 Job 31:26 f. throws light on the nature of one element of moon worship. The expression, "My hand kissed my mouth," means throwing a kiss to the moon, an act of adoration.

112 1 Kgs. 19.

solemn blood covenant had been made by which Yahweh became their own peculiar and distinctive God for all time.[113] In this covenant the blood of the sacrificial victim was sprinkled, half upon the altar which represented the deity in the rite and half upon the covenanting people themselves.[114] They who had before been independent entities now became one organic whole. Whereas Yahweh had hitherto existed independently of Israel, he now became incorporated into Israel. Yahweh covenanted to be their God and they covenanted to be his people and to have no other god in preference to him.

2. *Kadesh.* The very name *Kadesh* means "Holy," and it has already been noted that there was here a sacred spring called Enmishpat, the "spring of decision." [115] The Hebrew of Deut. 33:2 connects Meribah-Kadesh with Sinai, Seir, and Mount Paran.[116] For this and other reasons the place is generally thought to have been in the northeastern part of the Sinai Peninsula a little west of the Mount Seir Range. It was the rendezvous of the Hebrews for about a generation during the wilderness period of their history. Here, under Moses' direction, both the religious and the social life of the Hebrews gradually took shape.

The Nature of Worship in the Wilderness Period. 1. *The Tent of Meeting and the Ark of the Covenant.* The Ark was simply a box (Ex. *25:10–16), but it was the most revered emblem of the Yahweh religion, for to the Hebrew mind it symbolized the very presence of Yahweh himself.[117] It was carried by the Israelites on all their journeys, and after varied fortunes in Canaan it finally found a permanent location in the Most Holy Place of the Jerusalem temple. What the box contained is a matter of speculation, but in all probability some object which represented the deity, very likely a stone, or stones, originally taken from the sacred mountain, Horeb. Tradition asserts that they were stones inscribed with the Law, presumably the Decalogue in a brief form.[118] Num. *10:35 f. preserves the ritual chant to the Ark.

A deity must, of course, have his home, and naturally it would be similar to the nomad homes in which his people lived, i.e., a tent. Ex. *33:7–11 describes the simple "Tent of Meeting" which was set up just outside the camp wherever the people were encamped, e.g., at Kadesh, and which became their sanctuary. In this Tent of Meeting, Yahweh at divers times manifested his glory.[119]

[113] *Cf. supra*, p. 129.
[114] Ex. 24:6 ff.
[115] *Supra*, pp. 122 f.
[116] Cf. Moffatt and Chicago versions, *in loc.*
[117] Num. 14:43 f.; Josh. 7:6.
[118] Ex. 25:16, 21; Deut. 31:26; Heb. 9:4 (cf. Ex. 16:33 f.; Num. 17:10).
[119] The exceedingly ornate description of the Ark and Tabernacle in Ex. 35–40 is now generally interpreted as an idealized elaboration of much later centuries and is therefore disregarded here.

2. *Priesthood and Ritual.* It was necessary that there be some kind of priesthood to care for the sacred emblems (Ark and Tent), to regulate the approach of worshipers to Yahweh, and to interpret Yahweh's will to those who came "to inquire of Yahweh." Old Testament traditions usually connect this priesthood with Moses and his brother Aaron, but Ex. 33:11 assigns the position to Joshua.

People resorted to the Tent of Meeting to "inquire of Yahweh," i.e., to ascertain the divine will in matters of social adjustment for which there was as yet no precedent. The divine will was usually learned by the sacred lot. The objects used for this were the *ephod* and the *Urim* and *Thummim.* Just what these were and how they were employed can only be conjectured, for the Old Testament gives no definite information. The ephod may have been a ritual container, perhaps a sort of waistcoat, in the pockets of which the Urim and Thummim were kept. The Urim and Thummim may have been flat stones of which one side was much darker than the other, or possibly with some sort of inscription on one side. If both fell with the brighter, or inscribed, side up, it would mean an affirmative answer; if both of the other sides turned up simultaneously, the answer would be negative; if one of each, no answer was implied.[120] There is, of course, no certainty that these objects were employed in this way or even that their use can be traced back to the wilderness period.[121] Deut. 33:8 definitely asserts that the employment of Urim and Thummim in the sacred lot belonged to the priesthood (Levi). The most enlightening passage on this point is the Greek version of 1 Sam. 14:41, though it relates to the post-Mosaic time. It reads, "And Saul said: O Yahweh, God of Israel, wherefore hast thou not answered thy servant this day? If this iniquity be in me or in Jonathan my son, then, Yahweh, God of Israel, give Urim; but if it be in thy people Israel, then give Thummim."[122] 1 Sam. 23:6–12 tells of the use of the ephod in the sacred lot.

The ritual requirements demanded of the ordinary worshiper of this period are clearly revealed in Ex. *34:14–26 which is a very primitive decalogue enumerating specific things to do.

3. *The Passover.* The primitive nomad festival which was the prototype of the Passover has already been considered.[123] This primitive festival and what it originally signified became merged with the Passover festival commemorating the deliverance of the Hebrews from Egypt or, more exactly, the passing of the angel of death over Hebrew homes when the last plague struck down the first-born in every Egyptian home. An earlier, simpler form of celebration is

---

120 Cf. Oesterley and Robinson, *op. cit.,* p. 106.
121 But cf. Num. 27:21.   122 Cf. Moffatt and Chicago versions, *in loc.*
123 *Supra,* p. 126.

described in Ex. *12:21–27. In the course of centuries the Passover ritual became much elaborated and in some respects altered. Ex. *12:1–20 gives the regulations in force in this later period. The Passover was the Hebrew religious festival par excellence and remains such to this day with the Jewish people.

4. *Bull Worship.* Ex. *32 is a most informing narrative about the fashioning of a molten image of a calf at Sinai and the worship of it. The influence of Egyptian bull worship is here plain. Fortunately, Moses put a prompt stop to it as soon as he learned of it. Nevertheless it became a precedent for their institution of calf worship centuries later at the shrines of Dan and Bethel among the northern tribes of Israel.[124]

5. *The Bronze Snake.* The fashioning of this "seraph"[125] is directly attributed to Moses himself (Num. *21:4–9). This passage does not say that worship was offered to this serpent. But that it was and continued to be an object of worship for many centuries is implied in 2 Kgs. 18:4 where, in speaking of its destruction by King Hezekiah, it is said: "He brake in pieces the brazen serpent that Moses had made; for unto those days the children of Israel did burn incense to it."

The Ethical Aspects of Yahwism in the Mosaic Period. It was the ethical factor in Hebrew religion which ultimately made that religion unique in the ancient world and a permanent contribution to human civilization. Hebrew traditions consistently affirmed that Yahweh's demands upon his people were of a high, ethical quality, even from the beginning. The prophets Hosea and Jeremiah, five to six centuries afterward, looked back to the wilderness period of Hebrew life as most nearly approximating the ideal in religion.[126] In these later centuries, when ethical standards ran low and national life was corrupt, it was men of the wilderness imbued with the nomadic ideal who summoned Israel again to higher ethical standards. What was best in the ethical life of the Hebrews, these prophets regarded as the inheritance from the Mosaic era.

The Ten Commandments (Ex. *20:3–17) are commonly believed to embody the ethical consciousness of the Mosaic era, though originally very much briefer in form.[127] Certain of these regulations do accord well with the social life of nomads. To them two things are of vital importance, the purity of their blood and the sanctity of the life of the members of the tribe. The former is safeguarded by the

---

[124] *Vid. infra,* pp. 311 f.   [125] Cf. *supra,* p. 119.
[126] Hos. 2:14 f.; 11:1; 12:9; 13:4 f.; Jer. 2:2 f.
[127] For conjectures as to the original form, see C. F. Kent, *Beginnings of Hebrew History* (New York: 1904), pp. 185 f.; *ibid., Heroes and Crises of Early Hebrew History* (New York: 1908), p. 194; F. K. Sanders, *History of the Hebrews* (New York: 1928), p. 67.

seventh commandment (Ex. 20:14) and the latter by the sixth (Ex. 20:13). Moreover the social organization of the Hebrew nomads was patriarchal, and therefore reverence for the authority of the patriarchs, the fathers of the family, was a basic virtue, embodied in the divine command to respect parents (Ex. 20:12).

The ethical standards of the nomadic Hebrews were indeed praiseworthy. Notable among their virtues were: (1) Loyalty to one's own family, or clan, no doubt often solidified by group conflicts. Such loyalty was probably accompanied by a spirit of vengeance, at times raw and unrestrained. Such loyalty meant (2) the readiness of the individual to sacrifice himself for the accepted group *mores*. Josh. *7 is a dramatic picture of group *mores* in action. (3) Fidelity to a covenant.[128] (4) Courage in war. (5) Hospitality.[129] (6) Generosity. (7) An elemental, but strongly felt sense of justice. (8) Integrity of character and devotion to the people's welfare on the part of the men who judged their fellows.[130] (9) Temperance in matters of sex, due no doubt to the physically exacting character of desert life, which is free from the temptations that accompany the more complex and luxurious life of settled agriculturist and commercial communities.

All these moral virtues were regarded as necessary accompaniments of the one supreme religious virtue, i.e., exclusive devotion to Yahweh their God and fidelity to the Sinai covenant.

[128] Cf. *supra*, pp. 129 f.   [129] Cf. *supra*, p. 90.   [130] Cf. Ex. 18:21.

Chapter 9

THE WINNING OF THE HEBREW HOMELAND

The events described in this chapter cover nearly two hundred years, *circa* 1185–1000 B.C. This period witnessed the winning and settlement of the land of Canaan by the Hebrew tribesmen, the transition of these tribesmen from nomads to agriculturists with attendant advances in culture, and the initiation of the Hebrew kingship.

Sources for a History of the Period

Data for our knowledge of these two centuries are found mainly in the books of Joshua, Judges, and Samuel, with valuable supplemental material from contemporary records discovered in recent archaeological research. Joshua, Judges, and Samuel were not written as history, notwithstanding the fact that they are often referred to as historical books. They are apologetic rather than history, i.e., books which attempt to prove something, viz., that the Hebrew nation should never have made friendships with any of the prior inhabitants of Canaan but rather should have annihilated them and their religion. Jgs. *2 gives what may be called the author's philosophy of history. He interprets the career of the Hebrews during the settlement of Canaan as apostasy from Yahweh. Note how the formula of Jgs. 2:11–14 is repeated in 3:7, 12; 4:1; 6:1. The incidents narrated were selected because they supported this main contention. It is perfectly obvious, then, that documents such as these are inadequate for a complete historical picture, that they must be supplemented and balanced by all other available reliable data, and that in reading these Biblical books today one must seek to distinguish between the historical incidents related and the author's interpretation of the facts.

This statement leads to another fact of importance in using the Bible records as sources of history, viz., that the authors of the books in question were not the authors or originators of many of the stories and incidents related in Joshua, Judges, and Samuel, but that they copied them freely and apparently with few changes from much older works. Thus the vivid, spectacular, exciting exploits of the heroes and heroines of these books are probably very old stories which some scholars think almost contemporaneous accounts. But the explanations that victory or defeat, peace or war, followed inexorably and immediately upon undivided loyalty to Yahweh or worship of the Canaanite gods is the work of the later writer.

The New Leader: Joshua

"Hoshea, son of Nun," or Joshua, as he was renamed by Moses,[1] succeeded without opposition to the leadership left vacant by the death of Moses.[2] The name Hoshea means "deliverance"; the new name Joshua means "Yahweh is deliverance," a living reminder of the sworn covenant between Yahweh and the nation of which Joshua was official representative.[3]

Moses' choice of Joshua proved most felicitous. He was chieftain of the tribe of Ephraim,[4] a position which of itself marked him as a man of exceptional ability. He was one of the two scouts who urged direct attack upon Canaan from Kadesh.[5] Energetic, determined, resourceful, he was just the man to direct the advance into the Judean hills.

The Settlement of the East Jordan Country

The Moabites, who themselves originally came from the desert, had become an agricultural folk, settled east of Jordan. Some of the nomad Hebrews who had now filtered in among them gradually intermarried with the Moabites[6] and ultimately merged with them. Reuben, Gad, and part of the tribe of Manasseh were the clans which settled east of Jordan in territory taken from Sihon, king of the Amorites, and from Og, king of Bashan.[7] The account in Num. *32 of this settlement east of Jordan is at pains to point out that these tribesmen were still loyal to the whole confederation of tribes and that they helped their kinsmen fight for the west Jordan country.

The Winning of the West Jordan Country

The Crossing of the Jordan and the Capture of Jericho. Josh. *2-4, *6 describes the fording of the Jordan River, the establishing of a base at Gilgal, the sending of spies from that base to ascertain the situation in Jericho, and the attack upon, capture, and

[1] Num. 13:16.   [2] Cf. Num. 27:15-23; Deut. 34:9.
[3] Joshua was therefore the first of the Hebrew heroes to bear a name compounded with Yahweh.
[4] Num. 13:8.   [5] Num. 14:6-9.   [6] Num. 25:1-3a.
[7] Vid. supra, p. 105. In Deut. 33:6 Reuben is said to be dying, implying the disappearance of that tribe.

destruction of Jericho. At that time Jericho was a walled town of strategic importance because it dominated the main passes into the west Jordan highlands. From Jericho, three westerly routes radiate, one northwestward into central Palestine, one directly westward to Jerusalem, and one a little more to the south leading up to the plateau of Judea. Jericho was therefore the key to the land and whoever controlled it had access to the whole of Canaan.

The site of ancient Jericho was subjected to very careful excavation by the British archaeologist, John Garstang, between 1929 and 1936. The findings evidence that the city was destroyed by a terrific conflagration. On the basis of pottery fragments found at the site, Garstang dates the destruction of the city *circa* 1400 B.C. This places it at the beginning of the period covered by the Tell el 'Amarna letters.[8] This therefore integrates the destruction of Jericho with the Habiri invasion of Palestine. Interestingly enough, one of the 'Amarna letters, written by a certain Mut-Baal, mentions a *Ia-shu-ia* (Joshua) of the Gilead area.[9]

If Garstang's dating of the destruction of Jericho be accepted, then a difficulty in the problem of chronology becomes evident. We have indicated that the most probable date of the exodus is 1220 B.C.[10] Some interpreters claim that the exodus will have to be dated two centuries earlier, i.e., before 1400 B.C. Another interpretation is possible. We have pointed out that probably only a very few of the Hebrew clans went down to Egypt.[11] While they were down there, other Hebrew groups were occupying Palestine here and there. The clans which came from Egypt were joined by other groups which had not been in Egypt. The entry of these clans into Canaan marked what is technically termed the definitive conquest of Canaan by the Hebrews. This occupation of the land was therefore in process over a stretch of several centuries. The beginnings of it are to be noted in the stories of Abraham's migration to Canaan. Apparently it was at flood tide in the Habiri raids of the 'Amarna period. It reached its culmination when the clans from Egypt, with their attachés, settled in Canaan. The Bible writers fashioned all this into an Epic of the Conquest. Just as a sunglass will draw together many of the sun's rays and concentrate them on a single point, so the Bible writers gathered together what stories they could find about the Hebrews' occupation of Palestine and fashioned them into an epic which represents the whole diversified process as a single unified drive upon the land. The movement of the clans that went to and returned from Egypt furnished the framework for this epic. All the other incidents were fitted into this pattern, no matter when they happened. On this

8 *Vid. supra*, pp. 48 f.
10 *Supra*, p. 101.

9 He also mentions a Benjamin and a Job.
11 *Supra*, p. 94.

interpretation the story of Jericho's fall opens the narrative in the Book of Joshua because it was one of the most vividly remembered incidents of the early Hebrew raids upon Palestine. Drawing it down to a time subsequent to Moses was determined by literary necessity.

The Settlement of Southern Palestine. The west Jordan region was occupied by Hebrew tribes in three distinct areas, each separated from the others by chains of unconquered Canaanite cities. The southernmost section was taken by Judah and Simeon, aided by the Kenite clan. The account (Jgs. 1:1–21; Josh. 10; 13:2 f., 15:13–19, 63) shows that these Judah and Simeon tribes filtered in gradually. Historians are now of the opinion that these tribes entered directly from the south. Slowly they came into possession of the hill country south of Jerusalem, afterward known as Judah from the principal tribe settled there. Simeon later disappeared; it was doubtless absorbed by Judah.[12] These two tribes were cut off from the others by the isolated character of the Judean hill country and by a line of Canaanite cities along their northern frontier. These cities were Gezer, Aijalon, Shaalbim, and Jerusalem, which long remained unconquered by the Hebrews.[13]

The Settlement of Central Canaan. The tribes which settled in central Palestine were hemmed in on the south by the line of Canaanite cities mentioned in the preceding paragraph and on the north by another line of Canaanite strongholds—Dor, Megiddo, Taanach, Ibleam, and Bethshean,[14] fringing the Plain of Esdraelon. The principal tribes which settled in central Palestine were Ephraim and Manasseh, i.e., the part-Egyptian Joseph tribes. Affiliated with them was the little tribe of Benjamin, settled in the southern part of this central district right alongside the Canaanite fortresses.[15] Jgs. 1:22–29; Josh. 7–9 briefly sketch the conquest of this territory. From Jericho the Joseph tribes, under Joshua's leadership, advanced by the northwest road into central Canaan (the district we commonly speak of as Samaria), capturing Ai and Bethel on the way. Gradually they gained control of the whole area.[16]

Gen. *49:22–26 is a charming poem in praise of the Joseph tribes. It was written, of course, at a very much later time.

---

[12] Like Levi, Simeon was "divided in Jacob and scattered in Israel" (Gen. 49:7).
[13] Josh. 15:63; 16:10; Jgs. 1:35. Cf. G. E. Wright and F. V. Filson, *The Westminster Historical Atlas to the Bible* (Philadelphia: 1945), pp. 40, 45.
[14] Jgs. 1:27.
[15] Benjamin means "son of the right hand," which may mean "son of the south." Benjamin was the most southerly of the true Jacob tribes settled in central Canaan. Gen. 35:16 ff. represents Benjamin as the only one of Jacob's sons who was born in Palestine. This may imply a swarming of the clansmen after reaching Canaan.
[16] Cf. G. E. Wright and F. V. Filson, *op. cit.,* pp. 39, 44, 45, 105.

The Settlement of the North. The northernmost group of tribes—Issachar, Zebulun, Asher, and Naphtali—penetrated Galilee, the territory north of the Plain of Esdraelon. They were completely isolated from the other tribes by the line of Canaanite fortresses stretching across the southern edge of Esdraelon. Only a few details regarding this conquest appear in the Biblical sources (Jgs. 1:30–36; Josh. 11:1–15, 13:1, 4 ff.). Zebulun settled just north of Esdraelon, neighbor to the Phoenicians. To the eastward, bordering Lake Galilee, Issachar settled. North of these, respectively (Upper Galilee), were Asher and Naphtali. The little tribe of Dan settled at first in the north of the Shephelah where the valley of Sorek cuts into the Judean hills west of Jerusalem. It was an uncomfortable location, being in the area dominated by the Canaanite fortresses from Gezer to Jerusalem and jammed in between Philistines (southwest), Judahites (south), Benjaminites (east), and Ephraimites (north), all of whom were on the aggressive. Jgs. *18, an ancient story, narrates the migration of the Danites from this unfavorable area to the upper waters of the Jordan in the extreme north of Palestine.

The Nature of the Conquest

The conquest of Canaan is not to be thought of as a single short, swift campaign by a compact body of troops. It was a gradual process which lasted two centuries or more and which was carried on, as circumstances permitted, by groups acting more or less independently. Its fragmentary and gradual nature is well stated in Deut. 7:22, "Yahweh thy God will cast out those nations before thee by little and little; thou mayest not consume them quickly."

Josh. *11:1–15 is a realistic though gruesome picture of what the conquest was like. This chapter is a cross section of what was going on throughout the whole age. It reveals what ruthless barbarians the invading Hebrews were.

It is important to bear in mind the cultural contrast between the Canaanites and the invading Hebrews. The Canaanites were established agriculturists dwelling in cities, each city having its own king.[17] The Hebrews were nomads or near-nomads. At first they were satisfied to gain a foothold in the more hilly and rougher districts which were suitable enough for their shepherd life. The Canaanites fought stubbornly to retain possession of the farming districts but ultimately they succumbed to and were absorbed by the Hebrews.

Why the Hebrews Could Successfully Enter and Settle in Canaan. It is surprising that the Canaanites, who far outranked the

[17] *Vid. supra,* pp. 74 f.

Hebrews in knowledge of warfare and in military equipment, should have yielded so completely. Their war chariots, coats of mail, and weapons of every sort put them in a class with Egyptians, Babylonians, and Assyrians. There are four reasons for the success of the Hebrews. (1) The power of the Canaanites to resist invasion was at a minimum. Just prior to the Hebrew invasion, Canaan had been the scene of a devastating war between Egyptians and Hittites in which the nineteenth dynasty Egyptians were endeavoring to win back the territory in Palestine and Syria which had been lost by the impotent monarchs of the closing years of the eighteenth dynasty. This war, incidentally, left the Canaanites so weakened that they could offer no forceful resistance to determined invaders.[18] Moreover, the Philistines had since 1196 B.C. been pressing in upon Canaan, settling the coastal plain, and giving the Canaanites added trouble at the very time the Hebrew tribesmen were pushing in from the east. And of course the Canaanite princes were always engaged in feuds among themselves. (2) The Hebrews used tactics which rendered the Canaanite chariots and heavy armor worse than useless, for they refused to fight except in rough, broken territory where ambush and sudden raid could be most successfully employed. (3) Few Canaanites lived in the hill region and the dwellers on the plains were only remotely concerned about what went on in the mountains. At any rate, the Book of Judges indicates that the Hebrews suffered less from hostilities with the Canaanites than they did from depredations by marauders coming from the east Jordan region. (4) None of the great powers was in a position to interfere with Canaan. The Hittite war had been disastrous for all concerned. The Hittites retreated to the north. Egypt's days of aggression were over. Assyria did show her teeth when Tiglath-pileser I (*circa* 1115–1102 B.C.) made an advance as far west as Phoenicia (1104 B.C.),[19] but for two centuries after that there was no further show of aggression in the west. Thus all factors in the situation were favorable to the Hebrews.

Though the inhabitants of Palestine were not strong enough to keep the Hebrews out, they offered considerable opposition to their settlement. This is reflected and in part described in the Book of Judges.

The Nature of the "Judges"

The achievements of the Hebrews were in no small measure due to their leaders. Their penetration into Canaan was due to the masterful

---

[18] Certain strange but interesting verses (Ex. 23:28; Deut. 7:20; Josh. 24:12) speak of "the hornet" as clearing the way in Canaan so that the Hebrews could take possession of the land. "The hornet" may mean Egypt. The hornet was the symbol of the Pharaoh Thutmose III (1501–1447 B.C.).

[19] Cf. A. T. Olmstead, *History of Palestine and Syria* (New York: 1931), p. 292.

generalship of Joshua. The "judges" who followed him were merely local leaders who arose in times of crisis to assume command in their own and sometimes in neighboring tribes (Jgs. *2:16–23). The tribes in this period had no central government. They were separated by geographic barriers and intense clan loyalties. Consequently, sectional and tribal isolation was the rule, save as common peril led to temporary united action under some one of the so-called "judges." [20]

It is impossible to determine the dates and sequences of the "judges" mentioned in the Book of Judges. The author of the book seems to have selected his stories about "judges" according to a geographical scheme, aiming to give a sample from each area of the country and in connection with each of the enemy peoples who opposed the Hebrew settlement in the land. Thus Deborah and Barak are associated with the north and with the Canaanite opposition. Gideon is associated with central Canaan and with the repelling of Midianite raiders who came from the east but more remotely from the south. Associated with Eastjordania were Othniel, who expelled the Aramaeans,[21] Jephthah, who suppressed the Ammonites, and Ehud, who freed the Hebrews from the Moabites. Shamgar and Samson were associated with Philistine aggression in the southwest.

Overcoming Canaanite Opposition. Fearing the slow but persistent encroachments of the Hebrews, who evidently were fast crowding down from the hills into the farming territory and towns, the Canaanites reacted in counterrepressive measures which threatened to reduce the Hebrews to a state bordering on servitude.[22] Matters came to a climax in the famous battle described in prose and song in Jgs. 4 f., a battle from which the Hebrews emerged gloriously victorious. The poetic version (chapter 5) is a stirring ode commemorative of the great victory. Incidentally, this is one of the oldest extant poems of Hebrew literature.[23]

The Canaanite strongholds at this period were the city-studded fertile valleys. Of these, the Plain of Esdraelon was largest and richest. Here was fought the decisive battle described in Jgs. 4 f. Harosheth, one of the walled cities that fringed the plain, was the center of the Canaanite confederacy. Five of the Hebrew tribes—Ephraim, Benjamin, Naphtali, Zebulun, and Issachar, under the fiery exhortation of a prophetess named Deborah,[24] managed to raise an army of some 10,000 men. Against them were pitted the allied Canaanite forces, of unknown but evidently great size, including

---

[20] Cf. G. E. Wright and F. V. Filson, *op. cit.,* pp. 43–46.
[21] But cf. *infra,* p. 145, fn. 33. [22] Jgs. 4:1 ff.; 5:6 f. [23] *Vid. infra,* pp. 166 ff.
[24] The role played by Deborah shows that, in spite of woman's inferior social status (she was only a chattel), occasionally a woman of strong personal qualities could and did rise to a position of commanding influence.

900 armored chariots. Under ordinary circumstances the poorly armed Hebrews would have had no chance whatever against such overwhelming odds. However, two things were in their favor. One was the powerful religious bond under which they rallied, "To the help of Yahweh! To the help of Yahweh against the mighty!" [25] The other was that the Hebrew military leader, Barak of Kadesh-Naphtali, strategically placed his forces on the high ground of Mount Tabor on the north side of the plain. When a terrific rain storm had converted the Plain of Esdraelon into a veritable swamp, he hurled his lightly armed but extremely mobile forces down upon the deeply mired Canaanites, putting them to utter rout. Numbers of the Canaanites perished in the swollen waters of the Kishon, and their leader, Sisera, met his death ignominiously at the hands of a woman. This battle appears to have quite ended the Canaanites' efforts to keep the Hebrews out of the plains. Henceforth we find the two peoples living side by side in outward peace and apparent harmony. The harmony was no doubt helped on by the Philistine aggression, which was as much a menace to the Canaanites as to the Hebrews.

Overcoming the Opposition of the Midianites. Jgs. *6:1–6 is a graphic picture of Palestine overrun by hordes of marauding camel-nomads, Midianites and Amalekites from the barren tablelands of the Arabian Desert south and east of Canaan. These roving marauders made life wretched for the Hebrews, who by this time had given up their own roving habits to adopt the ways of settled agriculturists. At harvesttime these robbers made sudden, swift raids on one or another of the unprepared hamlets, seized the fruits of the season's toil, and then as swiftly withdrew to disappear in the vast desert wastes that fringe Palestine on the east and south. The situation became so bad, indeed, that the Hebrews could not openly winnow their grain. Gideon beat out his wheat in a wine press to escape being observed.[26] This intolerable situation was ended by the united effort of certain tribes that bordered the Plain of Esdraelon.[27] They were rallied by Gideon, a man of the little clan of Abiezer in Manasseh,[28] who was roused not alone by the economic disabilities under which he and others suffered but also by the stern duty of blood revenge, for these raiders had slain his brothers.[29] Fired by the war cry, "For Yahweh and for Gideon," [30] they drove the Midianites across the Jordan Valley and clear out of the country (Jgs. *6:11–8:12).

Gideon, in repelling the Midianites, was fighting the battle of the older inhabitants of Canaan as much as that of the Hebrews them-

---

[25] Jgs. 5:23.   [26] Jgs. 6:11.   [27] Jgs. 6:35.
[28] Jgs. 6:11, 15.   [29] Jgs. 8:18 f.   [30] Jgs. 7:18.

selves, which fact no doubt contributed to the fusion of Canaanites and Hebrews.

Gideon is typical of the "judges." He was leader in a particular crisis. His brilliant success gave him such prestige that the tribesmen immediately wanted to make him king.[31] Though refusing the royal title, Gideon apparently did rule as chieftain for the balance of his lifetime. At his death, one of his sons, Abimelech, conspired to succeed to the chieftainship. The story of this sordid conspiracy and its tragic outcome (Jgs. 9) is a true portrait of the rough life and crude standards of that age.[32]

Making Eastjordania Secure. Jgs. 3:7–11 is a brief account of how the Hebrews, under Othniel, checked raids by the Aramaeans.[33] Jgs. 3:12–30 tells of the aggressions of the Moabites who for a time pushed westward over the Jordan and practically subjugated the Hebrews of central Canaan. A left-handed Benjaminite named Ehud was the "judge" who ended that menace. Jgs. *10:6–11:40 recounts a vigorous war waged upon the east Jordan Hebrews by the Ammonites who claimed the region by right of prior possession. The Hebrews, on the other hand, claimed it by right of divine allotment, the gift of their deity, Yahweh. The tribesmen under Jephthah gained the victory.

The New Standard of Living

Houses. During the period of the settlement of Canaan, the Hebrews gradually gave up dwelling in tents and adopted the Canaanite custom of living in houses.[34] The simplest type of Palestinian house is the same today as it was in Old Testament times. They were and are insubstantial. Whenever a house collapsed, as it invariably did in time, the debris was simply leveled off and a new house was built on top of it. In very early times every man built his own house. In later Old Testament times expert builders or masons were employed on royal residences, on city walls, and on other buildings of size or importance.

Houses were usually of one story. They were usually square, and contained only one room, which was fairly large. Occasionally, a house

---

[31] Jgs. 8:22.   [32] Vid. infra, pp. 157 f.

[33] Some interpreters hold that it was not Aramaeans but Edomites whom Othniel repulsed. This view is based on translating "Cushanrishathaim" (Jgs. 3:8) by "double-dealing Cushite"; he was king of Aram. In Hebrew, the words for *Aram* and *Edom* are alike save for *d* and *r*, and these two letters are alike except that written *d* has a sharp corner while written *r* is rounded. Moreover, Othniel was "the son of Kenaz, Caleb's younger brother" (Jgs. 3:9), which associates him with the South near the Edomite frontier.

[34] Deut. 6:10 f. Cf. M. S. and J. L. Miller, *Encyclopedia of Bible Life* (New York: 1944), pp. 241–250.

belonging to some person of importance would have an upper room. Such was the house of Eglon, king of Moab, whom Ehud slew.[35]

The walls of houses were regularly three to four feet thick, built of common field stones or, in the more pretentious homes, of roughly dressed quarry stones. Sun-dried bricks were used by the poor. "Wrought stone," [36] i.e., stone carefully dressed, or "hewn stone, according to measure, sawed with saws," [37] was the most substantial material used. The mortar employed was made of clay, though bitumen was also sometimes used. Such a mixture of mud and slime for mortar became very soapy in rainy weather, and in heavy storms houses frequently collapsed. Sometimes the outside of a house was whitewashed. The foundation stones and the thresholds of houses were held sacred, and they were often laid with human sacrifices. That is, human beings, most likely children, were buried alive in jars under the stones to insure good luck to the owner of the house.[38] In time the Hebrews came to substitute lamps, symbolic of life, for human beings in such dedications.

The roof was usually flat. From wall to wall either tree trunks with branches and twigs or stout wooden beams were laid. Across these were laid small rafters upon which brushwood was piled, and then several inches of earth were added. Over all a coating of clay mortar was spread and either pressed down in showery weather with a small stone roller or pounded down with a board to make it watertight. Such a roof needed constant attention to keep it in condition. A steep outside staircase, with no protective railing, made access to the roof easy though not too safe. Around the edge of the roof ran a low battlement or parapet, a safety device which was in time made compulsory.[39]

The roof was used for domestic purposes. It was a handy place for drying linen and flax, figs and raisins. It was a comfortable place for sleeping in hot weather.[40] It was used on occasion for recreation,[41] for public proclamations,[42] for lamentation,[43] for prayer and meditation,[44] and for religious worship. There were altars on top of the roof chamber of Ahaz in Jerusalem,[45] and even idolatrous worship was carried on upon the housetops.[46] It was on such a roof, with its piles of drying flax, that the Jericho spies were hidden by Rahab.[47] No doubt people often found the roof an advantageous place from which

[35] Jgs. 3:20–23. [36] 1 Kgs. 5:17. [37] 1 Kgs. 7:9.
[38] Such threshold interment jars with bones of infants were discovered, for example, at Gezer and at Teleilat el-Ghassul east of Jordan. On the latter, cf. Nelson Glueck, *The River Jordan* (Philadelphia: 1946), pp. 233–237; C. C. McCown, *The Ladder of Progress in Palestine* (New York: 1943), p. 59.
[39] Deut. 22:8. [40] 1 Sam. 9:25.
[41] 2 Sam. 11:2. [42] Matt. 10:27; Lk. 12:3.
[43] Isa. 15:3; 22:1; Jer. 48:38. [44] Acts 10:9.
[45] 2 Kgs. 23:12. [46] Jer. 19:13; 32:29; Zeph. 1:5.
[47] Josh. 2:6.

to observe what neighbors were doing. One instance of this had fateful consequences.[48]

The few houses that boasted windows of any sort had them placed at least six feet above the ground. Such openings were small, but they might be large enough to let a man through.[49] They were closed, not with glass, of course, but with wood or latticework which could be opened when necessary. The poorer houses had no window openings at all. The idea was to restrict the light, thereby affording protection against the devastating summer sun.

The door was made of wood and hung upon projecting pivots of wood which turned in sockets in the threshold and lintel, something like our freely swinging doors between kitchen and dining room. The threshold [50] was of stone. The doorposts or jambs were simply square posts of either wood or stone. Doors were locked on the inside [51] by means of a square wooden bolt that was thrust horizontally into a socket fastened to the jamb. This bolt was hollowed out for a little more than half its length, and pins dropped from the socket into holes in the bolt. To unlock the door one "put in the hand by the hole of the door," [52] and into the hollow end of the bolt inserted the key, a piece of wood some nine inches long, with pins fastened on the top side at one end in such a way that, when the key was pressed upward, the pins entered the holes in the bolt, pushed up the pins of the lock, and made possible the withdrawal of the bolt. The key was often of great size, big enough even to serve as a stout club.[53]

The walls inside the house were commonly plastered with clay. In later and more opulent times, the homes of the wealthy had walls lined with cypress, fir wood, or cedar. King Ahab's ivory house was an extreme of luxury.[54] Amos speaks of "ivoried houses," which probably means houses with wooden panels inlaid with ivory.[55] The floor of the ordinary house was of hard, beaten clay. Houses of the better class were floored with cypress or other woods, like that of the Jerusalem temple.[56]

In all single-room houses the floor was built on two levels. The lower level, which was even with the entrance, harbored the domestic animals at night and in the winter. The higher level was for the family. It might be only eighteen inches above the other, or it might be a raised masonry platform resting on low-domed arches, eight to ten feet above the lower level and reached by a narrow flight of steps.

Among the arches of such a room the sheep and goats were kept in winter, shut in by bundles of brush piled in the arched entrances.

[48] 2 Sam. 11:2–5.
[50] Jgs. 19:27.
[52] Cant. 5:4.
[54] 1 Kgs. 22:39.
[56] 1 Kgs. 6:15.

[49] Josh. 2:15.
[51] Jgs. 3:23 ff.
[53] Isa. 22:22.
[55] Am. 3:15.

The rest of the floor space was for donkey, camel, or work cattle. Around the walls and suitably low against the ground, mangers were set; these were hollowed-out blocks of native limestone.[57] Sometimes there was a small raised platform on which the owner might sleep at night, partly because it was warmer near the animals and partly because he could better watch over the newborn lambs from there.

In the better homes the family level was lighted and aired by one or two windows which also served as an outlet for the smoke from the stove or fireplace. Fuel consisted of wood, dried grass, or dried manure. The more well to do used a brazier[58] or a firepan[59] in which charcoal was burned for warmth.

Household Furnishings. Near the hearth were the cooking utensils, which were commonly either "earthen vessels" or "vessels of wood" or, more rarely, of iron. Conspicuous among the earthen vessels were the water jars, or pitchers, in which water was brought from the village well, and the large jars which were used as containers of wheat, barley, olives, and fruits. The cruse was a smaller jar, with one or two handles, for holding oil or for carrying water on a journey. The bucket was a waterskin adapted for drawing water. Skins were also commonly used for keeping wine and milk. There were pots for cooking, either of clay or of bronze. Bowls were usually earthenware, though some were wooden. The kneading trough was simply a large wooden bowl.[60] Baskets were used for bread and fruits. There was commonly a hand mill of two stones, the lower stone embedded in a trough of sun-dried clay which served to catch the flour as it left the mill. There were flour sieves, cooking spoons, and cups. The most common iron cooking utensils were flat plates for baking or frying. There were also knives, originally of flint[61] but later of bronze, for cutting up meat,[62] and forks or "fleshhooks."[63] Occasional mention is made of silver and gold bowls, spoons, and goblets,[64] but these must have been very rare.

Other furniture about the house consisted of the housewife's bridal chest, a straw mat or woven woolen rug on the floor, and the bed and mattresses. The poor man slept on a mat of straw or rushes, on the floor in the one living room. He slept in his day clothes with his cloak wrapped about him.[65] In time it came to be not unusual for a house to have an "inner chamber" or "bed chamber," i.e., a separate room. The homes of prominent men were likely to have such. A bedstead was simply a wooden framework on which were spread

---

[57] Cf. M. S. and J. L. Miller, *Encyclopedia of Bible Life* (New York: 1944), pp. 26, 248, and Fig. 21.
[58] Jer. 36:22 f.
[60] Ex. 12:34.
[62] Gen. 22:6, 10; Jgs. 19:29.
[64] Num. 7:13 f.; 1 Kgs. 10:21; Est. 1:7.

[59] Zech. 12:6.
[61] Josh. 5:2.
[63] Ex. 27:3; 1 Sam. 2:13.
[65] Ex. 22:26 f.

cushions,[66] or "carpets," and "striped cloths." [67] During the day the bed was made up and used as a couch.[68] In the time of Amos the very wealthy had couches inlaid with ivory and furnished with "silken cushions."

Lamps were made of clay, with handles similar to those of our cups. There were two common types. One was open, like a saucer, with the rim pinched together on one side to form a channel for the wick. The other type was closed, except that in a saucerlike depression in the top surface there was a hole for pouring in the oil, and there was an opening for the wick at the side opposite the handle. A rag served as wick and olive oil was used for fuel. Such lamps held only a little oil and needed frequent refilling.

About the room were the distaff, spindle, and looms for making the family garments, and a chest for holding the latter.

The one room had to serve as kitchen, storeroom, living room, and bedroom. The family often used the stable part of the house when it was not needed for the animals. The housewife would cook or sew there, and the men would turn their looms, for this part of the room, being near the door, was comparatively well lighted. Especially was this important in winter. Guests were entertained in the animal quarters if there was no room in the upper part of the house. It was to such a house in Bethlehem that Joseph and Mary went when "there was no room at the inn." [69] They were not refused hospitality. The house undoubtedly being already crowded, they found lodging in the animal quarters, and so Jesus was cradled "in a manger." Sometimes the stable portion of the house was an old cave or cavern over which the house proper was built. Such a cave in the Church of the Nativity in Bethlehem is exhibited as the actual birthplace of Jesus.

The outer court was a walled enclosure that surrounded houses of the more pretentious sort. Goats, sheep, and cattle were penned within it. It often contained a cistern or well.[70] When it was desired to enlarge the house—e.g., because of the marriage of a son—one or more additional rooms were constructed on this court.

Food.   What was said in Chapter 5 regarding the diet of the Hebrews in the nomadic era is equally true of their life after the settlement in Canaan.[71] Bread was ever the staff of life. The type of baking pan used by the nomads [72] continued to be used, and now the oven came into vogue. One type of oven was bowl-shaped. Indeed, it was simply a large clay bowl with movable lid, inverted over stones. Fuel, heaped over this bowl, was burned and thus heated the bowl

[66] Am. 3:12.
[68] Ezk. 23:41.
[70] 2 Sam. 17:18.
[72] Cf. *supra*, p. 85.

[67] Prov. 7:16.
[69] Matt. 2:1–12; Lk. 2:1–20.
[71] *Vid. supra*, pp. 84 ff.

sufficiently to cook the batter when a thin layer of it was spread over the hot outside. Another type was the jar oven. Into a large earthenware jar, fuel was put and burned. When the jar was hot, the batter was spread on the inside walls to cook. From this jar oven was evolved the pit oven. This was shaped partly in the ground and then built up of clay, narrowing from the bottom upward and plastered throughout.

Breadmaking was always the work of women. Even when the profession of baker developed, this work consisted of baking the dough already prepared by the women at home.

Cereals and vegetables became staple articles of diet after the Hebrews had taken to agriculture.

Fruits began to come into general use. "Trees for food" was the quaint Hebrew expression for fruit trees.[73] (1) Olives were eaten either fresh or preserved in brine. Olive oil was used in cooking, serving the same purpose as butter and fat in modern cooking. It was mixed with vegetables, used in cooking fish and eggs, and in finer baking. Olive oil was often mixed with flour and shaped into cakes. It was often smeared on the baked cakes also. (2) Grapes, as a rule, were made into wine, the "fruit of the vine," but they were also dried into raisins. (3) Figs were, next to grapes, the most highly prized fruit. The early figs were considered the most delicious and refreshing. Figs were dried into clusters and pressed into cakes. (4) Other fruits of which we find mention were pomegranates, apples (probably the quince), mulberries (very likely from the sycamore or fig mulberry), cucumbers, melons, almonds, and nuts.

Honey was used in cooking as we use sugar. Much of the honey was probably made by boiling down dates. The natural product was found in hollows in rocks or in hollow trees.[74] Honey and oil were used together in baking sweet cakes. Ex. 16:31 compares the taste of manna with that of "wafers made with honey," and Num. 11:8 says manna tasted like "cakes baked with oil."

Meat was used sparingly and milk freely, as in the nomadic era.[75]

Breakfast, for the farmer or laborer, consisted of a small bit of bread with perhaps a few olives. The first real mealtime was about noon, when the hot climate compelled people to rest. It was a very simple meal of bread dipped in light wine (vinegar), and parched grain.[76] The principal meal of the day was in the evening, about sunset, when the workers "came in from the field." In early nomadic times they sat or squatted on the ground to eat their meals. After the

---

73 Lev. 19:23.
74 A jar shaped like a conical hive, found at Tell en-Nasbeh, evidences the practice of beekeeping. Cf. Millar Burrows, *What Mean These Stones?* (New Haven: 1941), p. 172.
75 *Vid. supra*, pp. 85 f.   76 Ruth 2:14.

settlement in Canaan, seats were sometimes used,[77] the food being placed on a low stand. Gradually the practice of reclining was introduced, until in New Testament times it was the regular custom and the expression "sitting at meat" is to be so understood.

Farming. Prior to their entrance into Canaan, the Hebrews were nomads and the activities of pastoral life made up their daily routine.[78] After their settlement in Canaan pastoral pursuits still retained a vital place in their life. Indeed, Palestine is better adapted to cattle raising and sheep breeding, especially in Judea, and many a settled agriculturist led a seminomadic life, turning aside from his flocks only at seasons of planting and reaping.

There were beginnings of agriculture in the nomadic period,[79] but it did not become an important occupation of the Hebrews until after they had lived some time in Canaan.[80] Yet husbandry was esteemed an honorable pursuit, an art which they regarded as learned from God himself,[81] to whom the land belonged.[82]

The most fertile districts were the great lowland plains and the plateau east of Jordan. In the broken hill country and on the plateau of Judea extensive agriculture was impossible. So steep are the hillsides that in many places terraces had to be built to prevent the washing away of the soil. The soil has been kept fertile through the centuries by the decomposition of the underlying limestone rock.

Irrigation was practiced to some extent, water wheels and ditches being used for the purpose. But agriculture in Palestine was, and still is, vitally dependent upon the "former rain" and the "latter rain." [83] The first rains fall in late October and November and soften the soil which during the long hot summer has been baked very hard. The weather from then on continues intermittently wet, but some fine days following the first rains give the husbandman his chance to plow and sow. The heavy winter rains saturate the soil. The rainy season continues until March and sometimes until April, and it is these "latter rains" which provide the necessary additional moisture to produce the harvest. The vintage and the fruit harvest depend especially upon these "latter rains." From mid-October to mid-April the farmer is engaged in plowing, harrowing, sowing, and weeding; and after mid-April he is engaged in reaping, carrying, threshing, and storing the grain.

The plow used by the Hebrews was not very different from the modern Syrian plow. It was a crude tool, made of oak, the bent parts

---

[77] 1 Sam. 20:25. [78] *Vid. supra,* pp. 86 f.
[79] Gen. 4:2; 26:12.
[80] Cf. M. S. and J. L. Miller, *op. cit.,* pp. 1–22.
[81] Isa. 28:26. [82] Lev. 25:23.
[83] Deut. 11:14. Cf. Nelson Glueck, *The River Jordan* (Philadelphia: 1946), pp. 128 f. for an account of an irrigation project in Eastjordania dating from Bible times.

being natural curves in the wood, held together by iron bands. The plowshare, which was small, merely scratched the ground a few inches deep. To it was fastened a single upright shaft with a short crosspiece to serve as handle. With one hand the farmer guided his plow, while with the other he wielded the ox goad, a light wooden pole with a vicious spike at one end with which to prod the oxen, and with a little spade at the other end for cleaning off the plowshare. The plow was drawn by two or more oxen or by asses. A religious law forbade to "plow with an ox and ass together." [84] Places which could not be plowed, e.g., gardens and vineyards, were worked with a hoe or a mattock.

Seed was scattered by hand and immediately plowed under. In the more developed agriculture, plowing and sowing were combined in one operation by fastening a seedbox to the plowtail, a pipe conveying the seed to the drill behind the share, where it was at once covered up. Sowing was toilsome work, hampered by uncertain weather. It was not counted a joyful task.

Growing crops were subject to many dangers such as blasting by the east winds, drought due to lack of the "latter rain," mildew, hailstorm, weeds (such as mustard, thistles, tares, and thorns), crows, sparrows, insects (such as palmer worm, locust, cankerworm, caterpillar), depredations of cattle, and fire.

Harvest, beginning as a rule about the middle of April, lasted about seven weeks until early June. Barley was the first crop to be harvested. Wheat ripened about two weeks later.

The grain was cut with a sickle of flint or bronze, about a foot below the ears. The stalks of grain were dropped by the reaper in handfuls and tied into sheaves by the binders. Sometimes, especially when crops were light and the stalks very short, the grain was pulled up by the roots. The corners of the fields were not reaped, but they, together with any sheaves overlooked by the binders, were left for the poor and the stranger.[85] The harvesting was done by the owners and their families, with the minimum of hired help. Ruth *2 is a delightful description of a harvesting scene.

From the harvest field the grain was transported on asses or in carts to the village threshing floor, where it was stacked in heaps. The threshing floor was a large flat rock (in the mountainous country) or a hard piece of ground (on the plains), suitably exposed to the breezes. The sheaves were first spread out over the floor; then from four to six oxen yoked together were driven around over the sheaves until the grain was separated from the straw. Laborers kept

84 Deut. 22 :10.
85 Deut. 24 :19 ; Lev. 19 :9 ; Ruth 2 :2-7.

stirring the straw with forks (having two or more prongs) to facilitate the threshing. The oxen were specially shod for the threshing,
a small iron shoe being fastened to each half of the cloven hoof because such a shoe prevented lameness and was more effective in
separating the grain. Oxen were not supposed to be muzzled when
treading the grain.[86]

Threshing was done more effectively by the threshing drag and
by the threshing wagon. The under side of the drag was notched or
studded with nails or sharp stone chips which, pressed down by the
weight of the driver, separated the grain and cut up the straw into
small lengths. The threshing wagon was simply a wooden frame
equipped with three or more rollers and a seat for the driver. When
the threshing was completed, the straw and grain were all heaped up
to await the winnowing.

The winnower, by means of a five- or six-pronged wooden fork
and a fan, which was really a kind of shovel, tossed the threshed
grain into the air when a wind of proper strength was blowing, which
was usually at night. The chaff and dust were thus completely blown
away, the straw blowing to one side in a pile and the grain dropping
back to the floor. Next the grain was sifted and stored in granaries
or "barns" and in cisterns or pits, the openings of which were covered
to protect against thieves and vermin. The straw became fodder for
the cattle. The chaff was burned for fuel.

The prophet Isaiah, in his "Poem of the Farmer" (Isa. *28:23–29),
idealizes the work of the farmer and its religious significance.

Interesting and sometimes unusual laws relating to agriculture
grew up in the course of time. The fields surrounding a village were
held in common by the villagers, who tilled them and shared the
produce in common. Thus, a neighbor's landmark, indicating the
boundary of his field, was not to be moved;[87] this, however, was
more a question of theft of crop than of land, for land was not
originally owned. Sowing a field with mixed seed and breeding
hybrids were forbidden.[88] Damages were allowed for burning a neighbor's field.[89] Straying cattle were to be restored to their owners.[90]
Of course there were no fences. A field was to lie fallow every seventh
year.[91] Land could not be permanently alienated from its holder; he
held his land in trust; it had come to him from his fathers and he
must preserve it for his children.[92] The wayfarer might pluck enough
of the standing grain to appease his hunger,[93] and the poor might glean
the fields.[94]

[86] Deut. 25:4.
[88] Lev. 19:19.
[90] Ex. 23:4; Deut. 22:1–4.
[92] Lev. 25:8–12.
[94] Lev. 19:9; Deut. 24:19.

[87] Deut. 19:14; 27:17.
[89] Ex. 22:6.
[91] Ex. 23:10 f.
[93] Deut. 23:25.

The vine was cultivated regularly upon hillsides not suitable for other crops. Isa. *5:1–7 is a poem whose analogies give a good description of grape culture. The vineyard was first fenced, then the stones were removed, and in the springtime the vines were cultivated with plow or mattock and pruned. Vines required several years' care before they bore fruit. When the fruit harvest drew near, the owner and his family moved out to the vineyard and lived in the watchtower, a small structure erected at a vantage point, from which the guardians watched for thieves and animals, particularly foxes and jackals. In the vineyard was a wine press cut in the solid rock, wherein the grape juice was extracted, which was afterward probably made into a kind of honey. Wine was made, but in that climate fruit juices quickly ferment and change to vinegar. The vine and the fig tree became symbolic of prosperity and contentment.[95]

The process of harvesting olives, still followed in Syria, is extremely damaging to the trees. The fruit gatherers beat the tree with sticks to knock off the fruit.[96] By so doing they destroy the tender shoots which would bear the next year's crop; hence the trees yield only every second year. An olive tree comes into bearing when about fifteen years old. Some olive trees survive to an extreme age, at least to three or four hundred years. The olives were run through a mill to extract the oil for commercial purposes, and the operation of the oil mills was quite an important industry.

Communities. There were no isolated homesteads in Canaan. Continual fear of marauding expeditions by desert tribes, who drove in their flocks among the standing grain and carried off grain and cattle, compelled the agriculturists to build their homes in clusters for the sake of security. This led to the formation of villages and cities. From these homes the men went out daily to till the surrounding fields.

Two factors determined the location of communities: (1) the presence of an adequate water supply; (2) the feasibility of defense. The water supply was all important. One or two springs were sure to be found in the vicinity of every community, where, "at the time of evening," the women drew water. Within the city were open pools or covered cisterns to store water against the long dry summer or against siege.

The defensive adaptability of a place was no less important. Cities were usually located on a spur of some mountain slope or on an elevation in the midst of a plain.[97] About the city were massive walls

---

95 1 Kgs. 4:25.
96 Deut. 24:20.
97 Cf. Josh. 11:13, "cities on their mounds."

of sun-dried bricks or stone or both.[98] The thickness of the walls varied from city to city and even in the same city, according to the height required. Some walls as much as twenty-six feet thick have been excavated. The height varied with the nature of the location. On top of the wall was a breastwork or battlement.

Walls were strengthened by buttresses, which often developed into towers, for towers at the corners of the walls were a great aid in defending the portion of wall between them. The strongest towers flanked the city gate.

The gateway was usually a passage forming a right angle through a tower which projected beyond the city wall, having outer and inner gates or doors.[99] The gates were two-leaved, massive, wooden doors, plated with iron or bronze to protect them against fire and battering. The bolts and bars and locks, in form not unlike those of dwellings but of massive proportions, were of wood, bronze, or iron.[100] At nightfall the gates of the city were closed,[101] and through the night watchmen were stationed on guard on the walls or went about the streets of the city.

Every city of importance had its citadel to which the citizens might flee as a last defense. It was the "strong tower" of the city.[102]

Dwelling houses were built right up to the city walls.[103] Streets were narrow, crooked, and dirty, with many blind alleys. At the intersections of the more important streets were the "broad places," the "markets" or "market places." The open space by a city gate was also a good place for specialized marketing. Hence such a place often had a special name, e.g., the "sheep gate," [104] the "fish gate," [105] the "horse gate." [106] In these open spaces the citizens gathered to discuss public matters, the elders to administer justice, the tax collector to receive the customs, and the children to play. The gate was for a city what the flat roof was for a house. Life about a city gate is admirably reflected in Job 29:7–10, 21 ff. Different quarters of the city came to have special names indicating the craft or profession of the residents there; e.g., Jerusalem had its "bakers' street," [107] "fuller's field," [108] and, perhaps, a "valley of craftsmen." [109]

[98] Num. 13:28; Deut. 1:28; 3:5; 9:1. At a later period facings of stone were placed both outside and inside the walls for additional strength. In the New Testament period the stones of the walls were laid in careful courses, e.g., at Jerusalem. In the wall of the temple area, stones measuring thirty by eight by three and one-half feet and weighing upwards of eighty tons are still to be found in place.

[99] Cf. 2 Sam. 18:24. The most impressive city gate known to archaeology is that at Tell en-Nasbeh (Mizpah). Cf. Millar Burrows, *What Mean These Stones?* (New Haven: 1941), pp. 147 ff. and Figs. 21–22; C. C. McCown, *The Ladder of Progress in Palestine* (New York: 1943), pp. 211 f.

[100] Jgs. 16:3 tells of Samson's tearing away the two leaves of the city gate at Gaza.

[101] Josh. 2:5, 7.   [102] Jgs. 9:51.   [103] Josh. 2:15.
[104] Neh. 3:1, 32; 12:39.   [105] Neh. 3:3; 12:39.
[106] 2 Kgs. 11:16; 2 Chr. 23:15; Jer. 31:40.   [107] Jer. 37:21.
[108] 2 Kgs. 18:17; Isa. 7:3; 36:2.   [109] 1 Chr. 4:14; Neh. 11:35.

2 Kgs. 4:8 ff. depicts how the hospitality of a certain Hebrew family prompted them to build a "guest chamber" where the prophet Elisha might find lodging when he came to town; the furniture of such a chamber, as noted in vs. 10, is interesting: "a bed, and a table, and a seat, and a candlestick." 1 Sam. 9:22 represents that there was a guest chamber at the high place in a certain community, presumably Ramah, where Samuel entertained Saul. Such guest chambers may have been the precedent for what, at some time, came to be a custom in Palestine, viz., of having village guest chambers maintained at common expense for the use of travelers.

Each city had its sanctuary or "high place," either inside the walls or outside on some adjoining hill.[110] No city would have felt secure without it.

The distinction between city and village was not one of size but rather of status, a city being the political and defensive center for a number of nearby affiliated villages. A city was related to its dependent villages as a mother to a daughter.[111] Some of the ancient cities that have been excavated did not cover more than fifteen acres.

Among the Canaanites the king was supreme in the administration of a city's affairs. In the time of the Hebrew monarchies the "elders of the city" administered the law.[112] There were freemen (i.e., the "men of the city," with their families), slaves (mostly captives of war), sojourners, and strangers (foreigners) in every place.

Social Conditions in the Age of the "Judges"

While the Hebrews were slowly giving up their nomadic ways, the old, free, independent spirit of the desert was still with them. The urge to wander was still in evidence, as shown by the story of the Danite migration.[113] It was a rough, unrestrained age. Clearly there was no central government at all during the two centuries. It must have been that two or more of the "judges" lived at the same time, ruling over different districts. Rarely, even in the time of common danger, did more than two or three tribes unite and fight shoulder to shoulder. Thus the Song of Deborah stingingly arraigns the tribes of Reuben, Dan, Asher, and the dwellers in Gilead for taking no part in the great battle of independence which it commemorates.[114] In short, in this period the tribes seem to have lost that sense of nationalism which Moses had worked to develop. The author of Judges illuminatingly remarks, "In those days there was no king in Israel: every man did that which was right in his own eyes." [115] It is a wonder they did not completely disintegrate.

---

110 1 Sam. 9:12.   111 2 Sam. 20:19; Josh. 15:32, 36, 41, especially 45.
112 Deut. 19:12; 21:3 ff.; Ruth 4:2.
113 Jgs. 18.   114 Jgs. 5:15 ff.   115 Jgs. 17:6; 21:25.

The crude state of their moral development is revealed in the sordid stories told in Jgs. *3:12–30, which recounts the cunning treachery of the Benjaminite Ehud, and in Jgs. *19–21 which tells of an inter-tribal warfare that almost exterminated the Benjaminites. There was, however, a better side to the life of the time. This is portrayed in the beautiful story of *Ruth and in the story of the birth and childhood of Samuel (1 Sam. *1–3). These stories vividly illustrate the manners and customs of daily life discussed on the foregoing pages.

The Canaanites were by no means exterminated. The summary in Jgs. 1 proves that to a large extent the land was still held by the Canaanites. This is not altogether to be regretted, for recent excavations in Palestine (e.g., at Kiriath-sepher) have shown that the Hebrew culture of the period was very low indeed and that it gained markedly in the exchanges with the Canaanites. In time the two peoples intermarried and became one race,[116] and the Canaanites disappeared because they became Hebrews.

The story in Jgs. *9 illumines the social conditions of the period. Gideon had a Canaanite concubine in Shechem (not his own home town). This was a marriage of the type wherein the wife remains with her parents, and occasionally her husband visits her, bringing a gift. The same custom is indicated in the case of Samson's marriage to the woman of Timnah,[117] and is implied in Samson's connections with the harlot and with Delilah.[118] The custom is a holdover from a matriarchal state of society. Gideon's son by the woman of Shechem was named Abimelech ("my father is king"). Organization under a local petty king was the Canaanite pattern, and after his repulsion of the Midianites the populace attempted to make Gideon a king. Perhaps this came about through the insistence of the Canaanite element in the population. Though open warfare no longer existed between the two elements in the population, there was, as the story reveals, deep-seated antipathy between the older Canaanite population (the people of Shechem in the story) and the more recent Hebrew settlers (represented in the story by the seventy sons of Gideon by his Hebrew wives). Abimelech based his appeal to the Shechemites on blood kinship,[119] his mother being a woman of Shechem. His slaughter of the seventy sons of Gideon reflects a Canaanite effort to assert control over the Hebrews. When Abimelech asked, "Whether is better for you, that all the sons of Jerubaal, who are threescore and ten persons, rule over you, or that one rule over you?"[120] he was casting aspersion on the Hebrew system of local government through tribal elders and urging the Shechemites to

---

[116] Jgs. 3:5 f. Cf. Gen. 38:2.
[118] Jgs. 16.
[120] Jgs. 9:2.

[117] Jgs. 15:1.
[119] Jgs. 9:2.

maintain the traditional Canaanite practice of community rule by a local king. The petty counterpolitical discord which the adventurer Gaal stirred up in Shechem against Abimelech is doubtless typical of the rivalry that existed among the Canaanites from of old.[121]

Peaceful relations did not always prevail among the Hebrew tribes themselves (Jgs. 9; *12:1–6; 20). They quarreled and fought with one another, thus making it easier for hostile neighbors to gain ascendancy over them. They could, however, act together when necessity forced them to do so. We have seen how they did successfully suppress enemy peoples in central and northern Canaan and in Eastjordania.[122] A century or more went by and there arose a threat of such compelling magnitude that in fear and desperation the Hebrews did enter upon a real union.

The Philistine Menace

Attention has already been directed to the Philistines and their culture [123] and especially to the fact that, at just about the time when the Hebrews began the conquest of the hill country of Judea, the Philistines were forcing their way from the coastal plain (which they had occupied since 1196 B.C.) into the Shephelah and dispossessing the Canaanites. What we find, then, is that two peoples, the Hebrews and the Philistines, were both seeking to gain control of Canaan. As soon as the Philistines had won the Shephelah, Hebrews and Philistines came to grips. Jgs. 13:1; 14:4b implies that *circa* 1100 B.C. the Philistines had brought the Hebrews into close subjection.

Conflict between the two peoples began soon after the Hebrews entered the country. There was a clash when Shamgar was "judge" in Israel.[124] "In the days of Shamgar the son of Anath, the highways were unoccupied, and the travelers walked through byways." [125] Philistine pressure was doubtless a leading cause for the migration of the Danites from the Shephelah region.[126] Relations between Danites and Philistines are reflected in the stories of Samson, a Danite hero.[127] The whole cycle of Samson stories (Jgs. *13–16) gives glimpses of the incidental, guerillalike warfare which characterized these clashes between Philistines and Hebrews. Samson, hero of these stories, scarcely deserves to be classed as a "judge." He was not in any sense a tribal or national leader. He simply harassed the Philistines by his tactics, but despite all he did the Philistine control steadily increased until, in a pitched battle, they overwhelmed the

---

[121] Vid. supra, p. 74.
[123] Supra, pp. 38 f., 78 f.
[125] Jgs. 5:6.
[122] Supra, pp. 143–145.
[124] Jgs. 3:31.
[126] Vid. supra, p. 141.
[127] Jgs. 13:2, 25. On the Samson stories, cf. R. H. Pfeiffer, *Introduction to the Old Testament* (New York: 1941), p. 318.

Hebrews and even captured the sacred Ark of the Covenant which had been carried into the conflict in the confident expectation it would assure victory (1 Sam. *4). The Ark symbolized the very presence of Yahweh, and its presence in the siege of Jericho had indeed brought victory to the Hebrews.[128] The loss of the Ark now meant to the Hebrews that their god had been vanquished by Dagon, god of the Philistines. Great, therefore, was the depression caused by this misfortune. Had it not been for the counterdisasters which presently befell the Philistines (1 Sam. *5 f.), faith in Yahweh might have been permanently impaired.

How completely the Hebrews were subjugated by the Philistines may be learned from 1 Sam. 10:5; 13:3, 23; 14:1, 11. Following this battle of Aphek, Philistine garrisons were stationed at important points in central Canaan, viz., Gibeah, Geba, and Michmash. 1 Sam. 13:19–22 shows either that the Hebrews were completely disarmed, or that they completely lacked iron weapons.[129]

The Philistine victories brought it home to the Hebrews that only by thorough organization and strong leadership could they hope to cope with their foes. It now became evident that either the Hebrews must get together against the efficiently organized Philistines or face complete and permanent subjugation. They determined upon national unity under a king.

Kingship the Solution of the Philistine Menace

Samuel and the Kingship. Samuel was held in honor by the Hebrews of central Canaan. His influence seems to have been about the only bond of union holding the tribes together (1 Sam. *7:15 ff.). 1 Sam. 7:5–14 (a narrative from a much later source than the rest of the account with which it is incorporated) describes a considerable victory over the Philistines in Samuel's time. This does not agree with the general picture of Hebrew subjection to the Philistines, and this battle must have been of less importance politically than one might otherwise infer. At any rate Samuel was getting old, and his sons proved to be worthless grafters (1 Sam. *8:1–5), so that the leading men among the people, "the elders of Israel," looked with grave concern upon the plight of their nation and finally asked Samuel to choose a king for them.

"We will have a king over us that we also may be like all the nations";[130] so reads the ultimatum of the heads of Israel to Samuel. This succinct statement indicates very clearly the existence of a developing nationalism. From their dealings and conflicts with sur-

---

[128] Josh. 6:6–20.   [129] *Vid. supra*, p. 79.   [130] 1 Sam. 8:19 f.

rounding peoples the Hebrews now saw clearly the advantage of strong national organization under a single ruler. It made for strength in war and for material prosperity. They realized the need of a forceful leader who, as they said, might both "judge us and go out before us and fight our battles." [131]

The principal achievement of Samuel was the inauguration of the monarchy. He was a maker of kings. He chose and anointed Saul, and, after him, King David, and so long as Samuel lived he was the power behind the throne.

A comparison of 1 Sam. *9:1–10:16; *11:1–15 with 1 Sam. *7:15–8:22; *10:17–24; *12 reveals two contrasting and seemingly contradictory attitudes toward the establishment of the monarchy. One set of narratives represents it as a real forward step taken with the full approval of and indeed upon the initiative of Samuel. The other set of narratives represents it as a great mistake, as a move greatly displeasing to Samuel. Why the difference? These narratives were written long after the events described, at a time when men looked back over years of experience under the monarchy and evaluated it variously. Some believed that the founding of the kingdom had contributed to the real national progress of the Hebrews. Others, thinking chiefly no doubt of the despotism of certain kings, e.g., of Solomon and of Ahab, considered the monarchy a retrogression from the good old days when men were free and families not subject to royal taxes, compulsory labor service, and forced enlistment in the army. The two views have been blended into one story. How the news of the decision to have a king was broken to the aged Samuel, and his pained reception of it, are told sympathetically in 1 Sam. 8. Recovering from the first bitter shock of disappointment, Samuel set vigorously about the new task that confronted him. If he could not himself rule, he could at least select the man who was to rule and thus insure the type of king who would with least harm guide the destiny of his beloved nation. To persuade all the tribes to accept his choice was a different matter, and despite Samuel's great influence, a part of the people at first withheld their allegiance from Saul. It was not until Saul had shown himself a really forceful and able military leader that opposition to him ceased and he was accepted wholeheartedly as king in fact as well as in name.

Saul—Kingship on Trial. 1. *Saul's Deliverance of an East Jordan Clan.* Saul's first opportunity to display his capacity for leadership was when the people of Jabesh-gilead, east of Jordan, were attacked by the Ammonites. 1 Sam. 11:1–11 tells how, in desperation over the brutal terms of surrender set by their conquerors, the men

[131] 1 Sam. 8:20.

of Jabesh-gilead appealed to all Israel, only to be met by futile lamentation. However, when word of their plight reached him, Saul, by a vividly suggestive though gruesome, primitive method of communication, summoned the tribesmen "throughout all the borders of Israel." [132] The instant response to this summons showed that here was the man who could stir them to a new sense of tribal unity and common endeavor. They rallied to Saul, marched to the rescue of their oppressed fellows, and completely routed the Ammonites. Saul thus proved his prowess. He was the man for the time, and "all the people went to Gilgal and there they made Saul king." [133] And when some of Saul's overardent partisans demanded, "Who is he that said, 'Shall Saul reign over us?' Bring them, that we may put them to death!", Saul won their hearts completely by declaring amnesty for all.[134]

2. *Saul Defeats the Philistines.* Saul's next objective was to secure release from the Philistine yoke. This was the real test of his kingly fitness. A brief but dramatic account of the struggle (1 Sam. *13:1–14:46) tells of the Philistines' aggressiveness, the near failure of Saul's efforts, and the turning of the fortunes of war through the skill and personal prowess of Saul's son, Jonathan, who, by his reckless daring, so fired the timid Hebrew forces that they attacked and drove the Philistines back to the coastal plain.

One incident in connection with this battle is of exceptional interest because it reflects so accurately the superstitious beliefs of the age. As he sent his men charging against the disorganized foe, Saul uttered a curse which all but cost the life of the innocent Jonathan, hero of the hour.[135] It reminds one vividly of the tragic death of Jephthah's daughter under strikingly similar circumstances. Had it not been for a violent popular protest and some sort of "ransom," [136] Jonathan would undoubtedly have been put to death in the mistaken belief that only so would divine wrath be averted.

3. *Other Achievements of Saul.* 1 Sam. *14:47–52 lists the successes of Saul in ridding Israel of enemies in other quarters, chiefly east of Jordan. The neighboring nations now learned to have a wholesome respect for Saul and the new Hebrew unity.

Saul's capital was Gibeah, a small but strong town a few miles north of Jerusalem, near Geba, the scene of Jonathan's exploit. I Sam. *22:6 ff. pictures Saul as a rough-and-ready chieftain, supported by a small retinue of loyal fellow tribesmen upon whom he evidently was able, by virtue of his royal position, to bestow grants of fields and vineyards as well as positions of tribal leadership. Saul

---

132 1 Sam. 11:7.
134 1 Sam. 11:12 f.
136 1 Sam. 14:45.

133 1 Sam. 11:15.
135 1 Sam. 14:24.

was far from being an absolute monarch. He represents a transition from the era of the "judges" to that of the monarchy. His kingdom centered in Benjamin and included Ephraim and Manasseh, in central Canaan, and Gilead, east of Jordan. He had a certain hold on Judah, evidenced by the fact that the men of Keilah, in the heart of Judah, remained loyal to him when much of Judah was disaffected.[137] There is no evidence that any other than the traditional tribal form of organization and government prevailed in Saul's day. In the sight of the tribes he was just about what they had asked for, someone to "go out for them and fight their battles." [138] To that extent, and that only, did they give him their allegiance.

4. *Saul's Decline.* Samuel was not only a maker but a breaker of kings, and the time came when Saul lost Samuel's powerful support. Samuel disagreed with Saul over the policy to be pursued in dealing with the Amalekites (1 Sam. *15). He apparently felt that Saul was lacking in whole-souled devotion to the cause of the kingdom, or at least that he was imperiling the nation by not obeying to the letter Yahweh's orders given through Yahweh's closest agent, i.e., through Samuel himself. So his charge against Saul was disobedience.[139] Behind all this we may discern Samuel's real reason for turning Saul down, viz., that Saul was assuming absolute power by presuming to arrogate to himself the priestly function.[140] Samuel was a "judge," and so was Saul.[141] Samuel was a prophet, and so was Saul.[142] So far the two were on a par. Saul was king, and Samuel was not. Samuel was a priest, and when Saul assumed to act in the capacity of a priest it made him superior to Samuel and absolute in Israel. This was more than Samuel could tolerate. With the friendship and support of Samuel forfeited, the decline of Saul set in. No king in those days could safely alienate the chief religious leader. Henceforth Samuel worked against Saul and selected a new king from an entirely different family and tribe, viz., David, son of Jesse, of Bethlehem in Judah (1 Sam. *16:1–13).

Saul's life from this point on is a story of tragedy mixed with flashes of nobility. Its black side was the implacable enmity between Saul and David, beautifully but tragically portrayed in 1 Sam. *18–24, *26. Even admitting that Saul had excellent reasons for fearing David, the picture of such personal persecution by the head of a nation is neither pleasant nor creditable. Manifestly Saul was emotionally insane in his later years. That he was highly emotional, impulsive, and precipitate in thought and act is clear from numerous indications. The Biblical historian explains this irrationality as due

[137] 1 Sam. 23:10 ff. [138] 1 Sam. 8:20 [139] 1 Sam. 15:22.
[140] 1 Sam. 15:15, 21. Saul would himself have presided over this sacrifice, in disregard of Samuel, just as he did on another occasion (1 Sam. 13:8–14).
[141] Cf. 1 Sam. 14:2. [142] 1 Sam. 10:9–13.

to the fact that "the spirit of Yahweh departed from Saul, and an evil spirit from Yahweh troubled (or, terrified) him." [143]

5. *The Death of Saul.* The Philistines, with whom Saul had dealt at the outset with some vigor, toward the close of his reign resumed their aggression and made a determined effort to resubjugate the Hebrews. The odds were in their favor, for Saul's persecution of David had made David an outlaw, and David attached himself to the Philistine Achish of Gath (1 Sam. *27). In their renewed assault upon the Hebrews, the Philistines manifestly counted on David's support (1 Sam. *28:1 f.) but later mistrusted him (1 Sam. *29).

Saul was a pitiful spectacle. Without David's support his cause was lost. He was defeated before he entered the battle. "When Saul inquired of Yahweh, Yahweh answered him not, neither by dreams, nor by Urim, nor by prophets." [144] Depressed by the feeling that Yahweh had deserted him, overcome by superstition and foreboding, he resorted to a necromancer at Endor (1 Sam. *28). The disheartening outcome of this séance sealed Saul's doom.[145] In the battle of Gilboa Saul fought valiantly but vainly until his cause was hopelessly lost, and then died by his own hand. The tragic tale is told in 1 Sam. *31, and in 2 Sam. *1:19–27 is David's "Lament over the Death of Saul and Jonathan," one of the most beautiful poems in the Bible.[146]

6. *An Estimate of Saul's Reign.* It must be conceded that Saul was an able man, and probably the best available when he was chosen. The Bible narrator, notwithstanding his partisanship toward David, has the following genuine praise for Saul:

> He fought against all his enemies on every side, . . . and whithersoever he turned himself, he put them to the worse. And he did valiantly, . . . and delivered Israel out of the hands of them that despoiled her.[147]

Likewise there is wholehearted admiration for the sublime courage of Saul and his son Jonathan in their last desperate battle, in David's lament of their death: "Saul and Jonathan were lovely and pleasant in their lives, . . . they were swifter than eagles, they were stronger than lions." [148] This is a splendid tribute from the man whom Saul hounded for so many years.

Wherein had Saul succeeded? (1) In extending the bounds of his kingdom. (2) In reducing the Canaanite strongholds to apparently only two, Gezer and Jerusalem. (3) In drawing the tribes together in a somewhat closer unity, including extension of authority over

[143] 1 Sam. 16:14.
[145] 1 Sam. 28:12.
[147] 1 Sam. 14:47 f.
[144] 1 Sam. 28:6.
[146] *Vid. infra*, p. 169.
[148] 2 Sam. 1:23.

the east Jordan tribes, as evidenced by the fact that after Saul's death, Mahanaim, across the Jordan, was selected as the capital by his son, Ishbaal. Saul's reign showed both the necessity and some of the advantages of kingship in Israel.

Wherein did Saul fail? (1) In the struggle with the Philistines. Though he checked them for a time, he did not break the Philistine yoke and therefore did not accomplish the main purpose for which the kingdom was established. Indeed, the political situation seemed almost as bad at the end as at the beginning of his reign. (2) In not achieving full national unity. Saul alienated the strongest man of the time, Samuel, and by jealously persecuting David, whom a different treatment might have converted into a tower of strength, he alienated both him and his powerful tribe of Judah. Nevertheless Saul was beloved by some, which is touchingly attested by the fact that the men of Jabesh-gilead, whose city he had saved as the first act of his reign, risked their lives to rescue his body and give it honorable burial.[149]

Philistine Overlordship Ended by David. Just how completely the Hebrews came under Philistine control at the death of Saul is not clear. The fact that the kingship was not interrupted suggests that the Philistine victory at Gilboa was not decisive. Within the ensuing decade or so, David fought several battles with the Philistines.[150] At times even David was hard pressed. Once he had to retire to the cave of Adullam for security when the Philistines forced their way up to the Judean Plateau. At least two battles were fought on the Plain of Rephaim southwest of Jerusalem. It was after the second of these engagements that the Philistines were driven for good and all out of the Hebrew domain. David ultimately pushed the warfare into Philistine territory and captured Gath, their leading city. With that event the Philistine menace came to an end and the integrity of the Hebrew nation was assured. The Philistines lasted on, of course, but never again did they attempt any major aggression against the Hebrews.

* * *

The Hebrews were in secure possession of their homeland. We now reach the third watershed of Hebrew history, viz., the creative work of King David in achieving Hebrew national unity.

[149] 1 Sam. 31:11 ff. Cf. Nelson Glueck, *The River Jordan* (Philadelphia: 1946), pp. 159–167.
[150] 2 Sam. 5:17–25; 8:1; 21:15–22; 23:9–17.

Chapter 10

CULTURE IN CANAAN IN THE ERA OF HEBREW SETTLEMENT

The era of the Hebrew settlement in Canaan was a rough-and-tumble time. The Hebrew tribesmen were crude indeed, and barbarous. The vandalism with which they destroyed things of culture in their anti-Canaanite passion has been made evident by the ruined ancient cities which have been uncovered in archaeological excavations. In this chapter our concern is only with the status of their literature and their religion in the twelfth and eleventh centuries B.C., since ultimately it was in these two spheres that the Hebrews made their creative contribution to human culture.

Literature

We have already noted the antecedents of Hebrew literature.[1] In the twelfth and eleventh centuries B.C. their literature was still in the prewritten stage. The spoken word, i.e., oral tradition, is just as truly literature as is anything written. There were, however, a few pieces of astonishing merit.

Although it was a crude age, we have to be cautious where we put the level of illiteracy, in so far as literacy means the ability of plain people to read and write. In Jgs. 8:14 it is recounted that Gideon captured a certain youth and made him write down, for Gideon's information, a list of the officials of Succoth. That Gideon could, at random, hit upon a youth who could write may have been just a streak of luck, but again it may attest a greater literacy than we might suppose. It is implied, of course, that Gideon could read the list after the boy had written it.

Stories. The exciting experiences of the era certainly provided abundant material for dramatic storytelling. The stories which we find in the books of Joshua and Judges undoubtedly existed only in the oral tradition throughout these centuries, though one scholar is of the opinion that "the original document of Joshua was written prior

[1] *Supra,* Chapter 7.

to 1030 B.C.," i.e., close to the time of Gideon.[2] Most of these stories are in the starred passages that were indicated in Chapter 9, *passim*.

Jotham's Fable. One piece of literature pertaining to this era introduces us to an additional literary type, namely, Jotham's Fable of the Trees (*Jgs. 9:8–15). A few critics regard it as a poem.[3] Prevailingly, however, it is construed as prose.[4] It is manifestly a piece of folk wisdom. Just when it originated it would be impossible to say. Its application to the situation in Jgs. 9 is due to the compiler of such folklore in the eighth century B.C.[5]

Riddles. As has been previously pointed out, Hebrew poetry does not depend on words that rhyme.[6] There are instances of rhyme, but they are occasional and coincidental, not a studied device. A very good illustration is Jgs. 16:24. The end words rhyme in the Hebrew, and the verse is translated in the Moffatt version so that the end words rhyme in English. Elsewhere in the Samson stories one meets with couplets which are riddles. Perhaps we would call such jingles verse rather than poetry. They are delightfully translated in the Moffatt version (Jgs. 14:14, 18; 15:16). Very likely, riddles of this sort were a delightful pastime in the era of the "judges" to folks on the social and cultural level of Samson.

The Ode of Deborah. We would scarcely anticipate that in this crude era we would come upon "the finest masterpiece of Hebrew poetry," but that is what Professor Robert H. Pfeiffer calls the Song of Deborah (*Jgs. 5).[7] Another scholar has called it "a work of genius, and therefore a work of that highest art which is not studied and artificial but spontaneous and inevitable." [8] Professor Pfeiffer holds that it was composed and written down immediately after the victory, i.e., *circa* 1100 B.C.[9] The author was therefore a contemporary of the stirring event of which he (or she) [10] sings. This makes the ode

---

[2] Cf. J. G. Duncan, *Digging Up Biblical History* (New York: 1931), I, p. 143.

[3] E. G. King, *Early Religious Poetry of the Hebrews* (Cambridge: 1911), pp. 14 f., arranges it in four strophes in the 3 + 3 meter throughout; W. O. E. Oesterley, *Ancient Hebrew Poetry* (New York: 1938), pp. 52 f., presents an arrangement with varying meter, some lines two-beat, some three, some four; George Adam Smith, *The Early Poetry of Israel in Its Physical and Social Origins* (London: 1927), pp. 90 f., thinks that its "rhythm is little, if at all, removed from that of prose." Nevertheless he prints it in four stanzas, in three-beat measure, with variations to two and four.

[4] The Moffatt and Chicago versions so print it.

[5] Cf. Robert H. Pfeiffer, *Introduction to the Old Testament* (New York: 1941), p. 330.

[6] *Vid. supra*, p. 112.   [7] *Op. cit.*, p. 326.

[8] George Foot Moore, *A Critical and Exegetical Commentary on Judges* (New York: 1910), p. 135.

[9] The Hebrew text is so corrupt that technical Hebrew scholars find it impossible to translate some of the verses. This very garbled condition of the text is evidence that it had been in writing a long time and corrupted in transmission before the editor of Judges incorporated it into his book.

[10] Not a few critics think the author was a woman, whether Deborah herself or another.

the oldest existing monument of Hebrew literature. It is a festival Te
Deum, lauding the mighty deed of Yahweh. "Bless Ye Yahweh" is
its theme (vs. 2) and its most appropriate title. In the following
arrangement, accents are indicated. The ode is in the three-beat and
four-beat rhythm. Its grandeur is not appreciated except when it is
read aloud.

² That leáders did leád in Isráel,
 That the peóple volunteéred,
  Bléss ye Yahwéh!

³ Heárken, O kíngs; prínces, give eár;
 Í to Yahwéh, even Í will síng,
 Will sing praíse to Yahwéh, the Gód of Isráel.

⁴ Yahwéh, in thine advánce from Seír,
 In thy márch from the lánd of Edóm,
 Eárth did quáke, the heávens were sháken,
 Yéa the cloúds poúred down wáter;
⁵ The moúntains trémbled befóre Yahwéh,
 At the présence of Yahwéh, the Gód of Isráel.

⁶ From the dáys of Shamgár ben-Anáth,
 From thóse days cáravans ceásed,
 Trávelers toók to the býpaths.
⁷ Víllages ceásed in Isráel,
 Coúntryfolk's wórk was húshed.
 Till thóu didst aríse, Deboráh,
 Didst aríse, a Móther in Isráel,
⁸ Was there shiéld or lánce to be seén
 Amóng forty thoúsand in Isráel?

⁹ My heárt to the leáders in Isráel,
 To the volunteérs of the peóple! Bléss ye Yahwéh!

¹⁰ Let ríders on táwny she-ásses recoúnt it,
 That sít on rich cárpets, and wáyfarers tóo,
¹¹ And hárk! at the wélls the laúghing of maídens;
 Thére they recoúnt the great deéds of Yahwéh,
 The great deéds of his árm in Ísráel.
¹² Awáke, awáke, Deboráh!
 Awáke, awáke, sing oút!
 Ríse, Barák, and leád cáptive
 Thy cáptors, O bén-Abinóam!

¹³ Then dówn to the gátes marched the nóbles,
 Yahweh's fólk márched down like héroes.

¹⁴ From Ephráim they rúshed to the válley;
After thée, Benjamín, with thy clánsmen.
From Machír came dówn the commánders,
And from Zebulún men wiélding the trúncheon.
¹⁵ With Deboráh were Íssachar's prínces,
To Barák was Náphtali lóyal,
Rushing fórth at his heéls to the válley.

In the tríbal divísions of Reúben
Deép were the seárchings of heárt.
¹⁶ Why sáttest thou stíll in the sheépfolds
To heár the flute-pláyings for flócks?
¹⁷ Gilead stáyed at hóme over Jórdan,   .
And Dán stays aloóf by the shíps;
Ashér sat stíll by the shóre of the séa
And stáyed besíde his creéks.
¹⁸ Zebulún is the clán that risked lífe to the deáth.
And Naphtalí on the heights of the fiéld.

¹⁹ Ón came the kíngs and foúght,
Then foúght the kíngs of Canaán
In Taánach by the broóks of Megíddo
But they toók no boóty of móney.
²⁰ From heáven foúght the stárs,
From their coúrses they foúght with Sísera.
²¹ The tórrent Kishón swept them óff,
The ón-rushing tórrent Kishón.
Bléss thou, my soúl, the míght of Yahwéh!

²² Then cláttered the hoófs of the hórses,
Off gálloped, off gálloped his chárgers.
²³ Cúrse ye, cúrse ye Meróz,
Cúrse ye, cúrse ye its dwéllers.
For they cáme not to the hélp of Yahwéh,
To the hélp of Yahwéh like héroes.

²⁴ Most bléssed of wómen be Jáel,
Of tént-dwelling wómen most bléssed.
²⁵ Wáter he ásked; mílk she gáve,
Lében she broúght in a lórdly bówl.
²⁶ She pút her hánd to the tént peg,
Her ríght hand to the wórkman's mállet,
She smáshed, she sháttered his témple,
²⁷ At her feét he sánk, he féll, he lay stíll,
At her feét he sánk, he féll,
Where he sánk, there he féll, deád.

²⁸ Oút through the window she gázed and excláimed,
Sísera's móther, oút through the láttice,

"Whý is his cháriot so slów to cóme,
Why tárrieth his cháriots' clátter?"
[29] Her wísest princésses make ánswer,
She ánswers hersélf her own quéstion:
[30] "Are they not fínding, divíding the spoíl?
A dámsel or twó for eách of the mén,
A spoíl of dýed stuffs for Sísera,
A spoíl of dýed stuffs brocáded,
Twó dyed brocádes for the néck of the queén."

[31] Só may they pérish, all thy fóes, O Yahwéh,
But be thy friénds like the sún going fórth in his míght![11]

Climactic Parallelism. The Ode of Deborah acquaints us with an additional variety of parallelism known as "climactic." The second line picks up the thought from the middle of the first line, i.e., it repeats part of the first, then carries the thought to completion. It is thus a variant form of synthetic parallelism. It is of the pattern a-b/b-c. For example (vs. 23):

For they came not / to the help of Yahweh,
     To the help of Yahweh / like heroes.

Climactic parallelism is present in vss. 5, 6, 7b, 9, 11, 12a, 12b, 18, 19a, 20, 23, 28.[12] Where this device of climactic parallelism is continued through two or more couplets in sequence, it builds up a stairlike parallelism. The Thunderstorm Psalm (29) illustrates this.[13]

David's Elegy Over Saul and Jonathan. Another masterpiece of early Hebrew poetry was composed at the end of the eleventh century B.C. It is King David's elegy over the death of Saul and Jonathan (*2 Sam. 1:18–27). It is hardly possible to question David's authorship of the poem. The profound emotion that permeates it shows that it came out of David's poignant grief under the impact of the distressing news of Saul's and Jonathan's death at tragic Gilboa. It is not a religious poem; indeed, God is not mentioned in it. It is a threnody, a noble voicing of genuine human grief. It should be read in the Moffatt and the Chicago versions.

---

[11] This arrangement is based principally on C. F. Burney, *The Book of Judges* (2d. ed.; London: 1919), pp. 94–176. Cf. George Adam Smith, *op. cit.*, pp. 81–93; E. G. King, *op. cit.*, pp. 6–15; W. O. E. Oesterley, *op. cit.*, pp. 43–50; C. F. Kent, *Narratives of the Beginnings of Hebrew History* (New York: 1905), pp. 320–323; R. G. Moulton, *The Literary Study of the Bible* (Boston: 1908), pp. 133–143; J. A. Bewer, *The Literature of the Old Testament* (New York: 1922), pp. 5–9; Robert H. Pfeiffer, *op. cit.*, pp. 325 ff. The *leben* mentioned in vs. 25 is a soured milk of the consistency of blancmange.
[12] Cf. Burney, *op. cit.*, pp. 169 f.
[13] *Vid. supra*, p. 19. Cf. Chicago and Moffatt versions.

The Deities That Were Worshiped

Pre-Hebrew Cults in Canaan. In the era of the settlement of Canaan, Yahwism was in conflict with Canaanite religion. Yahwism absorbed some elements from Canaanite religion, but there was much that Yahwism decisively repudiated.[14]

The names of several Canaanite deities are preserved in Old Testament place names which are compounded with them, which places were, in all probability, centers of the cults of these several deities. Among such deities was *Shamash,* the sun god, whose name is in Beth-shemesh (House of Shamash),[15] En-shemesh (Fountain of Shamash),[16] and Irshemesh (City of Shamash).[17] Another was *Ramman,* a weather god,[18] whose name is in Rimmon,[19] Rimmon-perez (Rent of Rimmon),[20] Gathrimmon (Winepress of Rimmon),[21] En-rimmon (Well of Rimmon),[22] Sela-ha-rimmon (Rock of Rimmon) ; [23] the proper name Hadadrimmon [24] expresses the identity of this god Ramman with the Babylonian Hadad, a thunder god. The name of *Barak,* a god of lightning, is preserved in Bene-barak.[25] The name of *Dagon* is preserved in Beth-dagon,[26] which shows that this deity was worshiped in Canaan before the arrival of the Philistines, who seem to have adopted Dagon as their deity. The name of *Nebo,* the god of writing, is preserved in Mount Nebo, the famous site from which Moses viewed the promised land.[27] The name of *Gad,* god of fortune, is preserved in Migdal-gad. (Tower of Gad).[28] The place names Beth-anath [29] and Anathoth [30] preserve the name of the goddess *Anat.*[31] Anat was a sister form of Ashtart, the mother goddess; the Anat worshiped at Bethshean was a serpent goddess; the Jews of Elephantine [32] compounded the name of Anat with Yahu, as Anat-Yaw, a type of father-mother deity. There were in Palestine numerous place names containing *Baal,* e.g., Baal-hermon,[33] Baal-hazor,[34] Baal-meon.[35] There was a place named for *Baalath* (Mis-

---

[14] For a discussion of the religion of the Canaanites in relation to the religion of the Hebrews in the light of archaeology, cf. W. F. Albright, *Archaeology and the Religion of Israel* (Baltimore: 1942), pp. 68–94.

[15] Josh. 19 :22.   [16] Josh. 15 :7.
[17] Josh. 19 :41.   [18] 2 Kgs. 5 :18.
[19] Josh. 19 :7.   [20] Num. 33 :19 f.
[21] Josh. 19 :45.   [22] Neh. 11 :29.
[23] Jgs. 20 :45.   [24] Zech. 12 :11.
[25] Josh. 19 :45.   [26] Josh. 15 :41.
[27] Deut. 32 :49.
[28] Josh. 15 :37. This god Gad was worshiped in Palestine until a very late time, according to Isa. 65 :11, which verse also mentions *Meni,* god of fate, possibly also an ancient Canaanite god.
[29] Josh. 19 :38.   [30] Josh. 21 :18.
[31] The expression "son of Anath" (Jgs. 3 :31 ; 5 :6) may be a formula for characterizing Shamgar as a valiant man of war rather than a statement of his parentage.
[32] *Vid. supra,* pp. 49 f.   [33] Jgs. 3 :3 ; 1 Chr. 5 :23.
[34] 2 Sam. 13 :23.   [35] Num. 32 :38.

tress),[36] the goddess of generation, and a place Baalath-beer (Mistress or Lady of the Well),[37] preserving, perhaps, a tradition of a water deity. An alternative form of the same name is preserved in Baalah,[38] and Mount Baalah.[39] There was a deity named *Salem,* whose name is in Jerusalem, which Barton interprets to mean "Salem directs." [40] There was discovered at Taanach, in 1903, a letter of the fifteenth century B.C., written in cuneiform, which contains the proper name Ahi-ya-mi which is the Babylonian equivalent of the Hebrew Ahijah. This is some evidence that the name Yahweh was known in Canaan before the coming of the Hebrews into the land.

One of the most interesting cults in pre-Hebrew Canaan was the serpent cult. Archaeological discoveries have revealed several images of the serpent goddess (usually Ashtart with a serpent entwined about her body),[41] models of serpents in pottery and bronze, pits (at Gezer) where sacred serpents were probably kept, little shrines with coiled serpents at the base, and a bowl with serpent design. The chief site of the serpent cult was Bethshean, which means "House of She'an," the old Semitic serpent deity. All this throws light on the presence of serpent worship at the Jerusalem temple until the time of King Hezekiah.[42]

Archaeological evidence also throws light on another interesting matter, viz., the Hebrew taboo of swine. The pig was the sacrificial animal of the pre-Semitic inhabitants of Canaan, as disclosed at Gezer, where little clay figures of swine, amulets made of the teeth of swine, and pig bones on an altar were found. The pig was also the sacred animal of the mother-goddess cult. This explains the Hebrew taboo; it was because the pig was the sacred animal of cults which the Hebrews abhorred.

Professor Barton interprets one of the Ras Shamra poems as a liturgy for the spring festival in Jerusalem in the time of Abraham, i.e., the twentieth century B.C.[43] It is his view that the ritual exactly fits the topography of the northern approach to ancient Jerusalem, as that approach was revealed in excavations in 1923–1924. The opening lines of the liturgy summon the gods to the festival. Then follows a vineyard hymn, the intent of which is to secure fertility to the vines. There follow directions for the admission of worshipers and for a

---

[36] Josh. 19 :44.   [37] Josh. 19 :8.
[38] Josh. 15 :29.   [39] Josh. 15 :11.
[40] G. A. Barton, "A Liturgy for the Spring Festival at Jerusalem in the Age of Abraham and Melchizedek," *Journal of Biblical Literature,* liii (1934), pp. 73 f.
[41] Cf. especially W. F. Albright, *The Archaeology of Palestine and the Bible* (New York: 1933), pp. 87 ff., for a description of these images.
[42] *Vid. supra,* p. 135, *infra,* p. 331.
[43] G. A. Barton, *Archaeology and the Bible* (Philadelphia: 1937), pp. 143 f., 534–540; *ibid.,* "A Liturgy for the Spring Festival at Jerusalem in the Age of Abraham and Melchizedek," *Journal of Biblical Literature,* liii (1934), pp. 61–75.

sacrifice for the fields, the chief feature of which is the slaying of a kid in the milk.[44] The favorable gods are again summoned, and the worshipers who are entering the sanctuary and pouring libations invoke the deity Salem to "come to the acceptable sacrifice." There follows a ritual for appeasing the unfavorable goddess Asherat, and a ritual to secure human offspring. The last of the poem deals with the gracious gods and their work in bringing agricultural blessings.

Yahweh a God of War. Persons are wont to think of their god or gods as most interested in the things that are of greatest concern to the persons themselves, and they believe that the gods are competent to help them in whatever constitutes their greatest need. The experience of the Hebrews from the time they left Kadesh until they were securely established in Canaan was one long story of conflict with enemy peoples. In the east Jordan country they had to battle with the forces of Sihon, king of the Amorites, and with Og, king of Bashan.[45] In both struggles they were victorious. Then there was the fighting which attended their entrance into Canaan under Joshua.[46] The most noteworthy incident was the presence of the Ark of the Covenant in the siege of Jericho (Josh. *6:6–20). The Hebrews, therefore, quite naturally came to think of Yahweh as a god of war; "Yahweh is a man of war." [47]

There once existed a "Book of the Wars of Yahweh," probably a collection of martial poems in which Yahweh figured as the central character. A quotation from this book is preserved in Num. 21:14 f., a brief description of the Arnon region east of the Dead Sea, the border of the Amorites which the Hebrews under Moses had reached after many vicissitudes.[48] It may be that this book rehearsed in poetic form the progress of the Hebrews through Eastjordania, the narrative being organized under the concept of Yahweh as a war god fighting his people's way through a hostile country.

Later on the Hebrews faced a yet more bitter struggle in the war against the allied Canaanites.[49] The decisive battle in this conflict was waged at Mount Tabor, and the famous "Ode of Deborah" (Jgs. 5) embodies the rallying cry of the Hebrews: "To the help of Yahweh! To the help of Yahweh against the mighty!" [50] Another important struggle of the period was that against the invading Midianites.[51] They were decisively repulsed by Gideon and his troops under the significant battle cry, "For Yahweh and for Gideon." [52] But by far the most instructive and fascinating narrative reflecting

[44] A rite forbidden to the Hebrews in Ex 23:19; 34:26; another sample of how the Hebrew taboos arose.
[45] Vid. supra, p. 105.
[46] Vid. supra, pp. 138 ff.
[47] Ex. 15:3; Ps. 144:1.
[48] Cf. Num. 20:14–21:13.
[49] Vid. supra, pp. 143 f.
[50] Jgs. 5:23.
[51] Vid. supra, pp. 144 f.
[52] Jgs. 7:18.

the concept of Yahweh as a war god is that of the taking of the Ark of Yahweh into battle against the Philistines, and its capture by the latter (1 Sam. *4:1–7:2). The capture of the sacred Ark, most precious symbol of Yahweh, was not only a smashing blow to the morale of the Hebrews, but a severe setback to the religion of Yahweh as well.

At a later time Saul carried into battle another symbol of deity called the ephod, with a victorious outcome.[53] What sort of thing the ephod was can only be conjectured. Jgs. 8:24–27 tells about Gideon making an ephod out of golden earrings and other jewelry, which plainly indicates that the ephod was some sort of image, being possibly merely whatever shape the molten metal took when it cooled, perhaps by being immersed in water, which shape would have been thought to be supernaturally fashioned. An image made this way would differ from a molten image which was formed by pouring molten metal into a mould. Jgs. 17:5; 18:14–20 tells of Micah's ephod, as well as his graven and molten images and teraphim. 1 Sam. 21:9 tells of the ephod at the sanctuary at Nob, which may have been the same one that Saul had carried into battle and which apparently had replaced the discredited Ark which at the time was in obscurity at Kiriath-jearim.[54] In other connections the ephod is described as though it were a garment.[55]

Here is the important element to be noted in the concept of Yahweh in this period: he is localized outside the land of the Hebrews, at Sinai. It is a case of a people's god not confined within the geographical boundaries of that people. This is a germinal idea that ultimately will become a doctrine of the universality of Yahweh.

The Baalim. The principal deities worshiped by the Canaanites were the *baalim*. The term *baal* means *lord* or *owner*. Each such baal was regarded as the master of a limited geographical area, to which his authority was restricted.[56] The baalim were separate and independent lords of local communities, though some seem to have exercised an influence beyond their own home towns, e.g., Baal-zebub, the god of Ekron. The Baal par excellence, the storm god, was regarded as cosmic in his scope.[57] The social basis of such a thought form is apparent. It has been pointed out that Canaanite social and political organization was distributive rather than centralized.[58] There

---

[53] 1 Sam. 14:18. Cf. RVmarg; also the Moffatt and Chicago versions, *in loc.*
[54] 1 Sam. 7:2.   [55] Cf. Ex. 28.
[56] This is one of the basic ideas underlying the narrative of the contest between the Hebrew prophet Elijah and the baal prophets on Mount Carmel (1 Kgs. 18). *Vid. infra*, pp. 233 ff.
[57] 2 Kgs. 1:3. Cf. W. F. Albright, *Archaeology and the Religion of Israel* (Baltimore: 1942), p. 116.
[58] *Supra,* pp. 33, 74.

were numerous city-states, each presided over by a local king. There was no one king of the land of Canaan. The same was true of their deities.

Thus the baalim were not clan gods but land gods. As distinguished from the *elim,* which were spirits of the open country,[59] the baalim were fertility spirits, i.e., essentially agricultural deities. The fertility of the soil, the germination of seeds, the control of rainfall, the fruition of the harvest were all conceived to be dependent upon the baalim, who must therefore be properly revered and worshiped.

Following their settlement in Canaan, the Hebrews took up agriculture and along with it naturally went the worship of the baalim. "They chose new gods." [60] The assertion that at Samuel's appeal they at one time "put away the baalim, and the ashteroth, and served Yahweh only," [61] only accentuates the obvious inference that ordinarily they did worship these other deities as a matter of course. There had been nothing in their previous experience that would lead them to suppose that control of the processes of agriculture might be under the dominion of Yahweh, a southern mountain and storm god, a wilderness guide, a "man of war." He was indeed on hand to help them fight against the Canaanites [62] and against the Midianites,[63] but, they reasoned, the growing of crops was not his concern but that of the baalim.[64] Indeed, had the immigrant Hebrews neglected to pay proper deference to the local baalim, their Canaanite neighbors would promptly have seen to it that they did so or else would have driven them out of the neighborhood, for the established residents of the land would by no means permit the presence of any people or things that might anger the deities and thus imperil their crops and indeed their very lives, as they believed.

It was only by slow degrees that the Hebrews came to believe that control of the processes of agriculture belonged to Yahweh. Just how far this changing conception had advanced before the time of the Hebrew monarchy cannot be definitely told, for the available data are from the time of the monarchy and later. That Yahweh controlled agriculture was the basic contention of the prophet Elijah against the prophets of baal (1 Kgs. *18). Hos. 2:5, 8 makes the same claim centuries later. Similarly, Isa. 28:29 declares that the art of agriculture "also comes from Yahweh of Hosts." [65] The idea of a deity's being attached to a land is interestingly illustrated in 2 Kgs. 17:24 ff., a tale of the calamities that befell the population which the Assyrian king Sargon settled in Samaria (720 B.C.) be-

---

59 *Vid. supra,* pp. 120 f.
61 1 Sam. 7:4.
63 Jgs. 7.
65 Cf. in full, Isa. 28:23–29.

60 Jgs. 5:8.
62 Jgs. 5.
64 Cf. Hos. 2:8.

cause they "knew not the law of the god of the land," and in Pss. 42 f.,
an exile's lament that in leaving his native Judah he had of necessity
left his god behind.

Ashtoreth.

The one divinity that is found in all parts of the Semitic race
is the mother goddess Ashtart, the Ashtoreth of the Old Testament, and the Astarte of the Greeks. In South Arabia she appears
as Athtar, in Ethiopia as Astar, in Moab as Ashtar, in Phoenicia
as Ashtart, in Syria as Attar, and in Assyria and Babylonia as
Ishtar. The fact that her name makes all the proper phonetic
changes in passing from one dialect to another proves that it is
primitive Semitic and that she is the most ancient of the greater
Semitic divinities.[66]

Ashtart was the chief goddess of productivity in the ancient world.
Consequently she was the guardian of births. She was the consort
and counterpart of Baal, the embodiment of the generative principle.
Archaeologists have dug up some interesting artifacts pertaining
to the mother-goddess cult. At Beth-shemesh was found a small
mould for making Ashtart heads, and also a double mould for making
two divinities, presumably Baal and Ashtart. At Gezer were found
terra-cotta plaques with figures of a goddess in low relief, presumably
the mother goddess or "queen of heaven." Such things make plain
what the prophet Jeremiah meant by the expression, "make her cakes
to portray her." [67] No end of figurines of the mother goddess have
come out of the soil of Palestine. We have already noted the suggestion
that the teraphim may have been such images of Ashtart.[68] There was
a temple of this goddess in Bethshean, where the Philistines hung
the armor of Saul.[69] This temple has been excavated in recent years,
and there was found a limestone stela with the figure of Ashtart
wearing two horns.[70]

For the Sidonian Ashtart, King Solomon erected a shrine which
stood until destroyed by King Josiah more than three centuries
later.[71] The plural of the word in the Old Testament is *ashteroth*,
and it is the worship of these fertility goddesses to which reference
is made in Jgs. 2:13; 3:7; 10:6; 1 Sam. 7:3 f., 12:10. The wide

[66] Lewis B. Paton, "The Cult of the Mother-Goddess in Ancient Palestine," *The
Biblical World*, 36 (1910), p. 27. The Biblical name Ashtoreth was formed by taking
the consonants of *Ashtart* and the vowels of the Hebrew word *bosheth*, which means
"shame." This was done, of course, to cast aspersion on the name of the mother
goddess. On a similar treatment of the name Baal, *vid. infra*, p. 210, fn. 35.

[67] Jer. 44:19.   [68] *Supra*, pp. 118 f.

[69] 1 Sam. 31:10.

[70] It reminds one of the place name Ashteroth-karnaim, "Ashtart of the two horns,"
in Gen. 14:5.

[71] 1 Kgs. 11:5, 33; 2 Kgs. 23:13.

prevalence of the Ashtart cult is attested by the preservation of the word in place names.[72]

Sacred Places

A belief in local deities inevitably leads to a belief that certain places are sacred to one or another of such gods, these being the places which the deities in question are supposed to frequent or to which they are believed to come to receive worship.

Shiloh. During the period of the "judges" the chief sanctuary of the Hebrews appears to have been at Shiloh. It was here that the sacred Ark was kept after the Hebrews settled in the land.[73] Archaeological excavation of the site has revealed no trace whatever of any pre-Hebrew occupation of Shiloh. Apparently the Hebrews chose a brand new site for their chief sanctuary. A consequence of this would be that the idea of Yahweh would not be confused with or assimilated to the idea of any other deity previously associated with that place. Religious festivals were held annually at Shiloh.[74] It was at this sanctuary that Samuel spent his youth (1 Sam. *3). It is spoken of as a temple, from which we may infer that some sort of permanent structure had replaced the Tent of Meeting of the wilderness period. After the disastrous loss of the Ark in battle with the Philistines, Shiloh evidently lost prestige as a central sanctuary and not long afterward the place was destroyed.

Local High Places. Local deities were worshiped at local sanctuaries called "high places," of which we find frequent mention in the Old Testament. The very name "high place" indicates that such sanctuaries were located on some natural elevation, either hilltop or mountain. They consisted of altars sacred to the deities, a large open court or a room where worshipers gathered for the sacrificial feasts, special places for the priests, places for storing the water for the ceremonies, and most important of all, a special shrine for the deity. Archaeological evidence indicates that at some sanctuaries images were used; e.g., at Gezer, statuettes of the nude mother goddess were found. In the Old Testament mention is made of the image of Dagon at Ashdod.[75] In general, the Hebrews seem to have dispensed with images, although the golden calves later set up at the sanctuaries of Dan and Bethel were images of deity, and the winged cherubim in the Jerusalem temple at least suggested Yahweh to the Hebrew mind.[76] We have already noted the snake and the bulls.[77]

---

[72] Josh. 9:10; 12:4; 13:12, 31; Gen. 14:5.
[74] Jgs. 21:19; 1 Sam. 1:3.
[76] Cf. Ezk. 10:18 f.

[73] 1 Sam. 4:3.
[75] 1 Sam. 5:2 ff.
[77] *Supra,* p. 135.

At the high places there was customarily found an upright stone pillar or *mazzebah*,[78] and in close proximity to it was an *asherah*, a sacred pole capped with an image of the goddess Asherah.[79] Sometimes an asherah was planted in the earth close to the altar.[80] The asherah was wooden.[81] Sometimes it was set up under living trees.[82] The asherah at Samaria evidently was famous.[83] One was installed at the temple in Jerusalem by King Manasseh [84] but was destroyed a few decades later by King Josiah.[85] These facts testify to the continuance of this religious practice throughout the period of the kingship. What the original idea behind the asherah was cannot be said. It was probably connected with tree worship and was a symbol of fertility.[86]

There is also mention of "houses of high places." [87] These may have been residences for the priests; or shelters for the images of the deities worshiped; [88] or rooms where sacrificial meals were eaten by the worshipers.[89] Very likely they were also chambers where religious prostitution was practiced, as evidenced by the prophets' condemnation of the practice at such places.[90]

The Nature of Ritual

Sacrifices and Feasts at the High Places. The most prominent feature of the worship at high places was the sacrifices. One type of sacrifice was of the nature of a communion with the deity, the idea being to renew or strengthen the bond uniting people and deity. In early times the eating of meat was a religious act, for the domestic animals belonged to the deity and their slaughter involved sacrifice. Therefore the victim was brought to the sanctuary and killed there; certain parts were burned, as representing the deity's share; a portion was given to the officiating priest, and the rest was eaten by the worshipers.

Another type of sacrifice was of the nature of a gift to the deity. To the baal, or "lord" of the land, of necessity went the first-born of the animals and the first fruits of the land, i.e., the first year's fruit borne by a tree and the first crop of a new field. From land which had previously yielded crops, the god's portion was the tithe, i.e., a percentage of the crop payable in kind. Most commonly, slaughtered

[78] *Vid. supra,* pp. 123 f.
[79] Cf. W. F. Albright, *Archaeology and the Religion of Israel* (Baltimore: 1942), pp. 78 f.
[80] Deut. 16:21, the prohibition testifying to the practice.
[81] Jgs. 6:26.   [82] 2 Kgs. 17:10.
[83] 2 Kgs. 13:6.   [84] 2 Kgs. 21:7.
[85] 2 Kgs. 23:6 f.   [86] Cf. W. F. Albright, *op. cit.,* pp. 78 f.
[87] 1 Kgs. 12:31; 13:32; 2 Kgs. 23:19. [88] Jgs. 17:5; 2 Kgs. 17:29.
[89] 1 Sam. 9:22.   [90] Am. 2:8; Ezk. 16:23–39.

animals (goats, sheep, and oxen) were thus offered as burnt offerings, the smell of the sacrifice being thought to be a sweet savor to the god.[91] Such gift sacrifices often were made to appease the displeasure of an offended deity as well as to retain a deity's favor.

Various occasions called for sacrifices which involved the killing of some animal, such as a marriage,[92] the weaning of a child,[93] going on a journey,[94] welcoming an honored guest,[95] the making of a solemn agreement,[96] the selection of a king,[97] consecrating warriors prior to a campaign,[98] and the like. Such sacrifice was performed not necessarily by a priest but by the head of a family.[99] Of course all of the participating group shared in the feast following the sacrifice. 1 Sam. *9:11–14, 22 ff. is a delightful picture of such a festal gathering in a village community.

One of the most instructive passages illustrative of religious ritual is Jgs. *6:19–32. Of the ritual acts there described, the pouring out of the broth is especially noteworthy.[100] Archaeological excavations have disclosed numerous prehistoric altars with cup holes in them. It is probable that libations were poured into these. In some of these altars there are channels which lead from these cup depressions to caves beneath. Perhaps the idea was that the blood or broth or other liquid of the libation could pass down to the earth spirits beneath. Anthropologists see in this a holdover from the age when prehistoric man dwelt in caves. 1 Sam. 7:6 mentions Samuel pouring out a libation at a religious assembly in Mizpah; the same verse mentions fasting as part of religious practice. Isa. *57:5–8 reflects the rites enacted at the high places.

One practice connected with the feasts and worship at the sanctuaries was the sacred dance. One of the most illustrative passages is 1 Kgs. 18:21 where the prophet Elijah asks his fellow Hebrews "How long go ye limping between the two sides?" The "limping" may be a satirical reference to the ritual dance steps of the devotees of the baal cult. Elijah's idea was that they couldn't dance to both gods at once. The Israelites danced in connection with their worship of the golden calf in the wilderness in the time of Moses.[101] Miriam and her women companions danced on the occasion of Israel's escape from Egypt,[102] which may reflect a primitive feature of the Passover celebration. Dancing was a feature of the annual vintage feast at

91 Gen. 8:21; Ex. 29:18, 25; 1 Sam. 26:19; Am. 5:21.
92 Gen. 29:22; Jgs. 14:10.
93 Gen. 21:8; 1 Sam. 1:24 f.
94 Gen. 26:26–31.
96 Gen. 31:54.
98 1 Sam. 13:9.
100 Vs. 20.
102 Ex. 15:20.
95 Gen. 19:3.
97 1 Sam. 11:15.
99 1 Sam. 1:25; 13:9. Cf. Lev. 1:1–5.
101 Ex. 32:5 f., 19.

Shiloh (Jgs. *21:19 ff.). King David danced when dressed in priestly attire and taking part in a religious procession.[103]

The Agricultural Festivals. The feasts were closely related to the agricultural calendar, occurring usually in the spring and autumn. In the spring came the *Feast of Unleavened Bread* (*Mazzôth*),[104] the idea of which was to end any contamination that had been transmitted from batch to batch through the year by throwing away all leavened bread and eating only unleavened bread until the new dough should begin to ferment of itself. Unleavened bread was the primitive type of bread of nomadic times, and this feast was a reminder to the Israelites of their ancient past, as was the Passover. Passover and Mazzôth come together at the time of the full moon of the spring equinox. The round form of the unleavened cakes may have come about in the remote nomadic past from some relation of the feast to moon worship.

About fifty days later in the spring occurred the *Feast of the Harvest*,[105] which was in the nature of a thanksgiving for the crops. Autumn festivals were designed to stimulate the fertility spirits to perform their tasks, thereby to insure the fertility of the soil. The climax of the festal year was the *Feast of Ingathering* at the close of the vintage season.[106] This marked the end of the old year and the beginning of the new.[107] Jgs. *9:26 f. affords a glimpse of a Canaanite vintage feast, and 1 Sam. *1:1–19 portrays a similar type of celebration by Israelites. The festivals were times of great rejoicing and abandon.[108]

The Worship of the Mother Goddess. Among the ancient Canaanites, Ashtart was worshiped at the out-of-doors high places. Whether at high places or at temples, the emblem of this mother goddess was a short cone-shaped stone, representing the female breast.[109] As the goddess of fertility she was worshiped by offerings in kind. Among the ancient Canaanites, newborn infants were sacrificed, very likely by smothering in sand and interring in earthenware jars, as evidenced by hundreds of such jars found at Gezer. The idea of sacrificing the first-born was to secure increased fruitfulness. In time substitutions came to be made, a lamp, the symbol of life, taking the place of the child.

As the goddess of love, Ashtart was honored by the exercise of the passion which she inspired, and chastity was sacrificed in her honor. The freedom of the sexual relation, which characterizes the

[103] 2 Sam. 6:14.   [104] Ex. 23:15.
[105] Deut. 16:9 f.; Ex. 23:16a.   [106] Ex. 23:16b.
[107] Ex. 34:22. The Hebrew year began in the autumn in pre-exilic times.
[108] Jgs. 21:21; Isa. 30:29; Hos. 2:11.
[109] Cf. Paton, *loc. cit.*, p. 31.

primitive matriarchal state of society, was continued in the *kede-shoth* or shrine prostitutes (literally, "holy ones") who were attached to the sanctuaries of ancient Canaan.[110] Ashtart herself was sometimes designated as Kadesh ("holy"). To the modern, such practices seem licentious. The ancients, however, regarded them seriously as of magical potency in securing good crops from the soil for they knew nothing about the scientific relation of cause and effect in agriculture.

Human Sacrifice. However gruesome the matter of human sacrifice may seem to us, the Hebrews were quite familiar with the practice, as evidenced in Gen. *22:1–19; Ex. 22:29; 1 Kgs. 16:34; 2 Kgs. 3:26 f.; 16:3; 17:17; 21:6; Mic. 6:7; Jer. 7:31. The valley of Hinnom, south of Jerusalem, was a Canaanite center of worship of Malik (Molech), the terrible deity to whom human sacrifices were offered by casting them into furnaces of fire. There is no evidence of any general or widespread application of this practice among the Hebrews in Old Testament times, although it certainly existed to some extent.

Domestic Worship. Jgs. *17 f., an old narrative about Micah's sanctuary, throws a flood of light on the conditions of Yahweh worship as it existed shortly after the settlement in Canaan. Images were no offense, and officiating at religious worship was not restricted to members of a priestly caste.[111] We find a similar situation in 1 Sam. 7:1; the presence of the sacred Ark made Abinadab's home a sanctuary and he made his son Eleazar a priest to look after it.

Sacred Persons

Priests. For the effectual carrying out of the ritual, a priesthood is necessary. It must not be supposed that in the era of the Hebrew settlement of Canaan there was anything like an official national ecclesiastical organization. Jgs. 17:5–13; 18:17–20; 1 Sam. 7:1 suggest the free and easy way in which the priesthood began and developed. The priests were local, as were the deities. Their functions included the assistance of the worshipers in their ritual, especially regarding sacrifices, tending the altar fire, offering the sacrifices which were made on behalf of the community as a whole, cleaning the sanctuary, and taking charge of the *ephod* and the *Urim* and *Thummim,* which were employed in the sacred lot. For their services the priests received portions of the sacrificial meat and such donations as might be made to them.[112] Unfortunately there were some priests

---

[110] Cf. Gen. 38:21. Cf. W. A. Irwin in Frankfort *et al., The Intellectual Adventure of Ancient Man* (Chicago: 1946), p. 235.
[111] Jgs. 17:5.   [112] Cf. Jgs. 17:10; 1 Sam. 2:19.

who abused their office (1 Sam. *2:12–17). Others, such as Eli and Samuel,[113] were men of genuine religious devotion and real force (especially Samuel) in the Hebrew social order.

The Sons of the Prophets. One of the most interesting phenomena of Hebrew religion in the period of the winning and settling of the Hebrew homeland, and later too, was the ecstatic behavior of the so-called "sons of the prophets." These religious enthusiasts existed in companies, and the term "son of a prophet" simply means that a man belonged to one of these bands. Interesting narratives about these sons of the prophets are 1 Sam. *9:1–10:16; *19:18–24; 1 Kgs. 18:4; 22:6; 2 Kgs. *2:3–18; *4:1–7, 38–44; *6:1–7; *9:1–10. Several observations are worthy of mention. (1) The prophetic ecstasy was sometimes induced by the aid of music.[114] (2) The prophetic ecstasy is described either as "the hand of Yahweh upon" the person[115] or as "the spirit of Yahweh upon" the person.[116] Psychologically, this conception of a supernatural force or spirit coming upon a man, impelling him to do things beyond his ordinary human power, is akin to the conception of *mana* which characterizes primitive religions, the term *mana* itself coming from the Melanesians. There is no Hebrew term corresponding to this but the essence of the idea is there, the spirit being conceived as sent out by Yahweh. (3) The phenomenon of mass prophecy frequently referred to among these sons of the prophets is akin to crowd psychology.[117] (4) A person in this prophetic frenzy was occasionally thought to be mad.[118] In such cases the prophet was supposed to speak in ecstasy, losing control of his own mind. In 1 Kgs. 22:20–23, Micaiah ben Imlah seems to consider the spirit of ecstasy as a lying spirit. (5) These sons of the prophets seem to have borne some special markings.[119] (6) On occasion they received pay.[120]

Apparently there were similar groups of baal prophets. 1 Kgs. *18:20–40 vividly portrays the ecstatic behavior of a company of 450 baal prophets in controversy with the Yahweh prophet Elijah. The inference that may be drawn from this is that the sons of the prophets were the ardent devotees of Yahwism and the uncompromising foes of baalism.

---

[113] 1 Sam. 3.
[114] 1 Sam. 10:5; 2 Kgs. 3:15.
[115] 1 Kgs. 18:46; 2 Kgs. 3:15; Ezk. 1:3; 3:14; 8:1; 33:22; 37:1.
[116] Num. 11:25 f., 29; 1 Sam. 10:6, 10; 11:6; 16:13; 2 Sam. 23:2; 2 Kgs. 2:9, 15 f.; Isa. 48:16; 61:1; Joel 2:28 f.; Ezk. 2:2; 11:5; 2 Chr. 24:20.
[117] 1 Kgs. 22:6; Num. 24:2 ff.
[118] 1 Sam. 18:10; Jer. 29:26; 2 Kgs. 9:11.
[119] 1 Kgs. 20:35–43; 2 Kgs. 1:8 marg.; Isa. 20:2; Zech. 13:4 ff. The children's taunt of Elisha, "Go up, thou baldhead" (2 Kgs. 2:23 f.), may have been in reference to some sort of tonsure.
[120] 1 Sam. 9:7 f.; 1 Kgs. 14:3; 2 Kgs. 5:15–27; 8:7–9; Am. 7:10–17.

The Hebrew word for prophet (*nabî*) means "one who speaks forth," a forthteller, a mouthpiece of another person with a mandate from that other person to speak in his stead.[121] This meaning of the term is clearly disclosed in Ex. *4:10–16; *7:1; Deut. *18:15–20; Jer. *1:6–9.[122] A prophet was usually a spokesman for God but not always, for Aaron was Moses' prophet, even as Moses was God's prophet.[123] As God's spokesman it was the function of the prophet to declare God's will for whatever situation the prophet was called upon to face.[124] The Hebrew word *nabî*, meaning spokesman, comes from a verbal root ending in the letter *aleph*. The same verbal root may end in the letter *ayin*, in which case it means "to boil (or bubble.)" Such a term used for a prophet would characterize his behavior as ecstatic or enthusiastic, an accompaniment of which might be a pouring forth of words with or without any meaning. Apparently the sons of the prophets were of this type; in none of the Bible passages pertaining to them are they credited with having anything of consequence to say. A prophet as spokesman was of a higher type. He was a man with a mind who had something to say. Moses was such a prophet. So was Samuel. The great prophets of Israel, whom we shall meet much later in our study, were such spokesmen for God.

1 Sam. 9:9 makes the interesting statement that "Beforetime in Israel, when a man went to inquire of God, thus he said, Come, and let us go to the seer; for he that is now called a Prophet was beforetime called a Seer." This affords an insight into a primitive element of Hebrew religion during the people's earliest days in Canaan. Two different Hebrew words are translated by "seer." One is *hôzeh*, which means "to gaze" or "to have a vision of." Such a person might observe the stars or the flight of birds in the sky or have visions in dreams. He was what we would now call an astrologer. The other word *rô'eh*, "to look upon," designates the diviner who inspected the entrails of a sacrificial animal. A person who did either sort of thing was regarded by his contemporaries as possessed of a supernatural insight into things; he could "see" things not visible to the ordinary mortal. Thus it was believed that Samuel could see where the straying asses of

---

121 W. F. Albright disputes this conventional explanation of the meaning of *nabî*. Its correct meaning, he holds, is "one who is called (by God), one who has a vocation (from God)." This call of God to a special mission, given to the prophet by direct inspiration, makes him a spiritually endowed leader, commissioned by God to preach warning and reform to the people. Cf. *From the Stone Age to Christianity* (Baltimore: 1940), pp. 231 f.

122 Cf. Jer. 15:19.   123 Ex. 4:16; 7:1.

124 In modern usage the word prophet commonly means a foreteller or predictor, and this meaning is often erroneously read into the Biblical word prophet. The English word prophet comes from Greek. The Greek *pro* means "on behalf of" or "in the place of," and the Greek word *prophetes* means one who speaks for another. It does not mean a predictor; for predictor the Greek word is *mantis*.

Saul's father were.[125] It is a far cry from this sort of thing to the great prophets who appeared in Israel from the eighth century B.C. onward.

The Relation of Religion to Ethical Conduct

The divorce of religion from morality is the distressing side of the picture of this period, for religion concerned itself only with such matters as have been mentioned in the foregoing. If the feasts were properly observed and sacrifices correctly and promptly offered so that the deities were kept in good humor, man was satisfied. Man's prime concern in religion was with material benefits. How man treated his fellow man, and whether social and moral wrongs were righted or not, were matters deemed to be outside the sphere of religion. The story in Jgs. *19:14–27 of the shameful abuse of the concubine is a ghastly picture of Hebrew morals in this period. What we would call official religious murder went on in human sacrifice, and what we would call sex immorality went on in the guise of sacramental fornication, utter sexual license prevailing at certain of the festivals, especially in the autumn. Religious practices which thus gave free rein to the human passions were bound to undermine the virile, social-ethical inheritance which Israel had from nomadic days.

One commendable moral quality characterized the time, viz., the sanctity which was attached to an oath. The form of oath used by the Yahweh worshiper is given in 1 Kgs. *17:1; Ruth 1:17; 2 Kgs. 6:31; the formula, "As Yahweh lives," guarantees divine support of the act, for a god who is "living" can punish a violator. The form for the believer in other deities is stated in 1 Kgs. *19:2. Fear of the terrible consequences to follow from perjury restrained men from taking the name of a god in vain. An element of the ritual of oath-taking is revealed in the Hebrew words *sheba,* "seven," and *shâba,* "to seven oneself," i.e., to take an oath. The implication is, perhaps, that the oath formula was repeated seven times or an appeal made seven times to the deity invoked.

Yahwism versus Baalism

Baalism went hand in hand with village patriotism. It exercised a disintegrating influence, separating village from village and city from city. The Canaanites had no sense of social solidarity. Their ideal was individualistic. The well-being of all was sacrificed to the prosperity of the individual. The Hebrews took over many things from

125 1 Sam. 9:6.

the Canaanites and were in grave peril of absorbing this disunity also. In fact, much of the unity Moses had succeeded in building up among the clans was lost in the early decades of life in Canaan. The unity Moses built up was founded upon the principle of loyalty to Yahweh.[126] The author of Judges, in contending that the era he described was an era of apostasy, was exactly right.[127] Baalism did make for disunity. The Hebrew social-ethical ideal always merged the individual in the group. The well-being of all was paramount in their thinking.

Yahwism made for such national coherence and well-being. It was in the name of Yahweh that certain tribes united under Deborah against the Canaanites.[128] It was in the name of Yahweh that certain others rallied to Gideon to drive off their oppressors. Yahwism was basic to the new unity that was desired by reason of the Philistine menace. Hence it was a priest and prophet of Yahweh (Samuel) who was asked to find a king, and to insure that Saul would be a true devotee of Yahweh he was put in touch with "a band of prophets" in order that "the Spirit of Yahweh" might "come mightily" upon him.[129] When Samuel later broke with Saul it was because Saul had been "disobedient to Yahweh" (1 Sam. 15), and in his place Samuel selected another devotee of Yahweh, David, "the anointed of Yahweh." In the next chapter we shall see how David brought about a real national unity of the Hebrews, not so much by his statesmanship and success in warfare as by firmly establishing Yahwism as the national religion.

126 Ex. 20:3.   127 Vid. supra, p. 137.
128 Jgs. 5:23.   129 1 Sam. 10:1-8.

Chapter 11

HEBREW NATIONAL UNITY

Hebrew national unity grew out of the crisis produced by the Philistine menace. The crisis called to the fore a man of destiny— David. It was David who put an end to the Philistine threat. David became the first real king of the Hebrews, exercising royal powers far in excess of those conceded to Saul and welding the tribes into a solid nationalism. David was the founder of a dynasty which continued in unbroken succession throughout the history of the kingdom of Judah. Thus there came to be associated with the name of David the most exalted hope which Hebrew thought ever conceived, the hope of the ideal ruler.[1] But alas! David also instituted policies which unleashed forces that led to the disruption of the very national unity he created and started the Hebrew nation on the road to ruin.

Sources for a History of the Period

The Biblical data for a history of the period under survey in the present chapter are in the books of First Samuel (commencing with chapter 16), Second Samuel, and First Kings (through chapter 11). Of this material, the most valuable part is 2 Sam. 9–20; 1 Kgs. 1–2, recognized by historians and literary critics alike as one of the finest historical documents to be found anywhere. The most valuable and trustworthy historical writing is that which comes from one who has himself witnessed the events he narrates or at least has derived his knowledge from such witnesses. It is strictly objective, i.e., it relates incidents realistically as they happened without attempting to point moral lessons or shape the facts so as to substantiate any theory of the author. The sketch of the career of King David was probably written in the reign of Solomon, very soon after David's death, by one who had intimate, firsthand knowledge of David's mature life and his reign.[2] This writer was not so well informed about the events, de-

---

[1] Cf. Isa. 11:1–10.

[2] As to the identity of this author, the most likely conjecture is Ahimaaz, son of Zadok. Only he and Jonathan, son of Abiathar, would tell about their adventure in hiding in the well in just the way it is told in 2 Sam. 17:17–21; certainly not the peasant woman who was an eyewitness of the incident. In the ensuing narrative in chapter 18, Jonathan has dropped out of the picture, but Ahimaaz has witnessed the

scribed in 1 Sam. 16 – 2 Sam. 8, connected with David's early manhood and his elevation to the kingship.

The material about Solomon in 1 Kgs. 3–11 apparently came from the "Book of the Acts of Solomon" mentioned in 1 Kgs. 11:41 but now no longer extant. This book was the work of some admirer of the king, and was probably written soon after Solomon's death. Much of the material is historically reliable but some is legendary and unimportant.

King David introduced the practice of employing an official royal recorder ("remembrancer") to keep the royal annals. Material from these annals is included in such passages as the summary of David's wars (2 Sam. 8); the census of David's generals and court officials (2 Sam. 20:23–26; 21:15–22; 23:9–39); and the list of his wives and sons (2 Sam. 3:2–5; 5:13–16). There were similar lists and summaries for Solomon (1 Kgs. 4:1–19). Temple records were similarly kept and upon them was based the narrative of the building of the Jerusalem temple (1 Kgs. 6 f.).

Several centuries after the events described, this material from the several original sources was gathered together by the editors of the books of Samuel and Kings and incorporated into a framework which determined the selection of material by its connection with the national religion. This editor's view is that the reigns of David and Solomon were glorious because they gave vigorous support to Yahwism, making it indeed the state religion.

The Rise of David to the Kingship

At the Court of Saul. The early life of David was closely intertwined with the fortunes of Saul. 1 Sam. *16:14–23 indicates that David's first connection with the royal court was as a harpist whose skillful playing restored balance to the deranged mind of his liege lord Saul. 1 Sam. *17 dramatically narrates David's daring exploit during the Philistine war in the Shephelah region when David defeated the Philistine champion, Goliath.[3] By this exploit David became not only a favorite with Saul and Jonathan but also the idol of the populace (1 Sam. *18:1–16). From then on David's fame eclipsed even that of the crown prince Jonathan who had been a popular hero since his brilliant defeat of the Philistines at Michmash.[4]

Saul's fondness for David, however, soon passed under a cloud. His growing madness made him insanely jealous of David, whom he

---

death of Absalom and runs to King David, though he refrains from telling the king the real facts (18:19–32). Cf. Robert H. Pfeiffer, *Introduction to the Old Testament* (New York: 1941), pp. 356 f.

 [3] 2 Sam. 21:19 credits Elhanan of Bethlehem with slaying Goliath.

 [4] 1 Sam. 14:1–46.

sought to kill by tricking him into the seemingly impossible venture of slaying a hundred Philistines, on the promise of marrying Saul's daughter, the princess Michal, as a reward.[5] David's unexpected success upset the king's calculation and the latter reluctantly carried out his promise. David thus became the king's son-in-law with a claim on the throne should Saul's sons die. This for Saul only added fear to jealousy, and "Saul was David's enemy continually," [6] with the result that David finally had to flee from the court to escape repeated plots against his life (1 Sam. *19:1–17). In all this it is a pleasant relief to find Saul's son Jonathan standing loyally by David, even to the extent of taking sides against his own father. The friendship thus established between David and Jonathan endured so long as both lived and has become the classic example of human friendship.

So "David fled, and escaped, and came to Samuel to Ramah, and told him all that Saul had done to him." [7] What Samuel had to say is, unfortunately, not recorded. Samuel was the real power behind the throne and it is evident that he had already come to the conclusion that Saul would no longer do as king.[8] Indeed, he had already anointed David (1 Sam. *16:1–13). Whatever Samuel may have advised David to do, it now became evident that reconciliation between David and Saul was out of the question (1 Sam. *20), and David therefore fled to the Negeb and became an exile, which was, under the circumstances, tantamount to being an outlaw.

David's Career as an Outlaw.   1 Sam. *21:1–28:2; *29, graphically portrays David's outlaw career in the Negeb, in the Wilderness of Judea (Jeshimon), and in the Shephelah. "And every one that was in distress, and every one that was in debt, and every one that was discontented, gathered themselves unto him; and he became captain over them; and there were with him about four hundred men." [9] David and this assortment of malcontents maintained themselves in Robin Hood style for several years.

In reality, David was leader of those who were for Yahweh. Shortly after the famous battle in which the Philistines captured the sacred Hebrew Ark, the city of Shiloh with its temple, which had housed the Ark, was destroyed. Apparently the Yahweh priests at that time fled from Shiloh to Nob, which became the headquarters of the Yahweh cult. Saul destroyed Nob and killed the Yahweh priests,[10] which was a colossal blunder, for it alienated from himself and arrayed behind David that fighting religious zeal which had rallied the Hebrews of Deborah's day "to the help of Yahweh against the

---

[5] 1 Sam. 18:8–28.   [6] 1 Sam. 18:29.
[7] 1 Sam. 19:18.   [8] 1 Sam. 15:23.
[9] 1 Sam. 22:2.   [10] 1 Sam. 22:18 f.

mighty," [11] and in Gideon's day to fight "for Yahweh and for Gideon." [12]

Saul hounded David relentlessly but without success. Twice David magnanimously spared Saul's life, and this because of David's idealistic conception of the kingship; for he regarded the king as "Yahweh's anointed." [13]

Finally, to escape Saul's relentless persecution, David went to Gath and attached himself to the Philistines, although he never forswore loyalty to the Hebrews. This situation became rather embarrassing for David when he actually set out as an ally of the Philistine Achish of Gath on a campaign against Saul. Luckily for David, the suspicions of some of the Philistine "lords" forced Achish to get rid of David before hostilities actually commenced.[14]

David Made King of Judah-Israel. Upon the death of Saul the people of Judah at once made David their king. He set up his capital in Hebron, most important city of that district (2 Sam. *2:1–7, 11). The fact that he had now been crowned king over Judah gave him no rights over the other tribes. He hoped, however, that the other tribes would follow Judah's example, and so he sent an ingratiating message to the people of Jabesh-gilead, the most devoted of Saul's supporters, with the idea of persuading them to set an example which the rest of the northern tribes would almost certainly follow.[15] But these overtures were rejected. Meanwhile the people of central Canaan and Gilead made Ishbaal (Ishbosheth), son of Saul, their king. Ishbaal's capital was Mahanaim in Gilead, and he ruled "over Gilead, and over the Ashurites (probably north of Esdraelon), and over Jezreel, and over Ephraim, and over Benjamin, and over all Israel." [16] The fact that Ishbaal moved his capital to the east Jordan area is evidence of how completely the Philistines had overrun central Canaan at the time of Saul's death. Moreover, a further reason for putting the capital there was the loyalty of the Gileadites to the house of Saul and the lack of support from the people of Judah who were ardent partisans of David.

Between these two little Hebrew kingdoms warfare raged for seven years, some details of which are recounted in 2 Sam. 2:12–4:12. David was ably backed by Joab, an exceptionally forceful leader, while Ishbaal was supported by Abner. Abner later revolted to David and was soon murdered by the ruthless Joab. Last of all, Ishbaal himself was murdered. It is likely that during all this period both kingdoms were subject to the Philistines, the latter not at all displeased to have the Hebrews thus fighting among themselves.

---

[11] Jgs. 5:23.   [12] Jgs. 7:18.
[13] 1 Sam. 24:6; 26:9.   [14] 1 Sam. 29.
[15] 2 Sam. 2:4–7.   [16] 2 Sam. 2:9.

After the death of Ishbaal representatives from all the tribes went to Hebron and requested David to be their king (2 Sam. *5:1–5). Manifestly they did not make an unconditional offer of the crown to David but specified terms to which David agreed in a most solemn and binding compact: "So all the elders of Israel came to the king to Hebron; and King David made a covenant with them in Hebron before Yahweh: and they anointed David king over Israel," [17] i.e., the king agreed to the terms which these elders of Israel stipulated and thereupon these elders anointed David king over Israel. They appear to have been at pains to safeguard the rights of their people, chief among which rights we may well infer (from what happened later) was the right to anoint or to refuse to anoint David's sons as his successors on the throne of Israel—"there is no inheritance in the son of Jesse." [18] In other words, David had not forced himself upon the nation. He was the popular choice, although it may have been a Hobson's choice; for they despaired of escape from Philistine oppression unless they submitted to a single leader. The Philistines had tolerated David as a vassal king over the little realm of Judah, but as king of united Judah and Israel such toleration was out of the question. So they promptly attacked and were as promptly defeated, as has already been noted.[19] Thus David put an end to the Philistine menace and was thereafter free to organize and develop his kingdom unhampered by fear of invasion.

National Consolidation and Expansion Under David

The Founding of a National Capital at Jerusalem. In our study of the Hebrew occupation of southern Canaan, it was noted that a line of Canaanite fortresses separated the tribes in the south from those in central Canaan.[20] By the time David became king, the Hebrews evidently had reduced all these strongholds excepting Gezer and Jerusalem (or Jebus, as it was called). David captured the latter city from the Jebusites, and made it his capital (2 Sam. *5:6–12). Gezer was not incorporated in the Hebrew kingdom until the reign of Solomon.[21]

It was a wise move on David's part to make Jerusalem his capital. It was so situated with respect to the tribes of the south and the north as to make it possible for the king to communicate readily with all parts of his kingdom. Moreover, the city had not previously belonged to any one of the tribes, and to make it the capital provoked a minimum of jealousy. It was also strategically located, hard to attack

---

[17] 2 Sam. 5:3.
[19] *Supra*, p. 164.
[21] 1 Kgs. 9:16.

[18] Cf. 1 Kgs. 12:16.
[20] *Vid. supra*, p. 140.

and easy to defend. At last the nation had a real center of political unity, "the city of David."[22]

David at once set about developing Jerusalem with a view to making it a real capital. The city wall had been breached in the capture of the city, and this he repaired; "David built round about from Millo and inward," i.e., from where the Millo rampart later stood.[23] He built a royal palace.[24] Wishing to make Jerusalem not only a political capital but a national religious shrine as well, David brought to Jerusalem the Ark of the Covenant which had been in obscurity for some twenty years.[25] This famous historical procession is described in picturesque detail in 2 Sam. *6:1–19. The sacred object was placed in a tent set up for the purpose, no doubt a revival of the historic Tent of Meeting.[26] A tent, however, no longer satisfied the people's sense of dignity and proper respect, since it savored of a bygone nomadism. David felt that religion had better be brought up to date, too, and therefore he contemplated building a temple in Jerusalem to house the Ark (2 Sam. *7:1 ff.). He never accomplished this, however, because he was too much occupied with wars.[27] But he did go so far as to acquire a site where the temple was later built by his son and successor, Solomon (2 Sam. *24:15–25).

The Extent of the Kingdom Under David. 2 Sam. 8:1–14; 10 records David's victories over his enemies on all sides and the territorial expansion of his kingdom. He began with a very small kingdom in Judah, extending in a north to south direction only from Jerusalem to Beersheba, an extreme distance of fifty-five miles; west and east it included only the district from the Shephelah to the Wilderness of Judea, about thirty miles. This little kingdom David expanded into a modest empire comprising the lands both west and east of Jordan, and extending from the Lebanon Mountains in the north to the very border of Egypt. Philistia, Moab, Ammon, Edom, the desert tribes, and the Aramaean states in the north were all brought to acknowledge David's overlordship. He not only held these people in subjection, but apparently commanded their loyalty, for some of David's ablest men were non-Hebrews; e.g., Ittai of Gath, a Philistine;[28] Uriah, the Hittite;[29] Zelek, an Ammonite;[30] and Ithmah, the Moabite.[31] David's vigorous and aggressive rule welded the Hebrews into a real state and gave them a place among the nations. David's

---

22 2 Sam. 5:9. Cf. G. E. Wright and F. V. Filson, *The Westminster Historical Atlas to the Bible* (Philadelphia: 1945), p. 97.
23 2 Sam. 5:9.   24 2 Sam. 5:11.
25 Cf. 1 Sam. 4:1–7:2.   26 *Vid. supra*, p. 133.
27 1 Kgs. 5:3.   28 Cf. 2 Sam. 15:19–22.
29 2 Sam. 11:6–11.   30 2 Sam. 23:37.
31 1 Chr. 11:46.

kingdom was the one nearest approach in ancient times to the development of an empire in the western horn of the Fertile Crescent. Such political expansion was possible because the tenth century B.C. was a period of both Egyptian and Assyrian weakness.[32]

The Organization of the Government Under David. In 2 Sam. 8:16 ff.; 15:37; 16:16; 20:23–26; 1 Chr. 27:33 mention is made of the important state officials whom David appointed. They were (1) the scribe, who was his secretary of state and doubtless handled the royal correspondence;[33] (2) the recorder, a word meaning "remembrancer," indicating that his function probably was to lay before the king such matters as required his personal attention, i.e., he served as a kind of chancellor; he probably also kept the official royal chronicles; (3) "the king's friend," his most helpful adviser; (4) two priests of the highest rank, undoubtedly also officials of state;[34] (5) an overseer of the labor gangs;[35] (6) a chief of staff of the army, who was David's own nephew, Joab;[36] and (7) a commander of the king's bodyguard, the Cherethites and the Pelethites (Cretans and Philistines); this was Benaiah, a Judahite.[37] This bodyguard, numbering 600, was composed of men who had been followers of David in his outlaw years. There were also two military orders, the "Order of the Three" and the "Order of the Thirty."[38] The military was headed by men upon whom the king could, because of their personal devotion to him, count in any crisis in which his person and power had to be insured, even and especially against disaffected groups of Hebrews as events later showed.[39] The army further included conscripts from the tribes of Israel, for which purpose, as well as for duty in compulsory labor gangs, David instituted a census.[40]

Throughout the kingdom purely local affairs were attended to by the elders. In any special matter calling for adjudication, the king deputed someone to act for him.[41] To the king himself an appeal could be carried directly by any citizen,[42] for he was at the head of the administration of justice.[43]

---

[32] Cf. W. F. Albright, *Archaeology and the Religion of Israel* (Baltimore: 1942), p. 130.

[33] The 'Amarna letters show what such a job was in an earlier age in Canaan. David's official correspondence would doubtless be in cuneiform characters; his scribe's name, Shavsha (1 Chr. 18:16; cf. Seraiah, 2 Sam. 8:17 and Sheva, 2 Sam. 20:25) intimates that he may have been a Babylonian, doubtless hired because of his skill to write in such characters.

[34] David's own sons were priests (2 Sam. 8:18), but with what relation to the chief priests is uncertain.

[35] 2 Sam. 20:24.   [36] 1 Chr. 2:16.

[37] 2 Sam. 8:18.

[38] 2 Sam. 23:8–12, 18–39. Cf. 1 Chr. 11:10–14, 20–47; 27:1–24.

[39] 2 Sam. 15:18; 1 Kgs. 1:8.   [40] 2 Sam. 24:1 f.

[41] 2 Sam. 15:3.   [42] 2 Sam. 14:4–24.

[43] 2 Sam. 8:15.

Despotism and the Menace of Division

David imitated the prevailing practice of royalty in his time by having a harem. In so doing he prepared a fruitful soil for intrigue. While in Hebron he had six wives,[44] and after becoming king in Jerusalem he took several others.[45] No doubt some of these were princesses from neighboring nations which were tributary to or allied with David, for such intermarriage of royalty was the approved way of cementing an alliance between nations. David thus introduced a practice which was carried to such an extent by his son and successor, Solomon, that it contributed to the disruption of the kingdom.

Like other Oriental kings, David could not avoid the temptation to play the despot. 2 Sam. 11 details one such incident which stands out sharply in the record of his numerous marriages, the sordid story of his adultery with Bathsheba. It is a typical instance of that brand of Oriental despotism which is based on the assumption that the common people have no rights which the monarch is bound to respect. Doubtless such an incident would have passed unnoticed in other realms, but in Israel it was a violation of the democratic and moral basis on which the kingdom had been founded. Popular rights were in this instance championed by the prophet Nathan, one of David's trusted counselors (2 Sam. *12:1–14). That a subject of the king, even though he were a counselor, would dare to condemn the king for his action is clear evidence of the democratic nature of the Hebrew kingdom and of the fact that the government was still regarded as a limited monarchy. What made David's act the more reprehensible was the fact that it included what amounted to official murder of the husband, Uriah.

The incident just discussed occurred during a war with the Ammonites. These Ammonites David virtually reduced to slavery,[46] and this, together with the fact that one of the chief officers of the realm was the overseer of the labor gangs, implies that David was fostering important building and other enterprises of national development and expansion. In such a program, however, the people may have scented a beginning of despotism.

How corrupting was the influence of the harem is evidenced in stories like that of Amnon's crime against his half-sister Tamar, and of the later murder of Amnon by Absalom in blood vengeance (2 Sam. 13). But most tragic of all is the story of how Absalom plotted against his own father to get the throne for himself while David was still alive (2 Sam. *15:1–12). It marks the first of a series

---

[44] 2 Sam. 3:2–5.   [45] 2 Sam. 5:13–16.
[46] 2 Sam. 12:31.

of rebellions which saddened David's later years and possibly hastened his decline and death.

It is reasonably certain that this particular rebellion had its roots in tribal jealousies, though other factors undoubtedly entered. The center of the revolt was Hebron and the entire support of the revolt was from Judah. Hebron had been David's first capital, and the men of Judah apparently resented the removal of the capital from there. But harem intrigue as to the succession was probably an even more important factor. Absalom's mother was a daughter of the king of Geshur.[47] He thus had princely blood in his veins from both parents, and very likely he felt that this gave him a special claim on the throne. For a time when this rebellion was at its height, David was forced to abandon Jerusalem and to flee across the Jordan (2 Sam. *15:13–16:14). On that occasion the once forceful king presented a wretched and pitiable spectacle. En route to the Jordan, David was vigorously cursed and pelted with stones, particularly by one Shimei, of the tribe of Benjamin.[48] Saul had been of that tribe. The rebellion ended with the death of Absalom, who was savagely killed by Joab (2 Sam. *18:9–33). At this David seems to have lost all grip upon himself. But, prodded by Joab, he finally pulled himself together (2 Sam. 19:1–8), assumed the reins of government, and issued a general pardon for all who had participated in the rebellion (2 Sam. 19:16–40). Judah was not easily reconciled (2 Sam. 19:11–15) but came around when David offered the post previously held by Joab[49] to Amasa, who had led the forces of Absalom.[50] But this was a compromise that satisfied nobody, as later events proved.

The favoritism to Judah, which had been the backbone of Absalom's rebellion, was resented by the northern tribesmen and they forthwith revolted under Sheba (2 Sam. *19:41–20:22). Sheba was of the Bichri clan of Benjamin and thus related to Saul. David ordered Amasa to gather his forces and put down this rebellion, but Amasa was so dilatory about complying that Joab suspected him of disloyalty. So he promptly slew Amasa, assumed command himself, and pursued Sheba into the far north of Palestine until he cornered him in Abel-beth-maacha. Confronted with the alternative of facing a desperate siege or of violating the law of asylum, the inhabitants of the town chose the latter. They slew Sheba, threw his head over the wall to Joab, and thus the rebellion ended. The kingdom of Judah-Israel had come perilously close to disruption on the very basis on which it was to break up a generation later.[51]

---

[47] 2 Sam. 3:3.
[48] 2 Sam. 16:5–14.
[49] 2 Sam. 19:13.
[50] 2 Sam. 17:25.
[51] Cf. 2 Sam. 20:1 f. and 1 Kgs. 12:16. *Vid. infra,* pp. 217–220.

The final item in this unceasing harem intrigue was the struggle over the succession to the throne, vividly recounted in 1 Kgs. *1. David was now advanced in years and his physical powers were fast failing. The question of the succession divided the nation's leaders into two parties. One party, including such important men as Joab, David's commander-in-chief, and Abiathar, the priest, favored Adonijah, David's oldest surviving son. But the right of the oldest son to succeed to the throne was not yet established in Judah. A king might make appointment, as was the case with any tribal sheikh, from among all his sons. Moreover, Adonijah, in gathering to his cause "all the men of Judah," [52] was attempting to make capital out of the old tribal lines of division. The other party favored Solomon, son of Bathsheba, David's favorite wife. In this party were counted such men as Nathan the prophet who for many years had been a trusted adviser of David; Zadok the priest; Benaiah the captain of David's body-guard; and the "mighty men." [53] In this contest of wits Nathan proved the shrewder, and his scheme for the anointing and proclamation of Solomon as king succeeded against the plot of the Adonijah party. It was a clever coup, so quickly put over that the people had little or no chance to assert their rights in the matter of their next king. David, however, in assenting to the coronation of Solomon, recognized the dual character of the Hebrew monarchy: "I have appointed him to be prince over Israel and over Judah." [54] Thus it came about that a younger son, Solomon, became king.

In his last days David was a sorry spectacle. His dying injunctions to his son Solomon were chiefly commissions to wreak vengeance on his (David's) enemies.[55] Most of these had been men who had defied the king's authority, and justly. That his dying injunction should have been to get even with these men shows how completely David had become obsessed by the spirit of the despot.

David's Contribution to the Nation

Next to Moses, who created the Hebrew nation, David was the greatest man Israel had yet produced. He was the real creator of the monarchy. He perfected the Hebrew national unity. To be sure he also introduced the forces which ultimately destroyed that unity, but never was the nation so much of a unit as in David's day. In no small

---

[52] 1 Kgs. 1:9. [53] 1 Kgs. 1:38.
[54] 1 Kgs. 1:35. L. W. Batten calls attention to the curious fact that the chronicler specifies two separate anointings of Solomon (1 Chr. 23:1; 29:22), and observes: "The first enthroning corresponds exactly to the record in Kings, but the second has no parallel in the early record. Is it possible that the chronicler has preserved an authentic tradition to the effect that David made Solomon king of Judah but that later Israel made him their king?" "A Crisis in the History of Israel," *Journal of Biblical Literature,* xlix (1930), pp. 55–60. [55] 1 Kgs. 2:1–10.

measure this was due to the charm and vigor of a winsome personality which evoked loyalty among his followers. He was a man of force and he was also, generally speaking, fair and just. He was an aggressive warrior. He silenced all the nation's foes and pushed the domain of the Hebrews to the widest bounds it ever knew. Internally, he perfected a strong, centralized government with a capital city which was a credit to the nation. The spoils of war and the gains of trade enriched the nation. His suppression of the Philistines broke their monopolistic control over iron, brought that metal into common use, and opened the way for Hebrew economic development. He founded *the* royal line, and though the kingdom was disrupted after the death of his son Solomon there never failed on the throne of Judah a king of the Davidic line so long as that kingdom lasted, except during the brief usurpation by Queen Athaliah.[56]

Solomon and Imperialism

The Murderous Disposal of Solomon's Rivals.   The baptism of blood which inaugurated the reign of Solomon is gruesomely narrated in 1 Kgs. 2:12–46. The trend during David's reign was in the direction of autocracy and in that atmosphere Solomon was reared. He inherited the very instincts of the despot. Placed on the throne by intrigue within the royal harem, he promptly displayed the spirit of the autocrat by putting out of the way every possible rival. He had no conscience about putting to death anyone he suspected of disloyalty. The first victim of his disfavor was his elder brother Adonijah, whose plot to seize the throne had been foiled by Solomon's supporters. Adonijah sought to marry one of the women of his father's harem. Solomon promptly and correctly interpreted this as treason because a king's harem was the property of his successor. Solomon therefore had Adonijah executed. Solomon next turned against the leading supporters of Adonijah's conspiracy. Abiathar, the priest, was deposed and banished to Anathoth. Joab, the intrepid commander-in-chief under King David, was the next to fall, foully murdered within the sacred precincts of the Tent of Yahweh, a fact which shows how utterly ruthless Solomon was. Solomon next ordered Shimei executed for disobedience to the king's command never to leave Jerusalem. This last execution completed the program of vengeance upon the men his father David had cursed in his dying hour.

Extent and Organization of Solomon's Kingdom.   Solomon inherited from his father an empire which extended on the northeast to the Euphrates,[57] on the southeast to the Gulf of Akabah, and

[56] *Vid. infra*, p. 238.   [57] According to 1 Kgs. 4:24.

on the southwest to Philistia and the border of Egypt. This empire began at once to shrink. The accession of a new king, especially if accompanied by disorders, was the time for discontented subject states to try to break away. Solomon's execution of Joab, the strongest warrior in the realm, was an added incentive to revolt.

The first of the subject states to break away was Edom.[58] Hadad of Edom, who had been an exile in Egypt since David had subjugated Edom, now returned and led a successful revolt. Edom's detachment from Solomon's rule did not disturb his control over the Arabah, the rift valley which extends from the Dead Sea southward to the Gulf of Akabah. Solomon's commercial enterprises demanded firm control of that region. As a matter of fact, all through the ensuing centuries it was vital for the kingdom of Judah to keep control of the route to Akabah, and those kings of Judah who kept or won back that control are the kings who are rated as great. The next to fall away was the Aramaean kingdom of Damascus. Its king, Rezon I, led a successful rebellion and established a kingdom which proved to be a thorn in the side of the Hebrews for the next two centuries, at times even reducing the Hebrews to subjection.[59]

Apparently this loss of territory was less damaging to Solomon's prestige than to his treasury. He made up for the loss of revenue by increasing the taxes of his own people and by reducing to slavery the descendants of the original inhabitants found by the Hebrews when they conquered and settled Canaan.[60]

Solomon possessed a great talent for organization. He expanded still further the system of national organization which David had begun. Solomon's machinery of government, described in 1 Kgs. 4:2–19; 9:23; 5:16 was as follows: two priests (4:2, 5) in addition to David's two (4:4); two scribes (4:3) in place of David's one; a recorder (4:3), "one who called to remembrance," i.e., not merely a chronicler but virtually a chancellor; a chief of staff of the army (4:4); a supervisor of the various officials (4:5); a "king's friend" (4:5); a superintendent of the palace (4:6); an overseer of the labor gangs (4:6); twelve internal revenue officers, one in each of the twelve administrative districts into which the kingdom was divided for purposes of taxation, three east of Jordan and nine west (4:7–19); numerous subordinate officials (9:23, 5:16). The king himself remained the supreme judge or ultimate court of appeal.[61] It was a simple but effective organization that met the needs of the time.

Solomon's Building Enterprises. Solomon's greatest contribution to the development of the nation was the building program

[58] 1 Kgs. 11:14–22.   [59] 1 Kgs. 11:23 ff.
[60] 1 Kgs. 9:20 f.   [61] Cf. 1 Kgs. 3:16–28.

which he carried out in Jerusalem and at other strategic points in his realm. Jerusalem he made into an imposing capital by erecting on the east hill a group of splendid buildings (1 Kgs. *5:1–6:10, 14; *7:1–12). Of these, by far the most significant and influential in Hebrew history was the temple, built upon the highest point of the capitol hill.[62] On the terraces below the temple were the other buildings: the king's palace (7:1), the House of the Daughter of Pharaoh (7:8), the House of the Forest of Lebanon, which was an armory (7:2; 10:16 f.), the Hall of Pillars (7:6), and the Throne Hall (7:7). All these buildings, which were made of most costly material,[63] added greatly to the beauty of the city.

Solomon further strengthened the defenses of Jerusalem. He built Millo (9:24), a fortress tower located at the site where David had breached the walls of the city when he captured it from the Jebusites. The wall of Jerusalem was extended (3:1; 9:15), perhaps that part which protected the east hill with its imposing buildings.

Outside the city of Jerusalem Solomon constructed six fortresses,[64] located at points strategic for controlling all approaches to the plateau of Judah and (what was even more important) for controlling the movement of caravans of commerce (1 Kgs. 10:14 f.). This latter was probably his chief purpose, for he doubtless levied toll on all passing trade, a customary practice in those days. A great trade route from Arabia northward to Phoenicia and Syria passed through Palestine. The westward branch of that route passed the head of the Gulf of Akabah. Solomon controlled that vital point since his kingdom extended southward all the way to Akabah. He therefore had a strangle hold on the very profitable spice trade that moved along that route. The visit of the celebrated Queen of Sheba, who came from a country in Southern Arabia 1,200 miles away, to the court of King Solomon in Jerusalem (1 Kgs. *10:1–10, 13) was in reality a sort of foreign economic commission in the interest of that spice trade. Solomon likewise built store cities and cities for his chariots and horses.[65]

Solomon's Commerce and Wealth. Solomon sponsored industrial and commercial enterprises that brought in wealth (1 Kgs. 9:26 ff.; 10:11–29). This trade was a royal monopoly and the revenue was much needed to support his numerous wives and extensive court.

---

[62] The complete description of this building and its erection is given in 1 Kgs. 5:1–9:9. A detailed study of this temple will be made in Chapter 17 in connection with a study of Hebrew architecture. Its religious importance will be considered in Chapter 12.

[63] 1 Kgs. 7:9–12.

[64] 1 Kgs. 9:15, 17 f.

[65] 1 Kgs. 9:19. The Hebrew word thus translated seems to have been a technical expression for horses used for military purposes, for either cavalry or chariots, and is so translated in certain other places in the Old Testament where the same word appears.

He carried on a lucrative trade in horses and chariots.[66] Egypt supplied the horses, the Hittites in the north furnished the market.[67] This horse trade was extensive and required large depots. The depot at Megiddo [68] is the best known of all because of the archaeological excavation of that place by the University of Chicago Oriental Institute in expeditions that have been made since 1925. A large complex of stables was uncovered, sufficient to accommodate 450 horses. In the stables the stalls are separated by huge square stone posts; the floors are paved with cobblestones and fitted with mangers and tie holes. Between the rows of stalls are cement-paved aisles. This horse trading of Solomon has a very ugly aspect. A later statute of limitation upon the authority of a Hebrew king prescribed that "he shall not multiply horses to himself, nor cause the people to return to Egypt, to the end that he may multiply horses." [69] The hideous implication of this is that horses were paid for with men, who doubtless were forced to serve the Pharaoh for a stretch of time as foreign slave labor. There can be little doubt that Solomon started the vicious practice which this law condemns.

Solomon established a merchant marine, with Ezion-geber at the head of the Gulf of Akabah as its home port.[70] The Phoenicians and Egyptians controlled seafaring commerce in the Mediterranean and to avoid trouble with them, Solomon kept out of those waters. Besides, Palestine didn't have any good Mediterranean harbor. Solomon's fleet traded along the coasts of the Red Sea to the south. Since the Hebrews knew nothing of navigation, Solomon had to man his fleet with Phoenician sailors.[71] This enterprise brought him enormous profit.

One of the most fascinating of recent archaeological achievements was the discovery by Professor Nelson Glueck, in campaigns made from 1938 to 1940, of copper and iron mines along the Arabah and the excavation of a considerable smelting plant at Ezion-geber.[72] The ores were mined and partly roasted in the Arabah, then transported to Ezion-geber where they were fully refined. At the plant, double rows of interconnecting air channels caught and utilized the strong winds which blow continuously from the north at that site. The artisans made nature do the work that otherwise would have necessitated a system of bellows. Artifacts found in the excavation disclose that a

[66] 1 Kgs. 10:26, 28 f. Cf. C. C. McCown, *The Ladder of Progress in Palestine* (New York: 1943), pp. 179–182.
[67] 1 Kgs. 10:26, 28 f. Cf. G. E. Wright and F. V. Filson, *op. cit.*, p. 48; W. F. Albright, *op. cit.*, pp. 134 f.
[68] 1 Kgs. 9:15.   [69] Deut. 17:16.
[70] 1 Kgs. 9:26. Cf. W. F. Albright, *op. cit.*, pp. 134 f.
[71] 1 Kgs. 9:27.
[72] Cf. Nelson Glueck, *The Other Side of the Jordan* (New Haven: 1940), pp. 50–113; McCown, *op. cit.*, pp. 294–299.

large variety of metal objects were manufactured there. Professor Glueck calls Ezion-geber the "Pittsburgh" of Solomon's kingdom. Now we can understand what objects were exported in Solomon's trading ships and bartered in remote lands for "gold, silver, ivory, apes, and peacocks." [73] It took three years for his navy to make a round trip to all its ports of call.

Though Solomon appears to have done almost anything to raise money to pay his debts, he didn't wholly succeed. King Hiram evidently had to foreclose, after waiting twenty years for his pay, and to settle this debt, Solomon turned over twenty cities of Galilee. But even this settlement failed to satisfy Hiram.[74]

Solomon's Imperialistic Policy. Solomon played the grand monarch in a way to give him international fame. The story of the visit of the Queen of Sheba is probably only a sample of what frequently went on in Solomon's intercourse with foreign nations, for wide contacts with foreign peoples are implied in 1 Kgs. 10:23 ff., "So King Solomon exceeded all the kings of the earth in riches and in wisdom," is the way the writer boastfully sums it up.[75]

All this splendor, however, was built upon an insecure foundation, viz., autocracy and iniquitous burdening of his people. He reduced them virtually to the status of serfs.[76] Such forced labor was hateful to them and they grew sullen and resentful. This arrogant policy proved in the end to be more than his little kingdom would stand.

King David started the practice of maintaining a harem, and his son Solomon completely outdid him. "Solomon loved many foreign women." [77] Numerous treaty alliances with foreign nations account for some of these marriages. Such alliances, made with a view to political advantage, proved to be of commercial and cultural advantage as well, bringing, as they did, contacts with older and more mature civilizations, notably that of Egypt. The most important of Solomon's international marriages was that with the daughter of the Pharaoh of Egypt. This is the first known connection the Hebrews had had with Egypt since the exodus, and in this case the Pharaoh may, indeed, have regarded Solomon as a vassal.[78] The enormous cost of maintaining Solomon's harem and court is indicated in 1 Kgs. 4:22 f.

The Conspiracy of Jeroboam. Solomon's imperialism, with its never-ceasing burden of taxation, strained the endurance of his subjects to the breaking point. The disaffection led to an attempt at revolt in the territory of Ephraim, the most powerful of Judah's rivals. The plot was hatched by Ahijah, a prophet of Shiloh, seat of

---

[73] 1 Kgs. 10:22. [74] 1 Kgs. 9:10 ff. [75] 1 Kgs. 10:23.
[76] 1 Kgs. 5:13 f. [77] 1 Kgs. 11:1. [78] Cf. 1 Kgs. 9:16.

a famous Ephraimite shrine. Having planned a revolution, Ahijah picked as his man to lead it an Ephraimite named Jeroboam, overseer of labor gangs in Ephraim. The story of the plot is vividly narrated in 1 Kgs. *11:26–40. The revolution was nipped in the bud. Solomon had dealt summarily with attempts at treason at the outset of his reign, and again he did so now. Jeroboam fled to Egypt for safety. The disruption of the kingdom was, however, only temporarily averted, for Solomon, with all his astuteness, was a shortsighted ruler.

The Achievements and Failure of Solomon

Solomon made Jerusalem a splendid city and a center of attraction to the world of his day. The temple was his one work of abiding value, for it provided a center for and gave stability to the national religion. In addition to the temple, a splendid group of government buildings, a city wall for Jerusalem where it was most needed, six fortresses at commanding locations, a fleet of commerce ships, industrial development, and the first scientifically planned tax system stand as the constructive accomplishments of his reign. For his time he was a merchant prince and an industrial magnate. He greatly developed the resources of his kingdom. Fortunately, throughout his reign peace prevailed, and this permitted the development of both commerce and culture. Solomon is also reputed to have been a patron of art and literature. He had a reputation for wisdom (1 Kgs. *3, *4:29–34), and his name was by later generations associated with the so-called wisdom literature (of which Proverbs and Ecclesiastes are examples).

On the other hand, Solomon's weaknesses were neither few nor trivial. He was selfish, overambitious, and out of sympathy with his people. He was a polygamist and the harem proved his undoing, as it had David's. Since it was looked upon as a matter of courtesy for the king to erect a sanctuary for a foreign wife that she might worship her own god, Solomon filled Jerusalem with shrines to all kinds of deities (1 Kgs. *11:4–13). He apparently worshiped with his wives too, and got so he could worship any god, which means that no god counted very much with him.

At this point Solomon was a sorry contrast to himself in the early days of his rule when he prayed earnestly for wisdom and sought to honor the god of his people by erecting for him a worthy temple. Without doubt this religious latitudinarianism was an offense to the more strictly religious element in the kingdom, and it is said to have been a cause for the disruption of the realm (1 Kgs. 11:11–13).

All in all, Solomon was a decided failure as a king, in that he did not promote the happiness and welfare of his subjects. He so tyrannized over them that at his death they were ripe for revolution.

Chapter 12

A CENTURY OF PROGRESS IN CULTURE

The era of David and Solomon was the high noon of Hebrew national life. What can be said of culture in this era? What of the social progress made in the tenth century? What literary advance, if any, can be discerned? What transformations did Hebrew religion undergo?

The Changing Social Pattern

The century that closed with the death of Solomon witnessed marked transformations in the cultural life of the Hebrews. Fusion with Canaanites went on apace. Contacts with the outside world through trade and diplomacy were fast altering the pattern of Hebrew civilization. Especially was this true of Jerusalem and the commercial cities of central Palestine and Galilee. It was much less true of Judah, and of Gilead, east of Jordan. The latter regions long resisted acculturation from outside and retained their primitive customs with little modification.

Conspicuous among the changes were the urban trend, the changed form of government, the fusion of religions, and a marked social stratification. All these changes have been brought into view in the preceding discussion of the political history,[1] and therefore only brief notice of them is required here.

The urban trend came about by the capture of Canaanite cities, by infiltration from country to city, and by intermarriage between Hebrews and Canaanites. The Biblical writers refer to this intermarriage only to point out certain regrettable religious consequences, but the biological effects of the fusion of races must have been of even greater import. One should therefore bear in mind that from this time forward the Hebrews, especially the urban ruling group, were in the nature of new hybrids. The fierce racial exclusiveness, which in the early days of the conquest of Canaan could glory in massacres of entire populations, was fast yielding to friendliness and tolerance which ever accompany closer social contacts.

[1] Chapter 11.

Along with the urban trend went certain occupational changes, particularly the adoption of agriculture and related pursuits. Most farmers lived in towns or villages [2] under conditions similar to those that have occasioned a like manner of living in parts of Europe and Asia down to recent times. The ordinary farmer toiled terribly for a living, and it was a very frugal living at that. Very few farmers became well-to-do, though some did.[3] The Hebrews seem to have been slow about taking up the arts and crafts, and presumably such occupations remained for some time longer in the hands of Canaanites save as intermarriage brought the offspring of some of these unions into the trades.

The change in the form of government has been amply discussed in Chapter 11, but we might remind ourselves that the Hebrews were in a dilemma. They were seeking a satisfactory substitute for the outgrown form of government by voluntary action of a loose federation of tribes or clans. The only apparent alternative was to place military power in the hands of one man from a particular tribe who thus could and almost certainly would use such power to favor the interests of his own tribe and kinsmen. The continued existence of the elders is proof that there was an attempt at preserving a sort of parliamentary check upon the king, but the scornful refusal of King Rehoboam (after Solomon's death) to accede to the request of these same elders proves how unadjusted were the powers of king and what passed for a parliament.[4] History is so replete with examples of the struggle between kings backed by armies and the unarmed representatives of the people as to make the Hebrew situation quite clear. Neither previous experience nor Mosaic legislation had prepared them to cope with the new governmental problem.

Equally far-reaching in its transforming cultural effect was the fusion of religions consequent upon the social intermingling and racial intermarriage.[5] The Hebrews both gained and lost by these religious interchanges. Undoubtedly they gained in a certain richness in the forms of worship, and probably also in thoughtfulness growing out of the need for justifying their own religious rites and ideas in the light of contrasts presented by the Canaanite cults. On the other hand, Hebrew life suffered from the absorption of licentious traits connected with the fertility cults of Canaan. The insidiousness of this process was such that its significance and seriousness were not immediately perceived. The more ethical Yahweh worship became deeply imperiled before effective resistance to baalism began a century or more afterward.

---

[2] Vid. supra, pp. 154 f.
[3] E.g., Nabal (1 Sam. 25:2 f.) and Ziba (2 Sam. 9:9 ff.; 16:1).
[4] 1 Kgs. 12:1–16.　　　　　[5] Cf. supra, Chapter 10.

The period of the united monarchy witnessed also a marked social stratification, a separation into ruling and ruled, into rich and poor. This trend, inevitable enough under any change from local units to united control, was given added impetus through the presence of Canaanite elements in the population, the Canaanites having been long accustomed to the idea of a rich and powerful reigning class.

One result of this class stratification was that in the cities the standard of living rose rapidly, while in the rural districts, particularly in the grazing hill sections, it remained practically at a standstill, giving rise to a new set of political, economic, and religious cleavages which from then on divided Hebrew from Hebrew in place of Hebrew from Canaanite.

The Dawn of Hebrew Literature

The Beginning of Hebrew Writing: The Alphabet. Just when the Hebrews began to write literature is not certainly known. The Babylonians were writing in cuneiform and the Egyptians were employing hieroglyphics centuries before the Hebrews appeared in history. Cuneiform was the medium of official correspondence throughout the Biblical world in the time of Joseph or a little thereafter, but there is no evidence that the Hebrews ever used it or the hieroglyphic or hieratic of their once Egyptian masters. Instead, as far back as available records extend, the Hebrews were using a kind of script with a true alphabet, now technically called the Old Semitic script.

Modern archaeological research has solved the problem of the origin of the alphabet.[6] Probably no one achievement has meant so much for the spiritual development of mankind as the invention of the alphabet, which now appears to have been made by a humble workman, presumably a miner, in the Sinai Peninsula, *circa* 1900 B.C. Neither Babylonian cuneiform nor Egyptian hieroglyphic writing had an alphabet. Both employed thousands of signs to express thought. Knowledge of such writing was therefore matter for a learned profession, the scribes. Struggling with the impossible complexity of such Egyptian writing, this plain workman of Sinai simplified the whole process by employing a few alphabetic signs to express what he wanted to say in the scratches he made on a mountain side.

This alphabet and style of writing spread north into the land of Canaan and was used there by Canaanites. In 1929 there was picked

[6] Cf. G. A. Barton, *Archaeology and the Bible* (7th ed., 1937), pp. 129 f.; Edward Chiera, *They Wrote on Clay* (Chicago: 1938), pp. 222–230; John W. Flight, "The Present State of Studies in the History of Writing in the Near East" in *The Haverford Symposium on Archaeology and the Bible*, Elihu Grant, ed. (New Haven: 1938), pp. 111–129; C. C. McCown, *The Ladder of Progress in Palestine* (New York: 1943), pp. 100–117; Millar Burrows, *What Mean These Stones?* (New Haven: 1941), pp. 180 f.

up on the site of ancient Gezer a broken jar handle on which were three letters in this Old Semitic script, "Ben-Y. . . .," manifestly only part of a word. The inscription had been scratched into the clay of the vessel before it was fired. The foremost experts on Palestinian pottery have pronounced this fragment to be a sample of Middle Bronze Age pottery, which definitely proves that the Old Semitic style of writing was in use in Palestine in the period 2000–1600 B.C.

In the land of Canaan this Old Semitic alphabet encountered the Babylonian cuneiform writing. The idea of an alphabet appealed to somebody as a good thing, he made cuneiform equivalents for the Old Semitic letters, and writing of this type came into vogue. The Ras Shamra tablets, which we have previously noticed,[7] were written in this way.

It was doubtless with such Old Semitic letters that the youth captured by Gideon was made to write down for Gideon's information a list of the officials and elders of Succoth (Jgs. 8:14).[8] One scholar understands "the pledge" which David was to take from his brothers for the foodstuffs (1 Sam. 17:18) to have been a written receipt.[9]

The Moabite Stone of the ninth century B.C. and the Siloam Inscription of the eighth century B.C., which we have previously noted,[10] were both inscribed in this Old Semitic script. Another interesting example of this handwriting is the inscription known as the "Gezer Calendar," dating from about the eighth century B.C. It purports to be a list of farmer's tasks, month by month for a whole year, which a farmer by the name of Abi had inscribed on a thin limestone slab. It reads as follows:

> A month of fruit harvest; a month of sowing; a month of after-grass; a month of flax harvest; a month of barley harvest; a month of everything else; a month of vine pruning; a month of fig harvest.

There is a square hole in this tablet by means of which it was hung on a peg. It is conjectured that it may have been a writing exercise rather than a needed reminder for a certain farmer Abi.[11]

Very interesting also is the name inscribed on an ossuary (receptacle for bones) dating from the Christian era and still using this alphabet in slightly modified form. It is the name *Yeshua,* the same as the name Jesus. It helps us to visualize how Jesus of Nazareth would have written his own name.[12] This Old Semitic script is in use even today by the Samaritans of Nablus, Palestine.

[7] *Supra,* p. 75.   [8] *Vid. supra,* p. 165.
[9] J. A. Montgomery, *Arabia and the Bible* (Philadelphia: 1934), p. 166.
[10] *Supra,* pp. 51–55.
[11] Cf. R. A. S. Macalister, *A Century of Excavation in Palestine* (New York: 1925), p. 249.   [12] *Vid. infra,* p. 491.

It is of added interest to learn that this same Old Semitic alphabet was the ancestor of our own, after the Greeks, introduced to it by the Phoenician merchants, had given it a few quirks and the Romans in their turn a few more. For example, the first letter of the Old

THE GEZER CALENDAR

Semitic alphabet (written 𐤀) was called *aleph,* "ox." The ox got its head twisted upside down, until, resting upon its horns (𐤀), it became our "A." The second letter (written 𐤁) was called *beth,* "house." In time its second room was enclosed (𐤁), then it got turned about and became our "B." When the Phoenician merchants said "aleph-beth," their Greek customers tried to mouth the words and got it "alpha-beta"; from this comes our English word "alphabet." [13]

The Earliest Hebrew Writings.   The first direct reference to writing among the Hebrews has to do with the Ten Commandments,

[13] On the evolution of the alphabet, cf. A. T. Olmstead, *History of Palestine and Syria* (New York: 1931), p. 243; Edward Chiera, *They Wrote on Clay* (Chicago: 1938), p. 226; Millar Burrows, *What Mean These Stones?* (New Haven: 1941), pp. 180 f.; C. C. McCown, *The Ladder of Progress in Palestine* (New York: 1943), pp. 100–117.

said to have been written on "tables of stone" and dating from the time of Moses.[14] This, however, is far from proof that they possessed a written literature so early; for a few "don'ts" don't make a literature. In fact it is highly improbable (quite apart from all direct evidence) that in the period of nomadic wandering and early years spent in the conquest and settlement of Canaan there should have been much attention paid to written records. They had little need of writing, for the oral traditions kept alive the heroic events of their experience. Num. 33:2 does credit Moses with keeping a log of the Hebrews' journey through the wilderness. Josh. 8:32 asserts that Joshua wrote on stones a copy of the law of Moses, and Josh. 8:35 says that Joshua read from "the book of the law." But even these constitute scant evidence for the existence of a real literature.

With the establishment of the kingship, however, and the subsequent flowering of national consciousness, the impulse to put achievements on permanent record gained attention and received official support. The peace which followed David's successful wars, the wealth which increased, especially under Solomon, and the leisure which followed in the train of these, all contributed to turn the minds of some Hebrews to cultural interests, which resulted in a literary awakening. Samuel is said to have written "On the Nature of the Hebrew Kingdom," [15] apparently a sort of constitution or charter for the newly adopted government. This may possibly be the same as the "Records of Samuel the Seer." [16] David had both a recorder and a secretary,[17] who doubtless kept the royal archives. It is possible to picture to ourselves what such royal archives may have been like because archaeologists have actually dug up some of the royal archives of kings of northern Israel (much later than David's time).[18] They were found in the king's palace. They consist of broken bits of pottery written upon with a carbon ink and a kind of brush pen. They are in the Old Semitic script. They relate mostly to matters of revenues and estates. Considerable literary activity during David's reign is implied in 1 Chr. 23:27, 27:24, and 29:29, these three verses naming no less than five different books: "The Last Words of David," "The Chronicles of King David," "The Records of Samuel the Seer" (referred to above), "The Records of Nathan the Prophet," and "The Records of Gad the Man of Vision." [19]

[14] Ex. 24:4; 34:1–4, 27. [15] 1 Sam. 10:25.
[16] 1 Chr. 29:29. [17] 2 Sam. 8:16 f.
[18] The ostraca found at Samaria, at first assigned to the reign of King Ahab (ninth century), but now assigned to the reign of Jeroboam II (eighth century). Cf. C. C. McCown, *The Ladder of Progress in Palestine* (New York: 1943), pp. 198 f.; Jack Finegan, *Light From the Ancient Past* (Princeton: 1946), pp. 155 f.
[19] It is quite possible that some or all of these were apocryphal works written long after David's time. The word in the titles of these books translated either "Words" or "Records" corresponds closely to our modern "Collected Works," i.e., of any author.

Solomon found use for two secretaries besides the recorder.[20] The complete story of his reign is said to have filled a book, "The Book of the Records of Solomon." [21] We need not suppose that such a "book," which in form was a handwritten roll, was anything so long as the average book of today, but it was most certainly a document

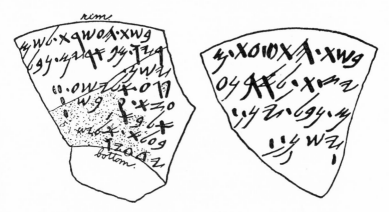

OSTRACA, BUSINESS RECORDS OF A KING OF ISRAEL

many times the length of the incidents related of King Solomon in the Bible. There is reason to believe that really important literary interest and activity existed in Solomon's time. 1 Kgs. 4:29–34, though an obviously exaggerated eulogy, implies writings on a considerable range of topics.[22] 2 Chr. 9:29 names three different works which the author apparently had at his disposal as sources for information regarding the reign of Solomon. They are: "The Records of Nathan," "The Prophecy of Ahijah the Shilonite," and "The Visions of Iddo the Seer."

All the writings mentioned in the preceding paragraphs are, of course, no longer extant. For that reason they are frequently referred to as "lost books." We can affirm little more about them than that they once existed and were known to the authors of the Bible books which contain mention of them. The nature of their contents can be only a matter of conjecture. They were manifestly prose writings. Happily, however, one excellent prose writing from the period of the united monarchy has come down to us, the account of David's reign in 2 Sam. 9–20; 1 Kgs. 1–2, which we have already had occasion to mention.[23] Modern historians and literary critics alike pay tribute

20 1 Kgs. 4:3.   21 1 Kgs. 11:41.
22 Psalm 88 is ascribed to Heman, and 89 to Ethan, both of whom are named in 1 Kgs. 4:31.
23 *Supra,* pp. 185 ff., *q.v.*

to the unknown Hebrew historian who produced this document about David's reign. It was a new thing in the world's literature. Nothing like it, which might have served as a pattern, is known to have existed in the literature of any other nation at the time. Here, then, we stand at a creative moment in the development of human literature.

What can be said about the poetry of the period? Among the now lost books mentioned in the Bible, two were manifestly collections of poems and they may have originated in the time of the dual kingdom or earlier. One is called the "Book of the Wars of Yahweh," from which a brief quotation is given in Num. 21:14 f.[24] The other book is called the "Book of Jashar" (meaning "The Upright"), from which quotations are given in Josh. *10:12 f.; 2 Sam. *1:18–27, the so-called "Song of the Bow," and in the Greek version of 1 Kgs. 8:12 f., as follows:

> The Lord established the sun in the heavens,
> But he chose to dwell in thick darkness;
> "Build my house, a house of habitation for me,
> That I may dwell therein forever."
> Is it not written in the Book of the Upright? [25]

King David is credited in Biblical tradition with being a poet and psalmist. In the Biblical Book of Psalms, the expression, "psalm of David," occurs in the titles of seventy-four of the psalms. Modern scholarly opinion holds that most of these psalms were later compositions assigned to David because he was the patron saint of this literary type. Some scholars hold that David must have composed some of the oldest of the psalms in order for later tradition to have given his name to the collection. However that may be, some of the very oldest of the psalms, probably as old as the time of the united kingdom, whether composed by David or not, are Pss. *7, *13, *18, *23, *24:7–10, *60:1–4, and *110 which should be read thoughtfully for an appreciation of the quality of Hebrew poetry in this era. 1 Sam. *30:24 preserves an utterance of David expressed in the rhythmic form that is characteristic of Hebrew poetry.

State Religion

The various beliefs and practices which characterized Hebrew religion in earlier centuries, as outlined in Chapters 8 and 10, continued in vogue in the period of the early monarchy. The outstanding development of the era was that Hebrew religion became a state religion. This had far-reaching consequences.

[24] Some scholars conjecture that the other poetic quotations in Num. 21:17 ff., 27–30 may also have been from the "Book of the Wars of Yahweh."
[25] See Leroy Waterman in the Chicago Version, *in loc.*

The Idea of Divine Beings. 1. *Yahweh*. The changing and developing social experience of the Hebrews gave rise to different conceptions of Yahweh in the successive epochs of Hebrew history. In the beginning, Yahweh was regarded as a mountain *El*,[26] manifesting his presence at Sinai in the volcanic activity of that mountain—in earthquake, fire, storm, and such. After the covenant at Sinai, the Hebrews believed that Yahweh accompanied them as a wilderness guide on their treks through the deserts.[27] Moreover, he fought their battles for them, against Amalek, against the Amorites, and against the inhabitants of Canaan whom he helped the Hebrews to dispossess. Thus he came to be thought of as a god of war.[28] Then came the readjustment due to the Hebrew settlement in Canaan and the absorption of Canaanite manners and customs, including religion. Yahwism triumphed over baalism, and so Yahweh came to be regarded as the god to whom the land really belonged. He sent the rain and the crops. Indeed, Yahweh *was* baal, i.e., *lord* of the land.

Thanks to the vigorous rule of David, the Hebrews had at last achieved a place in the sun. No nation in antiquity was regarded as a real nation that did not have a national god. For that reason David made it evident to all the world that the Hebrews did have a national god, and that Yahweh's residence was in the capital city, Jerusalem. Immediately after the capture of Jerusalem from the Jebusites, David took the significant step of bringing the Ark of the Covenant to the city and installing it there in a suitable tent.[29] The proof that Yahweh was in very deed the national god of the Hebrews was immediately shown. David forthwith launched a series of military campaigns against more or less hostile neighbors, and "Yahweh gave David victory wherever he went." [30] The next logical step was to provide Yahweh with a suitable national shrine, and accordingly David projected the plan for the Jerusalem temple which was later built by Solomon.[31]

2. *Other Gods.* Because Yahweh was now the national deity of the Hebrews, it must not be supposed that they believed him to be the only god in existence. The other nations had their gods—Chemosh of Moab, Melek of Ammon, Rimmon of Syria, and others more distant.

From 1 Sam. 26:19 we learn that already in the days of Saul the belief had become current that Hebrew territory was "Yahweh's inheritance" and that outside this area one must perforce "serve other gods." Just which gods one was to serve depended upon what gods were thought to have jurisdiction over the particular area in which

---

[26] *Vid. supra,* pp. 120 f., 131 f.   [27] *Vid. supra,* pp. 131 f.
[28] *Vid. supra,* pp. 172 f.   [29] Cf. *supra,* p. 190.
[30] 2 Sam. 8:14. Cf. *supra,* pp. 190 f.   [31] Cf. *supra,* pp. 190, 197.

one found oneself. This thought appears amusingly and yet pathetically in a later century when the converted Syrian Naaman asks Elisha for "two mules' burden of earth" from Yahweh's soil, by means of which he may henceforth be able to worship Yahweh, i.e., by standing on this soil when he gets back to Rimmon's land.[32]

Along with this recognition of Yahweh as supreme within the territorial confines of the Hebrew nation, other gods were recognized as exercising distinctive powers within their own limited spheres, even in Palestine. These were, for the most part, the Canaanite baalim which by now had been generally assimilated into the national Yahweh cult. Despite the small amount of direct evidence available on this point, the fact that Saul's immediate family included such names as Esh-*baal* and Merib-*baal*,[33] and that one of David's sons was named *Beel*iada,[34] points conclusively to baal worship's being taken for granted at this time.[35]

Worship of the ashteroth, the cult of the mother goddess, continued in this period too. Indeed, King Solomon gave official state recognition to this cult by the erection of a special shrine in Jerusalem [36] which lasted there for three centuries until destroyed by King Josiah.[37]

Teraphim continued to be in use, as instanced when Michal made use of one such idolatrous image to save David's life.[38] These, like many other religious symbols and practices which later came to be prohibited, persisted throughout most of the period of the kingship. Teraphim are mentioned as among the objects destroyed by King Josiah as late as 621 B.C.[39]

The ephod, behind which the captured sword of Goliath was kept in the shrine at Nob,[40] was probably also an image, similar no doubt to those made by Gideon [41] and by Micah.[42] The Bible gives no data by which to judge what an ephod looked like.

Quite clearly the worship of local and minor deities such as the baalim and the teraphim was not ordinarily regarded as disrespect to Yahweh, but quite the opposite was the case when Solomon, toward the close of his reign, built shrines to the national gods of Phoenicia,

---

[32] 2 Kgs. 5:17 f.
[33] Baal rewards. Cf. 1 Chr. 8:33 f.
[34] 1 Chr. 14:7.
[35] The name *Eshbaal* ("the man of baal," or, "baal exists") was corrupted to *Ishbosheth* ("the man of shame"). Cf. 2 Sam. 2:8 and elsewhere. The reason for such a change, which was made by a very much later generation, is to be seen in Hos. 2:17. Similarly the name of Jonathan's son *Meribbaal* (which, if the *meri* is Semitic, means "increase of baal" but, if the *meri* is Egyptian, means "beloved of baal") was corrupted to *Mephibosheth* ("dispeller of shame"). Cf. 2 Sam. 4:4 and elsewhere. *Beeliada* ("baal has known") is simply *Eliada* (God knowing). Cf. 2 Sam. 5:16.
[36] 1 Kgs. 11:5, 33.   [37] 2 Kgs. 23:13.
[38] 1 Sam. 19:13.   [39] 2 Kgs. 23:24.
[40] 1 Sam. 21:9.   [41] Jgs. 8:24–27.
[42] Jgs. 17:3 ff.; 18:14, 17, 20, 24.

Moab, and Ammon (1 Kgs. *11:4–8, 33). Here was a most flagrant
and intolerable affront to Yahweh's unique priority (1 Kgs.
*11:9 ff.).

Sacred Places. 1. *Local High Places.* Throughout this period, as
in the era of the settlement, the popular centers for worship were
the high places. Quite likely all communities had such sacred elevated
spots.[43] It was at such a high place that Samuel first became acquainted with Saul and decided that he was the best kingly timber
available.[44] It was at "the great high place" of Gibeon that Solomon
sacrificed "a thousand burnt offerings" and had his dream of such
religious import.[45] 1 Kgs. 3:2 explains that sacrifices at the high places
were a regular practice down to the time when Solomon completed
the temple, and from 1 Kgs. 15:14 it seems that not even the existence
of the temple greatly modified the practice.

2. *Famous Shrines.* The most noteworthy of the famous shrines
mentioned in this period are: *Mizpah,* where Saul was formally selected as the nation's divinely chosen king;[46] *Gilgal,* where the actual
crowning of Saul occurred and his elevation to the kingship was
formally ratified,[47] and where, at a later date, "Samuel hewed Agag
in pieces before Yahweh";[48] *Nob,* destroyed by Saul in a rage because
its priests had given aid to the escaping David;[49] and *Bethel,* a place
at which Samuel at one time gave judicial decisions[50] and which was
later elevated to the rank of northern Israel's royal sanctuary.[51]

3. *The Jerusalem Temple.* When David made Jerusalem his capital, one of his first acts was to transfer the Ark thither (1 Sam. 7:1 f.;
2 Sam. *6). Ps. *24:7–10 celebrates this historic procession. The
next logical step was to house this visible symbol of Yahweh's presence in a permanent building. This was David's intention[52] and was
at first approved by David's spiritual monitor, the prophet Nathan,[53]
but was later emphatically negatived by Nathan. He declared that
it was Yahweh's will that the actual construction be left to an
unnamed son of David (2 Sam. *7:3–17). This, of course, turned
out to be Solomon. Solomon is said to have chanted at the dedication
ceremony the quatrain, quoted on page 208, from the Greek version
of 1 Kgs. 8:12 f. The first line of this quatrain, "The Lord established the sun in the heavens," implies the association of sun worship with the Yahweh cult.[54]

---

[43] *Vid. supra,* pp. 176–180.
[45] 1 Kgs. 3:4 f.
[47] 1 Sam. 11:14 f.
[49] 1 Sam. 22. *Vid. supra,* p. 187.
[51] 1 Kgs. 12:32 f.
[53] 2 Sam. 7:3.

[44] 1 Sam. 9:13, 25.
[46] 1 Sam. 10:17–24.
[48] 1 Sam. 15:33.
[50] 1 Sam. 7:16.
[52] 2 Sam. 7:2.

[54] The connection of the sun cult with the Jerusalem temple is fully discussed by
F. J. Hollis in S. H. Hooke, *Myth and Ritual* (London: 1933), pp. 87–110.

In a later connection we shall give attention to Solomon's temple from the standpoint of its architecture.[55] It is important now to consider the equipment of the temple and its symbolism. The temple proper contained two chambers. The innermost room, the oracle (*debîr*), was the "Holy of Holies," or the "Most Holy Place." Here the Ark was placed and also the two huge cherubim whose wings overshadowed the Ark (1 Kgs. 6:23–28). The cherubim were the bearers of deity [56] and consequently symbolized the very presence of Yahweh in the Most Holy Place. In front (east) of this inner shrine was the other chamber, the *hêkâl* (temple), the Holy Place. Here was an altar of cedar upon which, in all probability, was placed the "showbread," or (better rendered), the "bread of the Presence." This represents a survival of the very ancient practice of propitiating a deity by providing him with a meal.[57] Also in the Holy Place were the lamp stands.[58] Possibly somewhere within the temple, but more probably out in the temple court where worshipers could see it, was placed the bronze snake,[59] the worship of which continued to be associated with Yahwism throughout the period of the united kingdom. In the court of the temple, and directly in front of the temple itself, was the altar of burnt offering [60] which functioned in the sacrifices exactly as did the altars in all sanctuaries and high places. To the south of the altar was the "brazen sea," resting upon twelve bulls, three facing toward each point of the compass (1 Kgs. 7:23–26). This evidences the association with Yahwism of the implications of bull worship. Arranged about the court were ten other lavers of bronze, which, like the brazen sea, contained water for the priests' use for ritual purposes. Somewhere in the temple court, probably flanking the porch, stood the two upright columns, "Jachin and Boaz" (1 Kgs. 7:15–22). Such pillars conventionally marked sacred places.[61]

The Nature of Worship. The beautiful prayer (2 Sam. *7:18–29) said to have been uttered by David, and the two others ascribed to Solomon (1 Kgs. *3:6–9 and *8:23–53), idealize the worship of the period. The usual worship was a matter of joy and feasting. Very characteristic of such worship, though on a special occasion, is the description of the ceremonies that took place when the Ark was escorted from the home of Obed-edom, who lived somewhere near Jerusalem, to the "city of David" (2 Sam. *6:12–21). The clamor

55 *Infra,* pp. 287 f.
56 Ps. 18:10. Cf. G. E. Wright and F. V. Filson, *The Westminster Historical Atlas to the Bible* (Philadelphia: 1945), p. 48.
57 The first mention of such holy bread is in 1 Sam. 21:1–6.
58 1 Kgs. 7:49.   59 *Vid. supra,* p. 135.
60 1 Kgs. 8:64; 9:25. Cf. R. H. Pfeiffer, *Introduction to the Old Testament* (New York: 1941), pp. 386 f.
61 *Vid. supra,* pp. 123 f. Cf. W. F. Albright, *Archaeology and the Religion of Israel* (Baltimore: 1942), pp. 139, 144.

of trumpets and shouting voices, the ecstatic leaping and dancing of
those in the procession, the slaughter along the way of great numbers
of sacrificial animals, and the royal blessing and largess at the conclusion of the ceremony are all typical of the prevailing ideas of worship at its best.[62]
Much less pleasant is the story told in 2 Sam. *21:1–14 of how
David permitted seven of the male descendants of Saul to be put to
death in the belief that only thus could an offended Yahweh be induced to end a three years' famine. This, together with the assertion
of 1 Sam. 28: 6, 15 that Yahweh, because deeply offended at Saul,
refused to answer him either "by dreams, or Urim, or prophets," so
that Saul was able to learn of the future only through the devious
and forbidden channel of a necromancer, portrays an age groping
in superstition, wildly joyous when their god was believed to be
favorably inclined, but cringing in abject fear when the deity was
thought to be in a mood of sullen anger. Such worship partook far
more of terror than of respect.

The Priesthood. In this period we observe an official ecclesiastical organization in the making. At the head of the whole Yahweh
cult stood the royally appointed priests. King David appointed two;
2 Sam. 20:25 gives their names as Zadok and Abiathar, but 2 Sam.
8:17 says they were Zadok and Ahimelech, the son of Abiathar.
What, if any, division of function there was cannot be told. According to 1 Sam. 21, a priest, Ahimelech, had charge of the ephod at
Nob; when he was slain by King Saul, his son Abiathar took refuge
with David.[63] Possibly this is the same one whom David, when he
became king, made official priest of the state cult, and if so, he may
have continued to look after the sacred ephod. The other official
state priest, Zadok, may have taken special charge of the sacred
Yahweh Tent in Jerusalem. Zadok and Abiathar continued as priests
under King Solomon,[64] and Solomon appointed two other official
priests, Azariah, son of Zadok,[65] and Zabud, son of Nathan.[66]
Apart from the official state priesthood there appears to have been
a private priesthood. King David himself functioned as priest when
the Ark of the Covenant was ushered into Jerusalem (2 Sam. 6:12–
15). "Ira the Jairite was a priest unto David"; [67] this would indicate
that the king had a private priest to minister to the royal household.
The same is implied in 2 Sam. 8:18, "David's sons were priests."

[62] Cf., further, 1 Kgs. 1:9, 19, 25; 3:4; 8:63–66.
[63] 1 Sam. 22:20. Father and son, Ahimelech or Abiathar, may have been confused in the transmission of the text.
[64] 1 Kgs. 4:4, but cf. 2:27, 35 where Solomon deposes Abiathar and appoints
Zadok in his place, evidently as chief priest.
[65] 1 Kgs. 4:2.   [66] 1 Kgs. 4:5.
[67] 2 Sam. 20:26.

Prophetic Leaders. The prophetic guilds known as the sons of the prophets, whose presence in Hebrew society we observed in our study of religion in the era of the settlement,[68] continued active during the period of the united kingdom. Besides these there are certain prophets properly so called, men of the caliber of Samuel, who exerted an active force in the national life.

One such was the prophet Gad, a counselor of David both before (1 Sam. 22:5) and after (2 Sam. *24:11–14) David became king. He is called "David's seer." [69]

Such a passage as 2 Sam. *24 throws a flood of light on the religious conceptions of the time. "The anger of Yahweh was kindled against Israel" (vs. 1), though why is not stated, "and Yahweh moved David" to take a census of Israel and Judah. David did so, but afterward, for some inexplicable reason, repented having done it (vss. 10 f.). At this point the prophet Gad appeared as spokesman of Yahweh's wrath, offering David a choice of three penalties for his sin: either seven years of famine, or three months of inglorious defeat at the hands of his enemies, or three days' pestilence in the land (vss. 11 ff.). David chose the pestilence, which is said to have destroyed 70,000 men. Now it is significant that the prophet Gad offered no protest over such a dire punishment of the common people for an offense committed by the king. The reason is easy to understand. Hebrew religious thinking was socially based. Whole tribes often suffered severely because of an offense committed by some one or a few of their group against another group, for which offense the other group retaliated in accordance with the age-old law of revenge. That Yahweh should thus retaliate presented no ethical problem to the mind of Gad or anyone else in his day. Religious thinking proceeded not upon the ethical but upon the ceremonial plane, and accordingly we are not surprised to find that Gad advised David to seek Yahweh's forgiveness and restored favor through purely ritualistic measures, which suggestion David carried out by erecting an altar on the threshing floor of Araunah the Jebusite and offering sacrifices thereon, as a result of which "Yahweh was entreated for the land, and the plague was stayed from Israel" (vs. 25).

Another prophet of the Davidic age was Nathan. He is represented as counseling with David concerning the proposed temple (2 Sam. 7:1–17), as criticising David's course of conduct toward Uriah the Hittite (2 Sam. 12:1–15), as giving to Solomon the name of Jedidiah, "beloved of Yahweh" (2 Sam. 12:24 f.), and as an active and shrewd leader of the harem intrigue by which Solomon became king in succession to David (1 Kgs. 1).

---

[68] *Supra*, pp. 181 ff.
[69] 2 Sam. 24:11. On seers, cf. *supra*, p. 182 f.

In the reign of Solomon there was another prophet similarly active in practical politics; so active, indeed, that he plotted the disruption of Solomon's kingdom. He was Ahijah of Shiloh (1 Kgs. 11:26–40).

In fact, all the prophets of this period were powerful political forces. It was no doubt partly a sense of personal responsibility for national politics that led certain of these prophets to champion the cause of special groups within the nation. Thus Ahijah is portrayed as a champion of the common people. Nathan was similarly a champion of the plain man in his protest to King David over the official murder of Uriah the Hittite. The prophets were against luxury in living and ornateness in worship, and for this reason Ahijah and, we may assume, others were outraged by Solomon's policy.

Moral Progress

Some significant germs of a future ethical development are observable in the era of David and Solomon. (1) The prophetic leaders discussed in the foregoing section are the most noteworthy feature of the time. The future of religion was with them. Their championing of the welfare and rights of the plain people of the land is a foretaste of what we shall in future chapters repeatedly observe when the great prophets rise as champions of the common people against tyranny and in favor of the simple life of earlier days. (2) From the most ancient of days, the principle of blood revenge had been basic in Hebrew group relations.[70] 2 Sam. *21:1–14 represents David himself as authorizing the carrying out of this law of the blood feud in what turned out to be a sordid, wholesale hanging. But quite a different picture is presented by 2 Sam. *14:1–21. By clever indirection a wise woman of Tekoa gets King David to take a position whereby he is obliged not only to protect her son against "the avenger of blood" but also to permit the return in safety of his own son Absalom, who, after murdering his brother Amnon, had fled to Geshur to escape blood revenge at the hands of David's other sons. Henceforth the operation of this blood vengeance must have been less stringent. Indeed, it was most likely during David's reign that "Cities of Refuge" were instituted.[71] Such cities were places of asylum to which one guilty of manslaughter, i.e., not intentional murder, might flee to escape the avenger of blood. While the evidence as to the number of such cities is perplexing, it would appear that ultimately there were six (Num. 35:11, 13 ff.; Deut. 4:41 ff.; 19:7–10; Josh. *20:2, 7 ff.). (3) By far the most advanced ethical thinking of the age is evidenced by that con-

[70] Vid. supra, p. 129.
[71] Cf. W. F. Albright, *Archaeology and the Religion of Israel* (Baltimore: 1942), pp. 124 f.

temporary of David, the author of 2 Sam. 9–20; 1 Kgs. 1–2, in his account of David's adultery with Bathsheba and the murder of her husband, Uriah.[72] The author's condemnation of the king's act pervades the whole narrative. Specifically, he recounts the prophet Nathan's reproof of the king (2 Sam. *12:1–15). Despite David's crudities and follies, he himself was morally sensitive in advance of his age, for he felt that his conduct with Bathsheba was wrong and that he must put Uriah out of the way before marrying her. By the standards of the age, any king was considered to be well within his rights to snatch the wife of any of his subjects if he wanted her, and he didn't feel called upon to justify his act to her husband or to anybody else. That David should have felt otherwise, and that his biographer should have given this moral tone to the narrative, is evidence of a power making for righteousness among the Hebrew people.

[72] *Vid. supra,* pp. 185 f., 207 f.

Chapter 13

DIVISION AND CIVIL WAR

We have come to another (the fourth) watershed in Old Testament history, viz., the disruption of the Hebrew kingdom ensuing upon the popular assembly held at Shechem in 931 B.C. Once a unified kingdom! Henceforth separation—Judah and Israel—and divided they fall!

The Disruption of the Kingdom

The Popular Assembly at Shechem: 931 B.C. The people of northern Israel tolerated Solomon with what grace they could so long as he lived. With his death they felt that the hour had come to seek redress for their grievances. They meant to have at the very outset an understanding with Rehoboam as to what rights they were to be allowed and how heavily they were to be taxed. Therefore when he came to Shechem to be made king by Israel, they presented their petition. The story of this popular assembly is told with dramatic power in 1 Kgs. *11:43–12:24. It was one of the truly great occasions of history when human liberties have been asserted in the face of tyranny.

Rehoboam prudently asked for time to consider the request. He took counsel, first with the old men. These were doubtless men who remembered the days before David had assumed that autocratic attitude which developed to such an offensive degree under Solomon. These older men knew that the king was the creature of the people, for it had been a popular demand that led to the institution of the kingdom in the first instance. These elders held a sound theory of the kingship, viz., that the king was the servant of the people,[1] and that the welfare of the people was paramount. Moreover, they understood the basis on which the kingship rested, viz., that the monarchy was a dual monarchy and that being Solomon's son did not give Rehoboam any claim to the throne of Israel; in other words, that for northern Israel there was "no inheritance in the son of Jesse," exactly as the northerners asserted.[2] Rehoboam himself surely must have known this too, for he had come to Shechem to be made king by Israel. The

---

[1] 1 Kgs. 12:7. [2] 1 Kgs. 12:16.

elders therefore advised the king to grant the people's demands. But from these experienced elders Rehoboam turned to the young habitués of the court who, like himself, had grown up amid the luxury of Solomon's display [3] and had imbibed the autocratic spirit of the monarch. Their idea of the kingship was that of an Oriental despotism which assumes that the common people exist only to serve the monarch and that they have no inherent rights which the monarch is bound to respect. In their opinion, any such request as the people now made to the king should be rejected emphatically and with severity. They therefore advised the king to increase the burdens of the people.

What the young men advised the new king to do was probably what he intended to do anyhow, and he therefore refused the people's petition in words that can scarcely be surpassed for impudence and brutality: "My father made your yoke heavy, but I will add to your yoke; my father chastised you with whips, but I will chastise you with scorpions." [4] The result was what might have been expected in the already tense situation. Shouting bitter defiance (1 Kgs. 12:16), the ten northern tribes seceded from the dual Hebrew kingdom by refusing to make Rehoboam their king. They selected as king Jeroboam the Ephraimite who returned from Egypt, whither he had fled when his earlier plot to secede from Judah was discovered by Solomon.[5] To suppress the new revolt, King Rehoboam resorted to force, and to crush the uprising he sent the most hated man in all the land, Adoram, overseer of the labor gangs in which the people had been forced to serve. Inflamed by this fresh affront, they stoned Adoram to death. Upon this, King Rehoboam fled in terror to Jerusalem. He next assembled an army to march against the northerners, but was dissuaded from venturing upon a suicidal civil war by the prophet Shemaiah. It is interesting to note that the revolution was originated by a prophet, Ahijah,[6] and that it manifestly commanded the sympathy, if not the actual support, of the prophetic party even in Judah.

Causes of the Disruption. 1. *Economic.* Undoubtedly the most active immediate cause of the disruption was the discontent of the people over excessive taxation and forced labor. The heavy burden of expense laid upon the people because of Solomon's enormous harem, his elaborate and luxurious court, and his pretentious building enterprises was more than his little kingdom could finance. He virtually reduced his fellow countrymen to the status of serfs and they were forced to serve in the royal labor gangs in the Lebanons.[7] Indeed,

---

[3] Doubtless wasting their time toying with the imported "apes and peacocks" (1 Kgs. 10:22).
[4] 1 Kgs. 12:14.   [5] Cf. *supra,* pp. 199 f.
[6] 1 Kgs. 11:26–40.   [7] 1 Kgs. 5:13–16.

they may have been subjected to the more heinous treatment of being exported to Egypt to pay for the horses and chariots which Solomon was buying there; [8] in Egypt they would have been forced to serve a stretch of time as mercenaries of the Pharaoh. Solomon's wealth is proverbial, but it was wealth gained at the cost of human life and liberty.

2. *Political.* Solomon's imperialism outraged the people's traditional instincts for freedom and democracy. Saul had been a choice of the people. So had David. But the people had no say as to the succession of Solomon, and they were given no voice in the selection of Solomon's successor. The northern tribes had already lost prestige to Judah when the royal succession passed from the house of Saul to the house of David. For the succession to become hereditary at this time would forever preclude the possibility of any other tribe's, especially the leading northern tribe of Ephraim, having the honor of furnishing the king. The slumbering jealousy was fanned into flame by the favoritism of David and Solomon toward Judah. 1 Kgs. 4:7–19 lists the twelve administrative districts into which Solomon divided the kingdom for purposes of revenue, and Judah is conspicuous by its absence from this list. Such glaring favoritism toward the king's own tribe looked suspiciously like an overlord-subject relationship rather than united tribes on equal footing. The rich and powerful tribe of Ephraim would be the more sensitive on this point because of the centuries-old rivalry between it and Judah.

In the past the people had maintained some measure of check upon the king's acts. There is a hint of this in the incident of the people's saving Jonathan from death in consequence of Saul's foolish vow,[9] although Saul may have been very glad of this "redemption." Nathan the prophet had dared to call in question an act of David,[10] but Solomon had brooked no such interference, nor would Rehoboam, as is manifest in his amazingly stupid, shortsighted, and impudent attitude in insulting the very people over whom he wished to rule.

3. *Social.* Jealousy, grounded in the differing racial traits and inherited customs of the northerners (the Joseph tribes) and the southerners (the men of Judah), was age-old and deep-seated. The south was conservative; the north was progressive and independent, ready to experiment. This was due partly to their differing geographical locations, for Judah was isolated from the rest of the world, whereas the land north of Judah was wide-open to the influences of the outside world, being crossed by the trade routes that followed

---

[8] Deut. 17:16 forbids this practice, the prohibition being evidence that it was done by certain Hebrew kings. Solomon may have originated it.
[9] 1 Sam. 14:45.   [10] 2 Sam. 12:1–7.

the great plains along the coast and Esdraelon. All this conspired to accentuate temperamental differences that already existed.

We must also keep in mind that these Joseph tribes proudly traced their ancestry to an Egyptian high-priestly family, and that they undoubtedly preserved certain distinctive social institutions or habits which served as reminders both to themselves and others of this hereditary uniqueness. It takes but little in the way of quaint mannerisms to keep human groups apart.

4. *Moral and Religious.* Solomon's idolatries must have been an offense to loyal Yahweh worshipers in the south as well as in the north. In all probability this was what alienated the prophets from him. We read of no prophet's having real influence at court in the reign of Solomon. Very likely, prophets were not welcome because they would not approve the king's course. So offensive indeed did the situation become to one of them, Ahijah, that he deliberately plotted with Jeroboam to disrupt the kingdom. Another factor making for religious jealousy and resentment was that the costly temple in Jerusalem, built largely by northern labor and taxes, was of little use to the northern people on account of distance and difficulties of travel. Moreover, so far as the Jerusalem temple affected their interests at all, apart from the increased taxes for its maintenance, it was mainly to cast in the shade their own local shrines.

Quite apart from the immediate occasion, it is altogether likely that deep-seated religious differences had long existed between the north and Judah. One evidence for this is the fact that, directly after the disruption, Jeroboam established in the northern kingdom sanctuaries for worship apparently more in accordance with the thinking of the people of the north.

The Situation After the Disruption

Relative Economic Resources of the Two Kingdoms. The economic advantages were wholly with the northern kingdom. Israel's territory covered five times the area of Judah. The boundary between the kingdoms was along a line from Aijalon to Michmash, marked mostly by steep gorges. Only the main highway north from Jerusalem was easily passable. Israel had twice the population of Judah. Moreover, Israel was much the wealthier because she had far greater natural resources, for within the confines of the northern kingdom were practically all the fertile farm lands possessed by the Hebrews at this time. Again, through Israel ran the great highways by which the caravans of commerce traveled from Egypt to Syria and the east. In this way Israel was brought into close contact with international trade and profited thereby. Judah, in contrast, was rocky and barren. Situated high up in the southern hills, it was isolated from the highways of world commerce and all chance for profit.

The Social Results of the Division. 1. *For Judah.* The population of Judah, while smaller than that of Israel, was much more homogeneous because of tribal consciousness, for it comprised virtually but a single tribe, Judah,[11] though a part, at least, of Benjamin seems to have affiliated with it.[12] This gave the southern kingdom a certain unity and stability which the northern state did not possess. Along with this greater homogeneity went a conservative quality of mind which also made for stability. On the other hand, Judah's geographical isolation made for narrow provincialism. Probably the greatest asset which Judah possessed, and certainly the greatest single unifying force, was the dynasty of David. In Judah there was not one change of dynasty so long as the kingdom lasted. Only once was a dynastic murder attempted in Judah.[13] It was a serious loss to Judah, however, that her interests early diverged from and often were antagonistic to those of her sister kingdom.

2. *For Israel.* Israel's greatest social asset was the pioneering and progressive spirit of her people. Her openness to the commercial world enabled her to reap large advantage from this receptiveness of mind so that she early became as cosmopolitan as Judah was provincial. On the other hand, Israel lacked that stability which comes from the unifying force of loyalty to one royal house, and revolution and even anarchy were frequent visitors throughout the history of the kingdom. This was to prove the ultimate undoing of the northern kingdom. During the two centuries of Israel's existence there were no less than nine different dynasties totaling nineteen rulers.

The Religious Situation. 1. *In Israel.* The break with Judah severed Israel completely from the Jerusalem temple. Jeroboam was quick to sense the hazard involved in this, and he took prompt steps to offset it. 1 Kgs. *12:25–33 describes the establishment of the two sanctuaries at Dan and Bethel. Jeroboam's motive in this undoubtedly was political. He wished to keep his people from going to Jerusalem to worship at the temple, lest by mingling there with the Judeans they forget their differences and the severed kingdom become reunited under Judah. The temple of Solomon had not existed for so very long and therefore had not taken such a deep hold upon the people that their interests could not be transferred to the new shrines. The temple in Jerusalem was a building of dazzling splendor, and no doubt Jeroboam did what he could to make the royal sanctuary at Bethel a

---

[11] 1 Kgs. 12:20.   [12] 1 Kgs. 12:21.   [13] 2 Kgs. 11:1.

place of splendor and attractiveness to offset the appeal of the Jerusalem temple.

2. *In Judah.* Judah retained the temple built by Solomon. As the centuries passed, this temple grew in importance in the life of the people and gained a prestige which no sanctuary in the north ever had. The south believed firmly that there ought to be but one "house for Yahweh," by which they meant the one in Jerusalem that contained the sacred Ark and the other treasured emblems of Yahweh. For King Jeroboam to assert that the northern kingdom held the "gods that had brought them up out of the land of Egypt" was to offend every fiber of Judah's faith. True, the south was permitting the worship of other gods than Yahweh (at least, there is no reference to the demolition of any of the shrines mentioned in 1 Kgs. 11:5–8), but they of Judah insisted that it was Yahweh alone who was responsible for the escape from Egypt and that he dwelt right there in the Jerusalem temple. Here were claims and counterclaims destined to leave a train of bitterness for centuries to come.

3. *The Prophetic Repudiation of Jeroboam.* Jeroboam's scheme was shrewd but shortsighted. It fostered a religious syncretism which undermined religious convictions and brought about a retrogression from the lofty ethical standards which Moses had set. It sowed seeds of moral and religious decline that ultimately brought ruin to the kingdom. This was "the sin which Jeroboam sinned and wherewith he made all Israel to sin." This mistaken policy of Jeroboam lost him the support of the prophetic party. 1 Kgs. *13:1–14:20 is an interesting narrative that brings out one prophet's violent opposition to Jeroboam, the very man who virtually made him king, the prophet Ahijah. Ahijah pronounced doom upon Jeroboam and his house. To contemplate the extermination of one's entire family line was considered the worst fate that could befall one.

The author of 1 Kings, being a man of Judah, may not have done full justice to the situation he describes, but so far as the records go it is interesting to observe how he attributes to Jeroboam's religious policy the whole series of calamities which befell northern Israel and which culminated in her downfall. He rarely misses an opportunity to point out how king after king of the north "walked in the way of Jeroboam the son of Nebat, who made Israel to sin." [14]

Political Results of the Division. Politically, the disruption was both a gain and a loss. It was a gain from the standpoint of the future spiritual growth of the nation in that it checked the growth of autocracy. Had the policy of Rehoboam prevailed, the Hebrew

---

[14] 1 Kgs. 15:3, 30, 34; 16:19, 26, 31; 22:52; etc.

kingdom would almost certainly have developed into a despotism. However, for the preservation of democracy, a terrible price was paid, no less than the destruction of the national unity created by David. Instead of a single state which could have presented a united front to outside foes and which might have grown increasingly greater as a world power, there were now two petty states, each no bigger and no more powerful than any of its neighbors. Worse yet, the mutual jealousy that had always existed was now intensified to a point which prevented united opposition to external foes and started both on the road to ruin. The immediate sequel to the disruption was a half century of warfare between the two kingdoms.

The Fifty Years' War Between Judah and Israel

The Outbreak of the War.   1. *The Reign of Rehoboam in Judah: 931–914* B.C. The reign of Rehoboam in Judah was marked by two events of importance. One was the invasion of Judah by Sheshonk I (Shishak) of Egypt, a Libyan usurper who had dethroned the Pharaoh whose daughter Solomon had married.[15] Sheshonk's object was plunder rather than conquest. Sheshonk set up a monument at Megiddo, a part of which, bearing his name, was discovered in recent years. In Egypt, he inscribed on a wall of the temple of Karnak, in Egyptian hieroglyphics, an account of his plundering raid upon Palestine. He looted the Jerusalem temple of much of the treasure put there by Solomon. This plundering must have left Rehoboam bankrupt. With an empty treasury and a shrunken territory, the southern kingdom had a poor start.

The second event of importance was the outbreak of a long war with Israel. The advantage seems to have been with Rehoboam. He apparently pressed Jeroboam of Israel so hard that the latter was compelled to shift his capital from Shechem to Penuel, east of Jordan.[16] Further details of Rehoboam's reign are given in 1 Kgs. 14:21–31.

2. *The Reign of Abijam in Judah: 914–912* B.C. No event of importance is recorded of the reign of Abijam, son of Rehoboam. 1 Kgs. 15:1–8 merely states that the war with Israel continued throughout his reign.

3. *The Reign of Jeroboam I in Israel: 931–911* B.C. Little is said about the reign of Jeroboam in Israel, and what is said is mostly adverse. Consideration of the religious organization which he instituted in northern Israel appears in a later chapter.[17] He fared

[15] 1 Kgs. 14:25 ff.   [16] 1 Kgs. 12:25.
[17] Chapter 17; and *vid. infra,* pp. 310–315.

badly in the war with Rehoboam of Judah. Jeroboam first made Shechem his capital. Then he shifted to Penuel, doubtless as a war measure. Subsequently his residence was at Tirzah,[18] a community praised at a later time for its beauty.[19]

The War at Its Height. *Asa in Judah: 912–872 B.C. Nadab (911–910 B.C.) and Baasha (910–887 B.C.) in Israel.* Jeroboam was succeeded by his son Nadab, who was assassinated after he had reigned for about one year. The leader of the conspiracy which overthrew Nadab was a man named Baasha, from the tribe of Issachar. Whether anything save tribal ambition was behind this assassination is not known, but it was premonitory of a long list of bloody revolutions and changes of dynasty that were to convulse the northern kingdom and bring it to ruin. Baasha celebrated his accession to the throne in the conventional way by complete extermination of the "house of Jeroboam" which he had supplanted (1 Kgs. 15:25–31). But Baasha really was an aggressive and capable ruler. Jeroboam's removal of his capital may have been construed as a tacit admission of fear, which thereby became a factor in the fall of his dynasty. However that may have been, Baasha immediately made a vigorous thrust against Judah. He successfully blockaded Judah by building a fortress at Ramah and stopping all communication between the two states (1 Kgs. 15:16 f.).[20]

Asa countered by appealing to Ben-hadad, king of Damascus, for aid. Asa sent a rich present to Ben-hadad[21] to bribe the latter to break a treaty with Baasha and help Asa out of his difficulty with him. The details of this are candidly related in 1 Kgs. 15:18–22. Along with his bribe, Asa sent Ben-hadad this diplomatic note: "There is a league between me and thee, between my father and thy father;[22] behold, I have sent unto thee a present of silver and gold; go, break thy league with Baasha, king of Israel, that he may depart from me." It was an amazing proposition to consider a treaty a mere scrap of paper, but it was quite in keeping with the diplomacy of the age and evidently the author of the Kings narrative saw nothing to apologize for. On the contrary he warmly commends the southern king: "Asa did that which was right in the eyes of Yahweh, as did David his father."[23] One wonders what may have been the exact nature of the league between Baasha and Ben-hadad. Probably it amounted to Baasha's paying Ben-hadad blackmail. Since Ben-hadad was out for money, he stood open to the highest bidder, "and Ben-

---

18 1 Kgs. 14:17. 19 Cant. 6:4.
20 Cf. Jer. 41:9. 21 1 Kgs. 15:18.
22 What the nature of this league was cannot be told. It may have dated back to Solomon's time, being possibly an understanding between him and the Aramaeans.
23 1 Kgs. 15:11.

hadad hearkened unto King Asa." Thus Asa purchased temporary relief. He destroyed Ramah, the fortress which Baasha had built, and then erected two fortresses of his own, Geba and Mizpah, as a protection against Baasha. This apparently put an end to Baasha's show of military power. Asa's league with Ben-hadad was a stupendous blunder. It gave the Syrian a permanent excuse to plunder, and Judah suffered for it heavily in later years.

2 Chr. 14:9–15 refers to one other attempted invasion of Judah during Asa's reign by a certain "Zerah the Ethiopian." Zerah penetrated nearly to Hebron but was overwhelmingly defeated and driven back into the Philistine plain. This Zerah cannot be identified.

The author of the Book of Kings was more interested in the religious attitudes and doings of the various kings than he was in the political history as such. His commendation of Asa is therefore uncommonly strong. He credits him with having been the first king to attempt to do away with the foreign cults and idolatrous practices instituted by Solomon. Asa even went so far as to depose the queen mother for having made an idolatrous image.[24] His unusually long reign of forty years was no doubt considered one of the divine rewards for his conduct.

Revolution and Anarchy in Israel. In the latter part of Asa's rule over Judah, virtual anarchy broke loose in Israel (1 Kgs. 16:8–22). The policy of murderous usurpation which Baasha inaugurated bore bitter fruit for his son and successor, Elah (887–886 B.C.), who was murdered in a drunken brawl by one of his own generals, Zimri. This was such a particularly revolting murder that the name Zimri thereafter became a synonym for regicide.[25] Zimri was a descendant of Saul in the sixth generation.[26] His coup was therefore an attempt to revive the Benjaminite dynasty. Zimri marched on Tirzah, the capital, took it and established himself there. But his triumph was short-lived. He was king for just one week. The army in the field, which happened at the time to be fighting the Philistines at Gibbethon, promptly elected their general named Omri to be king and marched on Tirzah. Besieged and outnumbered, Zimri committed suicide. But this by no means ended the civil turmoil. Though Omri had been hailed king by one part of the army, another part backed a certain Tibni. The consequence was four years of bitter civil warfare that ended with Tibni's death. Only then was Omri accepted by all Israel (1 Kgs. 16:21 f.).

End of the War Between Israel and Judah. Friction between Israel and Judah lasted throughout the reign of Omri of Israel (886–

---

[24] 1 Kgs. 15:13.   [25] Cf. 2 Kgs. 9:31.
[26] Cf. 1 Chr. 8:36; 9:42.

875 B.C.) and into the reign of his son Ahab (875–854 B.C.). There is, however, no record of actual hostilities. The old antipathies were wearing down. In the end the feeling of enmity between the two gave place to an alliance, entered into by kings Ahab of Israel and Jehoshaphat of Judah (872–849 B.C.). The decisive factor that brought this about was the aggression of Damascus against all Palestine. Confronted by a common peril, "Jehoshaphat made peace with the king of Israel." [27]

[27] 1 Kgs. 22:44.

Chapter 14

THROUGH CONFLICT TO PROSPEROUS PEACE

This and the next chapter deal with the era of the two Hebrew kingdoms, Israel and Judah, which began their separate careers after the disastrous assembly at Shechem in 931 B.C.[1] The study of this era will be simplified if we bear in mind the climactic events toward which the history moves. These are the downfall of the northern kingdom of Israel in 722 B.C. and the downfall of the southern kingdom of Judah in 586 B.C. Our aim is so to present the trend of events as to bring into clear view the major causes of these great national catastrophes.

The most important cause of all was political, and there were two phases to it, external and internal. The external factor was the westward aggression of Assyria, which was determined to incorporate the entire Fertile Crescent into her empire. After the collapse of Assyria, the same policy continued under the Chaldean Empire. The internal factor was the lack of cohesiveness which characterized the small states in the western part of the Crescent. Their only hope of successfully withstanding the Assyrian menace lay in united action. They did occasionally get together, but never for long. Much of the time they fought among themselves. We have already noted the half century of warfare between Israel and Judah.[2] In the present chapter we shall note the long-continued wars between the kingdom of Damascus on the one hand and Israel on the other.

No truly great events happened in Judah until after the fall of Israel. In the present chapter, therefore, our attention is focused upon the northern kingdom as we survey the period from 886 to 745 B.C. It was a period of turmoil for Israel. Social and religious upheavals contributed to dynastic overthrows in Israel and revealed that internal weakness which portended the ultimate doom of the nation. In the first half of the eighth century B.C., Assyria relaxed her effort at westward conquest, which enabled both Israel and Judah to enjoy a period of peace and prosperity.

---

[1] *Vid. supra,* pp. 217 f.   [2] *Vid. supra,* pp. 223–226.

Sources for a History of the Period

The source material for a history of the period under survey in this chapter is found principally in 1 Kgs. 16–2 Kgs. 15. The author of the Kings narrative, writing sometime after 621 B.C., did not write history for history's sake but history for the sake of religion. Not everything that happened mattered, and so he selected for narration such incidents from the career of the two kingdoms as would illustrate his religious theory, viz., that national well-being and permanence depended exclusively upon undivided loyalty to Yahweh and worship at Jerusalem, and that national ruin followed inevitably upon disloyalty to Yahweh and worship at the high places. He uniformly condemns all rulers of Israel on religious grounds, viz., because they worshiped the golden calves set up by Jeroboam I. The rulers of Judah are praised or censured according to whether or not they removed the high places in furtherance of the centralized national worship of Yahweh at the Jerusalem temple.

Obviously such a narrow theory of interpretation does not give an adequate picture of the career of the two kingdoms. Fortunately we can amplify the story on the basis of data which have come from archaeological research, principally Assyrian records and the Moabite Stone, as will appear in the subsequent discussion.

The era of great national prosperity both for Israel under Jeroboam II and for Judah under Azariah (Uzziah) is illumined by writings of the highest possible historical value, viz., the works of the prophets Amos and Isaiah. These books contain the sermons preached by these prophets in their effort to correct evil conditions of the time, and they therefore throw a flood of light on the economic, social, ethical, and religious situation.

Israel Under Omri: 886–875 B.C.

Foreign Relations. 1. *With Phoenicia.* One significant event of the reign of Omri was an alliance with Phoenicia. Ethbaal (Ithobaal), a priest of Ashtart, had seized the throne of Sidon by violence, the sort of thing Omri himself had done in Israel. Since Sidon dominated the other Phoenician cities, an alliance with Ethbaal was masterly. This Phoenician-Israelite alliance was ratified in conventional fashion by an interstate marriage between the crown prince Ahab of Israel and the princess Jezebel, daughter of Ethbaal. This alliance doubtless fostered trade reciprocity in a way that was favorable to both states, for Phoenicia controlled the sea and Israel at least partly controlled the caravan routes. Moreover, the alliance was of advantage, especially to Israel, in view of the renewed aggressiveness of Assyria and Damascus. There were, however, momentous aftereffects of this marriage, as will be seen later.[3]

2. *With Damascus.* In the relations between Israel and Damascus, Omri suffered some reverses (the precise nature of which is not even suggested) which forced him to cede several cities to the Syrian king, in addition to granting the Aramaeans special trading rights in Samaria.[4]

3. *With Moab.* Omri campaigned in Eastjordania with marked success. From the Moabite Stone we learn that Omri completely subjugated this area.[5] The Mesha inscription reads in part as follows:

> Omri, king of Israel, oppressed Moab many days because Chemosh was angry with his land. . . . Omri took possession of the land of Medeba and dwelt therein throughout his own days and half his son's days, forty years. But Chemosh restored it in my days. . . . Now the king of Israel had built Ataroth for himself; but I fought against the city and took it. . . . Also, the king of Israel had built Yahas, and he lived in it while he was fighting me. But Chemosh drove him out from before me; and . . . I took it and annexed it to Dibon.

Other Achievements of Omri.   Omri was a truly great king. Evidence of this is seen in the fact that in Assyrian inscriptions for a century and a half after Omri's death the northern kingdom, Israel, is referred to as the "Land of Omri." Indeed, on one such Assyrian monument, the black obelisk of Shalmaneser III, Jehu is called a "son of Omri," though actually he was the one who overthrew the dynasty of Omri in 842 B.C. So great was the impression Omri made upon mighty Assyria! It is astonishing, therefore, that the Bible record pays such scant attention to his achievements. The only thing of importance mentioned is the founding of the capital at Samaria.[6] This was a far-sighted move, for the location was a well-chosen hill dominating the environing plains for a considerable distance, thus permitting no cover to approaching enemies and rendering the capital almost impregnable. Omri gave a strong unity to the northern kingdom and a marked impulse to the development of the nation's resources. The "house of Omri" was the one strong dynasty of all that ever ruled Israel.

The Double-Headed Menace to Israel— Syria and Assyria

Assyria's Initial Threat: The Advance of Ashurnatsirpal II in 876 B.C.   Toward the close of Omri's reign there appeared upon

---

[3] *Vid. infra*, pp. 233–237.   [4] 1 Kgs. 20:34.
[5] Cf. *supra*, p. 53.   [6] 1 Kgs. 16:24.

the horizon a menace that was to grow more and more ominous and ultimately destroy Israel. This was the expansion of the ambitious and virile empire of Assyria. We have already noted that Tiglath-pileser I (1115–1102 B.C.) penetrated the west as far as Phoenicia.[7] After that, Assyria kept away from the Mediterranean until the savage Ashurnatsirpal II (884–859 B.C.) revived the policy of aggressive imperialism. After vigorously suppressing all opposition to himself in the regions south, east, and north of Assyria, Ashurnatsirpal turned toward the Mediterranean (*circa* 880 B.C.) on a plundering expedition. His advance through these previously unconquered lands appears to have been unopposed, possibly because his diplomatic agents during the immediately preceding years had succeeded in putting into power in some of those lands pro-Assyrians who submitted to the great sovereign as soon as he put in an appearance. Reaching the Mediterranean about 876 B.C., Ashurnatsirpal made an especially successful and lucrative raid on Phoenicia. His boastful record reads thus:

> The tribute of the kings of the seacoast, of the inhabitants of Tyre, of the inhabitants of Sidon, of the inhabitants of Gebal [Byblos], . . . of the city of Arvad that lies in the midst of the sea, silver, gold, lead, copper, copper vessels, garments of bright colors, cloth . . . I received.[8]

He attacked neither Israel nor Judah. Perhaps Omri hastened to offer him tribute.

Assyria's Westward Aggression Under Shalmaneser III: 859–824 B.C. 1. *An All-Syria Alliance Against Assyria.* For twenty years after the campaign of Ashurnatsirpal, Assyria made no further move westward. Then Shalmaneser III, a vigorous campaigner, undertook the extension of Assyrian dominion over the entire Fertile Crescent. He engaged in no less than twenty-six campaigns, several of them against the west. The mere approach of his well-nigh invincible armies was enough to overawe all but the strongest and most daring of lesser sovereigns. To the kingdom of Israel it was a menace of such magnitude as to call for the utmost alertness and energy on the part of King Ahab, inasmuch as Israel would have to bear the brunt of any invasion from the north.

From 1 Kgs. 20 it appears that a war had been going on for some time between Israel and Damascus and that at one point in the conflict the tide of battle so favored Ben-hadad of Damascus that his troops penetrated to the very gates of Samaria. There, however, he

---

[7] *Supra*, p. 142.
[8] *Annals of Ashurnatsirpal II.* Cf. G. A. Barton, *Archaeology and the Bible* (7th ed.; 1937), p. 457. The lack of any mention of iron is interesting.

and his thirty-two allies were completely routed, whereupon they retreated to Aphek in the Hauran. Thither Ahab energetically pursued them, engaged Ben-hadad once more in battle, and administered a smashing defeat to their demoralized forces. Ben-hadad, with a rope about his neck, begged for mercy. With what at first thought seems incomprehensible leniency, Ahab granted the petition. He subjected the Syrian king to none of the indignities to which captives were then customarily treated. He did not even exact an indemnity of the conquered country. Instead, the two kings pledged alliance! Why such surprising developments? Manifestly it was due to the approach of the Assyrians. Ahab was both farsighted and clearheaded. Above all else he desired a buffer state between himself and Shalmaneser III. A grateful Ben-hadad was his best security!

2. *The Battle of Karkar: 854* B.C. This alliance between Israel and Damascus was, according to Assyrian records, only part of a larger coalition of twelve small Syrian states. The leading states were Damascus, Hamath, and Israel. Of the three, Israel, in the person of King Ahab, furnished no small part of the brains. Israel's contribution in troops was about the same as that of the other two. From the Shalmaneser inscription it appears that Ben-hadad furnished some 1,200 chariots, 1,200 cavalry, and 20,000 infantry; Irkhuleni (of Hamath) 700 chariots, 700 cavalry, and 10,000 infantry; while Ahab contributed 2,000 chariots and 10,000 foot soldiers. The minor allies furnished smaller contingents of chariots, infantry, and camels. These allied forces met the mighty Shalmaneser at Karkar, near the Orontes River, in 854 B.C. It was a sanguinary battle. More than 20,000 are said to have been left dead on the field, an indication of the desperate effort the thoroughly alarmed allies made to check the Assyrian invader. Evidently they succeeded. Though Shalmaneser claimed victory, it is quite apparent that the battle was a draw for the Assyrian army proceeded no farther and thereafter for five years Shalmaneser kept out of Syria.[9]

Israel Under Ahab: 875–854 B.C. Judah Under Jehoshaphat: 872–849 B.C. Ahab, as may be inferred from what has already been said, was an even greater king than his father Omri. Problems which dimly appeared in Omri's reign became acute under Ahab, and the latter usually met them with rare shrewdness.

Ahab showed a keen interest in the promotion of trade. From hints in the Moabite Stone and in 2 Kgs. 3:4, we find that (for the first part of his reign at least) he exchanged wool, which he got as tribute from Moab, for the products of Tyrian weavers and dyers. After the victory over Damascus described in 1 Kgs. 20, he com-

[9] Cf. Barton, *op. cit.*, pp. 457 f.

pelled the Syrian king to cede to Israel trading rights in the city of Damascus. Further, it appears that the defensive and commercial alliance with Tyre was continued. That all this brought about unprecedented prosperity and wealth is attested by the magnificent palace, ornamented with ivory, which Ahab built in Samaria.[10]

Judah likewise prospered in this period. Jehoshaphat seems to have been just as able a ruler as was his father Asa. From 2 Chr. 17:11 we learn that he apparently extended his sway over part of Philistia and some portion of Arabia, for he received from those regions tribute in money and in flocks. His merchant-marine undertaking, however, was a complete loss, for the ships by some accident were all wrecked before they ever left port.[11]

As an ally of Ahab in a battle against an army of Damascus, Jehoshaphat narrowly escaped with his life (1 Kgs. 22:30–33). On a later occasion Jehoshaphat was an ally of Ahab's son, Jehoram,[12] in an attempted punitive campaign against revolting Moab, a campaign that turned out disastrously, as the Moabite Stone and 2 Kgs. 3:27 reveal. About the same time, and possibly as part of the same war, according to the author of Chronicles, occurred a joint invasion of Judah by Moabites, Ammonites, and certain others, doubtless those who had been paying tribute to Jehoshaphat but who now sought to throw off this yoke. Evidently some terrible disaster came upon the invaders when they were about halfway between Hebron and Jerusalem so that they left without joining battle, but the exact nature of the disaster is obscure (2 Chr. 20).

The War of Allied Israel and Judah with Damascus. 1. *The Occasion of the War.* Immediately after the battle of Karkar, the alliance between Ahab and Ben-hadad came to an end. It was evidently no more than an emergency truce, entered into until the Assyrians were driven back. There was, however, one clause in the treaty agreement which gave Ahab a plausible pretext for reopening hostilities. This was a promise by Ben-hadad to restore to Israel a number of cities that had been taken from her in the days of Omri. Ramoth-gilead was one of those cities which Ahab particularly wanted, perhaps because of its strategic location. Ben-hadad ran true to form by repudiating his pledge and refusing to give up this city. Ahab went to war about it.

In anticipation of just such a war, Ahab and Jehoshaphat had entered into an offensive and defensive alliance, cemented by the marriage of Ahab's daughter, Athaliah, to Jehoshaphat's son, Jehoram.[13]

---

[10] 1 Kgs. 22:39.   [11] 1 Kgs. 22:48 f.

[12] The student will avoid confusion by bearing in mind that each kingdom had a king Jehoram and a king Ahaziah, viz., Israel: Ahaziah (854–853 B.C.); Jehoram (853–842 B.C.). Judah: Jehoram (849–842 B.C.); Ahaziah (842 B.C.).

[13] Cf. 1 Kgs. 22:1–5; 2 Kgs. 8:18.

2. *The Disastrous Outcome.* Before actually marching into battle, Ahab, upon Jehoshaphat's earnest insistence, consulted a whole array of four hundred Yahweh prophets (1 Kgs. *22:5–28). This illustrates what an influence the prophets wielded in political affairs. These prophets advocated war, all save one, Micaiah ben Imlah. They assured the kings that Yahweh would deliver Ramoth-gilead to them. But Micaiah, pressed for an honest opinion, declared with intense earnestness that he could only see "all Israel scattered upon the mountains, as sheep without a shepherd," and he pronounced doom upon the king.[14] There was wisdom in Micaiah's advice. Ahab's move was stupid. To be sure, from the standpoint of Ahab and Ben-hadad, i.e., from the standpoint of individual interests, of selfish nationalism, Ahab had right on his side, for Ben-hadad's act was in violation of treaty. But from the larger and broader standpoint of internationalism, Ahab was wrong. The weakness of the Syrian states lay in the fact that they could never hold together for long nor work together for one another's interests. Although Ahab had been a leader in bringing about the alliance of these states, he was now simply undoing his own work and destroying both fact and spirit of international co-operation. He paid for his folly. The Hebrew forces were defeated, and Ahab lost his life (1 Kgs. *22:29–40). By this victory Syria once again secured an advantage which she was to press vigorously against Israel for the next fifty years, at one time reducing Israel to such a condition that the Bible narrator remarks of the army, "the king of Syria destroyed them and made them like dust in threshing." [15]

Civil War in Israel

Some twelve years after the death of Ahab, the northern kingdom passed through a baptism of blood such as it had never before experienced. The causes leading up to this revolution were complicated, but among them, one in particular stands out clearly: the increasing disaffection of a strong religious group headed by the afterward famous prophets Elijah and Elisha. Along with the alienation of this group went a succession of military reverses that gave power to the Yahweh loyalists in their attack upon the reigning houses.

Tyrian Baalism in Israel. Omri's alliance with Phoenicia, a seemingly astute political move, bore an unforeseen crop of internal problems for both Hebrew states. This alliance had been formed originally for commercial and political purposes, the latter being the dual threat from Assyria and Damascus discussed on the pre-

---

[14] Vss. 20 ff.   [15] 2 Kgs. 13:7.

ceding pages. Phoenicia had always been friendly toward the Hebrew states, had apparently kept her pledges, and consequently had been counted an ally worth having.

The Tyrian alliance brought with it a train of consequences disastrous to the best in Israel, particularly in religion and ethics. Queen Jezebel was an ardent worshiper of Baal-Melkart, the god of Tyre, and naturally brought that worship with her when she became Ahab's queen. Nor was this without precedent, for Solomon had openly recognized the Sidonian deity Ashtart.[16] In Jezebel's case, however, there was this difference: she was not the type of person to be content merely with the privilege of worshiping in her own way. She was a fanatic, bent on propagating her religion in Israel, even to the supplanting of the worship of Yahweh. Accordingly she built temples to her Baal everywhere she could, and gave to the priests of Baal such prominence at court as she was able to bring about. This could not fail to arouse resentment and fear in the strict Yahweh element, the group convinced that the nation's one hope of safety lay in undivided loyalty to Yahweh. Hence the policy of Jezebel and Ahab arrayed the Yahweh prophets solidly against the royal house in Israel. Elijah, the leader of this movement, was a sturdy champion of the older Hebrew traditions, especially of single-hearted loyalty to the nation's god and the inalienable rights of the individual Hebrew family. Because of this he vigorously opposed Jezebel's efforts to propagate baalism (1 Kgs. *17–19). Elijah launched a movement which had for its objective the complete rooting out of the hated foreign cult. These attacks by Elijah upon Tyrian baalism in turn roused Jezebel to a relentless persecution of the Yahweh prophets. How drastic this was may be inferred from the discouraged words attributed to Elijah in a moment of despondency: "The children of Israel have forsaken thy covenant, thrown down thine altars, and slain thy prophets with the sword; and I, even I only, am left: and they seek my life, to take it away." [17] But Elijah was not a person to give up. Realizing that the task would not be finished in his own day, he solemnly charged Elisha to see it through.[18]

Despotism Rampant. The coming of Jezebel gave fresh impetus to the trend toward autocratic despotism. This evil had been checked in a measure when the northern tribes refused Rehoboam as king; it now reared its head boldly under the influence of the Tyrian queen. Jezebel had grown up in an atmosphere of despotism, for her father, though a priest, had by bloody methods usurped the throne of

[16] 1 Kgs. 11:5.   [17] 1 Kgs. 19:10.
[18] 1 Kgs. 19:15–21. Cf. 2 Kgs. 2:1–14.

Phoenicia. Jezebel had the very spirit of tyranny in her blood and did her best to instil that spirit into Ahab, and with a measure of success. The rights and interests of the common people were gravely jeopardized by her highhandedness, as to which the story of Naboth (1 Kgs. *21) speaks volumes. Naboth's refusal to sell his vineyard, even to a king and even after the king had made him a generous offer, was, according to Hebrew ideas, well within his rights. Apparently Ahab recognized it as such and did not intend to press the matter until Jezebel became incensed at the very idea of a king's being thwarted in any wish by a mere subject. On a framed-up charge and perjured testimony she had Naboth condemned to death and then with brutal callousness said to Ahab: "Come, take possession of the vineyard of Naboth the Jezreelite that he refused to sell you for money; for he is not alive, but dead." Here again Elijah proved champion of the sturdy old Hebrew virtues of fairness and justice. Further, Elijah was doubtless actuated by the age-old principle of blood vengeance. The blood of Naboth cried for vengeance, and if there was no one of his next of kin to exact it, then Yahweh, through his prophets, must avenge him. Intercepting the king, Elijah boldly charged him with murder and called down upon his head the worst curse of which a Hebrew could conceive, the extermination of the family line.[19] To Ahab's credit be it said that he received the rebuke with a humility that later won for him partial mitigation of the curse.[20]

Military Reverses and Political Failures in Israel and Judah. Undoubtedly a potent factor in the mounting disaffection toward the reigning houses was the series of military reverses and loss of territory that began with the death of Ahab at Ramoth-gilead. So long as Ahab's star was in the ascendant, no effective protest against him, his policies, or his family was possible. The fateful battle against the Syrians changed all this. Thereafter the Yahweh prophets could assert without fear of successful contradiction that worship of the Tyrian god was bringing upon the Hebrew nation the same disastrous consequences that had attended the worship of the Canaanite baalim in the days of the "judges." Their argument was made the more unanswerable by a train of calamities which fell not only upon the kingdom of Ahab but also upon the kingdom of Jehoshaphat; for Jehoshaphat had admitted the Tyrian worship into his family through the marriage of his son Jehoram to Athaliah, daughter of Ahab.[21]

Both Ahab of Israel and Jehoshaphat of Judah had been defeated at Ramoth-gilead. Soon thereafter King Ahaziah of Israel (854–853 B.C.), son of Ahab, died from injuries received in a fall from

[19] 1 Kgs. 21:17–24.   [20] 1 Kgs. 21:27 ff.   [21] 2 Kgs. 8:16–19.

a house (2 Kgs. 1:2 ff., 17). He was succeeded by King Jehoram
(853–842 B.C.). Under Jehoram Israel lost Moab (2 Kgs. 3). Next it
saw its territory penetrated by a victorious Syrian army and its
capital, Samaria, subjected to a terrible siege (2 Kgs. 6:24–30).
Although the siege was unexpectedly raised because of the supposed
approach of strong reinforcements for the Israelites (2 Kgs. 7:3–15),
the prestige of the "house of Omri" must have suffered irreparably
by its inability to prevent the invasion.

In Judah a similar sequence of disasters piled up under Jehoram,
son of Jehoshaphat (849–842 B.C.).[22] Two subject states, Edom and
Libnah, successfully revolted from him.[23] Next, a force of Philistines
and Arabs, presumably also revolting subjects, ravaged Judah and
plundered Jerusalem, even carrying off the king's harem and all his
sons save the youngest.[24] Then the king himself was seized with a
loathsome illness from which he died within two years. This provided
the last needed bit of evidence that Yahweh had set himself against
the Tyrian-minded reigning house.[25] To deny Jehoram honorable
burial "in the sepulchers of the kings" was a crowning insult. Such
incidents were the rumblings of oncoming rebellion.

The Yahweh Loyalists Become a Political Power. For at
least a century after the time of Solomon, the worship of Yahweh
suffered decline despite the existence of the splendid Jerusalem
temple. This was due less to conscious repudiation than to casual
neglect ensuing upon official recognition of foreign cults. This governmental tolerance and protection long blocked whatever protest
the zealous Yahweh prophets might otherwise have made. Now, however, the time was ripening for articulate expression.

The loyal Yahweh group "whose knees had never bent to Baal
and whose mouths had never kissed him" numbered no fewer than
7,000 in the northern kingdom alone.[26] This is a very impressive
number when everything is taken into consideration. Such a group, if
organized, would be able to wield tremendous power and it was now
becoming organized.

Certain outstanding Yahweh prophets were showing increased interest and activity in politics. Elijah's sinister prediction of annihi-
lation for Ahab's entire family had been followed by a doom upon
Ahab's son Ahaziah.[27] That Elijah did not confine himself to mere
words but determinedly set about the overthrow of the reigning
house is attested in 1 Kgs. 19:15 ff. Though Elijah himself apparently never got far in the actual carrying out of his program of
revolution, the inference is clear that Elisha completed the task which

22 Cf. *supra*, p. 232, note 12.   23 2 Chr. 21:8 ff.
24 2 Chr. 21:16 f.   25 2 Chr. 21:11–15, 18 ff.
26 1 Kgs. 19:18.   27 2 Kgs. 1:2–8.

Elijah at death laid down. Elisha's undisguised hostility to King Jehoram of Israel was manifest when, on the fateful campaign against Moab, he curtly addressed the king in these words: "What have I to do with thee? Get thee to the prophets of thy father and to the prophets of thy mother. . . . As Yahweh of hosts liveth, before whom I stand, surely, were it not that I respect the presence of Jehoshaphat, king of Judah, I would not look toward thee nor see thee." [28] That this antagonism was mutual and venomous appeared later when King Jehoram vowed to get Elisha's head before the day was over, and Elisha in equal anger ordered the door bolted against the king's official agent.[29]

It was an easy step from such antipathy to overt political action.

Civil War and the Downfall of the Dynasty of Omri: 842 B.C. In 842 B.C. the revolution that had been brewing for years suddenly burst forth. While the main causes of this revolution are clear, one detail remains unexplained. This is Elisha's part in Hazael's murderous usurpation of the throne of Damascus (2 Kgs. 8:7–15). Apparently Elisha encouraged, if he did not actually instigate, Hazael to this deed. The most likely conjecture is that Elisha expected the change of Syrian rulers somehow to hasten the downfall of the hated "house of Omri," and that he desired this so intensely that he was prepared to drench his own nation with blood as part of the price. Hazael's accession was the signal for Jehoram of Israel, aided by Ahaziah of Judah (son and successor of Jehoram of Judah, 842 B.C.) to try for the recovery of Ramoth-gilead, the very same objective for which Ahab had lost his life some twelve years earlier.[30] As before, the battle went against the Hebrews. Jehoram, leading spirit, was wounded and retired to Jezreel to recover, leaving the army in charge of Jehu. Elisha recognized this as his long-awaited opportunity and sent one of his prophet followers to anoint Jehu as king of Israel in place of Jehoram. The army immediately backed Jehu and the revolution was over so far as change of rulers was concerned but not over in bloody reprisals. When at last they ceased there was not a person of the house of Ahab left alive! 2 Kgs. *9 f. tells the story in graphic and somewhat sordid detail.

The Aftermath of the Revolution. 1. *The Cost to Israel.* What were the results of such fanaticism? Certainly Tyrian baalism was checked, but at a frightful cost, for Jehu had killed off the leaders of the nation, those who by birth and experience were most familiar with the art of governing. Moreover, it put an end to friendship and alliance with Phoenicia and cut Israel off from profitable interchange

---

[28] 2 Kgs. 3:13 f.   [29] 2 Kgs. 6:31 f.
[30] 2 Kgs. 8:28. Cf. 1 Kgs. 22.

of goods with this affluent neighbor. The revolution throttled any progress in culture for a good long time, for the whole thing was a throwback toward nomadism, the ideal of the prophet Elijah. A further cost, the magnitude of which will appear more clearly later on, was a fresh aggressiveness on the part of Damascus, which in turn was due to a renewed advance by Assyria.

2. *Effects in Judah: Athaliah and Revolution.* Another outcome not anticipated by Jehu was the enthronement in Judah of Jehu's bitterest enemy, Athaliah, daughter of Ahab. Her son, Ahaziah, had been with his uncle Jehoram, of Israel, in the war for the recovery of Ramoth-gilead. Ahaziah's brutal assassination by Jehu was the price Ahaziah paid for being related to the royal family of the northern state. Immediately Athaliah learned of this assassination of her son, she executed a coup d'état of her own and "destroyed all the seed royal" (i.e., she supposed she had),[31] and mounted the throne herself. Thus it came about that Judah was ruled by a queen (842–836 B.C.) until Athaliah herself fell the victim of a counterplot. She was the only ruler Judah ever had who was not of the Davidic line.

Ultimately Jehu's act was condemned by thoughtful men. The prophet Hosea was one such.[32]

Athaliah's reign well illustrates how violence begets violence and helps to keep the spirit of revolution alive. By violence she gained the throne and by violence she lost it. Her hold on the throne even for six years was probably due to the support of a bodyguard of foreign mercenaries, the Carites (Carians),[33] backed by a substantial part of the people of Jerusalem, for she was tactful enough not to disturb the temple worship even though herself favoring baalism.

Athaliah's downfall was another Yahweh-party achievement, engineered by the chief priest Jehoiada, whose wife Jehosheba was sister to the murdered king Ahaziah. When Athaliah usurped the throne, Jehosheba managed to save the infant prince Jehoash from the general slaughter. After patient waiting and planning, Jehoash was hailed king in a well-planned and neatly executed revolution backed by "the people of the land" (2 Kgs. 11:2–20). Athaliah was put to death, as was also Mattan, the leading priest of Baal. The Baal temple in Jerusalem was completely destroyed in an effort to make the religious reformation complete and thorough.

The Period of Aramaean Oppression

Jehu's Acknowledgment of Assyrian Overlordship: 842 B.C.
In 842 B.C., the aggressive Shalmaneser III crossed the Euphrates

---

[31] 2 Kgs. 11:1.   [32] Hos. 1:4.   [33] 2 Kgs. 11:4.

on his sixteenth campaign. This time he advanced expressly to attack Hazael, king of Damascus. The western coalition that had checked Shalmaneser at Karkar some twelve years earlier had now completely broken up, leaving Hazael to oppose the Assyrian army alone and unaided. That he was able to halt Shalmaneser at this time is a great tribute to Hazael's energy and ability.

The advance of Assyria was as great a menace to Israel as it was to Damascus; yet Jehu for some reason did not join forces with Hazael. Instead, he made haste to pledge fealty to the Assyrian monarch, evidently deciding that it was cheaper to buy off Shalmaneser than to fight him. The Bible writers are quite silent on this chapter of Hebrew history, but the famous black obelisk of Shalmaneser III (now in the British Museum) portrays Jehu on his hands and knees, forehead touching the ground in front of Shalmaneser, waiting for the latter to place his foot on Jehu's neck in symbol of overlordship.[34] Behind Jehu in this picture are four Hebrew high officials, and behind them thirteen other Hebrews bearing the tribute which is thus enumerated on the obelisk:

> Tribute of Jehu son of Omri: silver, gold, bowls of gold, chalices of gold, pitchers of gold, lead, a royal sceptre, staves I received from him.[35]

Such was the cost of Israel's safety! Jehu had surrendered the liberty of his nation without a struggle.

Hazael's Revenge Upon Jehu.   For about five years, Jehu remained secure in the purchased protection of Assyria. Then, in 839 B.C., Shalmaneser returned to the attack upon the kingdom of Damascus. This time he was able to capture four Syrian cities though he failed to take Damascus. He took tribute from Tyre and Sidon but no mention is made of any exactions from Jehu, perhaps because Jehu was paying regularly or possibly because Shalmaneser withdrew before he could collect.

As it turned out, Jehu paid an even greater price for his choice of policy. As soon as Shalmaneser was out of sight, the infuriated Hazael launched a campaign of retaliation against the supine Jehu which was to last for almost half a century and to bring Israel perilously near to extinction. Attacking Israel vigorously, he quickly took from her all her east Jordan territory (2 Kgs. 10:32 f.). Then he turned to the west Jordan area and for a time it looked as if Israel would be completely subjugated by the Aramaean power.

---

[34] The same symbolic act is referred to in Josh. 10:24.
[35] Cf. Barton, *op. cit.,* p. 459.

Hazael's Oppression of Judah Under Jehoash: 836–797 B.C.
It is doubtful whether Hazael felt any personal animosity toward
Judah such as entered into his policy toward Israel. It is more
probable that he simply thought he saw a chance to extend sway

BLACK OBELISK OF SHALMANESER III [36]

over the rest of Palestine. At any rate, *circa* 810 B.C., we find him in
possession of Gath and moving upon Jerusalem. Only by stripping
the capital city of all movable wealth for a present to Hazael did
King Jehoash save Judah from worse ravages of war (2 Kgs.
12:17 f.).

[36] Oriental Institute cast of the famous obelisk inscribed with the expeditions
undertaken during the 31 years of his reign, also with representations of the kings
he conquered paying tribute to him. The second row from the top portrays King Jehu
of Israel offering his tribute. Original in the British Museum. Courtesy of The Oriental Institute, University of Chicago.

This exaction of tribute from Judah was the first of a long, long series of sorry experiences of this sort for the people of Judah. Throughout all the remaining centuries of Biblical history they will bow before the superior might of, and deliver up their treasures as tribute to, one after another mighty oppressor—Syria, Assyria, Chaldea, Persia, Greece, Rome.

End of the Aramaean Oppression.   Jehu died a political failure. Under his son Jehoahaz (815–799 B.C.), Israel's fortunes plumbed the depths of ignominy, of national weakness just short of political extinction (2 Kgs. 13:1–9). In the days of Ahab, Israel had been one of three mighty Syrian states able to block Assyria. But now the glory had passed from Israel, and Ben-hadad III, son of Hazael, "left not to Jehoahaz of the people save fifty horsemen and ten chariots and ten thousand footmen; for the king of Syria destroyed them and made them like dust in threshing."

Right at this point the fortunes of Israel suddenly changed for the better. The parenthetic remark of 2 Kgs. 13:5, "But Yahweh gave Israel a savior, so that they went out from under the hand of the Syrians; and the Israelites lived in their own homes as before," graphically describes the relief from constant fear of invasion that had hovered over the nation for half a century. The Assyrian Adad-nirari III, by campaigns in 804 and in 797 B.C., brought Syria, Phoenicia, and Palestine under his sway. Adad-nirari declares that his victories included

> Tyre, Sidon, the land of Omri, Edom, Philistia. As far as the Great Sea of the Setting Sun they cast themselves at my feet. Taxes and tribute I laid upon them. . . . Mari, king of Damascus [i.e., Ben-hadad III], I shut up in his royal city. . . . He embraced my feet, became my vassal.

The inscription goes on to tell of the huge indemnity paid to him.[37] That a conqueror who named "the land of Omri" as one of his tributary states could be thought of as Israel's "savior" [38] was doubtless because the peace which the Assyrian imposed upon turbulent Damascus was such a relief to harassed Israel that, in contrast to the previous plight of the nation, it seemed nothing less than salvation.

Jehoash of Israel (799–784 B.C.), who succeeded his father Jehoahaz, pressed the advantage which this sequence of Syrian reverses offered. In three decisive battles he won back from the weakened Damascus all the cities that had been lost to Syria by Jehoahaz (2 Kgs. 13:14–19, 25). This marked the end of the long and costly Aramaean oppression.

[37] Cf. Barton, *op. cit.,* pp. 462 f.
[38] The second part of Adad-nirari's name is explained as from the verb *nararu,* "to save." Possibly some sort of pun was taken seriously by the Biblical writer.

Recrudescence of War Between Israel and Judah

What was back of the senseless and suicidal war that suddenly flamed forth between the two Hebrew kingdoms is hard to comprehend. Temporarily relieved of pressure from Damascus, Amaziah of Judah (797–769 B.C.) invaded and conquered Edom.[39] Evidently friction of some sort grew out of this event, for in his caustic message to King Amaziah of Judah (2 Kgs. 14:9 f.) Jehoash of Israel bluntly accused Amaziah of having lost his head over his success against Edom. The version in 2 Chr. 25:5–13 gives a somewhat different picture. It charges Israelite mercenaries, whom Amaziah had hired and then immediately discharged, with plundering some border cities of Judah while Judah's army was engaged in Edom. This may have been the cause of the war. Even so, one marvels that either Hebrew state should have shown itself so wanting in ordinary political sagacity as to venture on a local war with Assyria still so menacing.

For Amaziah of Judah the war proved most disastrous. Jehoash of Israel plundered Jerusalem, took royal hostages, and demolished a large section of the city's fortifications (2 Kgs. 14:11–14). Judah remained a vassal of Israel as long as Amaziah lived. He was finally assassinated, evidently because of violent dissatisfaction with his policies and general conduct.[40] That it was repudiation of Amaziah personally, and not of the reigning family, is proved by the fact that the succession passed immediately to his son Azariah who is also called Uzziah.

The Great Era of Prosperous Peace

A Half Century of Assyrian Nonaggression: *Circa* 785–746 B. C.   Adad-nirari III was followed by three weak kings and a period of Assyrian decline. In this period such serious trouble developed for Assyria in the southeast with Babylon, and in the north with Urartu (Van), that control over the western dependencies was necessarily relaxed. A little later, shortly after 775 B.C., Shalmaneser IV did make an attempt to subdue Damascus. His successor, Ashurdan III, attacked both Damascus and the north Syrian city Arpad. Ashurdan's eighteen-year reign was a succession of calamities, and at his death Ashur-nirari V (755–745 B.C.) inherited a most impoverished empire which he in turn handed on to Tiglath-pileser III.

In a period of weakness such as this, one ordinarily expects to hear of numerous revolts among subject states. In the case of Da-

[39] 2 Kgs. 14:7. Cf. 2 Chr. 25:11 f.
[40] 2 Kgs. 14:19; 2 Chr. 25:14 ff., 27.

mascus, at least, its power had been so thoroughly broken by Adad-nirari that it seemed unable to recover. So for this period of approximately half a century Israel was enabled to pursue its way without fear of serious interference from either of its two dangerous enemies.

Israel Under Jeroboam II: 784–744 B.C. Freedom from external interference was accompanied by a rapid return of prosperity to the northern kingdom. Beginnings of this prosperity appeared when Jehoash of Israel launched three successful attacks against Ben-hadad III of Damascus and recovered much Hebrew territory. At Jehoash's death in 784 B.C., his son Jeroboam II, coming to the throne coincidentally with the death of the able Adad-nirari, was favored in that his entire reign fell within the period of Assyria's impotence.

The very brief summary of Jeroboam's reign (2 Kgs. 14:23–29) suggests that he promptly took advantage of this period of weakness in Assyria and Syria to extend the boundaries of his kingdom northward "to the entering in of Hamath" (i.e., probably, to the pass between Lebanon and Hermon), thus incorporating, no doubt, some territory that had previously belonged to Damascus. East of Jordan he conquered the Moabites and set the southern boundary of his kingdom at the south end of the Dead Sea. This was the largest area that the northern kingdom ever controlled and it made possible a fuller development of the natural resources of the country than had ever before been attained. With the flow of increased revenues into the royal treasury, ease and luxury rode in.

It is surprising that this, the most brilliant and prosperous reign in the history of Israel, should receive such scant notice in the Kings narrative, for it was the heydey of Israel and Judah alike. Apparently Jeroboam had a good counselor in the person of a Yahweh prophet named Jonah, son of Amittai, of Gath-hepher in Galilee.[41]

Judah Under Azariah (Uzziah): *Circa* 769–739 B.C.[42] Azariah (Uzziah) was a contemporary of Jeroboam II. Under him the southern kingdom enjoyed an era of territorial and commercial expansion and prosperity comparable to that of Israel. He was by far the ablest ruler Judah had yet had. The writer of Kings devotes only nine verses to his reign (2 Kgs. 14:21 f., 15:1–7), but the author of Chronicles dwells at length on his great achievements (2 Chr. 26).

---

[41] 2 Kgs. 14:25. Gath-hepher was about three miles from Nazareth.
[42] Azariah is credited with a reign of fifty-two years. It is impossible to find space for such a long reign in the total chronological scheme of the books of Kings, and many scholars therefore understand the fifty-two years to imply an overlapping of reigns, assuming that Azariah was, for some time, coregent with his father Amaziah, just as Azariah's own son Jotham was coregent with him for several years.

Azariah greatly expanded Judah's territory. In the west he crowded the Philistines into a yet narrower strip along the coast. East of Jordan he laid the Ammonites under tribute. On the south he pushed Judah's boundaries back even "to the entrance to Egypt."

His reign was also an era of commercial expansion. His father, Amaziah, had subdued Edom and opened a route toward Elath. Azariah took Elath and fortified it, thus giving Judah a commercial port. He fostered agriculture and animal husbandry, both tending to put the life of Judah on a sound economic basis.

Azariah also greatly improved the nation's military defenses. The fortifications of Jerusalem were strengthened, an adequate army was trained, and new and unusual engines of war were installed.[43] All these improvements were to stand the southern kingdom in good stead in after years.[44]

Economic, Social, and Religious Conditions. 1. *In Israel.* The internal conditions in Israel during the reign of Jeroboam are vividly portrayed by the prophet Amos. Here, with Amos, abruptly appears the first of the great prophets. He is never mentioned in the historical narratives but happily we possess his own writings, preserved by his faithful disciples.

Amos was a native of Tekoa in Judah (Am. 1:1), but his prophecies were directed against northern Israel. He was a stalwart champion of the poor and oppressed and a preacher of social justice (Am. *5:24).[45]

From Amos we learn that the profits of commerce and the spoils from conquered territories had brought about an era of extravagant luxury and soft living in Israel (Am. *3:15; *5:11; *6:4 ff.). The almost incessant warfare with Damascus from the time of Jehu on had been a heavy burden upon the citizens of Israel. It is the poor who always pay the bill for war. The result was that the middle class had been practically exterminated and the poor reduced to abject poverty, while the nobility had grown yet wealthier.

To add to their unfortunate condition, the poor were the victims of atrocious graft and vicious extortion. Often a man was obliged to sell himself into slavery to get food or to guarantee a debt no greater than the cost of a pair of sandals (Am. *2:6 ff., *3:10; *4:1; *5:11; *8:4 ff.). They were even unable to secure justice in the law courts (Am. *5:12 f.). What is worst of all, religion helped in no wise to secure justice or mercy (Am. 2:8). Materialism was triumphant.

---

[43] 2 Chr. 26:11–15.
[44] In the Negeb, one of Azariah's forts has been uncovered by archaeologists.
[45] A more detailed study of Amos, as well as the other prophets, will be made in Chapter 18.

In glaring contrast to the abject poverty of the masses, the religion of the time was characterized by most elaborate and luxurious
feasts at the shrines. The commercial prosperity which the nation
enjoyed was looked upon as the mark of Yahweh's pleasure and
favor. The continuance of his favor had to be guaranteed by costly
sacrifices. Ritual was wholly dissociated from morals. Religion was
thought to have nothing to do with moral conduct. This was what
aroused Amos and led him to denounce the official religion unsparingly (Am. *4:4 f., *5:4–7; *5:21–24).

Amos saw clearly that such conditions were surely leading the
nation headlong to ruin (Am. *8:8a). He made a great plea for justice (Am. *5:14 f., 24), but was cordially hated (Am. *5:10) and
was driven out of Israel (Am. *7:10–13). His preaching to all appearances was without effect in Israel. Nevertheless the doom which
he so clearly foresaw did speedily befall Israel. Following Jeroboam's
reign, Israel plunged to a convulsive epoch, some twenty years in
duration, and then to a violent end.

2. *In Judah.* Prosperity in Judah brought with it soft living and
luxury and consequent moral and social corruption, just as it had
in Israel. The corrupt social conditions in Judah are revealed by
the prophet Isaiah's denunciation of them. Isaiah became a prophet
in the year that King Azariah (Uzziah) died. Azariah was smitten
with leprosy and spent the last years of his life in a lazar house,
during which time (how long, we cannot tell) affairs of state were
administered by his son Jotham as coregent. Immediately upon the
great king's death, Isaiah began preaching social reform. Such passages among his earliest utterances as Isa. *2:6–9; *3:1–23; *5:7
show the prevalence in Judah of luxury and vice, of injustice and
tyranny, of loose women and demoralizing foreigners, and of corrupt
national leaders. In religion, Judah was nominally loyal to Yahweh.
Ethically there was little to choose between it and its sister state
on the north. Both were too prosperous, too comfortable, too smugly
complacent to pay attention to the warnings of their prophetic statesmen.

*   *   *   *   *

There is a "destruction that wasteth at noonday." Prosperous
though Israel and Judah were, both were due for a rude awakening.
The prophets denounced corrupt internal conditions in both lands,
proclaiming that such conditions foreboded ill to the nation. Far
more ominous for both countries was the renascence of Assyria following upon the accession of Tiglath-pileser in 745 B.C. This event
we mark as a new (the fifth) watershed in Old Testament history.

Chapter 15

THE ASSYRIAN ECLIPSE OF HEBREW NATIONALISM

The giant awoke. In 745 B.C., Assyria shook herself from the lethargy of nearly half a century and experienced a rebirth of power with the accession of the mighty Tiglath-pileser III, a general put on the throne by a rebellion at Nineveh. He is the same person as the Pul mentioned in 2 Kgs. 15:19. This monarch heard the call of the west and launched a drive for conquest that was continued by his successors until Assyrian sovereignty was acknowledged throughout the Fertile Crescent and in Egypt. This westward conquest by Assyria swept the kingdom of Israel off the map, for Israel fought. Judah submitted and survived.

Sources for a History of the Period

The source material for a history of the period under survey in this chapter is found in 2 Kings 16–23 and in the writings of the prophets Hosea, Isaiah, Micah, Zephaniah, and Jeremiah. The character of 2 Kings as a book of history has already been explained.[1] The writings of the prophets are, of course, documents of the highest value, preserving, as they do, the opinions of men who actually lived during this period. In addition to these writings, the annals of the Assyrian monarchs, as revealed by archaeology, illumine the history of the time.

Assyria Becomes Sovereign over Palestine

Israel's Submission to Assyrian Overlordship: 739–735 B.C.
Tiglath-pileser's initial demonstration was against Babylon, which he soon subdued, thereby protecting his kingdom on its southeast. Then he turned his attention to the west. In 743 he moved into Syria but en route was attacked on the right flank by Sarduris III, king of Urartu, an ally of the Syrian states. Tiglath-pileser turned to meet this attack, and completely defeated Sarduris. After that he pushed his westward campaign against Arpad, on the northern

[1] *Supra,* p. 228.

edge of Syria. Arpad fell in 740 and with its fall all opposition to Tiglath-pileser ended. The north Syrian states evidently lost heart.

Following this submission of north Syria, Tiglath-pileser campaigned in the Armenian Mountains, but from there he was obliged to return to southern Syria to suppress a revolt headed by a certain Azriyau of Yaudi, by some scholars identified with Azariah (Uzziah) of Judah.[2] If this identification be correct, it confirms the portrait given in 2 Chr. 26:6–15 of an extraordinary militaristic expansion of Judah under King Azariah. Back of this may have been a dream of restoring the glories of a Solomonic kingdom under Judah's domination, which Azariah may have hoped to bring about in the troublous times following the death of Jeroboam II of Israel. If so, Tiglath-pileser shattered the dream by destroying the Syrian confederacy in 739 B.C. In the Assyrian annals of Tiglath-pileser's reign there is no specific mention of indemnity demanded from Judah at this time,[3] but 2 Kgs. 15:19 f. names an enormous tribute which was exacted from Israel, the equivalent of one and one-half million dollars.

It should be noted that Israel was in the throes of anarchy when Tiglath-pileser made this exaction. Jeroboam II of Israel had been succeeded by his son Zechariah (744 B.C.), whose reign was cut short at the end of six months by the murderous hand of Shallum (2 Kgs. 15:8–12). Shallum lasted just one month (744 B.C.). He was in turn murdered by Menahem (744–735 B.C., 2 Kgs. 15:13–16). In the light of later events it is to be suspected that Shallum represented a political party which stood for resistance to Assyria, and that Menahem's frantic efforts were aimed at averting a more disastrous Assyrian punitive expedition. Menahem exacted the money from "the mighty men of wealth" who had piled up fortunes during the prosperous days of Jeroboam II and now lost their wealth through the same process of extortion by which they had taken it from the poor in Israel.[4] Laden with booty, and assured of the submission of Israel and the south Syrian states, Tiglath-pileser went home. For the next three years (738–735 B.C.) he was kept fully occupied in Media and in Armenia.

The Attempted Coalition of Syrian States Against Tiglath-pileser: 734 B.C. Menahem was succeeded by his son Pekahiah, who was assassinated by Pekah (2 Kgs. 15:23 ff.). The motive be-

---

[2] Cf. H. R. Hall, *The Ancient History of the Near East* (London: 1927), p. 463. Another interpretation identifies this Yaudi with a small independent kingdom of Y'di mentioned in Aramaic inscriptions found at Zenjirli. Cf. Sidney Smith, *Cambridge Ancient History*, iii, 36 f.; A. T. Olmstead, *History of Palestine and Syria* (New York: 1931), pp. 409, 435.

[3] Cf. Barton, *op. cit.*, pp. 463 f.

[4] *Vid. supra*, pp. 244 f.

hind this assassination was again the question of the national policy toward Assyria. Pekah, who represented the anti-Assyrian faction, promptly threw himself with might and main into the organization of a coalition to oppose Assyria. Rezin of Damascus and Pekah of Israel were the principals in this coalition. Tiglath-pileser was at the time (734 B.C.) engaged in a campaign in the north against the kingdom of Urartu.

Clearly the aid of Judah was counted on to make the coalition a success, for when King Ahaz of Judah (736–727 ? or 721 ? B.C.) refused to join the alliance and was backed in his refusal by the prophet Isaiah (Isa. 7:1–8), Pekah and Rezin went to the length of invading Judah and besieging Jerusalem in a desperate effort to force Ahaz into the alliance (2 Kgs. 16:5 f.). Whether the all-Syrian coalition might have succeeded had Judah joined it is, of course, a matter of speculation; as it was, Judah's defection doomed it to certain failure.

Ahaz of Judah Becomes an Assyrian Vassal: 734 B.C. This attack upon Jerusalem by kings Rezin of Damascus and Pekah of Israel came at a time when Ahaz was meeting with reverses on every side. The Edomites had rebelled and captured the port of Elath.[5] In the west the Philistines had invaded and annexed the Shephelah and the Negeb.[6] Consequently, when attacked by the two kings from the north, Ahaz was thoroughly frightened.

It was at this crucial point that Isaiah came to the fore. He was a statesman par excellence. He stood solidly for one political principle: Keep faith with Yahweh and with your pledged word and avoid all entangling alliances. Faith in Yahweh as the national deity of Judah was the basis of Isaiah's foreign policy. Any alliance with a foreign power implied that the god or gods of that foreign nation was or were more powerful than Yahweh. Such a thought was heinous to Isaiah, for Judah should have no other gods besides Yahweh. He urged Ahaz to keep out of the alliance with Israel and Damascus (Isa. *7:1–17), declaring that the king need have no fear of those "two tails of smoking firebrands." This was a picturesque way of saying that the career of those nations was just about over and that the situation called only for confidence.[7]

Ahaz, however, decided upon another policy, viz., to throw himself upon the protection of Tiglath-pileser of Assyria who was already on the march down the Mediterranean coast. By offering suitable tribute to the great Assyrian he could get him to attack Rezin and Pekah and thus relieve Judah (2 Kgs. 16:7 ff.). Isaiah saw the folly of such a policy and strove in vain to keep the king out of that

<hr>

[5] 2 Kgs. 16:6.   [6] 2 Chr. 28:18.   [7] Isa. 7:4.

type of alliance, for such an alliance meant a real entanglement as the event proved. Ahaz followed his own devices, however, and put his country under the heel of Assyria. No longer were the Judeans free men. Judah became henceforth a vassal of Assyria, and Tiglath-pileser received a handsome sum for doing what he intended to do anyway.

The Assyrian Conquest of Palestine: 734–721 B.C. 1. *Tiglath-pileser's Invasion of Philistia and Israel.* Very likely Rezin and Pekah were counting on Egyptian aid when they opposed Tiglath-pileser, but the latter promptly marched down the seacoast as far as Philistia and by this maneuver cut Israel off from communication with Egypt. After capturing Ashkelon and Gaza (734 B.C.), he attacked the Arab queen Samsi on the ground that she had intrigued with Ashkelon, drove her tribe into the interior, and then enlisted a friendly Arab tribe just south of the Dead Sea to act as a check on other tribes of the Arabian frontier. He next turned northward into the Plain of Esdraelon, attacked Israel, and ravaged all its territory from Esdraelon northward, as well as Gilead in Eastjordania (2 Kgs. 15:29). Tiglath-pileser states in his own annals: "As Pekah, their king, they had deposed, Hoshea I appointed king over them." [8] This amplifies the statement of 2 Kgs. 15:30 that Pekah was slain in a conspiracy headed by Hoshea, son of Elah. Thus was a tool and vassal of Assyria placed on the throne of Israel.

2. *The Fall of Damascus: 732 B.C.* Having rendered Philistia and Israel impotent to intervene, Tiglath-pileser turned to finish off Damascus, which he did with thoroughness and frightful devastation. In 732 B.C. the city fell and vast numbers of its people were taken into captivity. Rezin was put to death.[9]

3. *Judah Completely Subservient to Assyria.* Tiglath-pileser then summoned before him in Damascus all the vassal princes of Syria to receive from them their formal pledges of loyalty and to impose upon them the amount of indemnity they would have to pay annually. Among them was Ahaz of Judah.[10] One evidence of a vassal's fidelity was the adoption of the religion of the overlord. In accordance with this, an Assyrian altar had been set up at Damascus, presumably in the place of honor, and Ahaz, under what pressure can only be conjectured, had a careful replica of it set up on the site of the Yahweh altar at the Jerusalem temple (2 Kgs. 16:10–18). This meant that henceforth the Assyrian imperial worship was to take official precedence

---

[8] Cf. Barton, *op. cit.,* pp. 463–467, on the annals of Tiglath-pileser. Pekah is credited with a reign of twenty years, which perhaps can best be understood to mean that he was regarded as their leader by the anti-Assyrian faction since the troubled times began at the death of Jeroboam II.

[9] 2 Kgs. 16:9.   [10] 2 Kgs. 16:10.

of the state worship of Yahweh in Yahweh's own stronghold with Yahweh virtually dispossessed from his own temple! Even the temple furnishings were broken up to get at the brass with which to pay the tribute to Tiglath-pileser (2 Kgs. 16:17 f.). Ahaz was a religious degenerate. He was an out-and-out idolater who resurrected in Judah the heathenish practice of child sacrifice (2 Kgs. 16:3 f.).

Israel and Judah had now completely lost their independence. The Assyrian was master of the entire Fertile Crescent. Laden with tribute but without having attacked Egypt, he returned to Nineveh where he died in 727 B.C., leaving Assyria a greater empire than it had ever been before.

4. *The Assyrian Policy of Deportation.* The policy of deporting captives inaugurated by Tiglath-pileser merits special attention. 2 Kgs. 15:29 states that he deported captives from the conquered areas of northern Israel and Eastjordania, and 16:9 remarks of Damascus that he "carried it captive to Kir." These deported groups were not colonized in one place but were scattered about the empire. Doubtless captives from conquered areas in other parts of the empire were imported into the west. The Assyrian idea was to empty each conquered place of those who might later start a revolt there against Assyrian domination and to mix the captives up so thoroughly that they would be powerless to foment rebellion in the places where they were settled.

The Downfall of Israel

Political Anarchy and Intrigue in Israel. Following the death of Jeroboam II (744 B.C.) the decline of Israel was swift and complete. The last twenty years of Israel's existence was a period of anarchy and bloodshed. Of the six kings who reigned after Jeroboam, four were assassinated, one was captured and died in an Assyrian prison, and only one died a nonviolent death and was succeeded by his son.

A decisive factor in Israel's undoing was miscalculation as to the cohesiveness of the Assyrian empire. The sharp division of opinion among Israel's leaders as to the wise policy toward Assyria has already been touched upon.[11] Part believed that a firm front would preserve Israel's national integrity. Others felt equally certain that Assyria was irresistible and that only through submission could the horrors of invasion, bloodshed, and rapine be averted. Four changes of dynasty occurred in Israel over this very question.[12]

---

[11] *Supra,* p. 248.

[12] Zechariah was overthrown by Shallum on what was (presumably) an anti-Assyrian platform, inasmuch as Shallum was in turn killed by Menahem in a very obvious attempt to appease Assyria. The overthrow of Pekahiah by Pekah must have represented a second effort at defiance of Assyria, for Hoshea's accession is described as pro-Assyrian.

Tiglath-pileser III held his empire together by force alone. The death of that monarch (727 B.C.) was therefore a signal for revolt and among those who rebelled was Hoshea, whom Tiglath-pileser had made king of Israel in 730 B.C. There was, however, a more important factor making for rebellion than merely the death of an Assyrian king. About the middle of the eighth century B.C., a new Ethiopian dynasty arose in Egypt, bringing a fresh revival of power to that land. With a view to the consolidation of Egypt, the new Pharaoh tried to arouse the whole eastern Mediterranean region with plans for a campaign against Assyria. Evidently Hoshea thought that this time Egypt would really do something, for 2 Kgs. 17:4 states that he intrigued with So, king of Egypt.[13]

Economic, Social, and Religious Conditions in Israel Prior to the Downfall. We have, in a previous connection,[14] considered the economic, social, and religious conditions in northern Israel during the era of prosperity under Jeroboam II. Some idea of the social and religious situation during the turmoil that marked the closing years of the northern kingdom can be gained from the writings of two prophets who were contemporary with this period. One is Hosea, a native of the northern kingdom. The other is Isaiah of Jerusalem. These conditions are portrayed in such selections from their writings as Hos. *4:1–3a, 6–10; *5:1 f., 10–14; *6:4–10; *7:3–7, 11–16; *9:3, 5–9; *11:5 f.; Isa. *9:8–10:4; *5:26–29; *28:1–4. Additional light on the period is given in 2 Kgs. *17:7–23.

These passages reflect the same conditions of extreme poverty and unjust oppression of the poor as were denounced by Amos.[15] They show how morally corrupt society had become in the northern kingdom. The moral strength of the nation was dissipated in drunken revelry and licentiousness, and this was, all the sadder to relate, in connection with feasts at the religious shrines. Worship had indeed become largely an orgy of debauchery. Priests and princes alike were corrupt, and the nation was without real statesmen to lead it. The prophets denounced the vacillating political policies of the kings who entangled the nation in alliances, now with Assyria and now with Egypt, but efforts to effect reform were without visible results. Israel's internal corruption coincided exactly with Assyria's era of greatest power and aggressiveness. Israel's doom was fixed and there was no escape.

---

[13] So (also written Seve and Shabaka) was not really king at this time, unless perhaps he was a subordinate king of the delta region. He was son of the reigning Pharaoh Piankhi, and was by him made commander-in-chief of the Egyptian forces. It is with the latter title that he appears in the Assyrian records. Cf. H. R. Hall, *The Ancient History of the Near East* (London: 1927), p. 471.

[14] *Supra*, pp. 244 f.

[15] Cf. *supra*, pp. 244 f.

Siege and Fall of Samaria. Tiglath-pileser's successor on the throne of Assyria was Shalmaneser V (727–722 B.C.), a monarch concerning whose five years' reign little is known beyond the fact that most of it was consumed in a campaign to punish Hoshea of Israel for withholding tribute from Assyria and for intriguing with Egypt. Shalmaneser visited the west in 725 B.C. and took Hoshea prisoner, though where the latter was imprisoned and what his ultimate fate was are unknown. Samaria, capital city of Israel, was besieged for nearly three years. It is a tribute to the valor of the men of Samaria that despite all that had weakened their power they were able to hold out so long against the Assyrians. The city fell in 722 B.C. The Biblical account is exceedingly brief (2 Kgs. 17:5 f., 18:9 f.).

The Captivity of Israel. The records of Sargon II, who succeeded Shalmaneser in 722 B.C., state that after the capture of Samaria he carried 27,290 of the inhabitants captive, but that he allowed the remainder to retain their possessions, and further that he appointed a governor over them and exacted no more than the previous tribute from them.[16] The names of the places to which the captives were deported show that they were scattered in different parts of the empire, in accord with Assyrian policy.[17] These captives are known historically as the "lost ten tribes." They were lost in the sense that they were absorbed by the populations of the places to which they were exiled. In the circumstances it was impossible for them to retain their tribal or racial identity intact.

To take the places vacated by the deported Israelites, Sargon imported colonists from other parts of his realm (2 Kgs. 17:24) and settled them in Samaria. Assyrian annals reveal that these newcomers were tribes of Tamuda, Ibadid, Marsiman, Khayapa, and "distant Arabs" of the desert; i.e., there was a fresh infusion of nomad blood in Palestine, a fact of important social significance. Inevitably these people intermarried with the Hebrews who were left in the land, and from this mixture developed the people later known as the Samaritans. Because they were of mixed blood they were always despised by the Judean Hebrews, or "Jews." [18]

Anti-Assyrian Intrigue in Judah

Revolts Against Sargon II Throughout the Empire: 722–705 B.C. Sargon II of Assyria (722–705 B.C.) came to the throne just prior to the fall of Samaria. The capture of that city was the first event of importance in his reign. Immediately upon his accession Sargon was confronted by serious difficulties throughout his realm

---

[16] Cf. Barton, *op. cit.*, pp. 466 f.   [17] 2 Kgs. 17:6.   [18] Cf. Jn. 4:9.

which at that time extended over the entire Fertile Crescent. Both horns of the Crescent were seats of trouble. Babylonia in the east and Syria and Palestine in the west were centers of disaffection. In each locality intrigue was fostered by a rival power, by Elam in the east and by Egypt in the west.

In the east the Elamites backed Marduk-apal-iddin (known in Hebrew as Merodach-baladan) who seized Babylon and established himself as king. As soon as possible after the surrender of Samaria Sargon attacked these allies but met with a severe check. This reverse to the new Assyrian monarch was a signal for revolt throughout his empire.

In the west the king of Hamath headed a coalition of Palestinian peoples against Sargon in 720 B.C. Arpad, Damascus, and the remnant of Samaria were in this revolt. Sargon moved swiftly against these allies and defeated them at Karkar the same year. Then he made a beeline for Egypt because Egypt was behind the intrigue and her tool was Hanno, king of Gaza. Sargon therefore attacked Gaza and Hanno fled to Egypt. At this point an Egyptian army marched to the assistance of the Philistines but Sargon severely defeated it at Raphia (720 B.C.). Thus ended another disastrous attempt to get from under the Assyrian yoke. Apparently Judah did not join in this revolt. It was upon his return from this campaign that Sargon gathered up and transported the 27,290 captives of northern Israel.

The Near-Rebellion of 711 B.C.   1. *The Pro-Egyptian Party in Judah.* There were two political factions in Judah, the pro-Assyrian and the pro-Egyptian. Judah had been the vassal of Assyria since 734 B.C. (reign of Ahaz), and the pro-Assyrians stood for loyalty to the nation's overlord. The pro-Egyptians considered alliance with Egypt the more natural policy. Judah was near to Egypt, traded with Egypt, and her whole material welfare seemed to be bound up with Egypt. Added to this was the resentment felt over paying tribute to Assyria. The pro-Egyptians therefore fell easy victims to Egyptian intrigue. The political attitude of King Hezekiah of Judah (727 ? or 721 ?–693 B.C.) [19] at this time is nowhere either stated or implied, so that one may fairly infer that he took the safe course of siding neither with pro-Assyrians nor with pro-Egyptians.

[19] 2 Kgs. 18:1 implies 727 B.C. as the date of Hezekiah's accession; this is supported by 2 Kgs. 18:9 f., which plainly means that Hezekiah was, and for some time had been, king of Judah when Samaria fell in 722 B.C. On the other hand, Ahaz is credited with a sixteen-year reign, which would date his death and Hezekiah's accession in 721 B.C. Hezekiah is credited with a reign of twenty-nine years which works out correctly as 721–693 B.C. 2 Kgs. 18:13 further confuses the problem by implying 715 B.C. as the date of Hezekiah's accession.

2. *Egyptian Intrigue and Revolt in Palestine: 711* B.C. By 712 B.C.
Egypt was actively intriguing again. Three years earlier Sargon had
passed down the Mediterranean coast on a punitive expedition that
had included Tyre and Ashdod as parts of his objective. On this same
expedition he had campaigned in the Arabian Desert, subduing
numerous tribes, and had also pushed on as far as the border of
Egypt where he received gifts from the king of Egypt. Then, in
712 B.C., Shabaka, the Ethiopian, became master of Egypt and at
once set about stirring up the Palestinian peoples to revolt against
Assyria. No doubt his real aim was to ally these peoples with himself
in order to create buffer states between Egypt and the empire of
Assyria.

The revolt which followed centered at Ashdod and called for a
united movement against Sargon by Egypt, Philistia, Judah, Moab,
and Edom. It was an impressive scheme and might conceivably have
succeeded had not Sargon acted with such speed that before the
allies could get together his cavalry descended on Ashdod and administered a smashing defeat to the Philistines. Egypt was thus left
in a predicament, and to conciliate Sargon surrendered the king of
Ashdod to him as prisoner. The entire Philistine area now became
a province of Assyria and pro-Assyrian kings and governors were
appointed over its cities, exiles were deported and colonists imported.
Assyria took no punitive measures against the other confederates.

It was a lucky thing for Hezekiah, king of Judah, that Sargon
acted with such dispatch in this rebellion, otherwise Hezekiah would
have been altogether in it. Apparently Hezekiah's sympathies inclined more and more toward the pro-Egyptians.

Isaiah the prophet also did much to hold the king true to the
Assyrian alliance. This was not because Isaiah was a pro-Assyrian.
He belonged to neither political faction. He was simply acting upon
the principle that the nation should be faithful to its pledged word.
He also had sufficient insight to know that no good could ever come
from political intrigue. He especially knew how foolish it was to
depend on Egypt, "Lady Brag-and-Stay-at-Home" (Isa. 30:7); the
Revised Version puts it, "Rahab (Blusterer) that sitteth still," and
Moffatt still more picturesquely, "Dragon Do-nothing." This exhibits
Isaiah's contempt for Egypt and the pro-Egyptians. So strongly did
he feel about it and so desperately critical seems to have been the
situation at one time that he went over the head of the king in the
hope of convincing the people of the utter folly of revolting from
Assyria. For three years Isaiah went about the streets of Jerusalem
wearing the humiliating garb of a captive of war (the text says
"naked") to impress upon the people the certainty that the nation
would be carried into captivity if they revolted from Assyria

(Isa. 20:1–6), for he thought through the people to restrain the king and his counselors. Perhaps his efforts were really effective since Judah was not this time involved.

The Palestinian Revolt of 701 B.C. 1. *The Intrigues of Merodach-baladan.* At the conclusion of his campaign in the west in 711 B.C., Sargon returned to the east to deal with a difficult situation in Babylonia. For ten years he had permitted Merodach-baladan to rule Babylon without interference. The old Babylonian nobility had by now tired of this Chaldean usurper, and moreover the alliance between him and the Elamites had broken down. It was an opportune time for Sargon to strike. He forced the Elamites back into the mountains and then drove a wedge between them and their Aramaean allies. This left Merodach-baladan shut up in Babylon in the midst of a hostile population. In this dilemma he promptly retreated to his original home in Bit Yakin. Sargon drove him from Bit Yakin in 710 B.C., whereupon he fled to the marshes at the mouth of the Tigris-Euphrates. Though apparently disposed of, he lived to fight another day. Sargon established home rule in Babylon, setting up a line of Babylonian kings.

Sargon spent the remaining five years of his life in comparative peace. At Khorsabad, twelve miles north of Nineveh, he built an enormous palace and went there to live in 706 B.C. The very next year he lost his life in a skirmish with some border tribes and was succeeded by his son Sennacherib who ruled from 705 to 681 B.C. The death of Sargon was the signal for a general uprising throughout the empire. The king of Babylon was displaced by an adventurer and he in turn was dethroned by Merodach-baladan who seized the opportunity to return and establish himself in Babylon once more.

It was Merodach-baladan's plan to entrench himself in power by stirring up the nations at the western horn of the Fertile Crescent in order to divide Sennacherib's forces by simultaneous insurrections at both extremes of the empire. He decided that one promising place to start such intrigue was in Judah, for King Hezekiah was anti-Assyrian at heart. It happened that Hezekiah was at the time convalescing from a serious illness. Merodach-baladan sent emissaries to Hezekiah on the pretext of congratulating him upon his recovery (2 Kgs. 20). It appears that Merodach-baladan had already won to his cause the northern Arabians, at that time ruled by a Queen Iati'e, presumably the successor of Queen Samsi under whom the desert tribes had been paying tribute to Assyria.[20] Through the territory of these allies the embassy of Merodach-baladan crossed the desert to visit King Hezekiah. Their real mission was to foment

[20] Cf. *supra,* p. 249.

intrigue. They brought along a present (which of course means a bribe) to make their mission the more certain of success. Hezekiah fell an easy victim to their blandishments.

Merodach-baladan's return to power was short-lived. After ruling only nine months in Babylon, he was defeated by Sennacherib, who crushed the rebels, established his authority in lower Babylonia, and carried away a rich booty. This defeat of Merodach-baladan in the east did not, however, end the intrigue in the west.

2. *Judah Joins the Revolt.* The center of the western intrigue was Jerusalem. This was doubtless because at the time Jerusalem was the most nearly impregnable fortress in the west. We have already noted [21] to what perfection King Azariah carried the fortifying of Judah.[22] King Hezekiah now gave attention to the further strengthening of its defenses. Both 2 Kgs. 20:20 and 2 Chr. 32:30 mention Hezekiah's achievement in stopping the upper spring of Gihon and in building a conduit for bringing every drop of water from this spring inside the walls of the city to the pool of Siloam in order that Jerusalem might not be without an adequate supply of water in the event of siege. This conduit has already been described.[23]

All loyal Assyrian administrators of cities in the rebelling area were ejected at the outset of the rebellion. The king of Ashkelon, the military governor of Ashdod, and King Padi of Ekron were all ousted.[24] Padi was turned over to Hezekiah and by him imprisoned in Jerusalem. This had a twofold effect. It eliminated every ruler who was not in sympathy with the rebellion and it thoroughly committed Hezekiah to the revolt. Thus the other rebellious states made sure that this time Judah was in beyond withdrawal.

3. *Collapse of the Rebellion.* All Phoenicia, Philistia, Judah, and the east Jordan states of Ammon, Moab, and Edom were in the rebellion, and of course Egypt was behind it. As we have previously observed, the great weakness of these Palestinian states was their lack of cohesiveness. They never seemed able to hold together and work together for their common interests. This trait showed itself just as soon as Sennacherib put in an appearance (701 B.C.). The moment his army reached Phoenicia defections among the allies began. Phoenicia immediately submitted. The princes of Ammon, Moab, and Edom hastened to fawn upon the Assyrian and to offer him tribute. Sennacherib then marched down into the Philistine area. Egypt did make a fainthearted effort to assist the rebels, but to no effect, for the Egyptian forces were defeated by the Assyrians at El-tekeh near Ekron.

[21] *Supra,* p. 244.   [22] 2 Chr. 26:9–15.
[23] Cf. *supra,* pp. 53 ff.   [24] Cf. 2 Kgs. 18:8.

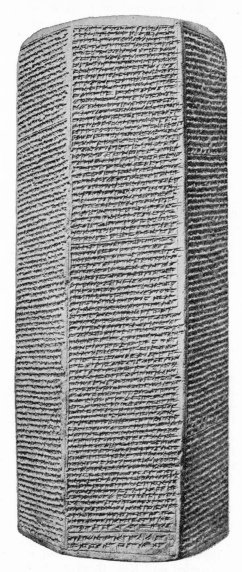

THE CYLINDER OF SENNACHERIB [25]

[25] A hexagonal prism containing a cuneiform record of the western campaigns of Sennacherib, including the expedition against Palestine in which he lost his army. Now in the Oriental Institute Museum, Chicago. Courtesy of The Oriental Institute, University of Chicago.

4. *The Siege of Jerusalem and the Devastation of Judah.* Judah was left to face the issue practically alone. Her territory was overrun and Jerusalem besieged. Hemmed in and with no help from allies, Hezekiah decided it was wise to make peace with Sennacherib and pay indemnity. 2 Kgs. 18:14 ff. specifies the amount paid, apparently all the treasure Hezekiah could scrape together. Hezekiah turned Padi over to Sennacherib, who reappointed him over Ekron after the capture of that stronghold. Thus the Assyrian won back the entire Philistine area.

Sennacherib now exhibited his characteristic duplicity. Notwithstanding his acceptance of the tribute Hezekiah had paid, he turned upon Judah and demanded the surrender of Jerusalem. He staged a demonstration before the walls of Jerusalem which threw the city into confusion. Surprisingly, Hezekiah refused the insolent demand and prepared to defend the city. The Assyrian version of this affair is contained in the fairly complete and carefully detailed account of this campaign of Sennacherib in Palestine in 701 B.C., as inscribed on the "Cylinder of Sennacherib," a six-sided, baked-clay cylinder in cuneiform script now in the Oriental Institute at the University of Chicago. It describes Sennacherib's campaign in Judah and states that he besieged and took forty-six of the strongholds and fortresses of Judah which he then turned over to the kings of Ashdod, Ekron, and Gaza. It further states that "Him [Hezekiah] himself, like a bird in a cage in the midst of Jerusalem, his royal city, I shut up." [26]

This, clearly, was a desperate crisis, and it looked as though Jerusalem were doomed. The populace was in terror, and Hezekiah at his wit's end. As a last resort he sent for Isaiah the prophet to ask his counsel.[27] Had he but followed Isaiah's advice in the first place he would not have been in his present fix. There were three stages to Isaiah's political policy. He had first counseled no entangling alliances, but this counsel had not been heeded. Instead, the alliance with Assyria had been made. Then Isaiah counseled fidelity to the nation's pledged word and aloofness from international intrigue (Isa. 30:1–17; 31:1–9), but again his counsel had not been heeded. He now counseled fidelity to Yahweh, for all he had to fall back upon was his trust in God. Yahweh, said Isaiah, had been "blasphemed" by the king of Assyria,[28] and for that reason was against Assyria and for Jerusalem. Apparently Isaiah had in mind the words of the Assyrian speech recorded in 2 Kgs. 18:19–25, 33 ff. So strong was Isaiah's own faith that he inspired the king and the people with con-

---

[26] For the full text of Sennacherib's inscription, in translation, cf. Barton, *op. cit.*, pp. 471 f.
[27] 2 Kgs. 19:2.
[28] 2 Kgs. 19:6.

fidence by declaring that the Assyrian would never take the city but that instead he "shall hear tidings and shall return unto his own land." [29]

What rumor Sennacherib may have heard is a mystery. Possibly he received some information about plotting against him by Bel-ibni, whom he had put over Babylonia in place of Merodach-baladan. At any rate, suddenly and unexpectedly he raised the siege and took his troops back to the east. 2 Kgs. 19:35 implies that some calamity befell the army of Sennacherib. Herodotus, the Greek historian of the fifth century B.C., says that Sennacherib's army camped on the border of Egypt and was infested with a plague of mice.[30] If so, the rodents in all probability brought the bubonic plague, which would have decimated the Assyrian army. Sennacherib left the west without invading Egypt and never returned.[31]

5. *The Aftermath in Judah—National Reforms.* Prominent in this period was the prophet Micah of Moresheth-Gath, a contemporary of the prophet Isaiah in the reign of Hezekiah. Micah lived in the country districts of Judah which had felt the full force of Sennacherib's devastating army. The terrible sufferings of these districts are reflected in Mic. *1:8–16. This prophet rightly laid the blame for all this suffering upon the corrupt national leaders in Jerusalem and declared that Jerusalem would surely suffer destruction in punishment (Mic. *3:9–12). The preaching of Micah, and no doubt of Isaiah as well, reinforced by the bitter experience through which the nation had just passed at the hands of Sennacherib, now led to a national upheaval.[32] 2 Kgs. 18:1–6 describes the religious reforms which King Hezekiah effected at this time.[33]

Judah's Loyal Submission to Assyrian Overlordship

Judah Loyal to Esarhaddon of Assyria: 681–668 B.C. 1. *The Character of Esarhaddon's Rule.* The first half of the seventh century B.C. saw the imperial star of Assyria attain its zenith, only to sink swiftly to its setting. The beginning of the century was marked by the

---

[29] Isa. 37:7 = 2 Kgs. 19:7, 32 f. The Kings narrative of this crisis of 701 B.C. in 2 Kgs. 18:13–19:37 is duplicated in Isa. 36–39.

[30] Book II, § 141. A translation of the passage is in Barton, *op. cit.,* p. 475.

[31] The difficulties of reconciling the Kings and the Isaiah accounts of the events of this crisis with one another and with the Assyrian annals have led some to the view that there was a second campaign of Sennacherib against Judah ten years later (691 B.C.). There is no mention of another western campaign in the Assyrian annals, and no other evidence is available to show whether or not there was such a campaign. It is possible the Bible writer has confused events of two or more campaigns. Cf. *The Cambridge Ancient History,* iii, 74, 278, 390.

[32] Cf. Jer. 26:18 f.

[33] It is barely possible that this had some connection with Isaiah's confident prediction that Jerusalem would not be taken by Sennacherib.

fiendishly cruel treatment of subject peoples by Sennacherib, the most
notorious of whose acts was the wanton sack of Babylon in 689 B.C.
Esarhaddon, who came to the throne in 681 B.C., brought in a new and
happier era for all concerned. His nature and policies were the
opposite of Sennacherib's. He restored Babylon and conciliated the
populace with the result that he had little difficulty in ruling that
province. In 678 B.C. he moved into the west and campaigned in
Phoenicia, all of which he subjugated save the island city of Tyre.
He then moved south and for two years was occupied with the subjugation of Arab tribes. His aim in this was to cut Egypt off completely from all her Palestinian allies. In 673 B.C. he invaded Egypt
and after several battles reached and captured Memphis. He made
Egypt into an Assyrian province governed by Assyrian officers. At
last Assyria had achieved its great ambition, the master, now, of the
entire Fertile Crescent and of Egypt.

2. *Judah Under Manasseh (693–639* B.C.). In dealing with the
small Palestinian states, Esarhaddon showed the same conciliatory
attitude he displayed toward Babylon and, at first, toward Egypt
also. He did demand tribute and he enumerates twenty-two western
princes who paid him such tribute, among them Manasseh, king
of Judah.[34] Manasseh remained loyal to Assyria throughout his long
reign. Manasseh was a young man just entering his twenties when
the campaign started which was to carry Assyria into Egypt. What
pressure was brought to bear upon him and what motives actuated
him are quite unknown. He bowed to Assyria and reestablished
the worship of the Assyrian deities, precisely after the fashion of
his grandfather Ahaz. The reasoning was simple. Judah was a part
of the Assyrian empire. If Judah was to share in Assyria's prosperity,
then Judah must worship Assyria's gods. Much the same results followed as in Ahaz's time. Material prosperity such as the nation had
not known for many a year convinced Manasseh of the rightness of
his choice. The faithful Yahweh prophets could only register their
disapproval and assert that doom would surely fall some day (2 Kgs.
21:10–15). But nobody listened to them particularly. Manasseh went
ahead with his Assyrian practices and literally filled Jerusalem with
Assyrian shrines and forms of worship (2 Kgs. 21:1–9, 16).

Judah Loyal to Ashurbanipal of Assyria: 668–626 B.C. 1. *The
Character of Ashurbanipal's Rule.* The first problem Ashurbanipal [35] had on his hands was a revolt in Egypt. He conducted two
campaigns, on the second of which he attacked and pillaged Thebes
in 662 B.C. So stunning was this act that the Hebrew prophet Nahum

---

[34] Esarhaddon's inscription, in translation, may be read in Barton, *op. cit.,* p. 476.
[35] Ashurbanipal is the same as the Osnappar in Ezr. 4:10.

a half century later refers to it as the outstanding calamity of its sort (Nah. 3:8 ff.). Ultimately Ashurbanipal was obliged to relinquish his control of Egypt, due to the rise of Psamtik I, founder of the twenty-sixth dynasty, who drove the Assyrians out of Egypt. By 645 B.C. Egypt was again independent.

Ashurbanipal also campaigned against Tyre, which had resisted the efforts of his father to take it in 675 B.C. Ashurbanipal captured and plundered Tyre and carried off captives. His most engaging problem, however, was in the east. His own brother, who was ruling Babylon as a vassal, thought to establish himself in an independent kingdom and precipitated a revolt which was put down with frightful cruelty.

There was an uprising against Ashurbanipal in the west. To catch the rebels by surprise, he made a remarkable forced march straight across the desert, a most unusual and difficult undertaking. He speedily defeated and plundered the rebels and carried many of them into captivity. Manasseh, king of Judah, may have been in this rebellion. 2 Chr. 33:10–13 says that Manasseh was taken to Babylon a prisoner but was later released and allowed to return to his kingdom, evidently after giving due assurance of his fealty. One of the books of the Apocrypha, *The Prayer of Manasses,* relates to this Babylonian imprisonment of the king. On the whole, Manasseh throughout his reign was loyal to his overlord and so his son and successor, Amon.

2. *Amon of Judah (639–638 B.C.) and a Revolution That Failed.* Amon lived for too short a period to effect much change in Judah even had he been so disposed, and there is no hint that he was. It is possible that religious motives had something to do with the assassination of Amon; if so, the plot failed (2 Kgs. 21:23 f.). The "people of the land" promptly rose against the conspirators, put them to death, and crowned Amon's eight-year-old son Josiah. It would seem, therefore, that Manasseh's policy was highly popular.

3. *Judah Under Josiah (638–608 B.C.).* For the first half of his reign Josiah evidently followed the policy laid down by Manasseh. When, in 621 B.C., Josiah was at last stirred to attempt a sweeping reform, Yahweh's temple, the pride of Solomon's reign, was in sad need of repair. To so low an ebb had the worship of Yahweh fallen! The so-called "Great Reformation of 621 B.C." was the most noteworthy event of Josiah's reign. We shall give it closer attention in Chapter 18.[36]

There were a few loyal souls in this period who stood firmly against all foreign worship, though their number we have no means

[36] *Vid. infra,* pp. 332 ff.

of knowing. Two there were with the courage to speak out boldly and with conviction, the prophets Zephaniah and Jeremiah, whose words, written in Josiah's time, have come down to us. There was little chance of their being listened to so long as the nation prospered and no signs of desolating war could be seen. Zephaniah might voice his conviction that Yahweh would yet "visit the men that are settled on their lees, that say in their heart, 'Yahweh will neither do good or evil.' " [37] but there were few to listen. Then in 626 B.C., for a brief time it did look as though his prediction might be fulfilled, and the Hebrew nation had a real fright. Bursting suddenly through the mountainous region of central Asia Minor came the hardy Scythians, sweeping down the eastern Mediterranean coast, plundering and pillaging, until they reached the Philistine plains. Judah was thoroughly alarmed.

[37] Zeph. 1:12.

Chapter 16

THE DECLINE AND FALL OF JUDAH

Coincidental with the Scythian invasion came the death, in 626 B.C., of Ashurbanipal, the last great sovereign of Assyria. Following his death the decline of Assyria set in and the once mighty empire went swiftly to its doom. Nineveh fell in 612 B.C. The last vestige of the Assyrian empire was obliterated at the battle of Carchemish in 605 B.C. The decline and fall of Assyria and the rise of the new Babylonian empire furnish another (the sixth) watershed in Old Testament history. With the rise of Babylon to world dominion, Judah's doom was sealed.

Sources for a History of the Period

As in the last two chapters, we are dependent upon the Book of Kings (2 Kgs. 24–25), the writings of the prophets, and archaeological monuments. Of the prophets, Jeremiah gives us many illuminating details about the closing years of Judah. Nahum and Habakkuk reflect the time of Assyria's fall, but give us no historical information.

The Decline and Fall of Assyria

Factors Leading to the Fall of Assyria. 1. *The Scythian Invasion in the West.* Assyrian dominion west of the Euphrates River ended with the invasion of that area by the Scythians. According to Herodotus,[1] these barbarous hordes, under their king Madyes, poured down out of the northwest on an expedition of plunder. Just when they first began to raid the possessions of Assyria cannot be learned. Herodotus states that their domination over Asia lasted twenty-eight years. The death of Ashurbanipal occurred *circa* 626 B.C. and at just about that same time these ravaging hordes worked their way down the Mediterranean coast at least as far as Philistia. Everywhere the peoples were panic-stricken at their approach. Judah was thoroughly alarmed. In Zeph. *1:14–18 and Jer. *1:1 f., 13–19;

[1] Book I, §§103–106.

*4:5–6:26, the prophets express their fear that the approaching terror will overwhelm Judah. This did not happen, however, for at the border of Egypt the Scythians were turned back by Psamtik I (663–609 B.C.) either by arms or (more likely) by a gift of gold. The Scythians were out for plunder only and had little interest in organizing conquered areas.

2. *The Alliance of Medes and Chaldeans in the East.* In the century preceding the fall of Assyria, the Medes had been settling the mountains east of Assyria and north of Elam. Here they were joined by other hordes from the region of the Black Sea in the time of Esarhaddon. The weakness of Assyria, apparent long before Ashurbanipal's death, stirred these peoples into action and they began a series of attacks upon the declining empire.

The death of Ashurbanipal was the signal for revolt in Babylonia. Within a year Nabopolassar, leader of the Chaldeans, seized the throne of Babylon and began hostilities against Ashur-etil-ilani, son and successor of Ashurbanipal. This monarch's reign soon ended in disorder; his successor, Sin-shum-lishir, was of no consequence, and then another son of Ashurbanipal, Sin-shar-ishkun by name, came to the throne. He proved utterly unable to cope with the forces of the Medes and the Chaldeans. Nabopolassar then set out to incorporate Assyria within his own Babylonian realm. He was thwarted in his first two attempts to reach Nineveh, first when Egyptian reinforcements came to Assyria's rescue, the second time when he was repulsed in an attack upon Ashur, the old Assyrian capital. On a third invasion he effected a junction with the Median Cyaxeres just after the latter had taken Ashur singlehanded (614 B.C.), and the two together then mapped out a campaign which was to bring about Nineveh's fall.

The Fall of Nineveh (612 B.C.) and the End of the Assyrian Empire (605 B.C.). The outlook was black for Assyria. Sin-shar-ishkun in desperation sought help from both Scythians and Egyptians, but it was a vain hope. The Scythians double-crossed him. Nineveh was famed for its riches. Probably the prospect of rich booty to be secured in the city was the inducement held out to the Scythians by Cyaxeres. At any rate he won them over and they joined him and Nabopolassar in the final assault on Nineveh. Inestimable booty was carried away and the city was turned into "ruined mounds." The Assyrian empire had indeed proved to be not a civilizing force but an unmitigated scourge.

A remnant of Assyrians escaped from Nineveh and fled to Haran. There Ashuruballit was made king. With his shattered forces he could only await attack, hoping for aid from the Egyptians, Assyria's allies at this time. Before they arrived Nabopolassar attacked and devastated Haran. Ashuruballit retreated westward until joined by the Pharaoh Necho of Egypt and his troops. Together they counter-attacked the Babylonian army but were defeated. The struggle dragged on, however, until 605 B.C., when Nebuchadrezzar, son and successor of Nabopolassar, administered a smashing defeat to Ashur-uballit and his Egyptian ally Necho at Carchemish. Necho returned to Egypt as hastily as he could with the remnant of his army. The Assyrian empire was a thing of the past.[2]

Judah Under Egyptian Overlordship

The decline and fall of Assyria had led to a brief Egyptian over-lordship over Judah. The powerlessness of Assyria to exercise effec-tive control over any of the west at this time inevitably transferred whatever vestige of authority might be left over Palestine to Assyria's ally, Egypt. When, therefore, Necho marched through Palestine on his way to aid the Assyrians, he naturally summoned Josiah, king of Judah, to meet him. Josiah obeyed the summons, "and Pharaoh Necho slew him at Megiddo, when he had seen him." [3] The state-ment, "when he had seen him," suggests an interview rather than a battle. Possibly Necho wanted to make sure he was leaving no foe behind him to cut off the possibility of retreat and, not liking Josiah's attitude, put him to death. Possibly Necho dreamed of a revival of Egyptian empire such as had existed in the fifteenth century B.C.

After the death of Josiah the "people of the land" again showed their power and made Jehoahaz, a son of Josiah, king (608 B.C.). After a rule of only three months, however, he too was summoned by the Pharaoh Necho to Riblah on the Orontes, the Egyptian's headquarters, there to declare his attitude toward Egypt and Assyria. Evidently dissatisfied with Jehoahaz's declarations, Necho put him in chains and sent him a prisoner to Egypt (2 Kgs. 23:31 ff.). In his place on the throne of Judah Necho put another son of Josiah, Eliakim, whose name he changed to Jehoiakim, the fact of a changed name evidencing to the nation of the Judahites that Pharaoh was now their suzerain. The disgust of the prophet Jeremiah over these

[2] The translation by Mr. C. J. Gadd, of the British Museum, in 1924, of a previously unread cuneiform tablet which treats of the period 616–609 B.C. reveals that the Egyptians and the Assyrians were military allies during this period, that Nineveh fell in 612 B.C., but that thereafter the Assyrian rule was transferred to Haran where it survived until the battle of Carchemish ended Assyria's existence and Egypt's overlordship over Palestine. The bearing of Gadd's tablet on the historical situation is fully discussed by I. M. Price, *The Monuments and the Old Testament* (Philadelphia: 1925), pp. 343–346.

[3] 2 Kgs. 23:29.

changes of rulers in Judah is expressed with unconcealed frankness in Jer. *22:10–19. Necho demanded a heavy tribute from Judah, and this was promptly collected by Jehoiakim from "the people of the land" (2 Kgs. 23:33 ff.), a fact confirming the conjecture that "the people of the land" were a political party not in favor of Egypt.

The Chaldean Conquest of Judah

The Pro-Egyptian Jehoiakim: 607–597 B.C. Revolts Against Nebuchadrezzar. The battle of Carchemish marked the end of one world empire, the Assyrian, and the beginning of another, the Chaldean or "New" Babylonian empire. The rise of this new Babylonian kingdom under Nabopolassar has already been considered.[4] The defeat of Assyria and Egypt at Carchemish made this new Babylonia overlord of the entire Fertile Crescent.

After his defeat at Carchemish, Necho, with the wreck of his army, beat a hasty retreat. Jehoiakim, facing the political necessity of a change of masters, swore fealty to Nebuchadrezzar and appears to have remained loyal to him for three years. During these years Nebuchadrezzar remained in the east, making secure his hold on the throne of his father Nabopolassar who had died in 605 B.C.

In Judah intriguing went on apace. Jehoiakim was at heart an out-and-out pro-Egyptian for he owed his throne to Egypt. Therefore after three years of apparent submission to Nebuchadrezzar, he withheld tribute and came out in open rebellion (2 Kgs. 24:1 f.).

The prophet Jeremiah seems to have been the one clearheaded individual in Jerusalem during this period. He saw the consummate folly of revolting against Nebuchadrezzar and declared that it would precipitate the ruin of the city and the exile of its inhabitants. Naturally he was branded a traitor for taking such a position, for the idea was abroad in Jerusalem that no matter what the people did the city was beyond reach of harm. This doctrine of the inviolability of Jerusalem was doubtless due to a misinterpretation of the prophet Isaiah. Back in the year 701 B.C. when Sennacherib was at the gates of Jerusalem, Isaiah had declared that Yahweh would deliver the city and the Assyrian would not set foot in it.[5] Actually it turned out that way, and this deliverance gave rise to the notion that Yahweh never would let harm come to his city. When, therefore, Jeremiah declared that Jerusalem would be destroyed, the prophets and the priests demanded his life as a traitor. He was saved only through the intervention of the princes and that part of the people who recalled that their forefathers had not killed the prophet

---

[4] *Supra,* p. 264.   [5] Cf. *supra,* pp. 258 f.

Micah for saying the very same thing (Jer. *26:1–19, *36; Mic. *3:12).

The First Captivity: 597 B.C.   In order to quell the rebellion in Judah, Nebuchadrezzar first sent marauding bands of Chaldeans, reinforced by Aramaeans, Moabites, and Ammonites (probably subject conscripts), who carried on a kind of guerilla warfare, ravaging the countryside. Some months later he moved against Judah with his main forces. The sudden death of Jehoiakim (597 B.C.), just after Jerusalem had been invested by the Chaldean army, threw heavy responsibilities upon his son and successor Jehoiachin (Coniah), a lad of eighteen. After carrying on for three months he surrendered in order to save the city from total destruction. The unfortunate young king was carried to Babylon into exile.[6]

Besides the king, Nebuchadrezzar carried some ten thousand of the people to Babylon as captives. Those thus deported were the leaders of the nation, the princes and the mighty men of valor, and the craftsmen, all who were "apt for war." The motive behind this was, of course, to cripple Jerusalem, to make sure it would be less likely in the future to be a center of insurrection, by taking away those who had brains enough to plan rebellion and those who had might enough to attempt rebellion (2 Kgs. 24:8–16).[7] None but the poorest of the people of the land were left behind. The prophet Jeremiah was an exception. He was left in Jerusalem undisturbed,[8] doubtless because Nebuchadrezzar considered him a peacemaking influence since he had had sense enough to see and declare the folly of defying Babylonia.

The Rebellion of Zedekiah: 588 B.C.   Probably Nebuchadrezzar believed that severity at the start meant a docile Jerusalem afterwards. At least he tempered his severity with what may have been intended as royal graciousness, for although he deported Jehoiachin he left a member of the royal family in control, a third son of Josiah, by name Mattaniah, twenty-one years old. Mattaniah's name he changed to Zedekiah and by the latter he afterward appears in the Bible records (2 Kgs. 24:17).

It was an impossible task that Zedekiah faced. Since all who had any ability or experience in administering affairs of state had been taken into captivity, it was the rabble who came into possession of the land and whatever property of value Nebuchadrezzar had left. These promptly developed all the arrogance of the newly rich. They

---

[6] Archaeology has shed new light on Jehoiachin's fate in Babylon. Cf. W. F. Albright, "King Joiachin in Exile," *Biblical Archaeologist* (December, 1942), pp. 49–55.

[7] Nebuchadrezzar may have desired the craftsmen for work in great Babylon which he was building.

[8] Jer. 27:1.

concluded that they were especially favored of Yahweh because he had spared them along with the supposedly inviolable city. Thus believing that they had the divine approval upon them, they continued their senseless course. To rule such a populace was almost hopeless.

Nevertheless Zedekiah succeeded in keeping loyal to Nebuchadrezzar for four years. Then intrigue captured the situation. Jer. 27:1 ff. refers to the presence in Jerusalem of ambassadors from Edom, Moab, Ammon, Tyre, and Sidon, agents who were clearly attempting to incite Zedekiah to rebellion. Evidently because of this fraternizing, Zedekiah was ordered to Babylon to explain his conduct.[9] Nebuchadrezzar apparently became convinced of Zedekiah's personal loyalty, or else forgave him, for Zedekiah was continued on the throne of Judah. Nevertheless the voice of the siren of revolt proved too much for him to resist. Jer. *28 f. suggests the terrific pressure that was forcing Zedekiah bit by bit toward rupture with Babylonia. The state of tension in Judah at the time is reflected in the Lachish Letters, found at Tell ed-Duweir in southwest Palestine, which were written just prior to the final siege of Jerusalem. In the ninth year of his reign he finally rebelled.[10]

This rebellion was instigated by Egypt. In that year (588 b.c.) Hophra-Apries came to the throne and promptly set about to recover Palestine for Egypt. Zedekiah became his willing tool. Jeremiah tried his best to keep the king from such folly, declaring that rebellion would precipitate the utter ruin of the city, but his efforts were in vain (Jer. *27).

The Capture and Destruction of Jerusalem: 586 B.C. The end came swiftly and terribly once the revolt started. Nebuchadrezzar's troops marched against the rebels and besieged Jerusalem. Terror filled the city. King and people now felt that the worst Jeremiah had predicted was coming true (Jer. *21:1–10). As a gesture to win the favor of Yahweh, if haply he might save the city, they set free their Hebrew slaves. Then suddenly the siege was raised and Nebuchadrezzar's army departed.

The real reason for this departure was that Egyptian troops had appeared in Palestine as part of Hophra's move to conquer the Phoenician coast (Jer. 37:1–10). At last it seemed as if Egypt were really going to do something. But right here the leaders in Jerusalem showed almost unbelievable inhumanity and stupidity; those who had set their slaves free promptly seized and enslaved them again. Jeremiah denounced this perfidy unsparingly (Jer. *34:8–22). Mean-

---

[9] Jer. 51:59.
[10] 2 Kgs. 25:1. Cf. G. E. Wright and F. V. Fïlson. *The Westminster Historical Atlas to the Bible* (Philadelphia: 1945), pp. 105 f.

while the Chaldeans made quick work of driving back the Egyptians and then returned to the siege of Jerusalem.

As a part of the general political blundering, Jeremiah was imprisoned as a traitor. He was accused of trying to desert to the enemy and of breaking down the morale of Jerusalem's defenders by advising the king to surrender to the Chaldeans. Zedekiah himself, however, did seem to have more confidence in Jeremiah than did his officers for though he let Jeremiah be imprisoned, the king hung on the prophet's words hoping that the prophet might tell him Yahweh would spare the city (Jer. *37:11–38:28).

The defenders of Jerusalem fought with desperate courage born of a realization of the terrible fate that awaited them if they fell into the hands of the enemy. For a year and a half the city held out. In July, 586 B.C., the walls were breached and the Chaldean troops poured into the city. Zedekiah, with a small bodyguard, managed to slip through the enemy lines, trying to reach safety in the east Jordan highlands. He was overtaken and captured near Jericho (2 Kgs. 25:1–5). The captive king was taken to Riblah on the Orontes, Nebuchadrezzar's headquarters, there to receive his sentence. He was first made to witness the execution of his two sons, and with this as the final visual image his memory might retain, his own eyes were put out and in chains he was taken to captivity (2 Kgs. 25:6 f.).

Jerusalem was doomed. It had long enough been a source of trouble for Nebuchadrezzar and his patience was exhausted. This time he intended that it should never rise again. So the city was sacked and the temple burned. The account in 2 Kgs. *25:8–21 needs no comment save to say that so thorough was the destruction that for a century and a half the city lay a mass of desolate and uninhabitable rubble.

The Second Captivity: 586 B.C.   Not only Zedekiah's sons but seventy of the leading citizens were also executed at Riblah (2 Kgs. 25:18–21, Jer. 39:1–9). The remaining inhabitants of the city, the deserters, and many others made up the sad procession to Babylon, there to join their fellow countrymen who had been taken into captivity eleven years earlier. None were left but the poorest of the land to be vinedressers and husbandmen, poorest in mental caliber and poorest in social heritage (2 Kgs. 25:11 f.). The city "sat solitary that had been full of people." [11]

The People Left in Judah.   Over the people left in the land, shattered fragments of the kingdom, Nebuchadrezzar placed as governor one Gedaliah, a native Judean, grandson of Shaphan (presumably the pious scribe of Josiah's time).[12] His headquarters were

[11] Lam. 1:1.   [12] 2 Kgs. 25:22.

at Mizpah, a small town located on a commanding height some six miles northwest of Jerusalem.

Jeremiah the prophet was one of those left. He was treated with the utmost consideration by the conqueror, being given his choice of going with the captives to Babylon or of remaining in Judah. He chose the latter, hoping still to be of service to his fellow Jews on their native soil, though he was indeed a prophet without honor in his own country (Jer. 39:11–14).

The Final Captivity: 581 B.C. The situation in Judah was impossible. One element of the rabble could not be brought to reason and immediately plotted rebellion. Gedaliah, as the appointee and representative of Babylonia, was murdered by Ishmael, a member of the royal family,[13] and civil war broke out. Then, through tardy fear of what Nebuchadrezzar might inflict upon them by way of punishment for this insurrection, the guilty parties fled to Egypt, dragging the prophet Jeremiah with them. The situation is graphically described in 2 Kgs. 25:22–26; Jer. 40:1–43:7. Just what Nebuchadrezzar did in view of this rebellion is not related, but Jer. 52:30 indicates that there was another deportation of captives from Judah in 581 B.C.

The Dispersion of the Jews

Thus did the Hebrew nation come to an end. From this time on there were three distinct divisions of Jews: (1) the Palestinian Jews, i.e., those left in the land, among whom colonists were settled by the conqueror; (2) the Jews of the Captivity, i.e., those who were taken to Babylonia in 597, 586, and 581 B.C., most of whom, together with their descendants, became merged with the Babylonian peoples; (3) the Jews of the Dispersion, known as the Diaspora, i.e., those who fled voluntarily to Egypt and eventually spread from Egypt through the whole Mediterranean world.

The destruction of Jerusalem and captivity of the Jews in 586 B.C. brings us to another (the seventh) watershed in Biblical history.

13 Jer. 41:1 f.

Chapter 17

HEBREW CULTURE UNDER THE KINGS

Hebrew history from the time of Solomon to the exile was packed to the full with political and economic changes. These were inevitably accompanied by correspondingly great changes in culture. War and peaceful commerce alternated, and both alike operated to introduce new racial elements, to alter social institutions, and to create new culture patterns and new standards of thought. Standing upon the ruins of Hebrew nationalism (586 B.C.) and looking backward over the centuries, we shall point out some of the most significant of these changes, both in the field of material things and in the realm of institutions and ideals.

Occupations

The occupations in which the people of a nation engage are an index of the inventiveness, resourcefulness, skills, and ambitions of such people. By this test we are able to appreciate the Hebrews for what they were.

Agriculture and Pastoral Pursuits. Herding and farming continued to be the basic occupations throughout this period. To be a stock raiser or to cultivate broad acres was, generally speaking, to belong to the higher social level. These were not occupations exhibiting much progress either in tools employed or methods adopted. In fact it was this rural population, the herders in particular, which stood out conspicuously as the bulwark of conservatism and resistance to change throughout the centuries.

Artisans and Craftsmen. As city life developed, craftsmanship likewise developed. In the simple villages of the rural regions the artisans were few in number and variety, and they exchanged their wares according to their own homely needs. In response to the city's call, however, these village artisans gradually drifted townward. Thus the specialized crafts, with their accompanying guilds of craftsmen, came into being. The native Hebrew craftsman was inferior, both in his skill and in the quality of his product, to the worker of Canaanite descent or of Phoenician origin.

The apocryphal Book of Sira (Ecclesiasticus), written in the second century B.C., contains a delightful poem (*38:24–34) which discusses the social importance of the plowman, the engraver, the smith, and the potter in comparison with the importance of the scribe. The poet says that "without these shall not a city be inhabited," but they nevertheless "shall not be sought for in the council of the people; . . . they shall not sit on the seat of the judge; . . . neither shall they declare instruction; . . .

> But they will maintain the fabric of the world;
> And in the handiwork of their craft is their prayer.

1. *Clayworking.* The modern Biblical scholar can hardly assent to Sira's view of the inferior social value of the potter. No other workman of antiquity has contributed so much to human civilization as he. The potters do indeed "declare instruction" to the modern archaeologists, for the use of ceramics as a means to knowledge of early human societies is one of the most important phases of archaeological research. The products of the potters had the good fortune to get broken, and where the pieces fell, there they lay for three millennia or more waiting to be rescued from the ancient rubbish heaps by the modern scientific diggers who piece them together and interpret their story of ancient society. Such potsherds are the archaeologist's one most certain clue to the date of any community which is dug up.[1] One eminent American archaeologist even trained himself, under the crime detection bureau of a large city, in recording and interpreting fingerprints and applied this to broken jar handles some five thousand years old, finding it of value in determining strata of civilization. This is only part of "the eloquence of potsherds"; they were even used by kings for stationery in Old Testament times.

The craft of the potter did not develop until some time after the Hebrews had settled in Canaan for in nomadic life and for some time thereafter animal skins and wooden vessels were preferred to the breakable clay vessels. With the adoption of settled habitations the use of pottery increased.[2] There are numerous allusions to the potter and his work. He trod the clay with his feet,[3] shaped the vessels on a wheel,[4] and afterward fired them. Some clay vessels were glazed. Jer. *18:1–12, in a prophetic sermon based upon the potter at his work, gives interesting details of such a craftsman's methods.

---

[1] Cf. W. F. Albright, *From the Stone Age to Christianity* (Baltimore: 1940), pp. 20–23.
[2] *Vid. infra,* p. 290.   [3] Isa. 41:25.
[4] Jer. 18:3. An actual potter's workshop was found in a cave at Tell ed-Duweir (Lachish). Cf. Jack Finegan, *Light From the Ancient Past* (Princeton: 1946), p. 127.

Brickmaking and bricklaying were unskilled occupations. The moist clay was first tramped and kneaded,[5] then pressed into a mold and set to dry in the sun. Sometimes finely chopped straw was mixed with the clay as a reinforcement. Ex. 5:7–19 is the familiar story of the Hebrew brickmakers, under Egyptian taskmasters, using straw in the sun-dried bricks.

2. *Carpentry.* The first carpenters mentioned in the Old Testament are some foreigners imported to build a house for King David.[6] At that time the Hebrews were evidently quite unskilled in the craft. Two centuries later, however, when the temple was being repaired, it was Hebrews who did the carpentry work.[7] The carpenter included among his tasks not merely what we understand as carpentry, but also cabinetmaking, wood carving, and the like. As to tools, Isa. 44:13, in an interesting description of a carpenter making a wooden idol, mentions a measuring line, a pencil, planes, and compasses. Other carpenter tools named are axes,[8] hammers,[9] and saws.[10] Holes were made by the primitive device of working a drill with bow and string, just as is still the method in parts of the Orient today.

3. *Masonry.* Masons were "hewers of stone" [11] as well as builders. They even quarried the stones for their own construction work.[12] Among their tools are mentioned the plumb line or plummet,[13] the measuring reed,[14] and the hammer.[15] The best masons of the period came from Phoenicia,[16] and to this day the masons of Lebanon are the most skilled in all Palestine and Syria.

4. *Metalworking.* Mines were found in the Lebanons, along the eastern border of the Arabah,[17] in the Sinai Peninsula, and in Egypt. Lebanon was especially rich in iron. The poem in Job *28:1–11 pictures the hazardous work of the miner and reads as though it was based on close observation of the mining process. Num. 31:22 mentions every metal referred to in the Bible—gold, silver, brass, iron, tin, and lead.

In the earlier period of Hebrew history the chief metalworker was the "worker in brass." [18] Phoenicians were acknowledged to be the best craftsmen in brass and copper,[19] no doubt Hebrews acquired the trade from them. Bronzeworking flourished most extensively in the time of the united kingdom, due to the fact that, as booty from

---

5 Nah. 3:14.
7 2 Kgs. 12:11.
9 Jer. 10:4.
11 2 Sam. 5:11; 1 Chr. 22:15.
13 2 Kgs. 21:13; Am. 7:7.
15 Jer. 23:29.
17 *Vid. supra,* pp. 198 f.
19 1 Kgs. 7:13 f.

6 2 Sam. 5:11.
8 Jer. 10:3.
10 Isa. 10:15.
12 1 Kgs. 5:17; 6:7; Am. 5:11.
14 Ezk. 40:3.
16 2 Sam. 5:11.
18 Gen. 4:22; 1 Kgs. 7:14.

his successful wars, "King David took exceeding much brass,"[20] and King Solomon's luxurious buildings, especially the temple, were ornamented with bronze.

Smithing in iron apparently was once a Philistine monopoly[21] but after the Philistines were suppressed the Hebrews themselves developed the craft.[22] Workers in iron used hammer, anvil, and bellows.[23] One specialized item of metalworking was locksmithery.[24] Goldsmithing included beaten work,[25] engraving, casting,[26] overlaying,[27] and the making of the fine wire for embroidering.[28]

5. *Tanning.* Tanning was an important trade in Old Testament times because so many skins for holding liquids were needed. It was not an esteemed occupation for it entailed ceremonial defilement through contact with the skins of dead animals. The work was done only because it was so necessary. Tanning was essentially related to the making of clothing, shoes, girdles, and such articles.

6. *Cooks and Bakers.* As a professional class, cooks were to be found only in the houses of the well-to-do. Bakers even had a street in Jerusalem where they plied their trade.[29]

7. *Occupations Related to the Clothing Trade.* These included the weaver,[30] the embroiderer,[31] and the fuller.[32] The fuller's work, like the tanner's, was done outside the city limits; thus the "fuller's field"[33] was outside Jerusalem.

Spinning, weaving, and sewing were chiefly the work of women, but men also engaged in weaving. They spun wool, flax, goat's hair, and perhaps cotton and silk. Each family probably supplied its own materials. Wool and flax in combination were taboo.[34]

Trade and Commerce. The first important stimulus to trade was injected into Hebrew life by Solomon.[35] From then on it steadily expanded, bringing both wealth and wider social and international contacts to the Hebrews. International trade appears to have been subject to royal control and, of course, taxation.

The principal exports from Palestine were corn, oil, wine, balsam, spices, cattle, wool, and fish. Honey, balsam, wheat, and oil were

---

[20] 2 Sam. 8:8.
[21] *Vid. supra,* p. 79.
[22] Cf. Deut. 19:5; 27:5; 2 Kgs. 6:5; Jer. 17:1.
[23] Isa. 44:12; 41:7; Jer. 6:29.
[24] Cf. 2 Kgs. 24:14, 16, Moffatt Version.
[25] Jer. 10:9.
[26] Jer. 10:14.
[27] 2 Kgs. 18:16.
[28] Ex. 39:3.
[29] Jer. 37:21.
[30] 1 Sam. 17:7.
[31] Ex. 35:35.
[32] Isa. 7:3.
[33] 2 Kgs. 18:17.
[34] Deut. 22:11. Lev. 19:19 says *any* "two kinds of stuff." On professions and trades in Bible times, cf. M. S. and J. L. Miller, *Encyclopedia of Bible Life* (New York: 1944), pp. 340–355.
[35] *Vid. supra,* pp. 198 f.

sent to Phoenicia,[36] as also oaks from Bashan.[37] Spices, balm, myrrh, honey, pistachio nuts, almonds, and oil were exported to Egypt.[38] The principal imports mentioned were timber from Phoenicia;[39] grain, horses, and chariots from Egypt;[40] gold and silver, spices, timber, precious stones, ivory, apes and peacocks, gold and silver plate and ornaments, armor, and mules from Arabia, Ophir, and other distant countries;[41] and wool and sheep from Moab.[42]

Within the confines of the Hebrew kingdoms there was also a fairly brisk domestic trade; e.g., in salt from the Dead Sea, city manufactures sold about the country, and foodstuffs from the country, sold in the cities.

Merchants carried their own wares to market or directly to customers. International traffic was generally by caravans of camels,[43] asses,[44] mules,[45] oxen,[46] or even slaves.[47] Merchants engaging in such international trade had quarters assigned to them in the foreign cities.[48]

Trade and commerce necessitated measures, weights, and money. Originally, parts of the human body were used as units of measurement; e.g., the finger's breadth,[49] the handbreadth,[50] the span,[51] and the cubit.[52] A cubit, originally the distance from elbow to finger tip, equaled two spans; a span equaled three handbreadths; and a handbreadth equaled four fingers. Distance was measured in terms of the pace[53] and the "day's journey."[54] The "Sabbath day's journey" was about 2,000 cubits, i.e., the distance the Ark of the Covenant was supposed to precede the Israelites,[55] and therefore the distance it was figured they covered on a Sabbath when they approached to worship at the Ark. It was a little over half a mile. Area was measured in terms of the amount of ground a yoke of oxen could plow in one day[56] or in terms of the amount of seed required to sow the area.[57] The unit of capacity for dry measure was the *seah,* about one and one-half pecks, and for liquid measure the *hin,* about one and one-half gallons; and there were fractions and multiples of each.[58] Weight was indicated in terms of shekels, minas, and talents on the basis of 1 talent = 60 minas = 3,600 shekels. Apparently there existed no such thing as uniform and exact weights, judging from the hetero-

[36] 1 Kgs. 5:11.
[38] Gen. 43:11; Hos. 12:1.
[40] Gen. 41:57; 1 Kgs. 10:28 f.
[42] 2 Kgs. 3:4; Isa. 16:1.
[44] Gen. 42:27.
[46] 1 Chr. 12:40.
[48] Cf. 1 Kgs. 20:34.
[50] 1 Kgs. 7:26.
[52] 1 Kgs. 6:2.
[54] Num. 11:31.
[56] 1 Sam. 14:14.
[37] Ezk. 27:6.
[39] 1 Kgs. 5:8.
[41] 1 Kgs. 10:10–25.
[43] Gen. 37:25.
[45] 2 Kgs. 5:17.
[47] 2 Kgs. 5:23.
[49] Jer. 52:21.
[51] Ex. 28:16.
[53] 2 Sam. 6:13.
[55] Josh. 3:4.
[57] Lev. 27:16; 1 Kgs. 18:32.
[58] For a table of measures and their approximate equivalents, cf. M. S. and J. L. Miller, *Encyclopedia of Bible Life* (New York: 1944), p. 146.

geneous character of the numerous weights found by archaeologists, though we do read of a common standard and a royal standard or "king's weight." [59] The ordinary shekel was slightly less than half an ounce; the talent something over one hundred pounds.

Money was not in the form of coins [60] but of metal bullion, silver and gold, in weights of shekels, minas, and talents. The gold shekel was worth about $10, the mina, about $546, the talent, $32,805. The silver shekel was worth about 62 cents, the mina, about $31, the talent, $1,883. Money always had to be weighed, especially if the parties were strangers to each other. Merchants therefore carried two sets of scales, one to weigh the goods, the other to weigh the money. A very interesting light upon the inferior value which the Hebrews placed upon money is shed by Ex. 22:1, 7 (in the Covenant code, formulated in Solomon's time),[61] which imposes a fine for money theft less than half the fine for cattle theft.

Much trading evidently remained in the hands of Canaanites,[62] the basis of the contemptuous remark in Hos. 12:7. Many merchants were indeed notorious sharpers. Apparently short-weighting and shortchanging were common practices, judging from the prophet Amos's denunciation of such dishonesty.[63]

Manners and Customs of Daily Life

The picture of Hebrew home life and customs outlined on pp. 145–151 is valid also for the period of the kingship. This picture may be amplified by noting the chief manners and customs of daily life.

Birth. Children were highly valued in the home, especially sons, and childlessness was considered a reproach and a punishment. A newborn babe was washed in water, rubbed with salt,[64] and wrapped in swaddling clothes. The mother usually named the child,[65] but not always.[66] A mother was considered ceremonially unclean for forty days after the birth of a son and for eighty days after the birth of a daughter.[67] The first-born, if a son, belonged to Yahweh and had to be redeemed by a gift.[68]

Marriage. Marriage was a simple matter among the peoples of the Bible. Arrangements for a union were in the hands of the parents,

[59] The earliest known Jewish coins were issued in the fourth century B.C., i.e., at the end of the Persian period when Judah was an autonomous province. Cf. Millar Burrows. *What Mean These Stones?* (New Haven: 1941), p. 177 and Fig. 57; M. S. and J. L. Miller, *op. cit.*, p. 140; W. F. Albright in *Bulletin of the American Schools of Oriental Research*, 53 (February, 1934), pp. 20 f., and in the *Biblical Archaeologist*, ix, 1 (February, 1946), pp. 13 ff. and Figs. 8–9. *Vid. infra*, pp. 385 ff.
[60] 2 Sam. 14:26.   [61] *Vid. infra*, p. 284.
[62] Prov. 31:24 RVmarg.   [63] Am. 8:5.
[64] Ezk. 16:4. The idea was to protect the child against evil spirits.
[65] Gen. 29:32; 1 Sam. 1:20; 1 Chr. 4:9.   [66] Gen. 16:15; Ex. 2:22.
[67] Lev. 12.   [68] Ex. 13:12; 34:20.

the children having little choice. The groom's family usually took the
initiative, but now and then the bride's family, if influential, did so.[69]
A daughter was a valuable possession and a dowry was paid for her to
her father,[70] either in money or in work.[71] The money was paid at the
betrothal and it was therefore the betrothal which made her the wife
of her husband and was so regarded by law.[72] Sometimes there was no
ceremony beyond the betrothal,[73] but usually, especially in the later
part of the period, there were wedding festivities following the
betrothal.[74]

Burial. Death was the occasion for much wailing and lamentation, not merely by the family and friends of the deceased but by
professional mourners as well.[75] Wailing began immediately after
a person died. Quick burial was imperative because of the climate.[76]
It was a ceremonial defilement to have a corpse around or to touch
it.[77] The body was carried on a bier,[78] accompanied by a procession
of mourners, with the professional mourning women at the head,
loudly lamenting.[79] Such mourning customs as wailing, rending one's
garments, throwing ashes over one's head, and the like are explained
as due originally to fear of the spirit of the deceased, which had to
be frightened away, and in case it should return, that the living
might be unrecognizable to the spirit.[80] The form of lamentation
for an individual is given in Jer. 22:18;[81] in Lam. 1:16; 3:48 f. it is
applied to the afflicted nation of Judah; and in Ezk. 27:28–36 to
ruined Tyre. There was no religious service attending burial. Burial
was in an ancestral sepulcher if possible. In other cases a public
burying ground was used.[82] Stones were heaped up on ordinary
graves for protection,[83] and stones and pillars were set up occasionally as monuments to the dead.[84]

Reckoning Time. The time of day was indicated by certain characteristic expressions such as "sunrise"; "morning"; "the heat of
the day"[85] for noon; "yet high day"[86] for early afternoon; "the
cool of the day";[87] "the time of the offering of the evening obla-
tion";[88] "the time of evening," "the time that women go out to draw
water";[89] "sunset." Sunset began a new day. There is mention of a

[69] Ex. 2:21; Josh. 15:17; 1 Sam. 18:27.   [70] Gen. 34:12.
[71] Gen. 29:20.   [72] Cf. Deut. 22:23–27.
[73] Gen. 24:63–67.
[74] Jgs. 14 is an example of an older, somewhat unrefined type of marriage.
[75] Jer. 9:17 f.   [76] Gen. 23:1–4.
[77] Num. 19:11 ff.   [78] 2 Sam. 3:31.
[79] Jer. 9:17; Am. 5:16.   [80] Cf. *supra*, pp. 124 f.
[81] Cf. 1 Kgs. 13:30.   [82] Jer. 26:23.
[83] 2 Sam. 18:17; Josh. 7:26 for a reproach.
[84] Gen. 35:20; 2 Sam. 18:18; 2 Kgs. 23:17; Ezk. 39:15.
[85] Gen. 18:1; 1 Sam. 11:11.   [86] Gen. 29:7.
[87] Gen. 3:8; Cant. 2:17.   [88] 1 Kgs. 18:29, 36; Ezr. 9:4; Dan. 9:21.
[89] Gen. 24:11.

sundial, named for King Ahaz, who probably introduced it as a novelty.[90] The night was divided into three "watches." [91]

The days of the week were known by number, the seventh day being the Sabbath. A month extended from new moon to new moon. Prior to the exile, the months were designated by old Canaanite names, of which only four have survived: *Abib,* "the month of the ripening ears," the first month; [92] *Ziv,* "the month of flowers," the second month; [93] *Ethanim,* "month of perennial streams," the seventh month; [94] *Bul,* "rain month," the eighth month.[95] By the time of the exile the months had come to be known by numbers. From the exile on, the Babylonian names for the months were fixed in Jewish usage: (1) *Nisan* = March-April,[96] (2) *Iyyar,* (3) *Sivan,*[97] (4) *Tammuz,* (5) *Ab,* (6) *Elul,*[98] (7) *Tishri,* (8) *Marchesvan,* (9) *Kislev,*[99] (10) *Tebeth,*[100] (11) *Shebat,*[101] (12) *Adar* = February-March.[102] Since a lunar year was about eleven days shorter than a solar year, they added a thirteenth month, *Second Adar,* at intervals in order to keep the calendar in agreement with the seasons.

The seasons of the year were known according to the "former rain" (October) and the "latter rain" (spring equinox) [103] "seed-time"; "harvest," "summer," "winter." [104] Various methods of reckoning the beginning of a year were in vogue, some placing the beginning on the tenth day of the first month,[105] some on the tenth day of the seventh month,[106] indicating, possibly, a difference between a civil year and a religious festival year. Ultimately it became fixed for the first day of the seventh month.[107] Chronology was reckoned according to significant events.[108] or by the years of monarchs.[109]

Travel. Traveling was always for necessity, never for pleasure. As a rule, travel was on foot, but quite often it was by camel back,[110] or by asses [111] or mules.[112] People always traveled in their best clothes.[113] At night they were entertained in homes, which hospi-

---

90 2 Kgs. 20 :9 ff.; Isa. 38 :8.
91 Ex. 14 :24; Jgs. 7 :19; 1 Sam. 11 :11.
92 Ex. 13 :4.   93 1 Kgs. 6 :1.
94 1 Kgs. 8 :2.   95 1 Kgs. 6 :38.
96 Neh. 2 :1.   97 Est. 8 :9.
98 Neh. 6 :15.   99 Neh. 1 :1.
100 Est. 2 :16.   101 Zech. 1 :7.
102 Est. 3 :7.   103 Deut. 11 :14.
104 Gen. 8 :22.   105 Ezk. 40 :1.
106 Lev. 25 :9. Cf. Nelson Glueck, *The Other Side of the Jordan* (New Haven: 1940), pp. 191 f.
107 Lev. 23 :23 ff., Num. 29 :1 ff.
108 Am. 1 :1; Isa. 20 :1; Ezk. 1 :2; Ezr. 3 :8; Isa. 6 :1.
109 This variation in the beginning of years, their difference from our own way of reckoning, the overlapping of a monarch's first year with the last year of his predecessor, all unite to make the calculation of year dates for Old Testament history very perplexing.
110 Gen. 24 :64.   111 Num. 22 :22.   112 2 Sam. 18 :9.
113 Cf. the fascinating story in Josh. 9. The Gibeonites wear tattered clothing to deceive Joshua into supposing they had traveled "from a very far country."

tality they could claim as a right.[114] When traveling, especially to and from the great national feasts at Jerusalem, the people had their chief opportunity for wider social intercourse.

Bargaining. Trading had its peculiar customs. A buyer, upon approaching a seller, saluted the man before stating what he wanted. His salutation was a wish that the day might be happy and profitable to the seller, who thereupon returned the salutation with some good wish. The buyer then stated his real desire, though often he had a go-between make a preliminary overture.[115] There followed an animated banter about the price, the seller seeking to get as much as possible, the buyer to pay as little as possible, both finally coming to an agreement. A deal was concluded by the seller's naming the price and saying, "What is that between me and thee?" The purchaser would remark, doubtless in a tone of reluctant submission to an overcharge, though inwardly rejoicing in the good bargain he had driven, "It is naught; it is naught"; then, "when he is gone his way, he boasteth." [116] Picturesque descriptions of trading that proceeded according to the best conventions are in the account of Abraham's purchase of the cave of Machpelah (Gen. *23:5–16) and in the account of David's purchase of the threshing floor (2 Sam. *24:18–24; 1 Chr. 21:18–25). In each case the seller, following the fixed formula, told the purchaser to help himself for nothing. The buyer then avowed he would pay the full price. Finally after much shrewd talk, the two agreed on a price. It is interesting to note, in Gen. 23:17 f., that "all the trees that were in the field, that were in all the border thereof round about, were made sure unto Abraham for a possession." Otherwise Ephron could have legally claimed the fruit on those trees, even if Abraham did own the field. Isa. 55:1 may be an adaptation by the prophet of a huckster's street cry.

Courtesy in Social Relationships. The Hebrew people possessed a strong sense of personal dignity, and their attitude toward one another was characterized by extreme courtesy and respect. This courtesy manifested itself in certain formalities, especially that of salutation.[117] Every message, matter of business, or conversation was preceded by a salutation, and no one was excused from such courtesy. There were special greetings upon such occasions as the birth of a son, marriage, the return of a friend from a journey, receiving refreshment from a host, meeting a fellow traveler, paying respect to officials, and the like. The salute of reverence was to stand erect.[118] The prescribed ritual in seeking a favor was to kneel and clasp and

[114] Gen. 18:1–8; 19:2 f.; Jgs. 19:14–21.
[115] Gen. 23:8.   [116] Prov. 20:14.
[117] Cf. Gen. 32:17–20; 33:3 f.; 45:14 f.; 1 Sam. 25:23–31.
[118] Gen. 18:8.

kiss the feet of the person asked.[119] Relatives and friends kissed each other on the cheek.[120] Respect was shown by children to parents and by servants to masters by bowing and kissing the hand. They never failed to ask after the health of one another upon meeting,[121] and upon parting the word of farewell was a benediction.[122] For both hail and farewell, the salutation was, "Peace be unto you." [123] We may remind ourselves that the gracious custom of hospitality never passed out of Hebrew life.[124]

The Hebrew had a deep sense of social solidarity. He was first of all a member of his family, then of his tribe, and finally of his nation. What bulked largest in his thought and counted most with him was the welfare of his group, not his own individuality.

The Use of Leisure. The Hebrews were a serious people; yet there are many hints of an innate lightheartedness and readiness to play when they had a chance. Children played in the streets.[125] Weddings, the harvest festivals, and the religious feasts were the only holidays for adults. Jer. 31:12 f. characterizes the holiday mood. Most of this play seems to have been impromptu. They probably made up their dance steps as they went along. It is doubtful if there were any competitive sports in the sense that is generally meant by that term now, though 2 Sam. 2:12–17 would indicate that friendly contests of skill were not unknown. Neither is there any hint that they indulged in the brutal sport of "spectacles," or "baiting" of animals or persons, such as the Philistines brought with them from Crete, as revealed in the story of how Samson, after being blinded by his enraged captors, was forced to "make sport for them . . . when their hearts were merry." [126]

In the excavation of Tell Beit Mirsim (Kiriath-sepher) there was found a set of backgammon pieces consisting of five little three-cornered pyramids and five little cones, all of faience, and a die of ivory shaped like a truncated pyramid. The board on which the game was played did not come to light. These pieces were found on the level of 1600 B.C. Backgammon is still a favorite game with Syrians. It is not an idle play of fancy to think of the Biblical Hebrews playing the same game. Game boards, some as old as 2500 B.C., even 5000 B.C., have been found by archaeologists in Egypt and in Babylonia, one of the most exquisite being that of Queen Shub-Ad of ancient Ur.[127] No doubt the most common form of amusement was exchanging stories.

[119] 2 Kgs. 4:27. [120] Gen. 27:27; Ex. 4:27. [121] Ex. 18:7.
[122] Ruth 1:9, 14; 1 Sam. 20:42; 2 Sam. 19:39.
[123] Jgs. 19:20. The exact form of this greeting is used by the Moslems to this day.
[124] Vid. supra, p. 90. [125] Zech. 8:5. [126] Jgs. 16:25.
[127] Cf. Leonard Woolley, Ur Excavations (1934), ii, pp. 274 f., 277 f., and Plate 95; M. S. and J. L. Miller, op. cit., pp. 391 f.

Social Organization and Control

As we look back over the long period of the Hebrews' residence in Canaan, from the conquest and settlement to the end of the monarchy, the most impressive social fact is the profound cultural transition which the Hebrews underwent, from nomadism to agriculture and small village life to complex city life with its social classes and its vexing community problems. The first comers in Canaan settled in the hills and only slowly, with the lapse of many decades, filtered down to the plains. This cultural transition proceeded at an uneven pace, differing in different sections of Palestine. In barren and rocky Judah the Hebrews of necessity longest retained shepherd life. Central Canaan (Samaria) was the haven of the planter, and here the transition was more rapid. Galilee and Eastjordania rated somewhere between.

The Agrarian Basis of Hebrew Society. Basically, the Hebrews were a people of the soil. As a rule, farmers owned land in common. Yet an individual might own his own plot, title to which passed to his son. Basic to the Hebrew law of real estate was the idea that land was the inalienable property of the clan, held in fee from Yahweh, its real owner. Therefore if a Hebrew was for any cause compelled to sell any part of his patrimony, it became the duty of his next of kin to redeem it.[128] Instances of this law in operation are in Ruth *4:1–11 and Jer. *32:6–12. When the basic right of the individual landowner was violated by rich oppressors, there were likely to be prophets to denounce the injustice.[129] This basic principle operated on one memorable occasion with far-reaching national consequences (1 Kgs. 21).

The landowner usually worked his plot with the help of his own family and his slaves. There were but few hired laborers, and Deut. 24:14 f. shows how graciously their economic well-being was expected to be provided for. Slaves were numerous, but their social position was not by any means debased. They were members of the household of their master, shared his friendship, were often entrusted with great and delicate responsibilities, and joined with the family in the religious festivals. While most slaves were doubtless foreigners who had been either bought abroad or captured in wars, even the free Hebrew might be reduced to slavery, e.g., if unable to meet his debts.[130] But in the later days of the monarchy a vicious social oppression set in, when the wealthy expropriated the lands of the peasants and reduced large numbers to hirelings or slaves, as Mic.

---

[128] Lev. 25:23 ff.   [129] Mic. 2:2.   [130] Cf. Am. 8:6.

2:2 so tersely but vividly discloses. Yet the lot of such slaves was not hopeless; a praiseworthy law (Ex. 21:2–6) provided for their release after six years. But this statute, like so many others found in their law books, was evidently not enforced.[131]

The Status of the Family. As has already been pointed out,[132] the Hebrew family was the unit of all their social institutions. With them, however, the term family meant something more and different from what it does with us. It included all those persons—married or unmarried, slave or free—who belonged to the extensive households of the clan chiefs or "heads of houses," as they were called. Therefore a family corresponded more nearly to what we mean by a small clan.

In governmental affairs, each such family was entitled to one vote. This meant that the head of the family did the voting, and that in municipal affairs there were as many elders as there were families in the city. Even after they decided to have a king, the popular sentiment was strong for keeping every possible right and prerogative of the separate family.

Within the family circle, the authority of its head had so long been supreme as to retain most of the powers of a petty despot even after corporate statehood had been some time in existence. He continued to arrange all marriages, buy and sell all chattels (which might include members of the family), and discipline all its members as of old. He held the power of life and of death, although when community life and collective governmental control grew stronger these absolute powers of the family head were gradually modified.

Community Organization. In general, the Hebrew villager's world was the local community. As a rule each little community was self-sufficient; its folks made what things they needed, and bartered among themselves. The social horizon was scarcely farther off than the fringes of each little valley with its encompassing hills. Yet in spite of everything it was a relatively easy transition from nomadic social organization to neighborhood community, for the community simply replaced the clan and social control continued, as it had always been, in the hands of the elders.

Now and then the horizon widened. This was usually when exacting demands were forced upon the villagers, e.g., when hostile foes had to be dealt with. It was in this way that there came to be "judges," as we have seen, persons having no fixed status in the government but serving as local leaders to see their fellow Hebrews through a particular crisis. The elders managed local affairs. This

---

[131] Cf. Jer. 34:8–22, and *supra,* pp. 268 f.   [132] *Supra,* pp. 89 f.

supervision was mainly of a judicial nature. They also negotiated with the elders of other communities when occasion required. Sometimes harder questions arose, of more than routine significance; the elders then sought the help of the priest, who added a divine sanction to social adjustments.[133] Thus the influence of the priest was enhanced and on this basis it is easy to account for the rise of a man like Samuel.

The Rise of an Aristocracy. From the foregoing it is plain that Hebrew society was democratic in spirit and pretty much on one level, but there came a time when it became two-storied, and then three. After the kingship became well established, an aristocracy arose. Government became centralized at the capital city. The king appointed officials and they, with the friends they drew to themselves, cliqued together and formed an aristocracy made up of princes, nobles, priests, army officers and the wealthy. David created officials, Solomon added to their number, and in time "princes of the provinces" were fastened on Hebrew society. They represented not the people, but the king. The elders of the city likewise ceased to derive their authority from their community; it came down from the king. Furthermore, the elders' influence in judicial matters waned in proportion as the king became the supreme judicial power. Local military leaders, such as the "judges" had been, were replaced by the king's officers; the army, recruited from foreign mercenaries, put military force back of the aristocracy. Priests also moved up to the top social level, for they were likewise the king's appointees. Thus the masses were left behind. But they were not wholly voiceless. There arose prophets in Israel, men from the level of the soil, a herdsman like Amos, a farmer like Micah, who championed the cause of social justice against the iniquity of class distinctions and class oppression.

The quality of the Hebrew monarchy varied, naturally, with the personal characteristics of the kings. There were good kings and there were ravenous and unrestrained rulers who made the lot of the people bitter. 1 Sam. *8:11–17 is a commentary on the burdensome nature of the monarchy. Deut. 17:14–20 defines and restricts the king's powers and (vs. 20) states the Hebrew ideal regarding a king's status, "that his heart be not lifted up above his brethren." It deserves to be remarked that, in comparison with other contemporary oriental despotisms, the Hebrews enjoyed a good measure of personal freedom.

The Administration of Justice. There never were any formally constituted courts of law in the sense that we mean today. Justice

---

[133] The priests determined their judgments by employing the sacred lot, i.e., the *ephod* and the *Urim* and *Thummim*. Cf. *supra*, p. 134. Such a judgment was accepted by all concerned as the very will of Yahweh, as *Torah*, i.e., "direction," or "law."

was dispensed originally by the elders. They sat in the city gate [134] and heard accusers and accused before witnesses. Most matters doubtless were determined by the taking of an oath.[135] Under the monarchy justice was dispensed by the king and by judges. The Josianic reform in 621 B.C. abolished all local sanctuaries in the land and centralized religious worship at the Jerusalem temple. This meant that there were no longer the local community priests to decide matters of controversy and issue judgments. Therefore provision was made for lay judges (Deut. 16:18 f.), with further provision for a court of appeal at the central sanctuary (Jerusalem) composed of the Jerusalem priests plus a layman judge (Deut. 17: 8–11). Ultimately it came about that the priests were the sole custodians of the law.

1. *Law Codes.* There are two sets of laws in the Old Testament which belong specifically to the period of the kingship. One is the code of laws found in Ex. 20:23–23:19, commonly called the *Book of the Covenant* from the title by which it is referred to in Ex. 24:7. The formulation of this code is assigned to the early period of the monarchy, i.e., the time of Solomon. But the social conditions mirrored in it are those of the premonarchical period in Canaan, i.e., before the king became the commanding judicial figure which he did later on. This *Book of the Covenant* embodies the civil and criminal code of early Israel; Ex. 21:1–32 gives the laws relating to persons; 21:33–22:17, the laws of property; and 22:22–27 and 23:1–9, some noteworthy social laws. We shall consider the religious laws of this code in a later chapter.[136]

The other set of laws is found in the Book of Deuteronomy and belongs to a much later century than the *Book of the Covenant*. In the year 621 B.C., King Josiah of Judah ordered the Jerusalem temple to be repaired. In connection with this work a certain "book of the law" was found in the temple.[137] This book, called "this book of the covenant" in 2 Kgs. 23:21, became the basis for certain revolutionary religious reforms put through by Josiah (2 Kgs. 23:4–27). The book has not come down to us in the form in which it existed in 621 B.C., but is embedded in the Book of Deuteronomy, chapters 12–26, 28).[138] This "D" code is commonly understood to be the product of men who

[134] Am. 5:15. At Tell en-Nasbeh (Mizpah) an entire city gate was uncovered by archaeologists, with the stone seats where the judges sat. Cf. C. C. McCown, *The Ladder of Progress in Palestine* (New York: 1943), pp. 211 f.
[135] 1 Kgs. 8:31 f.; cf. Gen. 14:22; Deut. 32:40; *vid. supra*, p. 183.
[136] *Vid. infra*, pp. 305 f. The entire code is admirably discussed in J. A. Bewer's *The Literature of the Old Testament* (New York: 1922), pp. 30–42; also J. M. P. Smith, *The Origin and History of Hebrew Law* (Chicago: 1931), pp. 15–38.
[137] 2 Kgs. 22:8.
[138] *Vid. infra*, pp. 332 ff.; the "D" code is discussed in Bewer, *op. cit.*, pp. 121–135, and J. M. P. Smith, *op. cit.*, pp. 39–69.

were under the influence of the preaching of the great Hebrew prophets and who formulated the code during the time of King Manasseh.

Since at least three centuries separate the two codes, a comparison of them will show the progress in social standards during the intervening period. Such a comparison reveals that the horizons of social justice have indeed widened.

2. *Standards of Social Justice.* Taking the Hebrew legislation as a whole, we find that the ideas of social justice are of a remarkably high order and that they command universal respect when the conditions under which they operated and the abuses they sought to correct are fully understood. There is here much closer approximation to a true democratic spirit than appears in the Code of Hammurabi.[139] Hebrew law did discriminate between Hebrew citizens, unnaturalized foreigners, and non-Hebrew slaves, but the discrimination was mild for its age. There is, in fact, many a sign of an innate humanitarianism which only awaited an opportunity to express itself. Thus the iron law of blood revenge inherited from desert days was gradually mitigated by provisions for impartial and unimpassioned trials. Compare in this connection the implacable penalties of Ex. *21:12–17 with the much modified regulations of Deut. *19:4–13. Even the oft-quoted "eye for eye, and tooth for tooth" principle ought probably to be recognized as a *not more than* "an eye for an eye, and [*not more than*] a tooth for a tooth" limitation of the old savage blood vengeance spirit that gloated over a "seventy and sevenfold" retaliation.[140]

Similar social ideals, groping for expression in the later period of the kingship, may be seen in numerous other laws and appeals to the conscience that found their way into the Book of Deuteronomy. The following are typical of this social trend. There is the injunction that at every great harvest and tithing festival the servants, the orphans, and widows of the neighborhood, the propertyless Levites, and the casual stranger be all invited to the banqueting;[141] there is the command that every third year a tithe of the entire year's products be turned over for distribution among this same group of the nation's poor;[142] there is the appeal that Hebrew slaves, when set free at the end of the six years for which it was legally possible to hold them in servitude, be liberally supplied by their masters with food and animals for a fresh start in life for themselves;[143] and there is a

---

[139] On the Code of Hammurabi, cf. *supra,* pp. 47 f., 68 ff. For a comparison of the laws of Hammurabi with the Covenant Code and with the Deuteronomic Code as well, cf. Barton, *Archaeology and the Bible,* pp. 378–406.
[140] Cf. Ex. 21:23 ff. with Gen. 4:23 f.   [141] Deut. 12:17 ff., 16:10 ff.
[142] Deut. 14:28 f., with which cf. the older legislation of Ex. 22:21–24.
[143] Deut. 15:12–18, with which cf. Ex. 21:2–6.

judicial decision that the picking of grapes or grain *to be eaten on the spot* was not theft.[144] A similar import and motive is to be seen in the regulation that no one might be deprived of his millstone under any circumstances,[145] and in the prohibition against taking interest from a fellow Hebrew.[146] Ex. 22:25 has a regulation about the taking of interest, but it is less explicit than its later Deuteronomic parallel.

Other interesting laws that show a humanitarian trend are the following: that children might not be put to death merely because their parents had committed an offense that involved the death penalty;[147] that convictions might not be made on the testimony of less than two or three witnesses;[148] and that oxen might not be muzzled when at work on the threshing floor.[149]

3. *The Status of Women.* Evidence of progress in social standards is seen further in the laws which reveal the status of women. The early Covenant code deals first with the status of slaves (Ex. 21:2–6) and *next* with that of women (21:7–11)! A woman was a piece of property. If a man bought a wife, he could not resell her to another man; but if a man bought a slave girl, he could resell her to another Hebrew when he chose. That was the whole difference between the wife and the female slave. The seduction of a virgin is treated (Ex. 22:16 f.) in the group of offenses against property (Ex. 22:7–17) and is the last (!) item in the list.

Turning to the "D" code, we find a more enlightened conception of woman's status in that she is regarded less as a piece of property and more as a person. For example, in the release of Hebrew slaves in the seventh year, the Covenant code applies this only to men slaves;[150] "D" applies it to women slaves as well,[151] and furthermore prescribes considerate treatment for women captives of war.[152] Ex. 21:16 restricts the law against kidnapping to men; Deut. 24:7 does not. Again, Deut. 22:13–29 is a series of regulations safeguarding women and prescribing punishment for a guilty person, whether man or woman, without discrimination. Further, it was "D" that required a husband, when expelling a wife from his household, to give her a clean "bill of divorcement."[153]

In sum, this progress in woman's position in Hebrew society is to be seen in the fact that the authors who at a later time than 621 B.C. embodied the "D" code in our present Book of Deuteronomy, in their recension of the Ethical Decalogue (the Ten Commandments, Deut. 5:6–21) so worded the tenth commandment as to put "thou shalt not

---

144 Deut. 23:24 f.
146 Deut. 23:19 f.
148 Deut. 17:6.
150 Ex. 21:7.
152 Deut. 21:10–14.

145 Deut. 24:6.
147 Deut. 24:16.
149 Deut. 25:4.
151 Deut. 15:12–17.
153 Deut. 24:1–4.

covet thy neighbor's wife" before the command "thou shalt not covet thy neighbor's house." [154]

Admirable as was the *Book of the Covenant* (Ex. 20:23–23:19) in its obvious striving for strict and impartial justice, one cannot fail to be struck by its many significant omissions of laws and their social interpretations with which the later Book of Deuteronomy abounds. "D" is evidence that the insight of the prophets was making its influence felt at last.

Achievements in the Artistic

Architecture. Architecture has ever been one of the impressive evidences of civilization. The sky lines of our big cities, the stupendous constructions of architect and builder, the graceful lines that distinguish cathedral and towering church are things that impress the traveler with the quality of the mind that gave them birth.

In architecture, Hebrew talent appears to have been at its weakest. There never was developed a distinctive Hebrew style. Every important building that we know about, from Solomon's temple to the temple of Herod, was copied with little modification from Egyptian, or Phoenician, or Babylonian, or (in New Testament times) from Graeco-Roman patterns. Even tombs, such as those still extant in the valley of Jehoshaphat, near Jerusalem, point unmistakably to Egypt. When an especially magnificent structure was to be erected, a palace or a temple, the Hebrews sought foreign assistance, as in the case of Solomon's buildings.

The greatest achievement in building prior to the exile was the elaborate program of construction carried out by King Solomon in Jerusalem. This included the temple of Yahweh, the imposing halls of state, the luxurious palaces, the spacious courts, and the sumptuous furnishings.[155] Happily, this is all described for us in fascinating detail in 1 Kgs. *5–7 and in the much later composition, 2 Chr. 3 f.[156]

Of all these structures, the most important was the temple. Its dimensions, 90 feet long by 30 feet wide by 45 feet high,[157] make it seem insignificant in size to moderns accustomed to the huge cathedrals and churches which adorn some of our greater cities, until we realize that unlike modern edifices the temple was not a place for the assembling of worshipers. It was a dwelling place for Yahweh. Worshipers used the courts in front of the temple. The temple faced the east and contained two rooms. One was the most sacred shrine,

---

[154] Deut. 5:21. Cf. Ex. 20:17.   [155] *Vid. supra,* pp. 196 f.
[156] These narratives will be more interesting if read in a modern version, preferably the Chicago Version or the Moffatt Version.
[157] 1 Kgs. 6:2, reckoning one cubit as 18 inches; so both Chicago and Moffatt versions.

the oracle (*debîr*), known as the Holy of Holies, at the rear (western end) of the interior; the dividing partition was at a "space of thirty feet" from the rear.[158] The other room, known as the *hêkâl* (temple), the Holy Place, was at the eastern end of the building and was the nave into which the entrance opened directly. The Biblical narrative revels in the wealth and labor expended on this structure, the enormous blocks of stone, the cedar and olive-wood panels and carvings, the rich inlaid work of ivory and precious stones, the platings of precious metals, gold, silver, and bronze, and the two impressive bronze columns which adorned the porch of the temple.

Adjacent to the outer court which surrounded the temple were the other sumptuous buildings which Solomon erected. The dimensions of two of these are cited. The "Forest of Lebanon House" was 150 feet in length, 75 feet in breadth, and 45 feet in height. The "Hall of Pillars" measured 75 feet in length by 45 feet broad. The dimensions are not given for the king's palace, the "Porch for Judgment," or the "House for Pharaoh's Daughter," but the narrative does state that all these structures were on the same scale of grandeur.

All this is indeed very impressive, but it bears no testimony to any skill on the part of the Hebrews in designing or in mechanical arts. The skilled work was executed by foreigners imported from Phoenicia, special mention being made of a Tyrian half-breed Hiram (not to be confused with the Hiram who was king of Tyre) who fashioned the bronze furnishings and adornments of the temple. Hebrews performed only the heavy manual labor.

All other Hebrew structures—dwelling houses, city walls, and the like—followed the architecture of the Canaanite towns that were in Palestine before the Hebrew settlement began. Such towns were small and compact, built with a view to defense, and both surrounding walls and enclosed dwellings were planned for security rather than from considerations of the artistic. Upon some spur on a mountain slope or some elevation in the midst of a plain, thick and steeply sloping walls of sun-dried bricks or stone were placed in such position as to take advantage of the natural inclines, and then the enclosed area was almost completely filled with one- or two-room houses, packed tightly together with only the narrowest of alleys running among them. The cities were not planned; they happened.

In the great capital cities of Jerusalem and Samaria there were, of course, much stronger structures and much finer workmanship, especially in the additions and reconstructions of later periods. Archaeologists have, for example, laid bare the foundations of King

---

[158] 1 Kgs. 6:16.

Ahab's palace in Samaria. But in the earlier period of Hebrew residence in Canaan, and in the less important towns generally, the work was for the most part crude. They simply built the walls high enough, steep enough, and smooth enough not to be readily scaled either by hand and foot or by scaling ladders. In his devastating campaign of 701 B.C., the Assyrian Sennacherib states that he besieged, captured, and plundered forty-six of the strong, walled cities of Judah.[159] In very recent years archaeological excavations at Lachish, at Tell en-Nasbeh (Mizpah of Benjamin), and at Tell Beit Mirsim (Kiriath-sepher) have uncovered thick city walls; e.g., the west wall at Tell en-Nasbeh was twenty-six feet thick, the thickest and strongest wall yet unearthed in Palestine. In his *Annals,* Sennacherib testifies to the difficulty his soldiers experienced in taking such walled cities "by the use of earthen ramps and the onslaught of siege engines, [by] the attack of storming on foot, [by] tunneling, cutting, and breaches." Interestingly enough, 2 Chr. 32:5 states that Hezekiah, in fortifying Jerusalem's defenses to withstand Sennacherib's siege, "strengthened Millo." This Millo was either a rampart or a fortress tower that was built by Solomon.[160] A large city had an inner citadel or "strong tower" [161] to which the defenders could retreat for a last stand.

A city itself consisted almost exclusively of one-room, one-storied structures of sun-dried brick and mud. The few wealthier homes might be more pretentious in size and of common field stones filled in with mud. In rare instances roughly dressed quarry stones have been found. There were no yards. The houses were even built right up to the city walls so that the city wall formed one wall of the dwelling. Further economies of space, materials, and labor were effected by building a house up against a neighbor's so that one side wall served two structures. The houses had flat roofs which were much used for the additional floor space they provided.

The narrow streets also ran tortuously wherever the contour of the surface or the line of the city wall determined the line of the houses. At certain intersections, however, necessity decreed that the streets must widen out, and these were the "broad places" and "market places." [162]

Sculpture, Carving, and Related Arts. There is no evidence of the Hebrews having tried their hand at sculpture. In place of it they did a certain amount of casting of both human and animal figures, and also wood carvings, some of which they ornamented with metal overlay. Details of decoration of the temple give examples of

---

[159] *Vid. supra,* pp. 256 ff.
[161] Jgs. 9:51; 1 Kgs. 16:18.
[160] 1 Kgs. 9:24.
[162] Prov. 1:20; Jer. 5:1.

such surface decorations, of "carved figures of cherubim and palm trees and open flowers," [163] of "lions, oxen, and cherubim." [164] In the line of metal castings, the most famous examples are the twelve bronze bulls that stood in the temple court until its plunder by Nebuchadrezzar,[165] Moses' brazen serpent, destroyed by King Hezekiah in a moment of religious zeal,[166] and the two golden calves set up by King Jeroboam when Israel seceded from under the Jerusalem kings.[167] Famous examples of wooden figures with metal overlay are the two cherubim that stood in the innermost room of Solomon's temple.[168] They are described as golden, winged figures of (apparently) human form, whose elevated wing tips reached a height of about fifteen feet. The descriptions given are suggestive of kinship with Egyptian art. The horses of the sun, mentioned in 2 Kgs. 23:11, were probably of similar overlay. As to the quality of this art there is no longer means of judging, since all of it was doubtless plundered and melted up long before the Christian era.

Vastly more numerous were the figures in clay which ranged all the way from the ashteroth, which were little figurines of the goddess Ashtart [169] to huge idolatrous images like those used in the gruesome human sacrifices of the god Molech. Many such clay figures have been found in the ruins of Palestine, but not much can be said for any of them as works of art. Clearly the Hebrews did not excel in this direction either.

Pottery. In pottery, as in most of the other arts, the Hebrews of early times trailed behind their Canaanite contemporaries. As nomads of the desert they had been entirely satisfied with the unbreakable and durable leather "bottle" made from the whole skin of sheep or goat, and this type they retained through the centuries. They did finally adopt the earthen vessels made by Canaanites and Philistines but mainly for uses to which skins could not conveniently be put, and for holding stores of grain, dried fruits, and the like following the harvest. A fair amount of better made and more beautifully decorated vases, flasks, and cups made by Philistines and Phoenicians has come to light in the mounds of Palestine, but for the most part the Hebrews seem to have been content with the plain utilitarian varieties. Later on, when the Hebrew craftsmen included potters, their best products were of a decadent hybrid type, half Phoenician and half Canaanite in motif.

Textiles. In textiles the Hebrews preferred warmth and durability to all other qualities. Their tent coverings and outer garments

---

[163] 1 Kgs. 6:29, 32, 35.
[165] 1 Kgs. 7:25; Jer. 52:20.
[167] 1 Kgs. 12:28.
[169] Jgs. 2:13.

[164] 1 Kgs. 7:29, 36.
[166] Num. 21:9; 2 Kgs. 18:4.
[168] 1 Kgs. 6:23–28.

had also to be waterproof, for which reason they were commonly made of goat's hair, although wool was sometimes used. Such clothes were necessarily thick and heavy and were spun, dyed, and woven by hand on the simplest conceivable sort of loom in the home.

Linen and cotton weaves are also mentioned frequently, and even silk is named. Apparently all these were imported goods, at least in the earlier period of Hebrew history. They long symbolized luxury.

In one branch of the textile industry it now appears that the Hebrews did make creditable progress. This was in dyeing. Dye works of surprising extensiveness have been discovered in ruins that date from a comparatively early era, showing that the liking for the "coat of many colors" [170] was an ingrained racial trait. This age-old love of color has persisted to the present day in the striped cloak of the Syrian shepherd.

Home Furnishings.   In a one-room house that must shelter the family cow, sheep, and goat on cold, wet nights, one does not expect to find an abundance of furnishings or decorations. The average Hebrew home assuredly had little enough. Until Solomon built his palace, even royalty boasted next to nothing in the way of furniture. Amos, two centuries later, does refer to beds of ivory [171] and to silken bed cushions,[172] but these, undoubtedly importations possessed by few, have no bearing upon the study of Hebrew culture save to emphasize the improbability that these luxuries represented Hebrew art. The same may be said of the long list of feminine trinkets and toilet accessories named in Isaiah's ditty (Isa. 3:18–23).

The average Hebrew home was barren in the extreme. Unlighted save for one or two small openings high up toward the ceiling, and with only a bare dirt floor, one can almost count the separate articles of equipment upon the fingers. Aside from the jars and "bottles" holding the winter's supply of foodstuffs, there were only a stone mill for grinding the grain, a wooden or clay "trough" in which to mix the dough, a clay bowl on whose inverted bottom dough was baked (although a stone would serve just about as well), or possibly a small clay furnace, a knife of flint or bronze, one or two clay lamps, and a few flasks, small jars, and baskets for a day's supply of water, oil, fruits, and the like. Now and then there was a home with part of the floor boarded over. Occasionally one was found to boast a wooden bed. Ordinarily the average citizen slept in his day clothes, with just his cloak wrapped about him, on a straw mat spread on the dirt floor.

---

[170] Gen. 37:3. Cf. C. C. McCown, *op. cit.,* pp. 94 f.
[171] Am. 6:4.
[172] Am. 3:12.

Music and Dancing. People of strong emotions ever tend to express themselves through music, the dance, poetry, and dramatic action. The earlier Hebrew narratives suggest that these tendencies were deeply ingrained in Hebrew nature. They sang and danced in times of victory; they burst into song as they worked in the harvest field or when they found water in digging a well; they played and sang in religious ecstasy before Ark and local shrine; they improvised and acted out their great national and personal emotional experiences. All this was as natural to them as breathing. In some directions their art was crude and unfinished; in others it was remarkably fine; but much of it was, perhaps, just ordinary for those times.[173]

Their music was possibly the worst of their artistic efforts. From what can be learned about the art, all their music was of a loud and piercing nature, emphasizing rhythm, and lacking sweetness. Their musical instruments were evidently rather primitive even down to relatively late times, and were limited to stringed instruments of the small harp variety, wind instruments like the pipe and simple flute, and harsh percussion instruments like cymbals.

The harp and the lyre (psaltery) were the principal stringed instruments. Gen. 4:21 assigns the invention of the harp to Jubal. These instruments were chiefly used to accompany songs, generally of a happy character. They were used at feasts of the rich.[174] They were played in processions on certain occasions.[175] 1 Sam. 16:23 is an instance of the use of the harp for mental healing. The use of the pipe, or simple flute, is indicated in connection with religious groups,[176] occasions of national rejoicing akin to a holiday,[177] festal processions of pilgrims,[178] occasions of mourning,[179] and even at drunken revels.[180] A trumpet was used for giving signals in war,[181] for announcing important public events,[182] for sounding an alarm,[183] and the like.

It is doubtful if the Hebrews ever attempted anything in music beyond the solo and unison variety. As a rule the music of instruments was accompanied by singing and dancing. Laban regretted his son-in-law Jacob's stealthy departure and would have preferred to give him a send-off "with mirth and with songs, with tabret and with harp." [184] No doubt there were often occasions when a bard alone sang his

[173] Cf. W. F. Albright, *Archaeology and the Religion of Israel* (Baltimore: 1942), pp. 14, 125–128; O. R. Sellers, "Musical Instruments of Israel." *The Biblical Archaeologist,* iv, 3 (September, 1941), pp. 33–47; M. S. and J. L. Miller, *Encyclopedia of Bible Life* (New York: 1944), pp. 284–293.

[174] Am. 6:5; Isa. 5:12; 14:11.   [175] 1 Sam. 10:5; 2 Sam. 6:5.
[176] 1 Sam. 10:5.   [177] 1 Kgs. 1:40.
[178] Isa. 30:29.   [179] Jer. 48:36; cf. Matt. 9:23.
[180] Isa. 5:12.   [181] Jgs. 3:27.
[182] 1 Kgs. 1:34, 39.   [183] Hos. 5:8.
[184] Gen. 31:27.

ditty; Isa. 5:1 f. suggests an instance of this in the case of the prophet Isaiah. As a rule, however, singing was in chorus, either in unison or antiphonal. 2 Sam. 19:35 implies that King David had singing men and singing women at his court. Ex. 15:20 f. is a famous example of antiphonal singing, Miriam doubtless singing the first line: "Sing ye to Yahweh, for he hath triumphed gloriously"; the accompanying women responding: "The horse and his rider hath he thrown into the sea." From this beginning there was to develop (centuries later than 586 B.C.) the majestic rhythm of the psalms.

Dancing appears to have been entirely of the folk and ceremonial type and was evidently for the free release of emotions. The character of the dancing is revealed in the very words which refer to it which signify making merry, circling or whirling, leaping wildly or for joy. Anything like the modern social dance may be said to have been unknown. At the joyous sacrificial feasts, when crowds streamed into the sanctuary or into the open space about the village altar, dressed in gayest attire to eat and to drink and to make merry together, dancing before their deity was a natural adjunct. The dance of Miriam (sister of Moses) and the women of Israel, mentioned in Ex. 15:20 f. was possibly part of an ancient ceremony connected with the Passover. Isa. 30:29 assumes that the dance was a genuine part of an act of worship. Jgs. 21:19 ff. tells of the girls of Shiloh dancing in the vineyards at a festival which was a "feast of Yahweh." 2 Sam. 6:14 tells about the whirling dance of King David at the head of the religious procession in which the Ark was brought to Jerusalem. In 1 Kgs. 18:21 the prophet Elijah sarcastically asks the people, "How long go ye limping between the two sides?" The "limping" alludes to ritual dance steps performed about the altars. He meant that they couldn't dance to two gods at once.

A similar spontaneity is found in their folk songs and lyrics. They never wrote drama, so far as we know, but their literature is conspicuously dramatic.[185]

Literature

In two important realms of cultural interest the Hebrews were truly creative—in literature and in religion. Their literature is a religious literature. The Bible is indeed the masterpiece of all literature.

The Hebrews absorbed many an element of culture from the Canaanites, but not literature. True, Egypt and Babylonia had produced some fine literature before the Hebrews emerged into history, but this had only an indirect and meager influence on the Hebrews

[185] For a summary of archaeology's disclosure of art in the ancient world, cf. Millar Burrows, *What Mean These Stones?* (New Haven: 1941), pp. 124–197.

prior to 586 B.C. The Hebrew literature is an expression of their own genius and the stimulus to produce it was the urge of their own religious experience. Of the near neighbor nations that figured conspicuously in Hebrew history during the era of the kingship, not one bequeathed any literature to civilization. From Moab, only the Moabite Stone has survived; from Phoenicia, only some royal coffin inscriptions and the Ras Shamra tablets; from Damascus, nothing at all.

Lost Books. The beginnings of Hebrew literature in the era of kings David and Solomon have already been considered.[186] In their time the practice of having officially appointed recorders and secretaries to keep official state records was begun. Such records were modeled on the Egyptian and Babylonian court records. Such royal records were kept by the succeeding kings both in Judah and in Israel. A "Book of the Chronicles of the Kings of Judah" and a corresponding "Book of the Chronicles of the Kings of Israel" are referred to many times.[187] Also there is reference to genealogical records (presumably military enrollment lists) made in the time of King Jotham of Judah and King Jeroboam II of Israel, i.e., *circa* 745 B.C.[188] What were apparently other genealogical chronicles of some sort were "The History of Shemaiah the Prophet" and "The History of Iddo the Seer." [189] One naturally questions, however, whether much real literary merit attached to either of these.

The writer of the Biblical books of Chronicles cites several other books to which he had access. Some books which he quotes were evidently either editorial revisions of prior works or else writings of the exilic period pseudonymously ascribed to well-known persons of an earlier age. Of this character must have been the "Records of Jehu the Son of Hanani *which are inserted* in the Book of the Kings of Israel," [190] and also, in all probability, "The Visions of Isaiah the Prophet *in* the book of the Kings of Judah *and* Israel"; [191] both these elaborately descriptive titles imply that *some* one at *some* time had inserted *some*thing into whatever original writings he had before him. The second of these titles even hints at two stages of editorial manipulation, one when "The Book of the Kings of Israel" was combined with "The Book of the Kings of Judah," the other when to these was added "The Visions of Isaiah the Prophet." The author of Chronicles also refers to certain *midrashes* (i.e., journalistic treatments of historical events for didactic religious purposes),[192] and to

---

186 *Supra,* pp. 203–208.
187 1 Kgs. 14:19, 29; 15:7, 23, 31; 16:14, 20, 27; etc.
188 1 Chr. 5:17.   189 2 Chr. 12:15.
190 2 Chr. 20:34.   191 2 Chr. 32:32.
192 2 Chr. 13:22; 24:27.

"The Prayer of Manasseh in the Records of the Seers," [193] but most likely these were late works dealing with the period of the kings.

The superscription in Prov. 25:1, "Proverbs of Solomon which the men of Hezekiah King of Judah copied out," suggests a corps of trained copyists and possibly even a library in Jerusalem as early as 700 B.C. If such was the fact, it constitutes one more item to the credit of the influence of the culture which overspread Judah in the time of Ahaz, Hezekiah, and Manasseh, for libraries were a prominent feature of Babylonian and Assyrian culture and scribes were in constant employment along the Tigris from very early times. That Hezekiah was a patron of literature is also implied in the ascription to him of the authorship of a poem, a really fine religious psalm (Isa. 38:9–20).

These references to lost Hebrew writings, unverifiable as their datings are in many cases, do attest the existence of a large amount of literature before the exile. It is clear that the Hebrews had become a literary people of no mean accomplishment some time before the Bible itself began to take form. One wonders how much else once existed and disappeared without a trace. Though these books have all long since perished, nevertheless it is possible to form some estimate of the literary quality and the nature of the contents of some of them from quotations embedded in the Old Testament. In fact, the bulk of the stories found in the books of Genesis, Exodus, Numbers, Judges, Samuel, and Kings had already been written before the Bible books which now contain them were composed, and the Biblical writers simply copied freely and with little change of wording from the rich treasury of older Hebrew literature available to them. Stories like the creation of a helpmeet for man in Gen. 2, the fall of man in Gen. 3, the banishment of Hagar in Gen. 21, and the familiar stories about Jacob and Esau, Joseph and his brothers, and about David, Saul, and Jonathan, are typical of this splendid pre-Bible literature.

The Early Judean and Ephraimite Narratives. Hebrew hero tales and other narratives were evidently current for a time in two distinct collections, one written and circulating in the southern kingdom of Judah, the other making its appearance in Ephraim, as the northern kingdom of Israel was often called.[194] The southern collection of narratives is appropriately referred to as the Judean, or "J" for short. The northern collection, due to the fact that it is believed to have come from the prominent and cultured tribe of Ephraim, is regularly referred to as the Ephraimite, or "E" narratives.

[193] 2 Chr. 33:19.   [194] Hos. 5:9, 6:4; Isa. 7:2; Jer. 7:15; Ezk. 37:16; etc.

1. *The Early Judean Narratives* = "*J.*" *Circa 850* B.C. The "J"
writers show unmistakable partiality for the Judean kingdom and
Judean heroes. They exhibit greatest familiarity with events in which
the southern kingdom or the tribe of Judah took part, and they give
a major prominence to men of that tribe. The language of "J" is
vivid and forceful, abounding in graphic metaphor and concrete
imagery. There is much dialogue, which adds to the dramatic quality
of the narratives. "J's" characters stand out sharply and the stories
move rapidly to a climax.

The "J" writers, moreover, had a distinctive vocabulary and
phraseology. Sharp dialectic differences seem to have separated the
Hebrew tribes. For example, one story of the "judges" period (Jgs.
*12:1–6) hinges on the inability of the Ephraimites to pronounce the
consonantal sound *sh*. The best they could do was to say *s*. When
ordered to say "shibboleth" they gave themselves away by saying
"sibboleth." Had an Ephraimite tried to converse in modern English,
he could have pronounced *she* as *see, shin* as *sin,* and *lash* as *lass.*
Provincialisms are common in our day and doubtless were abundant
then. It follows that it is quite possible to fix the locality, and sometimes even the general period from which a given Hebrew narrative
comes, by listing the linguistic peculiarities which distinguish it.
It is by this method that scholars skilled in Hebrew have picked out
many narratives in the Bible which they are confident were written
early in Judah, and others written in Ephraim almost as early.

Most of the dialectic differences inevitably disappear in any
translation from Hebrew into English. An exception to this is the
name by which the Hebrew deity is referred to when the distinction
is brought out in such versions as preserve the Hebrew original
YHWH in the form of Jehovah or Yahweh, which in other versions
is paraphrased as LORD.[195] The "J" stories use YHWH as though
they assumed that mankind had always addressed God by that title.
There is just one passage which shows that they really knew dif-
ferently (Gen. 4:26), but even this asserts that in the days of Enosh
men "*began* to call on the name of YHWH." The Ephraimite
writers, on the other hand, show by their stories that they did not
believe the name Yahweh to have been in use among the Hebrews
at all until the time of Moses, in fact not until it was revealed to
him in the "burning bush" experience.[196] In all the "E" stories
down to Exodus, therefore, the name Yahweh is carefully excluded
and the generic word *God* (Hebrew *El* or *Elôhîm*) is used instead.
So when one is reading the book of Genesis and comes upon the
word Yahweh or Jehovah, one can be reasonably certain that one is

[195] *Vid. supra,* p. 131, fn. 109.   [196] Ex. 3:13 ff., 6:2 f.

reading part of a "J" narrative written in old Judea some twenty-eight centuries ago.

This "J" literature was available to the compilers of the Bible books and was one of the sources which those compilers incorporated into them when the time came that they were put into the form in which they have come down to us. "J" begins at Gen. 2:4b, and continues, interspersed with other sources, to 1 Kgs. 2, ending with the accession of Solomon to the kingship. "J" was compiled from traditions and writings much older than itself, the most notable of which is the story of David,[197] a masterpiece of the Hebrew narrative art. To gain a firsthand acquaintance with the "J" style at its best, it is suggested that one read Gen. *2:4b–4:16; *16:1 f., 4–14; *18 f.; *24; Jgs. *16; 1 Sam. *17; 2 Sam. *18.[198]

2. *The Early Ephraimite Narratives = "E." Circa 750* B.C. The "E" writers also had their distinguishing traits. Aside from linguistic differences, the detection of which must be left to Hebrew scholars, and aside from the way in which they played up their own northern heroes when they had opportunity to do so, their writings possess certain literary qualities which are quite unmistakable. The "E" literature exhibits a refinement of thought and of style which the "J" narratives measurably lack. The "E" conception of God is more spiritualized, less anthropomorphic. Their ethical sense seems more developed so that they are wont to apologize for or explain away ethical lapses in their leading characters in places where the "J" storyteller seems quite oblivious that any moral fault exists. The historical perspective in the north was also more acute than among the Judeans, as, for example, in frankly recognizing that their remote ancestors were out-and-out pagans.[199] The northern writers surpassed the Judeans in literary polish; perhaps it is for that very reason that the "E" narratives lack the force and gripping quality which the abrupt, incisive, rugged "J" stories commonly have. "E" is a bit wordier; action does not leap to a climax with quite the same furious impetuosity as in the "J" stories. The charm of "E" is in the greater restfulness of a smooth literary style.

For an appreciation of the style and atmosphere of "E" one should read Gen. *20; *21:6–21; *22:1–14 (which is the consummate example of "E's" narrative art); *31; Ex. *1:15–2:10; *32:1–6, 15–24; Josh. *24:14–24 (a sermon); Jgs. *9:6–21; 1 Sam. *1; *3.[200]

---

[197] 2 Sam. 9–20; 1 Kgs. 1–2. Cf. *supra*, pp. 185 f., 207 f.
[198] In the Moffatt translation, "J" passages are printed in italics for the books of Genesis and Exodus. For an excellent discussion of the scope and character of "J," see J. A. Bewer, *The Literature of the Old Testament*, pp. 60–73.
[199] Josh. 24:14.
[200] In the Moffatt translation, "E" passages are in ordinary print enclosed within single square brackets []. For a discussion of the scope and character of "E," see Bewer, *op. cit.*, pp. 74–86.

"E's" story commences with Abraham and parallels "J" in scope. "E" told many of the same stories as "J," and there is no better way to gain an impression of the difference in literary style and mental attitude of the two than to compare the way they tell such a story, for example, as that of Hagar and Ishmael in the wilderness. "J's" story is in Gen. 16:1 f., 4–14; "E's" in Gen. 21:6–21.

3. *The Combination of the Early Judean ("J") and the Early Ephraimite ("E") Narratives = "JE." After 720* B.C. Upon the fall of the kingdom of Israel, the literary treasures of the north became the heritage of Judah. Judean writers who appreciated the merits of the "E" literature combined it with their own native "J" literature, thus producing a new body of literature which is designated by the symbol "JE." An idea of how this combining was done can be gained by noting how the text of Genesis is printed in the Moffatt Version: "J" is in italics and "E" is in ordinary print in square brackets [ ].[201] A reading in this Moffatt Version of the Joseph stories (Gen. 37–48) will give a clear firsthand impression of how "J" and "E" are interwoven.

Just when this combining of "J" and "E" was done cannot be told with any certainty. One of the most likely times was the middle of the seventh century B.C. when Ashurbanipal was king of Assyria and Judah was a vassal of Assyria. Ashurbanipal, a patron of literature, collected in his palace at Nineveh an extensive library of copies he caused to be made of literature of all types at temples and elsewhere in his kingdom.[202] This cultural stimulus may well have spread to Palestine to prompt religiously minded Judean authors to gather together and copy their own native literary products and thereby make their contribution to this literary renascence which was in process in the empire. Surely both "J" and "E" would need copying by this time, for the skins on which they had been originally written would by now have disintegrated considerably. There was no point in simply recopying them as they were. They both went over the same ground. They could be so interwoven as to present one masterful narrative of the origin and career of the Hebrew nation from the prophetic point of view. It must be recalled that in Ashurbanipal's time Manasseh was king of Judah and the Yahweh prophets were suppressed. Though they could not speak publicly, they could and did write. They produced "JE" to glorify Yahweh.

---

201 A passage like Ex. 4:13–16 Moffatt prints both in italics and within single brackets to indicate that it was antecedently both in "J" and in "E," and consequently the same in "JE."
202 On the archaeological discovery and importance of Ashurbanipal's library, *vid. supra,* p. 72.

Other Early Narrative Sources. Akin to these early Judean and Ephraimite sources as to subject matter, general manner of treatment, and point of view, but for the most part later in composition, are such vigorous stories as those in 1 Kgs. *13:1–32; *14:1–28; *17–21; 2 Kgs. *1:2–17a; *2; *3:4–27; *4:8–37; *5; *6:8–7:20. They suggest the existence of a considerable number of vivid stories told about noted seers or prophets, mainly about their miraculous deeds and their activities in the political and social life of their day. "The Prophecy of Ahijah the Shilonite" may have been of this character (2 Chr. 9:20).

The Oldest Books of the Bible. We come now to the beginning of the actual writing of the Bible itself. The first complete Old Testament book to be written was, without a doubt, the prophecy of Amos, followed very closely in point of time by the prophecy of Hosea. These two books evidently date just before Tiglath-pileser III of Assyria commenced his famous campaigning in the west, *circa* 740 B.C., to destroy abruptly and with little warning the prosperous peace of the long reigns of Azariah (Uzziah) of Judah and Jeroboam II of Israel. Both Amos and Hosea felt certain that this era of peace could not last. Both believed that the prosperity of the preceding decades had been built on insecure foundations of injustice and immorality and had lasted so long only because of Yahweh's patience. Both were convinced that a day of divine reckoning was not far away and that it would fall upon Israel and Judah alike. But their impassioned warnings fell on the deaf ears of a people smugly complacent in their belief that the long-continued prosperity was the reward of divine approval. Unable to make a dent in this national assurance, Amos and Hosea put their addresses in poetic form and inscribed them in a book till time should prove to be their vindicator. That later events did so conclusively vindicate these men is undoubtedly the reason why their writings were not allowed to perish.

It is important to note that both Amos and Hosea wrote poetry. This fact is the key to an understanding of their message and to a full appreciation of their style and language. Like all great poets who thoroughly believe in the ideas and ideals they would impress upon their readers, they phrased their thoughts in the finest imaginative language of their age and race.

Eighth-Century Poetry. 1. *Amos.* Great poetry arises from great thinking and profound feeling. Amos was a shepherd of Tekoa, on the Judean wilderness frontier, ten miles due south of Jerusalem. Such a job in such a place gave him plenty of time to reflect upon

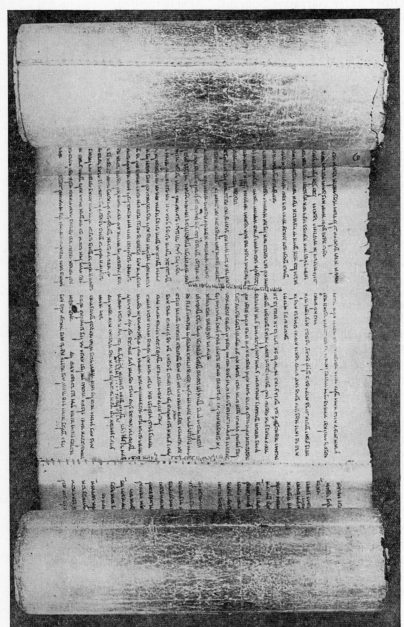

DEAD SEA SCROLL OF THE BOOK OF ISAIAH [203]

[203] The full column at the left contains Isaiah 40:2b–28a. The bottom line of the column to the right is the beginning of Chapter 40. From a photograph by Dr. John C. Trever, reproduced by courtesy of him and of the American Schools of Oriental Research.

the problems of his day, especially religion. His reflections generated within him a consuming passion for righteousness and social justice. On a feast day at the royal shrine at Bethel, in the northern kingdom, Amos blazed forth in an impassioned address which is one of the finest examples of oratory in the Bible. It is Am. *1:3–2:16, and should be read in some version which prints poetry as poetry ought to be printed, preferably the Chicago Version, or the Moffatt Version, or Moulton's *Modern Reader's Bible,* or the Jewish *Holy Scriptures.*[204]

One of the finest poems in the book of Amos is *3:2–8. This is best presented in the Chicago Version and should be read so as to note the changing meters which fit the moods of the thought (vs. 2; vss. 3–6; vss. 7 f.).

The three-beat measure, the usual cadence of lyric poetry, is abundantly present in the book of Amos. The golden gem of the whole book (5:24) is in the three-beat rhythm:

> Let jústice roll dówn as wáters,
> And ríghteousness as a míghty stréam.

The two-beat measure, which is rather staccato, expresses alarm. 3:8 is an instance:

> When the líon róars,
> Whó does not féar?
> When the Lord Gód spéaks,
> Whó will not próphesy? [205]

One of the peculiar rhythms of Hebrew poetry is the *kinah,* or dirge rhythm, the cadence of lamentation. It has three beats in the first line of the couplet, spoken with a rising inflection, and two sharp beats in the second line, spoken with a falling inflection. Am. 5:2 is an example:

> The vírgin of Ísrael is fállen,
> No móre shall she ríse;
> Forsáken she líes on her lánd,
> With nóne to upráise her.

The four-beat measure is marching rhythm, of which the best illustrations are to be found in Nahum 2:3; 3:2 f.

Amos thought in pictures. This is evidenced by the vivid imagery of 3:3–6 and the striking metaphors of 4:1 f.; 5:7,12,18 ff.; 6:12. Am. 8:2 contains a striking play on words: *qayits* = "basket of summer fruit," *qêts* = "end."

---

[204] The translation of 1917, published by the Jewish Publication Society, Philadelphia.

[205] Quoted from the Chicago Version.

Amos is one of the most virile and dramatic personalities of the
Old Testament. He was the first of the truly great prophets. His
significance for religion we reserve for the next chapter of our study.
In this present section we have tried to gain a literary appreciation
of the book which bears his name.[206]

2. *Hosea.* Hosea was a man of quite different type from Amos.
The thing that is best known about him is the tragedy of his family
life, on which he dwells in chapters 1–3. This registers a deep pathos
in his poetry. The finest poem in the book is *11:1–11. Examples of
his splendid metaphors are 5:12; 6:4; 7:4,6 f.,8 f.; 8:7; 9:10; 10:
1,4,7,11; 13:2,3,7. He is concerned with the same social and religious problems as Amos, and the thinking of the two is quite consonant. His religious significance will be considered in the next
chapter.[207]

3. *Isaiah.* Isaiah of Jerusalem was a majestic figure, an aristocrat,
an ardent patriot, an eminent statesman, an eloquent orator, a lyric
poet, and one of the greatest of the prophets. Chapters *1 and *2 are
among the best of his orations.

The poetry of Isaiah is of high quality. We have, in a previous
connection,[208] called attention to his "Poem of the Farmer" (*28:
23–29) and his "Song of the Vineyard" (*5:1–7). The latter should
be read again, preferably in the modern versions,[209] noting how it
flows along in the three-beat rhythm until vs. 7 when it changes
to the four-beat measure, suggesting Yahweh's tramping through
the worthless vineyard. 5:7 is a play on words: "He looked for justice
(*mishpat*), but behold oppression (*mishpah*); for righteousness
(*tsedhakah*), but behold a cry (*tse'akah*)." One of the striking poems
of Isaiah is in *17:12 ff., "The Roaring of the Peoples," [210] with its
instances of onomatopoeia.[211] 1:21 is a dirge. The vivid imagery of
Isaiah's thinking is to be observed in the metaphors he used in such
passages as 1:3,22,25,31; 5:24,29; 7:4,18,20; 9:18; 11:1,6 ff.; 17:6;
22:17 f.,25; 28:4,16 f.; 29:8; 30:14,27 f.,33; 31:5; 32:2.

4. *Micah.* Micah was a farmer who lived in Judah in the very
troubled period at the end of the eighth century B.C. when Sennacherib's army was ravaging the countryside. He laments the disaster
which has befallen the people and blames it all upon Jerusalem. No

---

[206] On Amos, cf. Bewer, *op. cit.*, pp. 87–93; Robert H. Pfeiffer, *Introduction to
the Old Testament* (New York: 1941), pp. 577–584.
[207] On Hosea, cf. Bewer, *op. cit.*, pp. 94–99; Pfeiffer, *op. cit.*, pp. 566–573.
[208] *Supra*, pp. 153 f.
[209] An even better arrangement of it may be found in Laura H. Wild's *A Literary
Guide to the Bible* (New York: 1922), p. 49.
[210] Cf. the Chicago Version.
[211] On Isaiah, cf. Bewer, *op. cit.*, pp. 100–117; Pfeiffer, *op. cit.*, pp. 415–481.

special greatness attaches to his poems, but his use of the *kinah,* or dirge rhythm, is worth noting in *1 :10–16; *2 :4 which are translated in such a way in the Chicago Version that the student will find it easy to read with the proper accents. In 1 :10–16 Micah indulges in a number of puns on place names; the Moffatt Version brings out these plays on words. Perhaps the finest poem of Micah is *6 :1–8, because of the dramatic character of the thought, in which the prophet presents, before the mountains as witnesses, a dialogue between Yahweh and the people.[212] Vivid metaphors are 1 :8; 3 :2 f.; 7 :1,4.

Seventh-Century Prophetic Books.   The seventh century witnessed the activity of four Hebrew prophets. The crisis occasioned by the Scythian invasion in 626 B.C. called forth Zephaniah and Jeremiah. Jeremiah continued his prophetic work until after Jerusalem fell in 586 B.C. The fall of Nineveh in 612 B.C. was the occasion of the Book of Nahum. When the world changed hands at the battle of Carchemish in 605 B.C., and the tyrant Assyria gave way to the oppressor Babylon, Habakkuk uttered his prophecies. We shall make a study of these men as prophets in the next chapter. In the present section we simply note some of the choice passages in each in order to gain an appreciation of their writings as literature.

1. *Zephaniah.* The finest thing in Zephaniah is the doom song in chapter *1. Its theme is the "Day of Yahweh" whose dreadful terrors are portrayed in language that haunts one long after the book is closed. Vs. 15 inspired one of the great hymns of the Christian church, the "Dies Irae" of Tommaso di Celano (A.D. 1185?–1255?).[213] Note the metaphors in 1 :12,17; 2 :2,14; 3 :3.[214]

2. *Nahum.* The thought of Nahum's poem is not elevated, but the language is vivid and dramatic. It is a picture of the siege and ruin of Nineveh, and the prophet fairly gloats over the prospect of its downfall. The whole poem might well be entitled "The Crash of Empire." He declares that all nations will "clap their hands" in vindictive exultation at the news of the tyrant's fall. Note especially *2 :1–10; *3 :1–7,18 f.[215]

3. *Habakkuk.* Habakkuk is often called the philosopher among the prophets. His poem in chapters *2 f. is reflective. Its theme is the might of evil in contrast to the enduring worth of righteousness. The golden gem of his thought is 2 :4b, "The righteous shall live by

---

[212] A good arrangement of this poem may be read in Wild, *op. cit.,* pp. 212 f. On Micah, cf. Pfeiffer, *op. cit.,* pp. 589–594.

[213] This poem may be found in Burton E. Stevenson's *Home Book of Verse* (New York: 1912), the Latin on pp. 3569 f., an English translation on pp. 3527 f.

[214] On Zephaniah, cf. Bewer, *op. cit.,* pp. 136 ff.; Pfeiffer, *op. cit.,* pp. 600 f.

[215] On Nahum, cf. Pfeiffer, *op. cit.,* pp. 594–597.

his faith," a thought taken up and expanded centuries later by the apostle Paul.[216] Observe the metaphors in 1:8,15; 2:1,11; 3:8,12.[217]

4. *Jeremiah.* Jeremiah was the most sensitive and sympathetic of the prophets. He was of priestly descent, a man of earnest moral and religious convictions, a devoted prophet of Yahweh for over forty years despite personal abuse and persecution. He probably died a martyr. He was a gifted poet; his poetic art can be seen at its best in the beautiful poems in chapters *9 and *31:2–6,15–21,31–34. One of the interesting features of Jeremiah's writings is his use of parables. Note especially the parables of the loincloth (*13:1–11), the wine jars (*13:12 ff.), the potter (*18:1–11), the broken bottle (*19:1–13), and the figs (*24:1–10). His use of choice metaphors is notable in 2:21–24; 4:3,11 f.,30; 5:8,16,26 f.; 6:4,9,29 f.; 8:7,17,22; 9:11,15, *21 f.; 10:22; 11:4,16,19; 12:9; 13:16 (marg.), *23; 15:18; 16:16; 17:1,11; 18:14; 19:3; 20:9; 22:24; 31:18,20 f.[218]

All these great souls were moved to speak and to write under the stimulus of stirring political movements and profound international changes beyond which their minds soared to the realm of the spiritual —to poetry, and to religion, and to ethical idealism. Of nearly every one of them we learn that their speeches were ignored or resented in their own day. In proportion as their tongues were forced to silence, the full power of their great natures found expression in beautiful and imperishable written speech.

Secretaries and Editors. The prophets were sometimes assisted in their literary labors by secretaries. Jeremiah had a man by the name of Baruch to do the actual writing for him.[219] It is a stirring picture that Jer. *36 conjures up—a prophet out of favor with king and court because he had dared to criticize official policies and to predict disaster for the nation; a rapt hour when a devoted disciple writes fast and furiously as phrase after phrase falls from the lips of his revered master; and another tense hour when, having read those trenchant lyrics to a vast concourse assembled for service in the great temple court,[220] Baruch hurries back to the waiting Jeremiah, while an enraged king slashes and burns the precious verses before he has listened to half of them.[221]

This Baruch was no nonentity. On one occasion he was accused of having influenced Jeremiah to take a position in a matter of public policy which Jeremiah might otherwise not have taken.[222] In fact, so great was Baruch's reputation, that in the course of time

216 Rom. 1–5.
217 On Habakkuk, cf. Bewer, *op. cit.*, pp. 139–142; Pfeiffer, *op. cit.*, pp. 597–600.
218 On Jeremiah, cf. Bewer, *op. cit.*, pp. 143–168; Pfeiffer, *op. cit.*, pp. 482–517.
219 Jer. 36:4, 32.   220 Jer. 36:9 f.
221 Jer. 36:23 f.   222 Jer. 43:3.

there grew up a tradition which credits him with the authorship of a number of books, one of which, bearing his name, is preserved in the Apocrypha. The fact that Jer. 51 closes with the note, "Thus far are the words of Jeremiah," has led many scholars to wonder whether Baruch may not deserve a larger share of credit for writing the book of Jeremiah than is generally supposed.

Whether or not other prophets had their Baruchs is not known, but one rather suspects that some of them had. It would seem that most of the prophets had some helpers or disciples who, either at the time of writing or later, added the explanatory comments about the prophets and the circumstances under which they preached or wrote, even if they did not, like Baruch, serve as secretaries. Such editorial notes appear, for example, in Am. 7:10–14; Hos. 1:2; Isa. 7:1 ff.; 20:1 ff.; 36–39.

The Rise of Rhetorical Prose. The "D" code, which appeared in 621 B.C. as we have already observed,[223] marks the rise of another type of literature which we may characterize as rhetorical prose. The full development of this type of writing did not come until after the exilic period was well advanced. As we observed, this was a humanitarian literature, written to produce a deeper and more sensitive social consciousness, a greater considerateness toward the poor and defenseless, a real humanitarian spirit in conduct, and genuine spirituality in religion. Of course all the great prophets from Amos to Jeremiah had stressed such qualities, but the Deuteronomic literature is different in style from nearly everything found in the prophets.

2 Kgs. 23:21 mentions a roll called "the book of the covenant" which brought about King Josiah's sweeping religious reformation.[224] This book is generally identified with the substance of Deut. 12–26, 28. From the description of the things which Josiah did, it is clear that he must have had before him a document which read just about as do parts of our present Book of Deuteronomy. The king was seized with terror upon hearing the book read, and there are parts of Deuteronomy which read that way.[225] Yet the most conspicuous trait of the book is its reasoned appeal to conscience, to the finer impulses of sympathy, gratitude, and generosity, not so much out of fear as because one would wish to be so treated were one placed in a like situation.[226] The classic example of the Deuteronomic appeal is in Deut. *6:4–13, with which should be read Deut. *4:31–39; both these passages, however, are probably exilic additions. They are

---

[223] *Supra,* pp. 284 f.   [224] *Vid. infra,* pp. 332 ff.
[225] E.g., 13:5, 8 ff., 15 ff.; 17:5, 12 f.; 19:21; 21:20 f.; 28:15–68.
[226] Cf. Deut. 12:19; 14:27; 15:7–11, 18; 16:12.

cited here only as indicating the ethical tone of this literature and this
rhetorical prose style at its best.

The Nature of a Hebrew Book. What would such a book as
those we have been discussing have looked like in 586 B.C.? For one
thing, a book might have been simply a basketful of broken crockery,
for potsherds were used for writing material, as evidenced by the
royal archives of King Jeroboam II which have been dug up,[227] and
by the Lachish Letters found in 1935 at Tell ed-Duweir in the
Shephelah; sixteen of these ostraca were in the stratum of debris
which marked the destruction of the city during Nebuchadrezzar's
invasion in 586 B.C.[228] Such ostraca would have made looseleaf pages
of a difficult sort to keep in order, and there is no telling how much
this may account for the confusion which characterizes the arrangement of material in some of the books. More usually, however, the
Hebrews wrote on skins. No doubt a considerable part of the work of
tanners and fullers was the preparing and bleaching of skins for
writing purposes. Such skins were joined to form a long strip and
rolled on a stick to make a book. The Old Testament frequently uses
the word "roll" for book. The size of such a book would be limited,
for it would soon become cumbersome and difficult to handle in reading. Probably the durability of such skins was not great, for the
process of preparation was by no means as efficient as that which
produces our modern sheepskins. Disintegration would cause the skins
to crack, and a book would fall to pieces, which would be just as
much of a problem to handle and arrange as were potsherds. It is
more likely, however, that such a book-roll consisted of sheets of
papyrus pasted together and rolled on a stick.[229] Jeremiah's book was
probably on papyrus, since the king so easily cut and burned it;
burning skin would have been malodorous. Such a book-roll would
have been, on the average, about thirty feet in length.[230]

What the writing looked like is easy to visualize, for the Hebrews
employed the Old Semitic script, examples of which are to be seen
on the Moabite Stone, the Siloam inscription, and Jeroboam's
archives.[231]

The very oldest extant Hebrew book is a scroll of Isaiah, dated by
competent experts *circa* 100 B.C. or even earlier. This book is one of
a collection (at least eleven) known as "The Dead Sea Scrolls." They
appear to have been part of the library of some as yet unidentified

[227] Cf. supra, pp. 206 f., Archives of kings of Northern Israel.
[228] Cf. C. C. McCown, *The Ladder of Progress in Palestine* (New York:
1943), pp. 137 ff.; Jack Finegan, *Light From the Ancient Past* (Princeton: 1946),
pp. 160–163 and Fig. 70.
[229] *Vid. supra*, p. 49.
[230] Cf. J. P. Hyatt, "The Writing of an Old Testament Book," *Biblical Archaeologist*, vi, 4, (December, 1943), pp. 71–80.
[231] Cf. *supra*, pp. 204, 205, 206, 207.

Jewish sect. For reasons now unknown, these scrolls were sealed in earthenware jars and cached in a cave high up on the cliffs near the north end of the Dead Sea. There they remained for more than 2,000 years until discovered by some wandering Bedouin in the summer of 1947. Some of the scrolls are now in possession of the Hebrew University of Jerusalem, others are at St. Mark's Syrian Orthodox Convent in Jerusalem. Officials of the latter institution have entrusted the study and publication of theirs to the American Schools of Oriental Research of Jerusalem. Some of the scrolls are on coarse parchment, others on leather. Pieces of such material were sewed together with linen thread. In some places patches of thin material were glued with pitch to the back of places that needed repair. The discovery of these scrolls is the most important Old Testament manuscript discovery ever made. Their study and interpretation will occupy scholars for a long time to come. The authenticity and pre-Christian antiquity of the scrolls have been confirmed not only by palaeographers but by the evidence of an archaeological excavation of the "Manuscript" cave at Ain Fashkha itself.[232]

The Language of the Old Testament. What would it have sounded like had we heard Baruch read his master's book to the people in the temple? [233] What strikes non-Semitic ears most strangely in hearing Hebrew spoken is the sound of the laryngeals (sometimes called gutturals), which only the Semitic throat can utter accurately. They impart a virility and ruggedness which give the language a character all its own.

What is the language like? The Hebrew thought in pictures, and consequently his nouns are concrete and vivid. There is no such thing as neuter gender, for to the Semite everything is alive. Compound words are lacking. In declining nouns there are only two cases, absolute and construct, the latter expressing a genitival relationship. There is no wealth of adjectives. Verbs are built up from a three consonant root and are highly inflected. There are two tenses, perfect and imperfect, which have to do not with order of time but with completeness or incompleteness of an action, whether it is in past, present, or future time. In sentence structure, verb comes first, followed by subject and object. Particles and conjunctions are few and consequently clauses are coordinate, following one another with the use of the simple "and." The resources of the language seem meager, but it nevertheless served as the vehicle of simple and majestic thought and gave to the world its greatest literature.

[232] Cf. *The Biblical Archaeologist,* xi, 2, 3 (May and September, 1948), pp. 21–23, 45–61; *Bulletin of the American Schools of Oriental Research,* 111 (October, 1948), pp. 2–24; 112 (December, 1948), pp. 8–23; 113 (February, 1949), pp. 6–35; 114 (April, 1949), pp. 5–12.

[233] Jer. 36:10.

The Bible in 586 B.C.   Having in mind the sequence of books in the English Bible as we have it, how much of the Bible was in existence in 586 B.C.? Any answer to this question must be qualified in advance by the remark that probably no one book of the Bible existed in its present form in the year 586 B.C. The nearest approach to this would be such a book as Amos; but Amos, like all the other literature written before 586 B.C., was subjected to reworking and editing after 586 B.C., i.e., in the exilic and post-exilic periods.

The first five books of the Bible (Genesis, Exodus, Leviticus, Numbers, Deuteronomy) are generally treated as a unit and called the Pentateuch. Some scholars prefer to add Joshua to this group and speak of the Hexateuch. All these books were built out of four basic documents. Of these source documents, "J" and "E" in their combined form "JE," and "D" (the heart of the Book of Deuteronomy) were in existence by 586 B.C.[234]

The bulk of the stories which make up the books of Judges and Samuel were in existence in 586 B.C., but to assert in what form would call for extended technical analysis. Some Old Testament scholars trace the "J" and "E" histories through these books.

The material comprising the books of Kings was produced in this period. Some scholars hold the view that a first edition of the Book of Kings was produced in the reign of King Josiah (638–608 B.C.). If so, it would have been another product of that widespread literary renascence of the last half of the seventh century, of which we have already spoken.[235]

The writings of the prophetic books Amos, Hosea, Isaiah, Micah, Jeremiah, Zephaniah, Nahum, and Habakkuk were produced by men whose names they bear, prior to 586 B.C., and, of course, subjected to editing, rearrangement, and additions in a later age. This last is especially true of Isaiah and Jeremiah.[236]

It is one thing for a writing to be in existence as a piece of literature, and another thing for it to be regarded as sacred literature or Holy Scripture. The process by which this comes about is a religious and not a literary process and is therefore reserved for consideration in the next chapter.[237] Suffice it here to state that of this literature all that definitely appears to have been regarded as "Holy" is "D," the "book of the covenant," which was the basis of Josiah's reformation and which by a solemn covenant was adopted as the sacred law of the nation (2 Kgs. 23:1 ff.)

[234] The fourth source document is "P". Cf. Bewer, *op. cit.,* pp. 259–279.
[235] *Supra,* p. 298.
[236] J. A. Bewer, *op. cit.,* pp. xii–xiv, gives a table of the historical development of the Old Testament writings.
[237] *Vid. infra,* pp. 334 ff.

Chapter 18

RELIGION: POPULAR AND PROPHETIC

Yahwism was established as the official state religion in the time of the united Hebrew kingdom.[1] The disruption of the kingdom in 931 B.C. was a political calamity of the first magnitude and it was a religious crisis as well, for it involved the exclusion of the seceding tribes from worship at the Jerusalem temple. How religion fared in the separate kingdoms and in surviving Judah after Israel went to her doom is our concern in the present chapter.

Popular Religion in Judah in the First Two Centuries After 931 B.C.

In general, the portrayal of the official state Yahweh cult given on pages 208–216 is valid for the period now under survey. Yahweh was the supreme national deity; the fine temple in Jerusalem practically assured that. But numerous high places with their characteristic pillars dotted the Judean countryside,[2] and shrine prostitutes evidently had a recognized part in the worship, save when an occasional spurt of reform was made.[3] Despite the commendation of kings Asa,[4] Jehoshaphat,[5] Jehoash,[6] Amaziah,[7] and Azariah,[8] it is obvious from the many qualifications accompanying these expressions of approval that the real character of worship did not materially improve in these two centuries. This impression is confirmed by the writings of such prophets as Isaiah and Micah who lived at the end of the period. In fact, when King Hezekiah carried out his religious reforms, *circa* 700 B.C., not only were the high places still in existence but the "brazen serpent that Moses had made" was being worshiped with the burning of incense.[9] The shrines to Ashtart, Chemosh, and Milcom, erected by Solomon in the immediate vicinity of the Jeru-

---

[1] Cf. *supra*, p. 208.
[2] 1 Kgs. 14:22 f.; 15:14; 22:43; 2 Kgs. 12:3; 14:3 f.; 15:4; etc.
[3] 1 Kgs. 14:24; 15:12 f.; 22:46. On the increasing paganism of the royal family of Judah, cf. W. F. Albright, *Archaeology and the Religion of Israel* (Baltimore: 1942), pp. 157 f.

[4] 1 Kgs. 15:11–15.
[5] 1 Kgs. 22:43, 46.
[6] 2 Kgs. 12:2–16.
[7] 2 Kgs. 14:3–6.
[8] 2 Kgs. 15:3 f.
[9] 2 Kgs. 18:4.

salem temple, were still standing as late as the time of Josiah (621
B.C.), more than three centuries after Solomon's death.[10]

Worthy of special note is the conception of Yahweh which pervades the "J" literature which appeared in Judah *circa* 850 B.C. In a
previous connection we have considered "J" from a literary standpoint. We must now consider it from a religious standpoint. It was a
religious writing and was designed to accomplish a religious, i.e., a
prophetic, purpose.

"J's" conception of Yahweh is vividly anthropomorphic.[11] It was a
real advance in religion to lift the idea of God from a theriomorphic
to an anthropomorphic level. In and around Jerusalem were plenty
of visible images to represent deity. There was a bronze snake and
there were bronze bulls right in the courts of the Yahweh temple,
and also the upright columns, Jachin and Boaz, which may or may
not have been capped by some symbol of deity. At the other shrines
around the city there were no doubt images of deity. The average
plain man of Judah doubtless asked, "What is Yahweh like?" The
only answer he would receive was that Yahweh dwelt in the Most
Holy Place of the temple (where the plain man himself could never
go) where the Ark was and above the Ark the cherubim. Moreover,
he would be told further that it was forbidden to make any image
of Yahweh or "any likeness of anything in the heaven above or the
earth below." But this prohibition did not inhibit "J" from fashioning a literary image of Yahweh and he fashioned a very realistic
picture of Yahweh to meet the plain man's need of such visual
imagery. He shows what Yahweh is like by showing how Yahweh
has been in action throughout the course of history. Though Yahweh
is portrayed in the "J" narratives in realistic anthropomorphic language, nevertheless he is depicted as the controller of the forces of
nature, the determiner of the destiny of his chosen people, and the
only god for them. They must therefore be loyal to him. He is essentially moral in character, a point which cannot be too strongly
stressed, and the demands he makes upon his people are demands of
righteousness.

There is little direct evidence on the subject of religious behavior
in Judah in this period. It probably was not markedly different from
what we find in Israel.

Popular Religion in Northern Israel: 931–722 B.C.

Deities. The secession of the ten tribes under the leadership of
Jeroboam I involved an immediate exclusion from worship at the

[10] 2 Kgs. 23:13.
[11] Cf. G. E. Wright, *The Challenge of Israel's Faith* (Chicago: 1944), pp. 65 f.

Jerusalem temple. Did that mean abandonment of all worship of
Yahweh as well?

Jeroboam promptly established two national shrines, at Dan and
Bethel, where "golden calves" were set up as visual images of the
deity (1 Kgs. *12:26–30). 2 Kgs. 10:29 intimates that there were
two calves in each place, and 1 Kgs. 12:32 speaks of the "calves"
(*pl.*) of Bethel. In Samaria, also, two calves were worshiped.[12] We
have already remarked upon the nature of bull worship in a previous
epoch of Hebrew history and its relation to the Egyptian cult of
Apis and Hathor.[13] Basically, it was a fertility cult and seems to have
been indigenous to Canaan. The mother goddess Ashtart was in one
form worshiped as a cow divinity, as reflected in the place name
Ashteroth-karnaim, "Ashtart of the two horns." [14] The place name
En-eglaim, "spring of the two calves," [15] may imply another seat of
such worship. The presence of the twelve bronze bulls in the court of
the Jerusalem temple, supporting the great bronze laver, shows that
the Hebrew mind assimilated this feature of religion to Yahwism. It
is probably, therefore, that Jeroboam and his contemporaries did not
design wholly to desert Yahweh but only made central another feature
of religion which certainly had a stronger appeal to the popular mind,
for instead of having a god hidden away inside a building where nobody could see him, the golden calves were out where the plain man
could look at them.

It is easy to see how each king in each nation would wish to have
Yahweh on his side, convinced as the rulers were of his invincible
power in battle. It is also easy to see how each party might reason to
its own satisfaction that Yahweh by right ought to be on *its* side;
Judah, because Yahweh's one and only temple was in Jerusalem,
Israel, because of the conviction that their secession was Yahweh's
own angry punishment of Solomon and Rehoboam.[16] Yet both kingdoms must have felt a certain measure of anxiety and uncertainty as
to which of them Yahweh would support in the event of war between
them, and on this assumption the readiness of Rehoboam to listen to
the prophet Shemaiah is quite understandable.[17]

On the basis of such considerations, some scholars regard the golden
calves placed in the shrines at Bethel and Dan as really intended to
represent Yahweh, just as the cherubim did in the Jerusalem temple. It is true that 1 Kgs. 14:9 accuses Jeroboam I of having "made
other gods and molten images" and of having cast Yahweh behind
his back. It is also true that 1 Kgs. 16:32 f. declares that Ahab,

---

[12] 2 Kgs. 17:16, though Hos. 8:5 f. speaks of only the "calf of Samaria."
[13] *Supra*, p. 135.   [14] Gen. 14:5.
[15] Ezk. 47:10.   .   [16] 1 Kgs. 11:31 ff.; 12:24.
[17] 1 Kgs. 12:21–24.

about a century after Jeroboam I, erected an altar for a Baal house at Samaria and made an asherah. Furthermore, according to 1 Kgs. 19:10, Elijah at one time complained that the Israelites had even thrown down Yahweh's altars and slain his prophets. But these are manifestly extreme statements which other evidence materially modifies. Thus Elijah, soon after his despairing complaint, was made to realize that there were even then no less than "seven thousand whose knees had never bent to Baal and whose mouths had never kissed him." [18] Again, 1 Kgs. 20 affirms that this same Ahab repeatedly defeated Syrian armies by the active aid of Yahweh, conclusively showing that Yahweh was recognized as Israel's national deity, at least as their god of war. Also, according to 1 Kgs. 21:27 ff., it was Yahweh who was noticeably touched by Ahab's humility toward him. No less than three of Ahab's children bore the significant names of Ahaziah Jehoram, and Athaliah. It seems obvious, therefore, that the northern kingdom did continue to worship Yahweh, though in a manner different from that followed in the temple of Jerusalem and perhaps for that reason the most vigorously disapproved by the southerners. These differences included the creation of an order of priests from the common laity,[19] the making of "molten images," [20] and, in the time of Ahab, the introduction of the worship of an entirely new cult, the god Baal-Melkart of Tyre, with his hundreds of priests under the active patronage of Queen Jezebel. Tyre was a mighty city of wealth whose far-flung commerce gave her contact with all nations. Doubtless the Tyrians thanked Baal-Melkart for this prosperity, and doubtless, also, Jezebel promoted the worship of this god in Israel that her husband's kingdom might similarly be prosperous and famous. It was for a like reason at a later time in Judah that the Assyrian religion was made official under kings Ahaz and Manasseh. This promotion of Tyrian baalism in Israel, it will be recalled, was what finally brought about the bloody massacres by Jehu in 842 B.C., aided and abetted by some of the more desperate and determined Yahweh prophets.[21]

After this revolution of Jehu it would seem that for the remaining hundred and twenty years of the kingdom of Israel the Yahweh religion had no real rival there. It is recorded of many of the kings of this closing century that they "departed not from the sins of Jeroboam the son of Nebat," but specific charges of apostasy from Yahweh are wanting. For the ultimate downfall of the northern kingdom in 722 B.C. the Biblical historian offers as his own explanation (2 Kgs. *17:7–23) that they had built any number of high places,

---

[18] 1 Kgs. 19:18. [19] 1 Kgs. 12:32 f.
[20] 1 Kgs. 14:9; cf. Ex. 20:23; 34:17.
[21] 1 Kgs. 19:15 ff.; 2 Kgs. 8:10–13; 9:1–10. Cf. *supra,* pp. 236 ff.

had "set up pillars and asherim on every high hill and under every green tree," had "offered sacrifices as did the nations which Yahweh had carried away before them," and had "served idols," this last being presumably a reference to the two calves.[22] Inasmuch as most of these offenses were committed by the people of the southern kingdom also, one is led to suspect that they were not generally held to be inconsistent with acceptable worship of Yahweh and that the condemnation is that of a later age.

Sacred Places in the Northern Kingdom. Unmistakably, Dan, near Israel's northern border, and Bethel, scarcely five miles from its extreme southern boundary, were the two chief shrines of the kingdom throughout its entire history. The golden calves stamped them as such permanently. Amos names both of these places,[23] though it is the nearer Bethel which most engages his attention and that of his contemporary, Hosea.[24] Bethel was the royal sanctuary of Israel. Amos and Hosea likewise mention Gilgal as in the same class with Bethel, but what gave Gilgal its prominence is not known.[25] Mount Carmel was a sacred site of obvious importance in the time of Elijah and Elisha, and possibly still so in the time of Amos.[26] Here occurred the famous contest between Elijah and the prophets of the Tyrian Baal (1 Kgs. *18:20–40), and here Elisha seems to have made his home.[27] But in addition to these famous shrines, singled out by name, the assertion of 2 Kgs. 17:9 f. that "they built them high places in all their cities" and "set up pillars and asherim upon every high hill and under every green tree" indicates that they by no means lacked for sacred places! Hosea, himself a sympathetic prophet of the north, acknowledges as much in 4:13.

The Character of Israelitish Worship. The conventional form of worship at these major shrines is vividly described or implied in the writings of Amos and Hosea. Outstanding features were feasting, music, and song.[28] There were daily morning sacrifices, and every third day tithes were exacted.[29] Sabbaths and New Moon days were observed as days of cessation from trade at least, but in an apparently grudging spirit.[30] Worship continued to be predominantly a thing of joy, a time of lightheartedness and freedom from care, a time of gala dress and holiday mood.[31]

Religious Behavior. Religion in this period had not ceased to have its harsh and unlovely aspects. Deception, lying, cruelty, and

---

[22] Cf. Hos. 8:4 ff.; 13:1 ff.; 14:3.   [23] Am. 4:4; 8:14.
[24] Am. 3:14; 4:4; 7:10–13; Hos. 4:15; 10:5; etc. On the shrine at Bethel, cf. W. F. Albright, *op. cit.,* pp. 172 f.   [25] Am. 4:4; 5:5; Hos. 4:15, 9:15.
[26] Am. 9:3.   [27] 2 Kgs. 2:25; 4:25.
[28] Am. 2:8; 5:21 ff.; 8:3, 10; Hos. 2:11; 9:4 f.
[29] Am. 4:4.   [30] Am. 8:5; Hos. 2:11.   [31] Hos. 2:13.

outright murder were not thought inconsistent with religious character. So we find a certain "old prophet in Bethel" lying outright
to a fellow "man of God" (1 Kgs. *13:11–32; cf. esp. vs. 18).
Similarly, in 1 Kgs. 22:22 f., Yahweh himself is represented as ap-
proving a "lying spirit in the mouth of all his prophets," while in
14:11, 16:3 f., and 21:21–24 he is pictured as purposing most horrible dooms for kings Jeroboam, Baasha, and Ahab, and for Queen
Jezebel. When Jehu carried through his unspeakably bloody "religious" revolution, Jehonadab, a Rechabite and therefore representative of the most conservative religious sentiment of the age,
asserted that his heart was as right as Jehu's.[32] And the Biblical
commentator finishes the whole sordid story of Jehu's shameless
treachery by adding: "And Yahweh said to Jehu, Because thou hast
done well in executing that which is right in mine eyes, and hast
done unto the house of Ahab according to all that was in my heart,
thy sons of the fourth generation shall sit on the throne of Israel." [33]
When people believe that God approves acts such as these, religion
has far to travel ethically. It is a relief, therefore, to find that at
least one voice was raised in vigorous protest, the voice of the gentle, kindly prophet Hosea. In his mind the "blood of Jezreel" was
an unforgivable blot upon the house of Jehu.[34]

Religion was beginning to show a finer side, a more sensitive
quality, the brilliant dawning of ethical consciousness. Hosea, who
belonged natively to Israel, is evidence of this. He vehemently
condemned the calves and the immoralities that were carried on wan-
tonly under the name of religious worship, together with the shallow-
ness of their idea of what it meant to be religious. Hosea had some
sympathetic hearers in Israel, at least those who preserved his sermons for the future. Evidence of this finer religious consciousness
that existed in some quarters in Israel is also seen in the point of
view which the so-called Elohist worked out in his compilation of
the "E" narratives.[35] "E" tells historical incidents, not for history's
sake but for the sake of religious lessons which he wishes to impart
to his own contemporaries. Compared with "J," the Elohist writes
from the higher ethical point of view.[36] "E" has a more spiritualized
conception of God. He does not have God appear in person, but
through dreams or visions or by angels. "E" tells the story of
Rachel's theft of her father's teraphim in such a way as to heap
contempt on the teraphim.[37] In his narrative about Aaron's making
of the golden calf at Sinai, "E" has a splendid opportunity to ex-

---

[32] 2 Kgs. 10:15.   [33] 2 Kgs. 10:30.
[34] Hos. 1:4.   [35] Cf. *supra*, pp. 297 f.
[36] Illustrated, e.g., in his version of "J's" story about Sarah (Abram's wife) in
Pharaoh's harem [J = Gen. 12:11–20; E = Gen. 20:1–17], and in his version of "J's"
story of Hagar [J = Gen. 16:4–14; E = Gen. 21:8–21], and elsewhere.
[37] Gen. 31:19, 32–35.

press his condemnation of calf worship, especially the giving of credit to a calf for delivering the people from Egypt (Ex. *32:1–6, 15–24). Such calf worship was, as we have noted, predominant in Israel in "E's" time, and "E" uses a historical incident to point out the essential folly of such worship. "E" is a thoroughgoing Yahweh loyalist and is keen to win his fellow Israelites to exclusive loyalty to Yahweh, nowhere better seen than in Josh. *24:14–24, a most admirable example of "E's" sermonizing. It is one thing to read this passage for whatever light it may throw on Joshua's time, and a different and much more illuminating thing to see mirrored in it not Joshua's but the writer's own time and appreciate this sermon as a strong appeal to the Israelites of the eighth century B.C. This appeal "E" reinforces when he comes to write up the career of Saul; this gives him an opportunity to stress obedience to Yahweh as the supreme religious virtue (1 Sam. *15:22 f.). True, "E" does not attack the local sanctuaries and the festivals carried on at them, but the sacred pillars and posts that marked such places "E" regards as memorials only, not as seats of the deity.[38]

It would appear, therefore, that before the fall of the kingdom, visions of deeper and truer meanings in religion had been caught by some whose own religious behavior, we may infer, was something far loftier, finer, and more admirable to modern minds than the examples chosen by the writer of the Book of Kings for inclusion in his narrative.

The Hebrew Conception of God Becomes Ethical

The conception of Yahweh as a national deity remained, of course, as long as the Hebrews were a nation. It is with the great prophets of the eighth century B.C. that there emerged the conception of Yahweh as an ethical deity whose demands are ethical and whose worship must be ethical. Four great thinkers, Amos, Hosea, Isaiah, and Micah, in the eighth century put an indelible impress upon Hebrew religion which in the course of time revolutionized its character.

The Religion of Amos, Prophet of Justice. We have already made the acquaintance of Amos and the few biographical details about him that can be gleaned from his book,[39] and we have gained an

[38] E.g., Gen. 28:18, 35:14, 20.
[39] *Supra*, pp. 244 f., 299 ff. As we now take up the study of the prophets, the following study pattern will assist the student:
(1) Biography. Such details as may be found in the prophet's own book and elsewhere in the Bible.
(2) Historical background. The times in which the prophet lived. Such material will be found in Chapters 14–16 of this text, especially pp. 242–270.
(3) The teachings of the prophet. What he had to say to his own age.
(4) Golden gems of the prophet's thought. The student should make a selection which should be committed to memory.

appreciation of the literary merit of his book.[40] We have likewise reviewed the history of the times in which he lived.[41] His prophetic work dates *circa* 750 B.C. We now wish to estimate his contribution to the development of Hebrew religious thought, especially the idea of God.

The one incident in the career of Amos which is high-lighted in his book is the occasion when he appeared at the royal Israelite sanctuary at Bethel on a feast day and addressed the group of assembled worshipers (Am. *7:10–17). How he came to be at an Israelite festival, particularly a festival at the royal Bethel shrine, chief rival of the Jerusalem temple, we can only conjecture. Possibly he went there to sell a few products at this favorable market, lambs for the sacrifices, wool for clothing. Or did he travel all those twenty-five or thirty miles with the deliberate intention of uttering stern denunciations upon a people who, he had come to believe, were straining Yahweh's patience to the breaking point? All that is clear is that upon a crowd of lighthearted, carefree merrymakers, whose confidence and gaiety had grown as year after year rolled around with unbroken peace and prosperity, Amos suddenly hurled his stinging censure. Startled and angered, the chief priest of Bethel, Amaziah by name, accused Amos to the king as a traitor and drove the prophet out of the country. Amos went back to the quiet of Tekoa, to his sheep, and to his thoughts, and then he wrote a book. His is the distinction of being the first of the writing prophets. We have writings about prophets before Amos, but no writings by them. Somebody must have gone along with Amos, attracted by his teachings. His sermon had not fallen wholly on deaf ears. Whether such disciples assisted Amos in the writing of his book (as Baruch assisted Jeremiah in a later century) we cannot know, but we certainly have them to thank for preserving the book for posterity. They are among the likely to be forgotten men of the Bible.

Amos definitely lifted religion from the ritual to the ethical level. The prevailing religious emphasis of the time was upon ritual, and elaborate and costly sacrifices and feasts characterized worship at the shrines. Amos denounced the prevailing cult practices (Am. *4:4 f.; *5:4 ff.; 21–25). In 5:25 he asserts that the essential element, historically, in Yahwism was not sacrifices and ceremonies. Amos implies that they were simply deluding themselves into believing that Yahweh liked that form of worship because they liked it so much themselves (4:5b). Amos's positive view is that the true religious attitude manifests itself in social righteousness (Am. *5:24). We have already seen wherein his conception of social righteousness consists.[42]

---

[40] *Supra*, pp. 299 ff.   [41] *Supra*, pp. 242–245.   [42] *Supra*, pp. 244 f.

Two hundred years earlier the prophet Nathan had rebuked David for his shameful betrayal of Uriah's confidence.[43] One hundred years before Amos the prophet Elijah had fiercely denounced Ahab for the official robbery and murder of Naboth.[44] But not until Amos do we find a carefully worked out religious philosophy based on consideration for the desperately needy, on impartial justice, and on righteousness. Amos's great exhortation, "Let justice roll down as waters, and righteousness as a mighty stream" (5:24), has itself been an everflowing stream of inspiration and power for social righteousness for twenty-seven centuries.

Amos's idea of God is also ethical. God's primary interest is in righteousness and justice. Amos set the idea of God forward a long way toward monotheism. Already Yahweh was the god of two nations, Judah and Israel. Amos could have preached for Yahweh in either nation. If the god of two nations, why not of more? Am. 9:7 affirms that Yahweh did guide other nations; he brought the Philistines from Caphtor and the Syrians from Kir, and Philistines and Syrians were the two most despised and hated enemies of the Hebrews. In chapter 1 Amos asserts that the power of Yahweh reaches out to other lands to punish Syria, Philistia, Phoenicia, Edom, Ammon, Moab. Amos did not in so many words affirm that Yahweh was the god of all the world nor did he deny the existence of other gods. But he did shatter the nationalistic idea of God.

Another important feature of Amos's religious thinking is his idea of the Day of Yahweh. Apparently down to Amos's time there existed a popular notion of a great day coming when Yahweh would destroy all the foes of his chosen people and usher in a new age of glorious prosperity in which they would see the realization of all their fondest hopes. It was to be a glorious holiday when Yahweh would subject the rest of the world to them. Amos turns this idea upside down and declares that the Day of Yahweh is to be a day of doom (Am. *5:18 ff.) in which Yahweh would visit punishment upon Israel (Am. *2:6 ff., 13–16; *3:2, 9–12; *4:12; 5:1 ff., *7:1–9; *8:3, 9–14; *9:1–4). The doom is not wholly unrelieved. There is hope for a "remnant" (Am. *5:15, cf. 5:3). The idea of a remnant is that of a small nucleus of spiritually minded and morally upright people around whom Yahweh can order the new day. We shall meet these ideas of the Day of Yahweh and the remnant again in other prophets.

Whether or not Amos thought his own Judah free from the same offenses he does not say. His one censure of Judah is the rather vague charge that they had "rejected the law of Yahweh and had

---

[43] 2 Sam. 12:1–15.   [44] 1 Kgs. 21. Cf. *supra*, p. 235.

not kept his statutes," [45] but with no further hint as to what that meant. We can feel confident, however, that a man so dynamic as Amos could hardly have failed to be a source of ethical inspiration in his own community or to make some sort of impress on his own state.

The Religion of Hosea, Prophet of Love. Hosea's prophetic work began not more than a decade after that of Amos, and possibly continued through the convulsive epoch that closed Israel's career.[46] In Hosea's day the northern kingdom had been enjoying at least a generation of unparalleled peace and material prosperity, and the people were celebrating the seasonal festivals to Yahweh and the baalim in the happy confidence that divine approval was upon all their acts. Hosea found himself unable to share this self-satisfied feeling. He felt certain, as had the prophet Elijah a century earlier, that Yahweh did *not* look tolerantly upon the worship of the baalim. Elijah had assumed that Yahweh approved the killing of those who were persistently disloyal to him, but Hosea held the very contrary. In fact, the most distinctive feature of Hosea's writings, surprising in view of the age in which they appeared, is the emphasis on the utter impossibility of Yahweh's feeling angry resentment or having a desire to punish and to hurt, let alone destroy, no matter how faithless and trying his people might be.

1. *The Tragic Domestic Life of Hosea.* How is the startling contrast between Hosea's concept of God and that of other men of his time to be explained? Judging from the prominent place which Hosea himself gives to a personal domestic tragedy (chapters *1 ff.), it was the transformation which this experience brought about in his own religious thinking that accounts for the revolutionary ideas Hosea held and taught.

So painful, and in certain details so nearly incredible, is the story which Hosea relates of his unfaithful wife and their helpless children that some have wondered whether Hosea may not have made up the story and given it this personal twist as a sort of parable by which to drive home the then utterly new idea of a boundlessly compassionate, sympathetic, understanding, and forgiving God. It seems more plausible, however, that just such an arresting and upheaving experience as this was needed to reverse in Hosea's mind the concept of God in which he had been nurtured. Some interpreters prefer to press Hos. 1:2 quite literally, and they understand Hosea to have gone and married a prostitute deliberately in order by such a sensational act to dramatize the message he wished to get across to

---

[45] Am. 2:4.   [46] Cf. *supra*, pp. 246–252.

the people.[47] This interpretation assumes that Hosea first got his idea of God, and then entered into this distressing marriage. But we are entitled to ask, "How did Hosea come by this idea of God?" This line of interpretation offers no answer to that question. Great ideas grow out of soul-searching experiences. Grant that Hosea first had an experience of tragedy in his marital relationship and found himself still loving Gomer and unable to cast her off utterly, and we have a basis in his experience for the origin of his idea of God. There is the possibility that Gomer had been one of the "sacred prostitutes" attached to some shrine, with whom Hosea fell ardently in love and married in all sincerity, not counting her past attachment to the shrine as any moral lapse on her part, but instead as an earnest religious consecration. It is difficult for us moderns to see how prostitution could ever have been regarded as sacred, but nevertheless it was. On this interpretation, after her marriage to Hosea the pull of her past was too strong for Gomer, and she went after other lovers, and this was not "sacred" adultery on her part. Whatever had been her past before her marriage, she did prove faithless to Hosea, but despite that he still loved her and could not let her go. This is the basic element in his experience. His very name, Hosea, means "salvation." [48]

Hosea's inability to cease loving the wife who so violated all wifely obligations must have been utterly inexplicable to himself on any natural basis. Then the thought filtered into his understanding that Gomer's conduct toward himself was exactly paralleled by the nation's conduct toward Yahweh (4:11 f., 14, 5:4). From that it was an easy step to the conviction that Yahweh was bringing upon him this unhappy chain of experiences as the only possible way by which a person could be made to put himself in God's place and get the divine viewpoint. For Hosea began to see that if he, a fallible human being, could feel such tenderness and understanding pity for the sins and follies of a headstrong, erring wife, surely God himself could not be less magnanimous and understanding toward a nation that was erring in ignorance.

2. *Hosea's Portrait of a Yahweh of Tender Love.* In some such way as just depicted, Hosea arrived at his conception that Yahweh was a God of love. He did not waste time arguing about the war-god fallacy but directed all his efforts to showing how Yahweh's known patience in previous centuries had been exactly characteristic of a loving husband and a tender father. And so with rare insight and delicacy of feeling he portrays Yahweh as giving expression to such

[47] Cf. J. M. P. Smith, *The Prophets and Their Times* (Chicago: 1925), pp. 56–59.
[48] *Vid. supra,* p. 138.

compassionate utterances as are found in *2:6 ff., 14, 19f.; *11:1, 3 f., 8 f.; *13:4 ff.; *14:1–8. There are few passages in all the Old Testament finer than these in their conception and interpretation of the divine. So impressive is this concept of God, now appearing in the Book of Hosea for the first time in literature, that Hosea is today commonly referred to as the "Prophet of Love." Hosea's ideas of God and religion are expressed most beautifully in *6:6 and *12:6.

The concept of a God of love was Hosea's most valuable but not his only contribution to the Hebrew idea of God, for he was the first thinker to urge clearly and convincingly that the disasters which follow wrongdoing need not imply anger and vengefulness in the deity, but loving guidance that utilizes pain to steer one from yet worse disasters (2:5b–7, 9, 11–16; 5:11–15; *6:1, 4 ff.; 7:1a).

It is interesting and significant that Hosea singled out the exodus and the wilderness experiences as the happiest period in the life of the nation and the one in which the nation had the least to regret; for it was then that the nation acted most like a trusting child under a father's loving protection (2:15; 11:1 ff., 12:9; 13:4).

Hosea's emphasis on God's tenderness and compassion in no wise leads him to portray Yahweh as an indulgent deity or one whose moral discrimination is blurred. On the contrary, Hosea was keenly alive to the ethical implications of religion and life (4:1 f., 11, 14; 6:6–9; 7:1 ff.). But like all truly great and noble characters, Hosea was able to hate sin without altogether despising the sinner.

Another of Hosea's distinguishing traits is his condemnation of idolatrous images (4:12, 17; 11:2; 14:3b). Here again he seems to have been a pioneer and an original thinker. Having in mind particularly the famous golden calves, he speaks of these images in terms of withering contempt (8:4b–6; 13:2 f., 14:8a). A religion which took itself out in kissing calves deserved such derision. The shrine that housed them, Bethel (literally "House of God"), he repeatedly refers to by the obnoxious nickname and half-pun *Beth-aven* [49] ("House of Panting Breath"), a phrase that carries the connotation of a place where tremendous efforts are put forth but with futile outcome (4:15; 5:8; 10:5). He means, of course, that all their zealous and costly worship before these images avails them not a thing in reality.

[49] The word *aven* is impossible to render accurately by any single word in English. In Isa. 41:29 it is rendered "vanity" in the sense of futility. In Hos. 9:4 the exact reading is "their sacrifices shall be unto them as bread of *aven*," evidently meaning unsatisfying or failing to give nourishment. Am. 5:5 expresses a similar thought in the last line, "and Bethel shall become *Aven*," which can only mean that Bethel is doomed to some sort of ruin. In Isa. 66:3 *aven* is translated "idol," showing that the word in time came to be accepted as a proper descriptive of idolatry as the very personification of futility and uselessness. On Hos. 5:8 see note 19 *supra*, p. 65.

This ability on the part of Hosea to sense the uselessness and folly of images with such clarity as to cause him to launch the prophetic attack upon their use is an additional tribute to his spiritual insight, his clear thinking, and his moral courage. It took centuries for this idea to capture the Hebrew nation so that it really did away with idolatry. But that day might have been longer postponed had it not been for Hosea's writings.

How did it come about that Hosea wrote a book? Doubtless for the same reason as with Amos—the encouragement of disciples who had been convinced by his preaching and whom we have to thank for preserving to posterity the prophet's great message. We have already made some observations upon the literary character of Hosea's book.[50]

The Religious Contributions of the Prophet Isaiah. It was not more than ten or fifteen years after Amos and Hosea addressed northern Israel when the youthful Isaiah began his ministry in Jerusalem. Amos and Hosea seem to have said their say and stopped. Isaiah continued his prophetic activity over a period of forty years.

Isaiah was the most majestic of the prophets. He was a citizen of Jerusalem and his prophetic career centered there, though he did have some things to say about conditions in Israel.[51] He was a married man and he speaks of his wife as "the prophetess" (8:3). He had two sons to whom he gave symbolic names, Shear-jashub, "a remnant shall return" (7:3) and Maher-shalal-hash-baz, "speed spoil, hasten prey" (8:3). Certain dramatic incidents in his career are depicted in his book. One is his vision in the Jerusalem temple (chapter 6). Another incident localized in the temple was of a wholly different sort; Isaiah was derided by the drunken priests and prophets and in reply he denounced them (Isa. 28:7–22). His memorable interview with King Ahaz "in the highway of the fuller's field" was fraught with far-reaching political significance (Isa. 7:1–17).[52] Isaiah was a poet, as we have already seen,[53] and perhaps 5:1–7 is best understood as a ditty which Isaiah sang on some occasion in the market place. Like many another of the prophets, he resorted to sensational behavior in order to dramatize his message. He went about the streets of Jerusalem "naked and barefoot three years" (20:1–4). On one public occasion he wrote upon a great tablet and had faithful witnesses to testify to it in order to convince the people of the imminent peril from Assyria (8:1 f.). He had disciples to whom he entrusted a book he had written containing his teachings (8:16 ff.). It is doubtless these disciples whom we have to thank for the preservation of Isaiah's poems

---

[50] *Supra*, p. 302.
[51] Isa. 9:8–10:4; 5:26–29; 28:1–4. Cf. *supra*, p. 251.
[52] Cf. *supra*, p. 248.   [53] *Supra*, p. 302.

and orations. In the critical year 701 B.C. when Jerusalem was be-
seiged by Sennacherib (Isa. 36), Hezekiah, the king of Judah, in
desperation sent to Isaiah for counsel. The prophet's memorable reply
to the king is recorded in Isa. 37. There is a tradition that Isaiah
died a martyr by being sawed asunder in the time of King Manasseh.[54]
Heb. 11:37 may be an allusion to his death.

Isaiah's prophetic career began "in the year that King Uzziah
(Azariah) died" (6:1), i.e., 739 B.C. The crucial historical events
to which Isaiah's career was related were 734 B.C when King Ahaz
deliberately made Judah a vassal of Assyria; [55] 722 B.C. when Samaria
fell and Israel was obliterated; [56] 711 B.C. when Hezekiah, king of
Judah, barely escaped being in the revolt against Assyria; [57] and
701 B.C. when Jerusalem was besieged by Sennacherib [58] and narrowly
escaped destruction.

1. *Popular Religion in Judah When Isaiah Began His Prophetic
Work.* The author of the Book of Kings gives a seamy picture of the
trend of religion when Isaiah was a young man. Under King Jotham
conditions are said to have remained much as they were under his
father Azariah (Uzziah). The author of Kings speaks in commendation of Jotham, although remarking that the high places were not
disturbed (2 Kgs. 15:34 f.). With the accession of Ahaz, however, a
drastic and startling change took place in the official religion. Within
a few months after Ahaz became king the Assyrians were sweeping
through Syria in resistless conquest, and when Damascus fell (732
B.C.) Ahaz made haste not only to swear allegiance to the Assyrian
monarch but also to adopt Assyrian worship as the official religion of
Judah in place of Yahweh worship (2 Kgs. *16:10–18).[59] An altar
to an Assyrian deity stood in the place of honor formerly occupied
by Yahweh's altar in front of the Jerusalem temple, and other
changes having the same general import were made. Assyrian religion was made official in Judah.

2 Kgs. 16:3 further informs us that Ahaz resorted to human
sacrifice, offering his own son. It does not say just when he did this
or why, but if it occurred (following the order in the narrative)
prior to his abject capitulation to Assyria and Assyrian worship,
one may well wonder if perhaps his sacrifice of his son may not have
been made (like that of the king of Moab referred to in 2 Kgs. 3:27)
in a last desperate appeal to Yahweh to keep the Assyrian invaders
away. If this be so, then apostasy from Yahweh might have seemed
to him logical when the Assyrian advances continued unchecked.

[54] In the Mishna, *Jebamoth* 49b (cf. *Sanhedrin* 103b) ; in the *Martyrdom of Isaiah*
5:11, a pseudepigraphic writing of the second century after Christ; and repeated by
Justin Martyr, *Dialogue with Trypho,* 120, A.D. *circa* 150.
[55] Cf. *supra*, pp. 248 f.   [56] Cf. *supra*, pp. 252 f.   [57] Cf. *supra*, pp. 253 f.
[58] Cf. *supra*, pp. 255–259.   [59] Cf. *supra*, pp. 249 f.

Strangely, there is no confirmation of this official repudiation of Yahweh anywhere in the writings of Isaiah. Isaiah refers to the use of idols,[60] but everywhere else he writes as though Yahweh were taken for granted and being honored as usual with rich sacrificial feasts. The popular conception of religion which rated ritual above righteousness Isaiah denounced in as strong terms as any Amos had used (Isa. *1:11–17). Isaiah is in harmony with Amos and Hosea in lifting religion to the ethical level.

2. *Isaiah's Temple Vision.* Isaiah *6 is one of the Bible's classic passages descriptive of an individual's mystical religious experience. The characteristic features of such experience are all present. The vision occurs at a sacred place, the Jerusalem temple. There is a theophany, or manifestation of the deity, who is both seen (vs. 1) and heard (vs. 8) by Isaiah. Isaiah reacts to the experience with the characteristic emotion of awe or fear (vs. 5). The outcome of the experience is a commission to ethico-religious service on the part of the prophet (vss. 8 f.). The steps of progress in Isaiah's vision are typical of the essential steps in the development of religion itself. The most elemental stage of religion is that of wondering appreciation, in which man stands in silent admiration before some awe-inspiring manifestation of the universe. Vss. 1–3 represent this phase of religion. The second stage of religion is that of fear and distress and arises when some crisis threatens the values of life and God becomes not an object of wonder and admiration but an obstacle to be feared. This is the religion of passive dependence before an obstacle which threatens destruction. Vss. 4 and 5 vividly portray this phase of religious experience. The third stage of religion is that of redemption, in which God is the savior of man. Vss. 6 and 7 most beautifully portray the Holy God taking the initiative in sending the seraphim to forgive and save Isaiah. To such divine grace the noblest type of response is not ritual performance but voluntary consecration of self to the active service of God. In all the ages since Isaiah, vs. 8 has been upon the lips of those who, having passed through some profoundly moving religious experience, dedicate their lives to spiritual service.

It is this vision that constituted Isaiah's call to be a prophet of Yahweh. The task laid upon him, as described in vss. 9–12, was indeed uninviting and disheartening, to give warning after warning to a people of unclean lips, unseeing eyes, deaf ears, and dull hearts over a period of years—a people he well knew would not heed his messages until a plundered country and ruined cities should drive home to them the realization that he had been speaking the truth. This chapter is undoubtedly an accurate reflection of Isaiah's lifetime of work—at

[60] Isa. 2:8; 10:11.

least to the time when King Hezekiah, in 701 B.C., with his country ravaged, forty-six of his chief cities and towns taken, and himself "shut up like a bird in a cage in Jerusalem," turned in desperation to Isaiah as the one man in the entire nation whose foresight had proved accurate (Isa. 36:1; 37:1-4). The charming but sad-toned lyric about Yahweh and his Vineyard in Isa. *5:1-7,[61] and the severe arraignment of the nation in 30:9-14, 16 f., throw further light upon Isaiah's expectations as to the probable responsiveness of the nation.

3. *Ethical Aspects of Isaiah's Views on Religion.* Isaiah assimilated into his thinking the ideas which Amos and Hosea contributed to Hebrew religion. We have seen that Amos was stirred by the conviction that God cared little for costly festivals but much for justice and righteousness that found expression in kindness and generosity toward the poor and unfortunate. The earliest preaching of Isaiah, between his call and the crisis of 734 B.C., was along much the same line, as may be seen in *3:13 ff.; *5:1-24 (especially vs. 16).[62] Ethical teachings, with the Old Testament prophets and later Jewish wisdom teachers, were often given in the form of "beatitudes" and "woes," the beatitudes being positive exhortations to righteousness and the woes being condemnations of vices. Sometimes these were put in the balanced form of antithetic parallelism, of which Isa. *3:10 f. is an excellent example. In 5:1-24 Isaiah makes repeated use of the "woe" form. Isa. *9:8-10:4 is a poem in four stanzas, each ending with the same refrain (9:12b, 17b, 21b; 10:4b), much on the line of Am. 4:4-11. We have seen how Hosea's thought of God centered in God's understanding and firm but tender love which the people did not know and therefore they perished for lack of knowledge. Isaiah has this very thought also (*5:13; cf. Hos. 4:6). Hosea's view that kindness rates above sacrifice (Hos. 6:6) is reflected in Isa. *1:11-17.

Isaiah specified what acts of conduct he considered unethical. His writings reveal the interesting fact that the traditional democratic ideal of a lot of small landholdings was being ignored in a system of accumulation of vast estates (5:8); that the rights of orphans and widows were being shamelessly violated even in the law courts (1:23; 10:2); that drunken debauchery characterized the life of the court nobility (5:11 f., 22; 28:7 f.); that violence and bloodshed, especially if it was against the lower classes, apparently went unchecked and unpunished (1:21 ff.; 3:14 f.; 5:18 ff., 23); that the women of Israel had become bold, modern, and vampishly wanton (3:16-24; 4:4); and that the very distinction between good and evil, right and wrong,

---

[61] Cf. *supra*, p. 154.
[62] Bewer, *op. cit.*, p. 117, arranges the passages of Isaiah chronologically.

had become confused (*5:20) resulting in an open cynicism toward divine retribution and justice (5:19, 28:14 f.). Personal unrighteousness and dullness to spiritual realities characterized the nation; they were "a people of unclean lips" (6:5). To such a nation Isaiah preached the necessity of personal and social moral redemption (*1:18).

4. *Isaiah's Concept of God.* Isaiah's creative contribution to the idea of God was the concept of holiness. "Holy, holy, holy, is Yahweh" (6:3). Yahweh is "the Holy One of Israel." [63] In the common religious thought of the time, the holiness of Yahweh meant his remoteness, his physical inaccessibility. He was a Holy God because he was separated from men, dwelling in the Most Holy Place of the Jerusalem temple where he could be approached only by certain men, the priests. Isaiah gave to this word *holy* an ethical content. God's holiness is his moral perfection, his transcendence. This "Holy One of Israel" is "Yahweh of Hosts," [64] whether the hosts of earth or the supernatural hosts. "The whole earth is full of his glory" (6:3). In the common view, Yahweh's glory meant his physical manifestation in fire and storm.[65] With Isaiah, Yahweh's glory is the manifestation of his holiness. He is "the King" (6:5) and rules in righteousness. Yahweh is so exalted, so powerful, so extended in his sway that even the mightiest of empires, Assyria, falls under his far-seeing control (*10:5 ff.). Assyria is the rod of Yahweh's anger (10:5), for whom Yahweh will whistle to come from the end of the earth to visit punishment upon Yahweh's own sinful people (*5:26–29). Amos had said that Yahweh guided Israel's enemies, the Philistines and the Syrians.[66] Isaiah extends this thought to include the worst of all their enemies, Assyria. To Isaiah, Yahweh is the exalted ruler of nations and the determiner of their destiny (Isa. *14:24–27), and when she shall have served Yahweh's purpose, arrogant Assyria will in turn be trodden under foot.

Isaiah did not deny the existence of other gods. Therefore monotheism has not yet been explicitly affirmed. But Isaiah's thought has moved in that direction. It is important to observe just what it is that is urging the thought of the prophets toward monotheism. It is the ethical urge, that basic moral idealism which demands that righteousness shall prevail in man and in the world. To achieve righteousness, man must have a God big enough to establish righteousness in the earth, big enough, that is, to bend Assyria, the mightiest nation on the earth, to his righteous purpose. And this is Isaiah's God.

[63] Isa. 1:4; 5:16, 19, 24; and often. Cf. O. J. Baab, *The Theology of the Old Testament* (Nashville: 1949), pp. 33 f.   [64] Isa. 6:3, 5; and often.
[65] Cf. Ex. 24:16 f.   [66] Am. 9:7.

5. *Political Aspects of Isaiah's Enlarged Concept of God.* The disaster of 722 B.C. which obliterated the kingdom of Israel was a crushing social and political calamity, but of far greater import was the peril to religion involved in the crisis. Israel claimed Yahweh as its national god and he had allowed his nation to perish. To the minds of many, therefore, not only of those deported into captivity but of those who remained in the land of Samaria, Yahweh was no god at all and they forever renounced Yahwism. In surviving Judah there were many no doubt who reasoned thus: "Yahweh never was the god of northern Israel. He is *our* god. His temple has not been harmed and we have come safely through. We are his chosen people." For this type of mind the evil day had only been put off until 586 B.C. The God of Isaiah was a bigger God than that. Samaria fell, not because Yahweh couldn't help it but because Yahweh willed it. The crisis of 722 B.C. stimulated the mind of the prophet to conceive of God in bigger than nationalistic terms.

Up to this time, loyalty to Yahweh had been accepted as axiomatic because of the belief that national security was bound up in Yahweh's expertness in war. Isaiah's broader view of God led him to develop the political theory that national security was assured simply by trusting Yahweh, doing righteousness, and remaining supremely indifferent to the threats and menacing activities of all outside powers. As already pointed out,[67] Isaiah's basic political principle was: Keep faith with Yahweh and avoid all entangling alliances. The meaning of this was that Yahweh's sway was so wide, his will so fair and just, and his power so unchallengeable that all that was essential was for a nation to live righteously and Yahweh would see to it that they were immune from invasion. Righteousness and loyalty to Yahweh guaranteed the integrity of the nation. This must have been the main thought behind such a passage as *30:15,

> Thus saith the Lord Yahweh, the Holy One of Israel,
> In returning and rest shall ye be saved;
> In quietness and confidence shall be your strength,

which one writer has called "a terse and splendid summary of Isaiah's gospel." [68] Precisely the same thought appears in 7:4a, 9b; *28:16; and *32:17.

Later generations attributed to Isaiah the doctrine that Zion (the holy city of Jerusalem) was inviolable, impregnable. They based this interpretation upon the confident prediction ascribed to Isaiah in the crisis of 701 B.C. (Isa. 37:33 ff. = 2 Kgs. 19:32 ff.) [69] that the

---

[67] *Supra*, pp. 248 f., 258 f.
[68] J. E. McFayden, *The Book of the Prophecies of Isaiah* (New York: 1910), p. 199.
[69] Cf. Isa. 14:24–27, 32; 29:1–8; 31:4 f.

king of Assyria would never enter Jerusalem nor so much as shoot an
arrow into it. It was easy to draw this inference because of the fact
that in the numerous invasions of Judah's soil, Jerusalem itself had
repeatedly escaped complete humiliation. Nowhere does he imply
that Yahweh's protection would be given because Zion was Zion—
that is, because Yahweh's own temple stood there—but only when a
nation was obedient to the divine laws of justice and righteousness,
as well as trusting.

6. *Isaiah's Optimistic Faith in the Future.* Isaiah takes up two
other doctrines of Amos. One is the idea of the Day of Yahweh,
which Isaiah delineates in the vigorous poem in *2:5–22.[70] The other
is the idea of the remnant.[71] This idea apparently held a central
place in the thinking of Isaiah, so much so that he named one of
his boys Shear-jashub, "A remnant shall return" (7:3). The thought
is that very few will survive the devastation of the coming Day of
Yahweh. The idea is developed in such passages as 4:2 ff.; 6:13;
17:4 ff.; 28:5; 37:31 f. which are generally regarded by Old Testament scholars as later insertions in the Book of Isaiah, although
Bewer considers 17:4 ff. a genuine passage [72] and it is a picturesque
expression of the idea. Isa. 28:16 expresses this idea of a remnant
under wholly different imagery; Yahweh lays in Zion a precious
cornerstone of sure foundation. What did Isaiah expect Yahweh
would build upon that foundation? What did he expect Yahweh
would do with the remnant after the Day of Yahweh had passed?
Did he speculate upon this problem and offer any answer to these
questions? If Isaiah himself did not, some kindred spiritual mind
was bound to do so, and did, and the answer is to be found in such
passages as Isa. *2:2 ff., *4:2–6, *9:2–7, *11:1–9, and *32:1–8, 15–
20. These passages express what is technically called "messianism."
Messiah is conceived of as that ideal person, usually an ideal ruler,
whom God would raise up to usher in the ideal age of the future.
The remnant is that group of spiritually minded persons upon whom,
as a nucleus, God can build the new and ideal order of the future
after the Day of Yahweh has swept unrighteousness off the earth.
This is the heart of Hebrew ethical idealism and the basis of it is
laid by the prophet Isaiah.[73]

The Prophecies of Micah. The Bible gives us no biographical
details about Micah nor is any one incident of his life high-lighted

---

[70] Cf. Am. 5:18 ff.; *supra*, p. 317.   [71] Cf. Am. 5:3, 15; *supra*, p. 317.
[72] *Op. cit.*, p. 117 fn.
[73] The writings of Isaiah of Jerusalem of the eighth century B.C. are found in the
first part of the Biblical book of Isaiah, i.e., chapters 1–39. The remainder of the
book, chapters 40–66, is known as the Deutero-Isaiah, and comes from a very much
later period, viz., the exile.

in his book. Mic. 1:1, 14 intimates that he was a native of More-
sheth near Gath, in the Shephelah. He was a farmer, and his book
everywhere reflects his peasant sympathies. The editorial superscription to his book (1:1) spreads Micah's prophetic career over the
same forty-year period as Isaiah's. Perhaps the editor who added
this superscription did so because he assumed that Micah must have
prophesied concerning Samaria before that city was taken by Sargon, in view of Mic. 1:5 f. It must be borne in mind, however, that
while Sargon did capture Samaria in 722 B.C., he did not destroy the
city. Two years later, in 720 B.C., Samaria was involved in another
anti-Assyrian revolt, at which time Sargon deported a great many
from Samaria into captivity.[74] Even at that time he did not destroy
the city but settled there a great many whom he had deported from
other corners of his empire. Samaria therefore continued to be a focal
point of sociological and religious problems to call forth utterances
from the prophets. What is said in Mic. 1:5 f. would have been
appropriate in the last decade of the eighth century.

The one historical situation to which Micah's career is definitely
related is the troublous period toward the end of the eighth century
when Sennacherib's army was ravaging Judah, culminating in the
siege of Jerusalem in 701 B.C.[75] Micah had firsthand knowledge
about the terrible sufferings of the poor in that chaotic period, for
he lived right in the heart of the devastated area. It was the poor
who were suffering for what the nation's leaders had brought upon
the country by their stupidity. The wealthy, landholding class had
"joined house to house and laid field to field" (as Isaiah had denounced, Isa. 5:8) by vicious oppression of the poor countryfolk of
Judah, and now that the Assyrians were ravaging the countryside
these same aristocrats were safe enough behind the walls of Jerusalem while the poor whom they had exploited were left out in the
country to bear the suffering of the invasion. Micah is almost savage
in his denunciation of the nation's leaders and the powerful upper
classes for the tyranny with which they oppressed the poor (chapters
*2 and *3). In the grimmest metaphor we have yet come upon Micah
says that they "eat the flesh of my people, and flay their skin from
off them, and break their bones, and chop them in pieces, as for the
pot" (3:3). To their shame, priests and prophets were serving for
revenue only (3:5, 11), and anyone who predicted materialistic
blessings would leap into favor. The ruin and wreckage thus brought
upon the whole nation Micah laments in that notable dirge (*1:8–16)
of which we have previously spoken.[76] The situation will lead to the

[74] Cf. *supra*, pp. 252 f.
[75] Cf. *supra*, pp. 255–259.
[76] Cf. *supra*, pp. 302 f.

destruction of the "holy city" which has been built up with blood and iniquity. To the pious protest of Jerusalem's leaders:

> Is not Yahweh in the midst of us?
> No evil shall come upon us! (3:11b)

Micah sharply retorted:

> Because of *you*, Zion shall be plowed as a field,
> Jerusalem shall become heaps,
> And the temple hill as a high place of a forest. (3:12)

Micah certainly harbored no illusion about an inviolable Jerusalem. This famous utterance of Micah was the means of saving the life of the prophet Jeremiah at a much later time (Jer. *26:18 f.). Indeed, Micah is the one prophet of whom it is recorded that by his preaching a king (Hezekiah) was directly moved to promote a religious reform (Jer. 26:19).

Micah may have lived on into Manasseh's reign, the religious character of which is reflected in Mic. 6:1–7:6. This passage and chapters 1 ff. are practically all of the book which came from Micah himself. The rest of it consists of additions made at a later time.

Micah contributed no religious idea which we have not already met in Amos, Hosea, and Isaiah. He assimilates their ideas in a grand passage which is a classic summary of the spiritual achievement of these eighth-century prophets (Mic. *6:6 ff.). This spiritual achievement consisted in definitely raising religion up to the ethical level. Vss. 6 f. portray ceremonial religion carried to the utmost possible extreme, human sacrifice, only to declare that it does not please Yahweh. Righteousness is above ritual. Yahweh is a righteous God. "He hath showed thee, O man, what is good; and what doth Yahweh require of thee, but to do justice [here speaks Amos], and to love kindness [here speaks Hosea], and to walk humbly with thy God [the human attitude toward the holiness of God which Isaiah preached]" (vs. 8). This verse expresses the essence of religion. It is graven as the motto of the alcove of religion in the Library of Congress, Washington, D. C. When he took his oath of office as President of the United States, Warren G. Harding kissed an open Bible with his lips touching this noble verse, Mic. 6:8.

The Religious Behavior of the Eighth-Century Prophets. These prophets were men who had profound experiences of a nature such that in them they perceived the guiding hand of God. One feature of their religious experiences is called "visions." Amos and Isaiah both had visions. Amos tells of visions of devouring locusts (7:1 ff.), blighting drought (7:4 ff.), a plumb line of judgment (7:7 ff.), and a basket of summer fruit (*qayits*) that symbolized an "end" (*qêts*) of the nation Israel (8:1 ff.). Isaiah had the famous temple vision (chapter 6). Hosea's experience took a somewhat different direction, a strange divine command to marry a prostitute (1:2, 3:1 ff.).

It may be that Amos's visions were woven of the ordinary fabric of life's experiences, all of them happenings he had noted and pondered upon in his home in the Tekoa Hills, which in his quiet communion with nature he had come to connect with Yahweh's warnings, a succession of hints of a growing divine displeasure. Isaiah's vision at the temple was primarily and emphatically mystical, a high-keyed emotional experience. Such experiences are not unusual in deeply religious natures in all religions. That both Hosea and Isaiah possessed deeply emotional religious traits is obvious. Both men gave their children strange, unlovely, symbolic names—Jezreel, in memory of Jehu's bloody days (Hos. 1:4); Lo-ruhamah, "Un-pitied," in token that the nation had sinned past redemption (Hos. 1:6); Lo-ammi, "Not-my-people," implying that Israel was no longer Yahweh's people (Hos. 1:9); Shear-jashub, "A-remnant-shall-return," hinting at the few loyal who might be saved (Isa. 7:3); and Maher-shalal-hash-baz, "Speed-spoil, hurry-prey," living reminder that the plundering was due to commence within a year or two (Isa. 8:1–4). To give children descriptive names was not uncommon. The name Immanu-el, "With-us-is-God," dramatizes the vainglorious boast of Judah's leaders as they scoffed at Isaiah's prediction of Assyrian invasion (Isa. 7:14, 16–25).[77] A set of names like the foregoing must have arrested attention in those days. That, of course, was what the parents wanted. Another striking feature of the behavior of the prophets is to be seen in the fact that Isaiah walked the streets of Jerusalem for three years in the garb of a captive of war ("naked and barefoot," as the Hebrew idiom has it),[78] a dramatized warning that captivity would be the penalty for alliance with Egypt instead of trusting Yahweh (chapter 20). Religion in that age was certainly an intense affair; the deities were not to be trifled with or lightly esteemed.

Official Religion in Judah: Apostasy and Reforms

Nominally, Yahwism was the official religion of Judah. In reality it was not so. Certain of Judah's kings, under stress of political expediency, made other cults, especially Assyrian cults, official in Judah. Other kings, roused by the prophets, reacted against such foreign cults and officially instituted religious reforms looking toward the re-establishment of Yahwism. For a century and a half, from the time of

[77] Scholars differ in their views as to whose child this Immanu-el was, whether the child of Isaiah himself, or (more likely) of King Ahaz himself, or of some other.
[78] Cf. Mic. 1:8.

King Ahaz and the prophet Isaiah to the end of Judah's career, the story of official religion in Judah is an alternation of apostasy and reforms.

Apostasy Under King Ahaz. The story of how King Ahaz made Assyrian religion official in Judah has already been considered.[79] The most revolting aspect of it all was the revival of the heinous practice of human sacrifice, the king himself setting the example.

Reforms Under King Hezekiah. 2 Kgs. *18:3–6 specifies certain reforms which were carried through at some point in the reign of Hezekiah, possibly in connection with his revolt from Assyria. Jer. 26:18 f. distinctly states that it was the preaching of the prophet Micah which roused King Hezekiah to this reform. Political revolt would certainly have included repudiation of the Assyrian cults.[80] Anyone possessing the courage to destroy a long-revered object like the bronze snake made by Moses might be expected to be thoroughgoing in the cleanup of the high places. Such conspicuous championing of the cause of Yahweh was probably the main reason why Isaiah so confidently backed him and urged him to steadfast defiance of Assyria in the war that inevitably ensued.[81]

Apostasy Under King Manasseh. With the accession of Manasseh, official religion promptly reverted to the policy adopted by his grandfather Ahaz. To evidence his political loyalty to Assyria, Manasseh reintroduced the Assyrian cults in Jerusalem.[82] The high places were rebuilt, polytheism was reestablished more firmly than ever, images were reintroduced, and the example of child sacrifice was again set by the king himself (2 Kgs. *21:1–9). From this time on, Ishtar, "Queen of Heaven," and all the host of heaven were worshiped in Judah just as in Nineveh. Ishtar (Ashtart), as the morning star, was worshiped as the goddess of war, and as the evening star, the patroness of love and harlotry. The astral deities were worshiped on the housetops, where altars were erected. Jer. 7:18, 44:17 mentions certain features accompanying such worship, such as the making of cakes to the "Queen of Heaven," burning incense, and pouring libations. Another feature was the singing of hymns.[83] Ezk. *8:5–18 is a vivid portrayal of the idolatry rampant in Jerusalem in the time of Manasseh and the last kings of Judah.

Manasseh was the arch idolater of Hebrew history. He even named his son after an Egyptian deity, Amon. The record states that "Manasseh shed innocent blood very much." [84] This may be a refer-

---

[79] Supra, p. 322.   [80] Cf. 2 Chr. 32:1.
[81] Cf. supra, pp. 258 f., 326 f.   [82] Cf. supra, p. 260.
[83] Cf. S. H. Langdon, Semitic Mythology (Boston: 1931), p. 25.
[84] 2 Kgs. 21:16, 24:3 f.

ence to human sacrifices which he inaugurated as a feature of his idolatry, or it may imply a murderous treatment of his political and religious opponents, especially the Yahweh prophets.[85] Certainly there is an ominous silence of prophets during the first three-quarters of the seventh century, B.C. Apparently there were no defenders of Yahweh zealous enough, courageous enough, and competent to rise to spiritual leadership in the face of the official disfavor which manifestly prevailed. At any rate, all that Hezekiah had accomplished seems to have been undone by his son. According to 2 Chr. 33:11–19, Manasseh experienced a change of heart after he had been arrested on orders from the Assyrian monarch, but the depth and permanency of this change are rather discounted by the statements in vss. 22 f. of the same chapter.

Manasseh's son Amon reigned too brief a time (two years) to accomplish much in the way of religious reform even had he so desired, and the Bible historian credits him with no such intention. His assassination left the eight-year-old Josiah suddenly in nominal control and for eighteen years more official religion remained much as it had been.

The Great Reformation Under King Josiah: 621 B.C. The most epochal of all the religious reformations in Judah was that which occurred in the eighteenth year of the reign of King Josiah (2 Kgs. *22 f.). The movement began with a plan to repair the dilapidated parts of the Jerusalem temple. In the course of the work a certain "book of the law" (in 2 Kgs. 23:2 also called the "book of the covenant") was found which was directly responsible for the reforms which the king carried out.

This book is technically referred to as the "D" code. We have already had occasion to note this book and its literary and social significance.[86] Its religious significance is our present concern. It finds its basis in that prophetic idea and interest which sought to lift religion from the ritual to the ethical level.

The movement was characterized by two leading features. On the one hand it sought to eliminate the baser practices then prevalent in religious worship by closing all shrine and sanctuaries outside of Jerusalem and centering worship in the temple where it could be strictly supervised and controlled (Deut. *12:1–14, 17 f., 26 f.). The code was doubtless elaborated in antipathy to the Assyrianizing policy that had long dominated the court of Jerusalem. On the other hand, it aimed to moralize a worship which up to that time had conspicuously lacked such emphasis, as shown in the charges of practically every prophet we have studied.

---

[85] Cf. Jer. 2:30.   [86] *Supra,* pp. 284 f., 305.

Child sacrifice, divination, augury, sorcery, necromancy, and other debased practices, of which frequent mention has been made by the prophets and Biblical historians, are squarely prohibited in Deut. 18:10 f. as "abominations" because of which Yahweh had driven out the Canaanites and which he would not tolerate in Israel. One of the most debased religious practices, rooted in the earliest Canaanite religious pattern, and continuing through the centuries, was sacred prostitution. Now at last this institution is forbidden in Deut. 23:17, as fine an illustration as could be cited of the moralizing of religion.

The Deuteronomic code aimed to put into practice some of the very principles for which the great prophets of the eighth century had stood: consideration for the poor, needy, and defenseless; freeing of worship from the worst of its licentious and superstitious elements; fresh emphasis on justice and kindness; and inculcation of worship based on love and gratitude rather than on fear and purchase of favor. One of the most notable provisions of the code, evidencing ethical advance, is in Deut. 24:16, the limitation of blood revenge to the actually guilty person. In 16:9–17 the slave, the casual passerby, the orphan, and the widow were to share in the joyous harvest festivals with the families of the wealthy. At the harvest season fields, orchards, and vineyards were not to be so closely gleaned as to leave nothing for these poorer groups (24:19–22). Lost property was either to be returned or carefully guarded for its owner, and no one was ever to shirk an opportunity to lend a helping hand to a neighbor in an emergency (22:1–4). Day laborers were to be paid daily, evidently because their need was often so desperate (24:14 f.), while a lender to a widow might not exact as security for the debt her very clothing (24:17 f.; cf. Am. 2:8). Acceptance of bribes by judges or any favoring of the social status of litigants was strictly forbidden (16:18 ff.). This appeal calls to mind the many charges of such corruption made by the prophets from Amos to Jeremiah.

By no means of least importance for the growth of ethical and spiritual sensitiveness, the Deuteronomist sought to build up in the hearts of the Hebrew people feelings of gratitude, loyalty, and affection by pointing out how the nation had never really *deserved* any of the things that Yahweh had done for them; how from the day when Yahweh had rescued them from their Egyptian bondage until then, they had been constantly in his debt; and that consequently the least they could do was to give him their undivided loyalty and affection and see to it that their children did not grow up without having impressed upon them what great things Yahweh had done for their fathers (6:10 ff., 20–25, 7:6–9).

This "D" code, which in 2 Kgs. 22:8 is called "the book of the law" and in 2 Kgs. 23:2 is called "the book of the covenant," was *the first piece of Hebrew literature to be elevated to the status of Holy Scripture,* which is what is meant by canonization. The book found in the temple made such an impression upon the king that he wished to know its divine status. He therefore sent to "inquire of Yahweh . . . concerning the words of this book which is found." [87] Inquiry was made of a prophetess named Huldah, who indorsed the book as being truly the word of Yahweh.[88] Thereupon the king gathered the people in a solemn assembly at the temple to hear the law read, after which both king and people entered into a solemn covenant to live up to it. Forthwith the king set about definite religious reforms to bring the life of the nation into definite conformity to what was written in a book. It was therefore a book set apart from other books of the time and esteemed on a different level. It was sacred literature.

The reforms which King Josiah carried through followed identically the lines laid down by King Hezekiah a century earlier. The main difference seems to have been that Josiah went a step farther in a deliberate effort so to defile the forbidden shrines and altars that never again (he hoped) could they be used for worship (2 Kgs. 23:6, 10, 13 f., 16, 20). To what extent these compulsory reforms touched the inner life and were permanent is an unanswered question. By centralizing religious worship in Jerusalem the Josianic reform divested the common people's everyday affairs of the religious import they had hitherto had. No longer was there open to the countryfolk that warm and helpful friendly intercourse with their local priest or man of God. Religion now meant a distant national shrine and an impersonal written law. These reforms met resistance, judging from what happened later, as evidenced particularly in the writings of the prophet Jeremiah.

Apostasy Under Judah's Last Kings. Following Josiah's violent death in 608 B.C.,[89] the religious policy of kings and people alike seems to have become vacillating. Probably they found it particularly difficult to adjust their religious philosophies to the rapid changes in political fortunes—the collapse of Assyria, the mercurial rise and eclipse of Egyptian overlordship, and a divided opinion as to whether the new Chaldean power might not duplicate the experience of Egypt. The author of the Book of Kings refers vaguely to these later rulers as doing "evil in the sight of Yahweh according to all that their fathers had done," [90] but he charges the fall of Jerusalem really to Manasseh's offenses.[91] From Jeremiah's writings, however, we deduce

[87] 2 Kgs. 22:13.
[89] 2 Kgs. 23:29.
[91] 2 Kgs. 21:10–15; 23:26 f.; 24:3 f.

[88] 2 Kgs. 22:14 ff.
[90] 2 Kgs. 23:32, 37; 24:9, 19.

the information that polytheism and idolatry continued rampant,[92] even to the fall of Jerusalem and after.[93] He comments with vehement distaste upon their facility for changing gods (Jer. 2:10 ff.). Even Zedekiah, who evidently had more respect for the opinion of Jeremiah than his immediate predecessors among the kings, is declared not to have "hearkened to the word of Yahweh which he spake by the prophet Jeremiah." [94] Such was the official attitude toward religion to the very close of Judah's history.

The Religious Leadership of the Seventh-Century Prophets

There is such ominous silence as to prophets in the seventy-five years which intervened between Isaiah and Jeremiah that some Biblical scholars infer that prophecy was suppressed in this period, perhaps even under the penalty of death. It may be, however, that for some obscure reason the age produced no really great, fearless characters. Whatever the explanation, it was not until the Scythians appeared along the Mediterranean coast in 626 B.C. that two prophets, Jeremiah and Zephaniah, are known to have challenged the existing religious order.

Zephaniah's Day of Yahweh.   About Zephaniah personally very little can be affirmed. The superscription to his book (1:1) traces his genealogy to his great-great-grandfather Hezekiah, presumably the king by that name. If he was thus of royal blood, the more significant is his condemnation of the princes and the king's sons (1:8). It may be inferred that he was a resident of Jerusalem from 1:4 ff., 12.

His prophecy finds its background in the Scythian invasion in 626 B.C.[95] The terror which the threatening invasion caused in Judah was interpreted by the prophet as Yahweh's punishment of the sinful nation. The imminent doom which threatens the nation is powerfully expressed in *1:2 f., which is the keynote of the book. Dire retribution threatens not only Palestine but Ethiopia and Assyria as well (2:12 f.). Nineveh is doomed to sink so low as to become grazing ground for cattle and a haunt of wild animals (2:13 ff.).

What are the offenses of Judah which, in Zephaniah's opinion, merit such extreme severity from Yahweh? It is Judah's apostasy, manifest in the unchanged baal worship and the worship of the stars and of Milcom (1:4 f.). Jerusalem itself is held in disdainful contempt (1:12), and her officials, her priests, and her prophets are flagrantly grafting and plundering (3:3 f., 7).

[92] Jer. 2:8; 11, 13, 27 f.; 7:17 f.; 19:13.   [93] Jer. 44:17 ff.
[94] Jer. 37:1 f.   [95] Cf. *supra*, pp. 263 f.

All of this threatening doom Zephaniah expressed under the imagery of the Day of Yahweh. His predecessors among the prophets, Amos and Isaiah, had dwelt upon this theme.[96] Zephaniah, in the blackest imaginable coloring, portrays the Day of Yahweh as a day of wrath, a day of dire punishment, a day of terrible destruction in which utter doom overtakes mankind (*1:14–18). We have already remarked upon the literary quality of Zephaniah's book.[97]

Closely associated with the doctrine of the Day of Yahweh in the preaching of Amos and Isaiah was the doctrine of the remnant which was especially stressed by Isaiah.[98] Zephaniah also holds this doctrine. This small group in society Zephaniah addresses as the "meek of the earth," and exhorts them to righteousness in the hope that "it may be ye will be hid in the day of Yahweh's anger" (*2:3). The hope of the remnant Zephaniah expresses in a poem of exquisite charm (*3:11 ff.).

What effect such preaching had in Judah is problematic. It may be that it helped create the attitude which was favorable to Josiah's reforms.

Jeremiah. 1. *The Life and Times of the Prophet.* We know more about Jeremiah biographically than about any other of the prophets. This is because his intimate friend and secretary, Baruch, wrote a biography of him which is incorporated into the Book of Jeremiah.[99]

Jeremiah was of priestly descent (1:1), a native of the village of Anathoth, four miles northeast of Jerusalem and within the territory of Benjamin. He never married for he did not have the heart to bring children into the world for such a time of suffering (16:1–4). His fellow townsmen of Anathoth once plotted against his life (11:18–23), perhaps because Jeremiah indorsed the reformation of 621 B.C. which by centralizing religion at the Jerusalem temple put the local priests at Anathoth and elsewhere out of their jobs. The incident caused Jeremiah to leave Anathoth and carry on his public prophetic work in Jerusalem.

In Jerusalem the prophet's work centered at the temple (7:1 f.), and we have glimpses of dramatic incidents which happened there. On one occasion a sermon he preached in the temple (26) so irritated a mob of priests, prophets, and people that they plotted to kill him; he was saved by the princes and elders who cited the preaching of Micah (26:16–19) to justify Jeremiah. Uriah, another prophet who evidently did the same as Jeremiah, was killed by King Jehoiakim (26:20–24). On another occasion Jeremiah brought some Rechabites

---

[96] Cf. *supra,* pp. 317, 327.   [97] *Supra,* p. 303.
[98] Cf. *supra,* pp. 317, 327.
[99] Jer. 19:1–20:6, 26–29, 32; 34–45. Bewer, *op. cit.,* p. 167, arranges the genuine passages of Jeremiah chronologically.

into the temple and tried to get them to drink wine (35). Their refusal gave Jeremiah the object lesson of fidelity to religious conviction he wished to drive home to all who witnessed the incident. Another time Jeremiah appeared in the temple with a wooden yoke about his neck (27 f.) as an object sermon to impress upon the people the fact that national bondage would result from the course the king and the nation were taking. Perhaps this happened in 593 B.C. when foreign agents were trying to incite Zedekiah to join a revolt against Babylon. A prophet, Hananiah, dramatically took the yoke off Jeremiah's neck and smashed it on the pavement and we can imagine that the crowd gave Jeremiah the laugh. Next day Jeremiah appeared in the temple wearing a yoke of iron; his idea couldn't be so easily disposed of. On one occasion he preached a vigorous sermon in the valley of Hinnom (19) which so irritated Pashur, the priest, that he put Jeremiah in the stocks for twenty-four hours (20:1–6), subjected to public humiliation.

Jeremiah dictated his sermons to his scribe Baruch (36) who read the sermons publicly in the temple courts. The matter was reported to the king, who, after hearing the book read, burned it.[100] The situation in Jerusalem was very tense after 597 B.C., Jeremiah was left behind when the captives were deported. He wrote a letter to the captives in Babylon (29) urging them to settle down for they would not soon return. His letter irritated Shemaiah, who wrote back to the priests in Jerusalem trying to stir up a plot against Jeremiah, but it didn't work. After King Zedekiah's revolt against Nebuchadrezzar, Jeremiah was imprisoned. It came about because Jeremiah tried to leave Jerusalem in an interval when the Chaldean army had temporarily withdrawn. Jeremiah had purchased a field in Anathoth, exercising the right and duty of redemption (32:6–15). He was bound for Anathoth to receive his inheritance when he was arrested on a charge of deserting to the Chaldeans (37). In prison he was secretly visited by the king, asking for counsel. Subsequently Jeremiah was cast into a dungeon to die but was rescued by Ebedmelech, an Ethiopian (38), the "good Samaritan" of the Old Testament. When Jerusalem was captured and destroyed by Nebuchadrezzar in 586 B.C., Jeremiah was released from among the captives about to be taken to Babylon and allowed to remain in Judah with Gedaliah, the governor (39 f.). After Gedaliah was murdered (41), Jeremiah advised the assassins and rebels against going to Egypt (42), but they went, and dragged Jeremiah with them against his wishes and protest (43). Jeremiah continued his preaching in Egypt (44), and died there, doubtless a martyr.

[100] Cf. *supra*, p. 304.

We have already spoken of the literary qualities of Jeremiah as an author.[101]

His public career as a prophet began at the time of the Scythian invasion in 626 B.C.[102] when Jeremiah made his first appeals to the nation (25:3). The dread Scythian marauders were sweeping down the Mediterranean coast scarcely ten miles from Judah's border. Chapters 2 to 6 are believed to have these invaders in mind, although the chapters were not written until fully twenty years had elapsed (chapter 36). Chapter *1 brings out the youthfulness and timidity of Jeremiah when the call to preach first came to him and tells how, step by step, Yahweh overcame the youth's reluctance and encouraged him for the thankless task of reforming critic. We are told among other things how a punning musing upon the name of a certain tree led him to think of Yahweh as a god ceaselessly awake, alert, watchful (1:11 f.) ; how a boiling kettle similarly suggested the idea that disaster, when it came, would certainly arrive out of the north (1:13 ff.) ; and how he reached the conviction that Yahweh had selected him to be a prophet even before he was born (1:4 f.). All this serves to class him with other great prophets as a man of mystical religious experiences.

The Scythians retreated without proving themselves the instrument of Yahweh's chastisement that Jeremiah expected. Josiah's reformation (621 B.C.) had been on trial only thirteen years when the king himself met a violent death (608 B.C.) at the hand of Pharaoh Necho.[103] Necho's own disastrous meeting with Nebuchadrezzar on the field of battle at Carchemish (605 B.C.) compelled Judah to transfer political allegiance from Egypt to the new Chaldean power.[104] The kings of Judah did not keep loyal to Nebuchadrezzar and thereby they brought about the capture of Jerusalem and the first deportation of captives in 597 B.C., and later the sack of the holy city in 586 B.C. and the deportation of additional captives.[105] Even after that there was an insurrection in Judah against the governor, Gedaliah, appointed by Nebuchadrezzar, as an outcome of which there was a third deportation of captives to Babylon.[106] The career of Jeremiah as a prophet thus spanned a period of more than forty years.

2. *Jeremiah's Restatement of Social-Ethical Religion.* One of the outstanding reform sermons of Jeremiah is sketched in chapter *7. It brings out with exceptional clarity the ethical emphasis which was characteristic of the great prophets. Standing at the entrance of the

---

[101] *Supra,* p. 304.
[102] The historical period covered by Jeremiah's career is that covered by Chapter 16, *supra,* pp. 263–270.
[103] 2 Kgs. 23:29.
[104] *Supra,* p. 266.
[105] Cf. *supra,* pp. 267–270.
[106] Jer. 52:30.

temple courtyard, Jeremiah spoke to everyone who approached to worship, in substance as follows:

> Change your religious creeds and your personal conduct if you hope to continue to live in this city. Put no confidence in fallacious and untrue slogans such as "The temple is Yahweh's." . . . Do you think you can steal, murder, commit adultery, swear falsely, burn incense to Baal, and pursue other gods you're not even acquainted with, do all these abominable things, and then come and stand before me in this house and say, "We are safe!"? (7:3 f., 8 ff.).

Jeremiah took the position that mere ritual is futile (6:20, 7:21–26) and that the temple was anything but inviolate. Calling attention to the fact that Shiloh, once the leading sanctuary of the nation and the home of the sacred Ark, had been destroyed by Yahweh's express will because of the wickedness of the people, he declared that precisely the same fate awaited the temple in Jerusalem and for the same reason (7:12 ff.).

Chapter 26 relates a remarkably similar if not identical experience dated in "the beginning of the reign of Jehoiakim" (vs. 1) ; i.e., just after the death of Josiah and the imprisonment of Jehoahaz in Egypt had left Judah in the hands of the profligate tool of Necho. Here again the same threat of making the temple like Shiloh is found (vss. 6, 9), but in this passage it is stated plainly that the execution of the threat is contingent on whether "they will hearken and turn every man from his evil way" (vss. 3, 12 f.).

Just how greatly such views as Jeremiah's differed from the official and popular conceptions, how furiously such views were resented, and how deadly dangerous it was to voice them openly are shown by Jeremiah's narrow escape from death at this time (26:8, 11, 14–19).

One wonders just when and to what purpose Jeremiah gave vent to the caustic implications of *5:1 ff. It almost seems as if it contained a bit of exaggeration, like Elijah's bitter cry that he was the only faithful one left, when really there were seven thousand.[107] When we reflect, however, upon the terrible suppression of free speech such as the incident of chapter 26 reveals, it seems little surprising if Jeremiah found it next to impossible to find another person with sufficient courage to exhibit an "honest mind" and "integrity" (as Moffatt's translation has it).

Jeremiah himself was one such courageous soul. He dared to express himself in forthright terms about kings and their kingly obligations; to declare that the king ought to set the example of strict integrity, impartial justice, considerateness toward orphans and

[107] 1 Kgs. 19:10, 18.

widows and toward foreigners, and that he should maintain order and refrain from extortion (*22:2 f.). He censured King Jehoiakim for having violated precisely these principles, in contrast to the laudable example set by his father Josiah (*22:13–17). And when, during the siege of Jerusalem, the slaveholders of the imperiled city repudiated their promises to let their Hebrew slaves go free, Jeremiah in biting language declared that "freedom" would then be given "to sword, to pestilence, and to famine" until those who had been guilty of breaking the most solemn of oaths taken in the name of the deity should be "tossed to and fro among all the nations of the earth" (*34:8–22). The ethical emphasis of Jeremiah's preaching may be seen in such additional passages as 2:22, 34; 3:1 f., 8; 4:*2, *14, 22; 5:*1 f., 7 f., *25–28; 6:13, 28; 8:6; 9:2–6; 13:*23, 25, 27; 21:12; 22:*3, *13, 15 f.; 23:10; 29:23.

3. *The Prophets Who Opposed Jeremiah.* Against the prophets of his own age Jeremiah was no less severe, and probably with reason. Some of them opposed him and blocked his efforts. Hananiah, for a time, wholly nullified Jeremiah's appeals to the nation not to commit the supreme folly of a second revolt (*27 f.). Hananiah was evidently one of a considerable group who were encouraging Jerusalem's leaders with false hopes of victory (14:13; 37:19) and who, Jeremiah declared, would in consequence themselves meet "sword and famine" (14:14 f.). Another was "Shemaiah the Nehelemite" whose clash with Jeremiah is described in 29:24–32. Such prophets were spiritually much more akin to the prophet Nahum, writer of the book by that name, who fairly gloats over the fallen Nineveh but who has not a word of criticism or warning for the sins of his own nation.

As to prophets in general, Jeremiah declared that they prophesied falsely (5:31) and that the people liked to have them do so. In 14:18b he says that prophet and priest are much in evidence in the land, but that they really "have no knowledge." The most sustained and complete arraignment of the whole prophetic group, however, is found in 23:9–40 which compares them and their utterances as "straw to the wheat" (vs. 28), and witheringly refers to their futile "He saith" (vs. 31) in contrast to the true word of Yahweh.[108] Apparently Jeremiah stood alone against the prophets of his generation.

4. *Jeremiah's Idea of God.* Isaiah, as we have observed,[109] almost reached the point where he could comprehend that Yahweh must be *the* God of the universe. Jeremiah's thinking traveled much the same

[108] Bewer, *op. cit.*, p. 167, assigns only vss. 9 ff. to Jeremiah. This implies that the rest of the chapter is a subsequent expansion of Jeremiah's view.
[109] *Supra*, p. 326.

road, but like Isaiah he stopped short of the ultimate step. In chapter 27 he develops the belief that Nebuchadrezzar of Babylon was actually Yahweh's "servant," to whom and to whose royal sons Yahweh had decided to give control of "all the nations" for a certain period (vss. 4–7). In two other places (25:9, 43:10) Jeremiah refers to Nebuchadrezzar as Yahweh's servant so that it is certain that he regarded this point an essential part of Yahweh's world plan and world outlook.

This does not mean that Jeremiah intended to imply that the mantle of the chosen people had passed from the Hebrews to the Babylonians. In 25:11–24 he makes it plain that as soon as Judah shall have learned its needed lesson through "seventy years" of chastisement, the other nations of the world, including Babylon, will have their turn at even severer disciplining. More than this, it is Jeremiah's picture of the future that there would be a glorious restoration (31:2–6, 15–21) and that a new and better covenant, written "in their heart," would thenceforth bind the nation to Yahweh in indissoluble fidelity (*31:31–34). That this was no mere flight of poetic fancy or figure of speech on Jeremiah's part is proved by his purchase of property at Anathoth, even when the final siege of Jerusalem was in progress, in the confident expectation that Judah and its people would yet be restored and flourish (32:1 f., 6–15, 36–44). Jeremiah had a deep, strong faith in God, and so he had faith in the future.

Choice passages in which Jeremiah's idea of God comes to clear expression are 1:5, 12; 3:*4 f., 12, 15, *19; *4:2; 5:3; *9:24; 11:20; 12:1, 15 f.; *14:8 f.; 15:16; 16:5, 19; *17:10; 18:6–10; *20:12; 31:*3, 20, *34. Yahweh is a god of love who loves mankind with an everlasting love (31:3). He is a god unto whom man is morally responsible (17:10). He is truth, justice, and righteousness, "and the nations shall bless themselves in him, and in him shall they glory" (4:2). In these passages Jeremiah almost voices a full monotheism. His supreme hope for the future is that man will call God "Father" and will not turn away from following him (3:19).

5. *Jeremiah's Doctrine of the Individual.* Jeremiah was a man of sorrows and acquainted with grief. His was a lonely life. He was despised and rejected by his fellow countrymen, an object of reviling and murderous plotting. The effect of such treatment was to throw him back upon himself and God alone. The pathos of his life is most feelingly portrayed in *15:10–18 in which he laments that he was ever born and even accuses Yahweh of untrustworthiness. Yahweh's gracious reassurance of the prophet is beautifully expressed in *15:19 ff. In *29:1 ff. and *31:33, two of the very finest passages,

Jeremiah expresses the inwardness of genuine religious experience. *12:1–6 sets forth the prophet's reflections upon his own loneliness and the abuse to which he was subjected. He raises a searching question which troubled not a few Hebrew thinkers subsequent to Jeremiah: "Wherefore doth the way of the wicked prosper?" (12:1).

Out of this experience was born one of Jeremiah's truly creative ideas, his doctrine of the individual. Man stands related to God as a man and not as a Jew. This was new. Yahweh had always been thought of as the God of the "chosen people." Whatever blessings the individual enjoyed were his because he belonged to the chosen nation. Conversely, responsibility was always conceived of as a group responsibility—the sins of the fathers were visited upon the children.[110] This was a convenient way for the fathers to shift their moral responsibility. "The fathers have eaten sour grapes, and the children's teeth are set on edge" became a proverb among them. But Jeremiah declares that the time will come when this proverb will yield place to a new ethical doctrine: "Every one shall die for his own iniquity: every man that eateth the sour grapes, his teeth shall be set on edge" (*31:29 f.; cf. 17:10). Here is a crystal-clear statement of the truth of individual moral responsibility, which truth is the basis of any valid ethics.

Habakkuk. We know nothing whatever about the biography of Habakkuk. Hab. *3:2–16 describes, in poetic form, a majestic theophany, quite comparable to the mystical religious experience of Moses at the "burning bush," [111] and to that of Isaiah in the Jerusalem temple.[112] This theophany was evidently the basic stimulus to Habakkuk's thinking and his prophetic activity (2:2 f.).

It may be inferred from his book that Habakkuk lived at the end of the seventh century B.C., and that his prophecy was uttered in Judah in that critical period which immediately followed Nebuchadrezzar's triumph at Carchemish in 605 B.C., when Judah passed from Egyptian to Chaldean overlordship.[113] The ruthlessness of the Chaldeans is portrayed in 1:5–11.

Isaiah had contended that Assyria was Yahweh's tool for inflicting punishment upon his renegade people and that when she had served Yahweh's purpose, ruthless and arrogant Assyria would herself be trodden under foot.[114] So it came to pass. Nineveh fell in 612 B.C. and Assyria was obliterated in 605 B.C., only to be replaced by equally ruthless and arrogant Chaldea. Was Isaiah's type of thinking still valid? Was Chaldea equally Yahweh's tool to punish his disloyal people? It would seem as though Yahweh's purpose had been ac-

---

110 Cf. Num. 16:31 f.; Josh. 7:24 f.; 2 Sam. 21:1–9.
111 Ex. 3; cf. *supra*, pp. 130 f.   112 Isa. 6; cf. *supra*, p. 323.
113 Cf. *supra*, p. 266.   114 Cf. *supra*, pp. 325 f.

complished when Josiah's great reformation was effected in 621 B.C. Why should Yahweh now wish to send the dread Chaldeans to afflict his chosen people? Hab. 1:12 probably voices the conventional view of the matter, that Yahweh did "establish him for correction." But to Habakkuk this is unthinkable and he challenges this doctrine (1:13). Habakkuk finds it difficult to think of the righteous God using the violent and wicked Chaldeans to afflict the righteous among his chosen people. He does not doubt that Yahweh is righteous or that righteousness will ultimately prevail. So he will patiently await the outcome of events to find the answer to his problem; "it will surely come" (*2:1 ff.). Habakkuk's greatest utterance is: "The righteous shall live by his faith" (*2:4), i.e., by his faithfulness or integrity. The real life of the upright man is not in outward circumstances or material prosperity; it is in his moral integrity. Here Habakkuk denies the conventional view that religion pays dividends in outward prosperity. Whatever the adversities of outward circumstances, the upright man maintains his moral integrity and his trust in God. This truth is voiced in Hab. *3:17 ff., one of the most beautiful passages in the Bible and one of the clearest statements of the essence of spiritual religion ever penned.

Progress in Religion to the Exile: A Summary

It is not a simple matter to measure religious progress. One can never be sure his measurements are accurate or that they do full justice to all aspects of the problem. What is true of one section of a people is not true of the rest. The teachings of forward-looking men are never a cross section of the popular religion nor even that of the conventional, orthodox, theological group. There is ever the drag of a retarded and superstitious stratum in every nation.

One can scarcely question the significance of the Hebrew writers' own criticisms of their past and present as the clearest evidence of a strong spiritual and ethical vitality. The prophets may not have changed significantly the popular conduct in their own or even the immediately succeeding generations. The number of complete converts to the prophetic way of thinking and acting was probably not very large. It took centuries for the leaven of their radical ideas to permeate society to the extent of really making a conquest of Hebrew thought. That is the way of human thought. The birth of ideals and their conquest of individual lives are decades, generations, even centuries ahead of their conquest over a whole nation.

We need not, therefore, be surprised or disturbed by the contradictions and contrasts in the picture of Hebrew religious life and thought down to 586 B.C. The vast majority of Hebrews were still thinking of God, or gods, in crude, realistic fashion or in terms of national interests and territorial boundaries. It is doubtful if many really saw much necessary connection between religion and ethics. Worship of the "Queen of Heaven" was the popular cult and could hardly have failed to retard the growth of ethics and morality. At the same time there were the cumulative attacks of men like Amos, Hosea, Isaiah, Micah, Zephaniah, and Jeremiah upon debased forms and practices that masqueraded under the guise of worship. And there was also the Deuteronomic movement, evidencing the existence of yet another group of spiritually minded men working toward the same end as the great prophets. It was the teaching of this small section of the Hebrew people which was preparing the nation as a whole to withstand the shock of Jerusalem's fall—a shock of the first magnitude because of their pivotal belief that the nation was Yahweh's sole realm, that the temple was his last citadel of defense, and that when temple and nation were both destroyed Yahweh was left a god without home and without people. That loss of faith was not complete and final was due principally to the changes in religious thinking to which the Hebrew nation was slowly becoming accustomed and adjusted—thanks to the great prophets.

Chapter 19

EXILE AND RESTORATION

In this chapter we are concerned with the sixth and fifth centuries B.C. The year 586 B.C. was a highly important watershed in Biblical history. From that date on the streams of Jewish life flowed in three directions: in Babylonian Judaism, arising from the exile; in Palestinian Judaism; and via Egypt in the Judaism of the Dispersion. Each group of Jews represented a different social class at the start and each lived under widely different conditions in the decades that followed. Nationality had ceased for the Jews but the virility of the race was unimpaired.

Through the long perspective of the centuries the significance of the exile and the restoration is not a little thrilling. Once already the Jews had survived the crash of empire which swept their brutal master, Assyria, into oblivion. Now we find them in exile, the subject people of the mighty Chaldean empire. In the present chapter we shall see that empire similarly swept into oblivion and the Jews survive the universal upheaval as the subject people of Persia. The Jews will survive the downfall of Persia and the overthrow of other empires after that, as future chapters will disclose. Out of their experiences of subjection and suffering in the exile emerged a literature, one piece of which is the noblest literature in all the Old Testament, the Second Isaiah, which sets forth a philosophy of history that integrates their own experiences of suffering and the rise and fall of world empires with the ultimate purposes of the Eternal God and the enduring values of life.

Sources for a History of the Period

There is no period of Biblical history more difficult to reconstruct than the period under survey in this chapter. It bristles with problems at every turn. The books of Ezra and Nehemiah are the principal Old Testament sources, but the sequence of events is difficult to disentangle and scholars are by no means unanimous in their interpretations. Some important inferences can be drawn from Haggai and Zechariah and scattered passages in other prophetical books. Some

345

archaeological monuments throw light on the period, one of the most notable being the Elephantine papyri already mentioned.[1]

Historical Development: 586–400 B.C.

New Situations Confronting the Jews After 586 B.C. 1. *The Jews Left in Judea.* Of the Jews left in Judea, but little need be said. Nebuchadrezzar considerately placed over them a governor of their own race, Gedaliah by name, but a hotheaded faction promptly assassinated him and then fled the country.[2] Many others emigrated from Palestine in the years which followed, mainly to Egypt. The remnant ultimately left in Judea was, therefore, a doubly sorry and disheartened lot. Unquestionably the Babylonians appointed another governor to succeed Gedaliah, and the Jews were ruled by such governors right along. Their near neighbors appear to have crowded in upon them and harassed them—Ammonites,[3] Moabites,[4] even the Philistines,[5] but most annoying of all, the Edomites.[6] Upon the removal of so many Judeans from Palestine into exile, the Edomites crowded west across the Arabah and up into Judea,[7] both because there was room for them there and because they were probably squeezed out of their former habitat east of the Arabah by the Nabateans, an Arab group which sometime in the sixth century B.C. pushed in from the desert. This coming in of the Nabateans is another instance of the oft-repeated intrusion of nomad groups from the desert into the Fertile Crescent.[8] The Nabateans in time developed a kingdom of considerable importance, with Petra as their capital.[9] Ultimately the Edomites (Idumeans in the Latinized form of the word) were incorporated into the Jewish Maccabean kingdom[10] and fused with the Jews. The Jews in Judea were probably not adversely affected by, though they surely must have been interested in, the principal events which transspired in the west, the long siege of Tyre by the Chaldeans (585–572 B.C.), Nebuchadrezzar's campaign against Egypt in 568 B.C., and Nabonidus's campaign in the west in 552 B.C. and his long stay in Teima.

[1] *Vid. supra,* pp. 49 ff.
[2] *Vid. supra,* pp. 269 f., 337.
[3] Reflected in Jer. 49:1–6; Ezk. 25:1–7.
[4] Reflected in Ezk. 25:8–11; Zeph. 2:8.
[5] Reflected in the later oracle of Joel 3:4–8.
[6] Reflected in Ezk. 25:12 ff., 35:1–15, 36:1–5.
[7] This movement of the Edomite clans is reflected in the genealogical lists of 1 Chr. 2, 4.
[8] *Vid. supra,* p. 24.
[9] Cf. Nelson Glueck, *The Other Side of the Jordan* (New Haven: 1940), pp. 40 f., 130 f., 133 f., 158–200; C. C. McCown, *The Ladder of Progress in Palestine* (New York: 1943), pp. 299–305; on Nabatean pottery, cf. C. H. Gordon, *The Living Past* (New York: 1941), p. 37.
[10] *Vid. infra,* pp. 418 f.

The city of Jerusalem remained ruined and largely abandoned for at least a century and a half. The chance for a Jewish rehabilitation appeared remote.

2. *The Refugees in Egypt.* Numbers of Jews found their way into Egypt in this period, were hospitably received, established Jewish quarters in several of the larger cities there, and prospered. Many of them attempted to transplant to this new home the pattern of life which they had lived in Judea, particularly on the religious side. Such was the case at Elephantine, where a Jewish colony constructed a temple to Yahweh very similar to the one in Jerusalem, showing that they believed Yahweh could be successfully worshiped outside of Palestine, just as did the faithful of the exiles in Babylonia. On the other hand there were some Jews in Egypt who forsook the faith of their fathers, just as did one faction of the Babylonian exiles. The Jews who settled near the Nile Delta were in this group. They repudiated Yahweh completely, impudently asserting that it was worship of him that had caused all their misery and disaster (Jer. *44; especially vss. 15–19).

3. *The Exiles Deported to Babylonia.* The exiles deported by Nebuchadrezzar in 597, 586, and 581 B.C. were colonized in Babylonia. The prophet Ezekiel mentions the fact that he "was among the captives by the river Chebar," [11] a large navigable canal running southeast from Babylon to Nippur through the heart of agricultural and commercial Babylonia. Ezekiel also speaks of the name of this place as Tell Abib, "the hill of the young ears of grain." [12] How many such communities there were we have no means of knowing.[13] These Judean exiles received from their Chaldean conquerors a more considerate treatment than that which the Assyrians had accorded the exiles of Israel. Those whom Sargon deported from Israel in 720 B.C. were scattered throughout the empire and eventually were assimilated with the peoples among whom they were settled, thus losing their Hebrew identity. They were "lost" tribes. The exiles of Judah, on the contrary, were colonized as a group and were thus able to retain their racial identity and also their Jewish customs and interests to a marked degree.

At the outset they were an unhappy group. The exiles of 597 B.C. believed that they would not be in Babylonia long. "False prophets" arose who declared that the exile would be over in two years and that within that period the kingdom of Nebuchadrezzar would be destroyed.[14] The effect of such preaching was to keep alive a spirit of

---

[11] Ezk. 1:1, Babylonian *Khebaru.*   [12] Ezk. 3:15.
[13] Ezr. 2:59; 8:15, 17 preserve the names of some.
[14] Cf. Jer. 28:11.

restlessness among the exiles. The prophet Jeremiah wrote a letter to the exiled group in Babylonia in which he declared that their exile would last for seventy years. In view of this he urged the captives to settle down in Babylonia, to build homes and establish families, and to work at rehabilitation of their fortunes (Jer. *29:1–14).

When Jerusalem was destroyed eleven years later (586 B.C.) and the second group of exiles reached Babylon, for a while their disappointment verged upon despair. Gradually they became adjusted to the new situation and most of them finally accepted it as inevitable.

Chaldea Supplanted by Persia as World Power. 1. *The Decline and Fall of the Chaldean Empire.* Nebuchadrezzar's vigorous rule came to an end in 562 B.C. He was the last great Chaldean ruler and at his death the empire's decline was rapid. Nebuchadrezzar was succeeded by an unworthy son, Amel-Marduk (the Evil-Merodach of 2 Kgs. 25: 27), who released Jehoiachin of Judah who had been kept in prison since 597 B.C. when Jerusalem was first captured.

After a rule of about three years Evil-Merodach was assassinated and was succeeded by his brother-in-law, Neriglissar, the Nergal-sharezer mentioned in Jer. 39:3, 13 as an officer who directed the disposition of Jerusalem after its fall in 586 B.C. He undertook to carry out the policies of Nebuchadrezzar but his able reign was cut short by death within five years (555 B.C.). The throne then passed to his young son Labashi-Marduk but after nine months he was deposed by the priestly party who made Nabuna'id (Nabonidus), a Babylonian of priestly descent, king.

Recent research has established the fact that Nabonidus spent much of his time in the west, where, after a successful military campaign, he established himself in Teima in Arabia [15] which he greatly beautified and made an outpost of his kingdom.[16] Affairs of state in Babylon were in the hands of the king's son Belshazzar, which explains why the latter is called king in Dan. 5:1. It was in the reign of Nabonidus that the Chaldean empire fell (539 B.C.).

2. *Cyrus and the Rise of the Persian Empire.* Cyrus the Great emerged in history in 559 B.C. as ruler of the little province of Anshan, a district in northwestern Elam just south of Media and east of the Zagros Mountains. Anshan was then under the overlordship of Media. When Cyrus revolted against his overlord Astyages, the Median army went over to him in a body, surrendering Astyages as prisoner. Cyrus apparently was the voluntary choice of the Medes as their king. The

---

[15] An oasis in the western Arabian Desert, east of the southern tip of the Peninsula of Sinai.

[16] Cf. J. A. Montgomery, *Arabia and the Bible* (Philadelphia: 1934), pp. 64 ff.; G. A. Barton, *Archaeology and the Bible* (7th ed.; Philadelphia: 1937), pp. 481–484.

empire's capital, Ecbatana, with all its treasure, came into possession of Cyrus practically without a blow. Thus within ten years Cyrus made himself master of the Median empire comprising modern Persia, northern Assyria, Armenia, and Asia Minor as far west as the river Halys.

After two years spent in organizing the empire Cyrus moved westward, bent on conquest. After conquering northern Mesopotamia he attacked and defeated the fabulously rich Croesus, king of Lydia, whose kingdom extended from the river Halys to the Aegean Sea. Croesus' capital city Sardis henceforth became the center of Cyrus's power in the west, and from Sardis as a base the Greek cities and colonies of Asia Minor were speedily conquered by him.

Returning in 539 B.C., Cyrus advanced against Babylon, which opened its gates to him without a battle. Indeed, he seems to have been welcomed by the populace as a friend and benefactor. Thus Cyrus became master of all western Asia.

The fall of Babylon marked the end of Semitic world power. With the triumph of Cyrus, a new race, the Indo-European, came into world dominion and the political destiny of the world was thenceforth in the hands of that race. This, therefore, marks a new and very important watershed in Biblical history.

Cyrus was a born ruler of men. He inaugurated a new policy in the treatment of conquered peoples. Instead of tyrannizing over them and holding them in subjection by brute force, he treated his subjects with consideration and won them as his friends. He was particularly considerate of the religions of conquered peoples. The effect of this policy was to weld his subjects to him in a loyalty which made his reign an era of peace.

Cyrus's New Policy and the Return of Jewish Exiles to Palestine. Cyrus reversed the policy of previous conquerors in dealing with exiles. We have noted how the Assyrians scattered the exiles of conquered nations throughout the empire and how the Chaldeans continued the policy of deportations. Cyrus instituted a policy of unscrambling. Wherever he found peoples in exile, he permitted them to return to their native lands and resume their native customs and religion.

Happily, Cyrus left his own account of his conquest of Babylon on a clay cylinder inscribed in cuneiform, now to be found in the British Museum.[17] The Cyrus Cylinder reads: "All their populations I assembled and restored to their dwelling places." As to their native religions, the inscription states: "The gods [whose sanctuaries had

---

[17] Cf. I. M. Price, *The Monuments and the Old Testament* (Philadelphia: 1925), pp. 373 f., 378 f., and Fig. 35; G. A. Barton, *op. cit.*, pp. 484 f.

long lain in ruins] I restored to their dwellings and caused them to dwell there forever." Thus quaintly are we informed of a change of policy which was to have far-reaching effects in history. It was no doubt a firman in accord with this general edict that is quoted or paraphrased in Ezr. 1:2 ff., which led to the return of a company of Jews from Babylonia, described in Ezr. 1:5–2:2; 3:8 and technically called "The Return."

Judging from the Ezra account, Cyrus seems to have specially favored the return of the Jews, even to granting them generous aid. Perhaps he wished to have Jerusalem rehabilitated, for down through the centuries Palestine had been a buffer state between southwestern Asia and Egypt. Since Cyrus's next advance in conquest would naturally be toward Egypt, it would be to his advantage to have such a fortress as Jerusalem close to that country.

Not many Jewish exiles proved eager to rush back to Palestine. A half century in Babylonia had led the majority to sink their roots deeply in the land of their enforced adoption. Most of them had become bound to the new land by ties of marriage and friendship and by strong business connections. Moreover there had grown up in Babylonia a generation which knew not Palestine and for such Jews Judea, no longer an attractive place to live in, had no appeal. The pull of a powerful sentimental attachment was needed to induce any of them to return to Palestine and few felt this. Accordingly, the greatest difficulty was encountered in arousing enough enthusiasm to make up a party for the first returning group. It arrived in Judea some time after 536 B.C. under the joint leadership of Zerubbabel, a member of the royal Davidic line, and Joshua, a Zadokite priest.[18] It somewhat resembled a religious crusade.

Those who returned were eager to reinstitute the official worship of Yahweh in Jerusalem. Their first act was therefore to repair the altar of burnt offering and to renew the regular morning and evening sacrifices. They then observed the Feast of Tabernacles and other feasts in routine succession (Ezr. 3:1–6).

After this they started the reconstruction of the temple. The foundation stone was laid amid weeping and rejoicing. But they were destined not to get very far with the building. Certain adversaries, presumably the Samaritans, wished to share in the work, and when their proffer of help was refused by Joshua and Zerubbabel the "people of the land" blocked the work of building, doubtless by preventing the importation of timber, "until the second year of the reign of Darius," i.e., until 520 B.C. if it means Darius I (Ezr. 3:8–4:5, 24).

---

[18] Ezr. 1:8, 11; 5:14, 16 states that one Sheshbazzar, "prince of Judah," led the return and "laid the foundations of the house of God which is in Jerusalem." If he was the actual leader of the return, he disappeared in the obscurity of the period of 537–520 B.C., even as Zerubbabel mysteriously vanished.

Jewish Fortunes from the Death of Cyrus to the Time of Artaxerxes II. With the construction of the temple halted, the Jewish repatriates seemed to be settling down to a despondent inactivity when suddenly they were stirred to fresh life by a series of usurpations, bloodshed, and general disorder which shook the Persian empire to its foundations. Cyrus the Great died in 529 B.C. leaving the empire to his son Cambyses. The latter campaigned southwestward and added Egypt to the empire. On his way home in 522 B.C. he was erroneously informed that his younger brother Bardiya had seized the throne. In reality, Bardiya was dead, murdered at the instigation of Cambyses, and the new occupant of the throne was a pretender. It is not quite clear what caused Cambyses' death at this juncture, whether an accident, which is the view of the ancient Greek historian Herodotus, or suicide, which may be inferred (though not necessarily) from Darius's statement in the Behistun inscription.[19] Chaos ensued. Some nobles, learning that the new king was an impostor, slew him and made Darius king. Numerous pretenders claimed the throne and throughout the empire whole provinces sprang into revolt. Within two years Darius fought nineteen battles against nine different rivals, and by 519 B.C. he had established his authority and reduced the empire to order. Before this was accomplished, however, the disorder had evidently fanned the flame of hope among the Jews of Judea that once again they might set up an independent kingdom under Zerubbabel, the more so since Zerubbabel was of the royal line of David.[20] The prophets Haggai and Zechariah urged the people to complete the construction of the temple.[21] Upon this, an attempt was made by the Persian governor of Syria to stop the work. Perhaps he suspected the Jews of planning revolt. The Jews, however, claimed to be doing the work by authority of a decree of Cyrus. The dispute was referred to Darius, who caused the state records to be searched. The decree was found, as the Jews had maintained, whereupon Darius ordered Tattenai to assist the Jews in their enterprise. The work now went forward and in 516 B.C. the second temple, known as the temple of Zerubbabel, was dedicated (Ezr. 6:1–14a).

Zerubbabel meantime dropped out of sight and what happened to him is unknown. The disorders throughout the empire at the accession of Darius may well have aroused Jewish messianic hopes and there may have been an attempt to set up a Davidic kingdom with Zerubbabel as king. That Zerubbabel was regarded as messiah is clear from Haggai's reference to him as "Yahweh's chosen one." [22]

[19] Cf. G. B. Gray, *Cambridge Ancient History* (New York: 1926), iv, p. 173.
[20] Matt. 1:6–12.
[21] Hag. 1:1–11, Zech. 4:9.
[22] Hag. 2:23.

The crowning of Zerubbabel as king is implied in Zech. 6:11.[23] Though the Persian government was tolerant in its treatment of subject peoples, it could hardly have ignored such a crowning of a king by one of its subject states. Therefore the movement must have ended in tragedy, and it passed into oblivion save for the faint trace left in the textual difficulties of Zech. 6:11,14. With this tragedy, Jewish hopes of Judah's being ruled again by a prince of the house of David collapsed.

Another implication of the textual confusion of Zech. 6:11–14 may be that there was a coronation of both the king Zerubbabel and the high priest Joshua. Indeed they are alluded to in Zech. 4:14 as "the two anointed ones." If so, the disaster that befell Zerubbabel left the high priest as the local ruler of the Jewish community in Palestine. As a matter of fact, from this time forward the Jews, from their own point of view, were a theocracy ruled by God's anointed high priest. Politically they were, of course, ruled by Persian officers.

Such was the lot of the Judean Jews throughout the reigns of Darius (521–486 B.C.) and his son Xerxes (486–466 B.C.). The latter wasted his energy fighting the Greeks, with disastrous results. In 480 B.C. his fleet was defeated by the Greeks at Salamis, and the following year his army was vanquished at Plataea. All this is a commonplace of Greek history.

The next monarchs of Persia were Artaxerxes I (466–425 B.C.), Xerxes II (425–424 B.C.), Darius II (424–404 B.C.), and Artaxerxes II (404–358 B.C.). It is one of these two Artaxerxes who was renowned for his friendship for Nehemiah which resulted in the reconstruction of Jerusalem.[24]

The Rehabilitation of Judea by Nehemiah. Nehemiah is one of the great Old Testament characters to be ranked with men like Moses and David. The story of his career is dramatically related and with unusual detail in the Book of Nehemiah and in one passage from the Book of Ezra. Read in the following order, the events stand out colorfully and clearly: Neh. 1–6; Ezr. 4:6–23; Neh. 7:1–4,

[23] The Revised Version reads: "Make crowns and set them upon the head of Joshua, the high priest." Why should there be more than one crown set on Joshua's head? The Jewish Version reads: "Make crowns and set the one upon the head of Joshua." Upon whose head the other one was to be put is not stated in the text. In Zech. 6:14, in the phrase "And the crowns shall be," the verb "shall be" is singular. This implies that the subject was originally intended to be "crown." The Moffatt Version and the Chicago Version both translate Zech. 6:11, "Make a crown and place it upon the head of Zerubbabel." This makes not Joshua but Zerubbabel "the Branch" (a messianic term) of Zech. 6:12, "who shall build the temple of Yahweh," which squares with Zech. 3:8 and 4:7, 9. Further light comes from the Septuagint (Greek) Version of Zech. 6:13 which reads, "and the priest shall be at his right hand," i.e., upon the right hand of Zerubbabel who sits upon the throne.

[24] Which Artaxerxes it was is not indicated clearly in the Bible. Most Old Testament historians assume Artaxerxes I to have been meant, but some incline to Artaxerxes II as more in keeping with the known circumstances.

11:1 f.; 12:27–43; 13:4–31. By virtue of Nehemiah's energy, ability, unselfish patriotism, and personal integrity a new, live Judah came into existence. The restoration of Jerusalem, which had lain in ruins for a century and a half or two centuries, was begun, and an impulse was given which in the decades following carried this work to completion.[25] Ps. *48 is a poem celebrating the restoration of Jerusalem. Jewish confidence revived. A stable, semiautonomous government was established with Jerusalem as the center and this small area was gradually extended until it included a district about half the size the kingdom of Judah had been at the time of its fall in 586 B.C.

Cultural Changes in the Two Centuries Following Jerusalem's Fall

No people is culturally immune to the impacts of an altered environment. Such radical environmental changes as the Hebrews encountered in the exile could not fail to affect the currents of their life and thought profoundly. That they were so affected, there is ample proof.

The Social Situation in Judea in the Two Centuries Following the Fall of Jerusalem. No contemporary records have been found reflecting the life of the Palestinian Jews between 580 and 535 B.C., i.e., between the time when Jeremiah went to Egypt and the return of the first band of exiles from Babylonia. From numerous sources, however, it is possible to fill in the picture somewhat as follows.

The Chaldeans deported the better classes—the rulers, skilled artisans, and the like. Of the remainder, those emigrating to Egypt, of whom there were evidently many thousands, represent on the whole the next most energetic and enterprising of the population. This left in Judea the poorer and less ambitious of the Jews, those likely to succumb to despondency and submit to arrogant overlords in a spiritless way. The feelings of this group in the first bitter years of grief and despair are vividly reflected in the Book of Lamentations (Lam. 1:1–7, 15 and 2:6–12, 15 f.). The reference to prophets with their "false and foolish visions," by which the Jewish people had been deluded to their terrible cost,[26] evidences a sane new understanding which they admitted came to them all too tardily.

The deliberate and systematic breaking down of Jerusalem's walls, and the wrecking of temple, palace, and other buildings, had been almost inconceivably thorough. It set Judea back to pre-Davidic

---

[25] Possibly it was at this time that the second temple was completed, rather than earlier in 516 B.C. The Ezra narrative is very confusing on the point.
[26] Lam. 2:14.

times as to defenses, and left it open to attack and encroachment from all directions, with no citadel of last retreat anywhere in the land. In a certain sense it seemed that those early days of foreign encroachments had actually come back again, with the connivance or indifference of the Chaldean officials left in control, for in a later century are found Edomites, Ammonites, Samaritans, and even Philistines in positions of power and influence in the affairs of Judah. In fact, the Judean community was restricted to a few square miles of territory immediately around Jerusalem, owing to the Edomite encroachments on the south.[27]

How tenaciously the faithful held to their old forms and ceremonies is shown by the pathetic attempt of some to keep up the regular temple service as of old by bringing their cereal offerings and incense to the temple, even though it lay in ruins.[28] But the old joy was a thing of the past for them as for their exiled countrymen in far lands. Instead, fasting in sackcloth and ashes became the approved mode of worship and continued throughout the seventy-year period to the time of Zechariah (Zech. 7:1–5) and undoubtedly much beyond that period. Thus in the time of Malachi (probably the century after Zechariah) it is stated that they were still "covering the altar of Yahweh with tears, with weeping, and with sighing," [29] and that they had "walked in mourning apparel before" him.[30]

Another change of far-reaching significance was a new attitude toward non-Jews. Throughout most of the two centuries under survey there had been a large influx of migrants from surrounding areas. This led in the course of time to intermarriages, with inevitable social fusions and religious compromises. A similar commingling had already produced the Samaritans with their hybrid religion.[31] An analogous process was now going on in Judea, with the difference that in Judea the groups of returning exiles, because of the flaming patriotism that motivated their return and the sentimental attachment that bound them to their Hebrew past, served as a powerful check upon the denationalizing process. This spirit shows up clearly in Zerubbabel's curt refusal to accept the advances of "the adversaries of Judah and Benjamin" in the rebuilding of the temple in 520 B.C.[32] It reached its culmination, however, when Nehemiah officially banned mixed marriages (Neh. 13:23–30). He was horrified to discover that there were half-Jewish children who actually "spake half in the speech of Ashdod" (or Ammon, Moab, etc., as the case might be)

---

[27] *Vid. supra,* p. 346.   [28] Jer. 41:5.
[29] Mal. 2:13.
[30] Mal. 3:14.
[31] 2 Kgs. 17:24–41; cf. vss. 32 ff., 41.
[32] Ezr. 4:1 ff.

"and could not speak in the Jews' language" (vs. 24).[33] The vigorous measures to which he resorted raise a smile of tolerant amusement in our time, but it was hardly an amusing matter to Nehemiah and his contemporaries. Ezr. 9 f. throws additional light on this movement to secure a rigid Jewish exclusiveness.

On the economic side it is apparent that the Judeans were rather poverty-stricken right down to the time of Nehemiah. Neh. 5:2–5 portrays the oppressive economic situation. We would rather expect this in the decades that immediately followed Jerusalem's fall. The first contingent of returning exiles is said to have brought back considerable wealth,[34] but part of this was in the form of sacred vessels (which of course could not be used for other purposes) and much of the remainder was apparently spent almost immediately in temple repairs.[35] Following the time of Zerubbabel, the Persian governors of the country were either inefficient or corruptly indifferent to the rights and interests of their subjects, probably the latter. The system of expecting "presents" along with every grievance or for favoritism in some affair was taken as a matter of course by Persian officials and could not have failed to lead to gross misgovernment so far as the poor and uninfluential were concerned. The system is casually alluded to in Mal. 1:8 in a telling way. To bring home to his countrymen how foolish and shortsighted they were to bring sick and crippled animals for sacrifices, Malachi ironically suggested that they try presenting such a "gift" to their governor! "Will he be pleased with thee?" he caustically asks; "Will he accept thy person?" The answer was too obvious to admit of debate.

With the arrival of Nehemiah in Judea, however, a great change took place. Such energy, efficiency, and new spirit did he inject into the Judean community that within a few decades it became scarcely recognizable because of its new wealth, its reorganized government, and its rejuvenated atmosphere. By the middle of the fourth century B.C. Jerusalem had once more a significant status in the world. It was a city-state with a priestly ruler. Here was the dawn of a new era in which literature was once more destined to flourish.

The Changed Culture of the Jews in Egypt.   The culture of ancient Egypt to the time of Moses was briefly sketched in Chapter 4 (pages 60–66). In the six or seven centuries that elapsed between then and the exilic period, Egypt received much infusion of new racial blood, and twice dynasties from alien immigrant groups gained possession of the throne. Yet throughout these centuries the funda-

---

[33] The genealogical lists in 1 Chr. 2 and 4 evidence extensive non-Jewish elements in the population, as well as the semi-Edomite names elsewhere used by the Chronicler. Cf. S. A. Cook, *Cambridge Ancient History* (New York: 1925), iii, 405, 478 ff.
[34] Cf. Ezr. 1:4–11.   [35] Ezr. 2:69.

mental culture forms of the days of Joseph and Moses had maintained themselves with relatively few changes. So when the Judean
émigrés sought asylum in Egypt upon the fall of their own capital
in 586 B.C., they went to an environment which, in its externalities
at least, was not so very unlike that which had existed when the
Hebrew tribesmen were there a thousand years earlier. Yet there
were some differences. The influx of Libyans in the century preceding the reign of Solomon had been so great as finally to put a Libyan
family on the throne and to keep it there for two centuries. Immediately afterward the Negroid Nubians pressed in from the south,
until in the days of Isaiah they gained the throne of Egypt. Kings
So and Tirhaka of the Biblical records are two of their most brilliant
representatives, and it was the ability and energy of these two which
captivated some of Israel's leaders at the time.[36] Neither Libyans nor
Nubians seem to have introduced new culture into Egypt, but their
blood henceforth flowed strongly in Egyptian veins. In the latter half
of the seventh century B.C. there was a great influx of Greeks, mostly
mercenaries, partly also traders. Even these newcomers seem not to
have made much of a dent on the ancient culture forms of Egypt save
in the trifling particular that pictorial art became less stiff and more
lifelike. This is not to say that Egypt did not change. It did, but with
a conservatism which for the most part deluded itself into a belief
that it was not changing. The priestly class and the literati were the
dominant cultural forces and they held a worshipful adoration for
the past.

Toward other peoples Egypt was noticeably tolerant, possibly a
blending of condescension and indifference. The Hebrew refugees
found them friendly, at any rate. Whether it was part of the Egyptian
requirement that they settle in a restricted area, or just a generous
concession to the Jews to live close together in communities of their
own, the fact is that there were sizable Jewish quarters in several of
the important cities of Egypt not long after the fall of Jerusalem.
These Jewish sections must not be understood as having been ghettos,
which they were not. Many Jews were soon busily engaged in trade,
banking, and the like.

Undoubtedly numbers of these Jewish refugees became swallowed
up in the cosmopolitan racial currents of Egypt. Such loss of racial
and religious identity has ever been true of a certain percentage of
Hebrew migrants as of other races. Jer. 44 hints that such defection
may have been heavy in the case of some Jewish colonies in the
neighborhood of the Nile Delta. Occasional references are found also
to mixed marriages, in some of which Judaism gained adherents, in
others, lost.

[36] Cf. *supra*, p. 251.

Other Jewish groups in Egypt remained sturdily loyal to their racial heritage. Concerning one of these, a colony in Elephantine, much information has come to light by virtue of the papyri documents discovered near Assuan about the year 1900.[37] These documents date from the fifth century B.C. but also throw light on the preceding century. From them we learn that these Elephantine Jews were numerous and wealthy; that they had a fine temple to Yahu (shortened form of Yahweh) which was in existence some time before 525 B.C.; and that they were permitted by the Egyptian government to have their own law court, ranking equally with the Egyptian courts of law. The Yahu temple was built of hewn stone and was roofed with cedar wood, possibly brought from distant Lebanon in imitation of the original temple of Solomon. In front were stone pillars, and there were seven great gateways of hewn stone fitted with bronze-hinged doors. The usual gold and silver vessels for the temple service are mentioned, as are also the regular burnt offerings, cereal offerings, and incense burning. Such a temple, preserving as it did the old religious forms, must have proved one of the strongest of Jewish conservative forces. In Elephantine, at least, the Jews must have stood foursquare against influences that would bring change into their religion as they had known it before Jerusalem fell. We wish more were known of the outcome, of what happened to this colony later on and whether or not Judaism in the time of Christ was influenced by this group.

What is known of the religion of these Elephantine Jews presents some curiosities. They had other gods besides their national deity Yahu. There is mention of Ishumbethel, 'Anathbethel, Herembethel, and 'Anathyahu. The last of these names compounds Anath, a goddess, with Yahu; evidently she was regarded as the consort of Yahu. They had a priesthood; a variety of sacrifices is mentioned, as are the Passover and the feast of Unleavened Bread; and women shared in the worship.

Cultural Changes Among the Exiles in Babylonia. The situation of the Jews in Babylonia differed from that of the Jews in Egypt in important particulars, both environmental and psychological. Babylonia was so much farther away than Egypt, and contacts through trade and travel had been so infinitely fewer, that Babylonia was an utterly strange land to the Jews. Those deported to Babylonia in 597 B.C. were a highly selected group—the artisans and the ruling class. The latter in particular would find it most galling to suffer such abrupt loss of status and would, in addition, be a social type likely to react intensely to a changed environment. The artisan group would

[37] Cf. *supra*, pp. 49 ff. Cf. W. F. Albright, *op. cit.*, p. 168; R. H. Pfeiffer, *History of New Testament Times* (New York: 1949), *in loc.*

probably make adaptations much more readily. The wealth and culture of Babylonia undoubtedly differed much from anything they had anticipated.

1. *Economic and Social Transformation.* Babylonia offered them economic advantages far superior to Palestine. The extensive alluvial plain, irrigated by reservoirs and by intersecting canals, such as the Chebar, yielded abundant crops. Agriculture flourished at their hands, and they achieved a success impossible in rocky and barren Palestine. But commerce, even more than agriculture, beckoned with a wealth of opportunity. Soon we find the Jews of Babylonia engaging in trade and growing rich. Gradually they gave up agriculture.

Thus did this people once again undergo a profound social transformation. When they originally conquered and settled Canaan they were transformed from nomadic to agricultural life. Now the exile transformed them from agriculturists to traders. To the present day the Jewish people bear the mark the exile put upon them as the world's traders.

The exiles were not oppressed by their Babylonian conquerors. They were simply obliged to pay taxes. For the rest they were allowed to retain their own family and social customs, their own religion and education, and to prosper according to the degree of their own effort. The only restriction placed upon them was that they might not return to Palestine. Such glimpses as we have of the intimate daily life of the exiles touch mainly the changes that took place in their religious thinking and their habits of worship.

In Babylonia they came into contact with a culture which aroused their latent talents. They had known and feared Nebuchadrezzar as a conqueror. Now they came to know his greatness as a ruler and a civilizer. He it was who rebuilt Babylon into a city of magnificence. "Is not this great Babylon which I have built?" he boasted.[38] In Babylon and Borsippa he rebuilt more than twenty temples, of which the most notable were Ezida ("the enduring house"), national temple of the god Nebo at Borsippa, and Esagila ("the house of the exalted head"), the national temple of the god Bel-Marduk at Babylon. In Babylon this king erected his magnificent palace, as well as the famous hanging gardens, one of the Seven Wonders of the World, built for the benefit of his Median wife because she had become homesick for the mountains of her childhood home. Besides this, he strengthened the fortifications of Babylon, erecting a double wall with numerous towers, and along the river bank he constructed enormous quays to facilitate commerce. The massive foundations and well-built walls of many enormous buildings, together with broad, fine thoroughfares

[38] Dan. 4:30.

fronting them, have been unearthed by archaeologists, all evidencing the greatness of Nebuchadrezzar as a ruler. He was no less great as an administrator. He made laws for and governed the numerous provinces of the empire and ruled the thousands of government officials with consummate skill. He promoted agriculture and commerce in the interest of the people of his realm. All this awakened the Jews to new horizons. They came actually to prize citizenship in such an empire and were quick to avail themselves of all opportunities offered them in education, commerce, and government. They cast off the outworn shell of Judean provincialism and became a cosmopolitan people.

2. *The Religious Challenge of the Exile.* What effect did this political and economic transformation have upon the Jews religiously? We shall study this in detail later on,[39] but here one may note two things: (1) A great many gave up Yahweh worship entirely because they concluded that Yahweh was an impotent god or no god at all. Inasmuch as he had allowed his own dwelling place, the Jerusalem temple, to be destroyed and his chosen people to be carried into captivity, they decided to worship the gods of Babylon who were able to make their king and nation so gloriously prosperous. (2) There were those who remained loyal to Yahweh. Although there was no temple at which they might offer sacrifices, they could gather on the Sabbath in groups by the riverside to comfort one another in their sorrow, as revealed in the beautiful poem, "The Lament of the Captives" (Ps. *137). This psalm is an appealing lyric that breathes the tragic sadness of the loyal among the Babylonian exiles. It does not exactly question the possibility of worshiping Yahweh there, but it does show that the name of Yahweh was still linked with Zion and national boundaries in the mind of the poet, who had not yet come to conceive of or quite believe in *one* God over all the earth. Just how Yahweh's care and sway could reach to Babylonia they did not know, but some had a dawning faith that it did.

(a) *The Origin of the Synagogue.* They also gathered in homes to read their historical and prophetical writings for the comfort and inspiration this afforded. From such gatherings developed a lasting Jewish institution, the synagogue. Thus there grew up in Babylonia a new form of worship, replacing the ritual of sacrificial offerings that had been associated with the Jerusalem temple.

Specific data regarding the origins of the synagogue are lacking. Nevertheless it is quite evident that a worship institution of some sort developed early in the exilic period, quite unlike anything prior

[39] *Infra,* pp. 378–383.

to Jerusalem's fall, a worship characterized by searching self-examination, deep contrition, and solemn purposeful resolves. One was the lighthearted buoyancy of the old feasts and sacrifices. The exiles were now accepting the assertions of Amos, Isaiah, and Jeremiah that sacrificial offerings alone were far from adequate. Like the great prophets of the preceding century, the Jewish religious leaders as a whole were now looking to ethical conduct as their spiritual criterion. This marks a notable advance in religious thinking.

(b) *The Hope of Restoration.* Soon another belief made its appearance among them, the conviction that the exile had not ended their national life or severed the unique relationship implied in the divine covenant; that on the contrary a more glorious future awaited them as a people, that Yahweh was still their God, though a different being from what their fathers had (inadequately) supposed him to be. Probably some of them still thought in national terms and assumed that God's righteous reign over the earth would be by way of a restored Jewish kingdom having Jerusalem as its capital. Accordingly, these hopes for the future invariably focused upon a return to Palestine, the original Zionist movement. Passages in most of the prophetic books refer to this and predict it, e.g., Am. 9:11–15; Mic. 4:1–8; Isa. 11:11 f., 16; 14:1 f.; 27:13; Zeph. 3:20; Jer. 16:14 f.; 23:3–8; 30:8–11, 17–22; 31:4–9, 12 f.; 32:37–40; 33; Deut. 30:1–5. It was in accordance with this belief that the return under Zerubbabel and Joshua, about 535 B.C., occurred, and that Haggai and Zechariah prophesied so vigorously fifteen years later. It was distress over the failure of this group of the returned to realize their goal that led Nehemiah a century or so later to give up his comfortable position at the Persian court and devote himself to the rehabilitation of his beloved Jerusalem and Judea (Neh. 1:1–2:8). Ps. *126 is a brief but expressive lyric voicing the joy of the return.

3. *The Literary Stimulus of the Exile.* The development of such a type of religious service as that of the synagogue could not have failed to stimulate the study and appreciation of religious and ethical writings and to encourage the production of more of them. Babylonia's vast libraries, her respect for scholar and scribe, and her rich and varied poetic literature—odes, epics, hymns, and liturgical prayers— all must have been a powerful incentive to the Hebrew exiles to exhibit a literature not one whit inferior. Furthermore, the patriotic and sentimental desire to preserve for their children such firsthand memories of Judea and Jerusalem as were possessed by the older generations would operate in the same direction. They may even have felt a pardonable desire to impress their non-Hebrew neighbors with a favorable picture of the vanished culture and glory of their nation,

as did the Alexandrian Jews under somewhat parallel circumstances three centuries later. But whatever the causes, worthy or pardonable, the fact remains that in Babylonia the Hebrew exiles developed into a literary people and their religion into a religion of *the Book*. This was their one effective way of recapturing the past. Cut off from that past in a physical sense, their thoughts turned with a hitherto unfelt passion to biographies, to writings and sayings of their fathers, to patriotic exploits of unselfish courage, and to history as an imperishable record of their nation's experiences for weal and for woe.

This exilic period witnessed a marked impulse toward hymnology, though the actual fruitage may not have appeared until the second temple became a reality. It may be mere coincidence that a number of Babylonian hymns and religious lyrics resemble parts of the Hebrew psalms, but it is altogether possible that acquaintance with the often really beautiful Babylonian liturgy stimulated the poetically minded among the Hebrew exiles to a more critical appreciation of their own religious poetry and to its further production. Pss. 137 and 126, for example, bear unmistakable evidences of their exilic background.

Selections from Babylonian prayers, hymns, and penitential psalms, which will reveal their beauty and value, are given in G. A. Barton, *Archaeology and the Bible* (7th ed.; 1937), pp. 497–500, and by Morris Jastrow, Jr., in Hastings' *Dictionary of the Bible,* ext. vol., pp. 563–567, and elsewhere.[40]

Meritorious as are the choicer Babylonian hymns, they are far surpassed by the Hebrew psalm literature. Whatever of inspiration and stimulus the Hebrew exiles may have received from the Babylonian poems, there is no evidence of dependence in thought. The Hebrew poems are original and vigorous. There is nothing in the whole Babylonian liturgy comparable to such psalms as Pss. 8, 15, 19, 23, 24, 27, 29, 32, 33, 34, 42, 46, 48, 51, 63, 65, 67, 90, 91, 95–99, 103, 121, 139.

What is true of hymnology is true also of epic poetry, of which Babylonia produced not a little. As poetry, the Babylonian epics of creation, of man's search for immortality, of the great flood, and other heroic legends are decidedly good. From the ethical and spiritual point of view, however, they leave almost everything to be desired. If they stimulated the exiled Jews at all, it must have been by way of thrilling them with a realization of how much worthier were their own

[40] I. M. Price, *The Monuments and the Old Testament* (1925), pp. 437–444; C. H. Toy, in *Library of the World's Best Literature* (New York: 1896), i, 77–80; Morris Jastrow, Jr., *The Religion of Babylonia and Assyria* (New York: 1898), pp. 294–327; Emil G. H. Kraeling, in *Columbia University Course in Literature* (New York: 1928), i, 91 f., 93 ff.; Grace H. Turnbull, *Tongues of Fire* (New York: 1929), pp. 74–80; James H. Breasted, *The Dawn of Conscience* (New York: 1933), pp. 339 ff.

conceptions. One has only to compare the Babylonian creation epic with the creation epic in Gen. 1 to see this difference.

The Babylonian creation epic is named for its opening words, *Enuma Elish,* "When in the height." The poem consists of seven divisions, each of which is inscribed upon a separate tablet.

This poem reveals the beliefs of the Babylonians concerning the origin of the universe. It describes the evolution of the gods from the primeval chaos, and the conflict between the primeval forces of chaos, Apsu [41] and Tiamat,[42] in which conflict Apsu was subjugated by Ea, and Tiamat was overthrown by Marduk, who then proceeded to create the world and man.

The first tablet begins with an account of the birth of the gods.

When in the height heaven was not named,[43]
And the earth beneath did not yet bear a name,
And the primeval Apsu who begat them,
And chaos, Tiamat, the mother of them both,
Their waters were mingled together,
And no field was formed, no marsh was to be seen;
When of the gods none had been called into being,
And none bore a name, and no destinies (were ordained);
Then were created the gods in their midst.[44]

Lahmu and Lahamu were the first pair of gods brought forth, then Anshar and Kishar, and then other deities. Of these other deities, only the name of Anu is preserved in the text that has come down to us, but according to Damascius, a writer of the sixth century A.D., the poem also included a description of Bel and Ea, the other deities of the supreme Babylonian triad.

The birth of these gods represented the coming of order and system into the universe. This provoked Apsu's resentment because he could get no rest by day or night on account of the "way" of the gods. He resolved to "destroy their way," but was unsuccessful. Tiamat was not vanquished. She was again incited to rebellion by Kingu, whom she chose as her spouse and to whom she entrusted dominion over all the gods who came to her side for the conflict. Upon the breast of Kingu she laid the "Tablets of Destiny." She spawned eleven kinds of monster serpents to aid her in the fight.

[41] Apsu, the male personification of the force that ruled over primeval chaos, represents the sweet waters. Cf. Thorkild Jacobsen in Frankfort *et al., The Intellectual Adventure of Ancient Man* (Chicago: 1946), pp. 171, 180.
[42] Tiamat, the female personification of the force that ruled over primeval chaos, represents the sea.
[43] Cf. L. W. King, *The Seven Tablets of Creation* (London: 1902), Vol. 1, p. 3.
[44] The concept of the primeval watery chaos developed out of the condition that even yet prevails where the fresh waters (Apsu) of the two rivers, Tigris and Euphrates, mingle with the salt water (Tiamat) of the Persian Gulf, their silt (the first gods, Lahmu and Lahamu) settles, and new land is actually formed. *Vid. supra,* pp. 45 f., 111 f. Cf. Thorkild Jacobsen in Frankfort *et al., The Intellectual Adventure of Ancient Man* (Chicago: 1946), p. 171.

This new peril to the gods from Tiamat and her brood roused them to action, and in tablets II and III there is a description of the consultations of the gods who sought to recover the "Tablets of Destiny." Ea carried to Anshar, his father, the news of Tiamat's preparations for battle. Anshar sent Ea against the monster, but he could not prevail against her. Nor could Anu. After they had both failed in their attempts, Anshar called upon Marduk to become the champion of the gods who opposed the forces of disorder.

Tablet IV describes the conflict of Marduk with Tiamat. Arrayed in formidable armor, mounted on a chariot, attended by a host of winds, he advanced to the battle.

> He made ready the bow, his weapon chose;
> Slung a spear on his back and tied it fast.
> He took up the club, with right hand grasped it.
> At his side hung he bow and quiver.
> Then placed he the lightning before him,
> With flaming fire filled he his body.
> He fashioned a net to hold Tiamat's vitals;
> Set four winds, that naught of her escape.

Tiamat's helpers fled in terror. Alone she faced Marduk. He caught her in his net, drove an evil wind into her opened mouth, thrust her through with his spear. "He overcame her and cut off her life; he cast down her body and stood upon it."

Tiamat's attendant gods and monster brood were likewise conquered. Marduk recovered from Kingu the "Tablets of Destiny" and laid them in his own breast. After the conflict Marduk rested, and as he gazed upon Tiamat's dead body he "devised a cunning plan."

> He split her up like a flat fish into two halves;
> One-half of her he stablished as a covering for heaven.
> He fixed a bolt, he stationed a watchman,
> And bade them not to let her waters come forth.
> He passed through the heavens, he surveyed the regions (thereof),
> And over against the Deep he set the dwelling of Nudimmud.[45]
> And the lord measured the structure of the Deep.
> And he founded E-shara,[46] a mansion like unto it.
> The mansion E-shara which he created as heaven,
> He caused Anu, Bel, and Ea in their districts to inhabit.

Tablet V, it may fairly be supposed, contained some account of the creation of the earth and of vegetation. This tablet also gives an account of the creation of the heavenly bodies.

> He[47] made the stations for the great gods;
> The stars, their images, as the stars of the zodiac, he fixed.

[45] Title of Ea.   [46] Heaven.   [47] Marduk.

He ordained the year and into sections he divided it;
For the twelve months he fixed three stars.
The moon-God he caused to shine forth, the night he entrusted
to him.

He appointed him, a being of the night, to determine the days;
Every month without ceasing with the crown he covered (?)
him, (saying):
"At the beginning of the month, when thou shinest upon the
land,
"Thou commandest the horns to determine six days,
"And on the seventh day to (divide) the crown.
"On the fourteenth day thou shalt stand opposite, the half
(. . .)."

Tablet VI gives an account of the creation of man, the culmination
of Marduk's creative work. The reason for the creation of man is that
in the course of his work as creator, Marduk encountered a difficulty,
to solve which he "devised a cunning plan."

When Marduk heard the word of the gods,
His heart prompted him and he devised (a cunning plan).
He opened his mouth and unto Ea (he spake).
(That which) he had conceived in his heart he imparted (unto
him):
"My blood will I take and bone will I (fashion),
"I will make man, that man may . . .
"That the service of the gods may be established. and that
(their) shrines (may be built)."

The final scene of the creation story is depicted in the concluding
lines of tablet VI which describe the gathering of the gods in Up-
shukkinaku, their council-chamber, where they sing the praise of
Marduk.[48]

With the foregoing contrast the "Creation Epic" of Gen. *1:1–
2:4a with its stately, dignified, lyric prose. The balanced symmetry
of the narrative is admirable. Prologue is balanced with epilogue, the
first canto with the second, each stanza with its counterpart in the
other canto, two acts of creation on day three and two on day six.
Within each stanza an opening refrain is balanced by a closing refrain,

[48] For a translation of the entire poem, cf. G. A. Barton, *Archaeology and the
Bible* (7th ed.; 1937), pp. 279–294; I. M. Price, *The Monuments and the Old Testa-
ment* (Philadelphia: 1925), pp. 101 ff.; C. F. Kent, *Students' Old Testament* (New
York: 1905), i, 363–370; C. H. Toy, in *Library of the World's Best Literature*
(New York: 1896), i, 69–72. Cf. also Morris Jastrow, Jr., in Hastings' *Dictionary of
the Bible,* ext. vol., 567–573; *ibid., The Religion of Babylonia and Assyria* (New
York: 1898), pp. 410–451; *ibid., The Civilization of Babylonia and Assyria* (Philadelphia: 1915), pp. 427–443; Emil G. H. Kraeling, in *Columbia University Course in
Literature* (New York: 1928), i, 72–76; S. H. Langdon, *Semitic Mythology* (Boston:
1931), pp. 289–312; Thorkild Jacobsen in Frankfort *et al., The Intellectual Adventure of Ancient Man* (Chicago: 1946), pp. 168–183.

and in each stanza (except day two) there is a secondary refrain
which builds up to the climax of verse 31.

"IN THE BEGINNING"

(Gen. 1:1–2:4a)

Prologue: *The Primeval Chaos* (1–2)

Canto I	Canto II
The First Order of Creation	*The Second Order of Creation*

I

And God said:

Light (3–5)

And God saw that it was good

And there was evening,
And there was morning, Day I

II

And God said:

Firmament (6–8)

And there was evening,
And there was morning, Day II

III

And God said:

Land (9–10)

And God saw that it was good

And God said:

Vegetation (11–13)

Consummation of the First Order

And God saw that it was good

And there was evening,
And there was morning, Day III

IV

And God said:

Lights (14–19)

And God saw that it was good

And there was evening,
And there was morning, Day IV

V

And God said:

Life in the Firmament (20–23)

And God saw that it was good

And there was evening,
And there was morning, Day V

VI

And God said:

Life on the Land (24–25)

And God saw that it was good

And God said:

Man (26–31)

Consummation of All Creation

And God saw that it was very good

And there was evening,
And there was morning, Day VI

Epilogue: *The Completed Cosmos* (2:1–4a), Day VII

Not only does the Genesis Creation Epic differ from *Enuma Elish*
in poetic form, but a spiritual gulf separates the two. The latter is
as gross in concepts and feeling as the former is delicate and refined.
One is polytheistic and ethically sordid; the other monotheistic,
reverent, innately profound. The Genesis narrative is classed as an
epic because of its balance of thought and lyric prose, because of
the simple and sublime narration of the deeds of the Creator-God,
and because of its appeal to the emotions and to the artistic sense.
It depicts the creation as an orderly process, the work of a personal
intelligence, harmonious in all details, advancing according to a plan

which finds its culmination in the creation of man in the image of the divine.

Jewish Literature of the Sixth and Fifth Centuries B.C.

Precise dating of most books belonging to the later centuries of the Old Testament period is quite impossible. They were not dated by their authors, the internal evidence is indecisive, and Jewish tradition is vague. Nevertheless, one may feel reasonably confident that the writings discussed in the following pages originated between 586 and 400 B.C.

The Book of Lamentations. Lamentations consists of five distinct and separate poems, four of which (1, 2, 4, 5) have for their general background the destruction of Jerusalem and its temple, and for their theme the grief of the bereft sufferers and their petitions to Yahweh to raise them out of ignominy and distress, for starvation faced many and previous social status and refinements of culture had been ruined.

These poems of lament may have been composed decades or even generations after the fall of the capital. Their background seems to be the later years of bleak despondency, when long brooding over their unchanged servile lot had lowered Jewish spirits to a dead hopelessness.

The second and fourth are generally regarded as the oldest of the poems. Their author may even have passed through the horrors of the final siege and sacking of the city. The first and fifth come next in order of date, both quite clearly before the restoration of the temple but perhaps in the later period of decay and arrested development preceding Nehemiah's reforms. The third lamentation is not about the fall of Jerusalem at all but is a prayer for personal pardon and vindication in the eyes of cynical friends and neighbors. The author has suffered reverses which cause those who know him to mock and rejoice, and this poem is a humble prayer (precisely in the tone of Psalms 69 and 102, and using much the same language) for an improvement in the author's fortunes.

Odes 1, 2, 4, and 5 have close counterparts in Psalms 74 and 79. Odes 1–4 are composed in the *kinah,* or dirge meter, the rhythm of lamentation.[49] Odes 1–4 are Hebrew alphabetic acrostics, only a little less elaborate than Ps. 119.[50] This artificial structure is one reason for regarding the poems as having been composed in an era removed from the first keen mental agonies.

[49] *Vid. supra,* p. 301.
[50] The acrostic character of Lam. 1–4 and Ps. 119 is nicely exhibited in the Chicago Version. On Lamentations, cf. J. A. Bewer, *The Literature of the Old Testament* (New York: 1922), pp. 189 ff.; Pfeiffer, *op. cit.,* pp. 720–723.

Obadiah. The Book, or "Vision," of Obadiah bears no dating. Because of its reference to the sacking of Jerusalem in vs. 11, Obadiah is generally thought to have been written not long after that event, but it may well have originated at the time when the Edomites were hard pressed by the invading Nabateans.[51] It is a brief prophecy in poetic form, predicting doom on Edom for its heartlessness toward its brother Hebrew people when Jerusalem was plundered (vss. 10 f.). One infers from vss. 3 f. that when the book was written Edom's fortunes had been in the ascendant but were now threatened, for Obadiah predicts that the time will come when the "Mount of Esau" shall become subject to "Mount Zion" (vss. 17 ff., 21). The basic doctrinal ideas of Obadiah are the "Day of Yahweh" (vs. 15) and the holy remnant (vs. 17).[52]

Ezekiel. The reader of the Book of Ezekiel is baffled at the very outset by the datings given in 1:1 f. Vs. 1 dates his visions "in the thirtieth year." The thirtieth year of whom or what? Vs. 2 specifies the "fifth year of the exile of King Jehoiachin," which was 593 B.C. Modern translations, such as Moffatt's and the Chicago Version, print vss. 2 f. in square brackets, thereby indicating that these verses are regarded as interpolations. Nevertheless this date in vs. 2, supported by 33:21, is accepted by the conventional interpretation of Ezekiel as a work written by one of those deported to Babylonia in 597 B.C. The author of the book relates a number of visions (chapters 4 f.) in which he is transported "in the spirit" back and forth between Babylonia and Jerusalem, learns of the impending destruction of Jerusalem and the temple, and is made to understand how necessary that destruction is. Whereupon he tries to prepare the exiles for the final blow by a series of symbolic representations of the siege and fall of the city and the calamities to follow.

Professor C. C. Torrey construes "the thirtieth year" of 1:1 to mean the thirtieth year of King Manasseh of Judah (693–639 B.C.), and holds that there was an original book of Ezekiel, a pseudepigraphic book written in the third century B.C. but given a time-setting in the reign of Manasseh. On this view the prophet was portrayed as actually in Jerusalem, and the portrait of idolatry in Ezk. *8:5–18 was intended to characterize the religious situation in the time of Manasseh's apostasy. Professor Torrey holds that this original Ezekiel was subsequently amplified and made to fit the exilic period from 597 B.C. on.[53]

Very few biographical details are given about the prophet. He belonged to a priestly family (1:3) and was taken into exile in 597 B.C.

---

[51] *Vid. supra,* p. 346.   [52] *Vid. supra,* pp. 317, 327.
[53] Cf. C. C. Torrey, *Pseudo-Ezekiel and the Original Prophecy* (New Haven: 1930).

He was a married man, and lived in his own house (3:24) in Tell Abib (3:15). His wife died suddenly, 589 b.c. (Ezk. 24:1, 15–18). His public career appears to have extended over twenty-two years (1:2, 29:17).

Chapter *1 gives the prophet's vision of the transcendence of God, and is another instance of mystical religious experience such as we have observed in other prophets.[54] The omnipresence of God is what the prophet visualized in this chapter. Several such visions characterize this book (8:2 ff., 10, 11:22 ff., 37:1–14), the most elaborate of all being his vision of the new temple (40–47). Such visions were a frequent feature of prophets' experience.[55]

The allegory of the eagles and the vine (*17:1–10) introduces an interesting literary type which we have not previously met. The conclusion of the allegory (*17:22 ff.) implies the doctrine of the remnant and is similar to Isaiah's verse about the olive berries on the outermost branch (Isa. 17:6).

Chapter *18 is an essay on the principle of individual moral responsibility, a doctrine which Jeremiah had preached.[56] Ezekiel discussed this same theme again in 33:7–20. The "Lament over Tyre" (*27) is an excellent example of highly developed poetic art; Tyre is portrayed as a gorgeously outfitted merchant ship which is wrecked at sea. Chapter *34, the prophecy against the shepherds (i.e., the national leaders), with its portrait of God as the Shepherd of His people, is one of the incomparably beautiful chapters of the Bible.[57]

Haggai and Zechariah. Neither of these books is great literature. The two prophets are so closely linked in history and aims that it is well to study them together. Ezr. 5:1 f. implies that they worked in concert for the rebuilding of the temple, *circa* 520 b.c. Both expected some sort of Jewish state to be reestablished, under the joint control of a governor, Zerubbabel, and a high priest, Joshua. Beyond a reasonable doubt what both looked for was the restoration of a modified Davidic kingdom under divine sanction and protection.[58]

Haggai was the first to speak. He declared that they could expect no return of prosperity so long as they allowed the temple, God's house, to lie in ruins, and he urged its repair without further delay (1:1–11). This appeal met with a prompt response, but the results fell far short of what had been desired (2:3). Then, several months later, he made his final prediction: shortly there would come a great upheaval among the world powers; the mighty would be overthrown; Zerubbabel would become Yahweh's own "signet" in the world

[54] *Vid. supra*, pp. 116 f., 130 f., 323, 338, 342.   [55] Cf. *supra*, pp. 329 f.
[56] Cf. Jer. 17:10; 31:29 ff.; *vid. supra*, pp. 341 f.
[57] On Ezekiel, cf. Bewer, *op. cit.*, pp. 169–183; Pfeiffer, *op. cit.*, pp. 518–565.
[58] *Vid. supra*, pp. 351 f.

(2:20–23). This could have meant nothing less than that the Jewish nation was to be raised to acknowledged primacy among world powers.

The month preceding Haggai's prediction about Zerubbabel, Zechariah warned his fellow countrymen that unless they reformed their ways they might find themselves headed again for the same doom that overtook their fathers (1:1–6). After that, however, all his messages were words of hope and encouragement. In a series of symbolic visions he paints a picture of a glorious future for Judaism: the "horns that scattered Judah" would themselves be "cast down" (1:21); the people were not to concern themselves over Jerusalem's ruined walls, for Yahweh himself would be a "wall of fire" round about her (2:1–5); Zerubbabel would surely complete the building of the temple, the foundation of which was already laid (4:9); he would, in fact, become a crowned ruler working in close coöperation with the high priest Joshua (6:11 ff.). Lastly, a prediction of general hope is given (8:1–13), in which, from its list of joys to be anticipated, we can see what conditions were most lacking at the time it was written. All these chapters, to judge from the careful datings given, were written 520–518 B.C.[59] Zechariah experienced an interesting series of visions (1:7–6:8).[60]

A type of literature known as apocalypse appears in partly developed form in the Book of Zechariah. The term *apocalypse* literally means "revelation," but as applied to Jewish writings it invariably means a document which, while it might be a revealed matter to Jews, would be rather a thing of mystification and bafflement to non-Jews not initiated into the secrets of this type of literature, if indeed they paid any attention to it at all. Since the Jews were a subject people, such literature would have been seized as seditious by their overlords had the latter been able to read between the lines and recognize against whom the animus of such apocalyptical treatises was directed.

Thus in Zech. 1 and 6, written when the Jewish world was tense with expectancy, with mingled hope and fear over the outcome of the desperate civil struggle being waged for the Persian succession, the author veils his political activity from all except Jewish understanding by means of the cryptic symbolism of horses, horns, and smiths that went by fours. No close student of the history of the period will fail to see that Zech. 1:21 refers to Cyrus's overthrow of the Chaldean power some nineteen years earlier, or that it contains a veiled but unmistakable prediction that the Persian power is now in its turn about to collapse.

---

[59] Only chapters 1–8 of the Book of Zechariah are from this prophet. Chapters 9–14 are a much later composition, assigned by Old Testament scholars to the second century B.C., and sometimes referred to as Second Zechariah. On Haggai and Zechariah, cf. Bewer, *op. cit.,* pp. 234–242; Pfeiffer, *op. cit.,* pp. 602–612.

[60] *Vid. infra,* p. 393.

Subsequent apocalypses make abundant use of animal symbolism and of the dream vision (implied rather than named in Zech. 4:1 and elsewhere). An angelic personage who explains to the author the significance of the obscurer symbolism is another standard feature of this type of writing,[61] in marked contrast to the direct communication between God and man which is the regular representation of the older prophets.

The apocalypse has no particular literary merit, but it is extremely important for an understanding of the changing currents of Judaism. We shall see more of it in subsequent chapters.

Nehemiah.   The Book of Nehemiah has the distinction of coming originally from the pen of a high official, a capable and efficient man of affairs, a governor.[62] These memoirs are the simple, unadorned, forthright statements of a high-minded, patriotic young Jew who was fortunate enough to be made governor extraordinary of Jerusalem and vicinity for a term of years (or possibly two terms) [63] and who achieved phenomenal success in getting the rehabilitation of Jerusalem and Judea under way. With no waste of words he relates just how he happened to get the royal commission (1:1–2:8); how he managed his first task of making Jerusalem safe to live in once more (2:9–4:23; 6); how that, in turn, led to the discovery of certain grievous abuses which he promptly remedied (chapter 5); the methods and devices by which he induced a number of patriots to move into Jerusalem to live (7:1–4; 11:1 f.); and the series of reforms he put through by rather forceful means on his return from Babylonia for his second governorship (13:4–31).

The book is invaluable for the light it throws on the condition of Jerusalem in Nehemiah's day. The reluctance of the majority to take up residence within the city, even after security had been assured by repairs of the city walls, shows how unattractive it must have been for residential purposes. One is forced to conclude that Jerusalem was still a much ruined place. Perhaps what Neh. 11:1 f. implies is that a few of the more substantial buildings had survived the centuries, but that most of the old dwellings had been allowed to disintegrate in the swift way that the mud-walled and mud-roofed structure of the Orient does. Even after twelve years of vigorous leadership, Nehemiah discovered one family using part of the temple buildings for a dwelling. It was a half-foreign family at that! [64]

The physical condition of the temple in Nehemiah's day is not known. It is commonly assumed that the Darius in whose reign the rebuilding of the temple was finally completed (as predicted in

---

[61] Cf. Zech. 1:12 ff.   [62] Cf. *supra*, pp. 352 f.
[63] Cf. Neh. 13:6 f.   [64] Neh. 13:4–9; cf. 2:10.

Zech. 4:9) was Darius the First.[65] But a careful reading of Ezr. 6:14 f. implies that the reign of one Darius and one Artaxerxes had already elapsed when the final repairs were made. If that be true, then the completion of the temple repairs will have to be put at least as late as 419 B.C. In some ways this fits into the general picture of the social-historical situation much better than the assumption that the fully restored temple had been in existence for a century before the time of Nehemiah. But the present evidence is indecisive.

Other interesting information can be gleaned from the memoirs of Nehemiah. For one thing, it is clear that little or no attention was paid to Sabbath observance as a time of cessation from work in general. Farming and trade apparently went on as usual, and priests got so little income from offerings that they had to engage in agriculture like the rest in order to eke out a livelihood (Neh. 13: 10–22). There was also little race consciousness among the Palestinian Jews at that time, or at least far too little to satisfy Nehemiah, as 13:23–30 vividly shows.

Nehemiah's memoirs are to be dated in the latter part of the fifth century B.C. or in the early part of the fourth century, depending on whether the Artaxerxes was the first or the second of that name. About a century later the memoirs of Nehemiah were merged in a larger history which comprises 1 and 2 Chronicles and Ezra.[66]

Malachi. Malachi is another undated book. The name is merely a title adopted from 3:1, "Behold, I send *malachi* (my messenger) to prepare the way before me," rather than a personal name. From the contents of the writing one senses that the background of the book is the period of Nehemiah or very close thereto. The temple had been rebuilt, the sacrifices and offerings were once more going on regularly, but the inner life of the Jews was not showing up creditably. Neh. 5, 13, reflect the same conditions that are described in Malachi. Note in particular the absence of respect and reverence toward Yahweh charged by Malachi (1:6 ff., 14), the open cynicism (2:17; 3:14 f.), the social oppression (3:5; 2:10, 14), as well as the general unreliability in their pledged word and gross failure to live up to their pledged tithes (3:8).

Malachi was written in a time of depression, both in agriculture and in Jewish psychology. His solution of the problem is reform, by showing respect and reverence, by bringing only the perfect or the best in offerings, by a scrupulous keeping of promises whether made to God or to a spiritual brother (2:10), and by an unstinted giving of "the whole tithe" (3:10 f.).

Malachi makes the familiar prophetic threat of a "terrible day of Yahweh" that would "burn up" the stubbornly wicked (4:1). But

---

[65] Cf. Ezr. 4:5, 24; 6:15.   [66] *Vid. infra*, pp. 406 f.

then he adds the promise that before that day arrives Yahweh will give one last warning and will send this "messenger," his *malach* (3:1–3), probably the same person referred to in 4:5 as "Elijah the prophet." This was the prediction which made so great an impression on Jewish and Christian thought in a later century.[67]

Second Isaiah. Second Isaiah, or Deutero-Isaiah, is the name by which it has become customary to refer to the latter part of the Book of Isaiah, beginning with chapter 40, and some scholars include chapters 34 f. as well. These chapters reveal a totally different socio-historical background from that of the first part of the book, which is the basic reason for assigning it to a much later author than the eighth-century Isaiah of Jerusalem, who prophesied in the time of kings Ahaz and Hezekiah.[68] Many scholars date the Second Isaiah about 540 B.C. because of the references in 44:28 and 45:1 to Cyrus, whose rule affected Jewish history from 539 B.C. onward. Some, however, regard the name Cyrus in these verses as a much later conjecture inserted by a Jewish scribe. This view leaves the question of the date of composition open, including the possibility that it may come from a period toward the end of the fifth century B.C.

Nothing whatever is known about the biography of this prophet, not even his name. This only can we say, that among the prophets and poets thus far there has not arisen a greater than the Second Isaiah, the "Great Unknown." His primary aim was to rouse his despondent fellow Jews to strong, confident faith in their nation's future. He explained the exile as a part of God's plan to bring it about that other nations of the world should recognize himself as the one and only God, by compelling the chosen people to become the teachers of the other nations. The Hebrew nation had been woefully blind to what it really meant to be a chosen people, in that they supposed it implied that they had exclusive rights to the one God. They ought to have seen they were to be the world's religious teachers (*49:6). Because they had failed in this, calamities had overtaken them, specifically the exile. But now at last (whenever the poems were written), their sins had been more than atoned for (40:1 f.), they were actually serving as God's witnesses in the gentile world; presently their humiliations would be over, a glorious compensation would be theirs for all their physical sufferings and mental anguish.

Second Isaiah is poetry of an intensely lyrical character.[69] Isa. *35 is a paean of high anticipatory joy over a future so glorious that it

---

[67] It is referred to in Matt. 11:14, Mark 9:11 ff., and Luke 1:17 as having been fulfilled in John the Baptist. This, of course, was only in Christian circles. The Jews looked for a different fulfillment. On Malachi, cf. Bewer, *op. cit.*, pp. 254–258; Pfeiffer, *op. cit.*, pp. 612–615.   [68] *Vid. supra*, pp. 321–327.

[69] C. C. Torrey, *The Second Isaiah* (New York: 1929), fully discusses the poetic character of the book (pp. 151–204), and prints the full text of Second Isaiah in a way to exhibit its metric structure (pp. 223–276).

will make the cripple leap and run and the dumb burst into singing (vs. 6). Chapter *40 introduces Yahweh as the incomparable God, approaching Jerusalem most imposingly over a broad graded highway made by leveling mountains off into the valleys. In chapter *41 Yahweh begins to speak, at times addressing the gentile nations or "islands" (41:1), at other times his "servant Israel" (41:8). For the most part all from chapter 41 on is a recitative in the mouth of the Lord God Yahweh. Occasional bursts of song or of lyrical exhortation interrupt this speech, only to heighten the total emotional appeal; e.g., *42:10–13; *51:9 ff.; *52:7–10; *60:1 ff.

The Second Isaiah is the most creative thinker we have as yet met in the Bible. The sweep of his thought is truly thrilling.

1. *His Idea of God.* Yahweh is the only God (*44:6, 8, *45:5 f.),[70] the omnipotent creator of the heavens and the earth (40:26, 28),[71] the God of the whole earth (*54:5; *56:7),[72] and, of course, the God of Israel (43:15).[73] He is in control of history (41:2 ff., 48:3),[74] the eternal God (40:28; *57:15), the "first and the last" (41:4, 44:6),[75] whose word is eternal (*40:8).[76] He is Yahweh of Hosts (44:6; 54:5),[77] the Holy One (43:14 f.; 47:4; 54:5),[78] Redeemer (44:6; 47:4; 49:26; 54:5; 63:16),[79] Saviour (49:26),[80] King (44:6),[81] and Father (*63:16; 64:8). He "forms the light, and creates darkness; he makes peace and creates evil," [82] which doctrine is a thoroughgoing monism.

Toward this exalted and holy God, the proper human attitude is that of humility and contrition; he dwells in the hearts of such (*57:15).[83] He esteems righteousness above ritual fasting (58:5–9).

2. *God's Universal Purpose.* Commensurate with his nature as the universal sovereign, God's purpose for the world is the redemption of all mankind. This includes salvation for the gentiles (*45:22 f.; *49:6; *51:4 ff.; *52:10; *55),[84] and for the Jews (*45:17; *60).[85] He speaks tenderly of Jerusalem as Mother Zion, and of the exiles as her children (49:16–21; 51:17–20; *54:4–8).

3. *Yahweh's Servant.* Israel is God's servant to accomplish his universal purpose (41:8–16; 42:1–7, 18 ff.; 43:10; 44:1 f., 21, 26;

[70] Cf. 43:10 f.; 45:18, 21 f.; 46:9.
[71] Cf. 40:12, 22; 42:5; 44:24; 45:12, 18; 48:13; 51:13, 16; 66:1 f.
[72] Cf. 45:6, 11 f., 14, 22 f.; 49:1–13; 60:3; 66:18 f.
[73] Cf. 45:11, 15, 17; 54:7 f.
[74] Cf. 41:22 f., 25; 43:9; 44:6 f.; 45:1, 13, 21; 46:10 f.; 48:14.
[75] Cf. 48:12.   [76] Cf. 55:11.   [77] Cf. 45:13; 47:4; 48:2; 51:15.
[78] Cf. 40:25; 41:14, 16, 20; 43:3; 45:11; 48:17; 49:7; 55:5; 57:15; 60:9, 14.
[79] Cf. 41:14; 43:14; 44:24; 48:17; 49:7; 60:16.
[80] Cf. 43:3, 11; 45:15, 21; 60:16; 63:8.
[81] Cf. 41:21; 43:15.   [82] 45:7.   [83] Cf. 41:17; 50:10; 61:1; 66:2.
[84] Cf. 42:4, 6 f.; 45:14 f.; 49:22 f.; 52:15; 56:7 f.; 60:6–14; 61:11; 62:2; 66:18 f.
[85] This theme of the restoration of the Jews runs all the way through the poems. Cf. 40:2, 9; 41:14; 43:1, 5 f.; 44:22 f., 26, 28; 46:13; 48:20; 49:5 f., 12 f., 22 f.; 51:3, 17–23; 52:3, 11 f.; 54:5; 61:4–9; 62:10 ff.; 63:7 ff.; 66:18 ff.

45:1–5, 13; *49:1–9; 50:4–11; *52:13–53:12; 55:4 f.; 62:1–9). The Jews had always regarded themselves as the chosen people, and this was conventionally interpreted to mean that they were God's special favorites, chosen for benefits which were denied to the rest of mankind. Second Isaiah uses the word "chosen" of Israel as Yahweh's servant.[86] They were chosen, not for special favors, but for special service.

Passages 44:1 and 49:3 specifically identify Israel as the servant, and presumably this was the Second Isaiah's idea in all of the "servant passages." In some of them, however, the servant portrait is highly individualized. This is doubtless due to the same pattern of thinking which individualized the stories of the experiences of whole groups, for example in the nomadic period, as the experiences of eponymous heroes, the patriarchs.

4. *Vicarious Suffering.* What perplexed the Jews was the calamity which befell them in the exile, and the adversity and suffering which continued to be their portion in Judah in the centuries which followed the restoration. Conventionally, this was explained as punishment for the nation's sin, and the Second Isaiah shares this view (42:24).[87] Second Isaiah offers a new explanation, namely, that such suffering is vicarious and redemptive (42:19–25; 48:10; 49:4, 7; 50:5–9; *53:4–12). This doctrine was something utterly new [88] but it rested upon a principle that was very ancient and very basic in Hebrew life and thinking, the principle of corporate solidarity.

From the most ancient times Hebrew thinking was socialized. The individual had no rights of his own apart from his family. He was, indeed, not an individual but a member of his family. He enjoyed such rights, privileges, and esteem as the entire group enjoyed, and by the same token he shared the responsibilities of the whole group.[89] He bore the blame which attached to the whole group for any evil done by any member of the group, and even though innocent himself, he bore whatever punishment was exacted of his group if the punishment happened to fall upon him. By his stripes the whole group was saved. This was also true of the particular family in relation to the whole tribe, and of the individual tribe in relation to the whole nation. Now the Second Isaiah extends this doctrine to its universal implication. It is true of the individual nation in relation to the whole world. Thus he explains Israel's suffering as on behalf of the whole world. It satisfied the demands of justice, paid the penalty for the sins of all mankind, and would accomplish the redemption of the

86 41:9; 43:10; 44:1.
87 Cf. 42:22; 43:25–28; 44:21 f.; 46:8–13; 48:4, 8–12, 18; 50:1; 59:12; 65:8.
88 Cf. "New things do I declare," 42:9; 43:19; 48:6.
89 *Vid. supra,* p. 89.

world by bringing all mankind to be worshipers of the one and only God.

The Second Isaiah was an idealist who thought in terms of ultimates. God's ultimate purpose of salvation for all mankind meant the universal establishment of righteousness in the world. There are two sides to the ethical problem, the destruction of evil and the establishment of righteousness.

5. *The Destruction of Evil.* Second Isaiah vividly and unsparingly condemns evil (34; 42:15; 47; 48:22; 56; 57; 59) and depicts God's irruption into the world to punish and destroy evil (*59:15b–20; *64:1 ff.). One of the most powerful poems in the book is *63:1–6 with its vivid picture of Yahweh treading the wine press to stamp out evil. Second Isaiah thought not in generalities but concretely, and the concrete symbol of evil was Edom.[90]

6. *The New Jerusalem and the Ideal Future.* The other side of Second Isaiah's ethical idealism is his portrait of the new heaven and the new earth which God will create (*65:17–25; 66:22).[91] He does not think of this ideal as a glittering generality, but the concrete symbol of it is the new Jerusalem (35:10; 49:17–21; *51:11; 52:1 f.; 8 f.; *54:11–14; *60; *62; 65:18–25; 66:10–13).

7. *The Way of Holiness.* One of the vivid metaphors of Second Isaiah is the highway through the desert (*35:8 ff.; *40:3 f.).[92] The meaning of this is that there is a way which leads from the present through the desert area of evil and affliction to the ideal future, and that way is the way of righteousness. Those who travel this way are the redeemed (*51:9 ff.; *60:21 ff.; *62:12),[93] an idea analogous to the idea of the holy remnant which was expressed by certain of the pre-exilic prophets.[94]

8. *The Messiah.* The climactic idea of Second Isaiah is that of the Messiah (41:2–5; *42:1–9; *45:1–7, 13; 48:15 ff.; 52:7; 55:4 ff.; *61:1 ff.). The word *messiah* means "the anointed one," [95] The idea of the Messiah represents the highest ascent of prophetism, the most idealistic conception in Jewish thinking. The Messiah is that ideal person whom God will raise up to inaugurate the ideal age. In the thinking of the Second Isaiah, the Messiah is the ideal coming leader who will lead the redeemed over the highway to the new Jerusalem.[96]

Poetry such as this has tremendous power. Its creative imagination is so unusual and so marked; its portraiture of God so majestic,

---

[90] 34; 63:1–6.   [91] Cf. 45:8; 51:6, 8, 16; 61:10 f.
[92] Cf. 41:17 ff.; 42:16; 43:19 f.; 48:21; 49:9 ff.; 51:10 f.; 55:12; 57:14; 62:10; 63:13.   [93] Cf. 40:11; 41:17; 42:16; 46:3; 51:1 f.; 7 f., 16; 65:9.
[94] *Vid. supra*, pp. 317, 327.   [95] Cf. 45:1; 61:1.
[96] This idealistic conception, somebody, whether the Second Isaiah or a later hand, identified with Cyrus (45:1) and his mission of world conquest.

yet so humanly tender and appealing; its suffering servant concept
so luminous of the great problem of all undeserved suffering, whether
of nation or of individual; and its faith in the ultimate triumph of
righteousness and divine justice so exuberantly positive, that the
reader is irresistibly borne along on the swelling tide of poetic rhythm
and lyrical feeling. Such literature is immortal.[97]

The Holiness Code = "H." Chapters 17–26 of the Book of Leviticus make up a small law book which is technically called the
Holiness Code; it is designated by "H." The compilation of this
code was done sometime after 570 B.C. by an author who was akin
to Ezekiel in thought and form of expression. He is dominated by
two principal beliefs: (1) Yahweh is holy, i.e., physically remote
and inaccessible; and (2) Yahweh's people must be holy, i.e., they
must avoid everything that is taboo. These ideas are clearly stated
in Lev. 20:26.

The holiness emphasized in these laws is a ritual rather than an
ethical holiness. There are nevertheless some notable social-ethical
principles enunciated (Lev. *19; 25:14, 17–25, 35–40, 44 f., 47 ff.,
53, 55). Indeed, Lev. 19:17 f. may be regarded as the loftiest principle of social ethics to be found anywhere in the Old Testament:
"Thou shalt love thy neighbor as thyself." Jesus of Nazareth did so
regard it.[98]

Lev. *26 is a splendid sample of "H's" hortatory style. "H" was
ultimately incorporated into the Priest Code, "P."

The Priest Code = "P." As has been pointed out in the preceding pages, following the restoration, Judah was a Persian province.
Local affairs passed into the hands of the high priests in Jerusalem.
Judah was a theocracy. God's rule was mediated through the priests,
his visible representatives. All life pivoted upon the temple ritual.
The place of this ritual in history had then to be interpreted to the
people so that they would understand the origin and sanctity of the
laws and cordially accept the entire ceremonial and legal system.
This task was undertaken by the writers of what is known as the
Priest Code, or "P," another of the basic source documents that
make up the Pentateuch. History is treated in four world epochs
in order to show the origin of what the priestly writers consider the
four most important ceremonial institutions. The first epoch is from
the creation to the flood. The creation story is told in a passage of
unsurpassed grandeur (Gen. *1:1–2:4a), the very finest thing "P"
wrote, and in a style markedly superior to the rest of "P."[99] At the

---

[97] On Second Isaiah, cf. Bewer, *op. cit.,* pp. 200–213; Pfeiffer, *op. cit.,* pp. 452–
481.
[98] Mark 12:31.   [99] *Vid. supra,* pp. 364–366.

close of the creation the Sabbath was instituted, the first of the ceremonial institutions. The second epoch is from the flood to Abram. After the flood the prohibition against eating blood, second of the ceremonial institutions, was imposed (Gen. 9:1–6). The third epoch is from Abram to Moses, within which the ceremonial institution of circumcision was begun in the time of Abram (Gen. 17). The fourth epoch began with Moses, in whose time the Passover was instituted (Ex. 12:1–14, 28). Thus God's will was revealed in four definitely marked stages, the final revelation being that of the law to Moses.

The passages noted in the preceding paragraph are samples of the literary style of "P" at its best. The document is readily detected by its priestly and ritualistic point of view. For the most part the style is dry and formal, abounding in tables of genealogies, dates, and such.[100]

"P" originated *circa* 500 B.C. in Babylon, but the composition and editing of it extended into the fourth century B.C. It brings to a climax the historical development, within the Old Testament period, of one important phase of religion, viz., the ceremonial. For "P" the sacrificial cult was religion. Yet in an amazing and doubtless wholly unintentional way, "P" shows how the religion of Judaism could exist without the priestly cult. For in his law of the Passover, "P" makes it a family festival, and the killing of the paschal lamb is described as a secular act which need not be performed at Jerusalem but may be consummated anywhere (Ex. 12:1–10). Ultimately, in A.D. 70, the Jerusalem temple was destroyed and the whole priestly cult disappeared forever from Judaism. Today the Passover remains Judaism's chief feast and is celebrated wherever there are Jews.

The Completion of the Torah. The close of the period under survey in this chapter practically saw the completion of the centuries-long process of composition, compilation, and editing which produced the Jewish Torah, also called the Pentateuch or the Law, i.e., the first five books of the Bible. Four basic source documents have entered into the formation of these books. "J" originated *circa* 850 B.C. in Judah,[101] and "E" in Israel, *circa* 750 B.C.[102] These two were combined in "JE" sometime after the downfall of Israel in 722 B.C.[103] "D" originated *circa* 621 B.C.[104] Then, sometime after the fall of Judah in 586 B.C., "D" was expanded and combined with "E" to form "JED." "P" originated *circa* 500 B.C. The combining of "JED" with "P" gave the completed work "JEDP," which is the Torah. Though minor changes may have been made subsequently,

---

[100] For a good presentation of the Priest Code, cf. Bewer, *op. cit.*, pp. 259–278; Pfeiffer, *op. cit.*, pp. 188–209.
[101] *Vid. supra*, pp. 296 f.
[102] *Vid. supra*, pp. 297 f.
[103] *Vid supra*, p. 298.
[104] *Vid. supra*, pp. 284 f., 305 f.

the books of Genesis, Exodus, Leviticus, Numbers, and Deuteronomy had reached the form in which we now have them in our English Bible.

Other Literary Activity of the Period. In this same period of the exile and restoration there went on further editing or supplementing of the books of prophetic history known as the *Former Prophets* of the Hebrew canon—Joshua, Judges, Samuel, and Kings. Such additions were chiefly in the nature of deuteronomic material and the deuteronomic interpretation of God in the history of the nation.[105]

It is also fairly certain that some psalm and proverb writing was done within the period, though which psalms and which proverbs would be difficult to assert. Few bear any precise marks of date, and the ascriptions of authorship in the titles of particular psalms are generally regarded as later conjectures.

Considerable additions to the great prophetic books were also made at this time, such as the concluding chapters of the Book of Jeremiah and (in all probability) many, if not most, of the passages of future hope which now soften the predictions of doom in the books of Amos, Micah, Zephaniah, and the like. (Cf. Am. *9:11–15; Mic. *4:7; Zeph. *3:8–20). The messianic prophecies of Isa. *9:1–7; *11 f.; *30:18–33; *32:1–8, 15–20; and *33 were for the most part written in this period, as were also the doom songs on Babylon and other nations in Isa. 13:1–14:23; 19; 21; and possibly 23.[106] The general doom song of Isa. 34, which goes with chapter 35, discussed in connection with the Second Isaiah, also comes from this period.

Postexilic Judaism

In order to get a picture of the religion of the Jewish people at the close of the period under survey in this present chapter, we may gather together and appraise the significance of various items mentioned in the foregoing sections.

The Idea of God. The exile made the Jews strict monotheists, and the doctrine of ethical monotheism came to full expression with the Second Isaiah (Isa. *40:12–26; *43:10 ff.; *44:6 ff.; *45:5; *46:9).[107] Yahweh was not just one among many gods. He was the only God. The corollary of this was that all the other supposed gods of the nations were only idols. Idolatry was denounced and ridiculed

---

[105] Cf. Bewer's chapter on "Deuteronomistic Historians," *op. cit.*, pp. 214–233.
[106] Cf. Bewer's chapter on "Exilic Poets and Prophets," *op. cit.*, pp. 189–199. On the poetic character of the dirge in Isa. 14, cf. Laura H. Wild, *A Literary Guide to the Bible* (New York: 1922), pp. 172 f.
[107] Cf. *supra*, p. 373.

by the great prophet of the exile (Isa. *44:9–19; *46:1–7). The exile forever cured the Jews of idolatry.

As to the character of God, he is "the Holy One." [108] Ezekiel emphasized the transcendence of God (Ezk. 1:26 ff.). The holiness of God was the central idea upon which Ezekiel's idealized pattern for a restored temple was based (Ezk. 40–47).[109] The Holy One dwelt apart within the Most Holy Place, and the gradations of courts around the temple were conceived to preserve the holiness of God by keeping the various classes of worshipers at different distances, according to their grades of holiness. Again, the idea of the holiness of God was worked out in the laws of the Holiness Code, as we have observed.[110]

Sanctuaries. 1. *The Jerusalem Temple.* The restored Jerusalem temple, often referred to as the second temple, or the temple of Zerubbabel,[111] was, of course, the central shrine upon which the minds of all Jews focused. Here the cult of sacrificial worship was centralized. To the Jerusalem temple all Palestinian Jews resorted at festival times, and it was the most devout desire of Jews outside of Palestine sometime to make a pilgrim journey to the holy land and the holy temple. The appointments of the temple were doubtless like those of Solomon's temple, though much less elegant.[112] The innermost room in Solomon's temple, the Most Holy Place, had housed the sacred Ark of the Covenant, but that holy emblem had been destroyed, along with Solomon's temple, in 586 B.C. Now the innermost shrine of the second temple was absolutely empty.

2. *The Synagogues.* Whatever the historic facts regarding the origin of the synagogue may have been,[113] certainly it held an important place in Judaism by the year 400 B.C. There was not one synagogue, but many, and not only in Palestine but in the Diaspora as well. The emergence and ultimate spread of synagogues in Palestine undid the mischief of King Josiah's reformation in 621 B.C. That mischief had been the destruction of all local high places in the land and centralization of religion in Jerusalem, the net result of which had been to eliminate religion from the local communities. The synagogue took religion back to the people in their home towns.

Worship. 1. *At the Temple.* The nature of worship at the temple can be understood by the one word—*sacrifice.* There were four types of sacrifices, viz., animal sacrifices, grain offerings, libations (drink offerings), and incense offering. Under the heading of animal sacrifices were the burnt offerings, including the continual burnt offering

---

[108] Isa. 40:25; cf. *supra,* p. 373.
[109] Ezekiel's projected plan for the temple never was carried out.
[110] *Supra,* p. 376.   [111] Cf. *supra,* p. 350.
[112] *Vid. supra,* pp. 211 f.   [113] *Vid. supra,* pp. 359 f.

(Lev. 6:8–13; Ex. 29:38–42),[114] sin offerings (Lev. 4; Ex. 29:36), trespass (guilt) offerings (Lev. 5; 7:1–10), and peace offerings (Lev. 3; 7:11–38). The basic idea of all such sacrifices was that of atonement or reconciliation between God and man. The highest expression of this thought was the Day of Atonement (Lev. 16), an annual atonement for all sin which might have been committed knowingly or unwittingly within the year, and a renewal of right relationship with God. The grain offerings were the meal offering (Lev. 2), and the showbread (Ex. 25:30; Lev. 24:5–9; Num. 4:7).[115] The libations were of wine (Ex. 29:40 f.; Num. 28:7 f.).[116] The incense offering was of sweet spices and was burned (Ex. 30:34–38; Lev. 16:12 f.).

There were sacrificial offerings by and on behalf of individuals, elaborately prescribed in Lev. 1–7. There were daily morning and evening sacrifices on behalf of the whole people (Num. 28:1–8). There were prescribed sacrifices for Sabbaths (Num. 28:9 f.) and New Moon Days (Num. 28:11–15). And there was a series of annual festivals, for each of which there was a prescribed ritual. *Passover* came on the 14th day of the first month, Nisan (Lev. *23:5; Ex. *12: 1–14, 21–28).[117] *Unleavened Bread* immediately followed, first month, 15th day (Lev. *23:6 ff.).[118] In the spring came the *Feast of Weeks,* or *Harvest,* culminating with *Pentecost* (Lev. *23:9–21).[119] *Trumpets,* or New Year's Day, now familiar to everybody as *Rosh Hashanah,* came the first day of the seventh month, Tishri (Lev. *23: 23 ff.).[120] The *Day of Atonement,* now familiarly known by its Jewish name, *Yom Kippur,* which was not a feast but a fast, came the tenth day of the seventh month (Lev. *23:26–32, *16).[121] *Tabernacles,* or *Booths,* or *Ingathering,* came the 15th day of the seventh month (Lev. *23:33–44).[122] In subsequent centuries we shall see other annual festivals added to the Jewish ecclesiastical calendar.

In addition to the foregoing there were two notable cyclical festivals, the *Sabbatical Year* (Lev. 25:1–7) every seventh year, and the *Year of Jubilee* (Lev. 25:8–12) every fiftieth year. In Jubilee year Hebrew slaves were liberated.

2. *In the Synagogue.* The core of worship in the synagogue was the reading of the Law, and Neh. *8:1–8 clearly reveals the ritual. First, Ezra was called upon by the people to read the Law (vs. 1). He stood upon "a pulpit (tower) of wood, which they had made for the purpose" (vs. 4). "All the people stood up" when he read the

---

114 Cf. Num. 28:3–6.   115 Cf. Ex. 35:13; 39:36; 2 Chr. 2:4.
116 Cf. Sir. 50:15. Libations of broth are referred to in Jgs. 6:19 f.; Isa. 65:4; and of water in 1 Sam. 7:6.   117 Cf. Num. 28:16; Deut. 16:1 f.
118 Cf. Ex. 12:15–20; Num. 28:17–25; Deut. 16:3–8.
119 Cf. Num. 28:26–31; Deut. 16:9–12.   120 Cf. Num. 29:1–6.
121 Cf. Num. 29:7–11.   122 Cf. Num. 29:12–38: Deut. 16:13 ff.

Law (vs. 5). Before reading, "Ezra blessed Yahweh, the great God," followed by an Amen-response by the congregation (vs. 6). At the conclusion of the reading came an interpretation of the Law (vs. 8) ; this ultimately became a regular feature, known as a *Targum*.[123]

The reading of the Law was followed (customarily if not invariably) by comments upon its meaning and its application to their life as a people, the opinions of the great prophets having much weight in such interpretations. Exactly what other features characterized the synagogue worship at this time it would be dogmatic to state, but it is inconceivable that it should not have included singing and prayer. Such prayer included confession of national sin with petition for forgiveness and restoration.

The Priesthood.   In the period of the second temple, Jewish ritual and ecclesiastical organization reached the culmination of their development. The pattern now achieved continued throughout all the rest of Bible times.

1. *The High Priest.* The pre-eminent person in the restored Jewish community in Palestine, both ecclesiastically and politically, was the high priest.[124] There were special personal qualifications for this office.[125] The high priest was regarded as the descendant of Aaron.[126] He was inducted into office by a special ritual of consecration,[127] wore prescribed vestments,[128] and performed special ceremonial functions not permitted to the generality of the priests.[129] The high priest performed a very special function annually on the Day of Atonement when, clad in special vestments for that occasion,[130] he entered the Most Holy Place of the temple (being the only person ever allowed to enter the most sacred chamber) and performed the ritual of atonement (Lev. 16).

2. *Priests.* Those who served in the office of priest had to be without physical defects,[131] and they were forbidden certain practices.[132] They wore prescribed vestments [133] and were inducted into office by special ceremonies of consecration.[134] Their duties were principally in connection with the offering of sacrifices,[135] but they also performed important duties in decisions about certain diseases, notably leprosy, and in performing the rites connected with the healing of those diseases.[136] They blew the trumpets on festal occasions.[137] They instructed the people in the ceremonial law [138] and also

[123] Cf. Luke 4 :20 f. ; Acts 13 :15.   [124] Cf. *supra*, p. 352.
[125] Lev. 21 :10–15.   [126] Num. 20 :23–29 ; 25 :10–13.
[127] Ex. 29 ; Lev. 8.
[128] Ex. 28 :1–38 ; 29 :5–9 ; 39 :1–31 ; Lev. 8 :6–9.
[129] Lev. 4 :13–21 ; 6 :19–23.   [130] Lev. 16 :4, 23.
[131] Lev. 21 :16–23.   [132] Lev. 10 :8 f. ; 21 :1–9.
[133] Ex. 28 :42, 29 :8 f. ; Lev. 8 :13.   [134] Ex. 29 ; Lev. 8.
[135] Lev. 1–7.   [136] Lev. 13 f.
[137] Num. 10 :10 ; Lev. 23 :24 ; 25 :9 ; cf. Ps. 81 :3.
[138] Lev. 10 :11.

pronounced the blessing upon the people (Lev. 9:22; Num. *6:22–27). They received various offerings.[139]

3. *Levites.* The Levites, though said to be in charge of the sanctuary,[140] were not permitted to enter it.[141] They were the temple servants, performing subordinate tasks in the courts outside the temple and doing everything except what the Law obliged the priests to do.[142] No other servants were allowed at the sanctuary.[143] They were dedicated by special ceremonies.[144] The Levites were in charge of the musical service of the temple.[145] A Levite served from his twenty-fifth to his fiftieth year.[146] They were supported from the tithe paid in to the temple.[147] There were forty-eight Levitical cities where they resided when not in service.[148]

The First Sacred Scriptures of the Jews: The Torah. In all our discussion of Hebrew literature thus far, we have sought to point out those things which interest students of any literature, viz., when these several books or documentary sources originated; who wrote them; why they were written; what contributions they made to developing Hebrew thought and culture. We now face another question: by what process did such writings come to be regarded as something more than literature, i.e., as Sacred Scripture?

The first definite milepost is the account of the discovery of "D" in the Jerusalem temple in the reign of King Josiah, 621 B.C. (2 Kgs. *22 f.). After this lawbook had been approved by the prophetess Huldah, the king gathered the people in an assembly to hear the law read, after which they entered into a solemn covenant to live up to it. Forthwith the king set about definite religious reforms to bring religious practices into conformity with what was written in a book.[149]

Not far from 400 B.C. occurred another event or movement which for the first time definitely gave to a section of the Bible that unique sanctity and authority which are associated with the Sacred Book. Due to the Biblical historian's omission of exact datings, particularly his repeated failure to mention which Artaxerxes he means, the precise date when, and the exact way in which, this process came about are obscure. All references, however, and later traditions as well, connect this movement with the names of Nehemiah and Ezra. Ac-

---

[139] Ex. 29:27 f.; Lev. 2:3, 10; 6:16 ff., 26, 29; 7:6–10, 31–36; 10:12–15; 24:9; Num. 5:9 f.; 6:19 f.; 18:8–32.
[140] Num. 3:5 ff. [141] Num. 4:20.
[142] Num. 3 f.; 8; 16. Cf. W. F. Albright, *op. cit.*, p. 109.
[143] Num. 3:9 f. [144] Num. 8:5–22.
[145] 1 Chr. 6:31 ff.; 9:33 f.; 15:16–24; 24 ff. Chapters 24 ff. describe other duties of the Levites besides their musical duties.
[146] Num. 8:23–26; cf. 4:3; cf. 1 Chr. 23:3, 24, 27.
[147] Num. 18:21–24.
[148] Lev. 25:32 ff.; Num. 35:1–8; Josh. 21:1–42; 1 Chr. 6:54–81.
[149] *Vid. supra,* pp. 332 ff.

cording to Ezr. 7:1–10 (with which read Ezr. 6:14), Ezra arrived in Jerusalem in the seventh year of an Artaxerxes. If this be the second Artaxerxes, then Ezra's arrival was in 398 B.C. Neh. *8–10 tells of a great general assemblage in "the broad place before the water gate" at Jerusalem at which some "law" was read and solemnly sworn to. At this meeting a group of priests, Levites, and forty-four princes signed a pledge to "walk in God's law which was given by Moses the servant of God, even to observe and do all the commandments of Yahweh our Lord and his ordinances and his statutes." [150] They agreed to sanction no more marriages with "the people of the land," nor to "buy . . . on the sabbath or on a holy day," and to "forego all claims for debt the seventh year." [151] They further drew up a set of self-imposed regulations by which they assumed responsibility for a more adequate and regular support of the temple worship through the adoption of a fixed schedule of tithes and offerings of various kinds (Neh. 10:32–39).

By *circa* 400 B.C., therefore, the Jews had accepted the Pentateuch,[152] i.e., the Torah, or Law, as their authoritative religious guidebook. This is what is meant by saying that the Law was canonized by this date. In the decades which immediately follow, we find the priesthood and the temple occupying a more and more dominating position in the life of the Judean community. The high priest soon demands tithes and dues as a legitimate tax perquisite, instead of merely accepting offerings and sacrificial gifts. Back of such demands there is manifestly some recognized law, and this can hardly be other than the books called the Torah. Henceforth, for orthodox Jews, the priest tends to wield authority equal to or even greater than that of the civil head.

Confirmatory of this general conclusion as to when the Law became authoritative is the fact that when the Samaritan schism occurred, shortly before 332 B.C.[153] the Samaritan priests took with them a copy of the Pentateuch as the lawbook.

The Essential Character of Judaism. From the foregoing it is evident that Judaism had become essentially a religion of the Book, a religion of law. This ideal, and the conception of God basic to it, are nowhere more lucidly expressed than in Deut. *4:1–40. To know and keep the law was the religious ideal for the Jew. This faith finds expression in what may be called the creed of Judaism, the Shema (Deut. *6:4–9; *11:13–21; Num. *15:37–41).

---

[150] Neh. 10:29.   [151] Neh. 10:30 f.
[152] On the canonization of "D" and the Torah, cf. R. H. Pfeiffer, *op. cit.,* pp. 50–58.
[153] *Vid. infra,* pp. 385 f.

Chapter 20

THE JEWS AND HELLENISM

In this chapter we are concerned with the fourth and the third centuries B.C. The latter half of the fourth century witnessed tremendous changes in the political and cultural conditions molding Jewish life and thought. The entire world of the Jews passed from under decadent Persian control to a new type of government and a manner of life and thought entirely unlike anything to which the Babylonian, Palestinian, or Egyptian world had ever before been accustomed.

Sources for a History of the Period

For the history of the Jews during the fourth and third centuries B.C., the documentary sources are meager indeed. There is no narrative of this period in the Bible itself, though some inferences can be drawn from Dan. 11. The chief source of information is the *Antiquities of the Jews* by the Jewish historian Flavius Josephus, who lived and wrote during the first century after Christ. This work, which consists of twenty books, traces Jewish history from its earliest beginnings. Josephus is full of gossip, superstition, and apologetic, but after allowance is made for these and the remainder is critically appraised, there does remain a considerable body of facts to illumine this obscure period in the history of the Jews.

Political Changes in the Fourth and Third Centuries B.C.

Judea During the Decline of Persian Rule. Around 400 B.C., the far-flung Persian empire showed unmistakable symptoms of decay. A weakened central government and a generally favorable (or possibly lax) attitude toward subject peoples continued until the end of the reign of Artaxerxes II (404–358 B.C.). By that time the fortunes of the Judean community had vastly improved over the low ebb of the preceding century; Jerusalem had evidently regained most of its old-time prosperity. A group of priests was in virtual control; that is to say, the Palestinian Jewish community was a hierocracy. In this earlier part of the fourth century a considerable return of Jews to

Palestine took place and Jewish hopes again grew strong for the realization of the long-awaited restoration of a Jewish kingdom.

With the accession of Artaxerxes III (Ochus, 358–338 B.C.), a radically different situation arose. This monarch was as energetic as his father had been easygoing, but whereas the elder Artaxerxes had been kindly, this young scion was shrewd, unscrupulous, and extremely cruel. His first act was a wholesale extermination of all members of the royal family who might by any possibility oppose him. From then on his reign was an unsavory and revolting story of bloodshed and shameless treachery. Three years before his accession Egypt had thrown off the weakened Persian yoke and had persuaded some of the Palestinian states to do likewise. Phoenicia was deeply involved in this revolt, and evidently Judea became compromised to some extent. Artaxerxes III put down the revolt with the utmost severity, though it took him upwards of ten years to do so. Sidon proved the most difficult and stubborn city of all. It held out until 348 B.C., and then, rather than surrender to one who had shown his perfidious character by massacring the deputation that went to him to sue for terms, the remnant of its defenders set fire to the city and burned its houses over their own heads. Tradition has it that no fewer than 40,000 Sidonians perished in this way! With Sidon obliterated, the brutal Persian turned his attention to Judea and to Egypt. Egypt was fully resubjugated five years later (343 B.C.), suffering a vengeance scarcely less appalling than Sidon's. Cities were sacked and temples ruined with all the ruthlessness of the Vandal plundering of Italy centuries later.

The few known details about what happened to Judea show that she suffered considerably. Jerusalem was invaded, the temple polluted in some way, a considerable number of people enslaved and deported to the province of Hyrcania, south of the Caspian Sea, and Jericho was destroyed. Oppression of the Jewish community kept up for about a decade. Psalms 74 and 79 may reflect the despair caused by these disasters.

Persia's last ruler, the third to bear the name of Darius, somewhat redeemed the tarnished character of the Persian kings, but he had the political misfortune to come to the throne (335 B.C.) [1] just as the youthful Alexander of Macedon started his world conquest.

It was about this time also that the rift between the Samaritan community and the Judean community widened into a gulf that has never since been bridged.[2] The Jewish historian Josephus (A.D. 37–100) dates this Samaritan schism in the high priesthood of Jaddua, who died a short time after the close of the Persian period. The schism

[1] Darius III succeeded Arses (338–335 B.C.).
[2] Cf. Neh. 13:28.

therefore occurred only a short time before Alexander conquered Palestine in 332 B.C. Josephus explains the occasion of the schism as follows.[3] Jaddua's brother, Manasseh, had married Nicaso, daughter of Sanballat II, satrap of Samaria under Darius III of Persia. At that time Manasseh was sharing the high priesthood with Jaddua. This was vehemently resented by the elders of Jerusalem, who demanded that Manasseh divorce his wife or else not approach the altar. Sanballat II took up the cudgels on behalf of his son-in-law and built for him a rival temple on Mount Gerizim in Samaria. A number of the priests of Jerusalem who were similarly involved in mixed marriages went with Manasseh to officiate at the Samaritan temple. The temple and services on Mount Gerizim were in many ways patterned after those at Jerusalem. The bitter hatred engendered in connection with this disruption constituted a serious obstacle to Jewish political development in the ensuing centuries.

Alexander's Empire and Hellenizing Program. Alexander the Great seized western Asia Minor in 334 B.C. In 333 he defeated a huge Persian army at Issus, in southeastern Asia Minor, not far from the Syrian border. In 332 B.C. he was master of Syria and Palestine, and by 331 B.C. he was master of Egypt. After pausing in Egypt long enough to found the new city of Alexandria as a memorial to himself, he advanced eastward, and in 331 B.C., at Gaugamela, in Babylonia, he destroyed the Persian army and thereby obliterated the Persian empire. He carried the Greek arms through Persia and into India as far as the Indus River. Then, back in Babylon once more, he suddenly died in 323 B.C. while still a young man of only thirty-three years. At the time of his death he was planning the conquest of Arabia.

Thus without warning or preparation, the Jews once more changed masters. It proved to be one of the most revolutionary events that had yet befallen them. Short as was Alexander's reign, within that period he planned and set in motion a vast, ambitious, Hellenizing program which was to go on with little loss of momentum long after his death and to become one of the most remarkable examples of acculturation that the world has ever witnessed. Alexander was something more than just another military conqueror. He was a pupil of the Greek philosopher Aristotle, and to this influence, no doubt, may be attributed the young Macedonian's ambition to spread the Greek civilization eastward until all peoples of the eastern Mediterranean world should speak one language, Greek, and Orientals and Greeks should be amalgamated in a new cultural unity.[4]

[3] *Antiquities*, xi, 7, 8.
[4] Cf. especially R. H. Pfeiffer, *History of New Testament Times* (New York: 1949), pp. 94–99.

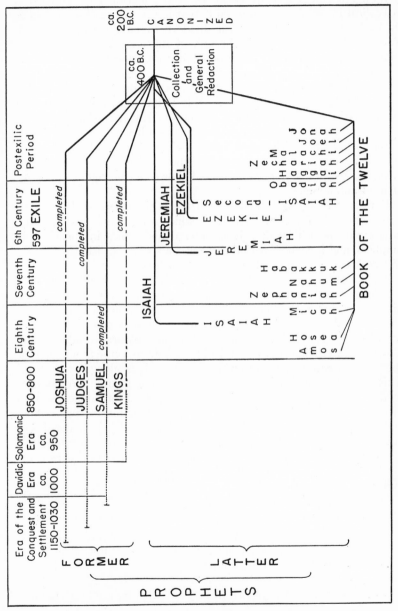

THE CANON OF THE PROPHETS

With Alexander's conquest we cross the meridian of Greenwich in Biblical history. Or, to use a different figure, we reach that watershed which constitutes the great divide between the Old and New Testaments. Henceforth and throughout the New Testament epoch, Biblical culture is to be understood against the background of Hellenism and appraised in relation to it.

The Egyptian city of Alexandria was located on the Mediterranean coast near the western apex of the Nile Delta. It was planned by the architect of the famed temple of Artemis (Diana), and built at royal expense regardless of cost. Alexander peopled it not alone with Greek colonists but also with Egyptians and Jews, each nationality being allotted its own particular quarter of the city and each group being given its own protecting city walls and allowed a considerable measure of local autonomy.[5]

For some reason, Alexander from the beginning treated the Jews with noticeable favor, the result of which was to win him a large measure of Jewish loyalty. Jews entered his armies in considerable numbers, and in a short period there was a strong Jewish assimilation of Greek customs and of the externals, at least, of Greek culture.

The youthful Alexander was undoubtedly sincere in his enthusiasm for things Greek and in his energetic efforts to engraft them over all his vast dominion. We know how splendid that culture was in the days of Plato and Aristotle and can therefore well appreciate Alexander's confident feelings. What he undertook to do was first of all to found a brand-new city in every country of his empire to serve as a model for the reconstruction and reordering of other cities along Greek lines. This included the building of gymnasia for games and contests modeled on the Greek order, of open-air theaters for public plays, of fine, stately, colonnaded buildings for the transaction of civic affairs, and the formation of municipal governments modeled on the democratic lines of the Hellenic city-states. Along with this program went every possible inducement for the adoption of Greek dress, the Greek language, Greek architectural styles in homes as well as public buildings, and Greek philosophy and manner of life generally. As will be seen later, this Hellenizing movement had a marked effect upon the Jewish people.

Greek Rule After 323 B.C. and Its Effects on Palestine. At Alexander's death his vast empire broke up into three main parts, divided among his generals, who are known as the Diadochi. One part, roughly comprising Greece, Macedonia, and an adjoining strip of Asia Minor, concerns Jewish history so little that it may be ignored

---

[5] Cf. especially A. H. Forster, "Propaganda Analysis Applied to Alexandrian-Jewish Apologetic," in H. R. Willoughby, *The Study of the Bible Today and Tomorrow* (Chicago: 1947), pp. 269–272.

here. A second part, comprising most of what had been the Persian empire westward and southward to Phoenicia, passed into the control of Seleucus, whose capital city was Antioch in Syria. This line of Antiochan rulers, therefore, came to be known as the Seleucids. The third part was Egypt, with Alexandria as its capital, and it was ruled by the Ptolemies. The two last-mentioned lines of rulers differed vastly in character and particularly in official attitudes toward subject peoples. The Alexandrian rulers came nearer to being the spiritual heirs to Alexander's benevolent rule for they ruled by favor rather than by fear. The policy of the Antiochan family, though for the most part not unduly harsh or severe, was nevertheless in noticeable contrast to that of the Ptolemies as a group. Between these two rival claimants for control of all Syria the Jews had a hectic time, and for a century and a quarter Palestine was a bone of contention between them.

Within the first twenty-five years after Alexander's death, Jerusalem changed hands no less than seven times! It then had a thirty-year breathing spell and had just settled down to what promised to be a restful prosperity when another struggle for possession began. Between 264 and 248 B.C. Palestine changed masters so often, and was so constantly suffering the horrors of armies marching one way or the other as the tide of victory inclined alternately to the Seleucids and to the Ptolemies, that no exact count is possible. Finally, in the closing years of the century, following a second thirty years' truce of cautious waiting, the stubborn contest for possession began all over again. The Alexandrian rulers finally gave up the unprofitable struggle and after 198 B.C. Palestine was left to the rude mercies of the Seleucids.[6]

Status of the Palestinian Jews During Late Persian and Early Greek Rule

The effects of this century and a half of constant war and fear of war, with almost uncounted changes in rulers, were incalculable.

The Economic Condition of Judea Between 350 and 200 B.C. One must bear in mind that Persian Judea, even in its more prosperous later period, was much more like a small county than a real state. At the maximum its dimensions did not greatly exceed fifty by twenty-five miles. Its population may not have been much if any in excess of one hundred thousand.

For fully a century and a half after 350 B.C. the economic fortunes of the community fluctuated with the many changes of ruler and the

---

[6] For a fuller discussion of the history of this period, cf. W. O. E. Oesterley in Oesterley and Robinson, *A History of Israel* (Oxford: 1932), ii, pp. 189–212.

frequent visitations by armies that tramped across its soil. Somehow it always managed to emerge with ample recuperative powers. Yet to amass any great amount of wealth was manifestly impossible, since sooner or later such wealth was bound to go for tribute or plunder. Perhaps this explains why, about 250 B.C., the entire assessment for the Judean community was only twenty talents as against 8,000 talents for Syria as a whole. Of course Judea was a tiny area, but an apportionment of only one-fourth of one per cent indicates either extreme poverty or a puzzling favoritism on the part of the reigning Ptolemy.

On the whole, and especially in view of the struggle that went on for the possession of Palestine, Judea fared rather well in the first century of Greek rule, for both Seleucids and Ptolemies competed for Jewish favor throughout much of this period. This Greek competition, however, worked unfavorably for the Judean community's prosperity in that it caused many enterprising Jews to emigrate to Egypt and (at a slightly later time) to Antioch also. The first known emigration to Egypt was a forced one (a deportation, in fact), shortly after 320 B.C., following the seizure of Palestine by the first Ptolemy. So happily did these deported Jews fare in Egypt, however, that later Ptolemaic rulers found that they were able to get all the Jews they needed in Alexandria and elsewhere by simply holding out persuasive inducements. It would appear that Jews were sought after in these outlying centers of Greek control, not merely to help colonize the new model Greek cities but to fill many clerical and minor governmental positions for which their proved industry and dependability admirably qualified them. But obviously such steady draining from the little Judean community of the capable, educated element affected Judea adversely. It was in this period of about three-quarters of a century that the taxes demanded of Judea by Egypt amounted to the trifling twenty talents already mentioned, and even this amount was protested and perhaps not always met.

In the second half of the third century B.C. the economic condition of the Judeans appears to have improved. At any rate, by *circa* 230 B.C. more taxes were being collected and paid into the Egyptian coffers. Possibly it was due to extortion, as revealed for example in Josephus's story of the highhanded procedure of the Jewish tax collector Joseph.[7] This Joseph was a nephew of the high priest Onias. Onias, by being dilatory about paying the twenty talents tax, had incurred the disfavor of King Ptolemy III Euergetes of Egypt (246–221 B.C.). Joseph went to Egypt, ingratiated himself with the king, and bid in the taxes for Palestine. At that time it was the custom to farm the taxes, i.e., sell to the highest bidder the legal right to collect the taxes in a province. Such collectors extorted from the people all they possibly

7. *Antiquities*, xii, 4.

could, retaining for themselves all they got in excess of what they had contracted to pay the king. In the present instance the highest bid was 8,000 talents, which Joseph, with a grand manner, doubled. The king granted Joseph a force of 2,000 soldiers to carry out the extortion. He did not hesitate to murder any who refused to pay and he confiscated their entire property. What wonder that Joseph became very wealthy during the twenty-two years he kept at this business!

This same story also reveals the extent to which some Jews went in adapting themselves to foreign customs. At Arak el-Emir, east of Jordan, is the extensive ruin of the white palace built by this Joseph's son Hyrcanus, evidence of the luxury some Jews were able to attain in this period. Judea suffered severely, however, in the closing years of the century and in the first year or two of the second century B.C., in the final bitter struggle between Antiochus III and Ptolemy V for possession of southern Syria and Palestine; so much so that when Antiochus was acknowledged victor in 198 B.C. he exempted Judea from all taxes for a period of three years to give it a chance to recover, and in addition made a liberal appropriation to help put the stricken district on its feet once more. Such was the bleak economic condition of Judea about 200 B.C.

Local affairs in Judea were in charge of the high priest, who thereby became supreme both in politics and in religion. Back of him was an Egyptian army to assure the collection of the taxes. Associated with the high priest was the *Gerousia,* or Senate of Jerusalem. The historical origin of this body is uncertain; possibly it grew out of the assembly of 150 leading citizens associated with Nehemiah at Jerusalem,[8] principally priests and elders. The Gerousia was the forerunner of the Jewish Sanhedrin, the most powerful governing body of Jews in New Testament times. The Gerousia was supposed to exercise a check upon the acts of the high priest, but there is reason to doubt that it proved very effective.

Social Effects of Hellenism Upon the Jews of Palestine.

The social complexity of Judaism in these later centuries increased so rapidly as to render it impossible to generalize accurately about the Jews as a whole. The new international horizons and multiplied racial contacts produced a people more and more reacting as individuals and less and less as racial units. While the old Hebrew nationalism continued to have exponents, of whom some were seemingly more ardent than any had been before them, on the whole, Hebrew nationalism was a thing of the past. That narrow provincialism which had pictured Palestine and Jerusalem as incomparably superior to all other countries and cities had been outmoded.

[8] Neh. 5:17.

This development shows up clearly only in the Hellenistic period, that is, beginning with the closing years of the fourth century B.C. Then many Jews became responsive to the attractiveness of the Greek culture, at first on the material side and then gradually on the intellectual and ethical side. Thus long before the close of the third century B.C. Jewish life, even in conservative Judea, had become vastly modified by the steady tendency to adopt Greek customs and Greek products. In Jewish colonies like Antioch such development was even more noticeable and there is evidence that the communication which these colonists kept up with the homeland operated toward this considerable Hellenizing of Judea.

Thus it came about that the Judean cities and towns joined the procession in improving the external appearance of their community life with broader streets, better buildings, neater and more orderly planning. Dwellings became more permanent in construction, more sanitary in appurtenances, and more homelike and comfortable through the addition of more and better furnishings. In dress, the old coarse and rather utilitarian garments and the colorful nomadic styles and tastes gave way, especially among the upper classes, to the more graceful Greek robes of finer materials and softer hues. The Greek decorative arts also won their way on their merit.

Likewise, social organization underwent considerable modification. In one respect it was a partial reversion to the more democratic type of the premonarchical days, for under Greek control a system of annual elections was introduced in which all citizens might participate. At the same time the social organization tended to class stratification, particularly to the emergence of an aristocratic educated and leisure class with a slave group doing most of the manual labor.

Another marked social change that resulted from Greek influence was a new interest in sports and games and a general joy in living. There lurked in this the danger of self-indulgence, particularly in the direction of conviviality and a relaxing of morals. The very hostility of some Jews to anything of this sort led others to renounce their Judaism and try to pass themselves off as Greeks.

In the Persian period Aramaic became the everyday language of the Jews. It was also the common language throughout the Persian Empire. It was spoken and written at Sardis (Asia Minor), in Assuan (Egypt), and on the borders of Baluchistan, as well as in Palestine. Aramaic was Hebrew modernized by contact with and borrowings from other languages. A good many Persian words were absorbed. Then in the Greek period the language of the Jews assimilated many words from the Greek. But alongside this Aramaic, the Greek language itself was adopted by the Jews, at first because it was compulsory in governmental affairs and in business and later because it signified education and because through it one could express ideas, especially abstract ideas, with greater accuracy than in the more primitive Hebrew. In time Jewish authors actually wrote some of their books in Greek. This was especially true of the Jews of the Dispersion, who knew only Greek. For their benefit as well as for the benefit of the gentiles who were unacquainted with the Hebrew Scriptures, the sacred writings of the Jews were translated into Greek, beginning about 285 B.C. under Ptolemy Philadelphus. The first part of the Bible to be translated was naturally the Pentateuch. This Greek version of the Old Testament is commonly known as the Septuagint.

Judaism in the Fourth and Third Centuries B.C.

The Idea of God and Other Supernatural Beings. The Hebrew concept of God had now become really monotheistic. The exile cured the Jews for all time of idolatry. Yahweh was the one and only God, a transcendent deity, the "Holy One," everywhere present.[9]

The idea of the transcendence of God had a corollary in the idea of supernatural beings, called angels, who function as intermediaries between God and man. For example, "the word of Yahweh" came quite directly to the great prophets, but not so to the prophet Zechariah; his conversation with Yahweh was through an intermediary angel (Zech. 1:12 ff.).[10] The Persian world view portrayed two supernatural hosts, good (angels) and bad (demons), waging a titanic struggle for the control of man and the world. The angels were the agents of Ahura Mazda, the good God, and the demons were the host of Angra-Mainyu.

In the literature of the postexilic period we meet for the first time the word "Satan" used as a proper name and applied to a supernatural being (Zech. 3:1 f., Job 1 f., 1 Chr. 21:1). The term "satan," in the general sense of "an adversary," "a satan," is found in Num. 22:22, 32; 1 Sam. 29:4; 2 Sam. 19:22; 1 Kgs. 5:4; 11:14, 23, 25; but in the Zechariah and Job passages it is "*the* Satan," i.e., "the Adversary" par excellence. The special function of this supernatural being was to report man's conduct to God. In a later age, as is very well known, "the Satan" came to be thought of as the evil spirit.

This Satan concept is an instance of the influence upon the Jews of Persian thought, which was essentially dualistic. It is nicely illustrated in the story of King David's census, of which there are two accounts. Apparently a devastating epidemic of disease swept

[9] *Vid. supra*, pp. 373 f., 379.
[10] Cf. Zech. 1:9, 19; 2:3; 3:1, 3, 5 f.; 4:1, 4 f.; 5:5, 10; 6:4 f.

Judea in David's time, not long after the taking of the census. The populace thoroughly hated the census anyhow, and so the pestilence was laid to the census. But what motivated David to take the census? One narrative (2 Sam. *24), written before the Jews had come into contact with Persian thought, says that "the anger of Yahweh was kindled against Israel, and he moved David against them." [11] This type of thinking was thoroughly monistic. Yahweh was responsible for both the good and the evil in the world, as Isa. 45:7 explicitly states. The mind that could hold such a view did not sense the ethical difficulty involved in making the good God responsible for evil. Persian thought did sense that difficulty and solved the difficulty by postulating the existence in the universe of two ultimate powers, good and evil, light and darkness, Ahura Mazda and Angra-Mainyu. The Jews assimilated this dualism from the Persians, and when the Chronicler's history was written,[12] the narrative of David's census was retold (1 Chr. 21), and the responsibility for the evil was removed from Yahweh: "And Satan (!) stood up against Israel, and moved David to number Israel" (vs. 1). Such dualism characterized Jewish thinking henceforth and through Judaism was transmitted to Christianity.

Worship at the Jerusalem Temple. 1. *The Worship of Sacrifice*. The Jerusalem temple continued to be, of course, Judaism's sanctuary par excellence. Here was centralized the ecclesiastical organization and the cult of sacrifice. We have already noted the general nature of this ecclesiastical and ceremonial system.[13]

Development had been toward a more and more elaborate and systematized liturgy, a more exacting system of tithing, and an increasing priest control. Since the sixth century B.C. the governor had acted as high priest and the office had finally become hereditary. This gave the high priest almost absolute power to levy taxes for the support of the temple. Such broad powers not infrequently led to gross corruption, to misappropriation of funds, to bribery, and, in one instance, to a peculiarly repugnant assassination, when the high priest Johanan murdered his own brother Joshua in the sacred temple precincts because Joshua was trying to secure the high-priestly office for himself through a Persian courtier.[14] The effect of having men of such character occupying the highest religious office can well be imagined.

The basic intent of the sacrificial cultus was admirable enough— to establish, maintain, and enhance harmonious relations between man and God. But the peril in the system was that it became for-

[11] 2 Sam. 24:1.
[13] *Supra*, pp. 380–382.

[12] *Vid. infra*, pp. 406 f.
[14] Cf. Josephus, *Antiquities*, xi, 7.

malized and externalized, which defeated its spiritual intent. It must have been deadening to the priests to be engaged continually in butchering animals, and such butchery could hardly have been edifying to the worshipers. The ultimate future of religion was not with the cult of sacrifice, for the final destruction of the Jewish temple (A.D. 70) put an end to this cult forever in Judaism. Happily there was a more lovely side to the temple worship.

2. *The Worship of Praise.* Whatever is vital and meaningful in religion is bound to come to expression in song, and the richest and most beautiful heritage of postexilic Judaism we possess is its songbook, the Book of Psalms. Many of the psalms bear annotations, the full meaning of which is not clear, but they are usually understood to be musical directions for singers and players.[15] The psalter was the hymnbook of the second temple. Let it be remembered that postexilic Judaism was a singing religion. Nothing whatever has survived to intimate to us what those ancient tunes were like, but the words of the songs are the cherished possession of Judaism and Christianity until the present day.

The pilgrimages to Jerusalem at the annual festival times were experiences of high joy to the Jews. They donned their best clothes and set out when the watchman gave the summons (Jer. 31:6). The pilgrim group was augmented by those who joined along the way. Here was opportunity for fellowship such as routine life did not afford. Onward they marched with music and song (Isa. 30:29). Perhaps Ps. 68:24 ff. indicates the formation of a festival procession when it became formal. What did they sing along the way? Pss. 120–134 constitute a group of pilgrim songs, called "Songs of Ascents," and are understood to be the songs sung en route to the national festivals. Pss. *121 and *126 are gems of this collection. Pss. *95 and *100 may well have been hymns sung when the group had reached the Holy City and was approaching the temple hill. Ps. *24 is a notable hymn for a festal procession,[16] and Ps. 118 is also a processional. No doubt different psalms were favorites at different festivals, but it would be difficult to distinguish which. One such is Ps. 81. Pss. 65 and *67 are clearly thanksgiving songs for harvest festivals, and Ps. *148 is a glorious hallelujah chorus. Ps. 150 enumerates the various instruments in the temple orchestra. The pageantry of the processions in the temple courts must have made a lasting emotional impression on the worshipers. And we can imagine the religious effect of hearing such triumphant hymns as Pss. 33, 99, 113, 135, 136, however much or little the generality of the worshipers may have

---

[15] Cf. Laura H. Wild, *A Literary Guide to the Bible* (New York: 1922), pp. 144 ff.
[16] Cf. the arrangement in Wild, *op. cit.,* p. 134.

shared in the singing, and the spiritual stimulation of hearing the hymns in praise of God, such as Pss. *46, *47, *48, *93, *96, *97, *98. At times the pilgrims came to the festivals with heavy hearts, when there had been widespread suffering throughout the nation or some distressing calamity. At such times their talk along the way deepened the bond of fellow feeling, and at the temple such psalms as 85, *90, 126 gave relief to their feelings, and consolation and strength to carry on.

Perhaps the limited economic resources of the Palestinian Jewish community imposed restrictions which prevented the ritual from becoming too costly, but nevertheless there were those who wished to bring the temple ritual up to a level of magnificence which tradition ascribed to the days of David, as portrayed in 1 Chr. 15 f., which, while it may idealize the situation in David's time, does reveal the situation in the time of the second temple.[17]

Worship in the Synagogues. We have already considered the emergence of the synagogue and its place in the religious life of the Jews.[18] Worship in the synagogue emphasized the reading of the Sacred Scriptures, instruction, exhortation, prayer, and singing. As we have already observed,[19] Judaism was a religion of the Sacred Book, and it was the Book upon which synagogue worship focused. There developed a professional religious class known as the scribes, made up of men who devoted the labor of their lives to the reading, copying, and interpretation of the revered writings. This bred in them a reverence for the five books of the Torah little short of adoration; this reverence we can sense from such poems as Pss. 19:7-14, 119. Their interpretations of the Torah (Written Law) were giving rise to an Oral Law which was to grow from more to more and to fill an increasingly important place in Judaism as "the tradition of the elders." The scribal idea was that religion consisted in perfect knowledge of the law and perfect observance of it to the minutest prescription. This ideal was noble enough, that life in its every detail should be lived according to the will of God, and it was this ideal that evoked the enthusiasm and devotion of the scribes. The peril that lurked in it was that of formalism, externalism, legalism.

The devotion of the scribes to the Torah was in large measure stimulated by their reaction against Hellenism. While many Jews were steadily assimilating more and more of Hellenistic culture, there were those who rejected and opposed it and who turned their

---

[17] Note that 1 Chr. 16:8–36 is made up of long quotations from Pss. 105 and 96, and short responses from 106; 1 Chr. 16:8–22 = Ps. 105:1–15; 1 Chr. 16: 23–33 = Ps. 96; 1 Chr. 16:34 ff. = Ps. 106:1, 47 f. On public worship in the temple, cf. Bewer, *op. cit.*, pp. 347–371.
[18] *Supra*, pp. 359 f., 381.   [19] *Supra*, pp. 383 f.

devotion to that which emphasized and cultivated their Jewishness. In the succeeding century this group precipitated into a party, the Hasidim or the Pious.

The Enlarged Bible: Law and Prophets. As we have observed, the Torah had been canonized *circa* 400 B.C.[20] At that time the writings of the Hebrew prophets and the books of prophetic history were in existence and were valued, of course, but were by no means esteemed as holy writings. During the two centuries following 400 B.C. the esteem for the prophetic writings mounted to reverence as they were continually used in the synagogues in connection with the Torah. As a result, by 200 B.C. the Jewish Bible contained a second grand division known as the "Prophets" (*Nebiim*). The books in this division were arranged in two groups of four books each: (1) the Former Prophets, comprising Joshua, Judges, Samuel, Kings;[21] (2) the Latter Prophets, comprising Isaiah, Jeremiah, Ezekiel, and the Book of the Twelve (the twelve being Hosea, Joel, Amos, Obadiah, Jonah, Micah, Nahum, Habakkuk, Zephaniah, Haggai, Zechariah, Malachi).

There was no formal assembly which ordained that these books should be called "Holy Scripture." It came about by natural development.[22] We can say that it was an accomplished fact by 200 B.C. on the basis of the prologue to the apocryphal Book Sira (Ecclesiasticus). In this prologue the translator states that he went to Egypt in 132 B.C. ("the eight and thirtieth year of Euergetes the king"),[23] and that he is translating into Greek a book written originally in Hebrew by his grandfather Jesus Ben-Sira. This grandfather must, therefore, have written his book at least a half century earlier or not long after 200 B.C. He says that his grandfather was much given "to the reading of the law, and the prophets, and the other books of our fathers," which was the equivalent of saying "the Bible and other books." He calls the Bible what it was conventionally called from 200 B.C. on, "the law and the prophets." This statement about Ben-Sira indicates that there were other Jewish books in existence in 200 B.C., but they were not yet considered holy writings. He names two of the grand divisions of the Jewish Bible. The third (the Hagiographa) is in the making.[24]

---

[20] *Vid. supra,* pp. 382 ff.

[21] Samuel and Kings were originally only one book each, because Hebrew was written without vowels and one large scroll apiece was sufficient. Greek was written with vowels, which made each book nearly twice as long. Hence the Septuagint divided each into two books.

[22] On the canonization of the Prophets, cf. R. H. Pfeiffer, *Introduction to the Old Testament* (New York: 1941), pp. 34–40.

[23] Euergetes was an honorary title of Ptolemy VII, 145–116 B.C. *Vid. infra,* p. 435, fn. 30.

[24] *Vid. infra,* Chapter 22.

Indeed, we can discern at this date (200 B.C.) the very process going on by which literature comes into being and comes to be esteemed as Holy Scripture, in the case of Psalms. Psalms had been originating over a long stretch of centuries and some of them originated later than 200 B.C. The use of the psalms in the singing of the temple, and no doubt in the synagogues also, was impressing their spiritual quality upon the minds of the Jews and gathering to themselves those emotional attachments which resulted in the Psalms becoming the next book after the Prophets to be esteemed as Holy Scripture. Two centuries later (and how much earlier we cannot say) the Bible was referred to as "the law and the prophets and the psalms." [25]

Ethical Emphasis in the Judaism of 200 B.C.   The Judaism of this period produced many admirable characters. No prophets are mentioned, but there seem to have been many whose personal religion was quite as ethical and lofty as was the religion of the great prophets. In fact, for one section of Judah's thinkers, the men of the so-called wisdom school, the dominant element in religion was the ethical. Moderation, self-control in all things, thrift, sobriety, benevolence, modesty, prudence, and purity were among the virtues emphasized. Reverence toward God was basic to their view of life but emphasis on formal worship is conspicuously absent from their teachings. It was these wisdom teachers, in fact, who carried forward the ethical emphasis of the great prophets.

The wise men or sages or teachers of wisdom, as they are variously called, were the educators of the day, men whose special interest lay in knowing and producing the kind of thought which is technically termed "wisdom." They were usually men of scribal training, but a Jew might gain a knowledge of the Hebrew language and the Sacred Scriptures apart from formal training. A man might be devoted to the law and also have an interest in wisdom, or a priest and devote time to wisdom, or neither legalist nor priest, for there were men without taste for law or ritual who gave their whole time and attention to wisdom. The aim of such men was to understand life and human experience, to find a way to realize ethical aspirations. They wished to live life worthily and to teach others to do so. They made a specialty of teaching the people.[26] These teachers of wisdom were the only philosophers Judaism produced.

Isa. 29:14 implies the existence of such wise men as early as the eighth century B.C., and Jer. 8:8 f.; 9:23; 18:18 indicates that they were recognized as a distinct class in Jeremiah's time, *circa* 600 B.C.

[25] Luke 24:44.
[26] For a detailed description of the career of the professional wise man, cf. Sir. 38:24–39:11. For the literary methods of the wise, cf. Eccl. 12:9–13.

Thus they were contemporaneous with the great Old Testament prophets. The dominant emphasis of the prophets was ethical. They were preeminently men of profound ethical insight. The passion which characterized their preaching was inspired by their appreciation of ethical values. After the period of prophecy was thought formally to have closed, the ethical impulse of prophecy continued to find expression in the teaching of wisdom.[27] Thus wisdom came to be the best type of prophetic activity in the late Persian and the Hellenistic periods of Jewish history. This wisdom type of study and teaching represented the line of general education. Jewish education was religious education. "The fear of the Lord is the beginning of wisdom"[28] was the basic principle on which the wisdom teachers founded their view of life. They sought to apply this religious wisdom to every nook and cranny of life. We have a fine picture of their method and aim in Prov. *1:20–23 and *8:1–5. The maxims which they gathered up, used in their teaching, and wrote out for future generations are preserved in the treasure house of wisdom called the Book of Proverbs.

The wisdom teachers were primarily interested in the individual in contrast to the nation. We have previously noted the emergence in Judaism of a doctrine of individualism with the prophet Jeremiah, who stresses the possibility of an individual relationship to God,[29] and in Ezekiel, who stresses the doctrine of individual moral responsibility.[30] This line of thought and teaching was carried forward by the wisdom teachers, whose concern was not with Jew but with men. Thus it happens that the concept Israel is quite lacking in the wisdom writings, for the wisdom literature is universalistic in its outlook and views all men as on an equality. True, it holds that the knowledge of Yahweh and of the law is the beginning of wisdom, but the outlook with these writers is not primarily nationalistic but universal and human. They are interested in man's capacities, his potentialities, and his duties as an individual.

The Wise Men of Israel are in a sense *Humanists*. Their point of view is universal and individual; they do not concern themselves with the religious relations and obligations of the Israelite as such, but only with those which pertain to him as a man, living under the rule of a perfectly righteous Governor of the world. . . . Wisdom represents a tendency of mind secluded in some way from the main currents of Hebrew piety, and containing the germs of a philosophy of life applicable to mankind everywhere.[31]

[27] Cf., e.g., Prov. 15:8; 16:6; 21:3, 27; 28:13.
[28] Prov. 1:7; 9:10.
[29] Jer. 31:27–34.   [30] Ezk. 18
[31] John Skinner, "The Cosmopolitan Aspect of the Hebrew Wisdom," *Jewish Quarterly Review*, xvii (1905), pp. 248 f. Cf. R. H. Pfeiffer, *Introd.*, pp. 34–40.

The Religion of the Plain Man. For the generality of the Jews, religion consisted in carrying out the conventional requirements—refraining from labor on the sabbath and on holy days, observing the prescribed festival and fast days, making pilgrimages to the temple, paying the enforced tithes and offerings, and attending worship in the synagogue. Then, as always, religion for the majority was conventional and external rather than inward and spiritual.

That a general disposition to lead a moral life existed, there is every reason to believe. The ideal righteous citizen is portrayed in Pss. *15; *24:3 ff.; and in Job *31 a poet has given us a portrait of the finest type of upright Jew. Many who cherished the moral ideal fell far short of purity or perfection, and the wisdom literature, notably Proverbs, is filled with counsels against various vices and exhortations to virtues. Such a Jew might sin, but he could also be deeply repentant and contrite in heart. Out of such a profound, inward experience came Ps. *51, one of the most spiritual of all the penitential lyrics in the psalter. Ps. *32 is of the same order.

How the plain man thought and felt about religion is revealed in the Book of Psalms, which is the plain man's book of devotions. Religious hymns do not express the ideas of the advanced thinkers or leaders of any age. They express what the average man feels in common with all others, and therefore hymns serve to unite all worshipers in a common bond of religious feeling and fellowship. Hence such hymns are on the level of the plain man. The Psalms range over the whole gamut of human experience.

The Inward Side of Judaism. The great prophets of the past had declared that true religion is not a matter of sacrifice, but of inward righteousness (Am. 5:21–25, Hos. 6:6, Mic. 6:6 f., Jer. 6:16, 20, 7:21 f.). The same sentiment is splendidly expressed in Pss. *40:6, 8, 50:8–15, *51:16. There were Jews in the fourth and third centuries (and later, too) whose religion was a matter deeply felt, earnest, sincere, inward, and spiritual. God was intensely real to such persons, and Ps. *139 portrays the God-consciousness of such minds, a splendid type of religious mysticism. There are many psalms which express this inwardness, notably Pss. *23, *25, *27, *34, 37, 39, *40, *42 f., 63, 77, 86, *91, *103, 142. The reading and singing of such psalms, and reflection upon the sentiments they express, nourished the religious life of the devout. It is in these songs of the inward life that something of enduring value came to expression. The poets who felt and wrote these lyrics bequeathed a priceless treasure to mankind. Their spiritual excellence commends them to the religiously earnest in every age.

But even the very finest religion of the time left something to be desired. Unfortunately the spiritual beauty of the Psalms is tarnished by the imprecatory psalms, notably Pss. 10, 55, 58, 69, and 109 (the most vicious of all). The imprecations of these poems cause us to shudder. We marvel that such sentiments could have found a place in religion. Manifestly the Jews did not know what to do about the problem of dealing with enemies. The solution of that problem had to wait for another two centuries until one should come who would say, "Love your enemies." [32]

Jewish Literature of the Fourth and Third Centuries B.C.

The Psalms. From the numerous references to the Psalms in the preceding section on religion, the student already has a good appreciation of the literary as well as the religious character of these poems. The psalter, i.e., the Book of Psalms, is really a collection of collections, and the entire process of writing and collecting them doubtless covered several centuries and included psalms written possibly as late as 100 B.C. Because the psalms are undated and ascriptions of authorship are late scribal conjectures or traditions, the exact century in which any particular psalm was written is extremely difficult to determine. It seems probable that the group of psalms called "Songs of Ascents" (120–134) originated in the late Persian or Greek period. The long elaborate alphabetic acrostic, Ps. 119, is another that can be safely put in these two centuries, as well as such markedly monotheistic hymns as Pss. 95–98, 100, 103, 104,[33] and 107. A number of older psalms were probably expanded.

The psalter as it exists today consists of five smaller books (Pss. 1–41; 42–72; 73–89; 90–106; 107–150), each such book ending with a doxology. The 150th psalm is a doxology in itself. Within these five books smaller collections or groupings are found, e.g., Pss. 42–49, 84 f., 87 f. are Korah poems; Pss. 50, 73–83 are attributed to Aspah; Pss. 120–134 are the "Songs of Ascents"; and Pss. 3–41, 51–72 are called Psalms of David. The fact that Ps. 53 duplicates Ps. 14, that Ps. 70 duplicates Ps. 40:13–17, and that Ps. 108 is simply Ps. 57:7–11 combined with Ps. 60:5–12, is evidence of this combining or accretion process. So, too, is the fact that books I, IV, and V refer to God regularly as Yahweh, whereas books II and III use El with equal

---

[32] Matt. 5:44.
[33] Professor J. H. Breasted emphasizes the resemblance of Ps. 104 to, and its dependence upon, the "Hymn to Aton" of the Egyptian Pharaoh Ikhnaton [vid. supra, p. 63] of the fourteenth century B.C. [Cf. *The Dawn of Conscience* (New York: 1933), pp. 282–284, 367]. Professor Breasted thinks that Ikhnaton's hymn spread, during his lifetime, to Palestine and Syria, where it was preserved in some Semitic dialect into which it was translated and in which it suffered modifications. Being thus preserved in western Asia through many centuries, the Egyptian poem, by reason of its monotheistic emphasis, influenced Ps. 104.

consistency. At the close of book II (Ps. 72) is the interesting and significant comment: "The prayers of David . . . are ended." [34]

Wisdom Writings. Certain psalms, some of which have been mentioned in various connections in the foregoing, are classed as wisdom psalms, especially Pss. 1, *8, 15, *19, 37, 49, 73, 103, 107, 119. Wisdom writers were usually poets, and it was quite in the order of things that ethical sentiments should have been sung. [35]

1. *Proverbs.* The Book of Proverbs was the standard work or text-book of the wisdom teachers. The book is a collection, or a collection of collections, of varying dates. There are at least five collections: 1–9; 10:1–22:16; 25–29; 30; 31; and to the second collection there are two appendices: 22:17–24:22 and 24:23–34. The Proverbs text circulated in different editions and with the material arranged in varying order, as evidenced by the Greek version in which the order is: 1–24:22; 30:1–14; 24:23–34; 30:15–31:9; 25–29; 31:10–31. In order of age, the collections are probably as follows: (1) 10:1–22:16; (2) 25–29; [(1) and (2) are of about the same age]; (3) 30–31 [appendices to 25–29]; (4) 22:17–24:34; [appendices to 10:1–22:16]; (5) 1:7–9:18; (6) 1:1–6.

The very oldest portion of the book is 22:17–24:22, a section which is manifestly taken from "The Wisdom of Amenemopet," an Egyptian book containing instructions for life, the date of which is not later than 1000 B.C. [36] One may conjecture that the Amenemopet collection found its way into Hebrew literature when King Solomon became son-in-law to the reigning Pharaoh. The older collections included in Proverbs are from the latter half of the Persian period. The Book of Proverbs as a whole is from the Hellenistic period, *circa* 250 B.C.

The book contains many a maxim which has come down to the present time with no lessening of its original force and appeal (e.g., 13:12; 15:1, 3, 17; 16:2, 18, 32; 19:17; 22:1, 6; 25:21 f.; 27:6; 28:1; 29:18). It abounds in clever thrusts at human weaknesses and an enjoyable humor, as evidenced in such passages as characterize the lazy and shiftless person (6:9–11; 10:26; 19:24; 22:13; 24:30–34; 26:14); the argumentative wife (21:9; 25:24; 27:15 f.); the indiscreet woman (11:22); the danger of wearing one's welcome out (25:17); interfering in others' quarrels (26:17); the bargain hunter (20:14); and the drunkard (23:29–35). In 30:15–31 is an interesting species of conundrum. *31:10–31 is a poem in praise of the model wife, a portrait to which the modern woman

---

[34] On the Psalms, cf. Bewer, *op. cit.,* pp. 340–390; Pfeiffer, *Introd.,* pp. 619–644.
[35] Consider the present-day vogue of such an ethical song as "I Would Be True," by Howard Arnold Walter.
[36] *Vid. supra,* pp. 65 f.

doubtless will not subscribe but which it will do her no harm to read. Especially beautiful on the literary side is the poem in praise of wisdom (*8:1–9:6). Chapters *3 and *4 on the same theme are of almost equal merit.[37]

2. *Job.* The Book of Job has evoked almost extravagant praise from literary critics. Carlyle said of it: "There is nothing written, I think, in the Bible or out of it, of equal literary merit." Certainly it stands with the Second Isaiah as the greatest work of art in the Old Testament.

In its present form, Job comes from the late Persian or possibly the Hellenistic period of Jewish history, but the basic poem (3–27, 29–31) is much older. The book is variously dated by scholars from 500 to 165 B.C.

Job belongs with the Jewish wisdom literature and is the greatest piece of such literature the Jews produced. It is a sustained treatise on the problem of human suffering, especially unmerited suffering. In order to appreciate the book one must bear in mind the conventional Hebrew belief that prosperity and adversity were rewards and punishments direct from God. The righteous prospered because of his righteousness and the wicked suffered for his sin. Nowhere is this view more simply or lucidly stated than in Ps. *1. In the conventional view, this basic belief was illogically converted into the view that all suffering was evidence of the sufferer's sinfulness, and all prosperity was evidence that the affluent man was *ipso facto* righteous. Poverty, sickness, disgrace, all indicated that a man, or else his parents before him, had sinned. The persistency of this conventional view is to be noted in an incident in the career of Jesus when a man born blind was brought to him with the query: "Who did sin, this man or his parents, that he was born blind?" [38] It is this conventional view which is maintained by the three friends of Job and denied by Job himself.

The book opens with a prose prologue (1–2) which depicts a scene at the court of Heaven where it is decided to put Job's uprightness to the test. As a consequence Job is stripped of wealth, children, and health. The prologue, therefore, proposes one reason for suffering: Suffering is a test of character, of moral integrity and purity of heart (1:11 f.; 2:4 ff.). This idea is skillfully worked into the body of the poem and placed in the mouth of Job himself in *23:10.

The main part of the book, which is poetry, opens with chapter 3 in which Job, in anguish, curses the day of his birth. Then follows a debate between Job and three friends, in three cycles (4–14, 15–21, 22–31). The three friends champion the conventional view that suffer-

---

[37] On Proverbs cf. Bewer, *op. cit.,* pp. 308–316; Pfeiffer, *Introd.,* pp. 645–659.
[38] Jn. 9:2.

ing is punishment for sin, and say that that is why Job suffers. Choice
passages which state this conventional view are *4:7–9, 17; 5:17 f.;
8:3–7, 20; *18:5–21; *20:4–29; 22:3–11, 29 f.; 27:13–23. Job denies
this orthodox dogma, most clearly in 9:22, 24; 10:1–15; 12:5 f.;
*21:7–21; 24:1–12. Job steadfastly insists upon his own uprightness
and integrity which merit no such fate as that which has befallen
him (9:21, 32–35; 10:7; 13:13–18; 16:12, 17 ff.; *19:4–27;
23:3–16; 27:4 ff.).

Following the debate come the speeches of a young man named
Elihu (32–37), by many scholars regarded as no part of the original because they add little or nothing to the views of the three friends.
They present only a variant of the conventional dogma, viz., that
suffering is a warning to restrain man from sin (33:14–30).

The grand climax of the book is a theophany (38:1–42:6) in
which God appears and answers Job out of the whirlwind. The poet
displays superb artistry by the way in which he prepares for the
theophany by putting into the mouth of Elihu, as the end of his
speech, a beautiful poem on the Greatness of God (*37:5–24), the
climax of which is vs. 22:

> Out of the north cometh golden splendor:
> God hath upon him terrible majesty.

Very likely this "golden splendor" is an allusion to the aurora borealis,
but it magnificently fits the author's purpose, for from of old the
presence of deity was thought to be manifested by fire, flame, or
light,[39] and this awe-inspiring golden brightness of Job 37:22 is an
extension of the same idea.

The speech of Yahweh is a recitative on the mysteries of the universe (38–41). By this, the author means to suggest that suffering
is an aspect of universal mystery; suffering and all mystery are inexplicable and are a revelation of God (13:16; 16:19; *19:25 ff.;
*23:3; *38 f.). By this theophany, God is portrayed as indeed having
upon him awe-inspiring majesty in the presence of which Job is
reverent and silent (23:15; 40:3 ff.; 42:1, 2, 3b, 4b, 5, 6).

Job *19:25 ff. has caused translators no end of difficulty.[40] The
thought is based upon the Hebrew idea of the *go-el,* the redeemer or
vindicator, the person who, as next of kin, had the duty of redeeming
the property of any poor man forced to sell,[41] or marrying the child-
less widow of a deceased man to whom the go-el was the nearest
living survivor.[42] Job says that he knows that his vindicator lives

---

[39] Cf., e.g., Ex. 3:2; Isa. 6:6.
[40] As can most clearly be seen by noting the changes in the Chicago Version in
the successive editions of 1927, 1931, and 1935.
[41] Lev. 25:25.   [42] Illustrated in the story of Ruth.

(19:25) and will ultimately justify him, and at the consummation of the poem God does prove to be Job's vindicator (*42:7).

The basic spiritual truth worked out in the Book of Job is that the pure in heart will see God. Job did. Whatever suffering befalls the pure in heart they may endure, for their inward, spiritual integrity is its own reward and the surest way to find God.

Whoever added the prose epilogue (42:7–17) could not bear to see the conventional dogma of the three friends defeated in the argument, as it had been, and consequently sought to prove the conventional view correct by making Yahweh give Job, in the end, twice as much as he originally owned.[43]

The excellence of the poetry in the Book of Job is seen in *9:5–15 and *37:5–24 on the Power and Greatness of God; *14:1–14 on the Frailty of Man; *28, in Praise of Wisdom; 29:1–30:1, 9 ff., Job's Mental Anguish; *31, on Social Ethics; *38 f., on the Mysteries of the World.

3. *Ecclesiastes.* Ecclesiastes also belongs with the Jewish wisdom literature. It is a miscellany of wisdom, part of it in prose, part in poetry. The book originated *circa* 200 B.C. The Hebrew title of the book is "Koheleth," a word about whose meaning there is dispute, but the favored interpretation is "gatherer" or "collector." In 12:9 ff., Koheleth is said to have been a collector of wisdom teachings. When the book was translated into Greek, the translators rendered Koheleth by the Greek "Ecclesiastes," a term which means "one who summons an assembly" or "a member of an assembly" of any sort. The English translators rendered it inadequately by "Preacher."

Some interpreters trace in Koheleth the influence of the Greek philosophies of Stoicism and Epicureanism, though others deny any definite influences of these in the book. Certainly the Jews had by the time this book originated been long enough in contact with Hellenism to have reacted to Greek ways of thinking. What we seem to have in Koheleth is Jewish religion sicklied o'er with a pale cast of Greek thought.

At the very outset (1:2) Koheleth states his thesis that there is nothing to life but vanity (transitoriness or futility); he frequently reiterates this theme and concludes on the same note (12:8). All is a futile, ceaseless round (*1:2–9) in nature and in human experience. It is impossible to solve the whole mystery of things (3:11; 7:24; 8:17; 11:5), so why try? Koheleth found in life a great many things which perplexed him (3:10 f., 16; 4:1; 5:8 f.; 6:1 f.; 7:15; 8:9, 14; 8:16–9:1; 9:2 f., 11; 11:5 ff.) and made him a skeptic and a pessimist. "Who knows what is good for man in life, all the days of his vain life

---

[43] Job 42:10. On Job, cf. Pfeiffer, *Introd.,* pp. 660–707.

which he spends as a shadow?" (6:12). Wisdom is futile (1:18), but it is preferable to folly (2:13; 7:12). The getting of material possessions is futile (2:4–11), but it is a source of satisfaction (5:19). There is no immortality (2:14 ff.; 3:19 f.; 9:2 f.), but life should be lived joyously and to the full (9:4; 11:7). Koheleth's basic philosophy of life is that a man should eat and drink and find satisfaction in his work, which is a gift of God, (2:24; 3:12 f., 22; 5:18; 8:15; 9:7–10, 11:7–10), and always observe the golden mean (7:16 ff.) and have regard for the fitness of things (*3:1–8). Skeptic though he was, Koheleth did not deny the existence of God or the power of God, but he did deny any providential care of God for the righteous (7:15) and regarded God as capricious (5:1–9), an idea which probably grew out of a consideration of the capriciousness of the rulers of the age (8:1–9).

The book concludes with a golden gem which is one of the most exquisitely beautiful poems in the Bible, "The House of Life" (*11:9–12:7) an incomparable picture of old age.

Koheleth has been called "the gentle cynic." He was gentle, perhaps, in not damning all life outright, but a cynic, certainly, in leaving immortality and fine idealism out of his philosophy.[44]

The Chronicler's History (Chronicles-Ezra-Nehemiah). In a previous chapter attention was directed to the central place which the priesthood and ritual held in Jewish life and religion in the post-exilic period.[45] The Palestinian Jewish community was a hierocracy, with the high priest at the head of both religious and civic affairs. At the temple the sacrificial cultus was preeminent, and basic to it was the Priest Code ("P"). The doctrine was held that national prosperity was conditioned upon perfect conformity of the community to the temple and the cultus and the ceremonial law. The dogma arose that it must always have been so; that in the past the prosperity of the nation, when it had prospered, must have been because the Judean kings had loyally fostered the cultus; the adversities which had befallen the nation must have been due to apostasy from the sacrificial cultus. It occurred to one mind (or possibly to a group of like-minded writers) thoroughly steeped in this dogma to rewrite the history of his people and nation, from Adam to the time of the second temple in the Hellenistic period, according to this dogma. This writer is technically called the Chronicler, and his literary product, the Chronicler's history, comprises the Biblical books of I and 2 Chronicles, Ezra, and

---

[44] The skepticism was toned down by orthodox Jewish revisers of the book (3:17; 8:11 ff.; 11:9; 12:1a, 13 f.; cf. also 4:5; 5:3, 7a; 7:18b, 19, 26b, 29; 10:1 ff., 8–15, 18 f.; 12:7b), which accounts for the place of the book in the canon of the Scriptures. On Ecclesiastes, cf. Bewer, *op. cit.*, pp. 330–339; Pfeiffer, *Introd.*, pp. 724–731.

[45] *Vid. supra*, pp. 380–382.

Nehemiah. What he wrote is not history at all; he uses historical facts only to illustrate his dogma, and he makes the facts over to suit it.

The Chronicler copied copiously from the books of Samuel and Kings, as well as from the memoirs of Nehemiah.[46] The Book of Ezra is by some scholars held to be a creation of the Chronicler himself, and by others it is regarded as a prior set of memoirs which, like the memoirs of Nehemiah, the Chronicler took over and adapted to his new work. The Chronicler also adds a few incidents which are of admitted historical value. For the most part, however, his supplemental material is either dry genealogical lists or lengthy descriptions of elaborate liturgical temple services which he pictures as having been participated in by priests, Levites, and guilds of singers as early as the time of David.[47] Such a portrait is not historical. The desire of the Chronicler to enhance the temple liturgy of his own day must have led him either to draw upon his imagination or to be unduly credulous of an embellished tradition of the past.

From the fact that this Chronicler's history refers to high priests down to about 300 B.C., it obviously was not written before then but probably several decades later.[48]

Books Exhibiting Contrasting Attitudes to Non-Jews. From the days of Nehemiah on, the Jews were sharply divided over the question of the right attitude toward the gentile world. Some Jews urged an uncompromising aloofness. Others urged that all nations were under the care and love of a common God. Perhaps the question seems simple to us today, but it was not so then.

Representative of the spirit of exclusiveness are the books of Joel and Esther. Their exact dates are not determinable, but they seem to fall within the fourth and third centuries B.C.

1. Joel presents one of the very finest poetical compositions in the Old Testament in the incomparable description of the locust plague in chaps. *1 f. The realism and accuracy of the description can be appreciated by reading John D. Whiting's account of "Jerusalem's Locust Plague" (of 1914) in the *National Geographic Magazine* for December, 1915, which furnishes an excellent commentary on Joel. The principal idea of Joel is the Day of Yahweh.[49] This idea had had an important place in the thinking of the prophets Amos,[50] Isaiah,[51] and Zephaniah.[52] It is an idea which appears to have been stirred up by reflection upon some disastrous incident. For example, it was the

---

[46] Cf., e.g., 1 Sam. 31 with 1 Chr. 10; 2 Sam. 5:1–10 and 23:8–39 with 1 Chr. 11; 1 Kgs. 15:1–8 with 2 Chr. 13; and 2 Kgs. 22:3–7 with 2 Chr. 24:8–12.
[47] 1 Chr. 15:4–24, 16:4 ff., 37–42.
[48] On the Chronicler's History, cf. Bewer, *op. cit.*, pp. 280–302; Pfeiffer, *Introd.*, pp. 782–838.
[49] 1:15; 2:1 f., 11, 28–32; 3:14 f.   [50] *Vid. supra*, p. 317.
[51] *Vid. supra*, p. 327.   [52] *Vid. supra*, p. 336.

threatening possibilities involved in the Scythian invasion of 626 B.C. which gave Zephaniah his black picture of the "Dies Irae." The disaster accompanying a locust plague turned Joel's mind to the same thought. Joel's Day of Yahweh is a judgment of vengeance upon the foes of the Jews (*3:1–13), whereas with Amos, Isaiah, and Zephaniah the Day of Yahweh was to be a day of judgment upon Israel itself. The war cry of 3:10 and the bloodthirstiness of 3:11 ff., link Joel with the more vengeful and racially exclusive group in Judaism. Although he does call the Jews to repentance (2:12–17) and promises forgiveness and a prosperous future (2:21–27; 3:14–21), the triumphant climax of his prophecy is a paean of joy over the destruction of Judah's enemies (3:19 ff.).[53]

2. Esther is not regarded by scholars as history but rather as a historical novel or didactic romance composed sometime toward the close of the third century B.C. The story is manifestly a piece of religious propaganda to promote the observance by the Jews of the Feast of Purim (Est. 9:17–32) on the fourteenth day of the month Adar (February-March). Purim was not one of the ancient Jewish yearly festivals.[54] It may possibly have been a Persian festival which the Jews took over [55] and undertook to adapt to their own life.

The word God nowhere appears in the Book of Esther. The spirit of hate and vindictiveness permeating the book register an all-time low in Jewish ethical thinking. The type of mind that could feel and express such a spirit of revenge has come to our notice previously in the imprecatory psalms.[56] The Jews may well have been goaded into this attitude by the persecutions to which they were subjected in the time of Artaxerxes III. Joel 3:19 is evidence that there had been pogroms in Egypt and Edom. In the next chapter of our study we shall see the Jews subjected to a vicious persecution (in the second century B.C.) which precipitated a rebellion that won their political and religious liberty. In the time of that Maccabean rebellion the Book of Esther served the jingo spirit very splendidly, and from that time forward the place of this book and of the Feast of Purim were established in Judaism.[57]

Over against such writings as Joel, Esther, and the imprecatory psalms, stand two little books of opposite spirit, Ruth and Jonah.

3. *Ruth is another piece of didactic romance. The story is given a time setting in the period of the "judges" and is a charming picture

53 On Joel, cf. Bewer, op. cit., pp. 395 ff.; Pfeiffer, Introd., pp. 573–576.
54 Cf. supra, p. 380 f.
55 The names Mordecai and Esther are the same as Marduk and Ishtar, the chief Babylonian god and goddess. This may be purely fortuitous, and again it may suggest pagan antecedents of the Purim festival.
56 Vid. supra, p. 401.
57 On Esther, cf. Pfeiffer, Introd., pp. 732–747.

of Hebrew manners and customs. The time of composition, however, was in all probability the third century B.C. It was intended as an offset to the bigotry of extreme racial aloofness that set in after the time of Nehemiah. Nehemiah had ruthlessly banned all intermarriage of Jews with foreign women. This little novel would remind the Jews that the most esteemed ruler they ever had, their great King David, had foreign blood in his veins; his great-grandmother was Ruth, a Moabitess. The jingoist, versed in the law, would not relish the reminder that this foreign marriage was only three generations back of David, for the law prescribed, "A Moabite shall not enter into the assembly of Yahweh; even to the tenth generation shall none belonging to them enter into the assembly of Yahweh forever:" [58] By depicting such a lovely character as Ruth in the ancestry of the Davidic lineage, the author effectively controverted the dogma that foreign blood was necessarily an evil and detestable thing. The book was designed to promote a liberal attitude of interracial good will.

4. *Jonah is another story that directly and appealingly argues for a liberal attitude toward foreigners. It is also a didactic romance. It is given a time setting in the era of the Assyrian Empire, before the destruction of Nineveh in 612 B.C.[59] Of all the masters who had ruled over them, there was none whom the Jews had more reason cordially to hate than the Assyrians. The character of Jonah is a caricature of the self-righteous, 100 per cent Jewish jingoist of the post-Nehemiah age, who despised foreigners and could not conceive of their having any place in the concern of God. When told to go preach to the Ninevites, Jonah set out in exactly the opposite direction to get as far away from them as possible. When finally forced to go do his duty, he thoroughly relished shouting "Nineveh shall be overthrown," but when the Ninevites repented and God did not destroy them, Jonah resented God's forbearance. He would rather die than see such grace extended to the heathen.[60]

The basic idea of the Book of Jonah is an extension of the Second Isaiah's doctrine of Israel's mission as Yahweh's servant to spread his religion to the nations.[61] The Book of Jonah represents the very highest level which the idea of God reached in Jewish thinking prior to Jesus of Nazareth: God so loved the world, which included the Ninevites, that he sent his prophet unto them, that they might not perish, but be saved.

---

[58] Deut. 23:3. Ruth 4:18–22 is manifestly an editorial addition by some literalist who thought that he could offset the problem by naming ten generations of David's forbears on his father's (!) side. He missed the point. On Ruth, cf. Pfeiffer, *Introd.,* pp. 717 ff.

[59] There was a prophet Jonah in the time of the Israelite King Jeroboam II (2 Kgs. 14:25). Cf. *supra,* p. 243. Cf. Pfeiffer, *Introd.,* pp. 586–589.

[60] Jon. 4:8.   [61] Isa. 49:6, cf. *supra,* pp. 373 f.

The Song of Songs. Canticles, or the Song of Songs, is a collection of love lyrics. They are frequently interpreted as wedding songs that were sung at marriage feasts. The central theme is the love of a young man for a young woman. Their unmistakably erotic character is especially manifest in 5 :2–8; 7 :1–9. The book is invaluable for its revelation of the Hebrew as a man, a thoroughly human being, capable of ardent emotion. A fine sentiment is expressed in the thrice repeated refrain (2 :7; 3 :5; 8 :4) that true love is spontaneous. The golden gem is 8 :7.

> Many waters cannot quench love,
> Neither can floods drown it;
> If a man would give all the substance of his house for love,
> He would utterly be contemned.

How did such erotic literature ever find admittance to a canon of Sacred Scripture? The best answer is that proposed by Professor Theophile J. Meek who regards the Song as the survival of an early liturgy of the fertility cult which was taken over by the Hebrews from the Canaanites.[62] According to this view the Song, instead of originating in the late period of Judaism under survey in this chapter, is one of the very earliest pieces of Old Testament literature and was from its inception distinctly religious. Its place in the sacred literature of Judaism was rationalized by an allegorizing interpretation which viewed the lyrics as descriptions of the love of God for his chosen people. Christianity subsequently accepted the book by making a fresh allegorizing by which the bridegroom was made to stand for Christ and the bride for the Christian Church.

An Appreciation of the Literature of the Fourth and Third Centuries. 1. *Development in Poetic Style.* Notable changes in literary style and forms are observable in the postexilic period. The poetry assumes a more varied and more complex form; its artistry is more manifest and its phraseology more conventional. The earlier ruggedness of style and diction gives way to a smoother elegance which is best seen in the later psalms. Assonance, alliteration, and the refrain are common. A conspicuously effective example of the latter is found in Ps. 107 :1–32 where a double refrain occurs in vss. 6 and 8, 13 and 15, 19 and 21, and 28 and 31. Note also the refrains in Pss. 57, 67, and 80, and the somewhat similar liturgical responses in Pss. 118, 136, and 115 :9–18. Such an artificial form as the alphabetic acrostic, already mentioned as occurring in Lam. 1–4 and

---

[62] Cf. T. J. Meek, "The Song of Songs and the Fertility Cult," in *The Song of Songs, A Symposium,* ed. W. H. Schoff (Philadelphia : 1924), pp. 48–69; Pfeiffer, *Introd.,* pp. 708–716.

Ps. 119,[63] further attests the degree to which the writing of poetry had become a professional art with a certain regrettable loss of spontaneity.

Notwithstanding this tendency to reduce poetic composition to certain conventional forms, there is a lyrical feeling of such intensity and depth as to save the poetry of these centuries from being trite and commonplace. It is this feeling tone which gives to the psalms a freshness and individuality altogether lacking in the contemporaneous hymnology of surrounding peoples; it achieves a surpassing dignity and depth in the Second Isaiah and in the earlier chapters of Proverbs; it affords an exquisite beauty to the Song of Songs; and it attains its sublimest reach in the greatest of all Hebrew poems, the Book of Job. Add to these a considerable number of poems found in other books of the Bible which were reedited in these centuries (e.g., Isa. 11–14; 24–27; and Ezk. 27), and we observe that a most impressive total of fine poetry was produced at this time. It was really a golden age in Jewish literary achievement.

2. *Development in Prose Writing.* The most conspicuous developments in the prose writing of the period are the essay, the short story, and the Chronicler's History.

The best example of the essay in the Old Testament is the Book of Ecclesiastes. By essay is meant the rather formal and altogether personal reflections of a writer upon some theme that particularly appeals to him. The essayist has a style all his own. It is familiarly conversational. In this way he unfolds to his readers the successive steps which his reflective thinking has traveled and thus takes the reader into his confidence in a peculiarly intimate and understanding way. This is precisely what we find in the Book of Ecclesiastes. Its author is primarily interested in the *summum bonum* of life, i.e., the most worth while in life, that which will in the long run afford the deepest and most abiding satisfaction. He is tolerant and objective. His essay sparkles with humor and with trenchant but kindly observations on life, and it is the nearest approach to philosophical speculation in the Old Testament.

Quite different in tone and theme, but none the less an essay, is the Book of Ezekiel. Instead of being a collection of separate compositions, this is a most carefully ordered, logical, and systematic argument (i.e., essay) to prove that Yahweh is at work on a planned program by which he will in time become the God of all nations in an earth of peace and plenty.

The Hebrews were masters of the short-story art. This does not mean that they set out to develop the art of short-story composition.

[63] Cf. *supra*, pp. 366, 401. For further examples of acrostics, cf. Bewer, *op. cit.*, p. 346.

They would have been most surprised at the very suggestion that they were producing a literary type. It was just that the same forces and factors which made for the creation of the folklore type of literature tended also to the production of the good short story.[64] In fact, a short story can be folklore, or vice versa.

The criteria of the short story are unity of impression, a well-knit plot, few characters drawn with a few swift, sure strokes, and brevity. A good short story is therefore certain to be highly dramatic and, like the drama, secure its effect by means of pictures—a succession of swift, vividly objective scenes that flash naturally and without effort before the reader or listener.

Tested by these standards, the Bible is especially rich in narratives of the best short-story type. One may read story after story and discover scarcely a word or phrase that could have been improved upon or omitted without positive loss. None of these stories introduce unnecessary characters. The scenes are drawn with cameo sharpness, yet leave details to the free play of the imagination. Direct discourse, straight to the point, and unwasted movements in the action assure swift progress throughout.

Three books of the Old Testament are short stories: Ruth, Esther, and Jonah. The fact that all three made their appearance at this time is further evidence of the rich literary productiveness which characterized these centuries.

The Chronicler's History [65] represents a literary development which attained some magnitude and importance in the postexilic period. The style of the Chronicler is decidedly dry and uninteresting. His bulky narrative (Chronicles-Ezra-Nehemiah), padded with long lists of genealogies and minutely detailed descriptions of priestly duties, is tiresome and boring. Yet he does occupy a worth-while place among Old Testament writers if for no other reason than that he appreciated the memoirs of Nehemiah to the extent of incorporating them, apparently unchanged, into his otherwise prosaic work.

The Greek Translation of the Jewish Scriptures: The Septuagint. One of the most important literary activities of Jews in the third century B.C. was the translation of the Sacred Scriptures into the Greek language. This was the work of Jews in Alexandria, Egypt. This translation is commonly called the "Septuagint," which name is derived from a legend that seventy (Latin, *septuaginta*) Jewish scholars participated in the work of translation. This legend is recounted in the *Letter of Aristeas,* a Jewish pseudepigraphical writing which arose sometime between 130 and 70 B.C. Aristeas

---

[64] Cf. *supra,* pp. 107–112.
[65] Cf. *supra,* pp. 406 f.

states that the translation was made in the reign of Ptolemy II, Philadelphus, of Egypt (285–247 B.C.).[66]

Alexandria had been founded by Alexander the Great in 332 B.C. Special provisions were made for Jews in the city. They had their own district, with full civil rights and local autonomy. Jews flocked to Alexandria, and after a half century there were probably tens of thousands of them there in the time of Ptolemy Philadelphus. Such Jews adopted the Greek language, which was commonly spoken in Egypt as almost everywhere else, and they rapidly lost knowledge of Hebrew and Aramaic. Primarily for the benefit of such Jews, the Scriptures were rendered into Greek that believers might not become detached from the faith of their fathers. Of course this Greek translation made Jewish literature known to the gentiles also. Naturally the first part of the Bible to be translated was the Torah. The Prophets followed.

It should be noted that the Alexandrian Jews were not only translating the Palestinian Jewish literature into Greek but they were also producing literature of their own. This literary productivity of the Egyptian Jews became more extensive in the three centuries following 200 B.C. Standing at the year 200 B.C., what we have is this: the canon of Sacred Scriptures, Torah and Prophets, is acknowledged by both Palestinian and Alexandrian Jews; the literature which will ultimately constitute the third division of the sacred canon (the Hagiographa) is coming into being both in Palestine and in Egypt. Ultimately it will result in a larger canon in Egypt than in Palestine, larger by the amount of those books commonly called the *Apocrypha.*

[66] *Vid. infra,* pp. 438 ff.

Chapter 21

INDEPENDENCE WON AND LOST AGAIN

The Jews knew many masters in the course of their history. Their hope for political freedom never died out. For a time their dreams came true in the era known as the Maccabean Kingdom (143–63 B.C.), the heroic age of Jewish history. Then Rome came and Jewish independence ceased for two whole millennia. Not until A.D. 1948 did an independent Jewish state exist again in the land of Palestine. In that year the state of Israel was created by the United Nations.

Sources for a History of the Period

The apocryphal Book *First Maccabees* gives the history of the Jewish struggle for independence from 175 to 135 B.C. It is a sample of first-class historical writing of the period. The book was written around 100 B.C. by a Palestinian Jew who was devoted to the faithful, nationalistic, non-Hellenizing Judaism of the period. *Second Maccabees* does not continue the history where First Maccabees leaves off, but duplicates the first fourteen years of the same period, 175–161 B.C. It is much less important and trustworthy than First Maccabees. Much knowledge of the history of the period is derived from Josephus's *Antiquities of the Jews,*[1] books xii, 3–xvii, 8, and his *History of the Jewish War,* book i. There are some allusions to the period in Daniel 11 and possibly also in the Second Zechariah, parts of which are dated by some scholars in this period.

Palestine Under the Seleucids (198–143 B.C.)

Antiochus III, the Great (223–187 B.C.), ruler of the Seleucid kingdom, took Palestine from the Ptolemies in 198 B.C. Thenceforward, until 143 B.C., the Jews were under the rule of the Seleucids, although this rule was more nominal than real after the Maccabean revolt began in 168 B.C. Antiochus III also tried to conquer Egypt but was frustrated by the Romans. Thereupon he attempted to organize a Panhellenic league, hoping thereby to check the Romans,

[1] Cf. *supra,* p. 385.

but he was overwhelmingly defeated by the latter before his league could function.

We have little light on the Jewish situation under Antiochus III. What little there is indicates a disturbed state of internal affairs. 2 Macc. 3 echoes an unsuccessful effort of Heliodorus, chief minister of Seleucus IV (son and successor of Antiochus III), to confiscate the treasure of the Jerusalem temple for the king. The same chapter reflects contention among the Jewish leaders themselves.

Antiochus IV and the Attempt to Force Hellenism Upon the Jews. When Antiochus IV, Epiphanes (176–164 B.C.), grandson of Antiochus the Great, became king, the Jewish high priest Onias III was temporarily absent from Jerusalem, having gone to see the king, Seleucus IV. Taking advantage of this situation, Jason, a brother of Onias, bribed the new king to appoint him as high priest.[2] The Jews refused to recognize him, even though he was of high-priestly parentage. Three years later one Menelaus, who was not of high-priestly parentage, played the same game and by a large bribe got himself appointed high priest, thus ousting Jason. This outraged the orthodox Jews who would have none of him. This attitude of the Jews was interpreted as political disloyalty by Antiochus IV, for he considered that he had the right to elevate or depose anyone he chose in any of his subject domains, and Antiochus looked upon the Jewish high priest merely as local governor in one district of his empire. The religious character of the Jewish high-priestly office meant nothing to Antiochus. The Jews, however, had a different idea; they regarded the high priest as being divinely appointed, and no human power, not even a king, had any right to interfere with him. While Antiochus was on a campaign in Egypt (169 B.C.), a false rumor of his death was spread in Palestine. Jason led an uprising and ousted Menelaus. Antiochus interpreted this as open rebellion, and after his return from Egypt he wreaked a terrible vengeance on Jerusalem and plundered the temple (1 Macc. 1:20–28). Jason, of course, fled. Menelaus was confirmed in the high priesthood, but the Jews refused to have anything to do with him and Jerusalem was in disorder.

It was this condition of affairs that goaded Antiochus into his persecution of the Jews. Moreover, Antiochus ultimately failed in his Egyptian venture, which left him in a disagreeable mood. He turned his attention to the internal consolidation of his empire (1 Macc. 1:41 f.). There was in Jerusalem a considerable body of Hellenized Jews (1 Macc. 1:11–15) who were entirely agreeable to cooperating with the king in his program of still further Hellenizing Judea.

---

[2] Cf. 2 Macc. 4:3–6. Cf. R. H. Pfeiffer, *History of New Testament Times* (New York: 1949), p. 11.

The king sent a "chief collector of tribute" to Judea, who plundered and devastated Jerusalem (1 Macc. 1:29–32), to teach them who was king. The Hellenized Jewish element established itself in the citadel in Jerusalem and from that base attacked and slaughtered the orthodox Jews in the temple, polluted and laid waste the sanctuary, annulled the feasts, and brought Judaism into contempt (1 Macc. 1:33–40).

This situation among the Jews supplied Antiochus with all the pretext he needed. He had inherited his grandfather's Hellenizing ambition and now he set about with vigor to Hellenize Palestine and to force the Jews into conformity, particularly to compel them to give up their own religion and to adopt the Hellenistic cult, very likely the cult of Dionysus (1 Macc. 1:44–53). The Jews were forbidden to perform the rite of circumcision, to keep the Sabbath, or to read their Scriptures. *Epiphanes* means "the illustrious." His enemies dubbed him *Epimanes* ("the crazy"). His madness is seen in the extremities to which he goaded the Jews. At the Jerusalem temple, on the site of the altar of burnt offering, he caused to be erected an altar to Olympian Zeus (2 Macc. 6:2), and there swine's flesh was offered as a sacrifice (168 B.C.). This is what Daniel means by "the abomination of desolation." [3] It was this act that precipitated the Maccabean uprising (1 Macc. 1:54–64; cf. 2 Macc. 6).

Antiochus did something similar among the Samaritans, for at their temple on Mount Gerizim he erected an altar to "Zeus the Protector of Strangers" (*Zeus Xenios*) (2 Macc. 6:2).

This attempt to compel the Jews to conform to Hellenistic religion was, from Antiochus's point of view, an effort to force them into political loyalty. The acid test of a vassal state's loyalty to its overlord was the official adoption of the overlord's religion. In bygone centuries this idea accounted for King Ahaz's adoption of Assyrian religion for Judah,[4] and at a subsequent time King Manasseh's sponsoring of Assyrian religion in Judah.[5] It was an ill-advised attempt on the part of Antiochus, but in all fairness to him it must be admitted that Hellenism had spread so far, not alone in Syria but in Judea also, as to lend some support to Antiochus's idea that he needed only to apply firm pressure to bring all the Jews into the Hellenistic movement. His calculations were wrong, because he failed to reckon with the intensity of Jewish national and religious sentiment. The Jews were embittered and resisted unto death (cf. 2 Macc. 7). The resistance was at first passive. Then it burst into flame.

The Maccabean Revolt. The Maccabean war broke out when Mattathias, an aged priest of Modein, of the Jewish family of Has-

---

[3] Dan. 11:31.　　　　　　　　　　　[4] *Vid. supra,* pp. 249 f., 322, 330 f.
[5] *Vid. supra,* pp. 260, 331 f.

mon, murdered the Syrian commissioner who came to order him and all other villagers at Modein to sacrifice to Zeus. Those who rallied to Mattathias fled to the wilderness where their numbers were constantly augmented by new accessions. In the ensuing two years these revolutionaries defeated four Syrian armies and forced a fifth to retire to Antioch. Upon the death of Mattathias in 166 B.C., the leadership passed to his son Judas Maccabeus,[6] who recovered Jerusalem and purged the temple of its defilement so that in December, 165 B.C., the regular Jewish temple service was reinstituted with great rejoicing on the part of the Jews (1 Macc. 2–4, 2 Macc. 8:1–10:8).

This restoration and rededication of the temple was ever afterward commemorated by the Jewish *Feast of the Dedication*.[7] The Jewish name of this festival is *Hanukkah*. It was first observed exactly three years to a day from the time the temple had been desecrated by Epiphanes.[8] This festival lasted eight days, as did the Feast of Tabernacles, to which Hanukkah has other resemblances, notably the part played by lights.[9] Josephus states that the popular name of this festival was "Lights." [10] It is a good example of a Judaized Hellenistic religious observance and is evidence of how much Hellenism had been assimilated even by those who were opposing it. The festival incorporated certain rites from the cult of Dionysus, and the incense offerings at the doors of houses and in the streets were a transfer from the cult of Apollo.[11] What this means is that these Hellenistic cult observances were in vogue in Palestine at the time, and Jews were accustomed to join in them. The anti-Hellenizing Jews were now able to rationalize the Hellenism out of such practices by associating them with the rededication of the temple. The Hanukkah lamp, an adaptation of the Apollo oracle fire, was interpreted as a symbol of the law. The first observance in 165 B.C. was an occasion of almost delirious joy. Hanukkah has always been a joyous festival, and today is particularly regarded as a children's festival. The lighting of candles is a conspicuous feature of its ritual.[12]

Ps. *118 is by some scholars interpreted as the battle hymn of triumph over Epiphanes.

One of the important victories of Judas was over the Syrian general Nicanor in 161 B.C. (1 Macc. 7:26–49). This victory, which was

[6] The word "Maccabeus" is generally understood to mean "the hammer"; for other suggestions as to its meaning, cf. W. O. E. Oesterley, *A History of Israel* (Oxford: 1932), ii, p. 229.

[7] Cf. Jn. 10:22.   [8] 1 Macc. 4:52 ff.

[9] Cf. 2 Macc. 1:18.   [10] *Antiquities*, xii, 7:6, 7.

[11] 1 Macc. 1:55. Cf. Oesterley, *op. cit.*, pp. 232, 307.

[12] The Christian celebration of Epiphany, which is likewise characterized by the lighting of candles, represents a transfer of the same sort of rite from the same source. Cf. the number of practices connected with the observance of Christmas which have come from non-Christian sources and have nothing whatever to do with the birth of Jesus.

celebrated by the Jews with great rejoicing, became an annual festival known as Nicanor's Day, observed on the 13th of Adar (February-March). Second Maccabees was written (originally in Greek) to make propaganda for this festival and encourage its observance in the Dispersion. It fell on the day immediately preceding Purim.[13] Ultimately it was assimilated to the preparation for Purim, and Nicanor's Day disappeared from the Jewish festival calendar.

The War of Independence lasted from 165 to 143 B.C. Judas Maccabeus was leader from 166 to 161 B.C. He won religious freedom for the Jews (1 Macc. 5:1-9:22). His brother Jonathan, leader from 161 to 143 B.C., was a diplomat who took advantage of disputes about succession to the Syrian throne in such a skilful way as to win one concession after another until in the end he became the acknowledged civil, military, and religious ruler of Judea (1 Macc. 9:23-12:53). Simon, last of the brothers, succeeded as leader from 143 to 135 B.C. He won from Demetrius II of Syria Judea's complete independence in return for Simon's support of Demetrius (1 Macc. 13-16).[14]

The Period of Independence: The Maccabean Kingdom (143-63 B.C.)

The reign of Simon (until 135 B.C.) was peaceful and prosperous. He was an able sovereign, though he would not call himself king. Instead, he was proclaimed high priest, which office was from that time on made hereditary in the family of the Hasmoneans.

The Emergence of Pharisees and Sadducees. Under John Hyrcanus (135-105 B.C.), son and successor of Simon, a period of expansion began. John annexed Idumea, Samaria, and Perea to Judea and beautified Jerusalem. John was the first Jewish ruler to issue coins. His conduct as high priest was so offensive to the strict Pharisaic religionists that they demanded his resignation. This angered John and made him a partisan of the liberal Saducean party. Thus began the strife between the Pharisees and Sadducees which was in the end to prove disastrous to the Maccabean kingdom.

The men who stood by Judas Maccabeus were motivated by the desire for religious freedom. These men, known as the Hasidim, were ready to die rather than abandon their ancestral religion. So long as the struggle was for religious freedom they ardently fought the Syrians. As soon as religious freedom had been won, they quit

---

[13] Est. 9:19. *Vid. supra*, p. 408.

[14] On the history of the revolt under the successive leadership of the three brothers, cf. Oesterley, *op. cit.*, pp. 217–272; R. H. Pfeiffer, *History of New Testament Times* (New York: 1949), pp. 9–19, 463–472. On Maccabean and Herodian Palestine, cf. G. E. Wright and F. V. Filson, *The Westminster Historical Atlas to the Bible* (Philadelphia: 1945), pp. 73–76.

fighting, for they had no political ambitions. They believed that all effort should be bent toward keeping God's law, that thus the nation would become pleasing to him. The Pharisees were the successors of the Hasidim. Their clear and steady faith commanded the loyalty of the masses of the people. The word "pharisee" means "separatist," and it is conventionally interpreted as meaning separation from unclean things and persons. It may well be that separation from Hellenism and Hellenizers was a major motivation, but the origin of the term as the name of a group is obscure.[15] Within the group itself members were called *Haberim,* "neighbors" or "associates."

There were many Jews who appreciated Hellenistic culture and welcomed it yet remained steadfastly loyal to their own religion. These favored a policy of internationalism, believing that there were many advantages the Jews might gain through foreign alliance and diplomacy. Out of this group grew the Sadducees. The name "Sadducee" is derived from the personal name of Zadok, who was made priest by King David,[16] was continued by King Solomon, doubtless as chief priest,[17] and whose family exercised the priestly office continually thereafter.[18] The high priests of the Persian and Hellenistic periods claimed their descent and special authority from Zadok. They considered themselves the rightful rulers of the nation. Through control of the temple worship they had possession of the temple riches. They were the aristocrats, and seemed to the Pharisees to be worldly minded and lacking in real religious conviction. They were not so numerous as the Pharisees but seem to have been almost equally powerful. The common run of priests probably were not Sadducees.

The Disastrous Struggle Between Pharisees and Sadducees. Antagonism between the Pharisees and the Sadducees became so bitter that in the end it wrecked the Maccabean kingdom and forfeited the political freedom of the Jews.

For the quarter century following the death of John Hyrcanus, the Sadducees were dominant. Aristobulus I (105–104 B.C.) was a thoroughgoing Greek sympathizer. His major accomplishment was the annexation of Galilee. His widow married his successor, Alexander Jannaeus (104–78 B.C.),[19] a Sadducee and a vicious and vindictive despot. Jews who resented his conduct as high priest were massacred. A revolt of the Pharisees was cruelly suppressed. Bitterness of party feeling reached its height during his reign.

---

[15] Cf. Oesterley, *op. cit.,* p. 317. For a quite different explanation, cf. Shailer Mathews, *New Testament Times in Palestine* (New York: 1933), pp. 85 f.
[16] 2 Sam. 8:17; 20:25; *vid. supra,* p. 213.
[17] 1 Kgs. 4:4; cf. 1 Kgs. 2:27, 35; *vid. supra,* p. 213.
[18] Cf 1 Chr. 6:1–15. Oesterley, *op. cit.,* p. 322.
[19] Jannaeus = Jonathan, in Hebrew.

The Pharisees had their turn when Alexander was succeeded by his widow Alexandra, a pro-Pharisee. She reigned from 78 to 69 B.C., the second queen to rule over the Jews in all their history.[20] Once in power, the Pharisees misused their influence by taking revenge on their rivals. Though clouded by this revengeful spirit, the reign of Alexandra was nevertheless a golden era for Judaism. Then it was that the elementary schools were established (75 B.C.) under the stimulating leadership of her brother, Rabbi Ben-Shetach. The yearly temple tax for all Jews was also instituted in this period.

The End of Jewish Nationalism. Upon the death of Alexandra in 69 B.C., a period of civil war broke out between her sons Hyrcanus II and Aristobulus II which dragged on until 63 B.C. when the kingdom was annexed to Rome. Hyrcanus II, the elder of the two, held the high-priestly title throughout his mother's reign. He was a pro-Pharisee. His brother Aristobulus II was a pro-Sadducee. When Alexandra died, Aristobulus II seized the throne. There now appeared upon the stage a figure who was to shape politics in Judea for the next half century, Antipater the Idumean. Antipater persuaded Hyrcanus II to flee to Petra, a city in the Mount Seir Range about fifty miles south of the Dead Sea, there to seek aid from Aretas, the Nabatean king. With the help of Aretas, Hyrcanus II defeated Aristobulus II, whereupon the latter fortified himself on the temple mountain in Jerusalem.

Pompey, the Roman, was at the time campaigning in Pontus and Armenia, his objective being the extension of Roman authority eastward to the Euphrates River. Pompey's general, Scaurus, was in Syria when the civil war broke out in Judea. Scaurus ordered Aretas to withdraw from Judea, which left Aristobulus II in power, 67–63 B.C. The party conflict now grew from bad to worse until in the spring of 63 B.C. no fewer than three deputations appealed to Pompey, one representing Hyrcanus II, one Aristobulus II, and a third representing the Pharisaic party. The Pharisees asked that neither be recognized as king but that Judea be permitted to continue its old type of government under high priest and Gerousia. Pompey decided upon annexation to Rome. Hyrcanus II yielded to this, but the party of Aristobulus II held out to the bitter end. So when his forces were defeated, Aristobulus II and his family were carried off to Rome to grace Pompey's triumph.

The Roman Period

From 63 B.C. to the end of Bible times Palestine was under the rule of Rome. Throughout the remainder of our study, therefore, we

[20] *Vid. supra*, p. 238.

must consider the Jewish people, both in Palestine and in the Dispersion, and also the Christians in the light of their relationship to the Roman Empire.

Palestine Under Pompey (63–48 B.C.): The Rise of Antipater. Pompey appointed Scaurus governor of the Roman province of Syria. Scaurus reduced Palestine to order. Pompey made Hyrcanus II high priest, with the title of ethnarch,[21] as a reward for his nonresistance to Roman intervention. He was nominal ruler until 40 B.C. Antipater was made the adviser of Hyrcanus II and then Antipater became the real power behind the throne. Antipater's aim was to establish himself in the favor of Rome and this he succeeded in doing by rendering valuable aid to the Roman government in a series of revolts which broke out in Palestine. In 57 B.C. Alexander, son of Aristobulus II, escaped from Rome and started a Palestinian revolt. This was soon quelled by Gabinius, who had just been appointed proconsul of Syria. In 56 B.C. Aristobulus II himself escaped from Rome with his son Antigonus and instigated another revolt. This was likewise quelled by Gabinius, and Aristobulus II was sent back to Rome, although his sons were allowed to live in Judea. Then Alexander headed a third revolt which was suppressed with severe consequences to the revolters.

In the struggle between Caesar and Pompey for the mastery of Rome, Aristobulus II and his sons supported the cause of Caesar. While en route to Judea with troops furnished him by Caesar, Aristobulus II was poisoned. Alexander was beheaded at Antioch by partisans of Pompey. Though Antipater was supporting Pompey, he could not restrain Crassus, appointed proconsul of Syria in 54 B.C., from plundering the temple in Jerusalem, despite an oath not to do so. This infamy led to further disturbances among the Jews, which were quelled with severity in 52 B.C.

Judea Under Julius Caesar (48–44 B.C.). The struggle between Caesar and Pompey ended in Caesar's favor at the battle of Pharsalus in 48 B.C. Although up to this point Antipater had been a loyal partisan of Pompey, he cleverly succeeded in winning the favor of Caesar by valuable service in assisting Mithridates of Pergamum, an ally of Caesar, to cross the Sinaitic Desert and enter Egypt. Caesar continued Hyrcanus II in his figurehead titles of ethnarch and high priest, but made Antipater a Roman citizen and procurator of Judea. Thus Antipater became the recognized superior of Hyrcanus II. At the same time Caesar granted the Jews many privileges not only in Palestine but also in Alexandria and in Rome, not least among such privileges being full religious liberty.

21 An honorific title meaning "ruler of a people."

Without doubt, Antipater was thoroughly loyal to Rome and sincerely devoted to the civil and political good of Judea. But the Jews hated him because he had been an Idumean, and Jewish hatred of Edom was centuries old and ineradicable. Consequently Antipater had to deal with civil disturbances. Antipater appointed his son Phasael governor of Jerusalem and his son Herod governor of Galilee. Herod promptly distinguished himself by breaking up certain robber gangs which infested Galilee. He executed their leader, one Hezekias, for which act Herod was summoned to Jerusalem before the Sanhedrin [22] to stand trial for having presumed to exercise the right of capital punishment. Sensitive for its prerogatives, the Sanhedrin undoubtedly would have condemned Herod to death, but Herod went to Damascus to appeal to the Syrian proconsul Sextus Caesar, who promptly appointed Herod governor of Coele-Syria.

Judea Under Cassius (44–42) and Antony (42–40 B.C.). Caesar was assassinated by Cassius and Brutus, March 15, 44 B.C. Cassius went to Syria to claim the proconsulship of Syria and to collect tribute and troops. Thereupon Antipater and his sons, especially Herod, adroitly won the favor of Cassius by zeal in collecting the tribute. In return, Cassius made Herod procurator of all Syria and promised eventually to make him king of Judea. So when Antipater was poisoned by Malichus, 43 B.C., Herod promptly exercised his new powers by having the latter stabbed to death.

The withdrawal of Cassius from Syria left matters in Palestine in confusion. Then came the battle of Philippi (42 B.C.), a decisive defeat for Brutus and Cassius at the hands of Antony and Octavian (Augustus). Antony now controlled Asia. Herod, through bribery, promptly won Antony's favor so that he appointed Herod and Phasael tetrarchs and continued Hyrcanus II as high priest.

Judea Under Antigonus. Rome naturally desired to hold Palestine and Syria under firm control because this was the empire's easternmost outpost against the Parthians, a people who had thus far successfully defied the mistress of the world. The struggle between Antony and the assassins of Julius Caesar had left the eastern frontier of the empire unguarded and the Parthians promptly attacked. In 41 B.C. they captured Jerusalem and made Antigonus, the son of Aristobulus II, king and high priest, the last of the Hasmonean line to sit on the throne. The aged former high priest Hyrcanus II was treated with shameful indignity—his ears were bitten off that he might never again be high priest. (He was later murdered at the command of Herod the Great).

---

[22] *Vid. supra*, p. 391.

The sons of Antipater were now in dire straits. Phasael, seeing no hope of escape from Antigonus, committed suicide. Herod fled to Mount Masada, on the west coast of the Dead Sea. Leaving his family there heavily guarded, he made his way to Egypt and thence to Rome. There he urged Antony and Octavian to appoint Aristobulus III king of Judea [23] and himself (Herod) prime minister to Aristobulus III. But the Romans suspected the Hasmoneans: they had made trouble enough. Antony and Octavian offered the kingship to Herod, an appointment speedily confirmed by the Roman Senate.

The Rule of Herod the Great (40–4 B.C.). Herod was thus nominally king in 40 B.C., but it took three years of persistent fighting to establish himself as actual king of Judea. From Rome he returned to Palestine, landed at Ptolemais, and mastered part of Galilee and down the coast to Joppa. From there he marched to relieve his family at Masada. After that he mastered Idumea, Samaria, and Galilee and then laid siege to Jerusalem. After five months Jerusalem fell, in 37 B.C. Antigonus was beheaded.

Herod gave the Jews a strong and efficient government. His creed, inherited from his father, was loyalty to Rome no matter who was in power at Rome. So long as Antony's power in the eastern Mediterranean was supreme, Herod was loyal to him. After the battle of Actium in 31 B.C., Herod shifted his loyalty to Augustus who, appreciating Herod's worth, confirmed his appointment as a *rex socius* and extended his kingdom to include practically all of Palestine. Thereby Augustus set up on the eastern frontier of the Roman Empire a strong bulwark of defense against the Parthians.

Herod's admiration for the Graeco-Roman culture made him a great builder. In Antioch, Athens, and Rhodes he caused noble public buildings to be erected. Jerusalem, his capital, he adorned with a theater and an amphitheater where he celebrated games in honor of Augustus. He also erected or improved other buildings, the most important of which was the temple. In the year 20–19 B.C. Herod began the reconstruction of the Jewish temple, not because he loved the Jews or desired to honor their religion but because he thought the temple of Zerubbabel too shabby in comparison with the splendid new structures rising about it. Samaria and Caesarea he thoroughly reconstructed and adorned with magnificent buildings.[24]

Herod pretty well concealed his inner contempt for the Jewish people. He ruled them with an iron hand, and through the fear instilled by his spies and his soldiers he kept them in complete subjec-

---

[23] Aristobulus III was the son of Alexander (son of Aristobulus II) by Alexandra (daughter of Hyrcanus II).

[24] Cf. G. E. Wright and F. V. Filson, *op. cit.*, pp. 75, 98.

tion. Consequently his reign was an era of freedom from wars and disturbances, though the tax burden was almost intolerable.

Herod's family life was tragic. He had numerous wives and children. One of his wives was Mariamme, sister of Aristobulus III and granddaughter of Hyrcanus II, and therefore a Maccabean princess. Herod loved her devotedly, as well as her sons. Herod was victimized by intrigues in his family, between his mother-in-law Alexandra and his wife Mariamme, representing the Hasmonean faction on the one side, and his mother Kypros and his sister Salome, representing the Idumean faction on the other. Due to such intrigue, Herod put Mariamme to death. Made insane by this mistake, he launched a career of murder which led the emperor to say, "It is better to be Herod's swine than his children." Despised and hated by the people, in his dying hours he planned his most revolting crime. That there might be sincere mourning when he died (4 B.C.) he directed that all of the principal men of the nation be shut up in the hippodrome and at the hour of his death be set upon by troops and massacred. Happily his orders were not carried out. In the light of such butchery one is not surprised at the Gospel story of his slaughter of the infants of Bethlehem (Matt. 2:16 ff.), in order to put out of the way a possible rival claimant to his throne, for it was in the reign of this Herod that Jesus of Nazareth was born, 6 B.C.

THE HASMONEAN FAMILY TREE

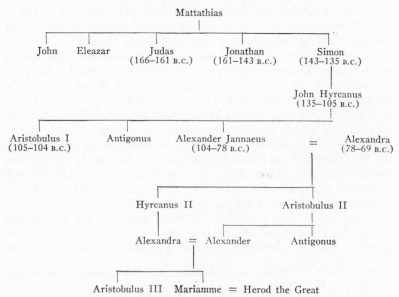

Mattathias

| John | Eleazar | Judas
(166–161 B.C.) | Jonathan
(161–143 B.C.) | Simon
(143–135 B.C.) |

John Hyrcanus
(135–105 B.C.)

| Aristobulus I
(105–104 B.C.) | Antigonus | Alexander Jannaeus
(104–78 B.C.) | = | Alexandra
(78–69 B.C.) |

Hyrcanus II   Aristobulus II

Alexandra = Alexander   Antigonus

Aristobulus III   Mariamme = Herod the Great

Chapter 22

JEWISH LITERATURE OF THE NEW TESTAMENT PERIOD

People are interested in other books besides the Bible. So were the Jews of the New Testament period. The present chapter attempts to indicate what such other Jewish literature was and the types of thought contained in it.

The term "New Testament Period" technically covers the three centuries from 200 B.C. to A.D. 100. The first two centuries B.C. are included because the experiences of the Jewish people and the character of their thought in those centuries are quite basic to any understanding of the first century after Christ, when Christianity emerged and produced its literature. The present chapter aims to give some appreciation of what Jews were reading and thinking when Jesus of Nazareth came into the world.

Foreign currents of thought, especially Persian and Greek, flowed in upon the Jews from the time of Nehemiah in the fifth century B.C. and Alexander the Great in the fourth century B.C. How such Persian and Greek thought patterns were assimilated by some Jews will become clear in this chapter. Other Jews reacted against such foreign influences with a revulsion of feeling which turned their minds more determinedly to their own Jewish past and enhanced their devotion to their own law.

The Completion of the Old Testament

Daniel. The Book of Daniel was called forth by the stirring times at the outbreak of the Maccabean rebellion when the Jews were being persecuted by Antiochus IV Epiphanes.[1] The author was an unnamed Judean, a Hasidist, thoroughly loyal to the strict, anti-Hellenizing Judaism of the time and faithful to Jewish customs. He wrote his book for the benefit of Jews of the same type, to encourage them to continue steadfastly loyal to true Judaism despite persecution and suffering. The author chose the name "Daniel" for the hero of the book after the Daniel whom Jewish tradition affirmed to be one of three men

[1] *Vid. supra,* pp. 415 f.

especially distinguished for their righteousness, the others being Noah and Job.[2] This legendary Daniel was also renowned for his wisdom.[3] Hence, in the Book of Daniel the hero is depicted as a sincerely devout young Jew, unswerving in his piety and wiser than all others of his time.

The author gave his book a time setting in the period of the Babylonian captivity of the Jews. The history of the period from Nebuchadrezzar to Antiochus Epiphanes is told in the form of visions. This recounting of history in the form of prediction is a characteristic device of the literary type known as "apocalyptic."[4]

Chapters *1, *3, *6 are stories which may be classified as religious fiction or didactic romance. Daniel is portrayed as one of four noble young Jews who in the midst of a foreign situation refuse to conform to foreign customs but remain loyal to their Jewish customs and thereby prove to be superior to other young men in health, wisdom, and skill. Obviously this is addressed to the youth of Judea in the Hellenistic period. The pull of Hellenism was very strong and conformity to Greek customs was quite the fashion. It was not easy for young Jews to resist this and cling to their Jewish customs, but superior health and morale were assured if they did. Of course they would be scoffed at and persecuted. Daniel's three friends were cast into a fiery furnace and Daniel himself was cast into a den of lions. Either metaphor, fiery furnace or lion's den, aptly characterized the situation in Judea in the time of Epiphanes. Daniel and his three friends came through the persecution securely because of the mystical presence and protection of God. God would equally protect those of Maccabean times who were loyal to him in the midst of persecution.

To stimulate the faith of the Jews and to encourage their steadfastness, this author predicted the doom of Epiphanes and the downfall of his kingdom, just as Chaldea and Persia, persecutors of the Jews in the past, had met their doom and the Jews had survived them. Of course the author could not state this openly, for to do so would not only have sealed his own doom but his book's as well, and would have intensified the persecution of the people. Consequently he resorted to cryptic language, talking about great images and beasts and horns, which hid his meaning from his enemies but not from his fellow Jews. This use of cryptic imagery is another characteristic of apocalyptic. By using such veiled language and by throwing it backward into the form of prediction made four centuries earlier, the author was able to convey his message to the second-century Jews.

Chapter 2 describes Nebuchadrezzar's dream of a great image which Daniel interpreted as representing four world empires

---

[2] Cf. Ezk. 14:14, 20.   [3] Cf. Ezk. 28:3.   [4] *Vid. supra*, pp. 369 f.

(Chaldean, Median, Persian, and Seleucid), and the last of the four was destroyed by "a stone cut out of the mountains without hands," which of course was the kingdom of the Jews. By this the author designed to assure the Jews that they would triumph over Epiphanes and establish an everlasting kingdom of their own.

In chapter 7 Daniel describes his vision of the four beasts, which mean the same four kingdoms. The fourth and most terrible of the beasts is more elaborately described (vs. 7). It had ten horns, meaning the ten kings from Alexander the Great to Demetrius (176 B.C.).[5] The eleventh horn of the beast, which emerged and plucked out three of the first ten horns, means Antiochus Epiphanes, whose three immediate predecessors, Seleucus IV, Heliodorus, and Demetrius, were "plucked out by the roots" in one year, 176 B.C. This eleventh horn persecuted "the saints of the Most High" (vs. 25) but after a period of subjection to him "they shall take away his dominion, to consume and destroy it unto the end" (vs. 26) and to replace it by an everlasting kingdom of their own (vs. 27).

Chapter 8 presents the vision of the ram with the two horns, and the he-goat and the desecrating horn. The two-horned ram is definitely identified as the Medo-Persian Empire (vs. 20). The he-goat is the Greek Empire of Alexander, and the great horn of this goat is the first king, Alexander himself (vs. 21). This great horn was broken and in its place came up four horns (vss. 8,22), meaning the four kingdoms of the Diadochi, or successors of Alexander. From one of these four horns branched out a little horn (vs. 9) which wrought devastation (vss. 10 ff.,24 f.) ; this means Antiochus Epiphanes. Again the doom of Epiphanes is foretold: "He shall be broken without hand" (vs. 25).

Chapters 10 f. present another vision of Daniel which gives the history of the Greek kingdoms so exactly that historians recognize it as a reliable historical source for knowledge of the period. This vision also culminates in an elaborate characterization of Epiphanes (11:21–39). The author gives several conjectures as to how long the persecution will last and when Epiphanes will meet his end (7:25; 8:13 f.; 9:25 ff.; 12:7,11), which are interpreted as meaning June, 164 B.C.[6]

In the second century B.C. the idea had arisen among the Jews that the age of prophecy had definitely ended. God had ceased to speak directly to inspired men but had now given his written law. In view

---

[5] Alexander (d. 323 B.C.) ; Seleucus I (312–281 B.C.) ; Antiochus I (281–261 B.C.) ; Antiochus II (261–246 B.C.) ; Seleucus II (246–226 B.C.) ; Seleucus III (226–223 B.C.) ; Antiochus III (223–187 B.C.) ; Seleucus IV (187–176 B.C.) ; Heliodorus (176 B.C.) ; Demetrius (176 B.C.). Heliodorus was the chief minister and murderer of Seleucus IV ; Demetrius was the son of Seleucus IV.

[6] On Daniel, cf. Bewer, *op. cit.*, pp. 410–419 ; Pfeiffer, *Introd.*, pp. 748–781.

of this dogma such a message as that which the author of Daniel sought to convey could not be put forth directly after the manner of an Amos or an Isaiah. Therefore writers of the apocalyptic type resorted to the predictive technique and put forth their message as a foretelling by some ancient worthy whose message, like Daniel, was "shut up and sealed till the time of the end" (12:9).

The Book of Daniel was the first notable book of apocalyptic and was a pattern for a literary type which had a vogue for about three centuries. The principal Old Testament apocalyptic sections are Isa. 24–27; Dan. 7–12; Zech. 9–14; Ezk. 37–39; Joel 2:28–3:21.

The Second Zechariah. Chapters 9–14 of the Book of Zechariah probably originated in the Maccabean era. The most notable passage is *9:9 f. with its portrait of Messiah. Undoubtedly the successes of the Jews in the Maccabean war aroused, among some at least, expectations of national greatness under a messianic king. The Second Zechariah is apocalyptic and 14:1–8 presents the idea of the Day of Yahweh in a novel way.[7] This author envisages the time when "Yahweh shall be King over all the earth,"[8] but regrettably he thinks of God's sovereignty in ritualistic terms rather than ethical.[9]

The Completion of the Hagiographa. The Book of Daniel was the very last book produced by the Jews of Palestine to secure a place in the canon of Sacred Scripture. It is manifestly a prophetic book, and yet the Hebrew Bible does not include it in the Prophets, the second grand division of the canon.[10] It is included in the third division of the canon, which is known as the Kethubim (*Hebrew*), or the Hagiographa (*Greek*), or the Writings.

One feature of the Jewish persecution under Antiochus Epiphanes was the forbidding of Jews to possess or use their Sacred Scriptures, and the destruction of such copies of those Scriptures as the inquisitors could find.[11] This had the effect of intensifying the regard which the Jews had for their Scriptures and they treasured them the more devoutly. Undoubtedly this helped to precipitate their feeling that the books which make up the Hagiographa were also sacred, as well as Torah and Prophets, although they never esteemed any other part of the Scriptures to be as holy as the Torah. Excepting Daniel, no book which originated after the year 200 B.C. found a place in the canon. This explains why so admirable a book as Sira (Ecclesiasticus)[12] is not in the Old Testament. Apparently Daniel was immediately popular and successful in stirring the Jews to faith

---

[7] On the Day of Yahweh, vid. supra, pp. 303, 317, 327, 336.
[8] Zech. 14:9. [9] Zech. 14:16–21. [10] Cf. supra, pp. 397 f.
[11] Cf. supra, p. 416; 1 Macc. 1:56 f. [12] Vid. infra, p. 434 f.

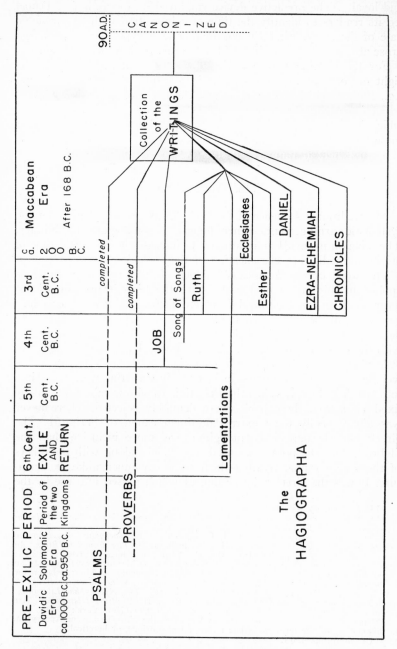

THE CANON OF THE HAGIOGRAPHA

and loyalty. The predictive device employed by the author of Daniel led its readers to identify the time of composition with the dramatic date of the story. First Enoch, another apocalyptical writing which arose at about the same time, did not secure a place in the canon.[13]

For the ensuing two centuries doubt was entertained about the right of some of the books to be in a canon of Sacred Scripture, e.g., Esther, which does not contain the name of God; Ecclesiastes, which is so patently skeptical and cynical; and the Song of Songs, which is so undisguisedly erotic. The question of the sacredness of these books and of the limits of the sacred canon was finally settled at a synod held at Jamnia, Palestine, A.D. *circa* 90.[14]

The Apocrypha

The traditional sequence of the books in the Apocrypha exhibits no systematic arrangement, either logical, chronological, or literary. The table on page 431 is an attempt to indicate the place and time of origin and a literary classification of the books.[15]

The word *apocrypha* means "hidden" or "stored away," and as applied to this group of Jewish books the term is prevailingly interpreted to mean "withheld from circulation because of secondary value." [16] All these books came into being after 200 B.C. which, as we have seen, was the limit of time for books of the Palestinian canon, with the exception of Daniel.[17] These apocryphal books circulated in Palestine and in the Diaspora (principally Alexandria, Egypt) as well. Those which originated in Hebrew in Palestine were translated into Greek in Egypt. When the Palestinian Hebrew canon was finally fixed (A.D. 90), these books were definitely rejected. There never was any formally fixed extra-Palestinian canon of Scripture. The Greek Old Testament (Septuagint) was more inclusive than the Hebrew. The Diaspora Jews used these books along with the others of the Hagiographa, treating them all pretty much alike as Scripture. It was the Greek Old Testament which passed into use by the

---

13 *Vid. infra*, pp. 445–452.
14 *Vid. infra*, pp. 556, 582; cf. R. H. Pfeiffer, *Introduction to the Old Testament* (New York: 1941), pp. 61–65.
15 The best translation is Edgar J. Goodspeed's *The Apocrypha, An American Translation* (Chicago: 1938), which is also included in *The Complete Bible, An American Translation*, published by the University of Chicago Press (Chicago: 1939). Dr. Goodspeed's *The Story of the Apocrypha* (Chicago: 1939) presents an introduction to each of the books and is an excellent companion to his translation for the beginner to use. Cf. also Wm. O. E. Oesterley, *An Introduction to the Books of the Apocrypha* (New York: 1935); Chas. C. Torrey, *The Apocryphal Literature, A Brief Introduction* (New Haven: 1945); Robt. H. Pfeiffer, *History of New Testament Times, With an Introduction to the Apocrypha* (New York: 1949).
16 There is a group of Christian books known as the New Testament Apocrypha. In this connection the term *apocrypha* means false, spurious, or heretical.
17 Cf. *supra*, pp. 426 f.

THE OLD TESTAMENT APOCRYPHA

Books of History

(13th)	First Maccabees,	Palestine,	*ca.* 100 B.C.
(14th)	Second Maccabees,	Alexandria,	*ca.* 75–63 B.C.

Books of Religious Fiction

(1st)	1 Esdras,	Alexandria,	*ca.* 150 B.C.
(3rd)	Tobit,	Alexandria,	*ca.* 200 B.C.
(4th)	Judith,	Palestine,	*ca.* 150 B.C.
(5th)	The Rest of Esther,	Alexandria,	*ca.* 100 B.C.
(8th)	Baruch,	Alexandria,	*ca.* 150–50 B.C.
	Additions to Daniel:		
	(10th) The Story of Susanna,	Alexandria,	*ca.* 100–50 B.C.
	(9th) The Song of the Three Holy Children,	Alexandria,	*ca.* 150–50 B.C.
	(11th) Bel and the Dragon,	Alexandria,	*ca.* 100 B.C.
(12th)	The Prayer of Manasses,	Alexandria,	*ca.* 150–50 B.C.

Books of Wisdom

(7th)	Ecclesiasticus (Sira),	Palestine,	*ca.* 190–170 B.C.
(6th)	Wisdom of Solomon,	Alexandria,	*ca.* 50 B.C.–A.D. 40

Apocalyptic

(2nd)	Second Esdras (Fourth Ezra),	Palestine,	A.D. 81–96

Christians as their Bible. This larger Old Testament was translated from Greek into Latin and has ever since continued as the Old Testament of the Roman Catholic Church.[18] From the time of the Reformation the Protestant Church has rejected and disregarded these books on the ground that the canon of Palestinian Judaism should be accepted as Holy Scripture rather than the Septuagint. Modern scholarship views these books not from a dogmatic or ecclesiastical standpoint but from a literary standpoint, and evaluates them according to their intrinsic worth. Indeed, the dogmatic Protestant attitude resulted in the obscuring of these books through neglect. Critical historical study has brought them to light again. The authors of these apocryphal books were Jews of scribal training or its equivalent, and were devoted to the faithful, loyal Judaism, mainly Pharisaism.

The Books of History. We have already had occasion to characterize First and Second Maccabees [19] and it is not necessary to give them further attention now.

[18] The Roman Catholic Church regards all books of the Apocrypha as canonical [they are styled "deuterocanonical"] excepting 1 and 2 Esdras and the Prayer of Manasses, which are styled "apocryphal."
[19] *Supra*, p. 414.

The Books of Religious Fiction. 1. *First Esdras.* This book is a repetition of the story of the rebuilding of the Jerusalem temple in the Persian period, based upon 2 Chronicles, Ezra, and Nehemiah.[20] There is only one original section in the book, an interesting piece of didactic romance, a discussion by three pages at the royal Persian court as to which is the strongest, wine, the king, women, or truth (*3:1–5:6).

2. *Tobit.* This book is named for the hero of the story who is depicted as a very pious Jew of Galilee, taken captive by the Assyrians, presumably in 720 B.C.,[21] to Nineveh, where he became an officer of the king (1:1–14). He made a visit to Media where he left a large sum of money in trust with one Gabael. He was benevolent toward his fellow Jews, particularly in burying the dead, for which he was ill-treated by the Assyrians. He was deposed from his position and his life was threatened. Through the intercession of a nephew, who was a high official under Esarhaddon, Tobit was permitted to go home to Nineveh. Through an accident he lost his sight, but was supported by his wife Anna, who spun material for merchants (1:15–3:6). In Ecbatana of Media lived an unhappy young widow named Sarah, daughter of Raguel, each of whose seven husbands had been killed on the wedding night by the demon Asmodaeus (3:7–17).

Apprehending that he would soon die, Tobit disclosed to his son Tobias the fact of his money in Media, and sent Tobias after the money, accompanied by a travel companion who gave his name as Azarias but who was in reality the angel Raphael, although neither Tobit nor Tobias knew that (4:1–6:17). On the way, Raphael proposed to Tobias that he should marry Sarah and dispose of the demon by making a smudge of the heart and liver of a great fish which Tobias caught in the Tigris River. When they reached Ecbatana they stayed with Raguel, and Tobias did marry Sarah and did dispose of the demon. Raphael continued the journey alone to get the money and returned to Tobias at Ecbatana (7 ff.). After celebrating the wedding feast, Tobias, with his bride, and the angel returned to Tobit at Nineveh. As Tobit greeted his son, Tobias squirted the gall from the same fish he caught in the Tigris into his father's eyes, which caused the white films to drop away so that he could see again. The angel Raphael made known his identity and ascended from their presence (10 ff.). The story closes with a prayer, which is a beautiful poem (13), and a prediction by Tobit of the overthrow of Nineveh (14).

[20] Chapter 1 = 2 Chr. 35 f.; 2:1–9:36 (excepting 3:1–5:6) = the book of Ezra; 3:37–55 = Neh. 7:73–8:13.
[21] *Vid. supra,* pp. 252, 253.

The purpose of this story was to inculcate religious faith and ethics of the sincerely devout type of Judaism. Didactic passages in which such teaching is most clearly set forth are 4:3–15; 12:6–21. The most remarkable verse of the book is 4:15, "What thou thyself hatest, do to no man." This is the earliest occurrence of the golden rule in all extant Jewish literature and the briefest form in which it has ever been stated, exactly four words in the Greek.

3. *Judith.* The word *Judith* means "Jewess" and is the name of the heroine of the story. The story is given a time setting in the reign of Nebuchadrezzar but the author is guilty of much historical confusion and once forgets himself and indicates that he is thinking of a situation in the time of the Persians,[22] presumably the time of Artaxerxes Ochus, who campaigned against Syria and Egypt, *circa* 350 B.C. The story is pure fiction. It represents ardent, patriotic Judaism and was written to stimulate patriotism and devotion. The story idealizes strict observance of the law and religious worship. Many prayers are interspersed through the story. The story may have been produced in the second century for use in the celebration of Nicanor's Day.[23]

The story represents Nebuchadrezzar as having waged a successful campaign against Media (chap. 1). He was angered because the countries in the west (Syria and Palestine) did not send armies to assist him. Therefore he sent a punitive expedition against them, under the generalship of Holofernes (2–6). The city of Bethulia,[24] residence of Judith, was besieged (7) and in a desperate condition because of lack of water and food. Judith, an attractive young widow, undertook to relieve the situation. Accompanied by her maid, she made her way to the camp of Holofernes, whom she deceived into supposing that the Jews of Bethulia were on the point of surrender (8–11). Holofernes made a great feast in honor of Judith and drank himself drunk (12). In the night Judith entered his tent, and as he lay in a drunken stupor she took his scimitar and cut off his head, which she and the maid took with them in the night to Bethulia (13). Next morning the Jews of Bethulia made a sortie against their enemies who, upon discovering the murder of Holofernes, were thrown into confusion and greatly despoiled by the Jews (14 f.). The story ends with a poem in praise of Judith (16).

4. *Additions to Esther and Daniel.* The so-called "Rest of the Chapters of the Book of Esther" are five sections which the Greek version adds to the book.[25] The purpose of these additions was not

---

[22] Jud. 16:10.   [23] *Vid. supra,* p. 418.
[24] A fictitious name. Some scholars think it means Shechem.
[25] One section precedes 1:1; the others are inserted after 3:13; 4:17; 8:13; 10:3.

only to amplify the story as told in the Hebrew but also to supply a religious element lacking in the book. This latter is particularly to be observed in the prayers which are put in the mouth of Mordecai and Esther in 13:8–14:19.

The additions to Daniel consist of three pieces. The *History of Susanna*, which is prefixed to the Book of Daniel, portrays Daniel as shrewdly and boldly showing up two perjurers who had falsely accused a virtuous woman of immorality. *The Song of the Three Holy Children* (inserted at Dan. 3:23) is an extended prayer and psalm of praise put in the mouths of the three young Jews when they were in the fiery furnace. *Bel and the Dragon,* which is added at the end of Daniel, represents Daniel as refusing to worship an image of the god Bel and as showing up the chicanery of the priests of Bel. Daniel similarly refused to worship a great dragon, and slew it, for which he was cast into the lions' den. The purpose of these additions obviously was to enlarge the story.

5. *The Book of Baruch (First Baruch).* This book purports to have been written in Babylon early in the exile by Baruch, friend and secretary of the prophet Jeremiah.[26] It contains a long confession of the sins which brought about the captivity, and a prayer for restoration (1:1–3:8). There is a passage in praise of wisdom (3:9–4:4) and an exhortation designed to comfort and encourage the exiles (4:5–5:9). Chapter 6 is a letter ascribed to the prophet Jeremiah, alleged to have been written to the captives in Babylon; it is a lengthy denunciation and ridiculing of the idols of Babylon. Such letters by Baruch and Jeremiah are, of course, pious fiction, a framework in which to express religious teaching.

6. *The Prayer of Manasses.* 2 Chr. 33:10–13 says that King Manasseh of Judah, for some offense against the Assyrian king, was taken a prisoner to Babylon but was later released.[27] Vs. 12 says that "when he was in distress, he besought Yahweh his God, and humbled himself greatly before the God of his fathers." This statement prompted someone to compose a prayer of deep repentance such as Manasseh might suitably have offered. Such a pious attitude, however, does not fit the arch idolater of Hebrew history who all but exterminated the religion of Yahweh from Judah.[28]

The Books of Wisdom. 1. *Sira (Ecclesiasticus).* Ecclesiasticus is exceptional among the wisdom books in that it definitely names its author, Jesus Ben-Sirach.[29] The prologue informs us that the book was originally written in Hebrew and that it was translated into Greek by the author's grandson. The prologue states that this grandson

---

[26] *Vid. supra*, pp. 304 f., 336 f.   [27] *Vid. supra*, p. 260.
[28] *Vid. supra*, pp. 331 f.   [29] Prologue; also 50:27.

came to Egypt "in the eight and thirtieth year of Euergetes the king," which was 132 B.C.[30] This definite dating would place the floruit of Jesus Ben-Sirach between 190 and 170 B.C., which is the date generally agreed upon for the composition of this book.

The proper Hebrew name for the book is *Sira* and it will be so designated here. When Sira was rendered into Greek, the Greek letter *chi* was affixed to indicate that it was an indeclinable noun, which accounts for the form of the name Sirach. The term "Ecclesiasticus" is generally understood to be the Latin adjective meaning "churchly," a term used to distinguish this book from the strictly canonical books. Some scholars maintain that this interpretation of the word does not apply to so early a period and they explain it as a Latinizing of the word "Ecclesiastes," which very term is the Greek name of an Old Testament book. The term Ecclesiastes, as we have seen,[31] means "gatherer" or "collector." Converting the term into an adjective would merely characterize Sira as that sort of book, and, as a matter of fact, Ben-Sira does characterize himself "as one that gathereth grapes," a gleaner of wisdom.[32]

Sira is one of the most delightful of the wisdom books produced by the Jews.[33] Sir. *1:1–20 and *24:1–22 are especially choice passages in praise of wisdom and should be compared with Prov. *8:22–31, for both authors present a similar view of wisdom as eternal.[34] Sir. *38:24–39:11 describes the work of a Jewish scribe (and the wisdom writers were scribes) and contrasts the importance of the scribe's career with that of the craftsman. Excellent passages to read for the flavor of Sira's thought and style are *6:5–17, on "Friendship"; *6:18–37, on "The Pursuit of Wisdom"; *15:11–20, on "Free Will"; *19:4–17, "Against Gossip"; *38:1–15, on "Physicians"; *42:15–43:33, on "The Works of the Lord"; *44:1–15, in "Praise of Famous Men." [35]

2. *The Wisdom of Solomon.* This book of wisdom is a product of Alexandrian Judaism. It is a pseudepigraphic work, i.e., a writing put out in the name of an ancient worthy. Pseudepigraphy was a literary form in vogue in this age, as we have already seen in Daniel and First Baruch and shall see further in the next section. In the

---

[30] There were two kings of Egypt to whom were given the honorific title of *Euergetes* (Benefactor), Ptolemy III, 246–221 B.C., and Ptolemy VII, 145–116 B.C. The latter also reigned as joint king with Ptolemy VI from 170 to 145 B.C. Ptolemy VII was, therefore, the only Euergetes to whom a thirty-eighth year could apply.
[31] *Supra*, pp. 405 f.   [32] Sir. 33:16 ff.
[33] On the Jewish wisdom books, *vid. supra*, pp. 402–406.
[34] *Vid. infra*, p. 436.
[35] On Ecclesiasticus, cf. W. O. E. Oesterley, *An Introduction to the Books of the Apocrypha* (New York: 1935), pp. 222–255; pp. 229–232 give a valuable table of the contents of Sira alphabetically arranged. The arrangement of the text of Ecclesiasticus in Moulton's *Modern Reader's Bible* is especially fine. Cf. also E. J. Goodspeed, *The Story of the Apocrypha* (Chicago: 1939), pp. 20–30.

wisdom literature Solomon's name was traditional, for the reason that the impulse to this type of literature first arose in Judah during his reign. He was the patron saint of wisdom, just as Moses was of law and David of psalmody. Hence the wisdom books, such as Proverbs, Ecclesiastes, and notably this one, were attached to his name. The author of the book was a Jew of Alexandria, probably about the middle of the first century B.C., who was truly and sincerely Jewish but who was also acquainted with Greek philosophical thought. This book, therefore, represents in a way the fusion of Jewish and Greek thought which went on among the Dispersion Jews in the Hellenistic age.

1:1-11 is an introductory section on the theme, "Love Righteousness." 1:12-6:11 is a discourse on immortality. This passage appears to be a direct answer to the cynicism and skepticism of Ecclesiastes and a refutation of the Epicurean attitude toward life. *3:1-9 and *4:1 f. are the choicest parts of the passage and affirm a clear faith in immortality.

6:12-11:1 is a panegyric on wisdom, well worth careful reading. 7:17-22 indicates that wisdom was thought to include reflection upon and analysis of external nature, i.e., what to us is physical science. 7:22 and 8:5 f. portray wisdom as the creator. In 7:23 ff. wisdom is regarded as a spiritual essence immanent in all things. Wisdom is an emanation from God (7:26), omnipotent (7:27), and the unifying principle in the world (8:1). Objective wisdom is equivalent to providence, and 10:1-11:1 points out the doings of wisdom on behalf of the ancient worthies of Israel.

11:2-19:22 is a glorification of Israel. *11:26 and *15:1 ff. express a beautiful idea of God and show the profound piety of the author. Chapters 13 ff. are a denunciation of idols, the fullest and most effective criticism of idols in all Jewish literature. This passage was apposite only to the Dispersion Jews. The Jews of Palestine had, after the exile, completely rid themselves of idolatry. But outside of Palestine, Jews were constantly meeting with the use of idols among the gentiles. Jews themselves were called atheists by gentiles because they had no visible symbols to worship. The author of this book expected, of course, that his book would be read by gentiles as well as Jews, and undoubtedly he hoped by this condemnation of idols to influence gentiles.

The Apocalypse of Second Esdras (Fourth Ezra). This book originated toward the end of the first century after Christ, and consideration of it is best deferred until we study the other important apocalyptical writings which arose in the centuries preceding it.[36]

[36] *Infra,* pp. 442-456.

The Pseudepigrapha

Besides the canonical and apocryphal Old Testament books, certain other Jewish literature of the New Testament period has survived. These books are commonly called the *Pseudepigrapha,* which term literally means "writings falsely assigned to some ancient worthy as author."[37] We shall not here name or discuss all these books. The standard treatise on the subject is R. H. Charles, *The Apocrypha and Pseudepigrapha of the Old Testament,* Vol. II (Oxford University Press: 1913). In general they fall into the same types as the classification we used in discussing the Apocrypha, and some of the more important of these pseudepigraphical books deserve attention.

Books of Religious Fiction. 1. *The Book of Jubilees.* This book, which originated in Palestine in the second century B.C. (135–105), has been preserved, not in the original Hebrew, but in Ethiopic. The author is unnamed, but he was manifestly a Pharisaic legalist. The book is a reworking of the story of Genesis, from the creation to the giving of the law on Sinai, and the opening chapter represents God as talking to Moses and giving him the material of this book. The history of Genesis is divided into Jubilee periods of seven times seven years each, plus the fiftieth, or Jubilee year.[38] This is what gives its name to the book.

Most of the book is dull reading. Certain elements in it are noteworthy. Its point of view is that the Torah, as given to Moses on Mount Sinai, represents the full revelation of God to mankind. Not only its ethical and social laws but its ritual requirements as well are part of a changeless and perfect order. It is therefore impossible to improve upon the Torah. There is strong emphasis upon observance of the Sabbath (2:25–33; 50:6–13), which reveals an important trend in Jewish thought and practice quite basic to an understanding of the situation in the lifetime of Jesus of Nazareth who came into conflict with the constituted religious authorities over this subject. A very significant feature of the book is the angelology and demonology, which had crept into Jewish thinking in the Persian period, as we have previously observed.[39] For example, a prince of angels called Mastema appeared before God (exactly as did the Satan in the Book of Job)[40] and secured permission to tempt Abraham to offer Isaac as a burnt sacrifice (17:16). Again, the malicious opposition of this same Mastema was the main cause of Moses's encountering so much difficulty in getting the Hebrews out of Egypt (48). This emphasis upon the activity of evil angels adroitly hints that the

---

[37] *Vid. supra,* pp. 435 f.
[39] *Supra,* pp. 393 f.

[38] *Vid. supra,* p. 381.
[40] Job 1:6; 2:1.

current trend toward Hellenism with its foreign innovations is the work of demons.

The book does not lend itself readily to quotation but it does contain one golden gem.

And the Lord saith unto Moses, I know their contrariness and their thoughts and their stiffneckedness, and they will not be obedient till they confess their own sin and the sin of their fathers. And after this they will turn to me in all uprightness and with all their heart and with all their soul, . . . and I will create in them a holy spirit, and I will cleanse them so that they will not turn away from me from that day unto eternity. And their souls will cleave to me and to all my commandments, and they will fulfil my commandments, and I will be their Father and they shall be my children. And they all shall be called children of the living God, and every angel and every spirit shall know, yea, they shall know that these are my children, and that I am their Father in uprightness and righteousness, and that I love them.[41]

2. *The Letter of Aristeas.* This piece of didactic romance, which originated in Alexandria, Egypt, 130–70 B.C., takes its name from a character in the narrative who is represented as a Greek officer at the court of Ptolemy Philadelphus in Egypt (285–247 B.C.). Aristeas writes to his brother Philocrates to explain the circumstances of the translation of the Pentateuch into the Greek language.[42] Demetrius, the king's librarian, proposed that the great library at Alexandria should contain a copy of the Jewish Law, which ought to be translated into Greek for the purpose.[43] Aristeas suggested that such a proposal would not be fitting until the Jewish captive slaves should be liberated, which the king did.[44] The proposal for a translation was thereupon adopted by the king and a letter was dispatched to Eleazar, the high priest in Jerusalem, making the request.[45] The high priest replied favorably.[46] Aristeas gives the names of the translators [47] and describes at length the elaborate gifts which the king had sent to Jerusalem along with his letter.[48] For the benefit of his brother Philocrates, Aristeas gives a description of Jerusalem and Palestine.[49] The translators, six from each of the twelve tribes, were dispatched with due instructions by Eleazar,[50] who makes an elaborate speech defending the Jewish Law.[51] The translators were royally welcomed at Alexandria,[52] and were elaborately banqueted by the king daily for a week. At each banquet the king put certain questions to these Jews, one to each man, which

[41] Jub. 1 :22–25 ; cf. Charles, *op. cit.*, p. 12.
[42] §§ 1–8. [43] §§ 9 ff. [44] §§ 12–27.
[45] §§ 28–40. [46] §§ 41–46. [47] §§ 47–50.
[48] §§ 51–82. [49] §§ 83–120. [50] §§ 121–127.
[51] §§ 128–171. [52] §§ 172–186.

questions were answered with wisdom and piety.[53] This setting furnished the author an excellent opportunity to introduce wisdom teachings, which are mainly Greek ethics mingled with Jewish piety. At the conclusion of the banqueting the Jews were escorted to the island of Pharos where they worked daily in quietness and seclusion for seventy-two days, when the work of translation was completed.[54]

The author of course intended the reader to accept the story at its face value as history but the account is pure fiction. The Septuagint translations may indeed have been begun in the reign of Ptolemy Philadelphus, but it was not done at the request of the king's librarian, nor was it done by Palestinian Jews, nor was the translation primarily designed for gentile readers. It was done by Greek speaking Jews of Alexandria for the benefit of their fellow Jews of the Diaspora that they might preserve the faith of the fathers. The author of the letter simply wove into this piece of fiction a story which apparently was current in the second century B.C.

The most pleasing part of the letter is the account of the table talk of the translators, especially as it discloses the type of ethico-religious thought which was current among the Alexandrian Jews. Some extracts will give the flavor of this thought. The most notable of all is the golden rule.

> What is the teaching of wisdom? As you wish that no evil should befall you, but to be a partaker of all good things, so you should act on the same principle towards your subjects and offenders, and you should mildly admonish the noble and good. For God draws all men to himself by his benignity.[55]
>
> What is the highest good in life? To know that God is Lord of the universe, and that in our finest achievements it is not we who attain success but God who by his power brings all things to fulfilment and leads us to the goal.[56]
>
> What is the true mark of piety? To perceive that God constantly works in the universe and knows all things, and no man who acts unjustly and works wickedness can escape his notice. As God is the benefactor of the whole world, so you, too, must imitate him and be void of offence.[57]
>
> To the king's question as to how he could despise his enemies, the answer was: "If you show kindness to all men and win their friendship, you need fear no one. To be popular with all men is the best of good gifts to receive from God." [58]
>
> To whom ought a man to show liberality? All men acknowledge that we ought to show liberality to those who are well disposed towards us, but I think that we ought to show the same keen spirit of generosity to those who are opposed to us that by

[53] §§ 187–300.   [54] §§ 301–322.   [55] § 207.
[56] § 195.   [57] § 210.   [58] § 225.

this means we may win them over to the right and to what is advantageous to ourselves.[59]

What is the fruit of wisdom? That a man should be conscious in himself that he has wrought no evil and that he should live his life in the truth.[60]

To whom ought men to entrust themselves? To those who serve you from good will and not from fear or self-interest, thinking only of their own gain. For the one is the sign of love, the other the mark of ill will and timeserving. For the man who is always watching for his own gain is a traitor at heart.[61]

3. *The Sibylline Oracles*. The most curious of all Jewish writings of the New Testament period is the *Sibylline Oracles*. Greek and Roman writers have familiarized us with the widespread belief in the sibyls, of which there were several. The word *sibyl* means "the counsel of God," and a sibyl was a woman in a cave who uttered prophetic words by divine inspiration. Such oracles were regarded as of great value, to be studied and carried out. The original sibyl was said to have lived in Erythrae of Asia Minor, on a section of the coast near the site of present-day Izmir. She was greatly revered and her utterances were carefully treasured over an extended portion of the Mediterranean world. By the third century B.C. these oracles appear to have been familiar to the Jews, at least to those Jews living in the more Hellenized parts of Egypt. *Circa* 150 B.C. one such Jew decided to capitalize these beliefs in a way to advance the cause of Judaism among non-Jews. So he published a new volume of Sibylline Oracles, cleverly purporting to be the authentic utterances of this most ancient sibyl of Erythrae. By interweaving certain fragmentary oracles accepted as authentic sayings of this sibyl with much more that emanated from his own fertile mind, he produced a document which represented the Greek sibyl as having predicted the rise of the Jews and the Jewish religion to world primacy. A sample of this ingenious piece of writing follows.

Now all were of one tongue, and they desired to ascend into the starry heaven. But straightway the Eternal laid great stress upon the blasts: then did the winds dash down the great tower from on high, and incited mortal man to mutual strife. Therefore men named the city Babylon. . . .

Now Cronos, Titan, and Iapetus were kings, the goodliest children of Gaia and Ouranos, whom men called Earth and Heaven. . . . And Cronos and Titan fought against each other; but Rhea and Gaia and garland-loving Aphrodite and Demeter and Hestia and fair-tressed Dione brought them to friendship. . . . Finally all the families of the Titans and of Cronos died.

[59] § 227.   [60] § 260.
[61] § 270. On Aristeas, cf. Charles, *op. cit.*, pp. 83–122.

Then in the circling course of time the Egyptian empire arose, then that of the Persians, of the Medes and Ethiopians and of Assyrian Babylon, then that of the Macedonians, again that of Egypt, and then that of Rome.

Then the message of the Great God fluttered in my breast, and bade me prophesy. . . .

First of all the house of Solomon shall hold sway, and the Phoenician invaders of Asia and of the islands as well, and the race of the Pamphylians, Persians, and Phrygians, and also of the Carians and Mysians and Lydians rich in gold. . . . And the terrible Phrygians shall perish; . . . after which evil shall come to the Persians and Assyrians, to all Egypt, to Lydia and the Ethiopians, and the Carians and Pamphylians. . . .

There is a city in Ur of the Chaldees from which comes a race of most righteous men. . . . These diligently practise justice and virtue. . . . They have just measures in country and city. . . . Neighbor does not remove his neighbor's landmarks, nor does a man of much wealth oppress his poorer brother. No one afflicts widows, but rather assists them, ever ready to supply them with corn and wine and oil. Always the wealthy man among the people sends a part of his harvest to those who have nothing. . . . To them alone does the fruitful field yield its fruit, even to a hundredfold.

But they too shall suffer evil, and shall not escape pestilence. . . . And then the God of Heaven shall send a king and shall judge each man with blood and flame of fire. There is a royal tribe whose family shall never stumble; and this tribe shall in the circuit of times have dominion and shall begin to raise up a new shrine of God. . . . Then the temple shall be again as it was before. . . .

O Hellas, who has put error in thine heart, that thou shouldst forsake the face of the Mighty God? Reverence the name of the Father of all and forget him not. . . . Cease thine arrogance. Supplicate the great heart of the Eternal. . . . And serve the Mighty God, that thou mayest have a share in these gifts.

For when the fated day shall arrive, and there shall come upon mortals the judgment of the Eternal God, . . . then Earth, the universal mother, shall give to mortals her best fruit in countless stores of corn, wine, and oil. Yea, from heaven shall come a sweet draught of luscious honey, . . . and the cities shall be full of good things, and the fields rich. Neither shall there be any sword or battle din; nor shall earth be convulsed any more with deep-drawn groans. . . . But a great peace shall be throughout all the earth, with king friendly to king, and a common law for all men. . . . For He above is God, and there is none else.

Rejoice, O virgin, and exult; for to thee the Creator of heaven and earth has given everlasting joy, and in thee shall he dwell, and thou shalt have eternal light. . . .

With this the oracle reaches its climax. To make such sentiments from the lips of a Greek prophetess sound plausible, the author makes the sibyl conclude:

> Mortals throughout Greece will doubtless call me a foreigner, the born of Erythrae, and shameless. Others will call me born of Circe, sibyl, a crazy impostor. But when all these things come to pass, then never again shall man call me crazy, but the prophetess of the Mighty God.[62]

We shall hesitate to pass judgment on the author or authors of these fraudulent documents if we reflect that such Jews were simply following the example set by the Greek and Roman Sibylline writers, for the latter had for generations been freely adjusting these old prophecies to meet the needs of their times. In fact it is a matter of record that the Roman government had for some time kept a book of Sibylline Oracles with which they practiced this very deception.

Precisely how influential the Jewish Sibyllines proved in making proselytes to Judaism cannot be said, but there are indications of considerable influence. And although they were out and out falsifications of so transparent a character that many must have been perfectly aware of the fact, it seems likely that their serious-minded author may have reasoned that they were predictions the sibyl would have made had she been able to read the future with the clarity she was popularly believed to possess. Viewed from this angle, the Jewish Sibyllines were not so unlike the literary device of putting in the mouths of historic characters speeches which they quite properly might have made.[63]

Books of Apocalyptic. We have already discussed the beginnings of apocalyptical literature among the Jews [64] and we have observed that Daniel was the first noteworthy book of this type.[65] Daniel was immediately popular, and from the time of its appearance to the end of the first century after Christ this type of literature enjoyed a considerable vogue among the Jews.

The Old Testament prophetic books contain an apocalyptical element. The prophets portrayed a glorious future which would see

---

[62] Sib. 3:100–818, *passim.* On the Sibyllines, cf. Charles, *op. cit.,* pp. 368–406.

[63] *Circa* 100 b.c. some Alexandrian Jew wrote a piece of fiction about an alleged persecution of the Jews of Palestine by Ptolemy IV Philopator after his success at the battle of Raphia in 217 b.c. The king himself was miraculously repulsed when he profanely tried to enter the holy temple in Jerusalem. Enraged, he ordered all Jews to be herded in the hippodrome and set upon by drunken elephants. This was miraculously prevented, which so affected the king that he turned patron of the Jews. It is purely fictitious, told in a profuse, artificial, and thoroughly uninteresting style. From being associated with 1 and 2 Maccabees this book got its title, *Third Maccabees.*

[64] *Vid. supra,* pp. 369 f.   [65] *Vid. supra,* pp. 426–429.

the sifting of Israel, all present evils eradicated, and the interests and activities of the present world purified and heightened. They were not mere visionaries but they related the future organically and ethically to the present. The predictive aspect of prophecy was carried forward by apocalyptic. In fact it was the reediting of unfulfilled prophecy which gave rise to apocalyptic. Ezekiel was one of the spiritual founders of apocalyptic because of his revamping of the unfulfilled predictions of Jeremiah[66] and Zephaniah[67] regarding the invasion of Judah from the north by a mighty foe into his speculative invasion of Palestine by Gog from the land of Magog.[68]

The word *apocalypse* is a Greek term which means "revelation." There are three senses in which the term apocalyptic is used. It designates a literary type. It designates the corpus of writings of that type. It designates the world view, or set of doctrinal ideas, embodied in such literature.

The following features characterize apocalyptic as a literary type. (a) It employs cryptic language. Animals, beasts, books, bowls, horns, images, seals, smiths, trees, weeks, ancient of days, abomination of desolation, scarlet woman are some of the terms employed. The object of this is to obscure the true meaning to enemies and thus to avoid trouble. But while such symbolical terms obscured the meaning to enemies, they were very revealing to the Jews themselves who understood what such terms were intended to imply. Yet if pressed by inquisitors for an explanation, they could pretend a quite innocent mystification. It was a protective device. (b) Apocalyptic is pseudepigraphic; i.e., it employs the device of assigning authorship to some ancient worthy in the far distant past. This again was a protective device, for it disclaimed responsibility on the part of the living author, who would have paid with his life had the inquisitors succeeded in identifying him. Pseudepigraphy was also a device for commending apocalyptical ideas to the Jews themselves. After the canonization of the Torah in 400 B.C., the belief was held that in the Torah God had given the final and complete revelation of his will; nevermore would he speak through a living prophet. Therefore anyone who published any prophetic literature would *ipso facto* be deemed an impostor. Pseudepigraphy circumvented this Jewish prejudice by assigning authorship to a well-known person who lived before 400 B.C., such as Enoch, Daniel, Baruch, and Ezra. (c) Apocalyptic employed the device of prediction for conveying its message. The message was not only assigned to an historical person of renown but was given a time setting in his era. It was represented as a foretelling at that remote time of what would come to pass in the future,

[66] Jer. 4–6.   [67] Zeph. 1:7.
[68] Ezk. 38:1–39:16.

and the readers would be well aware that the time of its fulfillment was their very own day. Inquisitors might wonder why the Jews were devoted to such old stuff, and thereby they were thrown off the track. (d) Apocalyptic employed dreams, visions, and angelic messengers as literary devices for disclosing the revelation which the apocalyptist desired to disclose to his age. (e) Apocalyptic was a literature called forth by persecution. Its object was to encourage the faithful to endure their trials and remain steadfastly loyal to their Jewish faith. It proclaimed the doom of their enemies (in concealed terms, of course) and the coming triumph of the Jewish people. This functioned as an incentive to loyalty and courage and faith.

As a corpus of literature, apocalyptic comprises the following. (a) The canonical Old Testament Book of Daniel.[69] (b) The apocryphal Old Testament Book of 2 Esdras, or 4 Ezra.[70] (c) Such pseudepigraphical books as 1 and 2 Enoch and 2 Baruch which are now to be discussed. There are other books not treated here, for it is not intended to make this presentation exhaustive but only illustrative. (d) The canonical New Testament Book of Revelation is the greatest of all apocalypses. The treatment of it belongs with New Testament literature.[71]

As a world view, apocalyptic embraces the past, the present, and the future in its scope. As a doctrine of the past it can be called a philosophy of history. It asks what the past reveals. It finds that certain crises of the distant past reveal God's catastrophic intervention in history to destroy evil and establish righteousness through a surviving remnant. It discerns a plan of God running through history. Thus Daniel deals with the present or the immediate past;[72] 1 Enoch deals with all the past preceding the life of Enoch;[73] 2 Baruch deals with the leading crises in the world's history down to Baruch's time;[74] the Sibylline Oracles take account of the course of history from the time of the Flood.[75] The cosmic purpose and plan of God, especially as it concerns the destiny of man and the world, is brought under survey in apocalyptic.

As a doctrine of the present (meaning, of course, the age when any such book was written) apocalyptic presents an ethical dualism. The present reveals good and evil in conflict, with evil growing from more to more, but there is a righteous remnant in the making. Indeed, apocalyptical literature urges people to righteousness and thereby seeks to create a righteous remnant to be available for God's use in the future.

[69] *Vid. supra,* pp. 426–429.
[71] *Vid. infra,* pp. 591 f.
[73] 1 En. 85 f.
[75] Sib. 3 :819–828.

[70] *Vid. infra,* pp. 455 f.
[72] Dan. 2 :31 f., 37 f.; 4 :7–12; 7 f.
[74] 2 Bar. 53, 56–69 ; *vid. infra,* pp. 454 f.

That phase of apocalyptic which deals with the future is technically termed *eschatology,* which literally means "the doctrine of last things," i.e., the future consummation. Apocalyptic and eschatology are not synonymous terms, though often erroneously so used. Apocalyptic is the more inclusive term. Eschatology is only one phase of apocalyptic. It sets forth what the future will reveal, namely, the climax of evil and its overthrow by God's catastrophic irruption again into history to renew the earth and establish righteousness forever.

There was variety and freedom in Jewish eschatological thinking. With some writers it found expression in highly figurative and fanciful forms. Eschatological ideas were not systematized or dogmatized. There were, however, certain conventional items common to the various eschatological programs, viz., the last evils; the coming of the messiah; the overthrow of evil, including the renewing (purification) of the earth; the resurrection; the judgment; the eternal awards of punishment for the wicked and eternal life for the righteous.

1. *First Enoch.* This book, sometimes simply called the Book of Enoch, was originally written in Hebrew in Palestine, afterward translated into Greek in Egypt, and from Greek was translated into Ethiopic, in which language only the text has survived. It is the work of several authors at different times and is composed of five principal fragments arranged in no logical order whatever. These component parts and the times of their origin are: chapters 1–36 (before 170 B.C.); chapters 37–71 (94–64 B.C.); chapters 72–82 (*circa* 110 B.C.); chapters 83–90 (166–161 B.C.); chapters 91–104 (104–95 B.C.).[76] This literature is chiefly eschatology, but certain parts of it, notably 91–104, contain splendid wisdom teachings. It is pseudepigraphic, put out in the name of the ancient worthy Enoch, who "walked with God"[77] and therefore had special opportunity to acquire supernatural knowledge. He "saw the vision of the Holy One in the heavens, which the angels showed me, and from them I heard everything, and from them I understood as I saw, but not for this generation, but for a remote one which is for to come."[78] This is the same sort of literary device as in Daniel, whose words were "shut up and sealed till the time of the end."[79]

We have noted how dualism came into Jewish thinking in the Persian period and led to the development of a doctrine of angels and demons.[80] An elaborate angelology is presented in 1 En. 20.

---

[76] These dates are those given by R. H. Charles, *The Apocrypha and Pseudepigrapha of the Old Testament,* ii, 170 f.
[77] Gen. 5:24.   [78] 1 En. 1:2.
[79] Dan. 12:9.   [80] *Vid. supra,* pp. 393 f.

And these are the names of the holy angels who watch: Uriel, one of the holy angels, who is over the world and over Tartarus; Raphael, one of the holy angels who is over the spirits of men; Raguel, one of the holy angels, who takes vengeance on the world of the luminaries; Michael, one of the holy angels, to wit, he that is set over the best part of mankind and over chaos; Saraqael, one of the holy angels, who is set over the spirits, who sin in the spirit; Gabriel, one of the holy angels, who is over paradise and the serpents and the cherubim; Remiel, one of the holy angels, whom God set over those who rise.

According to Gen. 6:1–4, the relationship of degenerate angels with the daughters of men brought evil on the earth. This suggestion was taken up by the apocalyptists and worked into an elaborate demonology as a solution of the problem of evil. 1 En. 6 presents such a view.

And it came to pass when the children of men had multiplied, that in those days were born unto them beautiful and comely daughters. And the angels, the children of the heaven, saw and lusted after them, and said to one another: "Come, let us choose us wives from among the children of men and beget us children." And Semjaza, who was their leader, said unto them: "I fear ye will not indeed agree to do this deed, and I alone shall have to pay the penalty of a great sin." And they all answered him and said: "Let us all swear an oath, and bind ourselves by mutual impreca-tions not to abandon this plan but to do this thing." Then swore they all together and bound themselves by mutual imprecations upon it. And they were in all two hundred; who descended in the days of Jared on the summit of Mount Hermon, and they called it Mount Hermon, because they had sworn and bound themselves by mutual imprecations upon it. And these are the names of their leaders: Samiazaz, their leader, Arakiba, Rameel, Kokabiel, Tamiel, Ramiel, Danel, Ezeqeel, Baraqijal, Asael, Armaros, Batarel, Ananel, Zaqiel, Samsapeel, Satarel, Turel, Jomjael, Sariel. These are their chiefs of tens.[81]

Demons were the spirits which proceeded forth from the souls of the giants born of the illicit union of the fallen angels with the daughters of men.

Evil spirits have proceeded from their bodies; because they are born from men and from the holy Watchers is their beginning and primal origin; they shall be evil spirits on earth, and evil spirits shall they be called. . . . And the spirits of the giants afflict, oppress, destroy, attack, do battle, and work destruction on the earth, and cause trouble. . . . And these spirits shall rise up

[81] Besides these, a considerable number of angels are named here and there in 1 En.

against the children of men and against the women, because they
have proceeded from them.[82]

The foregoing quotations are from that part of 1 Enoch which
originated in the second century B.C. They disclose what the second-
century Jewish mind was thinking and they enable us to understand
the background of Daniel, with its reference to Michael.[83] The Jewish
mind became thoroughly saturated with this angelology and demonology, and an appreciation of this fact is quite basic to any understanding of the background of the New Testament literature.

A reading of 1 Enoch will disclose what Jewish eschatology was
like. One of the most important items is the doctrine of Messiah.
The Old Testament reveals a trace of the messiah idea prior to
200 B.C.[84] Messiah is regarded as an ideal king through whom God
will achieve his purposes by endowing him with wisdom and power.
Messiah is regarded as the divinely provided and appointed agent
for bringing to pass the last things, chiefly the effective carrying
out of God's purpose.[85] The pre-eminent quality in the character of
the Messiah is that he is righteous. It is this which guarantees his
ability to carry out the righteous purposes of God.[86] Equally significant is his wisdom. It is by this quality that he succeeds in his work
of establishing righteousness. 1 Enoch says of the Messiah:

> Wisdom is poured out like water, and glory does not fail before
> him for evermore. . . . And in him dwells the spirit of wisdom,
> and the spirit which gives insight, and the spirit of understanding
> and of sight, and the spirit of those who have fallen asleep in
> righteousness.[87]

In 1 En. 90:37 f. Messiah appears as a lamb and transforms the
righteous into his likeness. 1 En. 37–71 terms the Messiah the
Christ,[88] the Righteous One,[89] the Elect One,[90] but most frequently
the Son of Man.[91]

Another important item in the standard Jewish eschatological
program was the intervention of God for the overthrow of evil and
for the renewing of the earth. Upon the ruins of the old world a new
order will rise. The new age is to be essentially good and eternal.
The doctrine of the renewed earth is present in Second Isaiah.

---

[82] 1 En. 15:9–12.   [83] Dan. 10:13, 21; 12:1.
[84] The most important passages on the subject of Messiah are: Isa. 11:1–10 f.;
9:2, 6 f., 51 ff.; Dan. 7; Mic. 5:2 ff.; Ezk. 34:11–31; Jer. 23:5 f.; Zech. 9:9 f.
The order in which these are cited is not chronological, but the order of importance; nor is this list intended to include all Old Testament messianic passages.
[85] 1 En. 49:4; 46:3; 47:3; 51:3; 62:2 f., 5; 69:27, 29.
[86] 1 En. 38:2; 53:6; 39:6; 62:2; 49:2; 48:4; 46:3; 71:14; 105:2.
[87] 1 En. 49:1, 3.   [88] 1 En. 48:10; 52:4.
[89] 1 En. 38:2; 53:6.   [90] 1 En. 40:5; 45:3 f.
[91] 1 En. 46:2–6; 48:2–10; 62:5–14; 63:11; 69:26–29; 71:14–17.

For, behold, I create new heavens and a new earth; and the
former things shall not be remembered, nor come to mind. But
be ye glad and rejoice forever in that which I create; for, behold,
I create Jerusalem a rejoicing, and her people a joy.[92]

For as the new heavens and the new earth, which I will make,
shall remain before me, saith Yahweh, so shall your seed and
your name remain.[93]

It is the same Jerusalem, only supernaturally transformed. Similarly
in Jubilees:

Mount Zion will be sanctified in the new creation for a sancti-
fication of the earth.[94]

In 1 Enoch the transformation of the earth is conceived as cata-
clysmic.

And the first heaven shall depart and pass away,
And a new heaven shall appear,
And all the powers of the heavens shall give sevenfold light.

And after that there will be many weeks without number for-
ever,
And all shall be in goodness and righteousness
And sin shall no more be mentioned forever.[95]

And I will transform the heaven and make it an eternal blessing and light:
And I will transform the earth and make it a blessing:

And I will cause mine elect ones to dwell upon it;
But the sinners and evildoers shall not set foot thereon.[96]

The doctrine of the resurrection of the dead is prominent in the
apocalyptical literature as one of the primary features of the eschatological program. This doctrine was clearly established and widely
held in later Judaism, i.e., after 200 B.C. The doctrine varies with
the different writers, some holding to the resurrection of the righteous
only, others maintaining the resurrection of all alike, good and bad.
The doctrine of a resurrection for all was a corollary of their doctrine of the day of judgment; all must arise from the dead in order
to present themselves before God for judgment.

The earliest definite expressions of the idea of a resurrection are:

Thy dead shall live; my dead bodies shall arise. Awake and
sing, ye that dwell in the dust; for thy dew is as the dew of herbs,
and the earth shall cast forth the dead.[97]

And many of them that sleep in the dust of the earth shall
awake, some to everlasting life, and some to shame and everlasting contempt.[98]

---

[92] Isa. 65:17 f.   [93] Isa. 66:22.   [94] Jub. 4:26; cf. 1:29; 23:26 ff.
[95] 1 En. 91:16 f.   [96] 1 En. 45:4 f.   [97] Isa. 26:19.
[98] Dan. 12:2.

The former passage is variously dated from 334 B.C. to *circa* 100 B.C. and by some is interpreted as applying only to the righteous, in view of the emphasis in the rest of the chapter.[99] The second passage (*circa* 165 B.C.) portrays a resurrection of some of the righteous and some of the wicked.

1 En. 6–36 presents a resurrection for all of the righteous and some of the wicked; the risen righteous eat of the "fragrant tree"[100] and thereby "live a long life," as did the patriarchs,[101] on the earth, which is cleansed from all oppression, unrighteousness, sin, and godlessness,[102] and all the children of men become righteous and worship God.[103] By this writer the resurrection life is portrayed in realistic terms of sense experience. Those wicked only are raised who have not been punished in this life.[104] According to 1 En. 87–90 the resurrection is for all the righteous and none of the wicked. In 1 En. 91–104 "the righteous shall arise from their sleep"[105] as imperishable spirits[106] to whom the portals of heaven are opened[107] and they "have great joy as the angels of heaven,"[108] being "companions of the hosts of heaven."[109] On the other hand, in 1 En. 37–71 the risen righteous are angelic in nature[110] and have "garments of glory,"[111] i.e., bodies.

> And in those days shall the earth also give back that which has been entrusted to it,
> And Sheol also shall give back that which it has received,
> And hell shall give back that which it owes,
> For in those days the Elect One shall arise,
> And he shall choose the righteous and holy from among them:
> For the day has drawn nigh that they should be saved.
> And the Elect One shall in those days sit on my throne,
> And his mouth shall pour forth all the secrets of wisdom and counsel:
> For the Lord of Spirits hath given them to him and hath glorified him.
> And in those days shall the mountains leap like rams,
> And the hills also shall skip like lambs satisfied with milk,
> And the faces of all the angels in heaven shall be lighted up with joy,
> And the earth shall rejoice,
> And the righteous shall dwell upon it,
> And the elect shall walk thereon.[112]

> And the Lord of Spirits will abide over them.
> And with that Son of Man shall they eat

[99] Especially vs. 2.
[102] 1 En. 10:20 ff.
[105] 1 En. 91:10; cf. 92.3.
[108] 1 En. 104:4.
[111] 1 En. 62:15 f.

[100] 1 En. 25:4 ff.
[103] 1 En. 10:21.
[106] 1 En. 103:3 f.
[109] 1 En. 104:6.
[112] 1 En. 51.

[101] 1 En. 25:6.
[104] 1 En. 22:10; 27:2.
[107] 1 En. 104:2.
[110] 1 En. 51:4.

And lie down and rise up forever and ever.
And the righteous and elect shall have risen from the earth,
And ceased to be of downcast countenance.
And they shall have been clothed with garments of glory,
And these shall be the garments of life from the Lord of Spirits:
And your garments shall not grow old,
Nor your glory pass away before the Lord of Spirits.[113]

In Jewish eschatology the oldest idea, and the basal idea, is that of a day of judgment, with which are associated two other ideas that are standard in Jewish apocalyptic, viz., eternal punishment for the wicked and eternal life for the righteous. The idea of a day of judgment grew out of the Old Testament conception of the Day of Yahweh. Down to the eighth century B.C. the popular conception of the Day of Yahweh was that of an unbroken era of national prosperity for Israel to be inaugurated by Yahweh's overthrow of the nation's enemies. With Amos the idea became that of a day of doom directed against Israel, a day of Yahweh's vindication not of the nation but of his own righteous purposes.[114] Isaiah similarly declared that the day was directed not only against Israel but against Judah as well.[115] The judgment of the nations was of course included in the judgment against the chosen people, but the conception of a world judgment is later than Isaiah. Zephaniah portrayed the Day of Yahweh as a day of wrath upon the whole world[116] from which a righteous remnant of Israel would survive.[117] With the exilic prophets, beginning with Jeremiah,[118] the conception of collective punishment for national guilt yielded to that of individual retribution in the judgment. Ezekiel portrayed a judgment in which the heathen are destroyed and a purged Israel emerges.[119] Joel approximated the idea of a final world judgment in his conception of Yahweh's judgment of the nations in the Valley of Jehoshaphat.[120] The idea of a universal final world judgment comes fully into view in Dan. 7. In the apocalyptical literature the judgment is variously viewed as taking place either at the advent of the kingdom or at its close. Judgment on the living and on certain classes of the dead at the advent of the kingdom is the view of 1 En. 6–36,[121] and 83–90.[122]

[113] 1 En. 62:14 ff.
[114] Am. 3:2, 11 f.; 5:1 ff., 5, 18, 27; 6:7; 7:11; 9:4. *Vid supra,* p. 317.
[115] Against Israel: Isa. 2:6–21; 8:1–4; 9:8–20; 17:1–11; 28:1–4. Against Judah: Isa. 1:10–17, 21–26; 3:1–15; 5:8–24; 28:14–22; 29:1–4; 30:8–17; 31:4. *Vid. supra,* p. 327.
[116] Zeph. 1:2 f., 8–18; 2:1–6; 3:8. *Vid. supra,* pp. 335 f.
[117] Zeph. 3:12 f.
[118] Cf. especially Jer. 1:11–16; 37:6–10; 25:15–24; 23:7 f.; 24:5 f.; 3:13, 19–25. *Vid. supra,* p. 342.
[119] Ezk. 38 f.   [120] Joel 3:1, 2, 12.
[121] Cf. especially 1 En. 10:1–13; 16:1; 19:1; 22:4, 11; 25:4.
[122] Cf. especially 1 En. 90:20–27.

Judgment on all rational beings at the beginning of the kingdom is
the view of 1 En. 37–71.[123] The judgment on all rational beings as
coming at the close of the kingdom is the view of Jubilees,[124] 1 En.
91–104,[125] and Psalms of Solomon 17;[126] also of 2 Enoch[127] and
4 Ezra.[128]

The judgment will be followed by the messianic kingdom. The
kingdom is conceived as one which will exist on the present earth
and as an everlasting state of material prosperity, in 1 En. 6–36.[129]
Despite the abundant sensuous imagery of this writer, there is a fine
ethical note.

> And in those days I will open the store chambers of blessing
> which are in the heaven, so as to send them down upon the earth
> over the work and labor of the children of men. And truth and
> peace shall be associated together throughout all the days of the
> world and throughout all the generations of men.[130]

1 En. 83–90 adds to this picture the conception of the New Jerusalem
as the center of this kingdom.[131] The idea of a messianic kingdom of
eternal duration on the present earth is abandoned by the writers of
the first century B.C. because of the dualistic element in their thinking
which set the things of earth and the things of heaven in sharp
antithesis. 1 En. 91–104 regards the messianic kingdom as of
temporary duration, concluding with the judgment.[132] A new heaven
is created, to share in which the righteous rise from the dead.[133] The
writer of 1 En. 37–71 regards the kingdom as a spiritual kingdom
enduring eternally in a *new* heaven and a *new* earth in which the
righteous will be like angels and will be companions of the hosts of
heaven.[134]

It is interesting to note how such an apocalyptical book includes
wisdom teachings within its scope, as seen in 1 En. 91–104, evidence
that wisdom and apocalyptic were not regarded as mutually exclusive thought patterns. An interesting pattern of such wisdom teaching in 1 Enoch is the "woe" form.

> Woe to those who build unrighteousness and oppression
> And lay deceit as a foundation;
> For they shall be suddenly overthrown,
> And they shall have no peace.

[123] Cf. especially 1 En. 41:1; 45:6; 63; 38:5; 48:9 f.; 62:12; 53:3 ff.; 54:1 f.,
6; 55:4; 38:3; 41:2; 45:2, 6.
[124] Jub. 23:11.
[125] Cf. especially 1 En. 91:12–17; 94:9; 98:10; 100:4; 103:8; 104:5.
[126] Especially vss. 27–30.
[127] 2 En. 7:1; 18:6; 39:2; 40:12; 48:8; 50:4; 51:3; 52:15; 58:4; 60:4;
65:6; 66:7.
[128] 4 Ezr. 7:31–44; 12:34.   [129] 1 En. 25:4 ff.; 10:7, 16, 20 ff.; 25:5.
[130] 1 En. 11.   [131] 1 En. 90:28–36.
[132] 1 En. 91:12–17.   [133] 1 En. 91:10, 16 f.; 92:3.
[134] 1 En. 58.

Woe to those who build their houses with sin;
For from all their foundations shall they be overthrown,
And by the sword shall they fall.

Woe to you, ye rich, for ye have trusted in your riches,
And from your riches shall ye depart,
Because ye have not remembered the Most High in the days
of your riches.[135]

Woe to you who acquire silver and gold in unrighteousness
and say:
"We have become rich with riches and have possessions;
And have acquired everything we have desired.
And now let us do what we purposed:
For we have gathered silver,
And many are the husbandmen in our houses.
And our granaries are full as with water."
Yea, and like water your lies shall flow away;
For your riches shall not abide
But speedily ascend from you.[136]

Woe to you who requite your neighbor with evil;
For ye shall be requited according to your works.

Woe to you, lying witnesses,
And to those who weigh our injustice,
For suddenly shall ye perish.[137]

There are many other similar woes. 1 Enoch does not make significant use of the "beatitude" form, although there is one fine example:

In those days blessed are all they who accept the words of wisdom, and understand them,
And observe the paths of the Most High, and walk in the path
of his righteousness,
And become not godless with the godless;
For they shall be saved.[138]

This lengthy discussion of 1 Enoch furnishes us a basis for understanding a type of thought and a whole body of literature which arose in the New Testament period, culminating in the greatest of all apocalypses, the Book of Revelation in the New Testament. In the light of this discussion it will not be necessary to go into extended detail with the other apocalyptical books.

2. *Second Enoch.* This book, sometimes called the "Book of the Secrets of Enoch," was originally written in Greek in Egypt, presumably at Alexandria, A.D. 1–50, and has been preserved only in Slavonic. It is representative of loyal, Pharisaic, non-Hellenizing

---

[135] 1 En. 94 :6 ff.   [136] 1 En. 97 :8 ff.   [137] 1 En. 95 :5 f.
[138] 1 En. 99 :10. On 1 Enoch, cf. Charles, *op. cit.,* pp. 163–281.

Judaism as carried on in Egypt, in distinction from the Alexandrian Hellenizing Judaism such as we encountered in the Wisdom of Solomon.[139] The aim of this writing was that the reader might learn "all the Lord's works, all that has been from the beginning of creation, and will be till the end of time." [140] In a dream, Enoch is conducted by two divine messengers through the seven heavens and on this tour he learns the secrets of the universe. The cosmic speculation of the Jews of the first century A.D. is revealed in this picture of the seven heavens. The blissful place of the righteous, who are characterized in chapter 9, is in the third heaven; and, strangely enough, the terrible place of torture of the unrighteous, who are elaborately delineated in chapter 10, is in the northern part of the same third heaven.

The most valuable part of the book is that which contains wisdom teachings (42–66). There are numerous beatitudes, which was a popular wisdom teaching-form.

> Then I spake: "My children: Blessed is he who fears God and serves him. And you, my children, learn to bring gifts to the Lord, that you may enjoy life. Blessed is he who judges a judgment justly to the widow and orphan, and helps everyone that is wronged, clothing the naked with garments, and to the hungry giving bread.
>
> Blessed is he who turns back from the changeable path and walks along the straight path.
>
> Blessed is he who sows the seeds of righteousness, for he shall reap sevenfold.
>
> Blessed is he in whom is truth, that he may speak truth to his neighbor.
>
> Blessed is he in whose mouth is mercy and gentleness.
>
> Blessed is he who understands the Lord's works and glorifies the Lord God." [141]
>
> Blessed is the man who opens his lips in praise of God of Sabaoth and praises the Lord with his heart.
>
> Cursed every man who opens his lips for the bringing into contempt and calumny of his neighbor, because he brings God into contempt.
>
> Blessed is he who opens his lips blessing and praising God.
>
> Cursed is he before the Lord all the days of his life, who opens his lips to curse and abuse.
>
> Blessed is he who blesses all the Lord's works.
>
> Cursed is he who brings the Lord's creation into contempt.
>
> Blessed is he who looks down and raises the fallen.
>
> Cursed is he who looks to and is eager for the destruction of what is not his.

---

[139] Seen also in 4 Maccabees and Philo. *Vid. infra*, pp. 462 ff.
[140] 2 En. 47:2.   [141] 2 En. 42:6–14.

Blessed is he who keeps the foundations of his fathers made firm from the beginning.
Cursed is he who perverts the decrees of his forefathers.
Blessed is he who implants peace and love.
Cursed is he who disturbs those that love their neighbors.
Blessed is he who speaks with humble tongue and heart to all.
Cursed is he who speaks peace with his tongue, while in his heart there is no peace but a sword.[142]

Such a balancing of blessings and cursings is patterned after the Old Testament model in Deut. 27:15–28:6.

3. *Second Baruch.* The city of Jerusalem was destroyed by the Romans in A.D. 70. The effect of this upon literature was twofold. For one thing it precipitated a final decision by the rabbis as to the limits of the Old Testament canon of Scripture, as we have already observed.[143] For another thing it called forth a number of apocalyptical writings. Such apocalyptists found an appropriate dramatic date in the previous destruction of Jerusalem by the Chaldeans in 586 B.C. What was more suitable than to assign such a book to a prominent character who lived at that time? Such a character was Baruch, secretary and friend of the prophet Jeremiah, to whom indeed a previous pseudepigraphical writing had been ascribed.[144] This second book of Baruch originated in Palestine in the period A.D. 50–90. It appears to be a composite of several sources. The principal topic of the book is the judgment, with the eternal destinies, that awaits mankind. There is some teaching regarding the Messiah and the resurrection. Like all apocalypses, this book was written to warn and exhort the wicked, and to encourage and comfort the righteous. 2 Baruch is entirely satisfied with the future outlook for Israel. The following quotations give the flavor of the book.[145]

For the righteous justly hope for the end, and without fear depart from this habitation, because they have with thee a store of works preserved in treasuries. On this account also these without fear leave this world, and trusting with joy they hope to receive the world which thou hast promised them.[146]

And it shall come to pass after these things, when the time of the advent of the messiah is fulfilled, that he shall return in glory. Then all who have fallen asleep in hope of him shall rise again. And it shall come to pass at that time that the treasuries will be opened in which is preserved the number of the souls of the righteous, and they shall come forth, and a multitude of souls

---

[142] 2 En. 52:1–14. On 2 Enoch, cf. Charles, *op. cit.,* pp. 425–469.
[143] *Vid. supra,* pp. 429 ff.
[144] *Vid. supra,* p. 434. There is a Third Baruch, an extra-Palestinian pseudepigraph in a Greek original, A.D. *circa* 100. Cf. Charles, *op. cit.,* pp. 527–541.
[145] Cf. Charles, *op. cit.,* pp. 490–519, *passim.*
[146] 2 Bar. 14:12 f.

shall be seen together in one assemblage of one thought, and the
first shall rejoice and the last shall not be grieved.[147]

In thee do we trust, for lo! thy law is with us, and we know
that we shall not fail so long as we keep thy statutes.[148]

In what shape will those live who live in thy day?
Or how will the splendor of those who are after that time con-
tinue? . . .
For the earth shall then assuredly restore the dead
Which it now receives in order to preserve them.
It shall make no change in their form,
But as it has received, so shall it restore them,
And as I delivered them unto it, so also shall it raise them.[149]

For though Adam first sinned and brought untimely death upon
all, yet of those who were born from him each one of them has
prepared for his own soul torment to come, and again each one
of them has chosen for himself glories to come. . . . Adam is
therefore not the cause, save only of his own soul, but each of us
has been the Adam of his own soul.[150]

Who can understand, O Lord, thy goodness?
For it is incomprehensible.
Or who can search into thy compassions,
Which are infinite?
Or who can comprehend thy intelligence?
Or who is able to recount the thoughts of thy mind?
Or who of those who are born can hope to come to those things,
Unless he is one to whom thou art merciful and gracious? [151]

4. *Fourth Ezra (Second Esdras).* This is one of the books in the
Apocrypha, but we deferred consideration of it until now in order
that we might appreciate it in its historical perspective.[152] 4 Ezra
originated in Palestine A.D. 81–96 and is given a dramatic date thirty
years following the fall of Jerusalem to the Chaldeans (586 B.C.),
which as a matter of fact was a whole century before Ezra's lifetime.
Ezra was famous as a scribe of Judaism and very likely his name was
chosen for this late first-century book in order to commend the book
to that element in Judaism which, at the end of the first century, was
turning away from apocalyptic toward what is technically called
rabbinic Judaism, which was strictly scribal and legalistic in character.

Chapters 3–14 are the original part of the book; 1 f. and 15 f. are
later additions. The material is arranged in seven visions. Ezra is
represented as going through an inward struggle, as bitter and as

[147] 2 Bar. 30:1 f.
[148] 2 Bar. 48:22.
[149] 2 Bar. 49:2; 50:2.
[150] 2 Bar. 54:15, 19.
[151] 2 Bar. 75:1–5.
[152] The four books of Ezra were (1) the Old Testament Ezra; (2) the Old Testament Nehemiah; (3) the apocryphal First Esdras; (4) the apocryphal Second
Esdras or Fourth Ezra.

earnest as that of Job, to maintain his faith in face of the disaster and suffering which had befallen the Jewish people in the loss of their temple and their nation. The material is altogether eschatological. The sinful state of man is ascribed to Adam's fall.[153] There is considerable emphasis upon messianism. A period of woes will precede the coming of Messiah.[154] His coming will be sudden, and his kingdom will last four hundred years.[155] Messiah's work will principally be to destroy the enemies of righteousness and to bring back the lost tribes to the holy land.[156] At the end of the four hundred years Messiah and all living beings will die, and creation will revert to primeval silence for seven days [157] after which will occur the general resurrection and the day of judgment.[158] In the final judgment only a few will be saved and it is this consideration that distresses Ezra who struggles to justify such a doctrine.[159] The purpose of such writing was, of course, to encourage men to righteousness and to deter men, if possible, from sin.

By the end of the first century after Christ the Jews lost interest in apocalyptic. It was not on the main line of Judaism, which was rabbinism, the legalistic interest which culminated in the Jewish Talmud. The first-century Christians carried forward the interest in apocalyptic and brought it to its climax in the greatest of all apocalypses, the Book of Revelation, a study of which belongs with Christian literature.[160]

The Psalms of Solomon. It is pleasing to know that Jewish interest in producing psalms did not end with the completion of the canonical Book of Psalms. The latest psalms to get into the canonical psalter were certain psalms which arose in the Maccabean period. The canonical psalms were ascribed to David. This new collection was ascribed to Solomon, perhaps because of the suggestion in 1 Kgs. 4:32 that Solomon's songs were "a thousand and five." This group of eighteen poems appeared *circa* 50 B.C., i.e., not long after the Roman conquest of 63 B.C. They are mainly petitions to God for help, comfort, and vindication, arising out of deep distress and perplexity of soul. Ps. Sol. 2:1 f., 5 evidently refers to the capture of Jerusalem by the Romans. It reads:

> When the sinner waxed proud, he battered down fortified walls,
>   And thou didst not restrain him.
> Alien nations ascended thine altar,
>   They trampled it proudly with their sandals. . . .
> It was set at naught before God,
>   It was utterly dishonored.

---

153 4 Ezr. 7:116–131.
155 4 Ezr. 7:26 ff.
157 4 Ezr. 7:29 f.
159 4 Ezr. 7:45–61; 7:132–8:3; 9:13–22.

154 4 Ezr. 4:52–5:13a; 6:11–28.
156 4 Ezr. 13:25–40.
158 4 Ezr. 7:31–44.
160 *Vid. infra,* pp. 591 ff.

Usually, however, these psalms express a triumphant faith.

God is a righteous judge,
    And he is no respecter of persons. . . .
For the Lord is good to them that call upon him in patience,
    Doing according to his mercy to his pious ones,
    Establishing them at all times before him in strength.
Blessed be the Lord forever in the sight of his servants.[161]

Why sleepest thou, O my soul,
    And blessest not the Lord?
Sing a new song
    Unto God, who is worthy to be praised.
Sing and be wakeful against his awaking,
    For good is a psalm to God from a glad heart. . . .
They that fear the Lord shall rise to life eternal;
    Their life shall be lived in the light of the Lord, and never end.[162]

O Lord God, I will praise thy name with joy,
    In the midst of them that know thy righteous judgments.
Thou art good and merciful, the refuge of the poor. . . .
When we are in distress we call upon thee for help,
    And thou dost not turn back our petition, for thou art our God.[163]

Turn, O God, thy mercy upon us, and have pity upon us;
    Gather together the dispersed of Israel, with mercy and good-
        ness;
For thy faithfulness is with us.[164]

Our works are subject to our own choice and power
    To do right or wrong in the works of our hands;
    And in thy righteousness thou visitest the sons of men.
He that doeth righteousness layeth up life for himself with the
        Lord;
    And he that doeth wrongly forfeits his life to destruction.[165]

Faithful is the Lord to them that love him in truth,
    To them that endure his chastening,
To them that walk in the righteousness of his commandments,
    In the law which he commanded us that we might live. . . .
For the ways of men are known before him at all times,
    And he knoweth the secrets of the heart before they come to
        pass.[166]

Lord, thy mercy is over the works of thy hands forever;
    Thy goodness is over Israel with a rich gift;

[161] Ps. Sol. 2:19, 40 f.   [162] Ps. Sol. 3:1 f., 16.
[163] Ps. Sol. 5:1 f., 7.   [164] Ps. Sol. 8:33 ff.
[165] Ps. Sol. 9:7 ff.   [166] Ps. Sol. 14:1, 5.

Thine eyes look upon them, so that none of them suffers want;
Thine ears hearken to the hopeful prayer of the poor;
Thy judgments are upon the whole earth in mercy;
Thy love is toward the seed of Abraham, the children of Israel;
Thy chastisement is upon us as upon a firstborn and only son,
To turn back the obedient soul from folly in ignorance.
May God cleanse Israel against the day of mercy and blessing,
Against the day of choice when he bringeth back his anointed.[167]

The last two lines of the preceding quotation are peculiarly interesting and significant because they show that when this psalm was written the expectation of a messiah was well established. He was pictured as one who was to be brought back, implying a belief that he had already been there at some previous time. The day of his return was to be a day of such gladness to the Jews that they were calling it "the day of mercy and blessing." Ps. Sol. 17 is one of the principal messianic passages in Jewish literature.

Behold, O Lord, and raise up unto them their king, the son of
David,
At the time in which thou seest, O God, that he may reign over
Israel thy servant. . . .
And he shall gather together a holy people, whom he shall lead
in righteousness,
And he shall judge the tribes of the people that has been sancti-
fied by the Lord his God.
And he shall not suffer unrighteousness to lodge any more in
their midst,
Nor shall there dwell with them any man that knoweth wicked-
ness,
For he shall know them, that they are all sons of their God. . . .
All nations shall be in fear before him,
For he will smite the earth with the word of his mouth forever.
He will bless the people of the Lord with wisdom and gladness,
And he himself will be pure from sin, so that he may rule a
great people.
He will rebuke rulers, and remove sinners by the might of his
word.[168]

Thus we see that nearly a century before Jesus of Nazareth embarked upon his public career there were Jews who were looking forward to a messiah of peace, one whose conquests were to be through the inner compulsion of truth and reason rather than through physical force.

Wisdom Writings. 1. *The Testaments of the Twelve Patriarchs.* Gen. 49 represents the patriarch Jacob on his deathbed bestowing

[167] Ps. Sol. 18:1-6.
[168] Ps. Sol. 17:23, 28 ff.. 38b-41. On the Psalms of Solomon, cf. Charles, *op. cit.*, pp. 625-652.

a parting benediction upon each of his twelve sons. A Jewish writer of the late second century B.C. (109–106) adopted this idea as a literary dress for a book of wisdom teachings and represented each of Jacob's twelve sons on his deathbed giving parting counsel and exhortation to his sons. Their testaments were their last solemn speeches just before death.

The book originated in Palestine. Its author was a devout Jew of the Hasidist or Pharisaic type. His purpose was to inculcate devotion to the basic Old Testament virtues.[169] Each of the twelve is idealized but not to the extent of denying some very human tendencies to sin. In fact, the author readily acknowledges serious flaws in his heroes but turns the flaws to excellent account in the exhortations put into their mouths in these deathbed speeches. Each patriarch rigidly judges and condemns himself by the standards of the Mosaic laws, thus implying that the patriarchs were aware of the principles involved in the Torah centuries before they were revealed to Moses. It is as if, in the hour of death, each patriarch said: "Here, my sons, is where I made the great mistake of my life. Take warning from my example." Then follows a noble exhortation, the luminous understanding of a soul at the portals of death. The teaching is all very simple and very earnest. Repeatedly the sins of hatred, lying, envy, lust, covetousness, retaliation, selfishness, and such are condemned, and the virtues of love, forgiveness, truthfulness, chastity, temperance, patience, self-control, and the like are exalted.

> Have compassion towards every man with mercy, that the Lord also may have compassion and mercy upon you. . . . For in the degree in which a man has compassion upon his neighbors, in the same degree has the Lord also upon him.[170]

> Unless ye keep yourselves from the spirit of lying and of anger, and love truth and longsuffering, ye shall perish. For anger is blindness, and does not suffer one to see the face of any man with truth. . . . Love the Lord through all your life, and one another with a true heart.[171]

> Walk in singleness of heart in the fear of the Lord, and expend labor on good works, and on study and on your flocks. . . . I adjure you by the God of heaven to do truth each one unto his neighbor and to entertain love each one for his brother.[172]

> Work righteousness, my children, upon the earth,
> That ye may have it as a treasure in heaven.
> And sow good things in your souls,
> That ye may find them in your life.[173]

---

[169] This book contains Christian additions here and there which are later insertions and attest the popularity of this book in early Christian circles.
[170] T. Zebulun 8 :1, 3.   [171] T. Dan 2 :1 f.; 5 :3.
[172] T. Reuben 4 :1; 6 :9.   [173] T. Levi 13 :5 f.

Most striking of all is the Testament of Gad. Like several of the twelve, Gad felt his chief regret to be the part he had played in the sale of his brother Joseph into slavery in Egypt.[174] Some of the patriarchs specify that it was envy which prompted them to do this thing, but Gad confesses that he had thoroughly hated Joseph. Deeply regretful, he warns his descendants in the following remarkable words:

> My children, hearken to the words of truth to work righteousness, and go not astray through the spirit of hatred. . . . Whatsoever a man does, the hater abominates him: and though a man work the law of the Lord, he praises him not; though a man fears the Lord, and takes pleasure in that which is righteous, he loves him not. He disparages the truth, he envies him that prospers, he welcomes evil-speaking, he loves arrogance, for hatred blinds his soul. . . .
>
> Beware therefore, my children, of hatred. . . . For as love would quicken even the dead, and would call back them that are condemned to die, so hatred would slay the living, and those that had sinned excusably it would not suffer to live . . . but the spirit of love works together with the law of God in longsuffering unto the salvation of men. Hatred therefore is evil, for it constantly mates with lying, speaking against the truth; and it makes small things to be great, and causes the light to be darkness. and calls the sweet bitter, and teaches slander . . . and all covetousness.
>
> And now, my children, I exhort you, love each one his brother, and put away hatred from your hearts; love one another in deed, and in word, and in the inclination of the soul. . . . Love one another from the heart; and if a man sin against thee, speak peaceably to him, and in thy soul hold not guile; and if he repent and confess, forgive him. . . . And though he deny it and yet have a sense of shame when reproved, give over reproving him. For he who denies may repent so as not again to wrong thee; yea, he may also honor thee, and be at peace with thee. And if he be shameless and persist in his wrongdoing, even so forgive him from the heart, and leave to God the avenging.[175]

Concerning this teaching of forgiveness in T. Gad as expressed in the passage just quoted, R. H. Charles states:

> It would be hard to exaggerate the importance of this passage. It proves that in Galilee, the home of the Testaments of the XII Patriarchs and of other apocalyptical writings, there was in the second century B.C. a deeply spiritual religious life, which, having assimilated the highest teaching of the Old Testament on for-

---

[174] Cf. Gen. 37.
[175] T. Gad 3–6, *passim*. On the Testaments of the Twelve Patriarchs, cf. Charles, *op. cit.*, pp. 282–367.

giveness, developed and consolidated it into a clear, consistent doctrine, that could neither be ignored nor misunderstood by spiritually minded men. This religious development appears to have flourished mainly in Galilee.[176]

The implication of this is that the Testaments of the Twelve Patriarchs circulated as a book of popular devotion in Galilee in the lifetime of Jesus of Nazareth, much as *Pilgrim's Progress* once did in America. People then, as now, had not only their Bibles to read (or hear read), but other religious books as well which nourished their religious life. What those other religious books were which the Jews read here and there, in Palestine and elsewhere, we can now appreciate, in view of the present chapter of our study.

2. *The Sayings of the Jewish Fathers (Pirke Aboth).* The Torah was canonized *circa* 400 B.C.[177] Questions arose as to the meaning of this written law, and there developed during the centuries a body of interpretation known as the "tradition of the elders" or the oral law. This body of tradition was itself put into written form A.D. *circa* 200 and is known as the Mishna,[178] one of the principal component parts of the Jewish Talmud.[179] One of the tracts of the Mishna is known as *Aboth* (Fathers), or *Pirke Aboth,* Sayings of the Jewish Fathers. It is customary among Jews to detach it from the Mishna and consider it as a treatise by itself, in six chapters. A total of sixty-five Jewish teachers are named in these chapters as authors of the sayings that are quoted. Some of these teachers lived as early as 200 B.C. Hence this teaching originated over a period of four centuries. They are representative of educational scribism, devoutly faithful to the Torah and zealous to inculcate Jewish religious ethics. Some of the fine sayings of this collection are the following:

> Say little and do much; and receive every man with the look of a cheerful face.[180]

> On three things the world stands: on judgment, on truth, and on peace.[181]

> Say not, when I am at leisure I will study; perchance thou wilt not be at leisure.[182]

> The day is short and the work is great, and the laborers are slow, and the hire is much, and the master of the house is urgent. It is not incumbent on thee to finish the work, and thou are not

---

[176] *Religious Development Between the Old and the New Testaments* (New York: 1914), p. 156.
[177] *Vid. supra,* pp. 382 ff.
[178] The word *Mishna* means "repetition," hence, "law learned by repetition."
[179] The other is the *Gemara* ("completion"), written in the sixth century A.D. and comprising the traditions which arose subsequent to the Mishna.
[180] Ab. 1:15.   [181] Ab. 1:18.   [182] Ab. 2:5.

free to desist from it. If thou hast learned much Torah, they will give thee much hire; and the master of thy work is faithful who will pay thee the hire of thy labor; and know that the giving of the reward of the righteous is for the time to come.[183]

Every one whose fear of sin precedes his wisdom, his wisdom endures; and every one whose wisdom precedes his fear of sin, his wisdom does not endure. Every one whose deeds are more than his wisdom, his wisdom endures. And every one whose wisdom is more than his deeds, his wisdom does not endure.[184]

Despise not any man, and be not captious at any thing; for you find no man that has not his hour, and no thing that has not its place.[185]

Be careful in teaching; for error in teaching amounts to sin.[186]

A wise man does not speak in the presence of one who is greater than he in wisdom; and he does not break in upon the words of his associate; and he does not hasten to reply; he asks according to the rule, and answers according to the subject; and he speaks on the first thing first, and on the last last; concerning what he has not heard he says, I have not heard; and he acknowledges the truth.[187]

Four types of them that sit before the wise: a sponge, a funnel, a strainer, and a sieve. A sponge, because it sucks up everything; a funnel, because it receives at one end and lets out at the other; a strainer, because it lets out the wine and keeps back the dregs; a sieve, because it lets out the coarse meal and keeps the fine flour.[188]

3. *Fourth Maccabees.* This book originated in Alexandria, Egypt, not earlier than 63 B.C. and not later than A.D. 38. The latter date has in its favor the fact that at that time the Roman emperor Caligula was persecuting the Jews of Egypt and this book was manifestly written to encourage Jews to resist their oppressors. The author is representative of that type of Jewish mind which fully accepted Greek philosophy while remaining thoroughly loyal to Jewish faith. He attempts to synthesize the two. His philosophical position is, "Reason I take to be the mind preferring with clear deliberation the life of wisdom. . . . While Reason is the guide of the virtues it is the master of the passions." [189] This proposition he illustrates by numerous examples taken from Jewish history, and he elaborates at great length the story found in 2 Macc. 6:18–7:41

---

[183] Ab. 2:19 f. The first sentence of this quotation (omitting "and the laborers are slow") is set in Hebrew letters in garnet-colored slate in a girdle about the dome of the library building at Union College, Schenectady, New York.
[184] Ab. 3:12 f.   [185] Ab. 4:3.   [186] Ab. 4:16.
[187] Ab. 5:10.
[188] Ab. 5:18. On Aboth, cf. Charles, *Apocrypha and Pseudepigrapha of the Old Testament,* ii, 686–714.
[189] 4 Mac. 1:15, 30.

about the aged Eleazar, and the seven sons and their mother who suffered torture and death, at the time of Epiphanes's persecution of the Jews, rather than Hellenize.[190] Because of this story the book was associated with 2 Maccabees and therefore it came to be known as 4 Maccabees.[191]

Philo and Josephus

A survey of the Jewish literature of the New Testament period would be incomplete without mention of the two most notable Jewish writers of the first century, Philo and Josephus, although it is not necessary to go into detail about their writings for they are not basic to an understanding of the New Testament.[192]

Philo was an Alexandrian Jew, born *circa* 20 B.C., died A.D. *circa* 50. He was a learned scholar, the only Jewish philosopher, properly so called, of Bible times. He heartily accepted Greek philosophy, particularly Stoicism, but was wholeheartedly loyal to Judaism. He sought to synthesize the two by showing that Moses and the Greek philosophers had meant the same thing.

The writings of Philo, which are in Greek, are numerous and cannot be definitely dated. A new edition of Philo's works containing both the Greek text and a fresh English translation is now appearing in the Loeb Classical Library.[193] For the flavor of Philo's thought and literary style, suggested passages (in the Loeb translation) are the following: "Concerning Noah's Work as a Planter" (vol. iii, pp. 213–305); "On the Migration of Abraham" (vol. iv, pp. 123–267); "On Abraham" (vol. vi, pp. 2–135); "On the Life of Moses" (vol. vi, pp. 274–595); "On the Ten Commandments" (vol. vii, pp. 7–95); "On the Special Laws" (vol. vii, pp. 307–331, 447–471); "On Courage, Humanity, and Repentance" (vol. viii, pp. 163–279); "Every Good Man Is Free" (vol. ix, pp. 2–101). A few gems from Philo's ethical thinking are set out below.

> Having learned, then, that in all that has to do with shewing honour to God, one work only is incumbent upon us, namely thanksgiving, let us always and everywhere make this our study, using voice and skillful pen.[194]

> There have been instances of a household or a city or a country or nations and regions of the earth enjoying great

---

[190] *Vid. supra*, pp. 415 f.

[191] Fourth because there was a Third Maccabees; *vid. supra*, p. 442, fn. 63.

[192] Except in respect to the doctrine of the Logos in Jn. 1. On this Philo is illuminating.

[193] By F. H. Colson and G. H. Whittaker. Vols. 1–5 published by G. P. Putnam's Sons (New York); vols. 6–9 by Harvard University Press (Cambridge). Vol. 10 will complete the series.

[194] "Concerning Noah's Work as a Planter," xxxi, § 131, Loeb Series, vol. iii, p. 279.

prosperity through a single man giving his mind to nobility of character. Most of all has this been so in the case of one on whom God has bestowed, together with a good purpose, irresistible power, just as He gives to the musician and every artist the instruments which his music or his art requires or as He gives to fire logs as its material. For in truth the righteous man is the foundation on which mankind rests. All that he himself has he brings into the common stock and gives in abundance for the benefit of all who shall use them. What he does not find in his own store, he asks for at the hands of God, the only possessor of unlimited riches; and He opens His heavenly treasury and sends His good things, as He does the snow and the rain, in ceaseless downpour, so that the channels and cavities of earth's whole face overflow.[195]

Love of learning is by nature curious and inquisitive, not hesitating to bend its steps in all directions, prying into everything, reluctant to leave anything that exists unexplored, whether material or immaterial. It has an extraordinary appetite for all that there is to be seen and heard, and, not content with what it finds in its own country, it is bent on seeking what is in foreign parts and separated by great distances.[196]

Be zealous therefore, O soul, to become a house of God, a holy temple, a most beauteous abiding-place; for perchance, perchance the Master of the whole world's household shall be thine too and keep thee under His care as His special house, to preserve thee evermore strongly guarded and unharmed.[197]

For beauty of body lies in well-proportioned parts, in a fine complexion and good condition of flesh, and short is the season of its bloom. But beauty of mind lies in harmony of creed, in concent of virtues. The passing of time cannot wither it, and, as its years lengthen, it ever renews its youth, adorned with the lustrous hue of truth and of consistency of deeds with words and words with deeds, and further of thoughts and intentions with both.[198]

Pride is also the creator of many other evils, boastfulness, haughtiness, inequality, and these are the sources of wars both civil and foreign, suffering no place to remain in peace whether public or private, whether on sea or on land.[199]

For in very truth he who has God alone for his leader, he alone is free, though to my thinking he is also the leader of all others,

---

[195] "On the Migration of Abraham," xxi, §§ 120 ff., Loeb Series, vol. iv, p. 201.
[196] *Ibid.*, xxxix, § 216, Loeb Series, vol. iv, p. 259.
[197] "On Dreams," xxiii, § 149, Loeb Series, vol. v, p. 377.
[198] "On the Life of Moses," Book III, xxvii, § 140, Loeb Series, vol. vi, p. 517.
[199] "On the Decalogue," ii, § 5, Loeb Series, vol. vii, p. 9.

having received the charge of earthly things from the great, the immortal King, whom he, the mortal, serves as viceroy.[200]

There is a peace-time war, no less grave than those fought with arms, a war set on foot by disrepute and poverty and dire lack of the necessaries of life, a war by which men are forced under duress to undertake the most servile tasks.[201]

For never will that soul surrender or suffer defeat which right reason has braced with principles firmly held.[202]

Do not do what any one is vexed to suffer.[203]

Flavius Josephus, the Jewish historian, was born in Jerusalem, A.D. 37 and lived to A.D. *circa* 100. During the great Jewish war of rebellion against Rome (A.D. 66–70), which resulted so disastrously for the Jews,[204] Josephus took a not very creditable part as head of the Jewish army in Galilee. After the year 70 he lived in Rome and wrote his several books, the *History of the Jewish War,* the *Antiquities of the Jews,* his *Autobiography,* and the treatise *Against Apion,* which writings are sources of valuable information as to Jewish history and culture. A new edition of Josephus's works containing both the Greek text and a fresh English translation is likewise now appearing in the Loeb Classical Library.[205] To get the flavor of Josephus's writings, H. St. J. Thackeray's *Selections from Josephus* [206] is recommended.

200 "Every Good Man Is Free," iii, § 20, Loeb Series, vol. ix, p. 21.
201 *Ibid.,* vi, § 34, Loeb Series, vol. ix, pp. 29 f.
202 *Ibid.,* xiv, § 97, Loeb Series, vol. ix, p. 67.
203 Ascribed to Philo by Eusebius, *Praeparatio Evangelica,* viii, vii, 6.
204 *Vid. infra,* pp. 554 ff.
205 Vols. 1–5 by H. St. J. Thackeray, after whose death the work was assumed by Ralph Marcus. To be complete in nine volumes. Vols. 1–4 published by G. P. Putnam's Sons (New York) ; vols. 5–7 (and presumably the remaining volumes) by Harvard University Press (Cambridge).
206 (London : 1919).

Chapter 23

PALESTINE IN THE FIRST CENTURY

Upon the death of Herod the Great, his kingdom was partitioned among three of his sons. Archelaus got Judea, Samaria, and Idumea. The emperor, Augustus Caesar, gave him the title of ethnarch, and had his rule been a success, Archelaus would later have had conferred upon him the title of king. But Archelaus proved barbarous, arbitrary, tyrannical, and utterly incompetent to deal with the delicate problems connected with ruling the Jews at this time. Resentment against him finally reached such a stage that a deputation of Jews waited upon the emperor Augustus to request that Archelaus be deposed. Such Jews doubtless thought a real Roman would be less extreme in his Hellenizing efforts than this son of Herod who was so keen to please his overlords. Augustus acceded to the request, and Archelaus was banished to Gaul (A.D. 6). The dominion of the deposed ethnarch was added to the province of Syria. Thus from A.D. 6 to 40 Judea was ruled by procurators.

A second portion of Herod the Great's territory, viz., Galilee and Perea, went to another son, Herod Antipas, with the title of tetrarch. He ruled from 4 B.C. to A.D. 39. His rule was moderately successful.

A third son of Herod the Great, Philip by name, was made tetrarch of the district east and northeast of Lake Galilee. He ruled from 4 B.C. to A.D. 34.

Political Divisions of Palestine

The Province of Judea Under Roman Rule. (After A.D. 6). The province of Judea included all of the west Jordan area south of Esdraelon, subdivided into eleven toparchies of which Jerusalem was the head. A toparchy was a major town and the adjacent country with its villages. Judea, being an eastern outpost of the Roman Empire and subject to frequent revolt, was placed directly under the emperor. The actual administration was in the hands of a procurator who was chiefly a fiscal agent for Rome. The capital was Caesarea, on the Mediterranean, this new port city being much more accessible to Rome than was Jerusalem.

Under the procurators, order was maintained not by regular Roman soldiers but by auxiliaries recruited from Samaritans and from Greek residents of Palestine. Jews were never required to serve in the Roman armies. In deference to the religious prejudices of the Jews, the Roman military standards were kept completely out of Jerusalem. With the one exception, that the robes of the high priest were kept in the tower of Antonia, complete religious toleration and consideration were shown the Jews at all times. On the whole, reasonable effort was made to avoid any semblance of oppression.

Collection and distribution of taxes were supervised by the procurator. The major tax was collected through the local Jewish sanhedrins in each of the eleven toparchies. As this money was turned over to the procurator, he retained what was needed to cover the cost of the provincial administration and authorized improvements and sent the remainder to Rome.

The customs tax was farmed.[1] The collector paid a fixed sum and then collected as much as he could above that sum as his own compensation. These customs included export and import duties on goods transported from city to city, on shipments to and from the province, market taxes, taxes on necessities such as salt, and tolls at bridges, harbors, and the like. Because of their extortions, these collectors, called publicans, were despised and hated by the Jews, and Jews who were publicans were the more heartily despised for being agents of their heathen conquerors.

In the administration of justice the procurator handled all cases involving gentiles, whether between gentile and gentile or between Jew and gentile. In ordinary cases the procurator was the final court of appeal except that Roman citizens could appeal directly to the emperor. Ordinary civil and criminal cases involving only Jews were decided by the local sanhedrins or were referred by them to the national Sanhedrin at Jerusalem. The procurator had the power of appointing and removing the Jewish high priests.

The Jerusalem Sanhedrin administered Jewish law covering civil, criminal, moral, and religious questions. Its civil authority was limited to Judea. It could make arrests and its authority over Jews, provided they did not possess Roman citizenship, was practically unlimited except in the matter of capital punishment, which required the procurator's approval. However, the Jews did have the right to kill on the spot any gentile who entered the sacred courts of the temple beyond the Court of the Gentiles.[2] The Jerusalem Sanhedrin consisted of seventy members. The high priest was its head.

---

[1] *Vid. supra,* pp. 390 f.
[2] *Vid. infra,* p. 577.

Apparently it was a self-perpetuating body, filling its own vacancies by members chosen from the ranks of the high-priestly families, the scribes, and the elders. The religious prestige of this body extended wherever there were Jews. But a few members of the Sanhedrin were Sadducees in the time of Jesus. It had been dominated by the Pharisees since the time when Herod the Great, following his victory over Antigonus in 37 B.C., slew forty-five of the Sadducee members of the Sanhedrin.[3]

Of the procurators who ruled Judea after A.D. 6, a special interest attaches to Pontius Pilate (A.D. 26–36) because of the fact that he was the one who condemned Jesus to death.[4] He is described as "of unbending and recklessly hard character."[5] He never understood the Jews or Jewish psychology. On one occasion he aroused their violent antipathy by an attempt to bring the Roman standards bearing the emperor's image into Jerusalem under cover of night. On another occasion he offended them by expropriating temple funds to extend an aqueduct into the holy city. In both cases Pilate did finally yield to protest, thereby averting serious bloodshed. On yet another occasion he actually set up votive shields in the temple, for which act he was condemned by the emperor himself. Finally, in the year A.D. 36, he was dismissed from office for peculiarly brutal treatment of some deluded Samaritans who had been induced to follow a false messiah.

Galilee and Perea Under Herod Antipas (4 B.C.–A.D. 39).

Galilee at this time was densely populated. The Galileans were an impulsive folk, loyal to Judaism but without fanaticism. They were markedly tolerant of Graeco-Roman culture and of things gentile. Yet restlessness pervaded the region because of the loss of political autonomy. Perea, east of the Jordan, was of little importance politically, since the important "ten cities" (i.e., Decapolis) were not included in the jurisdiction of Perea, nor were the prosperous farm lands stretching for miles around each of these cities. Perea, however, ranked next to Judea in purity of Judaism.

Herod Antipas legally bore the title of tetrarch, an official with somewhat less power than a king. He is so called in Matt. 14:1 and Luke 9:7; elsewhere he is usually referred to as king. On one occasion Jesus is reported to have characterized him as "that fox."[6] Since the Palestinian fox was a skulking, treacherous animal, given

---

[3] *Vid. supra,* p. 423.
[4] The first procurators of Judea were Coponius (A.D. 7–9); M. Ambibulus (9–12); Annius Rufus (12–15); Valerius Gratus (15–26); Pontius Pilatus (26–36); Marcellus (36); Marullus (37–41). On Pilate, cf. G. E. Wright and F. V. Filson, *The Westminster Historical Atlas to the Bible* (Philadelphia: 1945), pp. 84 f.
[5] Philo, *De Legatione ad Caium,* 38.
[6] Lk. 13:32.

to destroying or undermining the results of honest work, the caustic force of Jesus' metaphor is evident. An example of this fox-like trait is seen in the incident when, to win favor with the emperor, Antipas hurriedly and secretly forwarded to the emperor a private report of the successful termination of a certain embassage to the Parthians on which he and a general, Vitellius, had been dispatched, without waiting for Vitellius to share in drafting the report. Apparently Antipas gained his immediate objective, but at the price of Vitellius's enmity. When the latter became governor of Syria he evened off the score by bringing charges against Antipas which led to his banishment to Gaul in A.D. 39 by the emperor Caligula. Antipas forfeited popular esteem by his private life. In order that he might marry his niece Herodias, wife of his half brother Herod Philip,[7] he divorced his own wife, who was the daughter of the Arabian king, Aretas (9 B.C.–A.D. 40). It was this scandalous affair with Herodias that John the Baptist denounced.[8] Aretas later repaid this insult by joining Vitellius in preferring charges against Antipas, which brought about Antipas's political extinction.

On the whole, Herod Antipas gave his subjects a peaceful and prosperous rule. He was a noted builder. He rebuilt Sepphoris, a city just north of Nazareth, gave it a strong wall and fine public edifices and made it his first capital. Sepphoris had been completely destroyed by the Romans, assisted by Aretas of Arabia, as a penalty for a revolt headed by one Judas of Gamala shortly after the death of Herod the Great. As restored by Antipas, Sepphoris became "the ornament of all Galilee." Inasmuch as this rebuilding of Sepphoris was in progress during Jesus' young manhood, and since Nazareth was only an hour's walk from Sepphoris, it is conceivable that the carpenter of Nazareth found work there. Following the coming of Pilate to Judea (A.D. 26), Antipas built a new city on the shore of Lake Galilee, which he named Tiberias in honor of the emperor. Tiberias was provided with a strong wall, a palace, a stadium, and a fine colonnaded street. It was Graeco-Roman in plan and appearance. It was governed through a council of six hundred and a committee of ten, at the head of which was an archon. Antipas now made Tiberias his capital, despite the fact that it was not so large as Sepphoris. Other city improvements made by Antipas were the beautification of Betharampha, which he renamed Livias after the emperor's wife, and the building of the great castle of Machaerus east of the Dead Sea, in which tradition says that John the Baptist was beheaded.

---

[7] It is disputed whether Herodias's first husband was Philip the tetrarch or Herod Philip of Rome.
[8] Mk. 6:17 ff.

The Tetrarchy of Philip. The domain of Philip extended from Galilee and the Jordan eastward to the desert, and from the Yarmuk River northward to the foot of Mount Hermon. It included Iturea, Batanea, Trachonitis, Gaulanitis, and Auranitis. The capital was Caesarea Philippi, a Graeco-Roman city in the fertile, well-watered plain south of Mount Hermon. Philip built Bethsaida Julias in honor of the daughter of Augustus. Bethsaida means "house of fish"; the name intimates that the city was the center of a fishing industry. In personal character Philip was by all odds the best of Herod the Great's sons. His rule was benign. He developed the resources of his tetrarchy and promoted the best interests of his subjects. He aimed at peace and contentment and traveled about adjusting differences. He was Hellenistic in his sympathies and built a number of temples to pagan deities.

The Decapolis. The Decapolis was a league of ten Graeco-Roman cities scattered over Eastjordania. Each was a city-state modeled on the Greek order and independent of tetrarchs and procurators. The capital of the Decapolis league was Scythopolis, the ancient Bethshean, located just west of the Jordan River and about fifteen miles south of Lake Galilee where the transverse Plain of Esdraelon joins the Jordan Valley. The other cities belonging to the league were Pella, Gadara, Hippos, Dium, Gerasa, Philadelphia, Raphana,[9] Kanatha, and (for a while) Damascus. Most of them were in Perea. Roads ran from all of them to the chief city, Scythopolis. The Decapolis union dated from the time of Pompey and was instituted for military and commercial purposes. There were similar Hellenistic cities all over the region west of Jordan.[10]

Political Parties

As already observed, it is impossible to draw a hard and fast line between religious and political alignments among the Jews of Bible times. Hence the political parties here named in some cases also partake of a religious classification.

The Herodians. The Herodians were the supporters of the dynasty of Herod. When Archelaus was deposed (A.D. 6), the Jews were divided on the question of his successor. Some were satisfied with Rome's appointment of a procurator, while others preferred that another member of the Herodian family be appointed ethnarch in Archelaus's place. The latter group represented the party which

---

[9] The site of Raphana is unknown.
[10] On Palestine during the career of Jesus, cf. G. E. Wright and F. V. Filson, *The Westminster Historical Atlas to the Bible* (Philadelphia: 1945), pp. 82–86.

came to be known as the Herodians. The gospels mention them as making common cause with the Pharisees against Jesus.[11] Presumably the Herodians were pro-Hellenistic, since Herod had done more than anyone else to foster Hellenism.

The Zealots or Cananeans. This party began as a group of adventurers or militant patriots, heirs of the spirit of the Maccabees; later they crystallized into a party. The founders were a certain Judas of Gamala and a Zadduk, who together headed a misguided opposition to the census of Quirinius (A.D. 6). This census, of course, had to do with taxation, and the Zealots looked upon taxation by Rome as slavery. They had little difficulty in winning converts to their cause, for Galilee seethed with restlessness because of its subjugation to a foreign power. The more efficiently Rome governed Palestine, the more the Jews resented it. Their claim was that they wished to have no ruler but God. A certain Simon, one of Jesus' disciples, was a Zealot.[12] It was this Zealot party which kept alive the spirit of revolution and finally precipitated the rebellion of A.D. 66–70 against Rome, which ended in the destruction of Jerusalem and the Jewish state.[13]

The Pharisees. The Pharisees, while not primarily a political party, became such virtually by force of necessity. As Jews loyal to their religious past, they were patriots. They disliked the rule of Rome but considered it a just punishment for the sins of the nation. They believed that when the law should be perfectly kept the Messiah would come and Rome's sway would be miraculously brought to an end.

The Sadducees. The Sadducees, as descendants of the high-priestly families, were originally a religious group, but they had long been mixed up in politics by virtue of their civil powers. Since they got and held their wealth and power by virtue of Roman support, their policy was to keep on good terms with Rome. Thus they were diametrically opposed to the Pharisees politically.

Social Conditions

West of the Jordan there were approximately 6,000 square miles of territory on which there lived not over three million Jews. So many other nationalities were now in Palestine that only in Judea, Galilee, and Perea did a Jewish population and Jewish customs predominate. Galilee was more densely populated than Judea. Jerusalem probably did not exceed 100,000 in population.

[11] Mk. 3:6; 12:13. [12] Mk. 3:18; Lk. 6:15; Acts 1:13.
[13] *Vid. infra*, pp. 554–556.

Aramaic was the language spoken by the Jews. All other nationalities spoke Greek, the universal language of the Mediterranean world. Some Jews also used Greek, particularly those who had returned to Palestine after long residence abroad. There was a special synagogue in Jerusalem for such Greek-speaking Jews of the Dispersion.[14] Latin was the official language of the governing class, but it was not understood by the common people. Biblical Hebrew was used in religious services but this was no longer generally understood by the Jews, and Scripture lessons in the synagogue were orally translated into the vernacular Aramaic after being read in the original.

In cities such as Jerusalem, Caesarea, Sepphoris, and Tiberias were to be seen noble buildings towering above the flat houses of the natives. Small towns were very similar to the small Palestinian towns of today. Buildings were close together, streets were narrow, sanitary arrangements were nonexistent, and water was supplied by neighborhood springs or cisterns. Houses were no different from what they always have been—flat-roofed, usually one-roomed, and built of stone.[15] In the smaller towns the only public building was the synagogue, and not all towns had even one of these.

As to division into social classes, the most conspicuous cleavage was that into Jews and foreigners. The foreign influx had been very great under Herod the Great. Most Jewish communities became pretty generally mixed with this foreign element who brought in their own manners and customs. In consequence, foreign influence was very evident in business, amusements, types of building, politics, and religion. Yet despite this commingling there continued to be much mutual antipathy between native and foreigner, and this prevented rapid fusion. Another tendency to social stratification appeared in the gravitation of certain groups into the larger cities and of yet others into the small towns. Thus in the larger cities one found the bankers, the merchants, and the aristocracy of learning and public office; in the smaller towns were congregated the freemen and the menials. Beggars were everywhere. Slaves were fairly numerous, yet their number was decreasing in New Testament times due to the opposition of the Pharisees and the Essenes to human slavery.

Women continued to occupy a lower social position than men and were less thoroughly educated. Woman's sphere was distinctly domestic. Women could go about freely and were not compelled to be veiled. A wife could have property settled upon her by her husband. She might also hold a tenth of her dowry in her own right if arrangements for that were made at the time of marriage, but

---

14 Acts 6:9.
15 On dwellings and community life, cf. *supra*, pp. 145 ff., 154 ff.

if not distinctly specified in the marriage contract, all her property went to her husband.

Family life was generally monogamous, though this was by custom rather than because of any law requiring it. Polygamy was indeed practiced among the most wealthy. Marriage itself was a purely private affair as it had always been among the Hebrews. The families concerned made the arrangements and then a publicly witnessed passing of the bride to the house of her future husband completed the ceremony. A wife was the property of her husband, as had always been the custom among the Jews. The terms of a betrothal were made through a third party styled the "friend of the bridegroom." Betrothal itself consisted in the giving to the bride of a piece of money and a document specifying her future husband's promises and the amount of money to be paid to the bride's father, all of which was publicly announced. Usually also a wedding, similar in character to the betrothal ceremony, followed. It was not a religious ceremony, although it became customary to ask a priest, if one happened to be present at the time, to pronounce a benediction.

Divorce appears to have been much on the increase in New Testament times. Divorce, like marriage, was a private matter rather than one of law. It finally got so that divorces occurred for merely nominal causes, the only condition being that in case of divorce the husband had to pay back the dowry of his wife.

Children followed the status of the father. Boys were more desired than girls, as is practically universal in the Orient.

Education was primarily religious, the aim being to make good Jewish citizens and good servants of God. The system of elementary schools started by Rabbi Simon Ben-Shetach in Jerusalem *circa* 75 B.C. had been steadily extended until most Jewish youths had some sort of education. These elementary schools were held in the synagogues. The instruction, which was oral, was devoted almost exclusively to a study of the Scriptures, which were looked upon as adequate for the rudiments of history and science as well as religion. This continued to the age of ten. From ten to fifteen boys were taught the oral tradition and some further rudimentary science. Thereafter, if a boy planned to be a rabbi, which was what advanced Jewish education regularly led to, he went to the professional rabbinic school at Jerusalem. If a boy desired a liberal education, he had to go abroad to study, to Alexandria, or Tarsus, or Athens. The education of girls, such as it was, was almost exclusively of a practical, domestic character.

As for occupations, agriculture continued to hold the basic position, as in Old Testament times. This was particularly true of Galilee and Samaria which abounded in rich and fruitful farm land and were especially well watered. Judea was only moderately farmed. Perea, outside the areas included within the Decapolis, was mostly waste land.

Commerce was mostly in the hands of Greeks, though a few Jews did engage in trade. The chief commercial centers were Jerusalem, Caesarea, Sepphoris, Bethsaida, Chorazin, and the Decapolis union. Imports included fancy foodstuffs, dresses, and articles of luxury. Exports comprised agricultural products, oil, balsam, figs, salt, and fish. At Tiberias there was a market with a government inspector.

The industries were the manual trades which were now held in high esteem. Even the rabbis had trades. There was a rather extensive division of labor, with features frequently appearing in the guild system. The average wage for such labor was probably a denarius, i.e., nineteen cents, per day.[16] Of course its purchasing power was vastly greater than it would be today.

As to the learned professions, there were the scribes and the lawyers, between which it is difficult to distinguish. Physicians were numerous, though not commanding the fullest confidence, probably with reason. The prevailing belief was that disease was caused by demons, and consequently the physicians of the time resorted to charms and exorcisms and nauseous drinks to drive out the evil spirits. Bleeding was another common method of treatment. There was absolutely no knowledge of anatomy. Had the idea entered their heads, the fear of ceremonial defilement through the touching of a corpse would have proved an effective deterrent to any investigation in anatomy.

In architecture, sculpture, and painting no apparent progress had been made, doubtless due in part to the Old Testament prohibition against making graven images and other likenesses. So the new and remodeled buildings of the period, even those on the temple area, were Graeco-Roman in style.

The Status of Religion

To appreciate Jewish religion as believed and practiced in Palestine in the time of Jesus, one should read again the discussions of Judaism on pp. 378–384; 393–401. Supplemental to this, certain other matters require notice.

Religious Groupings. 1. *The Scribes*. The scribes were the professional interpreters of the law and were the backbone of Judaism. They were conscientious and logically exact in expounding the law

---

[16] Cf. Matt. 20:2.

in its minutest detail. They sought to set fine moral standards for their people but they overdid the matter and became pedants. They were the educators of the day and were often called lawyers,[17] or doctors of the law.[18] Most scribes were Pharisees.

2. *The Pharisees.* The historical origin of the Pharisees has been pointed out earlier in our study.[19] They constituted the largest and most influential group in Jewish society.[20] They were emphatically anti-Hellenizing and somewhat counteracted the liberalizing influence of the Greek element in Palestine with its indifference to Jewish religious rites and practices and its disregard for God, the law, the Sabbath, and the like. The Pharisaic ideal was a truly noble ideal, to live a life in full accord with the will of God. This was the basis of their zeal for the minutest regulations of both written and oral law. They either began as or developed into a fraternity with special vows and held themselves aloof from the common people, thereby earning for themselves the name Pharisees, i.e., "those who keep separate," perhaps at first a nickname.[21] Their doctrine became the orthodox Judaism.[22] They held that when the law should be perfectly kept the Messiah would appear and deliver the Jews from Roman domination. But unfortunately their tendency was to stress the outer forms of worship to the neglect of the inner spirit, and so they grew narrow, censorious, self-righteous, and conceited, while their insistence upon tithes and fees laid a heavy burden upon the poorer people. Not all Pharisees were of the unlovely sort, however. Noble exceptions were such men as Nicodemus,[23] Gamaliel,[24] and Saul (Paul) of Tarsus.

3. *The Sadducees.* The historical emergence of the Sadducees has been previously described.[25] They were friendly toward foreigners and wished to abolish all that made the Jews different from their gentile neighbors, i.e., they favored Hellenism. Their following was found mainly among the aristocrats. Far from sympathizing with the prevailing longing for release from Roman control, they actually wished to keep on good terms with Rome in order to retain their own power. In a way the Sadducees can hardly be called a religious sect since they were most distinguished by worldly traits rather than religious. They accepted only the written Torah and rejected the oral law, the doctrine of resurrection, and the current belief in spirits and angels.

---

[17] Lk. 11:45.   [18] Lk. 5:17.   [19] *Supra,* pp. 418 f.
[20] For a discussion of the various Jewish parties in Palestine cf. W. O. E. Oesterley, *A History of Israel,* vol. ii, pp. 314–328.
[21] Cf. Jn. 7:47 ff.; Lk. 18:9.   [22] Cf. Matt. 23:2.
[23] Cf. Jn. 3:1–15.   [24] Cf. Acts 5:33–40.
[25] *Supra,* pp. 426 f.

4. *The Zadokites.* This peculiar group represented a reform movement within Judaism. They were dissatisfied with the ineffectiveness
of Pharisaic religious leadership and were still more outraged by
the corruption of the Sadducean priesthood. They regarded themselves as the true Israel and were intensely zealous in their devotion
to the law, more so than any other group of Jews. They summoned
the people to repentance, to a very strict type of living, and to membership in their order which alone could deliver the nation from its
unhappy state, they believed. They emphasized messianism and eschatology. The chief center of this party appears to have been at
Damascus. The nature of their emphasis can be gleaned from a fragment of their literature which has survived and which was written
toward the close of the first century B.C.[26]

> God loveth wisdom:
> And counsel he hath set before him:
> Prudence and knowledge minister unto him.
>
> Longsuffering is with him
> And plenteousness of forgiveness
> To pardon those who repent of transgression.[27]

> To love every one his brother as himself, and to strengthen the
> hand of the poor and the needy and the stranger, and to seek
> every one the peace of his brother: To hold aloof from harlots
> according to the law: and that no man should commit a trespass
> against his next of kin:
> To rebuke every one his brother according to the command-
> ment, and not to bear a grudge from day to day, and to separate
> from all the pollutions according to their judgments.[28]

5. *The Essenes.* The Essenes were a monastic order who lived in
celibate communities. They had a solemn oath of induction into their
order and strict rules about frequent ceremonial ablutions, daily
labor, common meals, fasting, etc. Possessions were held in common.
They engaged in agriculture and handicrafts but would have nothing to do with commerce. Though forswearing marriage for themselves, they reared the children of others. In matters of doctrine they
represented an extreme Pharisaism, loyal to the Jewish religion and
meticulous in observance of the Sabbath but (curiously) rejecting
animal sacrifices. They believed in immortality but of the soul only.
They denied the resurrection of the body. Their principal com-

---

[26] *The Fragments of a Zadokite Work;* cf. R. H. Charles, *The Apocrypha and
Pseudepigrapha of the Old Testament*, vol. ii, pp. 785–834; R. H. Pfeiffer, *History
of New Testament Times* (New York: 1949), p. 58.
[27] Zad. 2:2 f.
[28] Zad. 8:17 ff.

munities were in the Wilderness of Judea but they were to be found elsewhere in Palestinian villages. They were complete pacifists in their attitude toward government.[29]

Among the "Dead Sea Scrolls" previously mentioned,[30] one is called by scholars "The Sectarian Document." It appears to have been the manual of discipline of some monastic Jewish sect. As yet the identity of this sect has not been established; the possibility of some relation to the Essenes or the Damascus-centered Zadokites is not excluded. This sectarian community appears to have regarded itself as the true Israel. The document contains an oath and a ritual of initiation of the sect. Initiates entered "into a covenant" and their ideal appears to have been "to keep the commandments of the Lord." Infringement of the rules of the community led to suspension or expulsion.[31]

6. *The Pietists.* Jewish society produced one class of people to whom religion was a genuine, earnest experience, people filled with a quiet devotional spirit, such as Zechariah and Elizabeth, Joseph and Mary, Simeon and Anna, Nathanael, Nicodemus, Joseph of Arimathea, the "rich young ruler," and the scribe who was "not far from the kingdom of God," to mention only some who are referred to in the Gospels.[32] It is perhaps scarcely accurate to speak of these as forming a religious group for they were quite unorganized, but the recognition of the existence of men and women of this type is most important if we are to appreciate the world of Jesus and do justice to the Jewish people of his day. These earnest individuals were on the whole indifferent to the mass of scribal laws. In them is to be found the hopeful side of a healthier popular religion. Their future hope consisted in looking forward to a spiritual redemption of Israel. Their consecrated spirit is revealed in the inspiring poem called *The Magnificat* (Lk. *1:46–55), which may have been a favorite hymn in this circle. They got their spiritual nourishment from the teachings of the psalms and the prophets. They were probably the "poor in spirit" to whom Jesus refers in such fervent commendation in the Sermon on the Mount.[33] They were the "Puritans" of the age.

7. *The Common People.* The masses among the Jews do not seem to have been particularly religious, though believing in religion and revering persons like the Pharisees, who passed for being very religious. Their attitude seems to have resulted from the fact that they

[29] On the Essenes cf. especially W. F. Albright, *From the Stone Age to Christianity* (Baltimore: 1940), pp. 288 f.; R. H. Pfeiffer, *History of New Testament Times* (New York: 1949), pp. 56 f.
[30] *Supra*, pp. 306 f.
[31] Cf. *The Biblical Archaeologist*, xi, 3 (September, 1948), pp. 58–60.
[32] Cf. Lk. 1 f.; Jn. 1:45–50; 3:1–15; Mk. 15:42–46; 10:17–22; 12:34.
[33] Matt. 5:3.

themselves could not hope to keep the law with its exacting burden of requirements. The Pharisees despised the common people both because of this general indifference to the law and also because, in consequence of this neglect of ceremonial, they became, in the eyes of the Pharisees, sinners whose very presence would defile both person and dwelling of the Pharisee. Plain people were as sheep without a shepherd.

The Temple. The temple as rebuilt and enlarged by Herod the Great was one of the most splendid religious buildings in all the ancient world. Begun in 20–19 B.C., the main part was completed within two years but the rest was still under construction during the period of Jesus' public career. In fact it was finished only shortly before its destruction in the great Jewish rebellion of A.D. 66–70.

The temple of Herod comprised a group of buildings with open courts and porches.[34] The temple proper contained two chambers and had a porch at the east end. The *Holy Place,* which was the chamber that opened directly off the porch, contained the altar of incense, the table of showbread (on the north side), and the seven-branched golden candlestick (on the south side of the room). In the rear of the Holy Place was the *Holy of Holies,* separated from the Holy Place by a heavy veil which was lifted only on the Day of Atonement,[35] on which day the high priest alone entered for one part of the sacred ceremony. To the Jew this was the most sacred spot on the face of the earth. In New Testament times the Holy of Holies was absolutely empty.

Directly in front of the temple was the *Court of the Priests.* Here stood the stone altar for the burnt offerings. Toward the south was an immense laver of brass, filled each morning with water. In this court the animals were killed.

Surrounding the Court of the Priests was the *Court of the Men of Israel.* This was a narrow court especially for the male worshipers.

The *Court of the Women* was larger than those already mentioned. It was used by both sexes, but this was as near as women could approach to the temple itself. Women continued to be relegated to an inferior status religiously. Indeed they were not even expected to keep the whole law. They were not obliged to recite the Shema or to wear the distinctive fringes on their mantles. They were not even permitted to wear phylacteries. In the Court of the Women special chambers were provided for lepers, Nazirites, and certain other groups. Here also were boxes for the money offerings.

[34] Josephus gives a full description of the temple in the *History of the Jewish War,* v, 5.
[35] Cf. *supra,* p. 380.

Outside the courts already described was the *Court of the Gentiles.* This court was surrounded by broad covered porches, such as "Solomon's Porch" on the east side.[36] These provided shelter in time of storm and also served as meeting places for instruction and discussion. The existence of this court was an effort to put into effect the Second Isaiah's ideal.

> The foreigners that join themselves to the LORD, to minister unto him, and to love the name of the LORD, to be his servants, every one that keepeth the sabbath from profaning it, and holdeth fast my covenant; even them will I bring to my holy mountain, and make them joyful in my house of prayer: their burnt offerings and their sacrifices shall be accepted upon mine altar; for my house shall be called a house of prayer for all peoples.[37]

This idealistic purpose was defeated because the court was cluttered with the stalls where cattle, doves, and other sacrificial offerings were on sale, and with the tables of the money-changers. No gentile was permitted to penetrate the temple area beyond this court. Violation of this rule permitted the Jews to strike down the offender on the spot without waiting for the procurator's consent to the death penalty.

The priests were assisted in the temple services by the Levites. There were twenty-four divisions of the priests, each on duty for a week at a time.[38] The priests received certain tithes and offerings as compensation.

Every Jew, upon reaching the age of twenty, paid an annual tax of one-half shekel into the temple treasury. Each morning and evening, sacrifices were offered on behalf of the whole nation. Josephus states that there was a daily sacrifice of two lambs and an ox for the emperor's welfare.[39] This must have been irritating to the Zealots. A constant succession of private sacrifices went on during the rest of the day.

The Synagogue and Its Worship. The synagogue, controlled by scribes and Pharisees, was the vital center of Jewish religious thought and life. In the time of Jesus it was required that there be a synagogue in every place where ten would agree to be regular attendants. The larger cities had several synagogues. The synagogue building was so constructed and arranged that the worshipers faced toward Jerusalem. At the end of the room which the worshipers faced was the *ark,* a chest or closet in which were kept the rolls of Holy Scripture in linen cases. In front of the ark was a curtain and before that a lamp which was always kept burning. The elders and the

[36] Jn. 10:23.
[38] Lk. 1:5, 8.
[37] Isa. 56:6 f.
[39] *History of the Jewish War,* ii, 10:4; 17:2 ff.

Pharisees occupied *chief seats* facing the congregation. There was a reading desk upon a raised platform. Control of the synagogue was vested in the council of elders. Officers of the synagogue consisted of (1) the *ruler of the synagogue,* who had the immediate management of the building and its services, and who sat in the "seat of Moses" during service; [40] (2) the *chazzan* or attendant,[41] who had charge of the sacred rolls, kept the building in condition, and administered the scourgings which were meted out to criminals by the local synagogue courts. The chazzan may also have served as village school teacher in the synagogue schools. (3) A third group of synagogue officials was the almoners who collected and disbursed the alms.

Synagogue services were held on all Sabbath mornings and feast days. Less formal services occurred on Sabbath afternoons, on Mondays, and on Thursdays. The order of worship included (1) the Shema (Deut. 6:4–9; 11:13–21; Num. 15:37–41) recited in unison with certain benedictions; (2) prayers, with responses by the congregation, standing; (3) a reading of passages selected by the ruler from the Torah and the Prophets, with an accompanying translation from Hebrew into Aramaic; (4) an address by any person selected by the ruler; [42] and (5) a benediction, provided a priest were present to give it; otherwise a prayer was substituted.

Hellenism in Palestine in the Time of Jesus

It must be borne in mind that Palestine contained many people besides Jews. The Jews were daily brought into contact with Greeks and Romans, and so were the Samaritans. The evidences of Hellenism everywhere stared the Jews in the face, thanks to the Herods, father and son. Josephus says of Herod the Great that "there was not any place of his kingdom fit for the purpose that was permitted to be without somewhat that was for Caesar's honor; and when he had filled his own country with temples, he poured out the like plentiful marks of esteem into his province, and built many cities, which he called Caesareas." [43] In Caesarea on the Mediterranean coast he erected an imposing temple of Caesar on an elevation "so that it was seen a great way off by those who were sailing for that haven." [44] This temple was "excellent both in beauty and largeness; and therein was a colossus of Caesar, not less than that of Jupiter Olympus, which it was made to resemble. The other colossus of Rome was equal to that of Juno at Argos." [45] The cult of emperor worship was not the

[40] Lk. 13:14; 8:41; Matt. 23:2; see Ex. 18:13. Cf. C. C. McCown, *The Ladder of Progress in Palestine* (New York: 1943), p. 272.
[41] Lk. 4:20.   [42] Acts 13:15.   [43] *History of the Jewish War,* i, 21:4.
[44] *Antiquities,* xv, 9:6.   [45] *History of the Jewish War,* i, 26:7.

only religious cult at Caesarea. Zeus, Poseidon, Athena, Apollo, Dionysus, Ares, Helios, Demeter, Heracles, Hygeia were all represented there and so was the Egyptian Serapis.[46]

The situation in Samaria was similar. Herod the Great rebuilt the city and renamed it Sebaste (Augustus), and he erected there a very large temple to Caesar which was surrounded by an extensive sacred area.[47] Remains of this temple can still be seen.

In the north, near the source of the Jordan, Herod the Great erected a white marble temple of Caesar, near Banias.[48] Doubtless this temple contained a similar image of Caesar. Within sight of this glistening temple occurred one of the most notable incidents in the career of Jesus and his disciples.[49]

All Jews were aware that the same Herod who had built these magnificent temples had also built their own white marble temple in Jerusalem. Jews knew very well what those temples to Caesar stood for, the deification of the emperor, and they knew too that every day at their own Jerusalem temple a sacrifice was offered for the emperor. But they would not tolerate any effigy of the emperor in the precincts of the Jerusalem temple and the attempts that were made to introduce it led to bitter disturbances.

Not only the emperor cult but the cult of Dionysus was also well established in Palestine, one of the most notable centers being at Scythopolis, the ancient Bethshean, situated eighteen miles east of Nazareth. In the lifetime of Jesus it was the chief city of the Decapolis. It is said to have surpassed Jerusalem in this period in both population and splendor. Its city walls had a circumference of nearly two miles, and many noble houses stood on the slopes of the hill and in the valley below. Culturally and commercially it overshadowed the entire district. The site of the city has been thoroughly excavated in recent years by archaeologists of the University of Pennsylvania. They reconstructed the Graeco-Roman period of the place from 300 B.C. to A.D. 200. The summit of the hill was crowned by a temple of Dionysus (Bacchus), erected by Demetrius I, king of Macedonia from 294 to 287 B.C. The temple appears to have housed a heroic statute of the deity, who was supposed to have been born there.

During the reign of Antipas Galilee was subjected to intensive Hellenization. We have already mentioned the noble cities which he constructed. Regrettably, no extensive archaeological work has as yet been done in Galilee to throw much needed light upon New Testament

---

[46] Cf. George Francis Hill, *Some Palestinian Cults in the Graeco-Roman Age* (London) published for the British Academy, p. 4.

[47] *History of the Jewish War*, i, 21:2. Cf. C. C. McCown, *The Ladder of Progress in Palestine* (New York: 1943), pp. 202 f.

[48] *History of the Jewish War*, i, 21:3.

[49] Cf. Mk. 8:27 ff.

times. It is hardly likely that emperor worship would have been omitted from Tiberias, which the ardently Hellenistic tetrarch built to honor the emperor. The eminent historian Mahaffy states that no outlying country in Alexander's empire was ever so thoroughly Hellenized as northern Palestine and Syria.[50] It is well to bear in mind that such things were in the environment of Jesus and his disciples.

[50] John Pentland Mahaffy, *The Progress of Hellenism in Alexander's Empire* (Chicago: 1905), p. 97.

Chapter 24

JESUS OF NAZARETH

"It was little by little and in different ways that God spoke in old times to our forefathers through the prophets, but in these latter days he has spoken to us in a Son," wrote a first-century Christian.[1] Little by little we have traced the development of the Biblical religion and literature. We have now reached the central personality of the Bible, Jesus of Nazareth.

Sources for a Knowledge of the Life of Jesus

There are no contemporary records of the life and teachings of Jesus. He himself wrote nothing. Nor have any documents been found to throw light upon his life and teachings which date within the generation that witnessed his life and death. One of his disciples named Matthew published a document called the "Sayings of Jesus." This we know from a second-century writer named Papias who states: "Matthew in the Hebrew (Aramaic) dialect compiled the discourses (*logia*) and each one interpreted them as he was able." This writing has not come down to us except as the Gospels of Matthew and Luke drew from it for the discourses they attribute to Jesus. Many of the apostle Paul's letters have been preserved but they are of little help in reconstructing a mental picture of the Jesus who walked and talked in Galilee.[2] So it happens that approximately forty years elapsed after Jesus' crucifixion before the first extant sketch of his life was written. This was the Gospel according to Mark.

The main sources for a knowledge of the life of Jesus are the four gospels found in the New Testament. These were written, in the judgment of most scholars, between A.D. 65 and 110, and in the following order: Mark, between 65 and 70; Matthew, between 70 and 80; Luke, between 75 and 85; and John, not later than 100.

Matthew, Mark, and Luke are called the synoptic gospels because they give a basically identical portrait of Jesus, agree in their

---

[1] Heb. 1:1. Quoted from the Chicago Version.
[2] Passages from Paul's writings which refer or allude to facts in the life of Jesus are Rom. 1:3; 9:3 ff.; 15:3; 1 Cor. 2:2; 9:5; 11:23–26; 15:1–11; 2 Cor. 5:21; 8:9; 10:1; Gal. 1:19; 3:1; 4:4; Phil. 2:5–8.

chronology, and exhibit extraordinarily marked identities of phraseology which prove a literary connection of the three. The Fourth Gospel, John, has little in common with the other three either as to incidents narrated, sayings of Jesus quoted, or total impression of the personality which Jesus exhibited in his words and deeds.

How did the synoptic gospels come to be so much alike? Why do they differ among themselves in just the way they do? These questions about the literary relationships of Matthew, Mark, and Luke constitute what is known as the synoptic problem. Practically every verse of Mark is found in one or both of the other synoptic gospels. Moreover, in the arrangement of their total mass of material, both Matthew and Luke follow Mark's outline. As to matter not found in Mark but appearing in the others, a surprisingly large proportion is common to both Matthew and Luke, indicating their literary dependence on a common source.[3] This non-Markan material found in Matthew and Luke is predominantly teaching material. The source (whether one document or many) from which the Gospels of Matthew and Luke drew this non-Markan teaching material is frequently referred to by scholars as the Second Source (Mark being the first source), or more commonly as "Q" (from the German word *Quelle,* meaning source).[4]

What we have in the gospels is essentially the following. A brief sketch of Jesus' life was written A.D. *circa* 70 by John Mark. This Mark is mentioned as a companion of more distinguished missionaries, Paul and Barnabas and Peter.[5] That Mark was an attendant of the apostle Peter, from whom Mark got his knowledge of the career of Jesus, is affirmed by the Christian bishop Papias of Hierapolis (already quoted) who, writing A.D. *circa* 135, quotes an earlier man, whom he calls "the Elder," as follows: "And the Elder said this also: Mark having become the interpreter of Peter wrote down accurately everything that he remembered, without, however, recording in order what was either said or done by Christ. [In what follows it is not clear whether Papias is still quoting the Elder or giving his own view.] For neither did he hear the Lord nor did he follow him; but afterwards, as I said, (attended) Peter, who adapted his instructions to the needs (of his hearers?) but had

---

[3] The literary relationships of the synoptic gospels are best exhibited in a synopticon in which the text of the three gospels is arranged in parallel columns. Cf. *Gospel Parallels—A Synopsis of the First Three Gospels,* published by Thomas Nelson & Sons (New York: 1949) ; E. D. Burton and E. J. Goodspeed, *A Harmony of the Synoptic Gospels in English,* published by Chas. Scribner's Sons (New York: 1917) ; or *Huck's Synopsis of the First Three Gospels,* arranged for English readers by Ross L. Finney, published by the Methodist Book Concern (New York).

[4] Many scholars restrict the application of "Q" to that discourse material which is common to Matthew and Luke and is not found in Mark.

[5] Acts 12:12, 25 ; 13:5, 13 ; 15:37 ff. ; Col. 4:10 ; 2 Tim. 4:11 ; Philem. 24 ; 1 Pet. 5:13.

no design of giving an account of the Lord's oracles (or *words*). So then Mark made no mistake while he thus wrote some things as he remembered them, for he made it his one care not to omit anything that he heard or to set down any false statement therein." [6] Mark's life of Jesus concentrated upon incidents that stood out sharply, both deeds performed by Jesus and things that happened to him, with some, but not much, of Jesus' teaching.

Within the decade following the appearance of Mark, the Gospel according to Matthew was written. This was based upon Mark's work, to which was added a very considerable body of Jesus' teachings. Whence was this teaching material derived? Its ultimate source may have been the Aramaic "Sayings of Jesus" written by the disciple Matthew, and perhaps this is why the new gospel was called by the name of Matthew. The Gospel according to Matthew also supplied as a preface certain stories about Jesus' parentage and infancy (chapters 1 f.). This made a fairly complete manual for use. by a generation of Christians who, for knowledge of what Jesus had said or done, could no longer appeal to anyone who had actually been with Jesus.

At the same time that Matthew appeared, or just a few years later, Luke wrote his "treatise," as he himself calls it. [7] This treatise comprised the Gospel according to Luke and the Book of Acts, which were originally one work, Luke-Acts. [8] The gospel portion was detached from the rest of the treatise early in the second century that it might be published with the other three gospels as a four-fold Gospel. As Luke explains in his preface (Lk. 1 :1–4), there had already been many attempts to write accounts of the events of Jesus' life. He assures Theophilus that he had tried to produce a document by which he might "know the certainty" of what he had been taught about Jesus. Apparently there was not the fullest confidence being placed in all the stories or accounts current about Jesus at that time. What Luke's gospel really does is to make use of Mark's outline with but little alteration, rearrange the discourse material Matthew had also used (though he got it not from Matthew but from the prior source) so as to give many of the utterances of Jesus new settings, [9] and to add a great deal of teaching material not found in Mark and Matthew (Lk. 9 :51–18 :14), conspicuous examples being the parable of the good Samaritan [10] and the parable of the lost son. [11] This Luke was the "beloved physician," companion and fellow worker of the apostle Paul. [12]

[6] Quoted in Eusebius, *Church History*, iii, 39.   [7] Acts 1 :1.
[8] Cf. H. J. Cadbury, *The Making of Luke-Acts* (New York: 1927).
[9] Cf. e.g., Matt. 5 :13 with Lk. 14 :34; Matt. 5 :25 f. with Lk. 12 :58 f.; and Matt. 6 :24 with Lk. 16 :13.   [10] Lk. 10 :30–37.
[11] Lk. 15 :11–32.   [12] Col. 4 :14; Philem. 24; 2 Tim. 4 :11.

Between the writing of the Gospel of Luke and the Gospel of John a period of perhaps twenty or twenty-five years elapsed during which Christians in various parts of the Roman Empire had been meeting severe trials and, in a few instances, martyrdom. This had widened the gap between Christian and non-Christian to such a degree as to lead to a fresh and better appreciation of the meaning of Jesus' life. The Gospel of John is a Christian's reinterpretation of the religious significance of Jesus that grew out of deepening personal experience.

Other ancient writers who refer to Jesus are the Jewish historian Josephus (in passages of doubtful authenticity) [13] and the Roman writers Tacitus,[14] Suetonius,[15] Pliny the Younger,[16] and Lucian.[17] None of them, however, contributes anything of value to our general knowledge. In fact they say little save to mention that there was such a person.

Jesus' Life Prior to His Public Career

The Name "Jesus." "Jesus" is the Greek equivalent of the Hebrew "Joshua," and means "Yahweh saves." [18] It was a name commonly given to children, and therefore when he was referred to as "Jesus of Nazareth," [19] or as "the Nazarene," [20] it was simply to distinguish him from others named Jesus.[21] Where he is referred to as "Jesus Christ" or "Jesus the Christ," it should be borne in mind that "Christ" is the Greek equivalent for the Hebrew word "messiah" and means "the anointed one," a term having a messianic significance, and therefore an honorific title applied to Jesus.

The Date and Place of Jesus' Birth. Jesus was born while Herod the Great was king.[22] Herod died in March or April, 4 B.C. Sometime prior to his death he had ordered the murder of the boy infants of Bethlehem who were "two years old and under." [23] This age limit obviously was intended to make sure that Jesus would not be overlooked in the slaughter and implies that Jesus was in his second year at the time. This intimates the year 6 or 5 B.C. as the date of Jesus' birth.

Each December, at the Buhl Planetarium in Pittsburgh, the pro-

[13] *Antiquities,* xx, 9 :1 ; xviii, 3 :3.
[14] *Annals,* xv, 44, written A.D. *circa* 115–117.
[15] *Life of Claudius,* xxv ; Suetonius lived A.D. 65–135.
[16] *Letters,* x, 96, written A.D. 111.
[17] *Death of Peregrinus,* 11, 13, written between A.D. 165 and 175.
[18] Cf. Matt. 1 :21.   [19] E.g., Lk. 18 :37.   [20] E.g., Mk. 10 :47.
[21] It has been suggested that there may have been some confusion about the name "Jesus" at the time of the trial before Pilate, the name of Barabbas being possibly Jesus Barabbas, whom Pilate was careful to distinguish from "Jesus who is called Christ"; cf. Matt. 27 :17, 22.
[22] Matt. 2 :1 ; cf. *supra,* pp. 425 f.   [23] Matt. 2 :16.

jector is run back to the year 7 B.C. and the demonstration for the public shows the changing aspect of the sky from November of 7 B.C. through May of 6 B.C. In February of 6 B.C. the three planets, Mars, Jupiter, and Saturn, appear in triple conjunction low in the western sky just after sunset. This verifies the calculation made by Kepler, who observed Jupiter and Saturn in close conjunction on December 17, 1603, and in the autumn of 1604, when they were still near each other, Mars passed Saturn and Jupiter. Scientific curiosity led Kepler to calculate how often that phenomenon happened, and he calculated an occurrence for 7–6 B.C. Such a planetary conjunction suggests an explanation of the "star of the east" at the time of Jesus' birth.[24] Another suggestion would identify the star of Bethlehem as a nova, i.e., a star that suddenly flares up only to fade away after a few weeks or months, such as the astonishing Nova Herculis of 1934–1935, which reached its maximum brilliance at Christmas time.

Lk. 2:1–4 dates the birth of Jesus "when Quirinius was governor of Syria," which was A.D. 6–9. There is some evidence that Quirinius at an earlier date was in service under the legate of Syria, though exactly when is problematic; 3–2 B.C. has generally been regarded as the date, though more recent research tends to push the date back to 11–8 B.C.[25] At that time Quirinius may have been dispatched to conduct a census in Judea, though there is no evidence of any such census having taken place before A.D. 6.

Again, Lk. 3:1, 23 has Jesus "about thirty years of age" in the "fifteenth year of Tiberius Caesar," which was A.D. 28 or 29. This would place the birth of Jesus in 1 B.C. The date would be three or four years after the death of Herod the Great, but it should be observed that Luke has no information about the wise men from the east or the slaughter of the Bethlehem infants.

Again, Jn. 2:20 associates a certain incident in the public career of Jesus with the forty-sixth year of the reconstruction of the temple, which would be A.D. 26 or 27, for the work was begun under Herod the Great in 20–19 B.C. Jn. 8:57 cites the remark, "Thou art not yet fifty years old," i.e., between forty and fifty. This would push the date of Jesus' birth back to *circa* 15 B.C. or even to 20 B.C.[26]

The date of Jesus' birth cannot therefore be determined precisely, but all things considered, 6 B.C. is the most probable.[27] Nor can the

[24] Matt. 2:2. Cf. "The Christmas Star," *Sky and Telescope,* vol. v, no. 2, whole no. 50 (December, 1945), pp. 7–8.
[25] Cf. Adolf Deissmann, *Light from the Ancient East* (rev. ed.; New York: 1927), pp. 5 f., for a discussion of the Quirinius inscriptions.
[26] Cf. A. T. Olmstead, *Jesus in the Light of History* (New York: 1942), p. 2. He favors the date 20 B.C.
[27] The Roman monk Dionysius Exiguus (died A.D. 556) was the first to suggest reckoning time as before and after the birth of Christ. Unfortunately he made a mistake in computing the year one as 754 A.U.C. Herod the Great died in 750 A.U.C.

particular day of the year on which Jesus was born be determined, for
there is not the slightest evidence in the gospels. The early church
celebrated the event on January 6, the date of the Epiphany of
Dionysus, which date is still celebrated by the Armenian church as
the birthday of Christ. The celebration of December 25 began in the
fourth century. December 25 was chosen for the following reason. It
was at that time (fourth century) believed that the universe was
originally created at the time of the spring equinox, reckoned as
March 25 in the Julian calendar. By similar reasoning it was held that
the inception of the new creation in Christ must have been on the
same day of the year, which would bring his birth nine months later,
at the time of the winter solstice, December 25. No doubt this date
commended itself to many Christians who had been converted from
the cult of Mithra, in which cult December 25 was celebrated as the
birthday of the *Sol Invictus* (The Invincible Sun).

Matt. 2:1–6 and Lk. 2:1–20 locate the birth of Jesus at Bethlehem. This was determined by the Micah (5:2) prophecy. All four
gospels testify that the family lived in Nazareth.[28] Luke represents
Nazareth as the home of Joseph and Mary before their visit to
Bethlehem,[29] and has them return there directly after the presentation
in the temple, i.e.. about forty days after Jesus' birth.[30] Matthew, on
the other hand, says nothing about their residence in Nazareth prior
to the birth of Jesus, and does not have them go there to live until
two years after his birth.[31]

The Narratives of Jesus' Birth. Narratives concerning the
birth of Jesus are found in Matthew 1 f., and in Luke 1 f. Why not
in the other gospels? It should be observed that the gospels were
written for the express purpose of convincing first- and second-
century minds (both Christians and pagans whom Christians desired to convert to Christianity) that Jesus was the Son of God.
"These are written, that ye may believe that Jesus is the Christ, the
son of God." [32] Definite stages of development in early Christian
thought on this subject are traceable. The first stage of belief seems
to have been that Jesus was Son of God from the time of his resurrection; he was "declared to be the Son of God . . . by the resurrection
from the dead." [33] This was the prevailing belief of the apostle Paul
and it accounts for his lack of emphasis on the earthly life of Jesus.
Paul's letters were all written before any of the gospels were written.
The next stage of development was to push the matter back in time to
the baptism of Jesus. This is the view of the Gospel of Mark,

---

28 Matt. 13:54; Mk. 6:1; Lk. 4:16; Jn. 1:45 f.; 7:41 f.
29 Lk. 1:26 f.; 2:4.
30 Lk. 2:39; cf. Lk. 2:22 and Lev. 12:1–4.
31 Matt. 2:19, 33.   32 Jn. 20:31.   33 Rom. 1:4.

written, as we have observed, before any of the other gospels.[34]
Mark states that his purpose was to trace the beginning of the gospel
of Jesus the Son of God,[35] and he commences with Jesus' mystical
experience at his baptism, emphasizing the voice which said, "Thou
art my beloved Son." [36] Mark manifestly knew nothing about the
miraculous birth of Jesus or he certainly would have included it in
his gospel, for it is the very sort of thing his gospel stresses throughout, i.e., emphasis upon the miraculous as proving that Jesus was the
Son of God. Papias stated that Mark "made it his one care not to
omit anything that he had heard." [37] It should be remarked, and it
will be discussed later,[38] that emphasis upon the miraculous was the
sort of thing which brought most certain conviction to people of the
time, Christian and pagan alike, for the miracle thought pattern was
the prevailing thought form of the age. Had the miraculous birth of
Jesus been a matter of common belief when Mark wrote his gospel,
he could not have left it out, for without it his gospel would not have
found acceptance by Christians and would not have survived. The
next stage in the development was to push the matter of Jesus' divine
sonship back to the time of his birth, and this is the stage of Christian
thought represented by the Gospels of Matthew and Luke. There
remained but one possible thing to do more, viz., to push the matter
back of Jesus' birth and make him the pre-existent Son of God, and
this is the stage of Christian thought represented by the Gospel of
John (chapter 1).

The dogma of the miraculous birth of Jesus has occasioned no
end of controversy. Into that controversy we do not need to enter.
Jesus was what he was no matter how he was born. The thoughts
which he thought and the influence he exerted are what primarily
concern us.[39]

Jesus' Residence in Nazareth. We moderns have a large interest in the life of Jesus during the silent years which preceded his
public career. The ancient Jewish mind, however, shared no such
interest. The life of Jesus was written up in typically Jewish fashion,
with narratives concerning his birth and infancy and then with
an account of his mature ministry. That is all that we have, for
example, in the Biblical accounts of Moses and Samuel.[40] Any reconstruction of the life of Jesus during the silent years can therefore

---

[34] *Vid. supra,* pp. 483 ff.   [35] Mk. 1:1.   [36] Mk. 1:11.
[37] *Vid. supra,* pp. 484 f.   [38] *Infra,* p. 511.
[39] The student who is interested in the controversy will find the matter fully
discussed in J. G. Machen, *The Virgin Birth of Christ* (New York: 1930), which
accepts the dogma, and in Paul Lobstein, *The Virgin Birth of Christ* (New York:
1903), which rejects the dogma.
[40] The likenesses of the Jesus infancy stories to those of Samuel in 1 Sam. 1 f.
are particularly interesting. Cf. especially the Samuel poem (1 Sam. 2:1–10) with
the Magnificat (Lk. 1:46–55).

only be in terms of the life of the average Jew of the time in the light of what is known about the social-historical situation, as discussed in Chapter 23. Specifically, we know next to nothing about Jesus prior to his public career. Luke alone speaks of the boyhood of Jesus and tells only one event (Lk. 2:40–52).

1. *Home Life.* The household of Joseph was apparently a normal Jewish family of the moderately poor but self-respecting type. Besides Jesus there were other children in the home, four brothers, James, Joseph, Judas, and Simon, and two or more sisters whose names are not preserved in the gospels.[41] Such a large family probably never enjoyed an abundance of good things and no doubt often felt the pinch of hard times. It is instructive to read the teachings of Jesus with a view to seeing how they may reflect the struggle for existence in his early home, which struggle helped to shape Jesus' attitude toward life; e.g., Matt. 6:25, 28, 31 f.; 10:29 (cf. Lk. 12:6). Tradition has it that Joseph died while Jesus was still a youth.[42] This obliged Jesus, the eldest son in the home, to assume the headship of the family and the burden of its support early in life.

We may understand that the parents of Jesus were sincerely religious and sturdily virtuous folk, quiet and unassuming about their religion, belonging no doubt to that class in Jewish society which we have designated the Pietists.[43] It is a pity that religious dogma has depreciated Joseph and that art has depicted him as a nonentity. A genuine tribute to his excellence of character is to be inferred from the fact that Father was the noblest epithet Jesus could use to describe the character of God, and we may well imagine that in his own home Jesus had seen the nobility of fatherhood exemplified.

2. *Occupation.* Jesus was by trade a carpenter.[44] The Greek word for *carpenter* means not only a worker in wood but also, in a broader sense, a builder, i.e., one who plans and directs constructive work. The tasks of such a craftsman in a small village like Nazareth would include the erection and repair of the simple structures that served for dwellings,[45] building barns, i.e., storehouses for grain, the making of simple furniture for homes, and the fashioning of tools, yokes, plows, and the like.

The teachings of Jesus abound in stories which reflect how his craft helped to shape his philosophy of life. Illustrations of this are his parable of the housebuilders (Matt. *7:24–27 = Lk. 6:47–49); his parable of the man who tore down his barns and built larger ones (Lk. *12:16–21); his parable of the man who set about building a

---

[41] Mk. 6:3 = Matt. 13:55.

[42] The last mention of him in the gospels is in connection with the visit to Jerusalem when Jesus was twelve (Lk. 2:41–50).

[43] Cf. *supra,* p. 477.   [44] Mk. 6:3; cf. Matt. 13:55.   [45] Cf. *supra,* pp. 145 ff.

tower without enough funds to complete it (Lk. *14:28 ff.); his interest in the foundations and structures of the temple area (Mk. *13:1 f. = Matt. 24:1 f. = Lk. 21:5 f.); and his parable about hiring laborers (Matt. *20:1–16).

There is no reason for supposing that Jesus worked at his craft in Nazareth only. Opportunities for employment were afforded him in nearby communities. At a half-hour's walk south from Nazareth was the largest village of Galilee, Japhia. North of Nazareth, an hour's walk, was Sepphoris, the largest city in Galilee where, during Jesus' young manhood, a huge building program was in progress under the patronage of Herod Antipas.[46] Here Jesus found something more than employment. He had firsthand contact with Hellenistic culture, for Sepphoris was "the ornament of all Galilee," and here he met and mingled with non-Jews, for Galilee had always been "Galilee of the Gentiles." [47] It is important to mark such diversified and broadening social contacts in the experience of Jesus during his formative years.

3. *The Education of Jesus.* We may understand that Jesus shared such education as was available to the average Jewish boy of the time.[48] Just how far his formal training went it is impossible to say. Certainly he could read and write.[49] The very first thing he would be taught as a child at synagogue school would be to draw the letters in the Shema.[50] He would have drawn the letters in the Old Semitic script. We have previously mentioned the interesting ossuary, dating from the early Christian era, which contains the name "Yeshua" in this script [51] and helps us visualize how Jesus would have written his own name:

$$\text{ישוע}$$

The language Jesus spoke was Aramaic, the vernacular of the Jewish people in Palestine in the first century. It is generally assumed that Jesus knew Hebrew, the language of the sacred writings.[52] Whether Jesus could speak and understand Greek can only be a matter of conjecture. Galilee probably was bilingual (Greek and Aramaic), and working in Sepphoris would certainly have brought Jesus into intimate contact with non-Jewish employees who spoke Greek. The gospels represent Jesus as carrying on conversations with non-Jews, e.g., with the Syrophoenician woman,[53] with Pilate,[54] and with the

---

46 Cf. *supra*, p. 469.
47 Isa. 9:1; Matt. 4:15.   48 Cf. *supra*, p. 473.
49 Lk. 4:16; Jn. 8:6.   50 *Vid. supra*, p. 384.
51 *Supra*, pp. 203–205. Cf. R. A. S. Macalister, *A Century of Excavation in Palestine* (New York: 1925), p. 252.
52 Cf. Lk. 4:16–21.   53 Mk. 7:24–29 = Matt. 15:21–28.
54 Mk. 15:2–5 = Matt. 27:11–14 = Lk. 23:3.

centurion, although this man may have spoken Aramaic, being presumably in the service of Herod Antipas.[55]

The Fourth Gospel represents that Jesus was addressed as Rabbi,[56] but in this gospel John Baptist is similarly addressed by his disciples.[57] Jn. 1:38 interprets the term as meaning "teacher," and it does not imply formal rabbinic training on the part of either John Baptist or Jesus. Indeed, Jn. 7:15 explicitly affirms Jesus' lack of such formal training.

Luke represents Jesus as having an eager and inquiring mind when a youth (Lk. 2:41–47) and affirms that "Jesus advanced in wisdom." [58] In the eighteen years that intervened between the boyhood visit of Jesus to Jerusalem and the beginning of his public career (Lk. 3:23), we may justly assume that his mind continued active and that a keen interest in religion stimulated him to study of and reflection upon Jewish Scriptures, canonical and other. He had three main ways by which he could enlarge his religious experience, increase his theological knowledge, and develop his idealistic thinking.

The first of these was the weekly services in the synagogue at Nazareth where Jesus was a regular attendant until he began his public career.[59] Here he heard the Scriptures read year after year. The Pentateuch was read in a cycle of Sabbath lessons completed once every three years. Selections from the Prophets were read at the services. Perhaps Jesus in his youth occasionally read the lessons in the synagogue. Children were encouraged to do so.

> When a preacher was present, he read the prophetical lesson, and in the absence of such a one the children read it, perhaps at greater length. For the prophetical reading was by nature a sermon, and as the service concluded with a sermon, the prophetical lesson concluded the service when no preacher was present.[60]

The passages read were translated into the vernacular Aramaic. Certainly Jesus would have had abundant opportunity to memorize some parts of Scripture and to know the substance of others. The synagogue was a place of worship and of teaching. Such teaching as Jesus heard in the synagogue year after year was assimilated into his own thinking.

A second educational advantage which Jesus had in the formative period was, of course, private study of the Jewish Scriptures. Copies of the Scriptures in the synagogue were available for reading. 1 Macc. 1:56 f. refers to the possession and use of private "books of the law" in the houses of certain devout Jews, and this

---

[55] Matt. 8:5–13 = Lk. 7:1–10.
[56] Jn. 1:38, 49; 3:2; 6:25.   [57] Jn. 3:26.
[58] Lk. 2:52.   [59] Lk. 4:16.
[60] I. Abrahams, *Studies in Pharisaism and the Gospels* (Cambridge: 1917), i, 4.

was not long before Jesus' time. There were probably only few such, however, owing to the cost of writing materials. Other literature besides the Law and the Prophets was in circulation, e.g., the books of the Hagiographa, i.e., the third division of the Hebrew canon, which books were not read in the synagogue services in Jesus' time. The gospel records reflect Jesus' acquaintance with Proverbs, Sira, and Ecclesiastes. One of the important books which originated in Galilee was the *Testaments of the Twelve Patriarchs*,[61] and this book of splendid ethical teachings functioned in religious circles in Galilee much as *Pilgrim's Progress* once did in America. Not only such a book as the *Testaments* but also the apocalypses, e.g., Daniel and 1 Enoch,[62] were popular books of edification of the time in Galilee, where Jesus derived his religious culture.[63] Jesus' thorough study of the Scriptures is evidenced by the way he handled the Scriptures in his teaching.

In the third place, Jesus, when growing up at Nazareth, would have had some opportunity to hear wisdom taught by the sages.[64] These sages were the thinkers of Judaism. They were less interested in the legal treatment of the Old Testament than were other scribes, less interested in the ritual at the temple, less interested in the administration of government or the law. They were concerned to understand life, to live it worthily, and to teach others to do so. They made a specialty of teaching the people. These wisdom teachers carried forward the ethical emphasis of the great Old Testament prophets.

Jesus' Call to Public Life

The Ministry of John the Baptist. It was a movement inaugurated by John the Baptist, described in Mk. *1:1–8 = Matt. 3:1–12 = Lk. 3:1–18, which stimulated Jesus to enter upon a public career. Mk. 1:9 definitely represents Jesus as attaching himself to the John the Baptist movement. What led him to do so?

There were several movements, political and religious, in vogue at the time, bidding for the allegiance of young Jews.[65] None of these movements seems to have appealed to Jesus. The one that would have thrust itself most insistently upon his attention as a youth in Galilee was the hot-headed Zealot movement which was chiefly localized in Galilee. This group definitely looked to the use of force to realize national aspirations. Such a course of action was futile and could only lead to ruin and the defeat of the very aspirations they

[61] Cf. *supra*, pp. 458 ff.   [62] Cf. *supra*, pp. 426, 429, 445–452.
[63] Cf. T. Gad 6:3 (*supra*, pp. 460 f.) with Lk. 17:3; Matt. 18:15, 35.
[64] Cf. *supra*, pp. 398 f.   [65] *Vid. supra*, pp. 470 f., 474–478.

cherished. Jesus could readily have foreseen that. Had not the neighboring city of Sepphoris been laid in utter ruin (shortly after the death of Herod the Great) by just such a course of action, an object lesson to any thoughtful Jew of what revolution would lead to? As a fact of history the Zealot movement did lead to exactly that in the year 70. The Zealot movement did not serve the social or religious well-being of the common people of the land.

The religious movement that would have been most definitely before Jesus' attention was Pharisaism. It was the teachings of the Pharisees that dominated the synagogues and therefore constituted the religious atmosphere in which Jesus grew up in Nazareth. The ideal of the Pharisees was truly noble, the ideal of all life adjusted to the will of God and lived in accord with God's will, an ideal of a whole people knowing the will of God through the law. There was a splendid ethical emphasis in Pharisaism which Jesus assimilated into his own teaching. But there was also an unlovely side to Pharisaism, its insistence upon minute legalism and the selfrighteousness to which it led. Apparently these phases of Pharisaism were repellent to Jesus. Plain people were of course welcomed to the synagogues if they chose to attend, but the masses of them did not choose to attend and were therefore without religious teaching.

John the Baptist was a dramatic personality quite like the Old Testament prophets, notably Elijah.[66] He was a prophet of doom, warning the nation of approaching destruction and urging repentance to avert the threatening judgment. Like the Old Testament prophets, John the Baptist threw the emphasis upon social righteousness (Lk. *3:10–15). John's preaching seems to have aroused widespread attention and to have drawn to him a large popular following.[67] There was an inner circle of disciples of John.[68] The movement survived the death of its founder for a considerable time. There was a remnant of the movement in Ephesus A.D. circa 55.[69] Ultimately the movement was absorbed in Christianity. This is why the gospels are at considerable pains to point out the subordination of John to Jesus.[70] To the present day John the Baptist is revered as a saint by the Mandaeans, a sect localized near the head of the Persian Gulf. Some historians regard this sect as a remnant of the John the Baptist movement but others contend that the sect is not older than the Mohammedan era, i.e., A.D. 622.

In John, ancient prophetism seemed to have been revived. It was the ancient prophets who had discerned God most clearly and had

[66] Matt. 11:14.   [67] Mk. 1:5 = Matt. 3.5.
[68] Mk. 2:18 = Matt. 9:14 = Lk. 5:33; Matt. 11:2 = Lk. 7:18 f.; Mk. 6:29 =
Matt. 14:12.
[69] Acts 18:24 ff. = 19:7.   [70] Cf. especially Jn. 1.

lifted the idea of God to the ethical level. They had made religion consist in righteousness rather than ritual. Their labors to promote righteousness among men had evidenced God in action. We may understand this as one reason why John's movement would have appealed to Jesus. The ancient prophets had always been concerned with the moral welfare of the common people. John the Baptist was similarly concerned. The plain people seem to have turned to him gladly.[71] This would have awakened a responsive chord in Jesus. He himself grew up among plain people and was one of them. He knew their problems and their needs and their lack of religious help and hope. He discerned that "they were as sheep not having a shepherd."[72] John's ministry was directed to the promotion of righteousness, both individual and social, and this purpose was dramatized in his practice of baptism, a ritual act of thoroughly ethical import.[73] John was an apocalyptist, i.e., he anticipated God's intervention to destroy evil[74] and establish righteousness. Doubtless this also appealed to Jesus, though Jesus differed from John in apocalyptic emphasis. What ought a high-minded youth like Jesus to have done about such a spiritual recovery movement as that of John the Baptist? As a matter of fact, Jesus joined the John movement,[75] for thus it became him "to fulfill all righteousness."[76]

The Baptism and Temptation of Jesus. The occasion of Jesus' baptism (Mk. *1 :9–11 = Matt. 3 :13–17 = Lk. 3 :21 f.) was for him a profound spiritual experience. We may classify it as a mystical religious experience, of which we have met several examples.[77] The experience is described in the gospels in terms of the prevailing thought form of the age. The Jewish world view posited a number of heavens above which the deity dwelt, and some Jewish teachers held that occasionally the heavens opened and the echo of the divine Voice (*Bath Qol,* "Daughter of the Voice") was heard.[78]

"Thou art my beloved Son, in thee I am well pleased (ie., thou art my Chosen)." What could such an experience have meant to Jesus ethically? An answer to this is doubtless to be found in terms of the Second Isaiah's conception of the Servant who was God's Chosen (Isa. *41 :8 f.; *43 :10; *44 :1 f.). We have observed that this prophet taught that the idea of a chosen people meant not chosen for special favors but chosen for special service.[79] It is along this line that the story of the temptation of Jesus (Mk. 1 :12 f. = Matt. *4 :1–11 = Lk. 4 :1–13) is to be understood. The force of the testing related to

[71] Lk. 3 :18.   [72] Mk. 6 :34 = Matt. 9 :36.
[73] Mk. 1 :4.   [74] Matt. 3 :12 = Lk. 3 :17.
[75] Mk. 1 :9 = Matt. 3 :13 = Lk. 3 :21.   [76] Matt. 3 :15.
[77] *Vid. supra,* pp. 116, 130 f., 323 f., 329 f., 342, 368.
[78] An instance of this is in Josephus, *Antiquities,* xiii, 10 :3.
[79] *Supra,* p. 374.

the proposition, "if thou art the Son of God." [80] Was Jesus to share the common lot of human kind or to be the recipient of benefits not available to all alike? Man must live by bread and must get it by toil; similarly man must face up to the dangers with which life is beset. Ought the specially Chosen of God to be relieved of this and be miraculously fed when hungry and rescued when in peril? Moreover, what ought a religious man to get for himself by being religious? Conventional theology of the time affirmed that religion and material prosperity went hand in hand and a man's material wealth was an index of his righteousness. It would not be too much, therefore, for God's Chosen One to expect to possess "all the kingdoms of the world" for himself.[81] Jesus rejected the whole proposition. Through a feeling of oneness with plain people he had come with them to John's baptism; he would continue to be one with them. As God's Son he was chosen for a special service to his fellow beings that they might all be sons of God (Matt. *5:45; cf. Lk. 6:35).

The career of John the Baptist was cut short by Herod Antipas, who caused the arrest of John,[82] no doubt because he regarded John as a dangerous agitator. The Jews cordially hated Rome, and Jewish national hope looked toward deliverance from the yoke of Roman domination. Any such popular gathering of people as that about John the Baptist would, in the eyes of the political rulers, furnish pretty inflammable material for revolution, and no doubt Herod's idea was to stop a revolution before it got started. Besides, the gospels indicate that Herod had a purely personal reason for antipathy toward John.[83] Mk. 1:14 = Matt. 4:12 indicates that it was after the arrest of John that Jesus began his own public ministry in Galilee.

The Galilean ministry of Jesus constituted the major portion of his public career. During the Galilean ministry Capernaum was Jesus' headquarters. Some commentators classify certain incidents in the career of Jesus as a "Border Ministry," i.e., a ministry in the districts bordering Galilee, viz., Phoenicia, the tetrarchy of Philip, and the Decapolis,[84] but this was really only an interlude in the Galilean ministry. It has long been customary to speak of a "Perean Ministry," but, strictly construed, the evidence does not indicate any such. The chief reason advanced for supposing there was such a ministry is that Luke inserts a long central section of teaching material (Lk. 9:51–18:14) at that point in the synoptic outline where Jesus has completed his Galilean ministry and goes to Judea.[85] All that can be made of this, however, is that Luke found this a suitable point at which to

[80] Matt. 4:3, 6 = Lk. 4:3, 9.   [81] Cf. Ps. 2:7 ff.
[82] Mk. 6:17 f. = Matt. 14:3 f. = Lk. 3:19 f.
[83] Mk. 6:17–20 = Matt. 14:3 ff. = Lk. 3:19.
[84] Cf. Mk. 7:24–8:30.
[85] Cf. Mk. 10:1 = Matt. 19:1 f.

introduce a large block of teaching material which he had not elsewhere put into his narrative and which he does *not* localize in Perea.
The conclusion of Jesus' public career was in Judea, and about this
we have the most detailed account of any phase of his career, i.e., the
narrative of the passion week (Mk. 11–15 = Matt. 21–27 = Lk.
19–23). The incidents narrated center mainly in Jerusalem.

Jesus' Public Life: Teaching

Jesus as a Teacher.   In Galilee, Jesus' public career was primarily that of a prophet and teacher. The most certain fact that we know
about Jesus is that he was a teacher. His ethical teaching shines
through every account of his life. He is represented thus in the oldest
sources. Mark, though himself chiefly interested in miracle working,
clearly represents that Jesus subordinated that element to his prophetic preaching (Mk. *1:38). Mark refers frequently to Jesus'
teaching, even though Mark himself gives but a limited amount of
Jesus' teaching (chapters 4, 10, 13). Mark records that Jesus was
saluted as "Rabbi" by his disciples,[86] and as "Teacher." [87] Mark
refers to the long tasseled teacher's robe which Jesus wore on which
the crowding people tried to lay hold.[88]

The conception of Jesus as a teacher and prophet is basic in the
Second Source, or "Q," [89] which source is indeed almost exclusively
teaching material. "Q" seems to have been an anthology of the wisdom sayings of Jesus after the pattern of Proverbs or the Sayings
of the Jewish Fathers.[90]

These sources depict Jesus as an itinerant teacher. He preached
in the synagogues, e.g., at Nazareth, Capernaum, and elsewhere. He
addressed people in the villages, not only in the synagogues but also
on the streets. He taught them about the countryside wherever he
chanced to meet them, by the lake, in the field, or on the hillside. This
method of Jesus was characteristically that of the wisdom teachers.[91]
"He saw a great multitude, and he had compassion on them, because
they were as sheep not having a shepherd; and he began to teach
them many things." [92] It was therefore a social interest that led Jesus
to go among the masses as a teacher.

Jesus' Disciples.   Jesus pursued his ministry in the manner of
friendship and intimate personal relationship. The synoptic records

---

[86] Mk. 9:5; 11:21; 14:45; as "Rabboni" in 10:51.
[87] Mk. 4:38; 9:38; 10:35; 13:1.
[88] Mk. 6:56; cf. Matt. 9:20; 14:36; 23:5; Lk. 8:44.
[89] Cf. *supra*, p. 484.
[90] Cf. B. H. Streeter, *The Four Gospels* (New York: 1925), p. 286.
[91] Cf. Elmer W. K. Mould, *The World-view of Jesus* (New York: 1941), pp. 1–33.
[92] Mk. 6:34.

give a unique degree of prominence to disciples in Jesus' ministry. He deliberately chose this method rather than any other for his work, for it was a customary method with Jewish teachers. He did not write books. He embodied in certain men the living spirit of his teaching.

The inner circle of Jesus' disciples included three men, Peter, James, and John.[93] These three and Judas, the traitor, are the only disciples of Jesus about whom any concrete information is given in the gospels. A larger group comprised twelve disciples. Their names are listed in Mk. 3:13–19 = Matt. 10:2 ff. = Lk. 6:12–16,[94] although the lists do not agree exactly and give a total of fourteen names. Luke mentions a company of seventy disciples.[95] Frequently there is mention of a "multitude" of disciples.[96]

Jesus' purpose in having disciples is stated in Mk. 3:14 f., "that they might be with him, and that he might send them forth to preach, and to have authority to cast out demons." All three synoptic gospels tell of a preaching tour by Jesus' disciples (Mk. *6:7–13, 30 = Matt. 10:5 = Lk. 9:1, 6, 10). Luke (*10:1–17) also speaks of a preaching mission of the "seventy" disciples.

It is important to see this conception of Jesus and his disciples as itinerant teachers in a larger social setting. Such itinerant teaching and preaching was a common phenomenon of the time in the Roman Empire. There is some likelihood that the Jews themselves carried on a propagandist movement in the extra-Palestinian area.[97] Of far greater significance however were the traveling philosophic teachers of the Mediterranean area. With genuine earnestness and zeal, these men journeyed far and wide with their message, calling the masses of mankind to a higher type of life. Such itinerant teachers were popularly called "philosophers." The whole emphasis of philosophy in the first century was ethical; its aim was the formation and guidance of moral character. The missionary philosopher was everywhere a familiar figure, with his long cloak and his staff and scrip, addressing the crowd wherever a crowd gathered. The crowd often jeered, but listened none the less, and found some help toward a way of life, for such itinerant preachers were not intellectuals but plain people themselves.[98] We have no specific records of the presence of any of these philosophic missionaries in Palestine. However, in view of their known practices of wide journeying, it would be strange

[93] Mk. 5:37; 9:2; 13:3; 14:33; etc.
[94] Cf. Matt. 9:9 = Mk. 2:14 = Lk. 5:27.
[95] Lk. 10:1, 17.
[96] E.g., Lk. 19:37. Acts 1:15 speaks of a multitude as "about one hundred and twenty."
[97] Cf. F. M. Derwacter, *Preparing the Way for Paul* (New York: 1930).
[98] Cf. Samuel Dill, *Roman Society from Nero to Marcus Aurelius* (New York: 1905), pp. 340 ff.

indeed if Palestine were the only part of the Mediterranean world where they did not go. There is certainly abundant evidence for an extensive Hellenistic culture in Palestine and especially in Galilee, as we have observed.[99] The significance of the foregoing is this: the craving of common people for ethicoreligious teaching was world-wide in the first century. The response to that stimulus was likewise world-wide, including the philosophic missionary propaganda in the Mediterranean area and the teaching ministry of Jesus and his disciples in Galilee and Judea, succeeded in time by the Christian missionary propaganda.

Jesus' Teaching Method. Jesus' teaching method is very apparent if one reads the Sermon on the Mount (Matt. 5 ff.). One may observe the following striking traits: (1) the use of many illustrations and figures from common life and experience; (2) a positive instead of a negative way of putting his ideas, the beatitude form of stating ethical truth being used to this end; (3) simple statements, easily grasped by plain people; (4) the use of the balanced poetic form; (5) the use of numerous similes, metaphors, and paradoxes. All these tended to make his statements of truth forcible and to impress them permanently upon the minds of his hearers.

A special feature of the teaching method of Jesus was his abundant use of the parable. A parable is a story out of life, told to illustrate and impress a religious teaching. Literally, the word *parable* means "thrown alongside"; i.e., a certain truth is thrown alongside life in order to make its meaning plain. There are notable instances of the use of parable in the Old Testament; e.g., Nathan's parable of the ewe lamb (2 Sam. 12:1–7); the parable of the wise woman of Tekoa (2 Sam. 14:6 f.); the parable told by the unnamed prophet to King Ahab (1 Kgs. 20:39 f.); Isaiah's parable of the vineyard (Isa. 5:1–7) and his parable of the farmer (Isa. 28:23–29). Lk. 4:23 gives "Physician, heal thyself" as a parable. As a rule, however, the gospel parables are larger stories. The parable of the soils (Mk. *4:3–25 = Matt. 13:3–23 = Lk. 8:5–18) is given in each of the synoptics in greater fullness than any other parable, which indicates that the gospel writers seem to have considered it the leading and model parable.

What was Jesus' purpose in using the parable teaching-form? Manifestly it was to make his meaning simple and easily understood. But Mk. 4:10 ff. = Matt. 13:10–17 = Lk. 8:9 f. gives a different view of the matter, making it appear that Jesus used parables in order to obscure his meaning from all but his immediate disciples. Such a point of view doubtless represents the gospel writers more than it

[99] *Supra*, pp. 480 ff.

does Jesus. It is unthinkable that Jesus would have deliberately sought to make his meaning obscure, but on the other hand it is quite thinkable that his meaning would have been understandable only to those genuinely interested and in sympathy with spiritual things, for they were the only ones who would be inclined to listen.

The Scope of Jesus' Teaching. In the synoptic gospels the teachings of Jesus are grouped in certain great blocks of material. In Matthew there are five such blocks quite distinctly marked off.[100] They are: (1) Matt. 5 ff., The Sermon on the Mount; (2) Matt. 10, Instructions to the Twelve Disciples; (3) Matt. 13, Parables of the Kingdom; (4) Matt. 18, Directions for Christian Behavior; (5) Matt. 24 f., Address on the Issues of the Future. Much of the material in these five sections is paralleled in either Mark or Luke. Luke gives a long block of teaching material (Lk. 9:51–18:14), much of which is not found in either of the other synoptics although some parts of it are paralleled in Matthew.

The Leading Ideas of Jesus' Teaching. Jesus was genetically connected with the thought life of his time. Many interpreters point out the resemblance of Jesus' teaching to other Jewish teaching of the age. Jesus' teaching, however, is not a mere echo of the common creed of the day. Old ideas, which had been little more than pious formulas (e.g., the Fatherhood of God), Jesus took with a new and profound seriousness. From the materials of thought which came to him from the past, he selected what he deemed vital and analyzed it into its essential principles, laying emphasis upon intrinsic values and inward motives. Jesus did not aim to construct a fresh system of knowledge. From the knowledge that was already available he selected that which he personally experienced as vital, and to this he imparted a spiritual dynamic which makes his teaching an inner and energizing principle that integrates the whole life of man.

1. *Jesus' Idea of God.* The evolution of the idea of God among the Hebrew people from earliest nomadic times has been one of the major lines of emphasis in this text. What did Jesus contribute to this most important of all doctrines of religion?

The Jewish people had by now come to esteem the sacred name Yahweh as the ineffable name, not even to be spoken, lest by mispronunciation or by improper tone of voice they should take the name of Yahweh in vain.[101] Consequently they resorted to substitute words, such as Lord (the term most frequently used),[102] the Most

---

100 It is interesting to note how each of these blocks is concluded by an almost identical formula, 7:28; 11:1; 13:53; 19:1; 26:1.
101 Ex. 20:7.   102 *Vid. supra*, p. 131, fn. 109.

High,[103] the Holy One (or Holy Spirit),[104] Redeemer,[105] Savior,[106] King,[107] Father,[108] Heaven.[109]

Jesus' term for God was "Father." The conception of God as Father was not a new thing in Judaism. It is found in the Old Testament,[110] in the Apocrypha,[111] and in the Pseudepigrapha. G. F. Moore's *Judaism* presents a surprisingly large and impressive collection of such passages.[112] All this to the contrary notwithstanding, the Jewish scholar Claude G. Montefiore finds an element of uniqueness in Jesus' use of the term Father for God. "It is apparently a fact that Jesus thought of God as his (and our) Father, and used the term Father for God more habitually and constantly than is the case with any one rabbi of whom we know. And this regular conception of God as Father, in proportion to the intensity and vividness of the feeling which suggested it, was something which may fitly be called original." [113] The conception of God as Father is one of the enduring values of Jesus' teaching. Indeed we may judge that he selected this idea just because of his perception of its ultimate worth, because it came alive in his own consciousness, expressing all that was most profound and sure in his experience of God.

Jesus' conception of God has a further attribute of enduring value, the *idea of redemption* as expressing the nature of God's activity in the world. The highest and best of Jesus' teaching regarding the divine Fatherhood is in the parable of the lost son (Lk. *15:11–32) which portrays fatherly love as a seeking love motivated by a redemptive purpose.[114] This conception Jesus based upon the idea of God in the Book of Jonah,[115] to which he referred in Matt. 16:4, "An evil and adulterous generation seeketh after a sign: and there shall no sign be given unto it, but the sign of Jonah." There is no added explanation or expansion of the saying. It means that Jonah is a sufficient sign of God at work in the world. In the Jonah story it was God who took the initiative in extending the benefits of his love to the (from the Jews' standpoint) undeserving Ninevites by sending Jonah to preach repentance to them. It is a clear and forceful picture of God acting. That is exactly the kind of attitude on

103 Cf. e.g., Lk. 1:32, 35, 76; 6:35.
104 *Vid. supra*, p. 373, and cf. Matt. 1:18; Lk. 1:35.
105 *Vid. supra*, p. 373, and cf. Lk. 1:68.   106 Cf. Lk. 1:47.
107 Cf. e.g., Matt. 5:35; 25:34, 40.   108 *Vid. supra*, pp. 341, 373.
109 Matthew regularly substitutes "kingdom of heaven" for "kingdom of God."
110 Ex. 4:22; Deut. 14:1; 32:6, 18; Hos. 11:1; Isa. 1:2; Jer. 3:19; 31:9; Isa. 45:11; 63:16; 64:8; Mal. 1:6; 2:10.
111 Sir. 23:1, 4; Wisd. 2:16; cf. 5:5.
112 G. F. Moore, *Judaism in the First Century of the Christian Era* (Cambridge: 1927), ii, pp. 201–211.
113 C. G. Montefiore, "The Originality of Jesus," *Hibbert Journal*, xxviii (October, 1929), p. 104.
114 Cf. especially vss. 20, 32.
115 *Vid. supra*, p. 409.

God's part toward man which Jesus set forth, a redeeming love which actively seeks man. That makes the world in which man lives a friendly world (cf. Matt. *5:45; Mk. *4:26–29; Matt. *7:7–11 = Lk. 11:9–11, 13; Matt. *6:25–34 = Lk. 12:22–31). This idea was to Jesus a dynamic conception. He experienced within himself the impulse to a redemptive ministry and this afforded him an insight into the nature of ultimate reality.

For Jesus, God was a clear, living, and present reality. The ethical and religious blend into one in his teaching. God, to him, is good and is to be found in the good. It is man's moral attitude toward life which makes men aware of the reality of God; the pure in heart see God.[116] This immanent God is trustworthy, the one most important force in the universe on which man can count. Jesus is concerned not with what man does but with what man gives God a chance to do through man's right religious attitude. This is basic to his exhortations to repentance and moral endeavor, "Be ye perfect as your Father in heaven is perfect." [117] God is to Jesus the ultimate reality, both present and to come. Jesus did not anticipate that the future would reveal anything essentially different from what he had already *realized* as an actuality in his own soul, the very nearness of God and the triumphant power of good. Jesus' conception of God as the ultimate reality, both present and to come, is reflected in his conception of the kingdom of God.[118]

2. *The Kingdom of God.* In order to appreciate Jesus' conception of the kingdom of God, it must be understood that the stress falls upon the word "God" rather than upon the word "kingdom." God's kingdom is God's manner of rule. Jesus is primarily concerned to teach what kind of king God is and is going to be. Jesus' theory of reality is: God is present and at work in his world. God is the Eternal. He rules now and he will rule in the future.

"And being asked by the Pharisees, when the kingdom of God cometh, he answered and said, The kingdom of God cometh not with observation, neither shall they say, Lo, here! or, there! for lo, the kingdom of God is within you." [119] This statement means that the kingdom of God is an existing reality awaiting discovery by those who take the right attitude toward it. Jesus made this point abundantly clear in parables illustrative of the kingdom, e.g., the parables of the leaven (Matt. *13:33 = Lk. 13:20 f.), the mustard seed (Mk. *4:30 ff. = Matt. 13:31 f. = Lk. 13:18 f.), and the seed growing secretly (Mk. *4:26–29). The parable of the leaven directs attention

---

[116] Matt. 5:8.   [117] Matt. 5:48.
[118] On Jesus' idea of God, see further, Elmer W. K. Mould, *The World-view of Jesus* (New York: 1941), pp. 77–98, 186 ff.
[119] Lk. 17:20 f.

to a present reality which, though hidden and though small, is nevertheless a force at work. When all is leavened, it is in quality just like
the small lump with which the housewife began. There is an inner
side to the process, a mysterious working. Similarly with the planted
seed, be it wheat or mustard seed, you know that in the end you will
have a harvest of what you sow, wheat or mustard. As illustrative of
the kingdom of God, the point of emphasis is not the smallness of
the beginning, and certainly not gradual development, but rather that
its essential nature is a present reality. You know what it is going to
be like in the eschatological climax because you may know what it is
like in the present, and Jesus' dominant concern is to teach what it *is*
like. Jesus views life *sub specie aeternitatis*. His ethical ideal is set
forth as that kind of life which characterizes those who now are sons
of God and which will be the kind of life all live in the fully consummated kingdom of God. The kingdom of God is like a treasure
hidden in a field (Matt. *13:44), or like a very valuable pearl which
awaits discovery by the persistent seeker (Matt. *13:45 f.). The
kingdom type of life is to be found in children (Mk. *10:14 =
Matt. 19:14 = Lk. 18:16); among the poor in spirit (Matt. *5:3); [120]
in the discerning scribe (Mk. *12:34); among repentant sinners
(Matt. *21:31); even among those of alien race (Matt. *8:5–11 =
Lk. 7:1–9).

The gospels state as the central theme of Jesus' preaching: "The
kingdom of God is at hand; repent ye." [121] Jesus' reply to the messengers from John the Baptist enumerates works which evidence the
existing reality of the kingdom (Matt. *11:4 f. = Lk. 7:22). Further,
the casting out of demons was evidence that "the kingdom of God is
come upon you." [122] "Seek ye first his kingdom" [123] implies that it is
something present. You do not have to wait for the future to reveal
what God is like. He is a living God, a present reality.

Jesus did not speculate concerning the eschatological details of
the kingdom. To do so would have been inconsistent with his own
faith. The same faith which the patient farmer displays toward the
future harvest for which he hopes and labors and waits is the faith one
may have toward the eschatological kingdom of God. Jesus revealed
his idea of the future kingdom in two choice parables, the ten virgins
(Matt. *25:1–13) and the talents (Matt. *25:14–30); [124] man is
here and now left on his own responsibility and in the future he will
be held to strict accountability.[125] "Of that day and hour knoweth no
one, not even the angels of heaven, neither the Son, but the Father

[120] Cf. Lk. 6:20.   [121] Mk. 1:15 = Matt. 4:17.
[122] Matt. 12:28 = Lk. 11:20.   [123] Matt. 6:33 = Lk. 12:31.
[124] Cf. Lk. 19:11–27.   [125] *Vid. infra*, pp. 509 f.

only." [126] The idea of the future kingdom of God is clearly reflected in "There are some here of them that stand by, who shall in no wise taste of death, till they see the kingdom of God come with power," [127] i.e., in its complete development and full strength; "Thy kingdom come"; [128] "Many shall come from the east and west, and shall sit down with Abraham and Isaac and Jacob in the kingdom of heaven"; [129] "I shall no more drink of the fruit of the vine until that day when I drink it in the kingdom of God." [130] The futurity of the kingdom is more pronounced in Jesus' teaching in the latter part of his ministry. Doubtless this was in view of his rejection by the people, which led him to stress the fact that only the direct intervention of God could achieve the consummation of the kingdom.

The essential idea of the kingdom of God is that in it there will be realized the highest moral and religious ideal, viz., the achievement of the ideal humanity in an ideal social order. Faith, repentance, and righteousness are the foundations upon which it rests and the conditions of entrance into it. Jesus considers that God's immediate purpose is the establishment of this ideal order. [131]

3. *Jesus' Emphasis on the Ethical.* The pre-eminent importance of the ethical in religion has been one of the major emphases in our interpretation of the development of the Hebrew religion. It was the great prophets, beginning with Amos in the eighth century, who brought the ethical to the fore. Their concern with the idea of God was to explain God's moral character. This also was Jesus' aim in his doctrine of God, as seen in the foregoing. The great Old Testament prophets were concerned with man's attitude toward God and his fellow men, rating ethics above ritual. The same is true of Jesus.

The Sermon on the Mount is a compendium of the ethical teachings of Jesus and sets forth "Jesus' Ideal of Life" as follows:

(i) The Ideal Attitude Toward Life (Matt. *5:1–12).
(ii) The Usefulness of the Ideal Life (Matt. *5:13–16).
(iii) The Superiority of Jesus' Ideal (Matt. *5:17–20).
(iv) The Difference which Jesus' Ideal Makes (Matt. *5:21–48).
(v) Jesus' Ideal in Religious Worship (Matt. *6:1–18).
(vi) What Jesus' Ideal Puts First (Matt. *6:19–34).
(vii) The Ideal Social Attitude (Matt. *7:1–12).
(viii) Man's Duty Toward Jesus' Ideal (Matt. *7:13–27).

A characteristic feature of the thinking of Jesus is his principle of inwardness. In his attitude toward the law (Matt. 5:17–48)

---

[126] Matt. 24:36 = Mk. 13:32.
[127] Mk. 9:1 = Matt. 16:28 = Lk. 9:27.
[128] Matt. 6:10 = Lk. 11:2.
[129] Matt. 8:11; cf. Lk. 13:29.
[130] Mk. 14:25 = Matt. 26:29 = Lk. 22:18.
[131] For a fuller discussion of Jesus' idea of the kingdom of God, cf. Elmer W. K. Mould, *The World-view of Jesus* (New York: 1941), pp. 151–162.

he regards the supremely important thing to be the inward motive which lies behind the external commandments.[132] Similarly, in his ideal of religious worship he emphasizes not the outward ritual act but the inner feeling and motive (Matt. 6:1–18).[133] His teaching is directed to the inner nature, to the soul of man, and it is the spiritual worth of man as a self which he makes central (Matt. *6:25). Jesus' belief in the inner, spiritual possibilities of every soul is revealed in his ideal for man, "That ye may be sons of your Father who is in heaven." [134] That is exactly what Jesus kept before him as his objective in all his teaching.

Another way of expressing what is meant by this principle of inwardness is to say that Jesus emphasized spiritual values. The term "spiritual" is not easy of definition. It is used as a general term to cover all ideal values, intellectual, aesthetic, ethical, social, and religious. All these values counted with Jesus, certainly, but his specific concern was with moral and religious values. Praiseworthy moral character is itself one of the most important elements in spirituality. Jesus exalted purity of heart, sincerity, humility, forgiveness, love toward enemies, self-sacrifice and generous service on behalf of others, especially the needy, and, above all, unworried trust in God. This emphasis upon the spiritual in the teaching of Jesus is very idealistic and is appreciated as such even by some who disclaim any effort to live by it. All bodily appetites and passions Jesus subordinated strictly to the higher nature of man. Material possessions, in his view, are not of intrinsic worth. Politics, he rated as inferior to righteousness. He stressed love to God and man, and faithful devotion to the moral ideal, as the very core of spirituality.

In his ethical teachings Jesus set forth an attitude toward God and life and destiny which may be termed "moral optimism," to borrow a phrase from D. C. Macintosh. Moral optimism means "a fundamental attitude of confidence in the cosmos, together with a full sense of man's moral responsibility. It expresses and is expressed in the conviction that if only a person's will is right, he need have no fear of anything the universe can do to him; no absolute or final disaster can come to him whose will is steadfastly devoted to the true ideal. . . . It would hold that if man does his best, the Supreme Power on which he is dependent will do whatever else needs to be done. . . . If one seeks first and in a rational way righteousness and other eternal values—the essential content of the 'Kingdom of God'— it promises that all that he needs will be his, and that being rightly

---

[132] Cf. especially Matt. 5:22, 28, 32, 37, 44.
[133] Especially vss. 3, 6, 18.
[134] Matt. 5:45.

adjusted at the center of his life, he need not even be afraid of them that kill the body and after that have no more that they can do." [135] Now it is significant that this explanation of moral optimism uses the language of the gospels, and while Professor Macintosh founds this moral optimism upon universal reason, he finds at the core of it certain of the principles of Jesus' teaching.[136] Jesus, however, expressed it in the simple religious terms of faith and love.

It was Jesus' view that the ethical principles he enunciated and stressed have ultimate survival value. They would survive the passing away of the age in which he was himself living. They would survive the judgment. They would be valid when the ideal should be fully consummated and eternal life in the kingdom of God should be an accomplished fact. Jesus' thinking was oriented toward the arrival of the ideal. This gives us a basis for appreciating the most difficult of the teachings ascribed to Jesus in the synoptic gospels, viz., his eschatological discourses.

4. *The Eschatological Teaching of Jesus.* Everything in Jesus' thinking pivots upon his ethical idealism, and this ethical idealism is the basic thing in the eschatological teachings ascribed to him in the synoptic gospels (Lk. *17:20–37; Mk. 13 = Matt. *24 f. = Lk. 21:5–36). On the representation of all sources, both ethics and eschatology are part of Jesus' teaching.[137] He could not have presented an effective ethical message to his age if he had neglected the thought of the ultimate realization of ethical values. He based his eschatology upon his ethics.

The central value in Jewish eschatology is righteousness. Righteousness is the condition of entrance into the kingdom. The kingdom is to be a kingdom of righteousness. Inwardly, Jesus felt a deep, intense appreciation of God and righteousness, a conviction of certainty that righteousness is and is to be supreme over evil. How could such an assurance find expression with a first-century Jew if not in the thought forms of his people and his age? He was bound to express himself in eschatological terms, just as we in the twentieth century are bound to express ourselves in evolutionary thought forms. The more intense the inner appreciation, the more vivid the outward expression. Hence the highly colored imagery of Jesus' eschatological discourses. Behind such imagery is the basic thing in the thinking of Jesus: his inner appreciation of righteousness and assurance of its ultimate supremacy.

[135] D. C. Macintosh, *The Reasonableness of Christianity* (New York: 1925), pp. 46 f. Quoted by permission of the trustees of Lake Forest University, owners of the copyright.
[136] Matt. 6:33 = Lk. 12:31; Lk. 12:5 = 10:28.
[137] On apocalyptic, *vid. supra*, pp. 442 ff.

Apocalyptic is basically concerned with two problems: the removal of evil from man and the world and the achievement of the ideal humanity. What did Jesus think about the problem of evil?

Jesus did not discuss the problem of evil in the abstract. He set forth his views in simple stories out of life, thus grounding his world view in actual common-sense experience. It is open to the simplest man to interrogate his experience and his environment. He has at hand all that he needs for shaping a philosophy of life. The parable of the wheat and the tares (Matt. *13:24–30) implies that nature's hidden forces are good and not evil. The farmer sowed wheat and trusted the earth for a harvest. It was an enemy that sowed the tares, i.e., the perverse willfulness of man directed nature's forces for evil ends. Growing together in the same field the tares were a challenge to the supremacy of the wheat and to the purposes which the wheat served. But at the final reckoning in the day of harvest the wheat triumphs. The tares are not burned just to get rid of them. The economy of living in Palestine forbade any such waste. Tares are bound in bundles for fuel and when so used they serve the real purpose of the wheat by assisting in the baking of the bread. This is a parable of faith in the supremacy of good and its ultimate triumph, as well as a parable of nonresistance. Jesus' basic dictum on the problem of evil is: "Resist not evil" [138] and "Love your enemies." [139] Forbearance of evil on God's part is not a sign of his incapacity nor of his indifference. By forbearance of evil and by forgiveness, evil is overcome. The parable of the lost son (Lk. 15:11–32) illustrates love in forbearance with the evil man, another example of nonresistance in operation.

Jesus' teaching about forgiveness is one of the finest examples of moral evolution that can be found in the history of thought. When we first meet man in the Bible he is acting upon the raw principle of unrestrained vengeance (Gen. *4:23 f.).[140] It was a step of moral progress when a restraint was put upon vengeance by the *lex talionis* (Ex. *21:23 ff.; Deut. *19:21; Lev. *24:19 f.). Crude as this "eye for an eye" philosophy seems to us today, we must acknowledge that when first promulgated it was a merciful provision. The thinking of Jesus carries this altogether away from revenge to nonrevenge, or nonresistance, or nonresentment (Matt. *5:38 f.), and even beyond this to unlimited forgiveness (Matt. *18:21 f.). From "seventy and sevenfold" revenge to "seventy and sevenfold" forgiveness—so far has the moral consciousness of man advanced within the scope of the Bible.

---

[138] Matt. 5:39.   [139] Matt. 5:44.
[140] *Vid. supra,* pp. 111, 285.

Jesus practiced nonresistance in his own ministry, as evidenced by his association with the religiously neglected publicans, sinners, and the diseased. Disease was looked upon as punishment for sin, the diseased person being *ipso facto* a sinful person.

In his own living Jesus identified himself with truth as he saw the truth. He found in Second Isaiah the principle that progress in the building of righteousness is founded on suffering that is vicarious. Jesus foresaw for himself opposition and martyrdom and for his disciples persecution. A first-century Christian writer said that Jesus "for the joy that was set before him endured the cross." [141] This is an appreciation of Jesus as one whose faith in the triumph of righteousness was such that he cheerfully identified himself with the cause of righteousness and took the consequences. This means that Jesus solved the problem of evil, not so much intellectually as practically and vitally.

In the standard view of first-century Judaism, evil would be removed in the coming age by its catastrophic overthrow through God's direct intervention. This conception was not an eccentric or tangential feature of Jewish thinking but was integrated with their philosophy of history. It was an adaptation of the theory applied to the original creation and the flood.

This conception is applied to the original creation by Second Isaiah (Isa. *51:9). The reference is to the ancient Hebrew tradition of Yahweh's contest with Rahab, the great dragon who personified the primeval chaos. By a mighty act of intervention, Yahweh overcame the forces of chaos and established the cosmos. This theory of course rested upon the Babylonian myth of Marduk's slaying of Tiamat, the Babylonian counterpart of Rahab, after which victory Marduk proceeded to create the world and man.[142]

In Jewish thought, Yahweh similarly rose up at the time of the flood to destroy evil (Gen. *6:5, 7). That this theory had an important place in Jewish thinking in Jesus' time is seen in the fact that 1 Enoch (37–71) expounds this view of the first world judgment in several fragments which deal mainly with the deluge.

Jewish eschatology applied this same philosophy to the future and declared that once again God would rise and by a mighty act of intervention overthrow the forces of evil and inaugurate a new age of righteousness. This is a conventional item in the general Jewish program of eschatological events. This conventional idea appears to have been Jesus' view also. It is definitely ascribed to him in Lk. *17:26 = Matt. 24:37.

141 Heb. 12:2.
142 *Vid. supra,* pp. 362 ff.

This theory is not inconsistent with Jesus' thought of God as a Father whose character is love and whose purpose is salvation, in view of which purpose he is forbearing with evil. Men may deliberately choose to continue in sin. What then? "The only absolute disaster to be feared is to be found in continued sin and its necessary personal and social consequences." [143] This is illustrated in the parable of the lord's vineyard (Mk. *12:1–9 = Matt. 21:33–41 = Lk. 20:9–16). Here is a picture of deliberate and willful evil behavior. In the end, after all other means had been exhausted, there was nothing for the lord of the vineyard to do but to come and destroy the husbandmen and give the vineyard to others.

This doctrine was not only ethically based but it functioned ethically. This portrayal of the ultimate destruction of evil was used by Jesus, as well as by other Jewish teachers of religion and ethics, as a powerful incentive for doing right. Certainly this hope, that righteousness soon would triumph and that all sin and evil would be forever banished, kept the Jewish people from despair in times of suffering under oppression and was an urge to self-sacrifice and heroic endeavor. So it was also to the primitive Christians.

In Jewish eschatology the basal idea is that of a day of judgment, which developed from the Old Testament conception of the Day of Yahweh, as has been pointed out.[144] The core of the idea is that history is leading up to a great transition. Jewish ethical impulse felt keenly the consciousness of sin as well as the urge to righteousness and demanded that righteousness prevail in man and in the world. The logical issue of such an ethical demand is that men will be held to accountability for their deeds. This is the ethical basis of the idea of the day of judgment. The judgment will sift out and conserve whatever is of ethical value in the present age and with this the new age will be integrated.

The day of judgment was the main theme in the preaching of John the Baptist. He regarded it as imminent.[145] The ethical test alone will be decisive at the judgment.[146] John therefore used this idea as a powerful incentive to right ethical conduct (Lk. *3:10–14).

The Synoptics present the idea of the judgment as a part of the eschatology of Jesus. Jesus explicitly disclaims the possibility of any knowledge concerning the day or the hour of the judgment.[147] Perhaps he considered it to be imminent, as did John the Baptist, to occur before the passing of the existing generation.[148] In any case it would

---

[143] D. C. Macintosh, *The Reasonableness of Christianity* (New York: 1925), p. 51. Quoted by permission of the trustees of Lake Forest University, owners of the copyright.
[144] *Supra*, pp. 450 f.   [145] Matt. 3:7, 10, 12 = Lk. 3:7, 9, 17.
[146] Matt. 3:8, 10 = Lk. 3:8 f.   [147] Mk. 13:32 = Matt. 24:36.
[148] Mk. 13:30 = Matt. 24:34 = Lk. 21:32.

come suddenly and unexpectedly.[149] It was characteristic of Jesus to emphasize the inward side of truth in his ethical teaching, and this is true of his parable concerning the judgment of the Son of Man (Matt. *25:31–46). The righteous are there depicted as not knowing what they had done to merit the kingdom. This parable is significant as showing the ethical basis of the judgment, which is according to deeds. Any view of the judgment would be impossible without the assumption of the punishment of the wicked. This appears as a conventional feature in Jesus' view and is likewise ethically based, as seen in the parable of the talents (Matt. *25:14–30).[150] This is a parable of judgment; the men are left on their own responsibility and they are held to account in the day of reckoning.

Jesus is not primarily concerned with the punishment of the wicked, but rather with the reward of the righteous. The ethical values which Jesus proclaimed in his teaching have ultimate survival value. That is what the judgment signifies. It signifies, however, not alone the survival of certain ethical values but still more *the arrival of the highest of all ethical values, eternal life in the kingdom of God.* It is in the direction of this that all of Jesus' thought is oriented. Not the judgment, but *beyond the judgment* is the determining consideration in the thought of Jesus. Jesus' thinking was oriented toward the arrival of the ideal; his ethical judgments were formed on the basis of enduring values; he regarded the world and life *sub specie aeternitatis.* It was the finest insight of Jesus that there were forces at work in his age making for the arrival of the ideal age. Upon these he threw all the weight of emphasis in teaching and endeavor in personal ministry. In his teaching he aimed to set out those values which would endure when his own age had passed away and the eternal world order of God's kingdom should be the ever-present order. Jesus did call upon his disciples to live the kingdom (i.e., the ideal) type of life in the age in which they lived, however unideal that age was. He considered his ideal valid for that age and for any age to come because he deemed it eternally valid. He perceived an ideal world in the making. Jesus regards God as actively at work now, accomplishing this purpose.

In its ultimate reach, Jesus' ideal is a social ideal. It is the ideal of God and man in perfect society. Apparently, Jesus could think of nothing beyond that. His teaching ministry was devoted to preparing men for participation in that divine society.[151]

---

[149] Lk. 21:34; Matt. 24:50 = Lk. 12:46.
[150] Cf. Lk. 19:12–26.
[151] For a fuller discussion of the eschatological element in the teaching of Jesus, cf. Elmer W. K. Mould, *The World-view of Jesus* (New York: 1941), pp. 99–150.

Jesus' Public Life: Miracles

The Definition of Miracle. Miracle was a prevailing thought pattern of the ancient world. Miracle evidenced to the ancient mind God's immediate activity in the world by intervention in the ordinary course of affairs. In that age nothing was known, of course, about the scientific method of explanation. Striking incidents were written up in a way to heighten the wonder element in them, and this was with the intent to establish faith in God.

The miracle thought pattern has given way to the scientific thought pattern which emphasizes cause and effect. This is what creates the difficulty in any modern understanding of miracles. The gospel accounts of Jesus' mighty works stress the miraculous, and it is not possible to get back of those accounts to the original incidents. A good many attempts to do so have been made, i.e., to rationalize miracles, in order to get at a natural explanation.

Dr. H. E. Fosdick in *The Modern Use of the Bible* surveys the various definitions of miracle which have prevailed in different ages, and offers as a modern definition: "A miracle is God's use of his own law-abiding powers to work out in ways surprising to us his will for our lives and for the world." [152] One recognizes at once that this is an attempt to bring into harmony with the newer scientific conception of the universe the older emphasis upon miracle as evidence for divine activity. Professor S. J. Case in *The Origins of Christian Supernaturalism* [153] discusses the miracle thought pattern in all its aspects, not only as we find it in the gospel miracles but also as it prevailed among all peoples, Christian and pagan alike, in the ancient world of Jesus' time. According to this view, miracle is seen to be a category of description and explanation employed by writers of the ancient world.[154]

Classification of the Miracles of Jesus. The miracles of Jesus fall into certain groupings, some of which occasion no surprise in the light of our present understanding of psychology and of the causes of disease, though others still baffle understanding on the basis of such knowledge as is possessed to date.

The following classification does not attempt to list all the gospel miracles, but only the types, with an illustration or two of each type.

---

[152] From H. E. Fosdick, *The Modern Use of the Bible* (New York: 1924), pp. 131–167. Quotation by permission of The Macmillan Company, publishers.
[153] (Chicago: 1946).
[154] On miracles, cf. Millar Burrows, *An Outline of Biblical Theology* (Philadelphia: 1946), pp. 130 ff.

1. *Nature Miracles.* The stilling of the storm (Mk. 4:35–41 =
Matt. 8:18, 23–27 = Lk. 8:22–25); the feeding of the multitude
(Mk. 6:30–44 = Matt. 14:13–21 = Lk. 9:10–17 = Jn. 6:1–13; Mk.
8:1–9 = Matt. 15:32–38).

2. *Healing Miracles.* (a) *The healing of bodily diseases:* The
paralytic (Mk. 2:1–12 = Matt. 9:1–8 = Lk. 5:17–26); the centurion's servant (Matt. 8:5–13 = Lk. 7:1–10); the woman with the
issue of blood (Mk. 5:25–34 = Matt. 9:20 ff. = Lk. 8:43–48); blind
Bartimaeus (Mk. 10:46–52 = Matt. 20:29–34 = Lk. 18:35–43).

(b) *The healing of mental diseases:* The Gerasene demoniac (Mk.
5:1–20 = Matt. 8:28–34 = Lk. 8:26–39); the demoniac boy (Mk.
9:14–29 = Matt. 17:14–20 = Lk. 9:37–43).

(c) *The resuscitation of the dead:* The widow's son (Lk. 7:11–17);
Jairus's daughter (Mk. 5:22 ff., 35–43 = Matt. 9:18 f., 23–26 = Lk.
8:40 ff., 49–56); Lazarus (Jn. 11:1–44).

3. *Works of Moral Redemption.* The sinful woman who anointed
Jesus' feet (Lk. 7:36–50); Mary Magdalene (Lk. 8:2; Mk. 16:9);
Zacchaeus (Lk. 19:1–10).

Essential Elements in the Miracles of Jesus. The conditions
essential to his mighty works, Jesus regarded as two: prayer and
faith. As to the need of prayer, in the case of the demoniac boy
whom the disciples tried unsuccessfully to cure (Mk. 9:14–29), Jesus
asserted that that particular form of malady yielded only to prayer.
Jesus is also said to nave uttered a prayer at the raising of Lazarus.[155]
As to the necessity for faith on the part of the persons benefited,
this appears as a feature emphasized in connection with each type
of miracle. It is mentioned in connection with the stilling of the
storm,[156] healing the paralytic,[157] healing the woman with the issue
of blood,[158] healing the centurion's servant,[159] giving sight to Bartimaeus,[160] raising Jairus's daughter,[161] and the conversion of the
sinful woman.[162] In all these instances, faith is seen to be a venture
on the part of a person to cooperate with a spiritual energy which he
believes will secure him a desired benefit.

Evaluation of the Miracles of Jesus. The performance of
miracles was by no means confined to Jesus, as is abundantly evidenced in the Bible. Many prophets of the Oid Testament times are
said to have worked miracles, the most detailed being those of Elisha
described in 2 Kgs. 2–8. In the New Testament period the performing
of miracles is repeatedly described or alluded to, both by Jesus'
disciples whom he sent out during his lifetime with that express in-

[155] Jn. 11:41 f.   [156] Mk. 4:40.   [157] Mk. 2:5.
[158] Mk. 5:34.   [159] Matt. 8:10, 13.   [160] Mk. 10:52.
[161] Mk. 5:36.   [162] Lk. 7:50.

junction [163] and by apostles and evangelists after Jesus' death.[164] Indeed, so far as curing demoniacs was concerned, Matt. 12:27 and Lk. 11:19 imply that some of Jesus' critics were accustomed to perform this type of miracle.

What, then, is to be said as to the uniqueness of the miracles of Jesus? In the first place it is to be noted that Jesus never used this power in his own behalf. Instead, there are indications that he actually tried to repress the tendency to herald him as a miracle worker.[165] In the second place, he affirmed that the working of such miracles was a permanent possibility. Thus he is quoted in the Gospel of John as having said, "The Father abiding in me doeth his works. . . . Verily I say unto you, He that believeth on me, the works that I do shall he do also; and greater works than these shall he do, because I go to the Father." [166] We must conclude, then, that Jesus was conscious that he possessed power that was released when faith and prayer were present and that others might and would possess the same power after him.

Jesus' Public Life: The Personal Influence of Jesus

Jesus valued personality above material things or institutions.[167] He stated this explicitly in connection with the incident of the healing on the Sabbath of the man with the withered hand: "What man shall there be of you, that shall have one sheep, and if this fall into a pit on the sabbath day, will he not lay hold on it and lift it out? How much then is a man of more value than a sheep!" [168] No institution, not even the Sabbath, equals in worth the human persons for whom it exists. "The sabbath was made for man and not man for the sabbath." [169] In another setting he declared to his disciples: "Ye are of more value than many sparrows." [170] Again, "Of how much more value are ye than the birds!" [171] In view of his principle of the supreme worth of persons, Jesus devoted his entire ministry to the redemption of persons. By his works of healing, he redeemed them from physical handicaps. By his teaching of wisdom, he redeemed them from ignorance and error. By his friendship, he redeemed them from their loss of hope because they were religiously neglected. By summoning them to a new life, he redeemed them from sin.

[163] Cf. Mk. 6:7; Lk. 9:1; Matt. 10:8; Mk. 6:13.
[164] Cf. Acts 3:1–10; 5:15 f.; 19:11 f.
[165] Mk. 1:38.   [166] Jn. 14:10b, 12.
[167] For a presentation of Jesus's view of Man, cf. Elmer W. K. Mould, *The World-view of Jesus* (New York: 1941), pp. 53–76.
[168] Mk. 3:1–6 = Matt. 12:9–14 = Lk. 6:6–11.
[169] Mk. 2:27.
[170] Matt. 10:31 = Lk. 12:7.
[171] Lk. 12:24 = Matt. 6:26.

This devotion of Jesus was not to humanity in the abstract. It was about individuals that he cared, for the reason that he believed they mattered most to God. He sternly rebuked any attitude of contempt toward another person. "Whosoever shall say to his brother, Raca, shall be in danger of the council; and whosoever shall say, Thou fool, shall be in danger of the hell of fire." [172] He was rated a friend of publicans and sinners and by that very attitude "Wisdom is justified." [173] Individual sinners received his sympathetic attention because no depth of moral degradation canceled the latent possibility of such a person becoming a child of God. Among the gospel stories illustrative of this are: the story of the call of Levi (Mk. *2:13–17 = Matt. 9:9–13 = Lk. 5:27–32); the story of Zacchaeus (Lk. *19:1–10); the story of the Samaritan woman at the well (Jn. *4:5–42); the story of the adulterous woman (Jn. *7:53–8:11); the story of the woman who anointed Jesus' feet (Lk. *7:36–50).

Jesus justified his attitude by remarking, "They that are whole have no need of a physician, but they that are sick. I came not to call the righteous, but sinners"; [174] "I came that they might have life, and might have it abundantly." [175] He illustrated his meaning in the parables of the lost sheep, the lost coin, and the lost son (Lk. *15). What he sought for above all else was to make bad men good. This aim he sought to realize through the law of love as the vital principle in human relations. "Thou shalt love thy neighbor as thyself," he said, quoting Lev. 19:18; [176] then he gave this old glibly recited law a matchless illustration in the parable of the good Samaritan (Lk. *10:29–37).

How often and in what a variety of ways this personal influence of Jesus made itself felt is illustrated repeatedly in the gospel narratives. There is the case of the official, Nicodemus (Jn. *3:1–21); of Mary and Martha (Lk. *10:38–42); of the rich young ruler (Mk. *10:17–22 = Matt. 19:16–22 = Lk. 18:18–23); and of his intimate disciples, as evidenced in the famous narrative of Peter's confession (Mk. *8:27–30 = Matt. 16:13–20 = Lk. 9:18–21).

The seriousness with which Jesus took this principle of the value of human personality is seen also in his attitude toward women (illustrated in the foregoing) and little children (Mk. *10:13–16 = Matt. 19:13 ff. = Lk. 18:15 ff.).

Jesus' ultimate thought on this point is to be observed in the idea that God's objective is the bringing to pass of a society of redeemed and God-like souls. Apparently he could think of nothing beyond that. It is in the light of that ideal of a society of "sons

---

[172] Matt. 5:22.
[174] Mk. 2:17 = Matt. 9:12 f. = Lk. 5:31 f.
[176] Mk. 12:31 = Matt. 22:39 = Lk. 10:27.

[173] Matt. 11:19; cf. Lk. 7:34 f.
[175] Jn. 10:10.

of God" that Jesus saw and evaluated persons in the present. To Jesus, the real man is the ideal man, the son of God, and the sons of God are sons of the resurrection.[177] This was Jesus' basis for belief in a life beyond death. He grounds that belief on the reality of the religious life and the goodness of God. God "is not the God of the dead, but of the living, for all live unto him." [178] If men belong to God, they share the life of God. God cannot be thought of as loving and caring for the righteous during their lifetime and then allowing them to be annihilated.

The Causes for the Martyrdom of Jesus

The gospels indicate that antipathy to Jesus set in very early in his public career.[179] There were numerous specific criticisms raised against him but in general they may be classed as ecclesiastical and political.

Jesus encountered the violent opposition of the Jewish ecclesiastical authorities. This was due to his disregard of the ceremonial in religion. From the time of the prophet Amos we have seen the ethical in conflict with the ritual. Ritual requirements and the prerogatives of the constituted ecclesiastical authorities were precious to the official religionists of Jesus' day. Jesus discounted and disregarded the ceremonial in religion and thereby drew to himself that opposition which led to his death.

Jesus had little interest in politics. It was not possible, however, that his public activity should escape the notice of the government. It was upon a false charge of sedition that he was ultimately condemned to death by the Roman authorities.

Jesus was accused of breaking the Jewish law, e.g., in ignoring the ceremonial washing before meals (Mk. *7:1–23 = Matt. 15:1–20; Lk. 11:37–41 = Matt. 23:23, 25 f.) ; in doing what was regarded as work on the Sabbath (Mk. *2:23–3:6 = Matt. 12:1–14 = Lk. 6:1–11; Lk. *13:10–17; Lk. *14:1–6; Jn. *5:1–18) ; in his free attitude toward the law (Matt. *5:17–48) ; and in his attack upon the oral law, i.e., the "tradition of the elders" (Mk. 7:1–23 = Matt. 15:1–20).

Jesus was accused of neglecting ritual fasting, which the scrupulous Pharisee claimed to do regularly twice a week.[180] So noticeable was this disregard of fasting by Jesus that his own disciples commented upon it (Mk. *2:18 ff. = Matt. 9:14 f. = Lk. 5:33 ff.). A clue to Jesus' attitude is seen in his remark about ostentation in fasting (Matt. *6:16 ff.).

---

[177] Lk. 20:36.   [178] Lk. 20:38 = Mk. 12:27 = Matt. 22:32.
[179] Mk. 2:1–3:6 = Matt. 9:1–17; 12:1–14 = Lk. 5:17–6:11.
[180] Lk. 18:12.

Jesus was accused of associating with sinners. At the feast given by Levi the publican (Mk. *2:13–17 = Matt. 9:9–13 = Lk. 5:27–32), the criticism was voiced so openly that Jesus was moved to vigorous defense.[181] On another occasion, when being entertained by a Pharisee named Simon, Simon's disapproval of Jesus' treatment of a sinful woman became so obvious that Jesus was moved to say some very plain things to his host (Lk. *7:36–50). On another occasion Jesus' singling out of Zacchaeus as his host for a night gave rise to the indignant murmur, "He is gone in to lodge with a man that is a sinner," [182] while both Matt. 11:19 and Lk. 7:34 record that he gained the name of "friend of publicans and sinners." By associating with such persons Jesus was attempting to right a great social wrong but the outcome was that he brought upon himself the accusation that he was a "seducer of the people" (Lk. *23:5, 14).

Jesus was accused of being in league with Beelzebub, the prince of demons, because of his success in casting out demons (Mk. *3:19b–30 = Matt. 12:22–45 = Matt. 9:32 ff. = Lk. 11:14 ff., 17–23). That is, they charged that his power came from an evil source. He was regarded as mentally deranged; "he is beside himself"; [183] "he hath a demon and is mad." [184]

Jesus was accused of blasphemy, that is, of making utterances which implied disrespect or lack of reverence toward God. He was thus accused because he said a certain man's sins were forgiven (Mk. *2:5 ff. = Matt. 9:2 f. = Lk. 5:20 f.), and on another occasion for admitting himself to be "the Son of God" (Mk. *14:61–64 = Matt. 26:63–66 = Lk. 22:67–71). A similar charge is referred to in Jn. *10:30–36.

Jesus was accused of refusing to give a sign in proof of his authority (Matt. 12:38–45 = Lk. *11:16, 29–32; cf. Mk. 8:11 f. = Matt. 16:1–4 = Lk. 12:54 ff.).

Jesus was accused of lack of respect for wealth (Lk. *16:14 f.; cf. Lk. 12:21; *14:12 ff.; Lk. *16:19–25; Mk. *14:3–7 = Matt. 26:6–11).

Jesus was accused of refusing to denounce Roman overlordship (Mk. *12:13–17 = Matt. 22:15–22 = Lk. 20:20–26). It was perhaps this conversation which was later (falsely) turned against him at his trial before Pilate (Lk. *23:1 f.; Jn. *19:12–15). It was on the charge of treason that he was tried and condemned to death (Mk. *15:1–15 = Matt. 27:2, 11–26 = Lk. 23:1–5, 13–25; Jn. 18:28–19:16).

181 Mk. 2:17 = Matt. 9:12 f. = Lk. 5:31 f.
182 Lk. 19:7.
183 Mk. 3:21.
184 Jn. 10:20.

The numerous grievances and charges against Jesus came to a tragic climax in his condemnation and crucifixion (A.D. 29 or 30).[185] The gospel accounts of the trial and death of Jesus are among the most dramatic and gripping passages in all the Biblical literature (Mk. *14 f. = Matt. 26 f. = Lk. 22 f.).

The Resurrection of Jesus

All the gospels give accounts of the resurrection of Jesus (Mk. 16; Matt. 28; Lk. 24; Jn. 20 f.). They all agree as to the central fact of Jesus' resurrection, but they differ so much regarding details that they are among the most difficult of gospel passages to interpret. Three things may be said. (1) These accounts are written in a way to emphasize the miracle aspect and our previously stated view regarding the miracle thought pattern is applicable to the resurrection narratives.[186] (2) Jesus' own view regarding immortality has been stated.[187] That "the sons of God are sons of the resurrection" certainly would apply to Jesus himself.[188] Manifestly this ethical argument held the foremost place in the earliest Christian preaching, for it is the basis of the apostle Peter's Pentecost sermon in which he declared that "it was not possible that he (Jesus) should be holden of death," [189] that is to say, it is unthinkable that such a personality as Jesus should be annihilated by death. This ethical consideration is also basic to the apostle Paul's extended argument in 1 Corinthians *15, the oldest New Testament passage about the resurrection. Paul argues for Christ's resurrection on the basis of the general resurrection of the dead (1 Cor. 15:12–17). (3) The disciples' experiences connected with the resurrection may be classed as mystical religious experiences and were the experiences which gave rise to Christianity.

[185] The Fourth Gospel represents that the crucifixion of Jesus occurred on the day before Passover, Nisan 14 (Jn. 19:14 ff., 31, 42; cf. Lk. 22:15 f.); the synoptic gospels put it on Passover day, Nisan 15 (Mk. 14:12–17; Matt. 26:17–20; Lk. 22: 7–14). All Christian tradition affirms that the crucifixion took place on a Friday. On the most probable calendar calculation, Nisan 14 fell on a Friday in A.D. 29, and Nisan 15 fell on a Friday in A.D. 30. Cf. S. J. Case, *Jesus, A New Biography* (Chicago: 1927), pp. 179 f., 282–286. A. T. Olmstead, *Jesus in the Light of History* (New York: 1942), pp. 279–281, fixes the date of Jesus' execution as April 7, A.D. 30.

[186] *Vid. supra*, pp. 511 f.
[187] *Supra*, p. 515.
[188] Lk. 20:36.
[189] Acts 2:24.

Chapter 25

THE RISE OF CHRISTIANITY

Today Christianity has the largest number of adherents of any of the world's living religions. There was a time when Christianity was a brand-new religion. In this chapter we aim to project ourselves back into that time. In the beginning Christianity was known as "the Way." Primarily this meant a way of salvation but it also included a way of life. We shall try to gain an appreciation of the inner life of those early groups which created Christianity.

The people with whom Christianity got its start were not conscious that they were launching a new religion. They did not keep memoranda of every incident connected with the beginnings of the new faith for they were unaware of the far-reaching significance of what was taking place among them. For about twenty years following the career of Jesus, the primary movement of Christianity was taking place unobtrusively. At the end of that period the new religion comes into full view, having its own peculiar name and calling into being a literature of its own. It is worthy of careful note and emphasis that it was the Christian religious life which produced the New Testament literature. This twenty-year period immediately following Jesus has been aptly called the "Epichristian Age." [1]

The Epichristian Age was followed by the Pauline period, extending to the death of the apostle Paul, A.D. 64. Christianity arose within Judaism but it was a vital, aggressive movement and early transplanted itself to the gentile world. That transplanting began in the Epichristian Age. The New Testament throws light upon only one phase of that expansion, viz., the missionary activity of Paul. By the end of Paul's career, Christianity was taking root in the Greek and Roman civilization around the Mediterranean basin, and assimilating what was vital in that civilization. This continued in the post-Pauline consolidation era until Christianity became altogether a gentile religion.

[1] For this term the author is indebted to Professor James Moffatt who, in an academic lecture, credited it to DeQuincey in Blackwood's Magazine, 1840.

Sources for a Knowledge of Christianity's Origin

The Writings of Paul.   Paul was the most eminent missionary of early Christianity. He founded many Christian churches in the North Mediterranean area. On numerous occasions he found it necessary to write letters to various churches, being at the time unable, usually because of pressing duty elsewhere, to visit in person the churches to which he wrote. It was this practical necessity which brought Christian literature into existence for these occasional letters by Paul are the earliest extant Christian writings. They are historical documents of the very highest value. First Thessalonians, written A.D. 50, has the distinction of being the oldest book in the New Testament collection. All the other letters of Paul were written between then and A.D. 64, the date of his martyrdom. The order in which the letters were written probably was: First Thessalonians, Second Thessalonians, Galatians, First Corinthians, Second Corinthians, Romans, Colossians, Philemon, Ephesians, Philippians. Some New Testament scholars question whether Paul wrote Second Thessalonians and Ephesians. First and Second Timothy and Titus are regarded as writings by Pauline disciples some time after Paul's death, expanding some surviving Pauline fragments. No scholar of repute now regards Hebrews as having been written by Paul.

The Book of Acts.   Acts was written by Luke, the author of the third gospel. Possibly these two books were originally one writing, Luke-Acts, composed A.D. *circa* 85–90, and at some time in the second century divided by copyists in order to put the first half with the other three gospels in a fourfold Gospel.[2] In Acts, the author Luke does not give exhaustive details about the rise and spread of Christianity. Indeed, the New Testament is silent concerning much that we wish for knowledge about, e.g., the spread of Christianity to Egypt and to Rome. Acts gives selected incidents which vividly depict how Christianity got its start and how it was spread by Paul in the North Mediterranean world. Luke says that in preparing his (gospel) "treatise" he knew and used other books as sources,[3] and he manifestly did the same in preparing Acts, especially the early part of the book. This Luke was a companion of Paul who refers to him as "Luke, the beloved physician."[4] In the latter part of Acts are several passages where the pronoun "we" is employed in such a way as to make it apparent that the author is traveling along with Paul,[5] giving us therefore vivid, firsthand information about a phase of Paul's career.

[2] *Vid. infra*, pp. 596.   [3] Lk. 1:1–4.
[4] Col. 4:14.   [5] Acts 16:10–17; 20:5–15; 21:1–18; 27:1–28:16.

Other New Testament Literature. All other New Testament books were, like Acts, written after Paul's letters, i.e., later than A.D. 64, some of them originating in the second century. They are valuable for the light they throw upon the post-Pauline consolidation era of Christianity. It should be borne in mind that the four gospels belong under this head. The gospels are usually read for information about the life and teachings of Jesus. They also can and should be read for the light they throw upon the nature of Christianity in the gospel-making period, i.e., A.D. 65–100.

The Inaugural Mystical Experiences

The Resurrection Visions. 1. *Individual Experiences.* 1 Cor. *15:5–8 is the primary historical account of the resurrection of Christ for it is older than any of the other gospel resurrection narratives. Paul, in vs. 3, asserts that this information was imparted to him by those from whom he learned the facts concerning the origin of the Christian religion. In this account of the resurrection appearances, the name of Peter (Cephas) heads the list. This means that it was a mystical experience of the disciple Peter which was the creative origin of Christianity. In all probability this experience of Peter happened somewhere in Galilee [6] probably not long after the crucifixion of Jesus.

What was the nature of this experience of Peter? Unfortunately the Bible contains no account of it. We are therefore dependent upon what can be inferred. At the end of the list enumerated in 1 Cor. 15:5–8 Paul includes his own experience. This implies that Paul considered his own experience as of the same nature and validity as Peter's or any of the others.[7] Therefore whatever we can make of Paul's experience psychologically may be affirmed of Peter's. The Book of Acts contains three accounts of Paul's vision of the living Christ on the Damascus road (*9:1–19; 22:6–21; 26:12–18). These narratives plainly belong in the category of mystical religious experience, of which we have noted several instances in the course of our study.[8] The characteristic elements are present: a theophany, i.e., a revealing of the divine reality; the overpowering emotion of religious awe; and the spiritual motivation to social-ethical service (Acts 9:5, 15; 22:10, 21; 26:16 f.), as in the case of Moses [9] and Isaiah.[10] It was a mystical religious experience of Moses which was the historical beginning of Yahwism.[11] Similarly, it was a mystical

---

[6] Cf. Mk. 14:28 = Matt. 26:32; Mk. 16:7 = Matt. 28:7.
[7] Gal. 2:8.
[8] *Vid. supra,* pp. 116, 130 f., 323 f., 329 f., 342, 495.
[9] Ex. 3:10.   [10] Isa. 6:8 f.
[11] Ex. 3; cf. *supra,* pp. 130 f.

religious experience of Peter which was the historical beginning of Christianity.

2. *Group Experiences.* 1 Cor. 15:5–7 mentions resurrection appearances to groups of varying size, to "the twelve," to "all the apostles," to "above five hundred brethren at once." Further narratives of such group experiences are found in Mk. 16; Matt. *28; Lk. *24; Jn. 20 f.; Acts *1:1–11. We recall that, similarly, the origin of Yahwism was attended by mystical experiences not only of the individual Moses but also of the group Israel.[12]

What did such experiences mean to the individuals and groups who had them? Reduced to its simplest terms, this meaning is to be found in their conviction that Christ was still alive and their discipleship had not come to an end and, further, that their fellowship and duties as disciples must be resumed. It was this conviction that rallied the disciples and created Christianity.

The Experience of the Holy Spirit at Pentecost. This is a second type of mystical religious experience connected with the origin of Christianity. The account is given in Acts *2:1–13. This narrative pertains to an experience of the Jewish Christian group in Jerusalem. The same type of experience is affirmed of a gentile Christian group in Acts 10:44 ff.; 11:15; 15:8.

Interest attaches to the accompanying phenomenon of glossolalia or the gift of tongues. Apparently this was a frequent and by some Christians much prized type of ecstatic behavior.[13] The person who spoke with tongues seems to have been in the grip of highly overwrought emotion or ecstasy, in which state he poured out a meaningless conglomeration of sounds.[14] Paul has much to say about it in writing to the Christians at Corinth (1 Cor. *12:6–11; *14:1–19). Paul had the good sense to try to divert this type of experience away from a mere expenditure of emotional froth into an ethical channel (the edification of others) and to bring it under the control of reason (1 Cor. 14:19, 26).

In a previous connection we discussed the nature of the religious behavior of the so-called "Sons of the Prophets" and compared it with what historians of religion term *mana*.[15] The ancient mind regarded such ecstatic behavior as immediately caused by the incoming of spirit from the realm of the supernatural. The Pentecost experience of the Christians was similar to this. The behavior of the group was characterized by high-powered emotion and when they came to interpret their own behavior they assigned its cause to the descent

---

[12] Ex. 19.   [13] 1 Cor. 14:5, 18, 23, 26; cf. Acts 9:17.

[14] J. B. Pratt, *The Religious Consciousness* (New York: 1920), pp. 183–187, discusses the nature of glossolalia as the modern psychologist views it.

[15] *Supra,* p. 181.

upon them of the "Holy Spirit." They were "pneumatic," i.e., spirit-filled.

The principle of control which Paul emphasizes is the principle of love (1 Cor. *13). It is important to observe the context in which Paul has set his matchless chapter on love by noting what he discusses just before (chapter 12) and directly after (chapter 14) his most famous and best known chapter. In Paul's thought the most genuine manifestation of the Spirit is to be observed in the Christian life of ethical integrity and altruistic service. This same principle of ethical and rational control, Paul applies to other types of ecstatic experience, as in 2 Cor. 12.

Primitive Christian Worship

The Early Christians' Jewish Connections.   Christianity began as a species of Judaism. The Book of Acts portrays the earliest Christians as thoroughly loyal to the central beliefs and practices of Judaism. Christianity in its initial period may be defined as Judaism with a plus. Briefly put, the plus consisted in the Christians' belief in the resurrection of Christ and their devotion to the person of Christ. What these beliefs involved will be considered more fully later.[16]

1. *With the Jerusalem Temple.*   The Acts narrative portrays the early Christian apostles as actively connected with the temple (2:46; *3:1–4:22), where they both worshiped and taught. We have previously considered that Peter's vision of the risen Christ took place in Galilee. It is likely that the resurrection visions of the others also occurred in Galilee. Why then did these disciples abandon Galilee for Jerusalem? For one thing, Jesus' own career had been cut short at the Jerusalem temple.[17] His followers evidently felt that discipleship must be resumed where it had been interrupted. But perhaps the reason which weighed most with them is to be seen in Mal. 3:1, "The Lord, whom ye seek, will suddenly come to his temple." They understood this to apply to Jesus, and the Jerusalem temple was, therefore, the logical place for them to focus upon. Any messianic movement was expected to take place in Jerusalem and the disciples plainly anticipated that Jesus would speedily return in power to inaugurate the kingdom of God.[18]

2. *With the Synagogues.* (a) *In Jerusalem.*   The first Christians lived as a loyal Jewish group in Jerusalem and doubtless worshiped at the existing synagogues. They did not form a synagogue of their own. There were in Jerusalem not only synagogues of the Pales-

[16] *Infra*, pp. 538–543.   [17] *Vid. supra*, pp. 515 ff.   [18] Acts 1:6.

tinian Jews but also special synagogues for the Diaspora Jews.[19] These Diaspora Jews were devoutly religious men who had returned to Jerusalem to live their last days in the holy city with its holy temple. Christianity was recruited from both groups of Jews.[20]

Palestinian Jews thought that Hellenistic Jews were religiously lax. There was antipathy between the two groups. This antipathy was transferred to Christianity [21] and created a problem within the Jerusalem Christian group. The problem was solved by the appointment of a committee of seven representatives of the Hellenistic group to look after the matter.[22] Of these seven representatives of the Hellenistic group, the most outstanding man of ability appears to have been Stephen. Acts *6 f. gives an account of Stephen's evangelizing activities in the Hellenistic synagogues in Jerusalem, of his speech and his martyrdom. Stephen appears to have been the first person to perceive the distinction between Christianity and Judaism, and the gist of his long speech is in 7:48, "The Most High dwelleth not in buildings made by human hands." This meant that Christianity was inconsistent with the temple worship. Stephen's speech and death forced the Christians to realize the need for thinking out their faith and their relation to Judaism for it was evident that they could not continue to be Jews.

(b) *In Damascus.* Acts 9:2 reveals that a Christian group was established quite early in Damascus and was closely associated with the synagogues there, and this verse implies, moreover, that Damascus was a very important center of the new sect since it was the place chosen by the arch persecutor Saul (Paul) to begin his anti-Christian activity. From whence did these Damascus Christians come? Acts gives no evidence that they had spread from Jerusalem to Damascus. They probably were recruited from the disciples made in the Decapolis by Jesus during his lifetime.[23] The Damascus group may also have included some who migrated thither from Galilee, including some who had seen or heard or been disciples of Jesus during his lifetime and possibly also some of that group of "above five hundred brethren" [24] who had shared the inaugural mystical vision of the resurrection,[25] for not all this group had gone to Jerusalem.[26] It is worthy of note that it was this Damascus Christian group which inducted into Christianity the most famous of all Christian apostles, Paul.[27]

(c) *In the North Mediterranean Centers.* According to the Acts narrative, Paul's missionary procedure in any community to which

[19] Acts. 6:9. [20] Acts 6:1. [21] Acts 6:1.
[22] Acts 6:5. [23] Cf. Matt. 4:25; Mk. 5:20; 7:31; and *supra,* pp. 496 f.
[24] 1 Cor. 15:6. [25] Cf. *supra,* p. 521.
[26] Cf. Acts 1:15. [27] Gal. 1:17; Acts 9:10–22; 22:10–16; 26:12–20.

he went was to preach first of all in the synagogue. As a rule, Paul's Christian message was rejected by the Jews and often there was trouble of violent character as a consequence. After such rejection by the Jews, Paul turned to the gentiles from among whom he won recruits to Christianity.

It is important to bear in mind who would be listening to Paul in any Jewish synagogue where he preached. His hearers would be of three sorts. There were those who were Jews by birth; these were the most ardently loyal to Judaism and very few of this group became Christians. Then there were the proselytes, who were Jews by religion but not by birth; in other words, gentiles who had been converted to Judaism. Some, but not many, proselytes became Christians.[28] In the third place there were the "God-fearers"; these were gentiles who attended the synagogues and helped support the synagogues but would not become Jewish proselytes.[29] Doubtless it was the monotheism and the noble ethical emphases of Judaism which attracted such God-fearers to the synagogues. What kept them from becoming proselytes doubtless was the Jewish insistence upon certain ceremonial requirements, such as the initiatory rite of circumcision and the observance of food taboos, and they were no doubt further deterred by the social disadvantages which Jews and proselytes suffered. In other words, the God-fearers were attracted by the ethical and repelled by the ceremonial. Such God-fearers readily became converted to Christianity, for the new religion, as Paul presented it, offered them all the high moral values they had found in Judaism without ceremonial obligations.

3. *Christianity's Ultimate Break with Judaism.* The Jewish Christians, in the main, appear to have regarded the new religion as a species of Judaism and the ethical teachings of Jesus as a new Torah. It was this interest which led to the preservation of the ethical teachings of Jesus. This is the motif of the Gospel according to Matthew, which is the Jewish Christian gospel, written by a Jewish Christian both for Jewish Christians and for non-Christian Jews that they might become converts to the new Way by understanding that Jesus was a new lawgiver, that his teachings were a new Torah, and that the faith of his followers was a higher Judaism.

The problem of early Christianity's relation to Judaism involved the question whether a gentile, in order to become a Christian, must first of all become a proselyte to Judaism and then become a Jewish Christian. Some Jewish Christians took the affirmative side of this proposition, e.g., James, the brother of Jesus and head of the Jerusa-

---

28 Acts 2:10; 6:5; 13:43.
29 Cf. Acts 10:2, 22, 35; 13:16, 26; 18:7.

lem Christian group.[30] Some of these were extremists in the matter and made considerable trouble. These extremists are known as the "Judaizers." Other Jewish Christians, notably the apostle Paul, took the opposite view. Judaism itself had always insisted that gentiles must submit to circumcision and food taboos in order to become Jewish proselytes, or remain forever outside Judaism. If Christianity had insisted upon the very same thing, then Christianity would have been merely a sect of Judaism and would have disappeared from history before the end of the first century, as indeed Jewish Christianity did. Paul took the ground that the message of Christ was for all mankind, that it transcended racial distinctions and customs, and that gentiles might become Christians without first becoming Jews. In Gal. *2 Paul has given us from his own pen a vigorous account of the controversy in which he engaged with Peter and James and others over this matter. Acts *15 gives an irenic account of how the matter was adjusted between the two parties. The importance of this controversy cannot be overemphasized. With the decision to admit gentiles to Christianity directly and not *via* Jewish ceremonial requirements, Christianity emerged as a separate and distinct and universal religion.

Primitive Christian Group Meetings. 1. *The Distributive Nature of Primitive Christianity.* Christianity began in many local groups. Group gatherings were in homes; [31] e.g., the home of John Mark's mother in Jerusalem,[32] the home of Lydia in Philippi,[33] the home of Titus Justus in Corinth,[34] the home of an unnamed Christian in Troas,[35] and Paul's house in Rome.[36]

In these local groups there were varieties of belief and practice. There were, e.g., the Jewish Christian and the Pauline varieties, already mentioned. A second-century Christian document known as the *Didache* represents another current, neither Jewish Christian nor Pauline, yet having distinctive features of both. One must not therefore assume a fictitious unity of organization or beliefs or practices in the early Christian churches.

2. *General Meetings for Worship.* 1 Cor. *12, *14 throws a vivid light upon the nature of worship in the church at Corinth. We have no means of knowing whether it was the same everywhere at the time. It is noteworthy that outsiders were present at the Christian meetings.[37] New converts to Christianity would have participated to some extent in what went on; they would have joined in the singing of the hymns and in saying the "Amen" at the end of the prayers; they would have heard some Scripture read and explained; they would

---

[30] Acts 15:5.
[32] Acts 1:12 f.; 2:2; 12:12.
[34] Acts 18:7.
[36] Acts 28:30 f.

[31] Acts 2:46.
[33] Acts 16:15.
[35] Acts 20:7 ff.
[37] 1 Cor. 14:23.

have witnessed the performing of miracles of healing; they would have marveled at and perhaps been caught up by the pneumatic behavior of some of those present, especially those who uttered tongues. Everything that went on would have impressed them with the belief that this was a group of Spirit-filled people.[38] Perhaps at some climatic point the entire group would have united in an ecstatic cry of "Abba," meaning "Father," the early Christian watchword.[39]

(a) *Modeled upon the Synagogue Ritual.* The very first Christians were Jews and it was only natural that when they met together as a Christian group for worship they should follow the worship pattern to which they were accustomed from their synagogue associations. The general nature of this synagogue ritual has already been discussed.[40]

Christian services were held on the Lord's Day, which is the first day of the week.[41] This was the distinctive Christian holy day because the resurrection of Christ took place on the first day of the week. We now commonly call this day "Sunday," which term was originally connected with sun worship. But the best and most distinctive Christian name for the day was and still is the "Lord's Day." It is important to differentiate the terms Sunday and Sabbath. The Sabbath was, and is, the Jewish weekly holy day, commencing at sundown on Friday and ending at sundown Saturday. The very first Christians, being loyal Jews, observed the Sabbath, and in addition to that, as loyal Christians, they observed the Lord's Day also. Gentile Christians of course observed only the Lord's Day; the Jewish Sabbath meant nothing to them. In the course of time Jewish Christianity died out, there being no more converts to Christianity from Judaism, for the Jews repudiated Christianity. Keeping of the Sabbath on the part of Christians therefore just naturally ceased, for Christianity became a gentile religion and the gentile Christians observed only the Lord's Day.

(b) *Singing.* The sources of our knowledge about synagogue worship do not mention singing; perhaps it is just taken for granted. Christianity from the start was a singing religion. The function of singing praise is to unite a group, and songs made for Christian solidarity.

All the early Christian hymns were sung to Christ. This is attested by Pliny, who says that the Christians "sang a song to Christ, *quasi deo.*" [42] Col. 3:16 mentions "psalms and hymns and spiritual songs." The psalms, of course, were those of the Jewish psalter and

---

[38] Cf. especially 1 Cor. 12:10, 28 ff.; 14:2 f., 16, 23 f., 26–30.
[39] Rom. 8:15; Gal. 4:6.   [40] *Supra,* pp. 479 f.
[41] 1 Cor. 16:2; Acts 20:7.
[42] *Epistulae* xcvi, § 7. It should be borne in mind that Pliny's letter originated in the same period as did the Fourth Gospel.

they were chanted antiphonally. Pliny again attests this: "We recite our songs antiphonally." [43] What, if any, distinction there was between hymns and spiritual songs it would now be impossible to state. A number of early Christian hymns are embedded in the New Testament. The best known are the *Magnificat* (Lk. *1:46–55), the *Benedictus* (Lk. *1:68–79), and the *Nunc Dimittis* (Lk. *2:29–32). Eph. 5:14 is regarded as a hymn, either a baptismal hymn or a hymn to the unconverted, that is, a very primitive hymn of the type in modern times called gospel hymns. 1 Tim. 3:16 is interpreted as a fragment of an early Christian creed which was no doubt sung. 2 Tim. 2:11 ff. is thought to be a fragment of an eucharistic hymn. Other passages regarded as hymns are Acts 4:24–28, Phil. 2:6–11, Col. 1:15 ff., Matt. 11:25 ff. = Lk. 10:21 f., Jn. 1:1–5, 9–13. [44] The Book of Revelation contains many songs which are stated to be songs sung in heaven and are to be interpreted as songs sung in the churches. The most interesting example is the *Song of the Lamb* (Rev. 15:3 f.). Others are Rev. 4:8, 11; 5:9 f., 12, 13; 7:10, 12; 11:15, 17 f.; 12:10 ff.; 19:1 f., 5, 6 ff.

(*c*) *Prayers.* Prayer was one of the vital features of early Christian worship. The model prayer was that which we know as the Lord's Prayer (Matt. *6:9–13 = Lk. 11:2 ff.). Worshipers customarily said "Amen" to the prayers said in Christian meeting. [45] Two types of posture in prayer are indicated. Pictures in the catacombs represent the Christians as standing in prayer with the hands held out; this is also implied in Lk. 18:11 and Acts 7:55. The other form was kneeling and prostration (Acts 7:60; 9:40; 20:36; 21:5).

(*d*) *The Shema and the Decalogue.* The repeating of the Shema (Deut. 6:4–9; 11:13–21; Num. 15:37–41) may have been taken over by the early Christians, especially the Jewish Christians, as a feature of their worship. This is intimated in certain gospel passages. [46] The same was probably true of the Decalogue also, as implied in the organization of the teachings of Jesus in the Sermon on the Mount (Matt. 5:17–48).

(*e*) *Readings.* The office of reader was one of the very early functions connected with Christian worship. [47] Passages from the *Septuagint,* i.e., the Greek Old Testament, were read. Indeed the Old Testament was highly prized by the early Christians for it was the only Bible they had. It was an ancient Scripture and its use gave to Christianity, a new religion, the guarantee of antiquity. The

43 *Ibid.*
44 Cf. B. W. Bacon, *The Gospel of the Hellenists* (New York: 1933), 114 f., 147, 313 f.   45 1 Cor. 14:16.
46 Mk. 12:29 f. = Matt. 22:37; Lk. 10:27.   47 Cf. Mk. 13:14 = Matt. 24:15.

early Christians may have had copies of selected Old Testament passages for their use. In the gospels one notes how frequently Old Testament passages are quoted with the remark that so and so "came to pass that the Scriptures might be fulfilled."

Letters received from the apostle Paul were read in worship by the churches to which they were sent,[48] and neighboring churches exchanged letters received from Paul.[49] Such letters were read not only when first received but repeatedly thereafter in order to digest their contents,[50] and it was just such repeated use in worship of what had originated as merely occasional letters that led ultimately to their being regarded as themselves Holy Scripture.[51] In this way the letters written not only by Paul but also by others [52] were used and esteemed and preserved by various Christian churches and ultimately found their way into the New Testament.

In the same way the *Gospels* were read in the worship services of the early Christians. The gospels were written for worship.[53] This fact accounts for the form and structure of the gospels, for they are made up of selections (often but not always coterminous with our present chapters) that were originally determined by their suitability for reading in church worship. Revelation was written to be read aloud to the church.[54]

The authors of none of the New Testament books had any idea they were writing Holy Scripture. They wrote something which they thought would assist fellow Christians in their worship. The repeated use of such writings in worship, in conjunction with the reading of the Old Testament which they did regard as Holy Scripture, led the Christian worshipers in time to regard these Christian writings as themselves being Holy Scripture. These Christian writings they referred to as "The New Covenant (Testament)" and thus distinguished it from "The Old Covenant (Testament)."

(*f*) *Exposition.* We can readily appreciate that at the meetings of the very first Christian groups the most important feature was the sharing of stories about Jesus, each one who had known Jesus personally telling what he recalled of the incidents he had witnessed and the teachings he had heard Jesus utter. As groups multiplied and new members were added who had never known Jesus, the function of recounting the gospel story became the more important, especially as the ranks of those who had known Jesus personally thinned out with the passing of time. The gospel storyteller came to be one of the most important functionaries in the early Christian churches.

---

48 1 Thess. 5 :27.
50 Cf. 2 Cor. 10 :10.
52 Cf. Rev. 1 ff., and the general epistles.
54 Rev. 1 :3.

49 Col. 4 :16.
51 Cf. 2 Pet. 3 :15 f.
53 Cf. Jn. 20 :31.

From the most primitive times storytelling had been one of the notable social institutions among the Hebrew people.[55] Storytelling became an art, and there came to be professional itinerant storytellers much as there are to this day among the nomads of Arabia. This institution carried over into Christianity and the man who could tell stories about the career and teachings of Jesus most enthusiastically went about from group to group. His very enthusiasm would mark him as a Spirit-filled man. We can well imagine that such a gospel storyteller was heartily welcomed upon his arrival and that the members of the local group would gather and listen far into the night to his stories,[56] for they had no other access to knowledge about the career of Jesus. In the New Testament such a gospel storyteller is known as an "evangelist," and the gospel story is called the "evangel" (Greek, *euangelion* meaning "good news").

With the passing of time there ceased to be any evangelists who had themselves known and heard Jesus. Evangelists of the second generation were dependent upon what they had heard in Christian meetings as their predecessors recounted the gospel story. The need became apparent for committing the gospel story to writing for the guidance of such evangelists, and this is how the synoptic gospels came to be written. The authors of the written gospels are commonly referred to as the Evangelists. Mark, e.g., wrote his gospel on the basis of what he remembered hearing Peter tell about Jesus.[57]

The telling of the gospel story led to discussion and interpretation, for the Christians would naturally understand the story in the light of their immediate social and religious experiences and problems. These experiences and problems of the Christian groups of the latter part of the first century shine through the written gospels.

Christian groups which received letters from Paul or others had plenty of incentive for discussion and interpretation. What did the apostle mean by this and that? We can guess that such letters as Romans and Ephesians were not comprehended at their first reading.

An address by some competent person was a regular feature of synagogue worship, and this carried over into Christianity also. The Book of Acts represents Paul as frequently addressing synagogue meetings and Christian groups. Paul's letters are frequently in the form of addresses, for as he dictated them to his scribe he no doubt was imagining himself talking to the group to which he was sending the letter. The books of Hebrews and James contain sermons by early Christian preachers. The style of public address reflected in these New Testament sermons has many features quite like the so-called Cynic-Stoic diatribe, which was the type of address in general use by non-Christian teachers and street-corner preachers of the age, of which the discourses of Epictetus are examples.

3. *The Christian Sacramental Meals.* Fellowship was one of the most striking features of the early Christian religion. The Christian church was conceived to be a family. The spiritual basis of this unity found expression in the word "Abba," which means "Father," and appears to have been a kind of watchword among the Christians (Gal. 4:6; Rom. 8:15). Christians called one another brethren, and this term corresponded to a real fact in their feelings and relations to one another. The early Christians therefore ate together as a family and this eating together meant to them not only fellowship with one another but also fellowship with God.

(*a*) *The "Agape" (Love Feast).* The *Agape* was the religious common meal of the Christians and occurred at the close of the day, for the reason that many Christians were slaves and therefore were not free until evening. Pictures of the *Agape* in the catacombs depict baskets, loaves, and fish. The *Agape* closed with the "holy kiss," [58] much as the members of a family now will kiss one another good night. This practice however was abused and was given up in the second century and a blessing of peace was introduced.

(*b*) *The "Eucharist" (Lord's Supper).* The term "Eucharist" means "giving thanks" and expresses the great gladness which characterized the early Christians in their group relations. Apparently the Lord's Supper followed the Love Feast at the close of day. The historical precedent was the last supper of Jesus with his disciples (Mk. 14:12–31 = Matt. 26:17–35 = Lk. 22:7–38). In 1 Cor. *11:23–26 Paul gives an account of the origin of the Lord's Supper. According to 1 Cor. 11, certain abuses arose in the Corinthian church in connection with the Love Feast and the Lord's Supper. The Lord's Supper therefore came to be separated from the *Agape* and held at a different time.

The conception of the Lord's Supper early changed from a memorial to a sacrament. Other religious cults of the first century had their sacramental meals in which it was verily believed that the worshipers, by ingestion, took into their very selves the presence and power of the lords of their respective cults.[59] Christianity, as it spread in the Mediterranean world, came into contact and competition with such mystery cults and some devotees from such cults became converted to Christianity. To the minds of such persons the Lord's Supper would seem to carry the same mystical implications. And indeed it seems to have been so regarded by Paul, for as he labors

---

[58] 1 Thess. 5:26; 1 Cor. 16:20; 2 Cor. 13:12; Rom. 16:16; 1 Pet. 5:14.
[59] Cf. 1 Cor. 10:21.

to differentiate the Christian communion from others (1 Cor. 10:14–31), he indicates that he regards the Christian communion as the mystical and realistic incoming of the presence of Christ into the self of the Christian communicant (especially vs. 16). The Lord's Supper is thus a sacrament of unity in the Christian church through fellowship with the living Lord, the body of the Lord being the mystical body of the church (vs. 17).

It appears to have been the practice of Christians at the communion table to "tell the story" of Christ's death.[60] Jews at their Passover recited the story of the ancient deliverance from Egypt, and the devotees of the mystery cults at their sacred meals recited the legends about their "savior gods."

4. *Baptism.* Baptism as a ritual rite was practiced by Christianity from the very beginning. It is plainly implied in the Pentecost narrative (Acts 2:38, 41) that there never was a time when the rite was not administered by Christians. The historical precedent upon which it rested was, of course, the baptism of Jesus by John the Baptist.[61] Paul, in 1 Cor. 12:13; Rom. 6:3, gives us to understand that he was baptized as a matter of course right after his conversion.[62] Baptism was by immersion, i.e., burial under the water (Rom. 6:3 f.), which symbolized the burying of the old man. Rising and coming out of the water symbolized the resurrection, rising to a new life in Christ. It also meant that the baptized had now come into full membership in the Christian group, in which all were on a social par because of their baptism, whatever their previous social status or their rating outside the Christian fellowship.

An interesting feature was proxy baptism for dead persons (1 Cor. 15:29). The motive behind this was the question which puzzled the first Christians, viz., what about those who had lived and died before the coming of Jesus and therefore did not hear his message or have opportunity to follow him? Early Christians did not want their loved ones absent from the society of the redeemed in the new world which they believed was soon to come and so they were baptized on their behalf.[63] No more did they want their children absent from the family of the redeemed in that new world which might break upon them at any moment. The gospel narrative about Jesus blessing little children intimates that the church in the gospel-making period was of divided opinion about admitting children; there were those who

---

[60] Such is the meaning of the Greek verb used in 1 Cor. 11:26 and customarily translated "proclaim."

[61] Mk. 1:9 ff. = Matt. 3:13–17 = Lk. 3:21 f.; cf. *supra*, pp. 495 f.

[62] Cf. Acts 9:18.

[63] This same interest at a later time led to the belief that Jesus, during the interval between his death and his resurrection, descended into the lower world and "preached to the spirits in prison" (Eph. 4:9; 1 Pet. 3:18 ff.); the idea later became incorporated in the Apostles' Creed in the phrase, "He descended into Hades."

rebuked their parents, but the prevailing view was that children should not be excluded but rather that it was to them that the kingdom of God really belonged.[64] This ultimately led to the practice of infant baptism.

Christian baptism was something more than the baptism of John. This is clearly brought out in Acts *19:1-7 where a group of John's followers was made to undergo a second baptism "into the name of the Lord Jesus." Apparently this phrase preserves the earliest ritual formula used in connection with baptism. The full trinitarian formula (Matt. 28:19) developed later. Christian baptism was all that John's baptism was, repentance and moral renewal, and more besides. What more besides is clearly intimated in the words put into the mouth of John the Baptist by the gospel writers, "He shall baptize you in the Holy Spirit." [65] Peter, at Pentecost, said, "Repent and be baptized . . . and ye shall receive the gift of the Holy Spirit." [66] At the conversion of Cornelius (Acts 10) "the Holy Spirit fell on all of them" (vs. 44) which Peter took as a sign that the rite of baptism could properly be administered. In other passages it is stated that the Holy Spirit came upon them through the laying on of hands subsequent to baptism.[67] The early Christian community was a community of Spirit-filled persons and baptism in the Spirit and entrance into the community went together.

Thus baptism came to be regarded as a mystical experience and to be interpreted in terms of the supernatural. Like the Lord's Supper, it passed from the stage of being regarded as a symbolic rite to that of a sacrament.

Early Christian Organization

The early Christian community was a brotherhood of Spirit-filled men. There was no respect of persons or distinctions in rank or formal organization of any sort. Mutual love and service were the ideals of their group relationships, in accordance with Jesus' teaching.[68] Yet of necessity, as their experience progressed, this very mutual service led to differentiation of functions and called forth leadership of one type and another. In 1 Cor. *12 Paul likens the Christian community to the human body with its various members and functions. Vss. 28 ff. of this chapter enumerate the several types of leaders in the church. Eph. 4:11 f. contains another slightly differing list.

The Ordinary Plain Members. Before the term Christian was coined, the early Christians were called by a variety of names. They

[64] Mk. 10:13–16 = Matt. 19:13–15 = Lk. 18:15–17.
[65] Mk. 1:8 = Matt. 3:11 = Lk. 3:16.   [66] Acts 2:38.
[67] Acts 8:16 f.; 19:6.   [68] Lk. 22:24 ff.; Mk. 10:35–45.

were known as Galileans,[69] as Nazarenes,[70] as saints (which is the term for Christians most numerously used through the New Testament), as disciples,[71] as brethren,[72] as believers,[73] as those that belonged to "the Way." [74]

Not for a dozen years or more after the start of Christianity was the name "Christian" coined. It originated in Antioch of Syria,[75] no doubt as a nickname bestowed either in malice or in derision. It is a term of Latin formation like *Sullani, Caesariani, Pompeiani,* all of which designated the partisan followers of those contestants for empire. Similarly, the Christians were dubbed the followers of a new pretender, "Christ." The term "Christ" is a Greek term, *Christos,* easily and doubtless often deliberately confused with *chrestos,* an adjective often used in the derogatory sense of "simple" or "silly." Because it was at the outset a contemptuous epithet, the Christians themselves were very slow to take up and employ the term. By the end of a century the name was fixed upon them and not inappropriately. It means "Christ's folk" and contains the term of central significance, "Christ." The Greek word "Christ" means "anointed one," and in Jewish usage it was a term of messianic import. In Jewish thought, Messiah was conceived to be that ideal person whom God would raise up and appoint as his agent in bringing to pass the ideal reality, namely, the kingdom of God. The very name of the religion, therefore, reveals the essence of its faith, viz., the idealism revealed in Christ and to be consummated through Christ.

Apostles. Acts 1:13–26 enumerates the names of the first apostles; they are the former twelve disciples, minus Judas Iscariot, whose position was filled by one Matthias. It is interesting to note that there were at least two men qualified to fill the place of Judas. By virtue of their previous relation to Jesus, these apostles were the pre-eminent persons in early Christianity. Many persons other than these twelve are referred to as apostles.[76]

Acts 6:4 describes the special ministry of the apostles as prayer and the ministry of the word. The term apostle means "one sent forth," and it was applied to those selected for missionary work. This may indicate that the term came into vogue when the missionary activity of the new religion had commenced. Acts 1:21 f. states the qualifications of an apostle to be first, that he had been associated with Jesus and the disciples ever since the baptism of Jesus by John, and second, that he had witnessed the resurrection of

[69] Acts 1:11; 2:7; 13:31.
[70] Acts 24:5.
[71] Frequently in Acts; cf. especially 11:26.
[72] Acts 1:15, and frequently.
[73] Acts 2:44, and numerously.
[74] Acts 9:2.
[75] Acts 11:26.
[76] Gal. 1:19; 1 Cor. 9:5; 2 Cor. 8:23; Rom. 16:7.

Jesus. This of course had primarily to do with the selection of a successor to Judas, but the second half of the qualification apparently was always required of an apostle. Specifically, it was a point of controversy as to the apostleship of Paul, who had not known or been with Jesus at all. He regarded his Damascus-road experience as a vision of the risen Christ [77] and therefore deemed himself fully qualified to be an apostle. Paul's right to be called an apostle was challenged by the Judaizers who attacked his reputation on this ground. Paul vigorously defended his apostleship in writing to the Galatian Christians [78] and likewise in writing to the Corinthians.[79]

Prophets. Christian prophets appear quite early in primitive Christianity.[80] Acts 15:32 seems to indicate that such prophets "exhorted the brethren." Such passages as Acts 19:6; 21:9 indicate that prophesying consisted in a kind of ecstatic behavior comparable to that of the early "Sons of the Prophets" of the Old Testament.[81] The most conspicuous aspect of such ecstatic behavior was "tongue-speaking." [82] Paul highly appreciated prophesying but was at considerable pains to lift it above "tongue-speaking," [83] and to bring it under the control of reason and especially of love.[84]

Without doubt the real center of interest and activity of the first-century Christian prophets is to be found in the sphere of apocalyptic. Apocalyptic, as we have previously observed,[85] is pre-eminently concerned with the issues of the future. This type of thought strongly appealed to the early Christians for their thinking was highly anticipatory. They looked forward to the return of Christ, to the establishment of Christ's kingdom and the realization of their ideals. Christian prophesying concerned itself with such apocalyptic forecasting of the future. The Book of Revelation is the example par excellence of this. It is designated an apocalypse by the very first (Greek) word in the book and is also called a "prophecy." [86] Its author is regarded as a "seer," [87] i.e., one possessed of an inward illumination which gave him insight into what the future would reveal.

Teachers. From the very outset of Christianity, an emphasis was laid on teaching, judging from the reference to "the teaching of the apostles" in Acts 2:42. Acts 13:1 mentions the presence of teachers in the church at Antioch. Paul rated teachers as next in importance after apostles and prophets (1 Cor. 12:28). We may reasonably assume that their chief function was imparting instruction in "the

[77] Acts 9:5; 22:8; 26:15; 1 Cor. 9:1.
[78] Gal. 1.
[80] Acts 11:27; 13:1.
[82] Acts 19:6; 1 Cor. 14; cf. *supra*, pp. 521 f.
[84] 1 Cor. 13:2, 8 f.
[86] Rev. 1:3.
[79] 1 Cor. 9.
[81] Cf. *supra*, pp. 181 ff.
[83] 1 Cor. 14:1-5.
[85] *Supra*, pp. 442 ff.
[87] Rev. 1:2.

Way of the Lord," [88] i.e., instruction about the career and teachings of Jesus. Perhaps the teacher would recite a story about Jesus, and the hearers would repeat it again and again until it was memorized. It was just such remembered fragments which constituted the materials of which the gospels were built up when they came to be written.

Evangelists. The nature of the service rendered by the early Christian evangelists has already been discussed.[89]

Elders, Pastors, Bishops, and Deacons. In the primitive Christian churches there were elders; e.g., in the Jerusalem church [90] and also in the churches which Paul established on the mission field.[91] We have been acquainted with the function of the elders in Hebrew society from the very earliest times; [92] it was only natural that the same institution for social control should carry over into the Christian groups. The Greek word for elder is *presbyter*. These presbyters were simply men of strong personality who took the lead in conducting the necessary business of the groups. These groups were brotherhoods of the Spirit. They acknowledged the authority of the Spirit wherever it manifested itself. Other than this, the only persons to whom the early Christians deferred as in any sense exercising authority over them were the traveling missionaries or apostles.

As Christian churches multiplied, ecclesiastical organization tended to come into being and to expand. The later writings of the New Testament reveal a system of church government in process of establishing itself. Pastors are listed in Eph. 4:11 among the early church officials. Such pastors replaced the traveling apostolic missionaries. There is mention of bishops, which means "overseers" (superintendents) [93] and deacons (assistants).[94] Undoubtedly the bishop was at first only an informal functionary overseeing the conduct of affairs in a local Christian group which recognized in its elders a number of leaders of equal standing. Presently the bishop came to be recognized as the chief authority in the group. Some misgiving and friction attended the coming of this new order of things and this is quite vividly revealed in 3 John which preserves the name of Diotrephes, the earliest Christian bishop we know by name. In the latter part of the first century Christianity came into conflict with heresy, which accelerated the fixing of the authoritative leadership of the bishop, who assumed the regulation of the preaching, teaching, and

[88] Cf. Acts 18:25.   [89] *Supra,* pp. 527 ff.
[90] Acts 11:30; 15:2, 4, 6, 22 f.; 16:4; 21:18.   [91] Acts 14:23; 20:17.
[92] Cf. *supra,* pp. 90 f., 160 f., 202, 282 f.
[93] Phil. 1:1; 1 Tim. 3:1 f.; Tit. 1:7.
[94] Phil. 1:1; 1 Tim. 3:8–13. Goodspeed in the Chicago Version translates "bishops and deacons" in these passages as "superintendents and assistants."

ritualistic observances of the Christian groups. The free Christian brotherhood of the earliest days of Christianity had given way to a Christian ecclesiastical organization.

The Seven. Acts *6:1–6 directs attention to an interesting problem growing out of attitudes which the Jewish Christians carried over from their Jewish relations into their Christian group relations. Palestinian Jews (the "Hebrews" of vs. 1) were extremely conservative and felt critical toward the Diaspora Jews (the Hellenistic Jews, the "Grecian Jews" of vs. 1) because the latter were appreciative of and responsive to the influences of the Graeco-Roman culture of the age. The Palestinian Jews felt that these Hellenistic Jews were not true Jews. This antipathy lies at the basis of the trouble reported in Acts 6:1–6. The needy of the Hellenistic Christian group were slighted in the distribution of the relief. The problem was adjusted by the appointment of a committee of seven Hellenistic Christians to attend to the relief. The incident is interesting as calling attention to the taproot of a difficulty that spread very widely in the first age of Christianity, viz., Jewish versus Hellenistic Christianity.

It is interesting to note that the seven were selected by a popular choice which was ratified by the twelve apostles. The special service of the seven was the care of the poor.[95] They were a sort of welfare board. The function of the seven was not, however, restricted to the administration of poor relief. They supervised the foreign-born converts in the Jerusalem Christian group and conducted an active propaganda among the Hellenists. Acts 6 ff. tells of the activities of the most famous of these seven Hellenistic leaders, Stephen and Philip. This Stephen was the first Christian martyr.[96]

The Unity of the Believers. 1. *The Idea of the "Ecclesia."* The New Testament Greek word *ecclesia* is commonly translated "church." The word church brings before the modern mind the concept of a thoroughly unified and centralized ecclesiastical organization. Christianity did indeed ultimately become such but to read this concept back into the early age of beginning Christianity is erroneous. The early Christian *ecclesia* was not an official church but a free community of the Spirit.

Jewish idealistic thinking had always distinguished between the actual Israel, which was the total nation of the Jews, and the true Israel, which was the "holy remnant" within the nation, the minority of the sincerely righteous few who were faithful to the higher calling of Israel, the small nucleus through which God would work

---

[95] These seven are the historical precedent for the modern church officials known as deacons in some Christian denominations.

[96] Cf. *supra*, p. 522.

out his purposes. It was this remnant that really was "God's peo-ple." The early Christians deemed themselves to be continuous with this "holy remnant." Indeed, as we have seen,[97] the name by which Christians are most commonly designated in the New Testament is "saints" which literally means "holy ones." The "holy remnant" which God had preserved in every age was now embodied in the Christian *ecclesia*. The Christians therefore regarded themselves as the heirs of all the promises God made to Israel, i.e., the spiritual, not the national, Israel.

Now the idea of the "holy remnant" had always been that of the small nucleus with which God integrated the new age or order of things when he intervened to overthrow evil and re-establish right-eousness on the earth. The Christian *ecclesia* was therefore a frag-ment of the future ideal order projected into the present. Or con-versely, the Christians threw in their lot with the future, the ideal order of things, and in the midst of an unideal present aimed to be an ideal society of persons. They were not an ecclesiastical or-ganization but a spiritual organism which the Holy Spirit indwelt and controlled. In the beginning, then, the only unity which bound together the multiplicity of Christian groups or churches was this unity of the Spirit.

2. *The Early Christian Communism.* The strong sense of spiritual unity which characterized the earliest Christians is revealed in the remark that "the multitude of them that believed were of one heart and soul." [98] From the very first the Christians deemed themselves to be members of a spiritual family,[99] and their use of the term "brethren" corresponded to a reality in their feelings toward one another. This feeling of love for all the brotherhood led to what is commonly referred to as the early Christian communism, described in Acts *4:32–5:11. A careful examination of the passage reveals that no such thing as a formal communism was established. In order to become a Christian no one was obliged to give up his property. But the passage does reveal that Christians felt such a bond of mutuality with all members of their group that any one possessed of property felt he should not retain his property, when to sell it would provide funds for the relief of needy Christian brothers. This arrangement probably began when the disciples gathered in Jerusa-lem after the resurrection. They were Galileans who had given up their occupations and in the large and strange city of Jerusalem they were without means of earning a living. So they shared their common possessions according to their simple needs. The Acts nar-rative singles out for special commendation for his high-minded

[97] *Supra,* p. 533.   [98] Acts 4:32.   [99] Cf. *supra,* p. 530.

devotion a disciple named Barnabas, later a zealous missionary. The narrative likewise tells of Ananias, whose pretense of devotion to the brotherhood was only a fraud.

3. *Paul's Near East Relief.* While no formal ecclesiastical organization bound the many Christian churches into a unity, a very practical measure of humanitarian relief did serve to make the gentile Christians conscious of their spiritual oneness with the Jerusalem Christians. The Jerusalem church suffered from chronic poverty, as evidenced in the passage discussed in the preceding paragraph.[100] Acts 11:27–30 tells of relief sent by the Christians of Antioch in Syria to the Jerusalem church during the widespread famine of the year 46. In the Jerusalem council, at which an accord was reached regarding Paul's gentile missionary work, the Jerusalem Christians wished that Paul "should remember the poor." [101] Acts and the letters of Paul reflect Paul's project of getting the gentile churches of his mission field to unite in a relief fund for the Jerusalem church, which fund Paul himself, accompanied by a relief committee from the gentile churches, took to Jerusalem (1 Cor. 16:1–6; 2 Cor. 8:1–4; 9:1–14; Rom. 15:25 ff.; Acts 24:17). It would be difficult to say how large a contribution this project of benevolence made to the advance of Christianity. It is a striking evidence of how the Christian movement united men for moral ends.

Early Christian Doctrine

The beliefs of the Epichristians all had to do with Jesus. They longed to express adequately their faith in Jesus. They were monotheists, to be sure, but they adored Jesus and found no expression too lofty to ascribe to him. All their thinking was Christ-centered. Their doctrine is technically called Christology.[102]

The Resurrection of Christ. Belief in the resurrection of Christ is what brought Christianity into being, as has already been pointed out.[103] That this was, at the outset, their belief of chief importance is evidenced by Acts 1:22 where it is prescribed that the one chosen to fill the place of Judas must with the others of the twelve "become a witness with us of his resurrection." 1 Cor. *15 is the classic passage which sets forth the doctrine of the resurrection of Christ. It was this belief and the mystical experiences connected with it which furnished the dynamic of Epichristianity. The attitude of the Epichristians toward Jesus did not consist merely in reverently remembering the

[100] Acts 4:32–5:11.   [101] Gal. 2:10; *vid. supra,* p. 536.
[102] Cf. Millar Burrows's chapter on "Christ," in *An Outline of Biblical Theology* (Philadelphia: 1946).
[103] *Supra,* pp. 520 f.

historical career and teachings of Jesus. They regarded him as still alive and they centered their thoughts on what he now was and how he was manifesting his power among them and how he would in the future reveal his presence and power.

The Future Coming of Christ. One of the very earliest ritual expressions used by Christians has been preserved for us in its original Aramaic form in the word *maranatha*.[104] The expression may be translated either "The Lord cometh," or "Come, O Lord." It seems to have been an Epichristian watchword. Its use testifies to the importance of their belief in the imminent return of Jesus.

The early Christians were apocalyptists.[105] They ardently longed for the "Parousia." [106] *Parousia* is the technical term which designates that time when God will, through his appointed agent, catastrophically intervene to destroy evil and establish his kingdom of righteousness. This is what the early Christians believed Christ was to do in the future. He would come as judge to destroy his enemies and establish his kingdom.

The practical consequence of this belief was the missionary activity which it inspired. Matt. *9 f. reflects the missionary activity of the Jerusalem church, endeavoring to convert the Jews before the Son of Man should come.[107] This belief was basic to the missionary activity among the gentiles that is recorded in Acts. It certainly was, at the outset, a foundation belief of the apostle Paul as evidenced by the letters to the Thessalonians. The prominence of eschatology in the thinking of the first-century Christians is evidenced by the eschatological discourse incorporated in the synoptic gospels [108] and pre-eminently by such a book as Revelation [109] which portrays what the rank and file of the plain members of the first-century church were thinking. Among the classic chapters of Revelation are the worship in heaven (4) ; the downfall of Rome (*18) ; the resurrection of the dead (20:11–15) ; and the new Jerusalem (*21:1–22:5).

In the beginning the Christians seem to have believed that the Parousia was very near.[110] The hope was never realized, and as the Parousia came to seem not near but more and more remote, the eschatological thought form tended to fall away and emphasis was shifted from the future coming of Christ to that new life in Christ and that fellowship with him which were a present reality.

The Messiahship of Jesus. The word *Christ* comes from Greek and means "the anointed one." It translated the Hebrew word for

---

[104] 1 Cor. 16:22. Another such term is *abba;* cf. *supra,* p. 530.
[105] Cf. *supra,* pp. 442 f., 507–510.
[106] Cf. Phil. 4:5 ; Heb. 10:37 f. ; Jas. 5:8 f. ; Rev. 22:20.
[107] Matt. 10:23.   [108] Discussed *supra,* pp. 506–510.
[109] Cf. *supra,* p. 534 ; *infra,* pp. 591 f.   [110] Matt. 24:34.

"messiah." The early Christians' belief that Jesus was the Christ led them to refer to him as "Jesus Christ" and in time simply as "Christ."

At the outset, the concept of messiahship was not applied to the historic career of Jesus prior to his death. In the earliest Christian preaching of which we have evidence, Peter's sermon at Pentecost (Acts 2:14–36), the historic Jesus of Nazareth was "a man approved of God unto you by mighty works" (vs. 22); God raised him from the dead (vs. 24) and "made him both Lord and Christ" (vs. 36). It was in his present, exalted state that Jesus had entered upon his office as Messiah, and they regarded the resurrection as evidence of this. At his future coming Jesus would fully carry out the functions which Jewish thought conventionally assigned to the Messiah, viz., to judge the world, to destroy his enemies, and to inaugurate the kingdom of God.

The earthly career of Jesus gave the early Christians difficulty in ascribing to him the role of Messiah. Jesus had been a teacher, and nothing in Jewish literature had led to any expectation that Messiah would come in the role of a teacher. It was expected that Messiah would come as a conquering hero to destroy his enemies, but the historic Jesus had been conquered by his enemies and crucified. The Christians had therefore to explain the cross. Isaiah's concept of the Suffering Servant (Isa. *52:13–53:12) afforded them the explanation they sought. To Epichristian thought the cross came to stand for something more than the martyrdom of Jesus. It meant his sacrificial death for all mankind's avail. "Christ died for our sins according to the scriptures." This, Paul says, is the explanation of the cross that was taught him when he became a Christian, and this was the very first item in his preaching to the Corinthians.[111]

The Lordship of Jesus. In so far as the Epichristians had any creed at all, it consisted of only two words (in Greek), "Jesus is Lord." In all probability this was the formula pronounced over a Christian at his baptism. Paul refers to the formula as the essential confession of the Christian faith (Rom. 10:9).

That the appellation "Lord" was applied to Jesus from the very start is attested by the use of the word *maranatha* and by the formula used in Peter's Pentecost sermon, "God hath made him both Lord and Christ." [112] In the beginning Lord was a title of reverence ascribed to Jesus. In the end it assimilated to itself all the implications of a cult divinity.

Throughout Old Testament times Yahweh was Lord of the Hebrews. Other peoples had their lords; e.g., *baal,* a term which means "lord" or "owner." In the first century there were many so-called

---

[111] 1 Cor. 15:3.   [112] Acts 2:36.

mystery cults in vogue in the Mediterranean world. As Paul put it, "there are gods many, and lords many," and he adds: "Yet to us there is one God, the Father, of whom are all things, and we unto him; and one Lord, Jesus Christ, through whom are all things, and we through him." [113] The loyalty and devotion of the Christians were exclusively rendered to Jesus Christ. In time, the Christians came to think of Jesus as a divinity to whom worship could be offered and the term Lord passed over into this sense.

The doctrine expressed in Peter's Pentecost sermon, that Jesus, "a man approved of God," was by the resurrection "made both Lord and Christ," [114] is a doctrine of apotheosis, i.e., Jesus began as a man and culminated by becoming a divinity. The same view is expressed by Paul when he says that Jesus "was of the seed of David according to the flesh" and that he was "declared to be the Son of God with power by the resurrection from the dead." [115]

Another type of doctrine prevalent in the thinking of the gentile world in the first century is known as "incarnation," i.e., beginning as a divinity and culminating by becoming man. Greek myths affirmed that many divinities came down to earth and mingled with humans. This was strikingly illustrated by an incident in the career of the apostle Paul and his companion the apostle Barnabas. The natives at Lystra said, "The gods are come down to us in the likeness of men," and they "called Barnabas, Zeus (Jupiter); and Paul, Hermes (Mercury)"; [116] and they wanted to offer sacrifice to them. On another occasion the natives of the island of Melita said that Paul was a god. [117] On a much higher plane, Hellenistic philosophical speculation affirmed that the Logos, i.e., Universal Reason, came to indwell certain men. This was an important belief of the Stoics. This doctrine of the Logos was taken over by the Jewish philosopher Philo, a contemporary of Jesus, and assimilated to Jewish thinking. It was easily assimilable to the Jewish doctrine of incarnate Wisdom. Prov. *8:22–31 portrays Wisdom as present with God when the world was created, either as a creative agent of God or as an onlooker. A similar view is presented in Job *28:20–28. In Sir. *1:1–9, *24:3–11, Wisdom is viewed as an emanation from the deity and is conceived of as eternal, having existed before the creation of the world, and always enduring, a kind of immanence in all nature, and in all peoples, especially in Israel. This type of thinking appealed to and was adopted by Christians for it furnished them another category for interpreting Jesus. Paul used this thought pattern in Col. *1:15 ff. It came to full expression in Christianity at the end of the first

---

[113] 1 Cor. 8:5 f.   [114] Acts 2:22, 36.
[115] Rom. 1:3 f. Cf. Millar Burrows, *An Outline of Biblical Theology* (Philadelphia: 1946), pp. 103 ff.   [116] Acts 14:11 ff.   [117] Acts 28:6.

century in the classic prologue to the Gospel of John (chapter *1)
which depicts Jesus as the incarnate Logos.

The Christian Idea of God.   Jesus' own idea of God was, of
course, at the heart of the Christian idea of God also.[118] The attribute
of God upon which early Christian thought delighted to dwell was
love. One of the most sublime chapters in the New Testament is
1 Cor. *13, Paul's hymn in praise of love. It is the view of some
interpreters that in this chapter Paul was delineating the character of
Jesus. What Paul saw in Jesus gave him insight into the nature of
God, and this immortal chapter is also a portrait of the love of God.
In Jesus' thought of God, the idea of redemption best expresses the
nature of God's activity in the world. To early Christian thought the
career of Jesus was a redemptive ministry and his death on the cross
was for the redemption of mankind. In the career and death of Jesus,
God wrought something for all mankind, namely, salvation. To Paul,
"God was in Christ, reconciling the world unto himself." [119] In Jesus
Christ could be seen what God was like and what God was doing in
the world. In a late first-century passage (1 Jn. *3 f.), God is defined
as love [120] and love is made the very heart of Christianity.

A favorite word in the apostle Paul's idea of God is "grace." Grace
means the free giving of God, God in action taking the initiative
in bestowing redemption upon mankind. By grace, Paul meant all
that Jesus meant by his doctrine of the Heavenly Father, and all
that the modern philosopher means by the idea of the universe being
friendly to man.

In Epichristian thought God was just as truly active through his
Holy Spirit in their midst as he had been in Jesus and was doing
the same thing, i.e., redeeming the world. Hence the reiterated emphasis upon the Spirit, the Holy Spirit, and the Spirit of Christ, the
Spirit of God. All these forms of expression meant the same thing to
the Epichristian mind. What came to expression in Jesus was coming
to expression in them. The Acts of the Apostles is really a book of the
Acts of the Holy Spirit. God present, God active, God redeeming—
that is what the early Christians believed had taken place in the career
of Jesus and was taking place in their own very midst.

The Christian Attitude Toward God.   To appropriate God's
grace, all that the Christian needs is the capacity to receive and
respond. This capacity is expressed by the word "faith." Faith is the
Christian's adventure in co-operation with that spiritual energy in
the universe which is known as the grace of God. "By grace have
ye been saved through faith; and that not of yourselves, it is the

---

[118] Cf. *supra,* pp. 500 ff.   [119] 2 Cor. 5:19.   [120] 1 Jn. 4:8.

gift of God," very well expresses Paul's view.[121] What is perhaps the most elaborate of all the writings of Paul, his letter to the Romans, is really a treatise on the text, "The righteous shall live by faith," [122] which is an idea taken up from the Old Testament prophet Habakkuk.[123] The heart of Paul's argument is contained in Rom. *7 f., another of the classic passages of the New Testament. Heb. *11:1–12:2 is another splendid passage on Christian faith.

Christian Ethics

The Ethical Teachings of Jesus. Jesus was pre-eminently a teacher, and the primary emphasis of his teaching was upon the ethical.[124] His teachings were cherished and preserved with remarkable fidelity by the Epichristians. The earliest Christian document about whose existence we have any knowledge was the collection of the "Sayings of Jesus" by Matthew, in the Aramaic language.[125] Interest in the ethical teachings of Jesus led to their ultimate incorporation and preservation in the gospels.

Christianity was, at the outset, known as "the Way," a way of salvation which included a way of life. There was a type of ethical living which was known as Christian. Early Christianity was indeed zealous in the matter of teaching its converts this way of life. It was interest in the ethical discipline of church members which led to the preservation of Jesus' teaching; the Gospel of Luke, for example, was written for a catechumen, Theophilus.[126] According as one and another type of problem arose in the group experiences of the early Christians, the teachings of Jesus were recalled. It was this which determined the form in which the teachings are preserved in the gospels. The gospels reflect living situations in the early Christian community and the problems they faced and the way in which they used the teachings of Jesus to solve their problems. For example, the way in which the parable of the soils [127] is told, with an interpretation of it added,[128] plainly indicates the problem of the unequal responsiveness, enthusiasm, and fidelity to the gospel message which members of the early church displayed; and the parable of the tares reflects the problem of unworthy members who got into the Christian churches.[129]

It was the ethical teachings of Jesus which once and forever determined the Christian morality. This was the heritage which the

[121] Eph. 2:8.
[122] Rom. 1:17.
[123] Hab. 2:4.
[124] *Supra,* pp. 504 ff.
[125] *Vid. supra,* p. 483.
[126] Lk. 1:3 f.
[127] Mk. 4:1–9 = Matt. 13:1–9 = Lk. 8:4–8.
[128] Mk. 4:13–20 = Matt. 13:18–23 = Lk. 8:11–15.
[129] Matt. 13:24–30.

early Christians received from Jesus and transmitted to all who came after them. Nothing else that happened in the first century can compare in far-reaching importance to that process by which Christians came to realize the necessity and desirability of putting the teachings of Jesus in writing, and thereby bequeathed to posterity its most priceless heritage.

The Ethical Sections of Paul's Letters. Paul's letters were addressed to concrete situations in the churches to which he wrote. Not being able to visit a certain church in person at the time, he writes what he would say if he were present, by way of helping toward a solution of the problems which the church is facing. In most of his letters Paul sees fit to include a section of ethical teachings. His aim in these sections is to restate the inner significance of the Christian morality and to apply it to the practical conditions his readers are facing. Some of the ethical sections which reveal the range of Paul's ethical thinking and the principles on which he based his teaching are 1 Thess. 4:1–12; 5:12–22; 2 Thess. 3:6–15; Gal. *5:13–6:10; 1 Cor. *6:12–7:40; *10; *13; Rom. 6:12 f.; *12:1–15:13.

Christian Wisdom Teaching. The nature of the Jewish wisdom type of teaching has come to our attention in previous connections.[130] Interest in this type of ethical teaching carried over into Christianity. Much of the teaching of Jesus is in the form of wisdom teaching, e.g., the Sermon on the Mount in Matt. 5 ff.[131] The book of *James is an example of Christian wisdom teaching.[132] It acquaints us with the type of first-century Christian who was concerned not at all with ritual or doctrine but only with those Christian ethical precepts which serve as a guide to everyday practical living.

---

[130] *Supra,* pp. 398 f., 402–406, 434 ff., 458–461.
[131] *Vid. supra,* pp. 497–510. [132] *Vid. infra,* p. 589.

Chapter 26

THE EXPANSION OF CHRISTIANITY

"I will give thee for a light to the gentiles, that thou mayest be my salvation unto the end of the earth." Such was Second Isaiah's vision of the world mission of his people.[1] Judaism produced a few kindred spirits, such as the author of the Book of Jonah,[2] but, on the whole, Judaism did not catch the vision; certainly not the Palestinian Jews. The Diaspora Jews, who were thrust out among the gentiles, made a feeble effort to commend Judaism to the gentile world but without success. Although some gentiles, known as the "God-fearers,"[3] were interested, only a few became Jewish proselytes.

Christianity did catch the vision. "Go ye therefore, and make disciples of all the nations" was from the start Christianity's ideal and program.[4] There was a man named Paul, zealous Jew of the Dispersion, trained to be a rabbi. Thoroughly disciplined in the Scriptures, as such a scribe would be, Paul was not ignorant of Second Isaiah's missionary ideal for the gentiles. In that hour of profound mystical experience which made Paul a Christian, this gentile missionary ideal welled up out of the depths of his sub-consciousness to the very center of attention with a driving force behind it which made him the great apostle to the gentiles. "It was the good pleasure of God to reveal his Son in me that I might preach him among the gentiles."[5] "Wherefore I was not disobedient unto the heavenly vision."[6] Thanks to the apostle Paul, Christianity became a universal religion with a world message and mission.

The sources for a history of the period discussed in this chapter are Acts and the Pauline Epistles in the New Testament; Josephus's *History of the Jewish War* and his *Antiquities of the Jews;* and the Roman writers Tacitus, Pliny, and Suetonius.

The Roman Empire in the First Century

When Christianity arose, the entire Mediterranean world was under a single ruler, the Roman emperor.[7] The first of the emperors

[1] Isa. 49:6.
[2] *Vid. supra,* p. 409.
[3] *Vid. supra,* p. 524.
[4] Matt. 28:19.
[5] Gal. 1:16.
[6] Acts 26:19.
[7] Cf. G. E. Wright and F. V. Filson, *The Westminster Historical Atlas to the Bible* (Philadelphia: 1945), pp. 77–81.

was Augustus (27 B.C.–A.D. 14) who, after defeating Antony and Cleopatra in the battle of Actium (31 B.C.), had made Egypt Roman territory and thereby ended a century of revolution and civil war which had convulsed the Roman dominions and had inaugurated what turned out to be two centuries of peace. A great statesman, Augustus organized the administration of the empire, put its finances on a sound basis, and greatly beautified the city of Rome. He first touched Jewish history when he and Antony appointed Herod the Great king of the Jews (40 B.C.).[8] Herod was steadfastly loyal to Augustus, thus enjoying his friendship and favor. Augustus again touched Jewish history importantly when at the request of the Jews of Judea he deposed the ethnarch Archelaus (A.D. 6).[9] The daily sacrifice offered at the Jerusalem temple for the welfare of the emperor and the Roman people was, according to Philo, originally a gift from Augustus.[10]

The second emperor, Tiberius (14–37), is mentioned in Luke 3:1. Though a skilful ruler he incurred the hatred of the Roman populace and during the last six years of his reign he stayed away from Rome, on the island of Capri. Because of some chicanery by certain Jewish rogues, Tiberius once ordered all Jews banished from Rome, though they later returned.[11] It was during his reign that Jesus was crucified and the apostle Paul was converted to Christianity.

Caius Caligula (37–41) was at first very popular in Rome because of his lavish expenditures. Long continued debauchery made him insane. Madly obsessed with the idea that he was divine, he demanded that he be worshiped. He ordered his statue erected in the temple in Jerusalem, which would have led to terrible consequences had it been done. Fortunately, the Syrian legate Petronius procrastinated, and Agrippa I, whom Caligula had made king of the Jews, being in Rome at the time, gave a banquet for Caligula, got the emperor in a good humor, and secured from him a reversal of the order. Caligula's cruelty and tyranny led to his assassination.

Though weak in character and personal qualities, Claudius (41–54) was devoted to the empire, tried to fill governmental positions with competent officials, and improved Rome with buildings and public works, e.g., constructing aqueducts to supply the city with water. He sought to improve the lot of slaves, and in his reign the murder of a slave by his master was rated a capital offense. He was religiously tolerant, holding that men should have the right to live in the religion of their own country and not be forced to transgress it, and in accordance with this attitude he issued an edict confirming

[8] *Vid. supra*, p. 423.
[9] *Vid. supra*, p. 466.
[10] Philo, *Legatio ad Caium*, § 40; *vid. supra*, p. 479.
[11] Cf. Josephus, *Antiquities*, xviii, 83 f.

the rights and privileges of Jews throughout the empire.[12] At a later time in his reign Claudius banished the Jews from Rome, a fact specifically mentioned in Acts 18:2. The Roman writer Suetonius states that this expulsion of Jews from Rome was because of Jewish rioting *impulsore Chresto,* "at the instigation of one Chrestus";[13] the name Chrestus may have been a misunderstanding of the name Christus,[14] so that Suetonius's statement may mean that the rioting was stirred up over the preaching of Christ among the Jews of Rome. It was during the reign of Claudius and of his successor Nero that the apostle Paul was energetically pursuing his missionary campaigns about which we read in the Book of Acts and was producing his letters which are preserved in the New Testament.

Nero (54–68), descended from the family of Augustus on both his father's and his mother's side, was the last emperor of the line of Augustus. His early education had been under the Stoic philosopher Seneca who, as Nero's chief minister during the first five years of his reign, made that part of Nero's rule both wise and successful. Victimized by plots and intrigue within his palace, Nero plunged into a career of vice and cruelty. Seneca was removed from office and banished; later he (62) killed himself at the emperor's command. Nero killed his wife and caused his mother to be assassinated. He was devoted to art, and he participated in dancing and singing contests, chariot races, and gladiatorial combats. His mad extravagance provoked disaffection both at Rome and in the provinces. A disastrous fire wiped out a large part of Rome in the year 64. One rumor accused Nero of starting the conflagration and another blamed the Christians. Nero sought to escape opprobrium by charging the Christians with the responsibility, and he instituted a persecution of Christians in Rome which was carried out with horrible torture, resulting in the death of many Christian martyrs. It was most likely at the time of this persecution that the Christian apostles Peter and Paul met martyr deaths in Rome. Rev. 13 is regarded as a fragment of Christian literature from this Neronian persecution, and the reference in vs. 18 to the beast with the number 666, which is "the number of a man," is a cryptic reference to Nero, the numerical value of the letters of *Nero Caesar* when written with Hebrew characters totaling 666. It was toward the end of Nero's reign, in the year 66, that the disastrous rebellion of the Jews in Palestine began.[15] Disaffection in the Roman provinces broke out in open revolt under the leadership of Galba, a Roman governor in Spain. The Roman Senate voted Nero's death, and he committed suicide in 68.

[12] Cf. Josephus, *Antiquities,* xix, 5:2.
[13] *Life of Claudius,* xxv.
[14] *Vid. supra,* p. 533.
[15] *Vid. infra,* pp. 554 f.

For a year after the death of Nero, leading military commanders contended for the throne and almost plunged the empire into another civil war. Within a year four emperors were crowned—Galba, Otho, Vitellius, and Vespasian. Vespasian secured the throne and restored peace in the empire. He had been appointed by Nero in charge of the Roman army to crush the Jewish rebellion in Palestine. When Vespasian was made emperor in 69, he left his son Titus to complete the war in Judea.[16] Titus ended the Jewish war, razed Jerusalem, and upon his return to Rome was given a triumph. The arch of Titus in Rome depicts the seven-branched golden candlestick, the table of showbread, and the priestly trumpets from the Jerusalem temple, carried by Jewish captives in the triumphal procession of Titus. Titus was associated with his father in the administration of the government, which assured his succession to the throne when Vespasian died in 79.

Titus was a benevolent ruler. During the two years of his reign (79–81) a succession of great disasters occurred, the destruction of Pompeii and Herculaneum, a great fire in Rome, and a devastating pestilence. He spent his own fortune as well as public funds in relief.

The fifteen years' rule of Domitian (81–96), a younger brother of Titus, was a time of prosperity for the empire. He was ambitious for power and suspicious of the Roman Senate and of many of his subjects, especially the Christians, whom he viciously persecuted. The Neronian persecution had been localized in Rome. The Domitianic persecution spread elsewhere over the empire. Domitian was a tyrant who insisted upon being paid divine honors by his subjects.

Vespasian and his two sons, Titus and Domitian, are known as the Flavian emperors. They were special patrons of the Jewish historian Josephus, who, after taking up his residence in Rome in the year 70, assumed the praenomen Flavius and is therefore known to history as Flavius Josephus. It was during their reigns that Josephus produced the writings which we have previously referred to.[17]

The reign of Nerva (96–98) was brief and kindly. He was succeeded by the great soldier-emperor Trajan (98–117) who revived the Roman military glory of the days of Julius Caesar. In the north, along the Danube, he conquered Dacia (Romania) and made it a Roman province. In the east, Trajan conquered the Parthians, who had continuously defied the Romans and defeated all attempts to subdue them. He added all the Fertile Crescent to the empire, but was forced to retreat by a rebellion in his rear and died in Asia Minor. Trajan gave his personal attention to an enormous volume of business pertaining to the colonies. This is disclosed in letters written to him by Pliny the Younger, governor of Bithynia in Asia Minor during his reign. One of these letters (x, 96), written in the year 111, pertains to the treatment of the Christians in his province and is of inestimable value for the light which it throws on the status of Christianity in the early part of the second century.[18]

The next emperor was Hadrian (117–138). Toward the end of his reign occurred the Jewish rebellion in Palestine under Bar-Cochba (132–135), the last desperate attempt of the Jews to win back their political independence. It cost Hadrian's army heavy losses to stamp out the rebellion. Jews were forbidden to enter their holy city and the very name of Jerusalem was changed to Aelia Capitolina. This made a difference with Christianity in Aelia, for Jewish Christianity disappeared and it was gentile Christianity which was established in Aelia after 135.

There was no aggressive persecution of Christians under Hadrian, nor under his successor, Antoninus Pius (138–161). The possibility of martyrdom was ever before the Christian because of his refusal to worship the emperor, but active, wholesale persecution of the Christians did not occur until the reign of Marcus Aurelius (161–180). The empire was then definitely on the decline and harassed by fighting without and fears within, Aurelius was intolerant of nonconformist sects, and the Christian church again underwent a baptism of blood. However, Christianity had by then developed an organization and a power which could not be conquered by the empire but would itself conquer the empire. That story, however, lies beyond the Biblical period.

Of the various provinces which made up the Roman Empire, some were responsible to the Roman Senate and some directly to the emperor. Syria was one of the latter. The chief administrator of a province was a proconsul or a legate. We meet with proconsuls in Acts 13:7–12; 19:38. Within a province there were subordinate officials known as procurators. Some of these were merely overseers of the emperor's property in provinces governed by proconsuls, but there was a higher type of procurator, such as the procurator of Judea, who was really the governor of a small country, was of equestrian rank, and had a military escort at his command. In the case of the latter type it was only when a very serious situation arose that a proconsul or a legate would interfere within such a procurator's country. There were two series of procurators in Judea, one of which we have already noted;[19] the other will be discussed presently.[20] Of the second series, two figure conspicuously in the career of the apostle Paul (Acts 23:24; 24:27).

[18] *Vid. supra,* pp. 525 ff.; *infra,* pp. 574, fn. 103; 575, fn. 110; 593.
[19] *Supra,* p. 468, fn. 4.   [20] *Infra,* pp. 551 ff.

Roman Rule of Palestine to A.D. 135

One by one the rulers of Palestine during the lifetime of Jesus passed from the stage. Philip, tetrarch of the lands across Jordan east of Galilee, died in 34. Pontius Pilate, procurator of Judea, who had condemned Jesus to execution, was dismissed from office in 36. Herod Antipas, tetrarch of Galilee and Perea, was banished to Gaul in 39. For a brief period of three years (41–44) all Palestine was again ruled by a king of the Jews, Herod Agrippa I, grandson of Herod the Great.[21]

Herod Agrippa I. As a youth, Agrippa was brought up in Rome in luxury and extravagance which ended in poverty. He fled from Rome to Judea and there, in order to escape his creditors, he sought refuge in an obscure place on the southern fringe of Judea. In despair over his bankrupt condition, he contemplated suicide, from which he was saved by his wife. Kypros interceded with Agrippa's sister, Herodias, who was the wife of Herod Antipas, and an appointment was secured for Agrippa to a minor administrative position in Tiberias. But Agrippa quarreled with Antipas and quit his job. In Damascus he found favor for a time with Flaccus, the legate of Syria. It ended when Agrippa's own brother, Aristobulus, charged him with accepting bribes. At the end of his rope in Palestine, Agrippa set out again for Rome. Cleverly eluding his creditors, he managed to get out of Palestine, and in Alexandria he borrowed a large sum from a Jewish official named Alexander, a brother of Philo the philosopher.[22]

In Rome he became a companion of Caius Caligula, an adopted grandson of the emperor Tiberius, and all seemed to be going well until he made the indiscreet remark one day, when driving in a chariot with Caius, that it would be a good thing if the emperor were dead. The chariot driver reported the remark and the emperor threw Agrippa into prison. Six months later Tiberius died and Caius Caligula became emperor (A.D. 37).

Caligula promptly released Agrippa from prison and made him king over what had been the tetrarchy of Philip and also the small tetrarchy of Lysanias in Lebanon. Agrippa remained in Rome until the year 39, when Caligula added to his kingdom what had been the tetrarchy of Herod Antipas, who was now banished because Agrippa had insinuated that Antipas was not loyal to the emperor.

---

[21] Agrippa's father was Aristobulus, son of Herod the Great by Mariamme the Maccabean princess (*vid. supra*, p. 424) ; Agrippa's wife Kypros was a granddaughter of Herod the Great through her mother Salampsio, daughter of Herod and Mariamme the Maccabean.
[22] *Vid. supra*, pp. 463 ff.

Agrippa rendered an invaluable service to the peace of Judea when he got Caligula to revoke the order that his statue be erected in the temple in Jerusalem.[23]

In 41 Caligula was murdered and was succeeded by Claudius, who was under some obligation to Agrippa. As a reward he added Judea and Samaria to Agrippa's kingdom. Agrippa was therefore now king over all the territory that had belonged to Herod the Great. His rule was successful, for he deferred to Jewish scruples, observed Jewish regulations, and sought to avoid giving offense in Jerusalem. Outside of Jerusalem he indulged in Graeco-Roman amusements. As a gesture to win the favor of the Jews, he persecuted the Christians, killed the apostle James (brother of John and one of the twelve), and imprisoned the apostle Peter.[24] Agrippa was stricken down by a mysterious disease on a state occasion at which he was addressed by his courtiers as a god (A.D. 44).[25]

Herod Agrippa II.   When Agrippa I died, the emperor Claudius at first thought to appoint Agrippa's only son, a youth of seventeen also named Agrippa, to his father's throne, but changed his mind. Four years later (48) young Agrippa was given by Claudius the little kingdom of Chalcis in the Lebanon area, which had belonged to an uncle named Herod. In 50 Agrippa exchanged this for what had been the tetrarchy of Philip and adjacent territory east of Galilee and the upper Jordan. The emperor Nero later added to Agrippa's kingdom some parts of Galilee and the Perean city, Julias, with its adjacent villages.

Agrippa's capital was Caesarea Philippi. He maintained a residence in Jerusalem where, of course, he had no authority, nor in Judea. He was not on good terms with the Jews. His own profession of Judaism was pretty thin and superficial. His reign was of no importance for Jewish history. It was during his reign that the disastrous Jewish war (66–70) occurred, though Agrippa had no responsibility for or connection with this war, but he did side against the Jews. Nor was his reign of any consequence to Christianity except that he figured prominently in an incident connected with the trial of the apostle Paul (Acts 25:13–26:32). Just how long Agrippa II lived is not certainly known; perhaps until the year 100.[26]

The Second Series of Procurators.   Since Agrippa II did not succeed his father as king of the Jews, the emperor Claudius again placed Palestine under the administration of procurators. Seven such

---

[23] *Vid. supra,* p. 546.   [24] Acts 12:2 f.
[25] Acts 12:19–23. On Agrippa I, cf. W. O. E. Oesterley, *A History of Israel* (Oxford: 1932), vol. ii, pp. 392–399.
[26] On Agrippa II, cf. Oesterley, *op. cit.,* vol. ii, pp. 425–428.

procurators ruled Judea from A.D. 44 to 66, when the Jewish war against Rome broke out.[27]

The first procurator was Fadus (44–48). He found Palestine in a state of unrest. All Jews were arrayed against the gentiles in the population, especially in Eastjordania, and the Jews themselves were divided into disturbing factions, principally fanatical Pharisees and extremist Zealots. Judea was infested with robbers, whom Fadus cleared out. He had to quell a number of disturbances, one of the most noted being a messianic revolt led by Theudas, whom Fadus beheaded. Fadus seized the vestments of the Jewish high priest and kept them in the tower of Antonia. This had formerly been the Roman practice, as we have noted.[28] In the year 36, however, the keeping of the robes had been turned back to the high priest by the Syrian legate Vitellius who intervened in Palestinian affairs to cause the deposition of the procurator Pontius Pilate. Fadus, therefore, had precedent in his favor, and he intended only an added measure of Roman control in the interest of peace. The Jews, however, resented the act and sent an embassy to Rome to appeal to the emperor that the vestments be left in their own keeping, which petition Claudius allowed.

The second procurator was Alexander, a nephew of the Jewish philosopher Philo. At most he served only a year (48). It was a year of famine in Judea.[29] For some insurrection, whether provoked by rioting due to the famine or not, Alexander crucified two sons of Judas of Galilee, the Judas who had led the revolt in A.D. 6.

Serious disturbances marked the administration of Cumanus (48–52). There was a gruesome massacre at Passover time of Jews who rioted because a Roman soldier had insulted the temple. There was a miniature war between Samaritans and Galileans which brought about the downfall of Cumanus. We have noted the deepseated hatred that had long existed between the Jews and the Samaritans.[30] Certain Galileans, passing through Samaria en route to a festival at Jerusalem, were attacked by Samaritans. The Samaritans had bribed Cumanus to disregard the attack. Since Cumanus would grant the Galileans no redress, they instituted reprisals. Though Cumanus punished the Galileans, the Samaritans had appealed to the legate of Syria. So had the Jews, complaining not only against the Samaritans for starting the whole affair but also against Cumanus for accepting bribes from the Samaritans. The matter was carried up to the emperor and, thanks to the influence of Agrippa II, Claudius banished Cumanus.

[27] Cf. Oesterley, *op. cit.*, vol. ii, pp. 428–439.   [28] *Vid. supra*, p. 467.
[29] Cf. Acts 11:27–30.   [30] *Vid. supra*, pp. 386 f.

Civil disorder was growing from bad to worse in Palestine and however efficient he might have been, the next procurator, Felix (52–60), had a bigger task than he could well handle. The country was terrorized by the Sicarii ("dagger carriers"), a sort of first-century "black shirts," who were urging the people to revolt and were perpetrating repeated assassinations. Messianic outbreaks were violent; one such disturbance, led by an Egyptian false messiah, is referred to in Acts 21:38. The high priest Jonathan, who was officiously patronizing toward Felix because he had helped Felix get his job, was assassinated. It is not clear whether this happened at the instigation of Felix or whether it was purely the work of the Sicarii. Felix definitely figures in the Bible narrative (Acts 24) because the apostle Paul was brought to trial before him. Some interesting things are there said about Felix. The orator Tertullus, addressing him, said, "By thee we enjoy much peace, and by thy providence evils are corrected for this nation" (vs. 2). And Paul said to Felix, "I know that thou hast been of many years a judge unto this nation" (vs. 10). These statements imply honest effort and some success in maintaining order, but nevertheless Felix was unable to suppress the Sicarii and quiet Judea so he was recalled by Nero.

Festus (60–62) likewise figures in the trial of St. Paul (Acts 25 f.). He appears to have been just and well balanced. His untimely death cut short his administration. Several months elapsed before the next procurator reached Palestine, and during those months the high priest Ananus presumed to rule the country and undertook to suppress the Zealots. He took measures against the Christians, stoning a number of them to death, including James, the brother of Jesus Christ and head of the Jerusalem Christians.[31] Except for this incident and the case of Paul before Felix and Festus, the Christians appear not to have attracted the attention of the authorities in Palestine during this period of civil disturbance.

Albinus (62–64) was thoroughly incompetent and corrupt and after two years was deposed. The Sicarii were ravaging the entire country, nobles were turning highwaymen, and rival high priests were carrying on a miniature war among themselves.

The disordered situation in Palestine had become intolerable and the time of explosion was at hand. The explosion came under the last and worst of the procurators, Florus (64–66), who allied himself with highwaymen, robbed cities, and goaded the Jews into rebellion. The incident which touched off the explosion grew out of a long-standing quarrel between the Jewish and the gentile residents of Caesarea. The Jews tried to bribe Florus but they lost their case

---

[31] Josephus, *Antiquities,* xx, 9:1.

when Nero decided against them and in disgust they quit Caesarea. Just when the Jews throughout the country were wrought up over the Caesarea incident, Florus had the stupidity to demand of the Jews seventeen talents from the temple treasury. The war was on!

The Jewish War (A.D. 66–70). 1. *The Basic Causes of the War.* Racial pride and national patriotism were deeply ingrained in the Jewish mentality. They were unwilling to be subject to a foreign power, though throughout the long centuries they had been forced to submit to one after another world ruler. No matter how efficiently or how beneficially Rome ruled them, they would not become reconciled.

The Jews were zealous for their national peculiarities. Some Jews in Palestine were willing to Hellenize, as did the Diaspora Jews, but the bulk of Palestinian Jews strongly maintained their Jewish laws and customs. Most of the difficulties experienced by the several procurators were due to conflict with such Jewish customs.

Moreover the Jews feared that Hellenism would submerge Judaism. The Maccabean struggle had been precipitated when Hellenism strove to crush Judaism.[32] The Jews of the first century feared a repetition of that by the Roman government, though as a matter of fact the Roman government never attempted and probably never intended any such thing.

2. *The Immediate Occasion of the War.* The steadily mounting dissatisfaction of the Jews with the Roman procurators has been discussed in the foregoing section. No procurator could have satisfied the Jews. The interracial disturbance at Caesarea, with its sequel, was what actually precipitated the war. The weakness of the emperor Nero in his last years made it seem that successful revolt was now possible. Again, the Jews themselves were divided into contending factions. Only the hotheads wanted war with Rome. The war fever raged chiefly in Galilee. Few Jewish leaders in Jerusalem favored it for they knew well enough what the only possible outcome would be. When such leaders saw that a revolt would be forced, they decided they had better assume control of the war so that they might bring it to an end with a minimum of damage and secure as favorable terms from Rome as possible.

3. *Reasons for the Failure of the War.* It was the most serious war the Jews ever waged but they were too few in number to have any chance for success. The Jews were not by nature of a military disposition. Because of their distaste for war they had been excused from service in the Roman army. They therefore had next to no military training and very poor equipment. Such small successes as

[32] *Vid. supra,* pp. 415 ff.

they did achieve were due to guerrilla tactics in which small bands fought on their own initiative. The Jews were split up into factions even during the war and spent their energy destroying one another, even destroying their own food supplies. They lacked efficient leaders and a really gripping motive for war. In the Maccabean revolution a truly great motive had inspired the Jews to fight for liberty. But all things considered, Rome had been fairly good to them and had they met Rome halfway, they might have enjoyed peace.

4. *The Course of the War.* The Jewish historian Josephus, to whose *History of the Jewish War* we are indebted for all that we know about the struggle, was himself leader of the Jewish army in Galilee the first year of the revolt. In the autumn of 66 the legate of Syria, Cestius Gallus, invaded Judea with a considerable force in an effort to restore peace. In an attempt to storm the Jerusalem temple he met inglorious defeat, suffered heavy losses, and fled from the country.

Nero assigned his general Vespasian to the task of subduing Palestine. He gathered an army at Antioch and spent the year 67 subduing Galilee. Josephus had to surrender to Vespasian, but adroitly won the Roman's favor and thereafter accompanied Vespasian on his campaign and acted on occasion as an intermediary in futile efforts to get the Jews to yield to the Romans. In the year 68 Vespasian subjugated Judea, Perea, Idumea, and Samaria, all of Palestine in fact except Jerusalem and a few other strongholds. He deliberately let Jerusalem alone to permit the three desperate factions which possessed the holy city to wear one another out.[33] These factions are to be distinguished from the populace of Jerusalem, which was victimized by the fanatics. The fact that Vespasian did let Jerusalem alone, and that no serious attempt was made against it until the fourth year of the war, intensified the belief of the fanatics in the inviolability of the sacred city. Consequently they made no preparation for defense against the Romans but engaged in mutual self-destruction.

In the year 69 nothing was done by the Romans to prosecute the war. Nero had died and Vespasian left Palestine for Alexandria to keep in touch with the situation in Rome where three emperors were striving for Nero's throne. The outcome was that Vespasian himself became emperor. When he left Palestine he placed the army there in charge of his son Titus, and to Titus fell the task of subduing Jerusalem.

[33] These factions were headed by different Zealot leaders. An interesting fact is that in the first year of the war, Menahem, last surviving son of Judas the Galilean who had started the Zealot movement in A.D. 6 (*vid. supra,* p. 471), appeared in Jerusalem and attempted to set himself up as king but perished at the hands of rivals.

5. The Destruction of Jerusalem (A.D. 70). Titus moved against Jerusalem in the spring of 70 and the siege lasted five months. The temple was captured in August. It was Titus's intention to spare the sacred building, but a soldier hurled a firebrand into the edifice and it went up in flames. The last stronghold of the Jews in the upper city was reduced in September, and the war was over except for a stronghold of Sicarii on Mount Masada, on the west shore of the Dead Sea, which was not reduced until two years later. Titus took Jewish captives to Rome, together with the sacred objects from the temple, and in the year 71 a magnificent triumph was given him in the imperial city. Jerusalem was as completely destroyed and as desolate as it had been when Nebuchadrezzar obliterated it in 586 B.C.[34]

6. The Aftermath of the War. The complete defeat of the Jews wiped out the Zealot party and nationalistic tendencies in Palestine. The Jews who survived the disaster realized how they had been duped by the fanatical nationalists. Henceforth, for sixty years, they submitted to the Roman authorities and kept the peace.

The complete destruction of the temple wiped out the Sadducean party, the priesthood, and the whole cult of sacrifice. The Pharisees survived, for they represented what had been best in Judaism. The rabbis established their center at Jamnia in the coastal plain, which place, and Tiberias in Galilee, were thenceforth the main centers of Judaism in Palestine. The Jerusalem Sanhedrin had also disappeared. Its function in Jewish society seems to have passed to the new school of rabbis at Jamnia. The institution of the synagogue survived, of course, and Jews were more than ever devoted to the law. At Jamnia, in A.D. 90, the limits of the canon of Jewish Sacred Scriptures were finally settled as we now know it in the Old Testament.

As for the Christians, the Jewish Christian group in Jerusalem left the city after the martyrdom of James in 62 [35] and before the siege of the city by the Romans. They were probably out of sympathy with the revolution. They settled at Pella, a little Greek town in Eastjordania. There was friction with the patriotic Jews because they had withdrawn. Gradually, in after years, the so-called Jewish Christian Church dwindled and disappeared. It was the gentile type of Christianity which became established in Jerusalem after the city was rebuilt in the year 135.[36]

The Rebellion of Bar-Cochba (A.D. 132–135). While the Palestine Jews kept the peace after the destruction of Jerusalem, not so the Jews elsewhere in the Mediterranean world. They had not tasted the sufferings that had befallen their Palestinian brothers and so were

---

[34] Vid. supra, p. 269. [35] Vid. supra, p. 553.
[36] On the Jewish war, cf. Oesterley, op. cit., vol. ii, pp. 440–459.

not tamed. During the half-century following the destruction of Jerusalem there were Jewish outbursts against Rome, some of serious proportions, in Alexandria, Libya, Egypt, Cyrene, Cyprus, and Mesopotamia.[37] In every case the uprisings were ruthlessly put down by the Romans. Prior to the war of 66–70, the Romans had been friendly disposed toward Jews. The war in Palestine and the uprisings elsewhere destroyed that friendship on Rome's part. Jews everywhere were viewed with suspicion and treated with severity.

The rebellion which burst forth in Palestine in 132 was sudden and unanticipated and amazingly unanimous on the part of the Jews. The emperor Hadrian issued an edict prohibiting circumcision, not meaning to offend the Jews, if indeed he took them into consideration. The prohibition was part of a larger restriction by which the emperor was trying to eradicate certain offensive practices in other quarters. The Jews regarded it as an attack upon their religious faith and practice. In another way, Hadrian unintentionally offended the Jews. Since Jerusalem had long lain in ruins and uninhabited, Hadrian planned to rebuild the city, call it Aelia Capitolina, and there erect a temple to Zeus. It apparently did not occur to him that the Jews still regarded the ruined site as their holy city. It had rankled in the Jews that ever since the destruction of the temple they had been forced to pay their historic temple tax to the Romans for the benefit of the temple of Jupiter Capitolinus in Rome. Their rancor now burst into fury. The passion of messianic hope was likewise aroused, for their self-appointed leader, Simon, Prince of Israel (the legend on his coins), claimed to be messiah, and his claim was acknowledged by Akiba, the most celebrated rabbi of the time. Quoting Num. 24:17, "There shall come forth a star out of Jacob, and a scepter shall rise out of Israel," Akiba named the leader Bar-Cochba, "Son of a Star." [38] Akiba even became the armor-bearer for Bar-Cochba. The Jews pursued the same tactics that were employed back in the Maccabean war. They scattered in small bands over the country, concealing themselves in the hills and carrying on a guerrilla war. It took the Romans three and a half years to locate and destroy all these hide-outs. Bar-Cochba and Akiba were both executed when they finally came into the hands of the Romans. Hadrian carried out his plan to build Aelia and peopled it with gentiles. Jews were forbidden even to enter the city on pain of death. This disaster was the final attempt of the Jews to re-establish a nation of their own in Palestine.[39]

[37] Cf. Oesterley, op. cit., vol. ii, pp. 400–424.
[38] Later rabbis, repudiating such a messianic claim, called him Bar-Koziba, "Son of a Lie."
[39] Cf. Oesterley, op. cit., vol. ii, pp. 459–463.

Social Conditions in the Roman Empire

Unity, organization, and power were the master words of the Roman Empire. The entire Mediterranean world, from the Atlantic to the Euphrates and from the Rhine and Danube frontier to the Sahara, with its multiplicity of races and nations, had been welded into a unity. Rome had the genius to retain what she conquered and to organize and administer it with skill and efficiency.

Primarily to facilitate the travel of officials of state to and from the provinces and Rome, a vast network of splendid roads was constructed, many of which are in existence and in use to the present day. Along such roads were mileposts, and inns where travelers found rest and fresh animals, and there were military guards to keep the highways safe. For the same reason Rome had swept all pirates from the sea. Officials of state were not the only ones to travel the highways and the sea. Merchants and craftsmen, seekers after pleasure and adventure, itinerant philosophers and missionaries, journeyed hither and yon. It was this splendid system of roads which made possible such a traveled career as that of St. Paul, which is depicted in Acts. Along those same highways the imperial postal service promoted intercommunication between widely separated places, and travelers carried letters for friends, such as Paul's letters which have been preserved for us in the New Testament.

Such facilities for travel brought about a mingling of the peoples of different races and nations and produced that cosmopolitanism which characterized the society of the empire. The cosmopolitan character of a city is nowhere better portrayed than in Acts 2:5–11, with its description of Jerusalem at Pentecost. The same condition prevailed in every large city. It is quite worthy of note that Christianity, according to Acts 2, was launched in a cosmopolitan setting, and according to the rest of Acts Christianity was carried from one great cosmopolitan center to another across the empire, Jerusalem, Antioch, Ephesus, Corinth, Rome. Christianity was not something done in a corner. Its ultimate triumph was in part due to the fact that it met the needs of humanity in the great centers where humanity was thickest and where needs were most acutely felt.

National and racial barriers broke down by reason of the ease of travel and intercommunication. One common language, Greek, was spoken everywhere. Judaism failed to become a universal religion because Jews in the Diaspora insisted upon maintaining their peculiarities of race and custom; such Jewish exclusiveness put them at a decided social disadvantage and this disadvantage deterred gentiles from becoming proselytes. In the empire all were one. In

Christianity all were one; there could not be Jew or Greek or barbarian or Scythian, bondman or freeman, male or female, but "all are one man in Christ Jesus." [40]

Men prized citizenship in such an empire. Men in the provinces obtained Roman citizenship sometimes by purchase, sometimes as a reward for service rendered the emperor, and sometimes by inheritance. Just what such citizenship meant and how highly it was prized is disclosed in Acts 22:25–29 where Paul, because he is a "Roman born," is treated with courtesy by the military tribune who had obtained his citizenship "with a great sum." Just how vigilant the Roman government was to protect a Roman citizen is portrayed in Acts 23 where Paul is given a huge military escort to save him from Sicarii and escort him safely to the procurator at the capital city, Caesarea. Every Roman citizen, in the interest of justice, had the right to appeal to the emperor. Perhaps the most fateful moment in the later life of Paul was when, in the presence of the procurator Festus, he uttered the words, "I appeal unto Caesar." [41] Roman citizenship saved one from degrading forms of punishment; hence St. Paul was executed by beheading, in contrast to St. Peter who, not being a Roman citizen, was crucified.

Society was divided into pronounced classes. There were the aristocrats of wealth and position, with abundance of leisure which was devoted mainly to self-indulgence and pleasure, resulting in materialism and vice, for there was little taste for or appreciation of the things of culture among the generality of such people. There were the intellectuals, devoted to literature and philosophy. The commonality of plain people struggled with the problem of existence and lived simple and commendable domestic lives. Their morale was undermined, however, by the presence in society of a vast multitude of slaves which so glutted the labor market and cheapened wages as to make it impossible for the industrious freeman to find ways to earn a good living. So he came, on the one hand, to despise manual work as proper only for slaves, and on the other to look to the government for doles of grain and money; he expected the government to feed and entertain him. Society was degraded by the vast horde of slaves who were recruited from all the provinces, chiefly as a result of conquest. Slaves, such as the Greeks, were often of high birth and splendid culture, far finer persons than their masters. Rome was not creative in culture; such culture as she acquired was assimilated from those she made slaves. There was little humanitarianism in Roman society and slaves were treated with brutality, though some of the emperors did seek to ameliorate their lot. A slave

[40] Gal. 3:28; Col. 3:11; Rom. 10:12.   [41] Acts. 25:11.

was required to be absolutely obedient and so he sought to please his master, usually by catering to his vices. Those slaves who came from the east introduced Rome to a multitude of new vices. Such slavery was the blackest spot in Roman civilization. One of the choicest letters of St. Paul was about a runaway slave, to his master Philemon, begging Philemon to receive him back for a reason which cut the very ground from under the institution of human slavery, "not as a bondservant, but more than a bondservant, a brother beloved, both in the flesh and in the Lord." [42]

Christianity was recruited from all classes in society. In the Christian groups which we meet in the New Testament we find both men and women, some well-to-do householders, who made their homes available for Christian meetings, some slaves, some traders and day laborers, and some so poor that they were dependent upon the Christian common meals. As Paul put it, "not many wise after the flesh, not many mighty, not many noble, are called," [43] but Christianity chiefly appealed to the plain man and especially to the submerged class. Not until the middle of the second century did Christianity begin to secure a following among the intellectuals.

The Roman genius was for law and organization. The government being altogether centralized in the hands of the emperor and his appointed executives, the generality of citizens had no civic responsibility. The populace looked to the government for social security, for food and entertainment, for protection, and for the care of the poor. Many of the emperors issued decrees providing for public constructions which constituted a work program. Such public works were a burden of expense which proved a disintegrating factor in the empire.

The trend of population was toward the cities where the masses gathered. As always, this resulted in impaired morale as the sturdy virtues of country life were sloughed off. In the large city the individual felt himself adrift in a strange world. He was altogether on his own initiative and responsibility. He was seeking an abundant life, to be sure. What he most needed was something to give life meaning and direction and force.

Such moral health as existed in the empire was principally to be found among the plain people of the middle class. On the whole, however, the state of morals was dark and distressing. St. Paul's starkly realistic picture of the morals of the first century in Rom. *1:26–32 is a concise and stinging indictment of the age.

Christianity spread in the empire as an idealistic social movement. It was profoundly concerned with human welfare. Its social ideal

---

[42] Philem. 16.   [43] 1 Cor. 1:26.

was the kingdom of God, conceived as a family, with God as Father and all men as brothers. That Christian brotherhood, by its comprehensive and supreme principle of the love of man toward man, unified Orientals and Occidentals in a fellowship which surmounted barriers of race and brought together on a common plane the rich and the poor, slaves and freemen, masters and servants. By teaching the sacrifice of self for the good of others, by seeking to establish justice in human relationships, by turning men away from the valuation and pursuit of material things to more spiritual interests, by elevating the ideal and practice of marriage and seeking to eradicate sexual immorality, by its condemnation of the vices of envy, strife, revenge, fraud, theft, drunkenness, reveling, pride, hypocrisy, and ostentation, by its inculcation of good will and the doing of good to all men, Christianity was emphatically a social movement. All over the empire there developed local groups of persons bound together in close Christian fellowship. Such persons found life idealistic, joyful, courageous, and hopeful. Their faith gave them assurance of eternal welfare in a coming perfect social order which was the kingdom of God. At the outset, Christian emphasis was apocalyptic; the catastrophic intervention of God to inaugurate his kingdom was stressed. By the end of the first century the catastrophic emphasis dropped away. The stress was placed upon those social principles of Jesus which united the Christians in a solid, permanent social organization which survived the decline and fall of the Roman Empire itself.

Religions in the Empire

Christianity did not grow up in a religious vacuum. It cannot be understood out of relationship to its religious environment. The Roman Empire was tolerant toward all types of religion, and Christianity in its expansion met with a variety of religious cults and movements other than Judaism.[44]

Local and National Cults. Everywhere throughout the ancient world there were local deities and cults. As the Christian missionaries went from place to place proclaiming the gospel message, they encountered such cults. The Book of Acts presents some vivid pictures of St. Paul in relationship to local cults, notably at Lystra (*14:8–18), where local priests sought to offer sacrifice to Paul and Barnabas; at Athens (*17:16–34) where Paul discussed the relationship of Christianity to the local shrines and deities before the

---

[44] Cf. S. J. Case, *The Evolution of Early Christianity* (Chicago: 1914), chap. vi, "The Early Christians' Contact with Gentile Religions," pp. 166–194.

Areopagus, the tribunal which passed upon religious matters; and at Ephesus, in the most vivid of all accounts of local cults (*19), that of the goddess Artemis (Diana).

From his study of ancient history the average student is fairly familiar with the gods and goddesses of ancient Greek mythology and with the fact that the whole Greek pantheon was imported into Rome and given Latin names.[45] For centuries before the Christian era men had criticized these anthropomorphic deities for their ethical deficiencies and faith in them had declined. Local myths everywhere did not differ very much from the Greek myths.

In the first century such local cults were on the decline. When an individual left home and migrated to Rome or some other big city, he cut loose from his old religious moorings and no longer enjoyed the religious benefits that had been his at home where he was under the immediate protection of his home-town gods. Loyalty to his native country and its gods was eclipsed. His new situation in the great empire which bound all nations and races into a unity called for a new form of patriotism and a new type of imperial religion, viz., emperor worship.

Emperor Worship. The historical antecedents of emperor worship extend into a remote past. The ancient rulers of Egypt were regarded as the incarnation of some god. In ancient Babylonia and Assyria the king stood in a very special relationship to some god, often being called the son of one of the gods. Even among the Hebrews the king was regarded as God's anointed and therefore his vicegerent on earth. In all such Oriental thought the king represented the gods and derived his authority and power from them, not from the people.

Greece and Rome had a different thought pattern, shaped by ancient Greek hero worship. A ruler was revered for his own achievements and at his death was apotheosized, i.e., elevated to the rank of divinity. Such was true not only of political rulers but also of persons of great distinction in other spheres; e.g., Aristotle erected an altar to Plato and there was a cult of Homer in Alexandria.

These two patterns of thought, incarnation and apotheosis, began to fuse in connection with Alexander the Great. During his lifetime he was honored as divine in the Orient, and after his death there arose a cult of Alexander. From then on the custom of worshiping the living ruler spread in Egypt, Syria, and Greece. In Egypt the Ptolemies were hailed as gods, or gods manifest, or savior gods, or benefactor gods, and the like. In Syria the Seleucids claimed to be, in every sense of the term, gods manifest in the flesh.

[45] Cf. Case, *op. cit.*, pp. 240–250.

When Julius Caesar defeated Pompey in the battle of Pharsalus in 48 B.C.,[46] he evoked the admiration of the Greeks of Asia and was hailed as a god manifest, a savior, a benefactor. Back in Rome exceptional honors were bestowed upon him during his lifetime, and after his death he was apotheosized by official decree of the Senate which declared him to be *Divus Julius*. After that, divinized rulers were *divi* rather than *dei,* i.e., men raised to the rank of divinity rather than originally gods incarnated in men. Augustus was accorded divine honors in the eastern provinces but declined such honors in Rome. His long reign, fraught with many benefits to the empire, so heightened the esteem in which he was held that after his death his official apotheosis only confirmed what had been going on during his lifetime. Tiberius was not assertive of the right to divine honors but Caligula did declare himself to be a god.

Domitian regarded himself as divine, and imperial orders issued in his name began with the formula, "Our lord and god." During the reign of Domitian the demand that the emperor be worshiped made serious trouble for the Christians and precipitated a widespread persecution.

The act of emperor worship consisted in sprinkling a few grains of incense or a few drops of wine on an altar which stood before an image of the emperor. Perhaps at our long remove from the situation we see in the act nothing different from standing at attention with removed hat before a statue of Abraham Lincoln or lifting the hand in salute to the flag or to some distinguished ruler of state, an expression of courtesy, respect, and patriotism. Possibly a good many people in the first century felt just that way about it but not so the Christians. They viewed the whole matter as one of religious worship, acknowledging the emperor as a deity and therefore being disloyal to God and Christ, and they refused to do it. Because they refused they were regarded as politically disloyal. The reason why Christians were persecuted was precisely that they were considered enemies of the state because they would not join in emperor worship. It was such worship that helped bind into a real unity the widely divergent elements that made up the Roman Empire. Emperor worship and the Christians' attitude toward it are basic to an understanding of two books of the New Testament which arose in times of persecution, viz., Revelation and 1 Peter.[47]

The Mystery Religions.   Widely diffused over the empire in the first two centuries of the Christian era were the mystery cults. They were the religions of the plain man in the pagan world. Principally

[46] *Vid. supra,* pp. 421 f.
[47] Cf. Case, *op. cit.,* chap. vii, "The Religious Significance of Emperor Worship," pp. 195–238. On Revelation and 1 Peter, *vid. infra,* pp. 591 ff.

emotional in appeal, they brought to plain people the sort of religious satisfaction they craved, a sense of intimate relationship with the lord of the cult, participation in his essential nature, and assurance of a life after death.

The various mystery cults have certain features in common. There is a lord of the cult, usually accompanied by a consort, his wife or sister, who mourns his death, which is caused either by accident or by self-mutilation. Her prayers effect his restoration to life. This sort of myth is a rationalizing and dramatizing of the action of life in nature, the death of vegetation in the autumn and its revival in the spring.

A member of a mystery cult was called an "initiate." Before initiation he underwent certain purificatory rites, notably baptism. Initiation included a witnessing of the mystery, i.e., a dramatization of the god's career and participation in a sacred meal. By such initiation the worshiper believed that he was assimilated to the very nature of the god himself and, through eating the flesh of the sacred animal, the god dwelt within him. He therefore felt strengthened to face the vicissitudes of life and felt assured that, like his cult lord, he too would live after death. As religions, they were sacramentarian.

1. *The Eleusinian Mysteries.* Best known of all the mysteries are those connected with Eleusis in Greece. The goddess Demeter represented Mother Earth. Her daughter Persephone was carried off by Pluto to the underworld. Mourning her daughter's loss, Demeter refused to give life to nature until Persephone was restored. An arrangement was entered into by which Persephone spent part of each year with her mother and part in the underworld.

2. *The Cult of Dionysus.* Dionysus personified the power of life in vegetation, and in Greece he was more particularly the god of the vine, Bacchus. In the Bacchic frenzy the devotee, filled with wine, believed he was infilled with the god himself and experienced an ecstasy of elation. In the Dionysiac festivals the devotees drank the blood and ate the raw flesh of the sacrificial victim which represented the god, thereby entering into participation in the life of the god himself. The sacrificial animal had to be eaten in great haste, lest the divinity escape, and this haste gave the festival a frenzied character. Similar worship characterized other mystery cults and Dionysus was assimilated to the nature of the lords of such cults, Attis, Adonis, or Osiris.

3. *Orphism.* The cult of Orpheus was a variant of the cult of Dionysus, who in Orphism is called Zagreus. He was devoured by the Titans, whom Zeus burned and whose ashes he scattered. These

became the source of divine life in the things of nature, especially in man. Man's soul, being thus essentially divine, could be purified of its bodily defilement through participation in the mystic rites of the cult, sacrifice, prayers, and libations. Long after the Orphic brotherhoods ceased as such, Orphic doctrines and practices continued over a widespread area of the empire, having been assimilated to other cults.

4. *The Cult of Cybele-Attis.* Cybele was a wild nature deity of Phrygia in Asia Minor, the source of life in nature as well as a mighty warrior. Cybele mourned the death of her consort Attis until he was restored to life. His triumph over death was the basis of the ritual performed in the cult. The worship of this cult was probably the wildest and most frenzied of any of the mysteries. In 204 B.C. this cult was, with great formality and circumstance, introduced into Rome by official action of the Roman Senate in order to insure victory in the Punic war.

5. *Syrian Mystery Cults.* In Syria there were a number of cults which did not differ greatly from the Cybele-Attis cult either in ideology or in ritual practices. A mother goddess was associated with a male deity whose death was mourned and whose resurrection was celebrated with great rejoicing. Such a cult was that of Ishtar and Tammuz, whose antecedents ran back into Babylonian religion. Still another was the cult of Aphrodite and Adonis, with two principal centers, Byblos in Syria and Paphos on the island of Cyprus. Yet another Syrian cult was that of Atargatis, known as the "Syrian goddess," and Hadad.

6. *Mithraism.* Persia contributed the cult of Mithra who was anciently the mediator between Ahura Mazda and man, a sort of messiah who was the foe of all evil and the savior of the righteous. Associated with him originally was a fertility goddess, Anahita, but ultimately Mithra alone was worshiped. Mithraism possessed an important doctrine of eschatology. Mithra ascended into heaven where he assists the souls of the righteous on their course through the seven heavens. He will preside over the final judgment, then return to earth, raise the dead, and put an end to the forces of evil. Mithra was depicted as a mighty hero and as such made a strong appeal to soldiers. Mithraism was probably Christianity's chief rival.

7. *The Cult of Isis and Serapis.* Osiris had been a beneficent king of Egypt who suffered a violent death. Isis was his wife who, after great wanderings and hardships, recovered his body and had it embalmed. Osiris then became king of the underworld. In the period of the Ptolemies, Osiris was identified with Serapis. Isis was a

mother goddess, the source of life and of civilization. Very sympathetic toward the sufferings of human beings, Mother Isis was one of the most revered deities of the ancient world. The cult of Isis and Serapis was widely spread over the Mediterranean countries from the third century B.C. throughout New Testament times.

A more detailed study of the mystery religions should be made by every student of New Testament times.[48] They were Christianity's competitors. People joined those cults because they offered certain desired values. In competition with such cults, Christianity had to offer the same values and greater. Why, for example, were miracles of healing and resurrection given such prominence in the gospels? Just because healing and assurance of life after death were two values most earnestly craved in the ancient world; because there were many cults offering those values of healing and immortality; and because the gospels must show that Christianity offered those values more abundantly and more assuredly. Let the student of the New Testament imagine himself a thoughtful gentile pondering whether he would join the cult of Isis, for example, or the Christian church. Why should he become a Christian instead of an Isiac? Or let him imagine himself a Corinthian, long since an initiate in the Eleusinian mysteries, inclined to become a Christian and being told that he must give up the other cult.[49] The shadow of the mysteries is in the background of 1 Corinthians. Such an attempt by the student to project himself into the first century will give an appreciation of the religious environment in which Christianity spread, of the impact of Christianity upon that environment, and of the reaction of that environment upon Christianity. The mysteries and Christianity alike were for plain people.

Epicureanism and Stoicism. Probably such religion as the intellectuals of the age possessed consisted in attitudes which grew out of one or other of the two systems of philosophy which were most prominent in New Testament times. It is not in order here to expound these philosophical systems but rather to indicate their religious significance.

For several centuries philosophers had been criticizing the Homeric mythology. Such anthropomorphic deities had no place in the system of thought which bears the name of Epicurus (341–270 B.C.). The Epicurean thought of the universe as made up of empty space and of material bodies subdivided into atoms. The gods of the Epicurean dwell in the empty ethereal regions among the innumerable worlds

---

[48] Cf. Case, *op. cit.*, chap. ix, "Hellenistic Religions of Redemption," pp. 284–330.
[49] Cf. 1 Cor. 10:21.

and have nothing to do with the creation or maintenance of the universe. They have nothing to do with human affairs but live an ideal life of perfect happiness wholly free from pain and disturbance and they are worthy of worship for that reason. In the ethics of Epicureanism the ideal for human life is pleasure, not merely sensual enjoyment but freedom from everything that would cause pain or disturbance to body or mind.

Far more important was Stoicism. The founders of early Stoicism were Zeno (336–264 B.C.), Cleanthes (331–232 B.C.), and Chrysippus (280–206 B.C.). Middle Stoicism was represented by Panaetius (189–109 B.C.), Posidonius (*circa* 135–51 B.C.), and Cicero (106–43 B.C.). In later Stoicism the great names are Seneca (*circa* 4 B.C.–A.D. 65), Epictetus (*circa* 50–130), and Marcus Aurelius (121–180). Acts 17:16–31 represents Paul in the city of Athens encountering "certain of the Epicurean and Stoic philosophers" and delivering a speech before the Areopagus in which speech no attention seems to be paid to the Epicureans but a very great deal to the Stoics. When Paul said of God that "in him we live, and move, and have our being" (vs. 28), he was stating exactly the Stoic idea of God. Further, when Paul cited to the Stoics "certain even of your own poets" as saying, "We are also his offspring," he was alluding to Aratus's *Phaenomenon* (§1) and to Cleanthes' *Hymn to Zeus* (line 5). Cleanthes' poem is one of the choice literary heritages of the past and should be read in full by every student.[50] The God of the Stoic gives life and purpose to the whole universe and especially fills man with rational soul. It is Reason (*Logos*) which unites man with God and with his fellow men. All men are therefore brothers. One sees in such doctrine how nicely adjusted Stoic thought was to the cosmopolitanism and individualism which characterized the social order of the first century in the Roman Empire. In ethics, Stoicism stressed the four cardinal virtues of wisdom, justice, courage, and temperance. One of the great seats of Stoicism was the university city of Tarsus, the home town of St. Paul. Paul was well acquainted with Stoic ethical thought and assimilated it to Christian ethics. Further, the Stoic doctrine of the Logos profoundly influenced Christian theological thought in certain quarters and finds its classic expression in the prologue to the Fourth Gospel (Jn. *1:1–18).[51]

[50] Cf. E. Vernon Arnold, *Roman Stoicism* (Cambridge University Press: 1911), pp. 85 ff.; *Library of the World's Best Literature* (New York: 1897), vol. 7, pp. 3784 ff.; *Columbia University Course in Literature* (New York: 1928), vol. 2, pp. 384 f.

[51] Cf. the poetic arrangement in three strophes of Jn. 1:1–18 in B. W. Bacon, *The Gospel of the Hellenists* (New York: 1933), pp. 243 f. On Epicureanism and Stoicism, cf. Case, *op. cit.*, chap. viii, "The Religious Significance of Philosophical Speculation," pp. 239–283.

Christianity in Palestine

In Galilee. Jesus lived his life in Galilee and the major portion of his public ministry was in Galilee.[52] The mystical religious experience of Peter, which launched Christianity on its way, occurred in all probability in Galilee, and so did the resurrection vision of those "more than five hundred brethren at once." [53] It amazes us, therefore, that the Book of Acts has nothing to say about Christianity in Galilee except for the single remark that "the church throughout all Galilee had peace, being builded up." [54] Recalling the multitude of disciples who had followed Jesus in Galilee, as well as the experience of the five hundred, we regret that Luke did not tell us the story of Christianity in Galilee. That the thousands of Jesus' followers in Galilee were allowed to drop into oblivion is one of the enigmas of history.

In Damascus. Luke's silence is likewise tantalizing because he merely indicates the existence of that very important Christian group which St. Paul first joined in Damascus.[55] It would seem to have been a base from which Paul carried on a missionary work in Arabia.[56]

In Jerusalem. Luke devotes chapters 1–7 of Acts to the story of the Christian group in Jerusalem. Much of this we have already discussed in Chapter 25. At the start, this Jerusalem group numbered about 120,[57] under the leadership of the twelve apostles. The place of Judas Iscariot among the twelve was filled by the selection of Matthias.[58] The head of this Jerusalem group was Peter,[59] and tradition says that he was so for twelve years.[60] Peter was the foremost spokesman of the group in preaching Christ to the populace (2:14–39; 3; 4:8–12).

Following the mystical experience at Pentecost (chapter 2),[61] the group increased in number to about 3,000.[62] A subsequent notice states that the number grew to 5,000.[63] Further growth beyond that, Luke indicates by the statement, "the number of the disciples multiplied in Jerusalem exceedingly," [64] but gives no more estimates in round numbers.

The headquarters of the Jerusalem group was at the home of Mary, the mother of John Mark.[65] Christian public activity centered at the temple (3:1–4:22) [66] and was unwelcome to the temple authorities

---

52 *Vid. supra,* pp. 496 f.
54 9:31.
56 Cf. Gal. 1:17.
58 1:15–26.
60 Cf. "The Preaching of Peter" and "The Acts of Peter," v, in M. R. James, *The Apocryphal New Testament* (Oxford: 1924), pp. 17, 307.
61 *Vid. supra,* p. 521.
63 4:4.
65 1:12 f.; 2:2; 12:12.

53 *Vid. supra,* pp. 520 f.
55 *Vid. supra,* p. 523.
57 1:15.
59 1:15.
62 2:41.
64 6:7.
66 *Vid. supra,* pp. 522 f.

so that Peter and other apostles were arrested and tried before the Sanhedrin on two different occasions but were released (4:1–31; 5:17–42).

The group lived a communal life, sharing all things in common (4:32–5:11).[67] These Jerusalem Christians were not only Palestinian Jews but also Hellenistic Jews of the Diaspora then residing in Jerusalem. They carried over into their Christian relationships the antipathy which marred the relationship between Palestinian and Diaspora Jews generally and this created a problem within the Christian group that was solved by the appointment of a committee of seven to represent the Hellenistic Jewish Christians (6:1–6).[68] The aggressive leader of this Hellenistic faction was Stephen, whose controversies with the Jews led to his martyrdom by stoning (6:8–7:60) and precipitated a persecution of the Christians by the Jerusalem authorities which caused the Christians to be "scattered abroad throughout the regions of Judea and Samaria, except the apostles" (8:1). The fact that the apostles were left undisturbed indicates that the persecution was directed against the Hellenistic element in the Christian group.

The group which remained in Jerusalem is commonly characterized as the Jewish Christian Church. Their point of view seems to have been that Christianity was only a subsect of Judaism, and therefore in order to be a Christian one must first be a Jew. What this implied for Christianity we have already discussed.[69]

The next head of the Jerusalem group after Peter was James, the brother of Jesus.[70] He continued in that capacity until his martyrdom in A.D. 62.[71] The Jerusalem group regarded itself as the parent church, which is why so much space is devoted to it at the beginning of Acts, conveying the impression that other Christian groups originated as a result of expansion from Jerusalem. As parent church the Jerusalem group presumed to exercise authority over Christian groups elsewhere, e.g., in Samaria (8:14–25), in Caesarea (11:1–18), and at Antioch (15:1–35; cf. Gal. 2), even issuing decrees for the gentile Christians to observe.[72] Their right to exercise such authority they rationalized as a special commission of Jesus to Peter, first head of the Jerusalem group.[73]

[67] *Vid. supra*, pp. 537 f.   [68] *Vid. supra*, pp. 523, 536.
[69] *Supra*, pp. 524 f.
[70] Cf. 1 Cor. 15:7; Acts 12:17; 15:13; 21:18; Gal. 1:19; 2:9, 12.
[71] *Vid. supra*, p. 553.
[72] Acts 15:23–29; 16:4.
[73] Matt. 16:17 ff. This moot passage, found only in Matthew, the Jewish Christian Gospel (cf. *supra*, pp. 524 f.), is plainly a Jewish Christian addendum to the original Markan narrative of the Caesarea Philippi incident (Mk. 8:27–30 = Matt. 16:13–16, 20 = Lk. 9:18–21) made for the reason indicated. The passage is not found in Mark, the Roman Gospel, based upon the preaching of Peter himself, whose interpreter Mark was (cf. *supra*, pp. 484 f).

This Jewish Christian group lasted in Jerusalem until the outbreak of the Jewish war, when the Christians removed from Jerusalem to Pella. After the fall of Jerusalem, groups of Christians of this type of faith were found here and there in the land but before long they ceased to be. After the year 70 Christianity in Palestine was gentile Christianity.

In Judea and Samaria. Acts 8–12 gives us glimpses of the spread of Christianity in Judea and Samaria. The gospel message was carried to Samaria by Philip the Evangelist, one of the Hellenistic committee of seven (*8:1–25). The interesting story of Simon the sorcerer acquaints us with an Oriental theosophist of a type destined at a later time to introduce heresy into the Christian movement. Philip also carried on his evangelizing activity along the coastal plain from Gaza in the south to Caesarea, capital of the country (*8: 26–40). The apostle Peter also carried on a missionary activity along the coastal plain (*9:32–11:18). The account of Peter's visit to Caesarea and his preaching there to the gentiles assembled in the home of Cornelius, the centurion, is intended by Luke to effect a transition to the story of the spread of Christianity to the gentile world. As the story stands, it would give Peter the credit of being the first to carry the gospel to the gentiles, but according to Gal. 2 that credit hardly belongs to Peter, and the incident of Peter's approach to the gentiles in Caesarea must have been subsequent in time to the event which Paul so hotly tells about in Gal. 2.

The brief persecution in Jerusalem at the time of Stephen's martyrdom had been at the hands of the Jewish religious authorities. Acts *12 gives an account of a persecution of the Christians by Herod Agrippa I which fell, therefore, between 41 and 44. In this persecution James, the brother of John, was killed, the first one of the original twelve disciples to die a martyr's death. Peter escaped from prison and so was spared.

Acts 11:19–26 transfers the scene of Christian missionary activity from Palestine to the gentile world, with Antioch in Syria as the chief center of gentile Christianity. It credits the founding of Christianity in Antioch to those Hellenistic Christians who were expelled from Jerusalem at the time of the martyrdom of Stephen (vs. 19).

St. Paul and the Spread of Christianity in the North Mediterranean World

St. Paul was the master mind of the apostolic age and after Jesus he is the most dynamic personality in the New Testament. The story of the spread of Christianity in the North Mediterranean world is the story of his career.

The Personality and Career of Paul. 1. *His Jewish Antecedents.* Paul was born A.D. *circa* 1 and died *circa* 64 at the time of the Neronian persecution. His birthplace was Tarsus in Cilicia,[74] which was "no mean city." [75] Tarsus was a university center, famed for its philosophy and general learning. Paul was "a Roman born," [76] which implies that his father had been granted Roman citizenship either by purchase or for some service rendered to the empire. Paul's parents, or an earlier generation, had migrated to Tarsus, possibly from Galilee.[77] Arising thus in one of the chief cities of the empire, Paul had that cosmopolitan sense and interest which so admirably fitted him to understand life in the great centers where he later introduced Christianity.

There is no doubt about Paul's Jewishness, for he emphasized it again and again.[78] Manifestly both parents were earnest, loyal Jews. The book of Acts up to 13:9 calls him "Saul" and after that "Paul." In his own writings he uses only the name "Paul." As a boy in Tarsus he could have had both names, Saul his Jewish name, Paul his Roman name, and being a Roman citizen he would have been given a Roman name.[79]

2. *Paul's Education.* Paul's earliest education was in his own home, which evidently was a typically devout Jewish home. He may have learned Aramaic in his childhood home, though he could have acquired it later when resident in Jerusalem; at any rate he could speak Aramaic.[80] It goes without saying that he knew Greek, for his letters were all written in that language. Any Jewish boy in the Diaspora would have spoken Greek. Presumably there was a synagogue in Tarsus where Paul learned to know the Jewish Scriptures and where he was trained in Jewish faith and practice. In the light of Phil. 3:5 we would not suppose that Paul was sent to a gentile school in his youth. While probably still in his teens he was sent to Jerusalem for scribal training under the celebrated rabbi Gamaliel,[81] successor of the famous liberal rabbi Hillel. Whether formally educated in a gentile school at Tarsus or not, the influence of his Hellenistic environment in Tarsus would have been penetrating, not only in his youth but in his maturer years, if he returned to Tarsus after completing his scribal training. Two features of the Hellenism of Tarsus are important to note; one was the local mystery cult of the divinity

---

[74] Acts 22:3.   [75] Acts 21:39.   [76] Acts 22:28.

[77] St. Jerome, A.D. *circa* 400, in his commentary on Philemon, has a tradition that Paul was born in Giscala in Galilee and that his parents were taken captive by the legions of Varus in the campaign of A.D. 4 and deported to Tarsus.

[78] Gal. 1:13 f.; 2:15; 2 Cor. 11:22; Rom. 11:1; Phil. 3:5.

[79] John Mark is another example of a Jew with both a Jewish and a Roman name (Acts 12:12); so also Joseph Justus (Acts 1:23) and Jesus Justus (Col. 4:11).

[80] Acts 21:40; 22:2.   [81] Acts 22:3.

Sandan, identified by Greek writers with Hercules, with ceremonies celebrating his "awakening" or "arising" (i.e., resurrection) ; the other was the fact that Tarsus was one of the chief centers of the Stoic school of philosophy.[82] Paul's letters evidence his thorough acquaintance with both these features of Hellenistic life and thought.

3. *Paul's Career as a Rabbi.* Between the completion of Paul's scribal training and his conversion, a period elapsed which Paul spent either in Jerusalem or more likely in Tarsus or elsewhere. At the end of that time we find him in Jerusalem, a zealous Jewish worker; "after the straitest sect of our religion I lived a Pharisee." [83] He was ardent in persecuting the Christians.[84] It is doubtful if Paul was in Jerusalem during the last week of Jesus' life and equally doubtful that he ever saw Jesus. He persecuted the Christians because he felt himself to be a defender of the faith of his fathers. Christianity was an independent, reforming movement, and Paul, with other Jewish leaders, took alarm and sought to repress it. Paul was present when Stephen was stoned to death and "was consenting unto his death." [85] Acts 26:10 represents Paul as saying that when the Christians he persecuted were put to death, "I gave my vote against them." Some interpreters hold this to mean that Paul was an official, voting a death sentence, but more likely its meaning is only that their death had his moral approval. Being a Diaspora Jew, Paul would not have been a member of the Jerusalem Sanhedrin.

Paul was unmarried.[86] He was afflicted with some physical malady to which he refers as a "stake in the flesh" as though a piece of wood had been driven into his body.[87] In Gal. 4:13 ff. he speaks of some trouble with his eyes. What such ailments were can only be a matter of speculation.

4. *Paul's Conversion to Christianity.* The year of Paul's conversion is variously calculated by interpreters; presumably it occurred sometime between 30 and 35. Paul refers to his conversion in Gal. 1:15 ff., and Acts gives an account of it three times (9:1–19; 22:6–21; 26:12–18). We have already discussed the nature of the experience.[88] It occurred near the city of Damascus, whither he was going to persecute the Christians. It completely changed Paul's life. He believed that the moral purpose of the experience was that he might preach Christ among the gentiles.[89]

5. *The Early Years of Paul's Christian Life.* Immediately following his conversion, Paul "went away into Arabia," [90] which un-

82 *Vid. supra*, p. 567.   83 Acts 26:5.
84 Gal. 1:13 f.; 1 Cor. 15:9; Phil. 3:6; Acts 7:58–8:3; 9:1 f.
85 Acts 8:1.   86 1 Cor. 7:1, 8.
87 2 Cor. 12:7–10.   88 *Vid. supra*, p. 520.
89 Gal. 1:16; cf. Acts 9:15; 22:21; 26:17.   90 Gal. 1:17.

questionably means that he at once began missionary activity in the Nabatean kingdom, with its capital city Petra.[91] He returned to Damascus, where Acts 9:20–25 indicates that he engaged in evangelistic activity. After three years, i.e., probably three years after his conversion, he visited Jerusalem where he spent a fortnight with Cephas (presumably Peter),[92] after which he went to his native Tarsus.[93] Undoubtedly he engaged in missionary activity in Tarsus and Cilicia for the next several years, perhaps ten in all. He worked there until he was summoned to Antioch by Barnabas.[94] He worked for a whole year at Antioch, and during the famine of 46 he and Barnabas made a trip to Jerusalem to carry relief to the needy Christians there.[95]

After his return to Antioch Paul began that series of missionary journeys from Antioch as a base which carried him clear across the North Mediterranean world to Rome, the story of which occupies all the rest of Acts from chapter 13 to the end.

St. Paul's Missionary Journeys. 1. *The First Missionary Journey.* Acts *13 f. is the narrative of Paul's first missionary journey.[96] His companions were Barnabas and John Mark. They sailed to the island of Cyprus, journeyed through the island, and sailed to Pamphylia on the mainland of Asia Minor. John Mark left the party at Perga in Pamphylia and returned to Jerusalem for some reason not stated.[97] From Perga, Paul and Barnabas went up to the Anatolian Plateau and evangelized the cities of Antioch in Pisidia (13:14–52), Iconium (14:1–6), Lystra (14:6–20), and Derbe (14:20 f.). The nature of Paul's missionary procedure in a community has already been discussed.[98] From Derbe they retraced their course over the same ground back to Pamphylia and sailed to Antioch in Syria (14:21–28).

The admission of gentiles into Christianity without requiring them first to become Jewish proselytes precipitated a controversy between Paul and the Jewish Christian group in Jerusalem. It necessitated a trip by Paul to Jerusalem to settle the matter. Paul's own account is given in Gal. 2; Acts 15 presents a different version. We have already pointed out the significance of this Jerusalem conference and of Paul's victory in the controversy.[99]

---

[91] Cf. Elmer W. K. Mould, "Paul and Petra," in *From the Pyramids to Paul,* ed. by L. G. Leary (New York: 1935), pp. 150–164.
[92] Gal. 1:18–24.   [93] Cf. Acts 9:30.
[94] Acts 11:19–26.   [95] Acts 11:27–30.
[96] On the geography of Paul's journeys, cf. Wright and Filson, *op. cit.,* pp. 87–91.
[97] 13:13. Paul evidently thought Mark a quitter, because he would not take him along later on the second missionary journey, which refusal caused a separation between Paul and Barnabas; cf. Acts 15:36–40.
[98] *Supra,* pp. 523 f.
[99] *Supra,* pp. 524 f.

2. *Paul's Second Missionary Journey.* Acts *15:36–18:22 tells
about Paul's second missionary campaign which carried him to the
continent of Europe. His companion at the outset was Silas; [100] they
later took on Timothy [101] and Luke. [102]

Starting from Antioch they traveled overland through Syria and
Cilicia, which enabled Paul again to visit his home town, Tarsus
(15:41). Passing through the Cilician Gates to the Anatolian Plateau,
Paul revisited the Galatian churches which he had founded on his
first journey (16:1–6). Paul aimed to go to Ephesus but was prevented for some reason or other (16:6). He then planned to go north
into Bithynia but was thwarted again (16:7). [103] They made their way
to Troas (ancient Troy) and sailed from there for Macedonia
(16:8–11).

The first place on the continent of Europe which Paul evangelized
was Philippi where he encountered the opposition of certain interests which were adversely affected by Christianity; Paul and Silas
were imprisoned and when released left the town (16:12–40). They
went next to Thessalonica where their preaching caused a riot which
obliged Paul and Silas to leave town under cover of night (17:1–10).
They went to Beroea but were followed thither by troublemakers
from Thessalonica (17:11–14). Paul had to leave Beroea but Silas
and Timothy continued the work there. Paul journeyed on to Athens
where he made his famous address before the Areopagus in the
presence of the Epicurean and Stoic philosophers (17:15–34). [104]
From Athens he went to Corinth. Not long after his arrival there,
perhaps three months later, he was joined by Silas and Timothy,
who came from Macedonia (18:5). The news which they brought
him caused Paul to write a letter to the Christians at Thessalonica. [105]
First Thessalonians therefore enjoys the distinction of being the oldest
book in the New Testament. After that Paul continued his Christian
work in Corinth for a year and a half (18:6–17). Toward the end of
his stay in Corinth disquieting news reached Paul from the churches in
Galatia concerning the disturbing Judaizers who had gone there after
Paul left, whereupon Paul wrote his famous letter to the Galatians. [106]

[100] Acts 15:40.   [101] Acts 16:1 ff.
[102] Acts 16:9 f. In vs. 10, note the sudden change from the third to the first
personal pronoun; this is one of the "we" passages of Acts (cf. *supra*, p. 519). The
implication is that Luke, the author of Acts, joined Paul's party at this point.
[103] We cannot help wondering by whom and when Christianity was introduced
into Bithynia, in view of the picture of Christianity in that province which we get
from Pliny the Younger's letters early in the second century; *vid. supra*, pp. 548 f.
[104] *Vid. supra*, p. 567.   [105] Cf. 1 Thess. 3:6.
[106] Some scholars hold that Paul wrote Galatians from Antioch between his
second and third missionary journeys (Acts 18:23). Had Paul been in Antioch
when the news about the Judaizers in Galatia reached him, it is doubtful if he
would have written a letter; he would have gone in person in all haste. Still other
scholars argue for Ephesus on his third missionary journey as the place and time
of the writing of Galatians, but that seems too late.

When Paul left Corinth he sailed over to Ephesus for a brief visit and thence sailed to Caesarea, "went up and saluted the church" (which probably means that he made a brief trip to Jerusalem), and then journeyed to Antioch in Syria (18:18–22).

3. *Paul's Third Missionary Journey.* Paul's third journey began at Antioch in Syria, took him through Asia Minor, Macedonia, and Greece, and ended in Jerusalem (Acts *18:23–21:16). From Antioch he traveled along the same route as on his second journey, revisited the churches of Galatia (18:23), and then went to Ephesus where he remained for three years. Paul's associates in the work of Ephesus were Timothy, Titus, Erastus, and Sosthenes.[107] At the end of the third journey Luke and several others were associated with Paul.[108]

Hellenistic religious cults met and mingled at Ephesus. Paul found there what appears to have been a small remnant of the John the Baptist movement (19:1–7).[109] There were also wandering Jewish exorcists (19:8–18). The cult of magic throve in Ephesus (19:19 f.) among Jews as well as gentiles. The books of magic were formulas sold about the country as charms against evil spirits and were worn as amulets or inscribed on doorposts, garden gates, and the like. A vast number of such magical papyri have survived to the present day; they make dreary reading! The emperor cult was there; there is reference to the local high priests of this cult, known as Asiarchs (19:31). Most important of all was the cult of the local goddess Artemis (Diana). Paul's preaching so undercut this cult that a riot was precipitated by the silversmiths who made the little Artemis shrines (19:23–41). This is the first instance of direct hostility to Christianity due to trade interests.[110] "All with one voice about the space of two hours cried out, Great Artemis of the Ephesians," [111] which probably means, not insensate yelling but the chanting of a long Artemis litany.[112]

Probably Paul was imprisoned for a time in Ephesus, due to the tense situation there. One wonders whether his remark made while there, "I fought with beasts at Ephesus," [113] implies an enforced combat in the arena.[114] In Acts 20:29 certain heretics at Ephesus

---

[107] Acts 19:22; 1 Cor. 1:1; 2 Cor. 1:1; 12:17 f.
[108] Acts 20:4 f.   [109] *Vid. supra,* pp. 494 f.
[110] Early in the second century, Pliny the Younger, governor of Bithynia, blamed Christianity for the lack of prosperity; the butchers' trade fell off because there was no demand for sacrifices. At a later time, in Arabia, the incense trade fell off, with similar complaint against Christianity.
[111] 19:34.
[112] It may have been a litany analogous to the long "Invocation of Isis," of which a very large fragment has survived. Cf. Bernard P. Grenfell and Arthur S. Hunt, *The Oxyrhynchus Papyri,* part xi (London: 1915), no. 1380, pp. 190–220.
[113] 1 Cor. 15:32.
[114] He does not refer to it again in his detailed enumeration of his missionary hardships in 2 Cor. 11:23–33.

are spoken of as "grievous wolves"; a fight with beasts might therefore have been only a figure of speech.

While located in Ephesus, Paul exchanged letters with the Christians in Corinth.[115] Thus arose First and Second Corinthians. Relations between Paul and the church at Corinth had become strained, and from Ephesus Paul made a brief trip to Corinth and back in an unsuccessful effort to straighten out the difficulty.[116] Nor did his letter settle the trouble, so he sent Titus to Corinth.[117] Before Titus returned, Paul left Ephesus for Troas, where he worked for a short time.[118] From there Paul crossed over into Macedonia, where he met Titus, presumably at Philippi, bearing the good news that the trouble in Corinth had been settled.[119] In great relief and joy Paul wrote what is incorporated in 2 Cor. 1–9. How long Paul spent in Macedonia at this time is not stated (Acts 20:1 f.). From there he went to Corinth (20:3).

During his three months' stay in Corinth Paul considered what his future plans for missionary work should be. He considered that his work in the eastern part of the Mediterranean world was done. (His statement, "From Jerusalem, and round about unto Illyricum [the area of Albania], I have fully preached the gospel of Christ," leaves us baffled, for there is no account whatever of any missionary trip to that region.[120]) He therefore planned to go west. For many years he had wanted to visit Rome.[121] Christianity was already established in Rome, and Paul would not "build upon another man's foundation"; he would only "preach the gospel where Christ was not already named." [122] Therefore he planned to go to Spain [123] and visit Rome en route. If he were to carry on missionary work in the west, he would need a base at Rome, just as Antioch in Syria had hitherto been his base. To prepare for his visit to Rome Paul wrote his Epistle to the Romans.

For some time Paul had been carrying on a practical philanthropic enterprise in the gathering of a relief fund among the gentile groups for the benefit of the Christians in Jerusalem.[124] That fund was now complete and from Corinth Paul took the fund to Jerusalem (Acts 20:3–21:16). En route he was advised to stay away from Jerusalem to avoid serious trouble (21:4, 10 ff.). But Paul was not deterred.

Paul the Prisoner. Paul said that he was "in prisons more abundantly" than any other Christian missionary.[125] Acts tells of his

---

[115] Cf. 1 Cor. 5:9; 7:1.
[116] Cf. 2 Cor. 12:14; 13:1.
[117] 2 Cor. 12:17 f.
[118] 2 Cor. 2:12 f.
[119] 2 Cor. 7:6, 13 f.
[120] Rom. 15:19, 23.
[121] Rom. 15:23.
[122] Rom. 15:20.
[123] Rom. 15:24. There is no good reason to suppose that he ever got there.
[124] 1 Cor. 16:1–6; 2 Cor. 8:1–4; 9:1–14; Rom. 15:25 ff.; vid. supra, p. 538.
[125] 2 Cor. 11:23.

imprisonment at Philippi (16:23–34) and we have indicated the likelihood that he was imprisoned in Ephesus. We have no means of knowing what other imprisonments Paul referred to in his statement, which was made before his final trip to Jerusalem.

1. *In Jerusalem.* Paul reached Jerusalem and promptly greeted the Christian leaders there (Acts *21:17 ff.). Presumably he delivered the relief fund to them, but there is not a single word of appreciation to Paul for this gift on which he had expended so much time and effort and on which he counted to bring about good will between the Jewish and the gentile churches.

The day after his arrival, Paul went to the temple with certain Jews who were to perform some purificatory rite for which Paul was to pay, a rite lasting a week (*21:20–27). An onset was made upon Paul by some Jews from the province of Asia who mistakenly supposed that the men with Paul were gentiles whom Paul had sacrilegiously led beyond the Court of the Gentiles into the Court of the Men of Israel. Notices were posted in Greek forbidding gentiles to pass beyond the Court of the Gentiles, and any Jew finding a gentile in the inner courts was privileged to strike him dead on the spot. One such inscription was discovered in 1871 and is now in the Imperial Museum in Istanbul.[126] It reads:

> Let no foreigner enter within the screen and enclosure surrounding the sanctuary. Whoever is found doing so will be the cause of his own death.

The incident precipitated a riot which the Roman military tribune hastened with troops to quiet (*21:27–40). He permitted Paul to address the mob (*22:1–21), but as they were the more irritated and demanded Paul's death, the tribune placed him under arrest (*22:22–29). Next day Paul made a speech in defense of himself before the Sanhedrin but to no avail (*22:30–23:10). For safety, the tribune placed him in the tower of Antonia. A plot, presumably by Sicarii, to assassinate Paul was reported by his nephew, whereupon the tribune sent Paul under heavy guard to the procurator Felix at Caesarea (*23:11–35). All this happened A.D. *circa* 58, in the time of Felix,[127] when Palestine was in a chaotic state.

2. *In Caesarea.* Paul, after a hearing by Felix, was kept in prison for two whole years (Acts *24). In the course of his hearing, Paul

---

[126] It is a limestone block, 22½ x 33½ x 14½ inches in size, and was discovered by Clermont-Ganneau. Cf. Adolf Deissmann, *Light from the Ancient East* (London: 1927), p. 80; Millar Burrows, *What Mean These Stones?* (New Haven: 1941), p. 269; Jack Finegan, *Light from the Ancient Past* (Princeton: 1946), p. 246 and Fig. 111.

[127] *Vid. supra,* p. 553.

happened to mention that he had come to Palestine "to bring alms to my nation, and offerings" (vs. 17), which aroused the cupidity of Felix who "hoped withal that money would be given him of Paul" (vs. 26).

Felix was succeeded by Festus as procurator of Judea in the year 60. Festus promptly examined Paul and proposed that Paul go up to Jerusalem to be tried there before Festus. Paul refused, and stood upon his rights as a Roman citizen and appealed to the emperor (*25:1–12). Festus had no option in the matter. He was obliged to send Paul to Rome but he was put to it to know just what sort of accusation to send to the emperor with the prisoner. Presently King Agrippa II came to Caesarea to greet Festus. Festus told Agrippa about the case and Agrippa expressed a wish to hear the prisoner, whereupon Paul pleaded his cause before the Jewish king (*25:13–26:32). Agrippa's judgment was that "this man might have been set at liberty, if he had not appealed unto Caesar." Once those fateful words, "Caesarem appello," escaped the lips of a Roman citizen, there was no retraction. The issue was forced.

3. *In Rome.* The narrative of Paul's journey as a prisoner to Rome, with its story of the shipwreck, is one of the most vividly dramatic passages in all the Bible (Acts *27:1–28:16). An interview with certain Jewish leaders of Rome is recorded (28:17–28). Besides that, all that is said concerning Paul's experience in Rome is that he "was suffered to abide by himself with the soldier that guarded him. . . . And he abode two whole years in his own hired dwelling, and received all that went in unto him, preaching the kingdom of God, and teaching the things concerning the Lord Jesus Christ with all boldness, none forbidding him." [128]

During the years of his imprisonment in Rome, Paul not only continued to preach but he also wrote letters to certain of his churches. Paul's letters to the Ephesians, Colossians, Philemon, and Philippians are commonly called the imprisonment epistles, and the conventional view is that they were written by Paul while a prisoner in Rome. Some scholars, however, consider it more likely that some of them were written from his prison in Caesarea or even in Ephesus.

Acts ends in a way most disappointing to the modern reader. Why did not Luke tell the outcome of Paul's trial? Was he acquitted or was he convicted and executed? The answer is the latter. Why, then, did not Luke say so? Because to do so would have defeated his purpose, which was to commend Christianity to the Roman world. If, after telling the story of Christianity's origin and spread to Rome, which is the subject of Luke-Acts, he had at the end

[128] Acts 28:16, 30 f.

pointed out that the chief hero of its spread had been put to death by the emperor as an enemy of the state, Roman readers would have turned away from Christianity in disgust. In a cryptic way Luke has indicated that Paul was dead at the end of the story, viz., in the farewell to the elders of Ephesus (Acts 20:17–38).

The Roman Empire was a vast domain. Judicial business for such a large dominion must have kept the imperial supreme court docket congested, which would account for the delay in settling Paul's case at Rome. The tradition is that Paul was beheaded at the command of Nero, probably in the year 64.[129]

Unto the Uttermost Part of the Earth

Acts 1:8 suggests the plan according to which, as we have just seen, Luke develops the story of the expansion of Christianity: "Ye shall be my witnesses both in Jerusalem, and in all Judea and Samaria, and unto the uttermost part of the earth." "The uttermost part of the earth" may have been a first-century equivalent to "Rome." [130] An apt title for the book of Acts, suggested by Professor James Moffatt,[131] is "How They Brought the Good News to Rome."

The New Testament does not make it clear just when or how Christianity first reached Rome. There were present at Pentecost certain "sojourners from Rome" [132] who probably carried the seeds of the faith back to Rome with them. In A.D. 50 the emperor Claudius banished a number of Jews from Rome for rioting, which was probably due to the preaching of Christ among the Jews of Rome, as we have already indicated.[133] Two such Jews expelled from Rome were Aquila and Priscilla, his wife, who found their way to Corinth where they became intimate friends of Paul.[134] The language of Acts leaves us in ignorance as to whether they were Christians before they reached Corinth or were converted there by Paul.[135] Paul's letter to the Romans attests that there was a fully established Christian group in Rome before he ever went there, and that it was a Greek-speaking group, for his letter was in Greek. A careful reading of Romans indicates that the type of Christianity established in Rome was neither Jewish, such as that of Jerusalem, nor Pauline, and part of the reason why Paul wanted to go to Rome was to bring the Christians there into harmony with his type of gospel.[136] After Paul did reach Rome, only part of the Jews there sided with him,[137]

---

[129] Cf. *The Acts of Paul*, x, 5, in M. R. James, *op. cit.*, pp. 293–296.
[130] Cf. Ps. Sol. 8:16.
[131] In an academic lecture.   [132] 2:10.
[133] *Supra*, p. 547.   [134] Acts 18:1 ff.
[135] They later were zealous Christian workers in Ephesus (Acts 18:24 ff.).
[136] Rom. 1:11.   [137] Acts 28:24.

and Col. 4:7–17 indicates that Paul had only a very small following in Rome if we accept the conventional view that Colossians was written from that city.

The New Testament says nothing whatever about the apostle Peter's connection with Rome, but apocryphal writings of the second century attest the tradition that Peter died a martyr thereby being crucified upside down,[138] even as such writings attest the tradition of Paul's martyr death at Rome.[139] There is no evidence that the martyrdom of Paul and Peter occurred on the same occasion, though they may both have been in the same year, 64, when Nero was persecuting the Christians of Rome. The martyrdom of these two pre-eminent apostles gave Rome a distinction which no other place had.

Christianity has always thrived when opposed and persecuted. Nero's persecution only accelerated the faith in Rome. The gospel began to radiate from Rome, due to the work of Christian evangelists. For the benefit of such evangelists, Mark, who had been the travel companion and interpreter of Peter, wrote his gospel, presumably at Rome.

When Luke wrote Acts (A.D. *circa* 85–90), Christianity was fully and firmly established at Rome and was spreading from there. Therefore he considered that he only need narrate how Christianity became established in Rome, the center of the empire, and he would have explained how it reached "to the uttermost part of the earth." In the way he told the story Luke has disclosed that spiritual dynamic which is in the very nature of Christianity and which has through all the succeeding centuries continued to take it to the ends of the earth. That story however belongs not to Biblical history but to church history.

A profound mystery surrounds one other phase of Christianity in the first century which contributed an important element in the spread of the gospel down through the centuries, namely, Christianity in Alexandria, Egypt. We are wholly in the dark as to when and how Christianity was planted there. The story of Pentecost specifies the presence in Jerusalem, on that occasion, of dwellers "in Egypt and the parts of Libya about Cyrene" [140] who may have carried the seeds of the faith to Egypt with them. Acts 8:26–39 narrates the conversion of the Ethiopian eunuch by Philip the Evangelist. This man was either a native Ethiopian, a would-be Jewish proselyte, and as such visited Jerusalem at festival time, or a Jew who held a high governmental position as treasurer of Candace's kingdom.[141] In either case

---

[138] *Acts of Peter,* xxxvii; cf. M. R. James, *op. cit.,* p. 334.
[139] *Vid. supra,* p. 579, fn. 129.   [140] Acts 2:10.
[141] Joseph and Nehemiah are examples of Jews who in earlier ages had become high government officials in foreign kingdoms.

he had nothing to do with Alexandria. Acts 18:24 f. gives us a hazy glimpse of Christianity being already in Alexandria. Apollos, an Alexandrian, had been taught "the way of the Lord" [142] and was himself able to teach "accurately the things concerning Jesus, knowing only the baptism of John." [143] When Paul, toward the end of his third missionary journey in Corinth, said that he had "no more place in these regions" [144] we can only wonder whether he considered Alexandria as a possible field of work but dismissed the idea because Christianity was already planted there and he did not wish "to build upon another man's foundation." That is all there is in the New Testament about the matter.

It is not until the end of the second century that Christianity in Alexandria comes into the full light of history and it is educational Christianity. Under Clement there was a flourishing Christian school there. In its beginning it was an instruction class for Christian catechumens, but young people became Christians who had been trained in pagan schools and so the Christian school expanded its program to give a broad education to Christian youth.

In the second and third centuries Alexandria was the intellectual capital of Christianity. "Textual criticism" is that branch of New Testament science which is concerned with the study of the original Greek manuscripts of the New Testament writings and the classification of such manuscripts according to types. One of the basic types of Greek New Testament text is known among scholars as the "Alexandrian." In Alexandria there existed a scholarly interest in the literature of the New Testament and in multiplying copies of the New Testament books. That scholarly interest produced at Alexandria, in the fourth century, one of the oldest, most valuable, and most basically important of all Greek manuscripts of the New Testament, the *Codex Vaticanus* (B), which is now in the Vatican library in Rome.[145] Possibly, also, the other one of the oldest Greek manuscripts of the New Testament, the *Codex Sinaiticus* (ℵ), originated at Alexandria.[146]

---

[142] The "Western" text adds "in his own country"; cf. D. W. Riddle, *Early Christian Life* (Chicago: 1936), p. 234.

[143] This Apollos was a Christian worker for a time in Ephesus and later in Corinth (cf. 1 Cor. 1:12).

[144] Rom. 15:23.

[145] Cf. K. Lake, *The Text of the New Testament* (London: 1928), p. 15.

[146] Either at Alexandria or at Caesarea; cf. Lake, *op. cit.*, p. 15.

Chapter 27

THE COMPLETED BIBLE

All the books of the Old Testament were in existence by the middle of the second century B.C.[1] "The Law, the Prophets, and the Psalms"[2] were esteemed as Holy Scripture,[3] and esteem for the sacredness of the books of the Hagiographa increasingly heightened until at the synod of Jamnia, A.D. *circa* 90, the last questions about some of the books were settled,[4] and the canon of the Jewish Holy Scriptures was closed.

Beginning in 285 B.C. with the Torah, the Jewish Sacred Scriptures were translated into Greek in the version known as the *Septuagint.*[5] In this version they were used by Jews of the Diaspora, such as Paul. The Septuagint was known and used by those Diaspora Jews who became Christians and thus it passed into use by the early Christians in their meetings for religious worship.[6] As a result of this process the Jewish Holy Scriptures became also the Christian Sacred Scriptures of the Old Testament.

In Chapter 24 the process was described by which the four gospels of the New Testament came into being,[7] and extensive selections from the gospels were starred for reading. In Chapters 25 and 26 the same was done for the Book of Acts.[8] In Chapter 25 numerous choice passages from the other New Testament books were starred for reading and it is now in order to consider the origin of those books.

The Epistles of St. Paul

All the writings of St. Paul are in the form of letters, and they are the oldest stratum of literature in the New Testament. All his letters were occasional, as we have pointed out.[9]

The Epistle as a Literary Form. Many thousands of letters written in the early centuries of our era have survived to the present. Some of them are the correspondence of emperors and high govern-

---

[1] *Vid. supra*, pp. 429 ff.
[3] *Vid. supra*, pp. 397 f.
[5] *Vid. supra*, pp. 412 f.
[7] *Vid. supra*, pp. 483 f.
[9] *Supra*, p. 519.

[2] Cf. Luke 24 :44.
[4] *Vid. supra*, pp. 430, 556.
[6]. *Vid. supra*, pp. 527 f.
[8] Cf. especially pp. 519 f.

ment officials; some are the letters of great authors; most of them
are the messages of plain people. It was in keeping with the spirit
of the age that the Christians should have exchanged letters. Paul's
letter to Philemon * is a gem of such correspondence and its structure
shows the pattern on which all his epistles were built.

Paul always starts with a salutation in which some of his intimate
associates often join as in Philem. 1 ff. Immediately there follows a
paragraph of thanksgiving in which Paul expresses affection for the
person or group to whom he is writing, as in Philem. 4–7. Then
follows a section in which Paul deals with the specific matters which
have called forth the letter, as in Philem. 8–20. This is often called
the doctrinal section of the letter for the reason that Paul thought
through every matter he discussed with reference to the basic beliefs
of the Christian faith. There follows next, in most of his letters, a
section of practical ethical advice and exhortation. The very close
of a letter is a benediction, as in Philem. 25, preceded by a paragraph of personal greetings, as in Philem. 23. At the end, some of
Paul's letters bore his signature in his own handwriting. As a rule,
however, he dictated his letters to an amanuensis.[10]

The Epistles of the Second Missionary Journey. 1. First
Thessalonians is the oldest extant letter of Paul. It was written
from Corinth just about the middle of the first century. The story of
the founding of the church at Thessalonica is in Acts 17:1–10.[11]
1 Thess. 1:9 f. states the sort of doctrine Paul emphasized when he
founded the church at Thessalonica. The Thessalonian Christians
had been enduring persecution (2:13–16) but had stood firm in
their faith (*3:7 f.). They were troubled about their loved ones
who had died (4:13–18) and about the coming again of Christ
(5:1–6). Passages which are choice expressions of Paul's thought
are *2:11, 20; *5:5, 8, 15–22.

2. Second Thessalonians deals with the coming again of Christ,
which the Thessalonians thought was near at hand. Paul's argument
in chapter 2 seems fantastic to a modern reader.[12] There is nothing
fantastic, however, about the common sense expressed in *3:10. 2:2
implies that someone had forged Paul's name to a letter which upset
the Thessalonians. Therefore Paul signed this letter at the very
end (3:17) that they might know what his signature looked like,
and he said that such a signature was "the token in every epistle." [13]

---

[10] Cf. E. F. Scott, *The Literature of the New Testament* (New York: 1932),
pp. 107–115.
[11] *Vid. supra,* pp. 574 f.
[12] The nature of this argument inclines some scholars to question the authenticity
of 2 Thess. The point is discussed by Scott, *op. cit.,* pp. 121–126.
[13] The same sort of subscription is to be found at the end of Gal., 1 Cor., Col.

3. Galatians is one of the major epistles of Paul. It deals with a great theme, "Christian Liberty." We have already discussed the controversy precipitated by the question whether gentiles could be admitted to Christianity without first becoming Jewish proselytes and the historical significance of Paul's victory in that controversy.[14] Gal. 2 makes Paul's position crystal clear. The controversy was not ended by the decision made at Jerusalem. Certain Judaizers went to the Galatian churches after Paul had left there. These churches Paul had founded on his first missionary journey (Acts 13 f.) and had revisited on his second missionary journey.[15] The Judaizers endeavored to get the Galatians to become proselytes to the Jewish law. This was the situation which called forth this vigorous epistle. In chapters 3 f. Paul deals with the subject of the law versus faith. The core of his argument is stated in *3:11, "No man is justified by the law before God, for the righteous shall live by faith." This sentiment about faith was first stated centuries earlier by the prophet Habakkuk.[16] The conclusion of Paul's argument is eloquently stated in *5:1–6. *5:13–6:10 is one of the choicest passages of Paul's ethical teachings.

The Epistles of the Third Missionary Journey. 1. *First and Second Corinthians.* The story of the founding of Christianity in Corinth is in Acts 18:1–17.[17] 1 Cor. 5:9 indicates that Paul had written a letter to the Corinthians before he wrote 1 Cor. It was a letter on the subject of sexual immorality. It is possible that a fragment of that letter is preserved in 2 Cor. 6:14–7:1 for this passage is on that subject and does not fit its context in 2 Cor.[18]

To that earlier letter the Corinthians replied (7:1), inquiring further about what Paul had meant, for a serious case of immorality had happened among them (5). They also asked his views about other problems which were troubling their group. In answer to this inquiry, Paul wrote First Corinthians. Factional divisions had developed at Corinth (1:10–17), one faction seeking to construe Christianity in terms of Greek sophistry (1:18–2:16); Paul's answer to factionalism (3 f.) stresses Christian unity, which is beautifully stated in *3:4–17. Some Christians at Corinth had been involved in lawsuits with one another (6). They were troubled by the problem of marriage and divorce and what should be done in the case of couples where only one partner was a Christian (7). They were religiously disturbed about eating meat which had been sacrificed

---

14 *Vid. supra*, pp. 524 ff.   15 *Vid. supra*, pp. 574 ff.
16 Hab. 2:4; *vid. supra*, pp. 303 f., 342.   17 *Vid. supra*, p. 574.
18 Read 2 Cor. 6:11–13; 7:2–4, and note how it all belongs together and how smoothly the thought passes from 6:13 to 7:2. Only some accident in the transmission of the text could have broken up such a passage by inserting a disharmonious passage on fornication.

to idols; after animals were butchered in sacrifice to a deity the meat was sold in the markets for general consumption. On the sacramentarian view of religion, a person who ate such meat thereby took into his body the very nature of the god to whom the meat had been sacrificed. Paul discussed this matter at length (8 ff.) for it gave him an opportunity to expound the doctrine of Christian liberty. In the exercise of Christian liberty, the principle of control, as stated in *6:12; *10:23, is the basis of Christian behavior in any age. Paul solved the transitory problem of eating sacrificial meat by a principle which is permanently valid, viz., regard for the good of other persons (*8:13; 10:24). The question of women being veiled in Christian meetings (11:2–16) and of disorderly behavior at the communion service (11:17–34) also perplexed the Corinthians. In his discussion of spiritual gifts (12 ff.) Paul rises to a height of eloquence not equaled anywhere else in his writings (*12:4–14:1).[19] Paul's discussion of immortality (*15) is likewise one of the finest passages in all his epistles.

In 2 Cor. 2:3 f., 9; 7:8, Paul refers to a letter which he wrote "out of much affliction and anguish of heart, with many tears," which letter made the Corinthians "sorry." Such a statement does not characterize 1 Corinthians and must refer to something else. The substance of that distressing letter is probably in 2 Cor. 10–13. Paul had been ungraciously assailed at Corinth (10) and he stirringly defends his apostolic rank and work (11). The enumeration of hardships he had suffered in his work (*11:23–33) is a choice piece of autobiography. As we have remarked, Paul interrupted his work at Ephesus to make a brief, but unsuccessful, trip to Corinth to settle the difficulty and later sent Titus to Corinth for the same purpose.[20] Titus succeeded, and when he reported to Paul in Macedonia, Paul promptly wrote a letter of joy and thanksgiving (*7:3 f., 16; *9:15) to Corinth, which is 2 Cor. 1–9. Some of the golden gems of thought in this letter are *3:17; *4:16 ff.; 5:17; *6:1–10; *8:9.[21]

2. *Romans*. The time, place, and purpose of Paul's letter to the Romans have already been explained.[22] In this letter Paul elaborates his basic doctrine of salvation by faith (*1:16 f.), which he also expounded in Galatians and which he based upon Habakkuk's doc-

---

[19] On the nature of tongue-speaking (glossolalia), which Paul discusses in 1 Cor. 14, cf. *supra*, p. 521.

[20] *Vid. supra*, p. 576.

[21] It is easy to see why, in the preservation of Paul's letters at Corinth, the painful letter should have come at the end of 2 Cor.; a reproving letter is likely to find its way to the bottom of the pile if indeed it be preserved at all. Paul's letters were reread for edification many times in the Corinthian group; after their reconciliation with Paul they would not have been disposed to bring out the painful letter very often. On the Corinthian letters, cf. Scott, *op. cit.*, pp. 127–144.

[22] *Supra*, p. 576.

trine that "the righteous shall live by faith." [23] Wisdom had not brought righteousness to the gentiles (1:18–2:11), though "God will render to every man according to his works . . . glory and honor and peace to every man that worketh good, to the Jew first, and also to the Greek: for there is no respect of persons with God." [24] Jews had founded their search for righteousness upon the law (2:12–3:20) but "by the works of the law shall no flesh be justified in his sight, for through the law cometh the knowledge of sin." [25] There is a higher way, the way of faith (3:21–8:39). Paul's reasoning is based upon his idea of God. Throughout this passage he emphasizes the grace of God. Grace means the attitude of free giving on God's part, God taking the initiative in bestowing redemption upon mankind. Faith is man's adventure in co-operation with the grace of God. Chapter *5 is an eloquent presentation of Paul's doctrine that "grace reigns through righteousness unto eternal life through Jesus Christ our Lord" by faith in whom the Christian is justified and has peace with God. The moral consequences of such faith are splendidly stated in *6:12 ff., 23. Paul reaches the climax of his argument in chapters 7 f., which are a sort of spiritual autobiography. In chapter *7 he depicts the inward conflict experienced in the search for righteousness through the law, which gives knowledge of the right but does not impart inner power to do the right. That such power is released by faith in Christ is the theme of chapter *8, which ranks with 1 Cor. 13 in beauty and power.

Rom. 9 ff. deals with the relation of Judaism and Christianity. Why the Jews should have repudiated Christianity was a problem which troubled Paul and apparently troubled those to whom he was writing in Rome.

Rom. *12:1–15:13 is a full and strong presentation of Paul's ethical teachings. It portrays the type of life which follows upon faith in Christ.[26]

Rom. 16 was probably no part of Paul's letter to Rome for in a place where he had never been he could hardly have known all the people it mentions. It was doubtless a separate letter (like Philemon and about as long), written probably at Corinth, commending Phoebe to the Christians in Ephesus where Paul was extensively acquainted.

The Imprisonment Epistles. 1. *Philemon.* We have already examined the structure of Philemon [27] and have stated the nature of its contents.[28] It is the briefest letter we have from Paul but one of the most significant ethically.

---

[23] Hab. 2:4; *vid. supra,* pp. 303 f., 343.
[24] Rom. 2:6, 10 f.   [25] Rom. 3:20.
[26] On Romans, cf. Scott, *op. cit.,* pp. 154–169.
[27] *Supra,* p. 583.   [28] *Supra,* p. 560.

2. *Colossians.* Paul did not introduce Christianity at Colossae, which lies about a hundred miles east of Ephesus, nor had he ever visited the Christian group there. His reason for writing to them was that he had heard, through Epaphras (1:7), of certain heretical teachings which were disturbing their faith in Christ. This heretical teaching seems to have been that Christ was only one among a host of cosmic powers, all of whom should be reverenced and worshiped, especially by observing legalistic requirements. Paul met this heresy by stating the cosmic significance of Christ (*1:9–23), viz., that he is supreme above all things in the heavens and on the earth. Paul exposes the errors of this heresy (2:8–23) and urges their firm faith in Christ (*3:1–4). There is a fine passage of ethical teachings (3:5–4:6).[29]

3. *Ephesians.* The Epistle to the Ephesians is one of the problem books of the New Testament.[30] The words "at Ephesus" are no part of 1:1 according to the oldest and best of the Greek manuscripts. Some interpreters hold that it was a circular letter with a blank space left in the salutation which was to be filled in with the name of the church to which it was given by the messenger delivering it. In Col. 4:16 Paul mentions that he had written a letter to Laodicea, with which the Colossians should exchange their letter. The letter to Laodicea has perished unless, as some interpreters maintain, Ephesians is that letter.[31] The real heart of the problem, however, is the great likeness of Ephesians to Colossians both in thought and in emphasis, and this leads some scholars to hold that Ephesians was written by someone later than Paul and based upon Colossians as a model. Professor E. J. Goodspeed suggests that some church leader in the last decade of the first century collected the letters of Paul and caused them to be copied and circulated together as a unit, and this leader composed what is now Ephesians as an introductory covering letter for the whole group, in the same way as Rev. 1:4–20 is an introductory letter covering the entire collection of seven separate letters to the seven churches in Asia (Rev. 2 f.).[32] According to such a view, Eph. 1:1 would be construed as the title of the collected letters of Paul, "Paul to God's people who are steadfast in Christ Jesus" (Goodspeed's translation); or, "Paul to the saints who are faithful in Jesus Christ" (Moffatt's translation).

Chapters 1 ff. set forth a high Christology, which concludes with a beautiful prayer (*3:14–19). 4:1–16 presents a doctrine of the church

---

[29] On Colossians, cf. Scott, *op. cit.,* pp. 173–176.

[30] Scott, *op. cit.,* pp. 179–185, discusses Ephesians and the problems it presents.

[31] Professor E. J. Goodspeed, however, identifies Philemon as the letter to Laodicea. Cf. his *An Introduction to the New Testament* (Chicago: 1937), pp. 109–124.

[32] Cf. E. J. Goodspeed, *New Solutions of New Testament Problems* (Chicago: 1928); also *The Meaning of Ephesians* (Chicago: 1933).

as the body of Christ.[33] 4:17–6:9 is a passage of ethical teachings and *6:10–20 is a noble exhortation to Christian steadfastness.

4. *Philippians.* Philippi was the first city on the continent of Europe where Paul planted Christianity.[34] There appears to have been a deeper intimacy between Paul and the Philippians than was the case with any other group. More than once they sent Paul gifts of money to supply his need and sustain his work (Phil. 4:15 ff.).[35] When Paul was in prison (chapter 1), the Philippians sent him another gift by Epaphroditus (4:10, 18). Epaphroditus became ill when with Paul, and as soon as he recovered Paul sent him back to Philippi (2:25–30) and this letter with him. Paul seems to be near the end of life (1:19–24). The Philippians have themselves been undergoing trials (1:27–2:18). Paul bitterly denounces certain "dogs" who have been troubling the group at Philippi (chapter 3); perhaps they were such Judaizers as made trouble also in Galatia. *3:7–16 and *4:4–13 are passages of great beauty.[36]

The Pastoral Epistles. 1 and 2 Timothy and Titus are commonly designated the Pastoral Epistles. They are among the problem books of the New Testament.[37] If the apostle Paul himself wrote them, he did so between the time when he arrived in Rome a prisoner and died in Rome a martyr, and that period of Paul's life is obscure, for Luke tells next to nothing about it in Acts 28. An alternative view is that they were written toward the end of the first century, long after Paul's death, being expansions of certain genuine Pauline fragments which had survived and which are incorporated in the Pastorals. For example, 2 Tim. 4:6–18 reflects Paul's situation as a prisoner not long before his final condemnation. Titus reads like a condensed form of 1 Timothy.

The Pastorals imply a type of Christian ecclesiastical organization (1 Tim. 3; Tit. 1) quite different from the more free and diversified Christian brotherhood reflected in the undisputed letters of Paul.[38] There is much warning against heretics (1 Tim. 4; 2 Tim. 3:1–4:4; Tit. 1). It was toward the end of the first century that conflict with heresy consolidated Christianity into an ecclesiastical organization. Gems of thought in the Pastorals are 1 Tim. *4:4 f.; *6:6–12, 17 ff.; 2 Tim. *2:15, 22–25; *3:14–17.

---

[33] Cf. Eph. 1:23.
[34] Acts 16:11–40; *vid. supra,* p. 574.
[35] Cf. 2 Cor. 11:9.
[36] On Philippians, cf. Scott, *op. cit.,* pp. 186–190.
[37] Scott, *op. cit.,* pp. 191–197 discusses the problem of the Pastoral Epistles.
[38] *Vid. supra,* p. 535.

The Christian Wisdom Book of James

In previous chapters we have devoted much attention to the place and importance of wisdom teaching in Judaism.[39] This wisdom interest passed over into Christianity. It was this type of interest which first prompted the collecting of the sayings of Jesus.[40] Toward the end of the first century, James, a Christian wisdom teacher, wrote a compendium of wisdom teachings as he had been accustomed to present those teachings in his sermons, for he was also a Christian preacher.

Three sources shaped the thought and style of James. (1) James was well acquainted with the Jewish wisdom literature, particularly the book of Sira.[41] (2) James echoes in a remarkable way the Sermon on the Mount.[42] (3) James understood the Hellenistic type of mind and employed the Hellenistic diatribe style in his sermons.[43]

We have had occasion to call attention to the presence throughout the Mediterranean world of the traveling philosophic teachers.[44] These simple, earnest men were actuated by a sincere devotion to the moral welfare of plain people. What they preached was Stoic ethics. They were street-corner preachers, and their style of address is known as the Cynic-Stoic diatribe. An appreciation of that style may be gained from the discourses of Epictetus.[45] Christian preachers also sought to reach and influence plain people, and adopted and adapted the prevailing type of popular address in order to teach the Christian way of life.

The book of James probably originated somewhere in the North Mediterranean world about the end of the first century. 1:1 was probably added by a later hand to give the whole a semblance of epistolary character. The "Dispersion" mentioned in 1:1 was probably intended to mean the spiritual Diaspora, i.e., the Christians, who were regarded as the new Israel; hence the book was intended for all Christians everywhere. There is no epistolary ending whatever.[46]

[39] Vid. supra, pp. 398 f., 402–406, 434 ff., 458–461, 493.
[40] Vid. supra, p. 497.
[41] Cf. 1:2 ff., 12 with Sir. 2:1–2; 1:5 with Sir. 18:18; 1:6, 8 with Sir. 1:28; 2:12 f.; 5:9; 1:9 with Sir. 3:18; 1:12 with Sir. 15:6, 1:13 ff. with Sir. 15:11 f., 20; 1:19 with Sir. 5:11; 1:23 with Sir. 12:11; 2:1–6 with Sir. 10:22 ff.; 3:2 with Sir. 19:16; 3:13–17 with Sir. 19:18–22; 4:6 with Sir. 10:7; 5:2 f. with Sir. 29:10; 5:5 with Sir. 27:13; 5:14 f. with Sir. 38:9–15. Also cf. 2:23 with Wisd. 7:27; 4:14 with Wisd. 2:4; 5:6 with Wisd. 2:12, 20.
[42] Cf. the beatitude form in 1:12 and cf. 1:20 with Matt. 5:22; 1:22 with Matt. 7:24–27; 2:5 with Matt. 5:3 and Lk. 6:20; 2:8 with Matt. 7:12 (also 19:19; 22:39); 2:10 with Matt. 5:19; 2:13 with Matt. 5:17; 2:18 with Matt. 7:16 f.; 3:12 with Matt. 7:16; 4:4b with Matt. 6:24; 4:11 ff. with Matt. 7:1–5; 5:10 with Matt. 5:12; 5:11 with Matt. 5:10; 5:12 with Matt. 5:34–37.
[43] Cf. 2:18; 3:8; 4:13, 15; 5:1.
[44] Vid. supra, pp. 498 f.
[45] Cf. W. A. Oldfather, Epictetus (Loeb Classical Library) (New York: 1926).
[46] On James, cf. Scott, op. cit., pp. 209–216.

Literature from a Time of Persecution

From the very beginning, Christianity met with opposition. There were numerous local outbursts against Christians principally on the part of Jews, such as those in Jerusalem which led to the martyrdom of Stephen,[47] of James the brother of John,[48] of James the brother of Jesus,[49] and the imprisonment of Peter.[50] Paul himself was a persecutor of the Christians before his conversion, and in the course of his missionary labors he aroused opposition which brought upon him imprisonment, the lash, stoning, and beating with rods.[51] Nero persecuted the Christians of Rome,[52] and there was a more widespread persecution under Domitian [53] and subsequent emperors.

Hebrews. That Hebrews was addressed to a situation in which Christians were suffering oppression is plain from 10:32–39; 12:2–11. Hebrews is designated an epistle, but there is nothing epistolary about it except the very end (13:22 ff.). It stands quite apart from all the other New Testament literature by the character of its Greek, its polished diction, and the nature of its thought. It is in the manner of oratory and probably was the sermon of a Christian preacher who, when he found he could not deliver it in person, appended greetings and sent it as a letter to the group for whom it was intended.[54]

The name of the author is unknown but judging from the contents of the book he was a Christian of Jewish antecedents, well acquainted with Alexandrian philosophical learning of the Philonic type,[55] thoroughly Hellenized, a man of literary culture. The concluding greeting, "The brethren from Italy salute you," [56] indicates that he was one of a group, perhaps of Roman Christians, who at the time were away from Italy, and it implies that the congregation for which the sermon was intended was somewhere in Italy, perhaps at Rome. It was written *circa* 85.

In order to understand the religious attitude of this author it is well to remind ourselves of the five main aspects which have always characterized religion.[57] For one type of mind, one phase of religion is pre-eminent; for another, another. For the author of Hebrews the ritual and priestly side of early Christianity were all important. He interprets Christ as "a merciful and faithful high priest in things pertaining to God . . . named of God a high priest after the order

---

[47] Acts 6:8–8:1.
[48] Acts 12:1 ff.
[49] *Vid. supra*, p. 553.
[50] Acts 4:1–22; 12:1–19.
[51] 2 Cor. 11:23 ff.
[52] *Vid. supra*, p. 547.
[53] *Vid. supra*, p. 548.
[54] Marks of its sermonic character are observable in 2:5; 6:9; 8:1; 11:32; 13:22.
[55] Cf. especially 1:1–4; 2:8–11. He might even have known Philo who wrote between A.D. 15 and 45. *Vid. supra*, pp. 463 ff.
[56] Heb. 13:24.
[57] *Vid. supra*, p. 116.

of Melchizedek." [58] He interprets Christ as the supreme and final
revelation of God to men (*1:1–4), and in a long dissertation he
compares Christianity with Judaism to show that Christianity super-
cedes and fulfills Judaism (1:5–10:18). Christ is interpreted not
only as high priest but as himself the sacrifice which effects eternal
redemption (9:14, 26). In what is one of the Bible's classic chapters
he urges his readers to a steadfast and energetic Christian faith
(*11:1–12:2).

Apparently the Christians addressed in this sermon had grown
sluggish (10:35) for the author seeks to stir them up to display
again such zealous leadership as once before they had shown in a
time of oppression (10:32–39).[59]

Revelation.   Revelation is the greatest of apocalypses. Apocalyptic
was a type of literature called forth by persecution.[60] Daniel, the
prototype of the apocalypses, arose at the time of the Maccabean
revolt when Epiphanes was trying to destroy Judaism and force all
Jews to adopt Hellenistic religion.[61] The destruction of the city of
Jerusalem by the Romans in 70 called forth the apocalypse known
as Second Baruch.[62] 4 Ezra (2 Esdras) arose in Palestine in the
time of Domitian's reign (81–96),[63] and it was then also that Revelation arose in Asia Minor (1:9). The exact title of the book is "The
Apocalypse of Jesus Christ" (1:1) but it is commonly called "The
Apocalypse (Revelation) of John" after its author.[64]

Chapter 13 is a piece of apocalyptic which arose in the time of
Nero's persecution and was incorporated into the later and larger
book. Chapter 17 evidences the time of Domitian. 6:9 f.; 17:6; 20:4
state Christians were suffering martyrdom. Rome is spoken of by
the cryptic name of Babylon the Harlot,[65] and the emperors are
alluded to as beasts.[66] The several references to the worship of the
image of the beast make quite plain what the persecution was about,
viz., the refusal of the Christians to submit to emperor worship.[67]

We have already explained the component ideas which make up
the apocalyptic thought pattern.[68] Revelation fits into that pattern.
The material is presented in a series of seven visions (1:9–3:22;
4:1–8:1; 8:2–11:18; 11:19–14:20; 15:1–19:10; 19:11–20:15; 21:1–
22:5). The purpose of the Apocalypse was to encourage Christians
to remain steadfastly loyal to the faith and endure the persecution

[58] Heb. 2:17; 5:10.
[59] On Hebrews, cf. Scott, *op. cit.*, pp. 198–208.
[60] On the characteristics of apocalyptic as a literary type, *vid. supra*, pp. 369 f.,
427 ff., 442 ff.
[61] *Vid. supra*, pp. 426 ff.   [62] *Vid. supra*, pp. 454 f.
[63] *Vid. supra*, pp. 455 f.
[64] The book itself gives no hint as to who this John was.
[65] Rev. 17:5.   [66] Rev. 17:9–13.
[67] Rev. 13:14 f.; 14:9, 11; 15:2; 16:2; 19:20; 20:4.
[68] *Supra*, pp. 443 ff., 507–510.

(*2:10), for they are assured of an eternal redemption (*7:14–17; *21:3 f.). As a world view, apocalyptic stresses two ideas: the ultimate overthrow of evil and the ultimate triumph of righteousness. In Revelation, the concrete embodiment of evil is Rome and the doom of Rome is portrayed in a passage of lyric grandeur (*18) comparable to Ezekiel's "Lament over Tyre" (Ezk. 27), and to the "Doom of Babylon" in Isa. 14. Even more gripping is the portrayal of the complete triumph of Christ and the judgment (*19 f.). The faith which girded the Christians to endure persecution was their profound and ardent conviction that "the kingdom of the world is become the kingdom of our Lord and of his Christ: and he shall reign forever and ever" (11:15). This faith inspires the author to conclude with the most rapturous vision of all, the consummation of the kingdom of God in the holy city, new Jerusalem (*21:1–22:5).

One striking feature of the genius of Christianity is disclosed in Revelation. The Christians went through that fiery trial of persecution singing. The book is punctuated throughout with songs which are sung in heaven which plainly must be understood to be hymns of the faith sung by the Christian groups in their worship.[69]

As literature, Revelation is highly imaginative and dramatic. It abounds in figures and images which are vivid, to which one frequently finds allusions in English literature.[70]

First Peter. The situation which we sense in 1 Peter is an organized persecution which is a "fiery trial" (4:12), widespread throughout the world (5:9). The specific area of persecution with which this epistle deals is the northern part of Asia Minor, the provinces of "Pontus, Galatia, Cappadocia, Asia, and Bithynia" (1:1). *4:12–19 makes plain what the persecution is about, viz., the Christians are persecuted just because they are Christians. Such a situation does not fit the time of Nero, for his persecution, while savage enough, was localized in Rome and his motive was to make the Christians scapegoats for the burning of Rome.[71] The persecution of 93–96 under Domitian did spread to the provinces and was directed against the Christians for their refusal to submit to emperor worship.[72] Revelation displayed a contemptuous attitude toward the emperor, but not 1 Peter; "Honor all men. Love the brotherhood. Fear God. Honor the king." [73] This makes a nice distinction. The Christians refused to perform emperor worship because from their point of view it dishonored God. In the eyes of the Romans, their refusal

---

[69] Cf. Rev. 4:8, 11; 5:12, 13; 7:10, 12; 11:15, 17 f.; 12:10 ff.; 15:3 f.; 19:1 f., 5, 6 ff.; vid. supra, pp. 526 f.
[70] Cf. 1:14 ff.; 3:8, 15, 20; 4:3, 6; 6:12–15; 7:13; 8:10; 9:7–10; 10:1; 11:4; 12:1–4, 14 ff.; 14:2, 15, 17–20; 17:3; 21:10–13, 18–21; 22:2. On Revelation cf. Scott, op. cit., pp. 274–284.   [71] Vid. supra, p. 547.
[72] Vid. supra, pp. 548, 591.   [73] 1 Pet. 2:17.

dishonored the emperor. 1 Peter's advice to "honor the king" was an attitude in harmony with Paul's teaching in Rom. 13:1–7 and was intended to save the Christians from seeming treachery toward the Roman government. Many scholars date 1 Peter in the reign of Domitian but some find a later date in the reign of Trajan even more fitting.[74] The basis of this view is the harmony between the picture 1 Peter presents and that presented in Pliny the Younger's famous letter about the Christians to the emperor Trajan (x, 16). In both alike their pagan neighbors are informers (2:12) against the Christians, not for crimes but for being Christians.

The basic aim of 1 Peter was to encourage Christians to remain steadfast in their Christian faith in a situation of oppression (*1:3–9). The whole epistle reads very much like an early Christian sermon addressed particularly to gentile converts to the Christian faith, who are "newborn babes" (2:2) coming to the Lord (2:4), who called them "out of darkness into his marvelous light, who in time past were no people but now are the people of God" (2:9 f.). The sermon falls into two principal divisions; 1:13–2:10 expounds the nature of Christian faith, hope, love, and righteousness; 2:11–5:11 sets forth the principles of Christian living. Addressed as it is to plain people, it presents Christianity in simple terms as a way of living.

If it was originally a sermon, 1 Peter was subsequently cast into epistolary form. "She that is in Babylon saluteth you" (5:13) probably means the Christian church in Rome. The authorship of this sermon or letter is one of the knotty problems of New Testament interpretation since it fits a situation so long subsequent to the death of the apostle Peter.[75]

Literature Directed Against Heresy

The Epistles of John.   These three small books are by the same author, who refers to himself as "the elder" in 2 Jn. 1 and 3 Jn. 1 but nowhere gives his name. 2 John and 3 John are real letters, quite in the style of many of the nonliterary papyri which have survived. 1 John has no epistolary beginning or ending but the author makes it quite explicit that he is writing.[76]

1. *First John.* 1 John is a miscellany of meditations not arranged in any systematic order. The object of the author is to condemn and correct certain heretical views which have led to a schism in his church (2:19). One such view was that of the docetists (seemists)

---

[74] The argument for dating 1 Pet. in Trajan's reign has been newly presented by D. W. Riddle, *Early Christian Life* (Chicago: 1936), pp. 144–153.
[75] For a discussion of 1 Peter, cf. Scott, *op. cit.,* pp. 217–223.
[76] 1:4; 2:1, 7 f., 12 ff., 26; 5:13.

who held that Jesus did not have a real physical body but only "seemed" to have one; therefore he could not suffer physically because he was a spirit-person. Such heretics minimized Jesus' death on the cross. The author condemns this view (2:22; 4:2 f.; 5:5). Another heretical view was perfectionism, the arrogant claim of certain Christians to be without sin (1:8 ff.). Another heresy was libertinism, i.e., the freedom to sin (3:3–10). All this heresy was an incipient type of Gnosticism. Gnosticism comes from the Greek word *gnosis* which means "knowledge." Such heretics justified their vagaries of behavior and belief on the basis of an alleged inner illumination, or esoteric knowledge, by reason of which they thought themselves to be superior Christians. In the second century Gnosticism worked considerable havoc in Christianity. In 1 John the reader notes the repeated use of the word "know" and especially the phrase "hereby we know" (2:3, 5; 3:16, 19, 24; 4:2, 6, 13; 5:2). In this way the author sought to set forth the tests of what he deemed to be true Christianity. Genuine inward spiritual illumination always leads to outward ethical conduct (*2:3; *3:1 ff.) and to sincere love for other Christians (*4:7–21).

2. *Second John.* 2 John is a brief letter addressed to "the elect lady," most probably meaning a certain church, warning against the heretics (vs. 7) and advising that they not be given a welcome or a hearing (vs. 10).

3. *Third John.* 3 John is addressed to an elder named Gaius, commending him for siding with the orthodox Christians (vss. 5–8) and complaining against a bishop named Diotrephes because he would not welcome or heed the visiting orthodox Christians.

Here is plainly revealed a situation in which certain Christian churches are at odds with one another. It happened probably early in the second century somewhere in Asia Minor.[77]

Jude and Second Peter. These two epistles have so much in common that they manifestly originated in the same sort of situation. Judging from the internal evidence, Second Peter (especially chapter 2) is an expansion of Jude, with adaptation to a somewhat later time and a larger circle of readers. They originated in the second century, and were directed against the heresy of Gnosticism.

1. *Jude.* Jude and James (vs. 1) were very common names. This Jude makes it plain that he writes at a time long subsequent to the beginning of Christianity (vss. 3, 17 f.). He contents himself with denouncing the heretics, some of whom he hopes may be saved (vs. 23). The thought in this epistle is on a plane very much inferior to

[77] On the Johannine epistles, cf. Scott, *op. cit.,* pp. 260–273.

the rest of the New Testament. Vss. 12 f. are packed with metaphors of interest from a literary standpoint. The closing benediction (vss. 24 f.) is the one beautiful thought in the epistle.

2. *Second Peter.* 2 Peter is pseudepigraphic,[78] put out in the name of the apostle Simon Peter. The author, however, makes it entirely plain that he lives and writes at a time long after the fathers who founded Christianity have died (3:1–4). This letter is one of several spurious books put out in the name of Peter; there was a *Gospel of Peter,* a *Preaching of Peter,* an *Acts of Peter,* and an *Apocalypse of Peter.*[79] This 2 Peter had a hard time to get into the Bible at all. There are some branches of the Christian church which never would accept it, and there are high-minded scholars today who think that it ought to be removed from the Bible. Its readers are urged to hold fast the faith (chapter 1) and reject heresy (chapter 2). The author also restates the doctrine of Christ's coming again, which had passed out of vogue (chapter 3). *1:5 ff. is a choice passage of Christian ethics.

Jude and 2 Peter have a historical value in that they reflect the age in which Christianity was consolidating into an ecclesiastical organization, and they reveal what it was that stimulated that consolidation, viz., the conflict with heretics. Christianity originated in a diversified manner among numerous local groups of spirit-filled and spirit-guided men. It was in the nature of the case that some groups might be erratic and tend to excess. In such a situation it became evident that there must be a definition of common Christianity. These latest books of the New Testament leave us in the midst of that situation.

The Canonizing of the New Testament

The foregoing survey has made us conscious of the existence of the several New Testament books as separate pieces of literature. How did it come about that these writings were gathered into a single collection known as the New Testament, and how did these writings come to be esteemed as Holy Scripture?

The Collection of Paul's Letters (*circa* 90). The letters of Paul are the oldest stratum of literature in the New Testament. They were written as occasion required and sent to their destinations, where they remained, scattered in communities across the North Mediterranean world from Asia Minor to Rome. Paul was

---

[78] On the nature of pseudepigraphy, *cf. supra,* p. 437.
[79] Cf. M. R. James, *The Apocryphal New Testament* (Oxford: 1924).

not consciously writing Holy Scripture. He was writing to Christian groups, he expected that his letters would be read in the meetings of the groups to which they were sent, and he directed that certain neighboring groups exchange letters.[80]

A given group probably reread its letter many times in successive meetings in order to make sure they understood Paul's meaning. In those same meetings they read the Old Testament Scriptures in the Septuagint Version. Thereby was fashioned in their minds an association of ideas which began the process that culminated in the esteeming of Paul's letters as themselves sacred literature.[81]

Paul died *circa* 64. Twenty-five years later there appeared the monumental work of Luke-Acts which depicts Paul as the heroic figure in the spread of Christianity but strikingly enough does not evidence any acquaintance with Paul's letters. Acts undoubtedly heightened the esteem in which Paul was held and stimulated a fresh enthusiasm for what he had accomplished. It also suggested to some unidentified Christian the idea of gathering together such letters of Paul as could be found among the various churches he had established and making copies of the entire collection to circulate among the churches.[82]

It is easy to see how this worked out, for in Rev. 1:4–3:22 there is a collection of seven letters of John, composed as a collection and sent as a collection to each of the churches; i.e., each church had not only the letter bearing its own name but all the others as well. This is exactly analogous to the circulating of the collected letters of Paul among the churches.[83]

---

[80] Cf. Col. 4:16.   [81] *Vid. supra*, p. 528.

[82] That unidentified Christian would have had to start with the knowledge that Paul had written letters, and there is nothing in Acts to suggest that Paul had done so. A reasonable case for identifying him as Onesimus can be made out. He certainly would have known about the letter to Philemon (vs. 10) and about the letter to the Colossians (cf. Col. 4:9 and note the identity of the persons mentioned in these two letters; cf. Col. 1:1; 4:10, 14 f., with Philem. 1 f., 23 f.). Possibly he also knew about Romans, if, as is commonly held, it was in Rome that Onesimus was converted by Paul (Philem. 10) and served Paul (Philem. 13). He would have had some contact with the church at Rome. Col. 4:16 contained all the suggestion necessary that Paul had written other letters besides. The Acts narrative would have directed him to all the places to which Paul wrote letters, Rome, Corinth, Thessalonica, Philippi, Ephesus, and the cities of Galatia. Unless he otherwise knew of the existence of the letters to Philemon and to the Colossians, nothing in Acts would have suggested seeking for them. On Goodspeed's theory that Eph. was composed as an introductory covering letter for the entire Pauline corpus when that corpus was published, Onesimus would have been likely to write just that sort of letter. He knew Col. most thoroughly (cf. Col. 4:9) and composed Eph. on the basis of Col., which explains the otherwise perplexing similarity between Col. and Eph. If, as some suggest, Eph. is that missing letter to the Laodiceans, Onesimus would have been sure to get hold of it. And if Eph. was a genuine letter of Paul sent to Ephesus in the first instance, Onesimus could not have missed locating it there. Cf. Edgar J. Goodspeed, *Christianity Goes to Press* (New York: 1940), pp. 49–59.

[83] The collection of the seven letters of John may have been suggested by the corpus of Paul's collected letters. So E. J. Goodspeed, *The Formation of the New Testament* (Chicago: 1926), pp. 22 f.

Churches which came into possession of copies of this Pauline collection now had a book of distinctly Christian literature which they read at their meetings in connection with the reading of the Old Testament Scriptures. It came to pass in time (certainly by the middle of the second century) that the two were esteemed on a par, i.e., that Paul's letters were regarded as inspired and therefore Holy Scripture. 2 Pet. 3:16 (written *circa* 150) refers to the Pauline corpus, "all his epistles," in connection with "the other Scriptures."

The Fourfold Gospel (*circa* 125). Knowledge of the career and teachings of Jesus was in the beginning transmitted orally. When the impulse to put the story of Jesus into writing arose, many took in hand to draw up such narratives.[84] The process by which those many were reduced to four was traced at the beginning of Chapter 24.[85] Each of the four was produced for the benefit of the community where it arose, Mark at Rome, Matthew at Antioch, Luke at Antioch or Ephesus,[86] John at Ephesus. The Fourth Gospel was the latest to arise (*circa* 100–110), and the motive to produce it seems to have been to reinterpret Jesus to the Greek world. It was the Gospel of the Hellenists.[87]

There could not be many gospels. The gospel was one. Nevertheless four gospels were in existence and apparently were well known. Not long after the Fourth Gospel appeared, the idea occurred to some unidentified Christian to publish all four as a unity, which was done, probably *circa* 125.[88] The combination was made just as it appears in our Bibles today; The Gospel:—According to Matthew, According to Mark, According to Luke, According to John. This of course necessitated detaching the gospel half from Luke's great book, Luke-Acts.

2 Peter reflects a knowledge and use of the fourfold Gospel by the author of that epistle (*circa* 150). Other Christian literature which arose around the middle of the second century, but is not included in the New Testament, similarly reflects acquaintance with the fourfold Gospel.[89]

Like the collection of Paul's letters, this fourfold Gospel was also read in the churches, along with the reading of the Old Testament Scriptures, and this is what prompted the appreciation of the Gospel as Holy Scripture just as it did the Epistles of Paul.

---

[84] Cf. Lk. 1:1.
[85] *Vid. supra*, pp. 483–486.
[86] Scholars differ regarding the provenance of Luke but the choice seems to lie between these two places.
[87] This is the title of the late Professor B. W. Bacon's posthumous treatise on the Fourth Gospel (New York: 1933).
[88] Cf. Goodspeed, *The Formation of the New Testament*, pp. 33–41.
[89] *Ibid.*, p. 37.

This process making for canonization, which began in New Testament times and is reflected in the New Testament itself, continued. The rest of the story is found in noncanonical Christian literature which arose in the second century and later.

The Canon of Marcion (144). Marcion, a native of Sinope in Pontus, Asia Minor, visited Rome in 140 and there came under the influence of Gnostic teachings. He felt that Christianity was too Jewish, that the Jewish Scriptures had no proper place in Christianity and that they should be removed. Not being able to bring the Roman church to his view, he withdrew in 144 and organized his followers into a separate church. The use of the Jewish Scriptures by Christians, he had sense enough to see, could not simply be uprooted; it had to be displaced. It was Marcion's brilliant idea that there should be a body of Christian Scriptures to substitute for the Jewish Scriptures. So he made such a collection to suit his purpose, choosing the Gospel of Luke and ten letters of Paul, viz., Galatians, 1 and 2 Corinthians, Romans, 1 and 2 Thessalonians, Laodiceans (which is what he called Ephesians), Colossians, Philippians, and Philemon.

Marcion's influence spread for a time but his movement finally came to an end. Nevertheless, to him belongs the credit for definitely starting a movement for official canonization of Christian Scriptures. If not the books he selected, then which ones should be in a canon? [90]

The Muratorian Canon (*circa* 200). During the second century a number of heretical sects sprang up within Christianity. This had the effect of precipitating the consolidation of the nonsectarian, or general, or catholic, churches under the leadership of the church at Rome. This catholic Christianity claimed for itself apostolic authority. This claim in turn precipitated the formation of a canon of Christian Scriptures that were of apostolic origin or authorization.

In the year 1740, L. A. Muratori discovered in a manuscript at Milan (written *circa* 800) a list of the books in use at Rome *circa* 200. The author of the list may have been Victor, who was bishop of Rome at that time. The list represents a collection of collections. The fourfold Gospel stands first. Next comes the Book of Acts, which is called "Acts of All the Apostles" and serves to bind the fourfold Gospel with the Pauline Epistles, which come next. The list of Pauline epistles not only has the ten which Marcion chose, but the three pastorals as well; i.e., the Muratorian canon has all thirteen so-called Epistles of Paul which are in our English Bible, although the order in which they are listed differs from that in our

[90] On Marcion, cf. Goodspeed, *The Formation of the New Testament*, pp. 42–49.

English Bible.[91] The Muratorian list includes Jude and 1 and 2 John, thereby attesting the beginning of the group known as the Catholic Epistles or the General Epistles. The list also includes the Revelation of John and two other apocalypses with remarks, viz., the Revelation of Peter, with the comment, "which some reject," and the statement that "The Shepherd of Hermas may be read but not publicly in church." Apparently there existed a tendency to form a collection of apocalypses which ultimately did not succeed. Interestingly enough, the Muratorian list contains the Wisdom of Solomon.

This Muratorian list is evidence that at the end of the second century the canon of New Testament Scriptures was settled with respect to the Gospels, Acts, and the Pauline Epistles. The area of the general epistles and of apocalypses was still debatable.

By the end of the second century also, the expression "New Testament" had been coined. It was first used by an unnamed writer in A.D. 192 in a tract against certain heretics.[92]

The Canon of Origen (*circa* 250). Attention has already been called to the important place which the city of Alexandria held in Christianity at the end of the second century.[93] We recall that the Jews of Alexandria were more liberal and inclusive with respect to the books which they included in the Hagiographa than were the Palestinian Jews.[94] Analogously, the Christians of Alexandria were more inclusive than the Christians of Rome with respect to the books which they regarded as making up the New Testament. This is apparent from the New Testament books which are reflected in the writings of Clement of Alexandria (*circa* 150–216), head of the Christian school at Alexandria from 200 to 202, and his successor as head of the school, Origen (*circa* 185–254).[95]

Origen gives careful attention to the books of the New Testament. He formulates two lists of books, those which are "acknowledged" and those which are "disputed." By "acknowledged" he means that he understands they are accepted by everybody; he lists twenty-two such books. By "disputed" he means books which he himself accepts but frankly admits that some others do not; there are seven of them.

The very oldest Greek New Testament in existence today is the *Codex Sinaiticus* (ℵ), now in the British Museum.[96] It was written about the middle of the fourth century, either at Alexandria or at Caesarea. It contains twenty-nine books, the very same books which

---

[91] The order is: 1 and 2 Cor., Eph., Phil., Col., Gal., 1 and 2 Thess., Rom., Philem., Tit., 1 and 2 Tim.
[92] Cf. Eusebius, *Church History*, v, 16:3.
[93] *Supra*, pp. 580 f.   [94] *Vid. supra*, pp. 429 f.
[95] Details regarding the N. T. books reflected in Clement and in Origen are given by Goodspeed, *The Formation of the New Testament*, pp. 80–97.
[96] *Vid. infra*, pp. 602 f.

Origen accepted as making up his New Testament.[97] Of the twenty-nine books in it, twenty-seven are the books of the canonical New Testament in our English Bible today, though in a different sequence.[98] The other two are the letter of Barnabas and the Shepherd of Hermas (an apocalypse).

That Origen should have called certain books "disputed" reveals to us just where the borderline of the canon lay in the first half of the third century. Some of the books had not yet gotten safely over the border. Origen's disputed books were James, 2 Peter, 2 and 3 John, Jude, Barnabas, and the Shepherd of Hermas. Barnabas and Hermas did not ultimately secure a place in the canon. Otherwise Origen's idea of the limits of the canon was that which finally came to pass.

The Canon of Eusebius (*circa* 325). One of the most famous Christians of the early centuries was Eusebius (*circa* 260–*circa* 340), bishop of Caesarea in Palestine. About 325 he produced his monumental *Church History* which is still extant. He discussed the New Testament books under three categories, "accepted," "disputed," and "rejected" books. The combination of the books he lists as accepted with those he lists as disputed makes up the roll of the twenty-seven books which finally did constitute the New Testament canon. The books he calls disputed are James, Jude, 2 Peter, 2 and 3 John. He lists Revelation as accepted "if it seem proper." [99]

The Canon of Athanasius (367). Athanasius (*circa* 295–373), bishop of Alexandria, wrote an Easter letter to the churches of his diocese in the year 367 in which he discussed the books of Scripture. The books he enumerates as making up the inspired Scriptures of the New Testament are the twenty-seven books as we know them, although he lists them in a different sequence.[100] "Let no one add to them or take away aught of them." [101]

After the time of Athanasius, opinion fluctuated regarding the right of Hebrews, Revelation, and the Catholic Epistles to be in the canon. Doubt about Revelation prevailed in the Eastern or Greek churches. It was the West that was doubtful about Hebrews. In both quarters alike there were those who felt uncertainty about the Catholic

---

[97] Origen taught at Alexandria until 231 or 232, when he was deposed, whereupon he went to Caesarea and established a Christian school there.

[98] The order is the same as in our English Bible except that Acts does not come until after Philemon and Hebrews comes between 2 Thess. and 1 Tim. Barnabas and the Shepherd of Hermas come after Revelation.

[99] Concerning Eusebius, cf. Goodspeed, *The Formation of the New Testament*, pp. 98–105.

[100] The catholic, or general, epistles follow Acts and precede the Pauline epistles. Heb. is listed with the Pauline epistles between 2 Thess. and 1 Tim.

[101] On Athanasius, cf. Goodspeed, *The Formation of the New Testament*, pp. 106–113.

Epistles.[102] But practically, the list of Athanasius settled the question. *Circa* 400 St. Jerome produced his Latin translation of the Bible known as the *Vulgate,* and he included in his New Testament the books of the Athanasian list. Thousands of manuscript copies of the Latin Bible have survived to the present and they attest the fact that for Western, or Latin, Christendom the limits of the New Testament had been settled by Athanasius in his festal letter of 367.

The Nature of a New Testament Book

The books of the New Testament were written in Greek and undoubtedly were first written upon papyrus.[103] A glance at 2 John and 3 John will give an impression of about how much matter could be written on a single sheet. For longer writings, sheets were pasted together to form a roll. The rubbish heaps of Egypt have yielded up thousands of nonliterary papyri in Greek, written in the early centuries of the Christian era. The kind of Greek in these papyri is known as the *Koine* and is the same as in the New Testament; i.e., the New Testament was written in the everyday language of the plain people of the first century. Only a few of these papyri are Bible fragments. In 1897 a papyrus sheet of the Gospel of Matthew, as old as the second century, was discovered. In 1934 there came to light a papyrus leaf containing a fragment of the Gospel of John, written before 150.[104] The Chester Beatty Papyri of the University of Michigan, found in 1930, are fragments of a beautiful uncial Greek Bible copied before 250.[105] No entire New Testament book written on papyrus has yet been found.[106]

At the beginning of the fourth century the use of parchment came into favor, especially for books which were to be preserved permanently. With the use of parchment the form of a book changed from a roll to a codex, i.e., a number of pages of parchment stacked up one on top of another and all bound together in book form. The choicest treasures which the world of Biblical scholarship possesses today are two uncial Greek codices of the Bible written in the fourth century. An uncial manuscript is one in which the Greek words are

---

[102] For the further story of the course of canonization after the time of Athanasius, cf. Goodspeed, *The Formation of the New Testament,* pp. 114–170.

[103] On the nature of New Testament books, cf. Jack Finegan, *Light From the Ancient Past* (Princeton: 1946), pp. 307–352; C. C. McCown, "The Earliest Christian Books," *Biblical Archaeologist,* vi, 2 (May, 1943), pp. 21–31; Bruce Metzger, "Recently Published Greek Papyri of the New Testament," *Biblical Archaeologist,* x, 2 (May, 1947), pp. 25–44.

[104] G. A. Barton, *Archaeology and the Bible* (7th ed., 1937), pp. 587 f.

[105] *Ibid.,* pp. 580 f.

[106] For an account of the Greek papyri and their bearing upon the New Testament, cf. E. J. Goodspeed, *The Making of the English New Testament* (Chicago: 1925), pp. 90–104.

written altogether with capital letters. All Greek Bible manuscripts from the fourth to the eighth centuries are uncials, as are also some of the ninth and tenth centuries. A cursive manuscript is one written in running hand. Some of the ninth- and tenth-century manuscripts and all written after the tenth century are cursive.

The chief glory of the Vatican library in Rome today is its *Codex Vaticanus* (B).[107] Nobody knows how it came to Rome but it is listed in the Vatican catalogue of 1481. It came to the attention of the scholarly world when the conquests of Napoleon brought it to Paris. It was afterwards returned to the Vatican. It comprises more than seven hundred leaves of the finest vellum, each a foot square, bound in faded red morocco. It is clearly and beautifully written, three columns to a page, forty-two lines to a column. Photographic facsimiles of it are to be found in many learned libraries over the world. It is a pandect, i.e., it contains substantially the entire Greek Bible. Certain parts of Genesis and the Psalms are missing, as is also the last seventh of the New Testament, i.e., all from Heb. 9:14 to the end. The books of the Apocrypha are intermingled with the Old Testament books.

The other uncial Greek Bible of the fourth century is the *Codex Sinaiticus* (ℵ),[108] now in the British Museum. It was discovered by a German scholar, Konstantin von Tischendorf, in the Monastery of St. Catherine on Mount Sinai, at the southern end of the Sinai Peninsula. In 1844, when he visited the monastery, he discovered forty-three leaves of a beautiful old manuscript in a scrap basket. He could not find the rest of it about the place, though he felt certain it was there. The monks gave him the forty-three leaves and he took them home. Unable to rid his mind of the notion that the rest of the manuscript must be somewhere around the monastery, he visited the place again in 1853 but without success. He went back again in 1859. He could not find it and ordered his camels for the return to Suez. The evening before his departure, the steward took him to his cell and showed him the manuscript he had sought so long, wrapped in a red cloth. In his excitement, Tischendorf stayed up all night to copy the Epistle of Barnabas of which no copy in Greek had hitherto been known to exist. The Czar of Russia had been the patron of Tischendorf's last trip to Sinai and it was arranged that the manuscript should be presented to him. It was placed in the imperial library in St. Petersburg, now Leningrad. After it got there, Tischendorf published a copy of it in facsimile type; subsequently a photographic facsimile was published. In 1934 the Soviet Govern-

---

[107] This letter (B) is the code designation by which this manuscript is known among scholars.
[108] This Hebrew letter Aleph (ℵ) is the code designation for *Sinaiticus*.

A PAGE OF CODEX VATICANUS [109]

ment sold the manuscript to the British Museum for 100,000 pounds. It is a magnificent pandect, written with stately letters on the finest of all vellum, i.e., that made from antelope skins. There are usually four columns to a page, forty-eight lines to a column. The most interesting fact about *Sinaiticus* is that it contains the whole of the New Testament and it is the only uncial Greek manuscript that does.

[109] The first page of the Epistle to the Romans. By courtesy of Prof. Jack Finegan, of the Pacific School of Religion, and of the Bibliotheca Apostolica Vaticana, Rome, Italy.

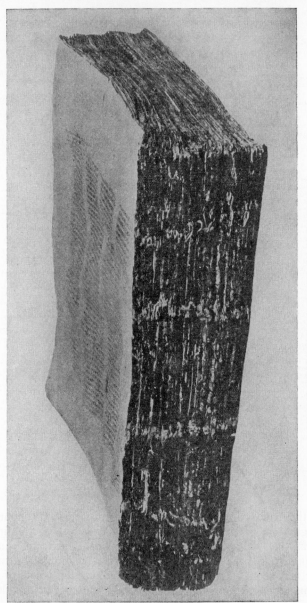

CODEX SINAITICUS BEFORE BINDING [110]

[110] Courtesy of the British Museum, London.

Textual criticism is that branch of New Testament science which seeks, from a study of the Greek manuscripts, to determine exactly what the original text of the New Testament was. These two manuscripts are the rock bottom of that science. Where *Vaticanus* and *Sinaiticus* agree on a reading, it amounts to certainty that that was the original reading.[111]

The Genealogy of the English Bible

The Latin Vulgate. Jerome (*circa* 340–420) was head of a monastery in Bethlehem for thirty-four years, from 386 to his death. He was a close friend of Pope Damasus (died 384), who commissioned Jerome to revise the old Latin versions of the Bible. There was a large number of such Bibles in existence, differing so greatly in their text that men were in confusion as to what was the true text. Jerome first revised the New Testament (383–385) on the basis of the existing Latin translations and their comparison with the Septuagint, not by making a fresh translation from the Greek. He could have done the latter had he chosen, for he was skilled in Greek. He next revised the psalter, then undertook the revision of the Old Testament from the Septuagint, and not finding that satisfactory, he translated the Old Testament anew from the Hebrew. The task was finished in 405. Jerome's Version became the standard Latin version of the Bible and for that reason is called the *Vulgate,* from the Latin *vulgatus* ("usual," "common"). It has ever since been the official Bible of the Roman Catholic Church. It was from the Vulgate that the Bible was first translated into English.

Early Anglo-Saxon Paraphrases. The old Anglo-Saxon poet Caedmon, in the seventh century, told in song the story of the creation of the world, the wanderings of the Israelites, and the story of Jesus as he had heard them from the monks at Whitby. This was the first presentation in our tongue of any part of Scripture, and it was paraphrase, not translation.

The definite beginning of translation was by the Venerable Bede, the father of English history. At the time of his death in 735 he was engaged in translating the Gospel of John from the Latin of the Vulgate into Anglo-Saxon.

King Alfred (*circa* 842–*circa* 900) prefixed a translation of the Ten Commandments to his code of laws which is known as the "Dooms of Alfred." There were renderings into Anglo-Saxon of other Scrip-

[111] For a brief account of the discovery of the ancient text of the New Testament, cf. E. J. Goodspeed, *The Making of the English New Testament,* pp. 52–67. The facts regarding the manuscripts and versions of the New Testament are presented very compactly by K. Lake, *The Text of the New Testament* (London: 1928).

ture portions from the psalter and from the gospels. There was nothing systematic about any of this.

The Wyclif Version (1382). John Wyclif (1320–1384) translated the Latin Version into English in 1382. He was aided by his pupil, Nicholas Hereford, who did most of the Old Testament. Wyclif organized the circulation of the Bible throughout England by itinerant preachers, trained to read and explain it to the common people, who, by ecclesiastical edict, were forbidden to possess any book of the Bible, especially in a translation, except perhaps the psalter. After Wyclif's death in 1384 his translation was revised and improved by his friend, John Purvey, in 1388, and it is this form of the Wyclif Version that is preserved in the copies which have survived until now.

Between Wyclif and the next great Bible translator, William Tyndale, three events profoundly affected the history of the Bible. One was the discovery of the art of printing by Johann Gutenberg who in 1450 turned out from his press in Mainz (Germany) a Latin Bible based on the Vulgate. The Bible was the first book ever printed. Wyclif's Bible had to be copied by hand, which took ten months of hard labor and cost the equivalent of two hundred dollars. The second epochal event was the fall of Constantinople to the Turks in 1453, which ended the Byzantine empire, and at the moment seemed a crushing disaster to Christendom. Scholars forsook Constantinople and fled westward. Their coming brought to western Europe a revival of arts and letters which led to the Renaissance and the Reformation. With that westward tide came scholars versed in the Greek and Hebrew languages. Until then the world had been content with the Latin Vulgate for a Bible. Scholars now set about to find Greek and Hebrew Bible manuscripts. The consequence of this was the third revolutionizing event, the publication of the first Greek New Testament in 1516 by the Dutch scholar Erasmus.

The Tyndale Bible (1525–1536). After Erasmus, it was possible for men who knew to go back of the Latin Vulgate to the original languages. This is what William Tyndale (1492–1536) did. He was "moved to translate the New Testament" because he "perceived by experience how that it was impossible to stablish the lay people in any truth, except the Scripture were plainly laid before their eyes in their mother tongue." Tyndale once remarked to a learned man, a foe of his work, "If God spare my life, ere many years I will cause a boy that driveth the plough shall know more of the Scripture than thou doest."

Tyndale's English New Testament was published in 1525, was eagerly read in England, and survived the most vigorous efforts of king and ecclesiastics to destroy it. In 1530 Tyndale published his translation of the Pentateuch, the first five books of the Old Testament, directly from the Hebrew, thus laying the foundations of the English Old Testament. Before his death Tyndale had completed the translation of the first half of the Old Testament directly from the Hebrew. He was imprisoned in May, 1535, in Vilvorde Castle, near Brussels. In a letter supposed to have been written by him in prison as winter was approaching, Tyndale asked for some of his warmer clothing from his former lodgings, a lamp to light his cell in the evening, and his Hebrew books that he might continue his translation of the Bible. A year later he was strangled by King Henry's executioner and burned. His end was miserable but his influence was far-reaching.[112]

The Coverdale Bible (1535). Myles Coverdale (1488–1569) was no such scholar as Tyndale. He did not go back to the original languages to make his translation. He stated that he "faithfully translated this out of five sundry interpreters." Two of these were Latin, two were German, and the fifth was the English translation of Tyndale. Coverdale was more an editor than an independent scholar, and although his work was largely secondhand it has the distinction of having been the first complete Bible in English. Coverdale included the Apocrypha in his Bible. The first edition of Coverdale's Bible contained a long and fulsome dedication to King Henry VIII. It was printed again in 1537 in London, with the imprint, "set forth with the king's most gracious license." This is the very king who killed Tyndale for the crime of translating the Bible into English.[113]

The Rogers Bible (1537). In 1537 appeared an English Bible under the name of Thomas Matthew, which name may only have been a fiction, for the translation was actually the work of John Rogers (1500–1555). Rogers was a friend and admirer of Tyndale and was his literary executor. The Rogers Bible is simply Tyndale's translation, so far as Tyndale had carried it, with the balance taken from Coverdale's Bible, i.e., Ezra through Malachi plus the Apocrypha. Sixty-five per cent of the Old and New Testaments was Tyndale's work. The Rogers Bible established the basic text of the English Bible and subsequent versions were chiefly revisions of this text.[114]

[112] For a fuller account of Tyndale's Version, cf. Goodspeed, *The Making of the English New Testament,* pp. 1–13.
[113] On Coverdale's Bible, cf. Goodspeed, *The Making of the English New Testament,* pp. 14–17.
[114] On Rogers' Bible, cf. Goodspeed, *The Making of the English New Testament,* pp. 17–20.

Taverner's Bible (1539). Richard Taverner (1505–1575) put out a Bible in 1539 which is nothing but Rogers' Bible with very slight changes. Though subsequently reprinted, it proved to be of slight influence.

The Great Bible (1539). This Bible takes its name from its size, for the printing of it was projected on splendid lines, since its production had been officially prompted by the king's minister, Thomas Cromwell. A second edition, printed in 1540, bore a preface written by Thomas Cranmer, the archbishop of Canterbury, from which fact this Bible is often called Cranmer's Bible. This 1540 edition also carried on the title page the notation, "This is the Bible appointed to be read in the Churches." Cromwell and Cranmer promoted the spread and use of this Bible among the churches. It was to be installed in the churches in a convenient place where people could have access to it. The size and cost prohibited plain people from owning copies. In a church, such a Bible was chained to the lectern, just as books in libraries were, to prevent their removal and make them accessible to the greater number of people. The Bible was now read eagerly by the English people, many in advanced years even learning how to read for the purpose. As a Bible it was merely a revision of the Rogers Bible and therefore continues the creative contribution which Tyndale had made to the English text.[115]

The Geneva Bible (1560). The Great Bible was too huge and expensive for common people to own and use conveniently. That defect was remedied by the Geneva Bible, so called because it was produced there by a group of English scholars in exile. It was a revision of the Great Bible on the basis of new Latin translations which had been published and improved Greek texts which were available. The latter half of the Old Testament was referred more directly to the Hebrew than was the case of any preceding English version. It will be recalled that Tyndale had died before completing his translation of this part of the Old Testament directly from the Hebrew. The New Testament in the Geneva Bible is only a revision of Tyndale. It was a small book, neatly printed in roman type instead of black letter, and for the first time in an English Bible the chapters were subdivided into verses. It attained great popularity among the English people for it was the Bible of the home. Copies of this Bible came to America with early settlers. It was the Geneva Bible which made the English a Bible-reading and Bible-loving people. This version is frequently called the "Breeches Bible" because of the

---

[115] On the Great Bible, cf. Goodspeed, *The Making of the English New Testament*, pp. 20–24.

way Gen. 3:7 is rendered, "They sewed figge leaves together and made themselves breeches." [116]

The Bishops' Bible (1568). The popular use of the Geneva Bible put the Great Bible at a disadvantage, so a revision of the Great Bible was undertaken under the leadership of Matthew Parker (1504–1575), Archbishop of Canterbury. So many of the revisers were bishops that the new version came to be known as the "Bishops' Bible." They knew Greek better than Hebrew and therefore their revisions in the New Testament showed better scholarship. The Old Testament was revised on the basis of the Geneva Bible. The use of this Bible in churches and in the houses of the bishops was promoted and displaced the Great Bible as the Bible officially appointed to be read in the churches, and it was so until 1611. [117]

The Rheims-Douay Version (1582–1609). Roman Catholics of England were at a disadvantage in not having an official English version of their own Bible. Therefore Roman Catholic scholars at the English college at Rheims (France) made an English translation from the Vulgate. The New Testament was published in Rheims in 1582 but lack of funds prevented the publishing of the Old Testament until 1609. By then the college had returned to Douay (France), which gave its name to this version. The sponsor of the project was William Allen (1532–1594). Most of the actual translating was done by Gregory Martin (died 1582). [118]

The King James Version (1611). King James I of England called a conference at Hampton Court in 1604 to deal with church matters. At the conference a proposal that the English Bible should be revised was made by Dr. John Reynolds, president of Corpus Christi College. The king took up with the idea and the work was assigned to committees of scholars, four groups working on the Old Testament and two on the New. The task undertaken was in reality a revision of the Bishops' Bible rather than a fresh translation from the original languages. The Bishops' Bible was to be "as little altered as the truth of the original will permit." Tyndale's, Rogers', Coverdale's, the Great Bible, and the Geneva Bible were "to be used when they agree better with the text than the Bishops' Bible." The finished product came from the press in 1611 and in subsequent years, down to 1769, it was frequently revised. Its use in the churches

---

[116] On the Geneva Bible, cf. Goodspeed, *The Making of the English New Testament,* pp. 25–31.

[117] On the Bishops' Bible, cf. Goodspeed, *The Making of the English New Testament,* pp. 32–35.

[118] On the Douay Version, cf. Goodspeed, *The Making of the English New Testament,* pp. 35–40.

was sanctioned but never authorized. Notwithstanding this, however, it is commonly spoken of as the "Authorized Version." It displaced the Bishops' Bible in the churches and in time displaced the Geneva Bible among the common people. The King James Version is still the best known and most widely used and therefore the most influential English Bible. The greatness of the King James Bible is due to the genius of William Tyndale, of nearly a century earlier, whose vigorous and rhythmic English was transmitted through the succession of Bibles (Rogers', Great, Bishops') to the great English classic, to which it gives tone and color. In the King James New Testament, nine tenths stand as Tyndale rendered it.[119]

The Revised Version (1881–1885). The oldest and basically most reliable Greek manuscripts of the New Testament were not known to the scholars who produced the King James Version. In 1682 one of the three greatest uncial manuscripts, the *Codex Alexandrinus* (A), reached England, a gift to Charles I by Cyril Lucar, Patriarch of Constantinople. It is now preserved in the British Museum. It rates in value next after *Vaticanus* and *Sinaiticus.*[120] Besides these three greatest manuscripts, others were discovered. This led to a better knowledge of the true Greek text of the New Testament, and critical editions of the Greek text appeared, vastly superior to the text underlying the King James translation. This was bound to lead to dissatisfaction with that translation. The English language itself changed considerably. Therefore during the two and one-half centuries after the publication of the King James version, a number of revised translations were published by private individuals, not a few of them in America.[121] The use of the King James Version was conventional but the need for an official revision was apparent.

At the Convocation of Canterbury in 1870, the movement was begun. On May 6 the organization of a group of scholars to undertake the work was authorized. The organization was promptly formed with two committees, one for the Old Testament and one for the New, and work was begun. American scholars were invited to assist in the project. The New Testament was published in England May 17, 1881, and the Old Testament May 19, 1885. Many of the suggestions of the American scholars were accepted and adopted either in the text or in the margin, but not all of them. Other readings preferred by the Americans were printed in an appendix. The

---

[119] On the King James Version, cf. Goodspeed, *The Making of the English New Testament,* pp. 41–51.

[120] *Vid. supra,* pp. 602 ff.

[121] An account of these private translations is given by Goodspeed, *The Making of the English New Testament,* pp. 68–79.

American scholars agreed not to publish a separate American edition, which would embody their preferred readings in the body of the text, for fourteen years. The American Standard Edition of the Revised Version was published in 1901. What this version is like is well known to the student of this textbook for it is the basic text of the English Bible recommended for use in this course and is the version from which quotations in this textbook have been taken unless otherwise specified.

The Revised Standard Version (1946–1952). In 1929 an American Standard Bible committee was appointed by the International Council of Religious Education, owner of the copyright of the American Standard Version. To date, thirty-one Biblical scholars have served on the committee. The work of revision was begun in 1937. The Revised Standard Version of the New Testament, the work of nine New Testament scholars, was published in February, 1946. Work on the Old Testament is progressing toward completion and publication of the complete Revised Standard Version of the Holy Bible is promised for 1952. This version designedly continues the line of the great versions from Tyndale through King James and American Standard.

Recent Translations. Translations into English continue to multiply, based upon enlarged knowledge of original manuscripts, which continue to be discovered at a surprising rate. Within the twentieth century new translations of the New Testament alone have appeared at the rate of one a year. It would be out of place here to list all these versions, but certain of them ought to be on the bookshelf of every thoughtful student of the Bible.[122]

1. *The Holy Scriptures,* according to the Masoretic text, published in Philadelphia by the Jewish Publication Society of America in 1917.

2. *The Holy Bible, A New Translation,* by James Moffatt, published in New York in 1924. His New Testament had previously appeared in 1913.

3. *The Bible, An American Translation;* the Old Testament translated by a group of scholars under the editorship of J. M. Powis Smith; the New Testament translated by Edgar J. Goodspeed. The Goodspeed New Testament appeared separately in 1923; the Old Testament in 1927; the two combined in 1931. To these was added Goodspeed's new translation of the Apocrypha (first published in

[122] For a discussion of modern-speech translations of the New Testament, cf. Goodspeed, *The Making of the English New Testament,* pp. 105–124.

1938) under the title, *The Complete Bible, An American Translation,* 1939.

4. New Roman Catholic Translations. The number of these which have appeared in recent years is significant. The important ones are (1) *The New Testament of Our Lord and Saviour Jesus Christ,* translated from the original Greek by Father Francis Aloysius Spencer, published in New York in 1937. (2) *The New Testament of Our Lord and Saviour Jesus Christ,* translated from the Latin Vulgate, a revision of the Challoner-Rheims Version, edited by Catholic scholars under the patronage of The Episcopal Committee of the Confraternity of Christian Doctrine, published in Paterson, New Jersey, 1941. (3) *The New Testament in English, A New Translation,* by Monsignor Ronald A. Knox, published in New York in 1945. At the present time other Roman Catholic scholars are turning out a new revision known as the *Westminster Version.* Parts of it have already been published and other parts are in preparation. Still others are working on a revision of the Douay Version.

Our English Heritage

It is a remarkable fact that the most important book in the English language, and the Bible is universally conceded to be that, was not originally composed in English at all. Our English language was practically created in the process of translating the Bible into the language of the common people.[123] The Bible has always had to be known through translation so far as plain people are concerned. The Old Testament was originally written in the Hebrew language, but the last of it had scarcely been produced before the Jews ceased to know and understand Hebrew except for the rabbis who were specifically educated in it. In Palestine, when the Hebrew Scriptures were read in synagogues an oral translation of their meaning had to be given in Aramaic, the language plain people knew and used. Jews living outside of Palestine knew neither Hebrew nor Aramaic; they used Greek, like the rest of the world, and for their benefit the Old Testament was translated, beginning *circa* 285 B.C., into Greek, the Septuagint Version. The use of this version passed over into early Christianity. The New Testament was composed in the *Koine,* the everyday language of plain people of the New Testament period, as has been abundantly proved by the many papyri which have in recent years been discovered. Presently it became necessary to translate the Bible into Latin, and, as we have seen, the Vulgate

---

[123] The same is true of modern German, which was largely the achievement of Martin Luther in the process of translating the Bible.

was the basic Bible down to the Reformation. The Reformation re-created the zeal to give the Bible to plain people in their vernacular, and has resulted in the translation of the Bible, in whole or in part, into every known tongue.

The English Bible has molded the inner character of our public institutions, it has inspired high achievements in literature and in art, it has ennobled the language of our daily life, it has been and is the beloved guide and companion of millions of persons of high degree and humble, and it has far surpassed in circulation any other book in the world.

GLOSSARY OF TECHNICAL TERMS

Agape. The early Christian Love Feast, or common meal; cf. p. 530.

Ain. Arabic word for spring.

Anakim. A people of giant stature located in southern Palestine when the Hebrews first came to the land; cf. p. 26.

Angelology. Doctrines about angels as intermediaries between God and man; cf. p. 393.

Anthropomorphism. Conceiving of God as having a bodily form like man.

Apis. Egyptian bull deity; cf. p. 103.

Apocalyptic. A literary type of prophetic "revelation"; the body of literature of that type; the set of doctrinal ideas expressed in such literature; cf. p. 443.

Apocrypha. Certain books found in the Septuagint, but not in the Hebrew Old Testament; cf. p. 431.

Apologetic. Literature which is written to establish a certain theory or doctrine; cf. p. 137.

Apostasy. The desertion of whatever religion was previously professed in order to adopt some other religion.

Apotheosis. The elevating of a human to the rank of deity; cf. p. 541.

Arabah. That part of the great rift valley in Palestine which lies immediately south of the Dead Sea; cf. p. 13.

Aramaic. The common (Semitic) language of the Jews from the Persian period to the end of Bible times; cf. p. 392.

Aramaean. Pertaining to that branch of the Semitic peoples which, from earliest times, was settled in Syria and Mesopotamia; cf. p. 21.

Aram Naharaim. Aram of the two rivers, i.e., Upper Mesopotamia, from the Euphrates to the Tigris.

Ark. The Ark of the Covenant; the sacred box or chest, presumably containing certain sacred relics, which symbolized to the Hebrews the immediate presence of Yahweh; cf. p. 133. Also, the chest or closet in a synagogue in which the rolls of the Holy Scriptures are kept; cf. p. 479.

Asherah. A sacred wooden post, possibly capped by a wooden image of the goddess Asherah, set up near the altar of a Canaanite high place; cf. p. 177.

Ashteroth. Plural of Ashtoreth, the Hebrew word for Ashtart, the mother-goddess.

Avvim. Early, presumably pre-Amoritic, people localized near Gaza on the southwest coast of Palestine; cf. p. 25.

Bedouin. Sometimes spelled Bedawin. Nomadic Arab of the desert east of Palestine.

Beit. Arabic word for house.

Bronze Age. 3000–1200 B.C.; cf. p. 59.

Cananeans. The Zealots, or revolutionist group in Palestine in the first century after Christ; cf. p. 471.

Canonization. The process by which Hebrew books came to be esteemed as sacred, i.e., as Holy Scripture; cf. p. 334.

Captivity. The deportation of the Israelites from the northern Hebrew kingdom to various parts of the Assyrian empire in 720 B.C., and the deportation of the Jews from Judah to Babylon in 597, 586, and 581 B.C.

Chalcolithic Age. The overlap of the Stone and Bronze ages of antiquity, 4500–3000 B.C.; cf. p. 59.

Cherubim. Winged figures above the Ark of the Covenant in the Most Holy Place of Solomon's temple in Jerusalem.

Chinnereth. Ancient name of Lake Galilee; possibly it means "harp-shaped"; cf. p. 12.

Codex. An ancient manuscript book of the Bible, written on sheets of papyrus or parchment stacked in a pile and bound together; cf. p. 601.

Cuneiform. Ancient Babylonian style of writing; the characters were impressed with a wedge on clay tablets, which were then hardened by baking; cf. p. 44.

Cursive. A Bible manuscript written in running hand; cf. p. 602.

"D." The Deuteronomic code, contained in the book of Deuteronomy, generally identified as the law book found in the Jerusalem temple in 621 B.C.; cf. p. 284.

Decapolis. Ten Hellenistic cities in Eastjordania, mostly in Perea, politically independent city-states, leagued together; cf. p. 470.

Demonology. Doctrines about demons as malevolent supernatural beings; cf. p. 393.

Devoted. Doomed to death or destruction; cf. p. 127.

Diadochi. The successors of Alexander the Great, i.e., his generals among whom his empire was divided; cf. p. 427.

Diaspora, or Dispersion. Jews outside of Palestine, principally in Egypt and the Mediterranean world.

Divination. Discovering secret knowledge, or foretelling the future by the practice of certain rites believed to be effective in securing a supernatural revelation; cf. p. 182.

"E." The early Ephraimite Narrative source of the Pentateuch, which originated *ca.* 800–750 B.C. in Ephraim, i.e., central Palestine; cf. p. 297.

Ecclesia. Greek word, commonly translated church, not to be understood as meaning a unified and centralized ecclesiastical organization, but rather a Christian group; cf. pp. 536 f.

Elohim. Hebrew word (pl.) translated God.

Emim. Early, presumably pre-Amoritic, people localized in Moab, east of the Dead Sea; cf. p. 25.

'En. Hebrew word for spring, or fountain; cf. p. 122.

Ephah. Hebrew dry measure, slightly more than one bushel.

Ephod. Some sort of image; also a type of waistcoat worn by priests; cf. pp. 82, 134, 173.

Epichristian Age. The twenty-year period immediately after the lifetime of Jesus; cf. p. 518.

Eschatology. That phase of apocalyptic which deals with the issues of the future; cf. p. 445.

Essenes. A monastic order of Jews in Palestine in New Testament times who lived in celibate communities, whose doctrine was an extreme Pharisaism; cf. p. 476.

Ethnarch. An honorific title meaning "ruler of a people"; cf. pp. 421, 466.

Eucharist. The Lord's Supper, the Christian sacramental meal; cf. p. 530.

Exile. The deportation of the Jews from Judah in 597, 586, and 581 B.C. to Babylon, and their residence there until permitted to return to Palestine in 538 B.C.

Exodus. The departure of the Hebrew tribesmen from Egypt under the leadership of Moses, *ca.* 1220 B.C.

Father of. A biblical expression used figuratively as a genetic formula to explain the origin of any social custom or institution; e.g., the origin of musicians was explained by saying that Jubal "was the father of all such" (Gen. 4:21) ; cf. p. 88.

Fertile Crescent. The territory stretching in an arc from Palestine northward along the Mediterranean coast to the Euphrates river, thence eastward to the Tigris, and southeastward to the head of the Persian Gulf; cf. p. 4.

Gerousia. The Senate of Jerusalem; associated with the high priest in the government of the Restored Jewish Community in the Hellenistic period; forerunner of the Sanhedrin; cf. p. 391.

Ghor. Arabic El Ghor, "the trough"; the Jordan valley.

Glossolalia. Tongue-speaking, ecstatic utterances accompanying certain highly emotional types of religious experience; cf. p. 521.

Gnosticism. A system of doctrinal beliefs emphasizing *gnosis,* or esoteric knowledge attributed to alleged inner illumination, a type of heresy which early Christianity confronted; cf. p. 594.

God-fearers. Gentiles who attended Jewish synagogues but would not become Jewish proselytes; cf. p. 524.

"H." The Holiness code, Lev. 17–26, produced in the exilic period, i.e., later than 586 B.C., and subsequently incorporated in the "P" code, *q.v.;* cf. p. 376.

Habiri. Lit. "boundary-crossers." Nomadic invaders and plunderers of Palestine in the fourteenth century B.C.; cf. pp. 29 f.

Hagiographa. Greek name for the third division of the Old Testament canon of Scripture; cf. pp. 428 f.

Hanukkah. Jewish Feast of the Dedication, commonly called the festival of "Lights"; cf. p. 417.

Hasidim. The Pious, the devoutly earnest Jews who resisted Hellenism and in the Maccabean revolt fought for their religious freedom; the forerunners of the Pharisees; cf. p. 418.

Hasmonean. Pertaining to the Jewish family of Hasmon, to which Judas Maccabeus belonged; cf. p. 424.

Hellenism. The fusion of Greek culture with oriental culture following the conquests of Alexander the Great; cf. pp. 386 f.

Henotheism. Exclusive worship of and devotion to one god, though not denying the existence of other gods; cf. p. 130.

Hexateuch. The six books of the law; a name applied to Gen., Ex., Lev., Num., Deut., Josh., when regarded as a literary whole; cf. p. 308.

High Place. A local village sanctuary, or place of worship, usually located on some elevated spot; cf. p. 176.

Hin. Hebrew liquid measure, *ca.* 1½ gallons; cf. p. 275.

Hurrites (Hurrians). A people of western Asia in the third and second millennia, B.C.; cf. p. 25.

Hyksos. "Rulers of Countries"; Semitic conquerors and rulers of Egypt, 1680–1580 B.C.; cf. p. 94.

"J." Early Judean Prophetic narratives, which originated *ca.* 850 B.C. in Judah; cf. pp. 296 f.

Jebel. Arabic word for mountain.

Jeshimon. "Desolation"; the wilderness of Judea; cf. p. 16.

Koheleth. Hebrew title of the book of Ecclesiastes, conventionally translated "preacher"; cf. p. 405.

Koine. The common, or everyday, kind of Greek spoken and written by plain people in New Testament times; cf. p. 601.

Leben. Soured milk, of the consistency of blancmange; cf. p. 168.

LORD (all caps.). In certain Bible versions (notably the King James, the Jewish, and the Chicago) the Hebrew word Yahweh is so rendered; cf. p. 131, fn. 109.

Lost Books. Hebrew books whose names are mentioned in the Old Testament, but are no longer extant; cf. pp. 207, 294 f.

Maccabees. The Jewish patriots of the family of Hasmon who led the Jewish revolt against the Seleucids, 168–143 B.C.; also the apocryphal books which tell about that revolt; cf. pp. 416 ff.

Mana. A Melanesian word signifying a supernatural force or spirit coming upon a man, impelling him to do things beyond his ordinary human power; cf. p. 181.

Mazzebah. Hebrew word for upright stone column marking a sacred place; cf. p. 123.

Mazzôth. Unleavened bread; cf. p. 179.

Mesolithic Age. The Middle Stone Age, i.e., *ca.* 12,000–8000 B.C.; cf. p. 59.

Messianism. Belief in the coming of an ideal, divinely appointed leader, usually thought to be a king, who will inaugurate the ideal age; cf. pp. 61, 327.

Monotheism. Belief in the existence of only one god.

Myth. A primitive, realistic story told to explain some belief; cf. p. 110.

Neanderthal. A valley in Germany in which were found parts of the skeleton of a very early type of man; cf. p. 24.

Necromancy. The practice of conjuring up and holding conversation with the dead in order to discover the future; cf. p. 128.

Neolithic Age. The New, or Late Stone Age, i.e., *ca.* 8000–*ca.* 4500 B.C.; cf. pp. 25, 59.

Nephilim. Name of an early people, presumably of giant stature, in Palestine; cf. p. 26.

"P." The Priest code, one of the basic sources of the Pentateuch, which was produced in the exilic period, i.e., later than 586 B.C.; cf. pp. 376 f.

Palaeolithic Age. The Old Stone Age, i.e., before 12,000 B.C.; cf. p. 25.

Pandect. A codex of the entire Greek Bible; cf. p. 602.

Papyrus. Writing material, produced in Egypt, and made from the papyrus plant; cf. p. 49.

Parallelism. Balance of thought, the distinguishing characteristic of Hebrew poetry; cf. p. 112.

Parousia. The time when God, through his messiah, will catastrophically overthrow evil and establish his kingdom of righteousness; cf. p. 539.

Patriarch. The father, or head of a family, in early Hebrew nomadic times; one of the Bible worthies of Genesis; cf. p. 91.

Pentateuch. The five books of the law, i.e., Gen., Ex., Lev., Num., Deut.; same as the Torah; cf. p. 308.

Pentecost. Harvest festival, fifty days after passover, in the spring; cf. p. 380.

Pharisees. "Separatists"; devoutly earnest Jews who were intensely loyal to the Jewish law, both written and oral; successors of the Ḥasidim, *q.v.;* cf. p. 419.

Polytheism. Belief in the existence of many gods, and the indiscriminate worship of them.

Potsherd. A fragment of a broken earthen vessel.

Procurator. A fiscal agent of the Roman emperor in a province, sometimes a governor of a small country, such as Judea; cf. p. 549.

Psalter. The book of Psalms.

Pseudepigrapha. Lit., writings falsely assigned to an ancient worthy as author; a body of Jewish literature which was produced in the New Testament period; cf. p. 437.

Publican. A tax collector.

"Q." The source, whether one document or several, of the discourse material (i.e., teachings of Jesus) common to the gospels of Matthew and Luke but not found in Mark; cf. p. 484.

Redemption. The ancient Hebrew custom by which the next of kin was in duty bound to purchase a piece of property which a man was obliged to sell; cf. p. 281.

Remnant. The spiritual minority which, according to some of the prophets, would survive the destruction of the existing age, and with which as a nucleus God would integrate the new age to come; cf. p. 317.

Rephaim. "Giants"; the early people of giant stature whom the Hebrews found in Palestine when they first entered the land; cf. p. 25.

Restored Jewish Community. Jerusalem and environs when rehabilitated after the exile; cf. pp. 352 f.

Sadducees. The high-priestly group in New Testament times; accepted only the written law, approved Hellenism and Roman rule; cf. p. 419.

Saints. Early name for Christians before the term Christian was coined; cf. p. 533.

Sanhedrin. The Jewish court of seventy members, presided over by the high priest, which administered the Jewish law; cf. pp. 467 f.

Scribes. Jews professionally devoted to the reading, copying, and interpreting of the Holy Scriptures; cf. p. 396.

Seah. Hebrew dry measure, *ca.* 1½ pecks; cf. pp. 85, 275.

Se'irim. "Hairy Ones"; a type of demons; cf. p. 119.

Seleucids. Seleucus, a general of Alexander the Great, and his successors as kings of Syria; cf. p. 389.

Septuagint. The Greek version of the Old Testament; cf. p. 412.

Seraphim. "Burning Ones"; a type of supernatural beings; cf. p. 119.

Shema. The ritual formula which is the basic statement of the essence of Judaism (Deut. 6:4–9; 11:13–21; Num. 15:37–41); cf. p. 383.

Shephelah. The lowland, or rolling country, between the coastal plain of Philistia and the hill country of Judah; cf. p. 16.

Showbread. Bread of the presentation, placed on the altar in the Holy Place of the Jerusalem temple; cf. pp. 380, 478.

Sicarii. Dagger carriers, or assassins, extremely fanatical Zealots in the time of the Jewish war, A.D. 66–70; cf. p. 553.

Sin. The moon god; cf. p. 121.

Son of. A biblical expression used figuratively to characterize a person as having certain qualities, or as belonging in a certain classification; e.g., "son of a prophet" does not mean that the man's father is a prophet, but that the man himself is, i.e., he belongs in the class, or to one of the groups of prophets.

Synoptic. Presenting a common view; applied to the gospels of Matt., Mk., and Lk.; cf. pp. 483 f.

Tell. Arabic word for hill, or mound; formed by the debris of several ancient towns which had been built each on top of the ruins of its predecessor.

Teraphim. Household gods; cf. p. 118.

Tetrarch. An administrative official, having somewhat less power than a king, appointed by the Roman government; cf. p. 468.

Theophany. An appearance and revelation of the deity, who is both seen and heard; cf. p. 116.

Theriomorphism. Representing the deity as having an animal form.

Torah. The Hebrew name for the first five books of the Bible, Gen., Ex., Lev., Num., Deut.; cf. pp. 382 f.

Uncial. A manuscript of the Greek Bible written with all capital letters; cf. pp. 601 f.

Vulgate. The Latin version of the Bible translated by St. Jerome A.D. *ca.* 400; cf. p. 605.

Wadi. Arabic word for a dry stream bed.

Watershed. Figuratively, an event, or series of events, which gives new direction to, or releases fresh energies in the course of historical development; cf. p. 96.

Yahweh. The name of the Hebrew deity; cf. p. 131.

Yahwism. The religion of Yahweh, i.e., the Hebrew religion as established by Moses.

Zadokites. A sect of Jewish religious reformers in New Testament times; cf. p. 476.

Zamzummim. Name of a shadowy, early people localized east of the Dead Sea; cf. p. 25.

Zealots. The militant patriots, or revolutionist group of Jews in Palestine in the first century after Christ; cf. p. 471.

Ziggurat. A Babylonian ramped tower of several stages, each smaller than the one beneath it.

Zin. A wilderness, part of the Negeb, south of Judea; cf. p. 17.

THE BOOKSHELF

I

Books which the student should use continually as tools for Bible study.

The Bible

HOLY BIBLE WITH APOCRYPHA. American Standard Version. New York: Thos. Nelson and Sons.

REVISED STANDARD VERSION OF THE NEW TESTAMENT. New York: Thos. Nelson and Sons, 1946. [Publication of the REVISED STANDARD VERSION OF THE OLD TESTAMENT is set for 1952.]

THE HOLY BIBLE—A NEW TRANSLATION, by James Moffatt. New York: Harper and Bros., revised and final edition, 1935.

THE COMPLETE BIBLE—AN AMERICAN TRANSLATION. J. M. P. Smith, editor of the Old Testament; E. J. Goodspeed, translator of the Apocrypha and of the New Testament. University of Chicago Press. [THE APOCRYPHA—AN AMERICAN TRANSLATION, by E. J. Goodspeed, University of Chicago Press, is separately available. This is the only English translation of the Apocrypha made directly from the original language.]

A Bible Dictionary

THE WESTMINSTER DICTIONARY OF THE BIBLE (one vol.). Revised by H. B. Gehman. Philadelphia. Westminster Press, 1944.

or

A NEW STANDARD BIBLE DICTIONARY (one vol.). Edited by M. W. Jacobus, E. E. Nourse, and A. C. Zenos. New York: Funk and Wagnalls Co., 3d revised edition, 1936.

or

DICTIONARY OF THE BIBLE (one vol.). Edited by James Hastings. New York: Chas. Scribner's Sons, 1921.

or

A DICTIONARY OF THE BIBLE (5 vols.). Edited by James Hastings. New York: Chas. Scribner's Sons, 1911.

A Bible Concordance

CONCORDANCE TO THE WHOLE BIBLE, by Alexander Cruden. Original, unabridged edition published by Fleming H. Revell Co., New York, 1930. (Various other editions of this work are to be had.)

or

CONCORDANCE OF THE BIBLE, by James Strong. London: Hodder and Stoughton, 1931.

Bible Maps

THE WESTMINSTER HISTORICAL ATLAS TO THE BIBLE. Edited by George Ernest Wright and Floyd Vivian Filson. Philadelphia: The Westminster Press, 1945.

For Extra-Biblical Source Material

ARCHAEOLOGY AND THE BIBLE, by George A. Barton. Philadelphia: American Sunday School Union, 7th ed., 1937.
Supplements Chapters 2, 3, 4 especially.
LIGHT FROM THE ANCIENT PAST, by Jack Finegan. Princeton University Press, 1946.

II

Reference Books

The student who wishes to read more widely on some line of interest stimulated by the study of this textbook may profitably turn first to the following books. The student who then wishes to read more widely still will consult the bibliographies in these books, as well as seek guidance from his (or her) teacher.

W. F. Albright, THE ARCHAEOLOGY OF PALESTINE. Harmondsworth, Middlesex, England: Penguin Books, 1949.
Supplements Chapters 2, 3, 4.
W. F. Albright, FROM THE STONE AGE TO CHRISTIANITY. Baltimore: The Johns Hopkins Press, 1940.
Supplements Chapters 2, 3, 4, 5, 6, 8, 10, 12, 18, 25.
J. A. Bewer, THE LITERATURE OF THE OLD TESTAMENT, New York: Columbia University Press, 1922; revised ed., 1933. Gives an excellent bibliography, pp. 437–448.
Supplements Chapters 7, 12, 13, 14, 15, 16, 17, 18, 19, 20, 22.
S. J. Case, THE EVOLUTION OF EARLY CHRISTIANITY, University of Chicago Press, 1914.
Supplements Chapter 26.
R. H. Charles, THE APOCRYPHA AND PSEUDEPIGRAPHA OF THE OLD TESTAMENT, 2 vols., Oxford University Press, 1913.
Supplements Chapter 22.
E. J. Goodspeed, INTRODUCTION TO THE NEW TESTAMENT, University of Chicago Press, 1937.
Supplements Chapters 24, 26, 27.
GOSPEL PARALLELS—A SYNOPSIS OF THE FIRST THREE GOSPELS. The text is that of *The Revised Standard Version of the New Testament*. New York: Thos. Nelson and Sons, 1949.
Supplements Chapter 24.
C. C. McCown, THE LADDER OF PROGRESS IN PALESTINE. New York: Harper and Bros., 1943.
Supplements Chapters 2, 3.
Madeleine S. and J. Lane Miller, ENCYCLOPEDIA OF BIBLE LIFE. New York: Harper and Bros., 1944.
Supplements Chapters 1, 3, 5, 8, 9, 10, 12, 17, 18.
W. O. E. Oesterley and T. H. Robinson, A HISTORY OF ISRAEL, in 2 vols. (vol. i, to 586 B.C.; vol. ii, to A.D. 135). Oxford University Press, 1932.
Supplements Chapters 5, 6, 9, 11, 13, 14, 15, 16, 19, 20, 21, 23, 26.
W. O. E. Oesterley and T. H. Robinson, HEBREW RELIGION, ITS ORIGIN AND DEVELOPMENT. New York: The Macmillan Co., revised ed., 1937.
Supplements Chapters 8, 10, 12, 18.

Robt. H. Pfeiffer, HISTORY OF NEW TESTAMENT TIMES, With an Introduction
to the Apocrypha. New York: Harper and Bros., 1949.
Supplements Chapters 22, 23, 24, 25, 26.

Robt. H. Pfeiffer, INTRODUCTION TO THE OLD TESTAMENT. New York: Harper
and Bros., 1941.
Supplements Chapters 9, 11, 14, 15, 16, 17, 18, 19, 20, 22.

Ira M. Price, THE ANCESTRY OF OUR ENGLISH BIBLE. Second Revised Edition
by Wm. A. Irwin and Allen P. Wikgren. New York: Harper and Bros.,
1949.
Supplements Chapter 27.

E. F. Scott. THE LITERATURE OF THE NEW TESTAMENT. New York: Columbia
University Press, 1932; excellent bibliography, pp. 297–303.
Supplements Chapters 24, 26, 27.

L. A. Weigle, THE ENGLISH NEW TESTAMENT FROM TYNDALE TO THE REVISED
STANDARD VERSION. Nashville: Abingdon-Cokesbury Press, 1949.
Supplements Chapter 27.

TABLE OF LITERARY TYPES

Allegory
The Eagles and the Vine (Ezk. 17:1–10) ; cf. p 368.

Apocalypse
Cf. pp. 369 f., 425 ff., 442–456.

Essay
Individual Moral Responsibility (Ezk. 18) ; cf. p. 368.
Ecclesiastes; cf. pp. 405 f., 411.
Ezekiel; cf. p. 411.

Fable
Jotham's Fable (Jgs. 9:8–15) ; cf. p. 166.

Folklore
Cf. pp. 109–112.

Historical Writing
Cf. pp. 137, 185 f., 228, 519 f., 578 f.

Legislation
Cf. pp. 284–287.

Oratory
Cf. p. 301. Am. 1:3–2:5.
Paul's speech at Athens (Acts 17:22–31), cf. p. 567; his speeches in self-defense (Acts 22, 26) ; cf. pp. 576 f.
Early Christian sermons (Jas., Heb., 1 Pet.) ; cf. pp. 589–591, 592 f.

Parable
Nathan's parable of the ewe lamb (2 Sam. 12:1–7) ; cf. p. 192.
The loin cloth (Jer. 13:1–11) ; cf. p. 304.
The winejars (Jer. 13:12 ff.) ; cf. p. 304.
The potter (Jer. 18:1–12) ; cf. pp. 272, 304.
The broken bottle (Jer. 19:1–13) ; cf. p. 304.
The figs (Jer. 24:1–10) ; cf. p. 304.
Hosea's marriage (Hos. 1–3) ; cf. pp. 318 f.
Parables of Jesus; cf. pp. 499 f., 502 f., 507, 509 f., 514.

Poetry
The structure of Hebrew poetry; cf. pp. 112–114, 165, 301, 410 f.
Folk songs; cf. pp. 111 f., 114.
War songs; cf. p. 114.
Poetry in the eleventh century B.C.; cf. p. 165.
Poetry in the time of David and Solomon; cf. p. 208.
Poetry of the prophets; cf. pp. 299–303, 324, 372–376.
Books of poetry: Lamentations, cf. p. 366; Psalms, cf. pp. 395 f., 400 ff.;
Job, cf. pp. 403 ff.; Song of Songs, cf. p. 410.
Poems discussed in this text:

p. 19	The Thunderstorm Psalm (Ps. 29).
p. 87	The Shepherd Psalm (Ps. 23).
p. 87	In Praise of Pastoral Life (Prov. 27:23–27).

Rhetorical Prose

Riddles

Story

Special Discussions of Literature

PRINCIPAL PERSONS	EPOCHS	SOURCE BOOKS
	20th century B.C.	
Abraham Isaac Jacob Joseph	THE PATRIARCHAL PERIOD *or* THE PRE-MOSAIC ERA	Genesis
	1220 B.C.	
Moses	THE EXODUS AND THE WILDERNESS WANDERING *or* THE MOSAIC ERA	Exodus Numbers Deuteronomy
	1185 B.C.	
Joshua Samuel Saul	THE WINNING OF THE HEBREW HOMELAND *or* THE CONQUEST AND SETTLEMENT OF CANAAN	Joshua Judges I Samuel 1–15
	1000 B.C.	
David Solomon Ahijah	HEBREW NATIONAL UNITY—THE DUAL KINGDOM OF JUDAH–ISRAEL *or* THE UNITED HEBREW KINGDOM	I Samuel 16–31 II Samuel I Kings 1–11 I Chronicles 11–29 II Chronicles 1–9
	931 B.C.	
Omri, Ahab Azariah, Jeroboam II Elijah, Elisha	THE TWO HEBREW KINGDOMS *or* THROUGH CONFLICT TO PROSPEROUS PEACE	I Kings 12–22 II Kings 1–15:16 II Chronicles 10–26
	745 B.C.	
Amos, Hosea Isaiah, Micah Zephaniah, Nahum Jeremiah	THE ASSYRIAN ECLIPSE OF HEBREW NATIONALISM *or* THE ASSYRIAN MASTERY OVER PALESTINE	II Kings 15:17–23:37 Amos, Hosea Isaiah, Micah Nahum, Jeremiah Zephaniah II Chronicles 27–35
	605 B.C.	

PRINCIPAL PERSONS	EPOCHS	SOURCE BOOKS
	605 B.C.	
Jeremiah Habakkuk	THE END OF HEBREW NATIONALISM *or* THE DECLINE AND FALL OF JUDAH	II Kings 24–25 Jeremiah Habakkuk II Chronicles 36
	586 B.C.	
Jeremiah Ezekiel Second Isaiah	THE BABYLONIAN EXILE	Jeremiah Ezekiel, Obadiah Second Isaiah
	539 B.C.	
Nehemiah Ezra	THE PERSIAN PERIOD *or* THE RESTORED JEWISH COMMUNITY	Second Isaiah Haggai, Zechariah Nehemiah, Malachi Leviticus
	332 B.C.	
	THE GREEK MASTERY OF PALESTINE *or* THE JEWS UNDER THE PTOLEMIES AND THE SELEUCIDS	Proverbs, Ecclesiastes Wisdom of Solomon Sira, Joel, Esther Ruth, Jonah
	168 B.C.	
Judas Maccabeus	THE MACCABEAN KINGDOM	I and II Maccabees Daniel
	63 B.C.	
Jesus Peter Paul	THE ROMAN PERIOD	The Gospels Acts Pauline Epistles
	70 A.D.	

A CHRONOLOGICAL CHART

OF

BIBLICAL HISTORY TO A.D. 100

Items in Bold-Faced Type Have Special Significance for Religion.

Items Blocked in Are Titles of Epochs and Watersheds.

PATRIARCHAL PERIOD

HAMMURABI

ABRAHAM   Middle Bronze Age 2000–1500

JOSEPH: Late Bronze Age 1500–1200
               Hebrew Migration to Egypt

               HABIRI Enter Palestine, *ca.* 1360

HYKSOS in Egypt
(*ca.* 1680–1580) ?

IKHNATON (1375–1358) ?

RAMSES II (1292–1225)   MOSES

MERNEPTAH (1225–1215)

1225 ——— 1225

| The Exodus, *ca.* 1220 | THE EXODUS AND THE WILDERNESS WANDERING |

Covenant at Mt. Sinai

Kadesh Reached
Futile Effort to Enter Canaan from the South
War with Amalekites   Iron Age, from 1200
Korah Rebellion

630

1200 — 1175 — 1150

Migration from Kadesh to Eastjordania

Philistines
Settle Southwest
Palestine

THE WINNING OF THE HEBREW HOMELAND

Principal Judges and their Accomplishments

OTHNIEL Expels the ARAMAEANS

JOSHUA Leads the Hebrews
into Canaan, *ca.* 1185

EHUD Frees from MOABITES

SHAMGAR Repulses the PHILISTINES

P
H
I
L
I
S
T
I
N
E
S

T
R
Y

T
O

C
O
N

1125 ————————— 1125

1100 ————————— 1100

1075 ————————— 1075

Q
U
E
R

C
A
N
A
N

DEBORAH and BARAK Defeat Allied CANAANITES

GIDEON Stops Raids of MIDIANITES

JEPHTHAH Checks Aggression of AMMONITES

P
H
I
L
I
S
T
I

N
E
S

SAMSON Clashes with PHILISTINES

T
R
Y

1050 — 1050

1025 — 1025

1000 — 1000

TO CONQUER CANAAN

SAMUEL

Philistines Complete Masters of Palestine

SAUL (*ca.* 1015–*ca.* 1000)

"King" over Benjamin, Ephraim, and Manasseh
Ammonites Driven from Gilead
Philistines Defeated at Michmash by Jonathan
David Forced into Outlawry and Brigandage

Philistines Regain Control—Battle of Mt. Gilboa

HEBREW NATIONAL UNITY—THE DUAL KINDGOM OF JUDAH-ISRAEL

ISHBAAL
King of Israel

DAVID (*ca.* 1000–*ca.* 970)

King of Judah, *ca.* 1000
King of Judah-Israel after
Assassination of Ishbaal, *ca.* 993
Philistines Decisively Defeated
Jerusalem (Jebus) Taken and Made Capital
Subjugation of Moab, Ammon, Zobah, Edom

975 ——————— 975

Absalom's Attempted Usurpation
Sheba's Rebellion—Attempt at Secession of Israel
Adonijah's Attempt to Seize Throne

SOLOMON (*ca.* 970–931)

Alliances with all Neighbor States   Revolt of Edom
Organization of Revenue System   Revolt of Damascus

Construction Work { Temple
             Palace
             Strategic Fortifications

Industry, Trade, and Commerce Fostered

950 ——————— 950

Attempted Revolution by Jeroboam, Incited by **Ahijah**

The Assembly at Shechem 931   THE TWO HEBREW KINGDOMS

Disruption of the United Hebrew Kingdom

JUDAH   ISRAEL

REHOBOAM (931–914) 17   i/ 22 (931–911) JEROBOAM I

SHESHONK I..........invades Judah............and Israel

925 ——————— 925

ABIJAM (914–912) 3
ASA (912–872) 41

Half
Century
of

War

between

Alliance with
Damascus
against Israel

ii/   2 (911–910) NADAB
       24 (910–887) BAASHA
           Ramah Fortified BENHADAD I
           Galilee Invaded and
               Ramah Razed

900 ——

Judah Invaded by
Zerah of Ethiopia

Judah
and
Israel

iii/   2 (887–886) ELAH
    7-days (886) ZIMRI
iv/   12 (886–875) OMRI
    Samaria Made Capital
    Alliance with Phoenicia
    Subjugation of MOAB
    876 Tribute Paid to . . . ASHURNATSIRPAL II
                (884–859)

—— 875

JEHOSHAPHAT (872–849) 25

E

L

I   Judah
   and
   Israel
J   become
A   Allies

Edom Subjugated

H   E

Judah & Israel Defeated by Syrians
Invasion of Moab & Ammon Fails

22 (875–854) AHAB

Wars with Benhadad
Jezebel Promotes
Baalism

Westward
Campaign of
SHALMANESER III
(859–824)

ca. 855 Syrians Defeated
854 Battle of Karkar

2 (854–853) AHAZIAH
12 (853–842) JEHORAM

875 ——

JEHORAM (849–842) 8
Edom Wins Independence
Jerusalem Taken by Philistines
   and Arabs
AHAZIAH (842) 1
QUEEN ATHALIAH (842–836) 6
J(EH)OASH (836–797) 40

L   Moab Wins Independence
   Samaria Invaded by . . . . BENHADAD II

I   v/   28 (842–815) JEHU
     842 Pays Tribute to
     Assyria

S   Long and
   Disastrous
   War

HAZAEL

—— 850

825 ———————— 825

Repair of Temple

H   with

A   Damascus

17 (815–799) JEHOAHAZ

ADAD-NIRARI III
(812–782)

Syrian Invasion
Jerusalem Spoiled

End of Syrian Oppression

800 ———————— 800

16 (799–784) JEHOASH   BENHADAD III
Recovery of Territory
from Damascus

AMAZIAH (797–769) 29
Resubjugation of Edom

Judah defeated in War for Supremacy by Israel
(Jerusalem wall partly razed)

41 (784–744) JEROBOAM II

Assyrian

PERIOD

775 ———————— 775

AZARIAH [UZZIAH] (769–739) 52   OF   National Expansion   Non-Aggression
Military Expansion

GREAT

PROSPERITY

JOTHAM Co-regent

ASSYRIAN ECLIPSE OF HEBREW NATIONALISM

750 ——— 725 ——— 700

Assyrian Rulers

TIGLATH-PILESER III (745–727)
SHALMANESER V
(727–722)
SARGON II (722–705)
SENNACHERIB (705–681)
ESARHADDON (681–668)

Hebrew Kings and Events

JOTHAM (739–736) 4

½ (744) ZECHARIAH
1 month (744) SHALLUM
10 (744–735) MENAHEM
Tribute Paid to Assyria
2 (735–734) PEKAHIAH
20 (734–730) PEKAH
Galilee and Eastjordania Lost
9 (730–722) HOSHEA
726 Joins Tyre in Revolt against Assyria

Fall of Damascus 732

AHAZ (736–727? or 721?) 16
Judah Invaded by Pekah and Rezin
Judah Becomes a Vassal of Assyria
Assyrian Religion Made Official
HEZEKIAH (727? or 721?–693) 29

AMOS
HOSEA

724 Siege of Samaria Begins
722 Fall of Samaria
720 Deportation of Captives
END OF THE NATION ISRAEL

MICAH
ISAIAH

720 Egypt Defeated at Raphia by Assyria
711 Egypt Incites Palestinian Revolt Against Assyria

Siloam Conduit Cut
705 General Palestinian Revolt Against Assyria
701 Judah Ravaged and Jerusalem Besieged by Sennacherib

Religious Reforms
MANASSEH (693–639) 55
Assyrian Overlordship Again Acknowledged
Assyrian Religion Again Made Official
Prophets Repressed

H

637

675 —————————— 675

ASHURBANIPAL
(668–626)

673–670 Egypt Con-
quered by Assyria
669 Assyria Forced
Out of Egypt

662 Egypt Recon-
quered by Assyria
Thebes and Memphis
Destroyed

650 —————————— 650

Manasseh Arrested for Disloyalty, but later Restored to Throne

645 Egypt Regains
Independence

AMON (639–638) 2
JOSIAH (638–608) 31

626 Scythians In-

NABOPOLASSAR

ZEPHANIAH   J

625 —————————— 625

vade Philistia

621 **Great Reformation**

JEHOAHAZ (608) ¼
JEHOIAKIM (607–597) 11

NECHO of Egypt is Overlord of Judah until Defeated at
Battle of Carchemish 605

NAHUM   E

of Babylon
Becomes Dominant
in the East
612 Nineveh Falls

HABAKKUK   R

End of Assyria
605 NEBUCHADREZZAR
Rules
Chaldean Empire

HABAKKUK   E

602 Judah Revolts Against Chaldea

600 — 575 — 550

THE BABYLONIAN EXILE

JEHOIACHIN (597) ¼
597 *First Deportation of Captives*
ZEDEKIAH (597–586) 11
588 Judah Again Revolts

Temple Destroyed

M

I

A

H

586 Fall of Jerusalem

Second Deportation of Captives
END OF THE NATION JUDAH
Gedaliah Governor of Judah (586–581)
581 *Third Deportation of Captives*

EZEKIEL

CYRUS THE GREAT
559 King of Anshan

Colonies of Jewish Refugees in Egypt

OBADIAH

SECOND ISAIAH

549 King of Media and Persia

Jewish Temple at Elephantine

546 Cyrus Conquers Asia Minor
Edomites Settle in Southern Judea

539 Conquest of Babylon by CYRUS THE GREAT

THE PERSIAN PERIOD

538 Return of Exiles from Babylon to Judea
Under leadership of
JOSHUA and ZERUBBABEL

(529–522) CAMBYSES

Egypt Conquered by Cambyses

639

575 — 550

A CHRONOLOGICAL CHART OF BIBLICAL HISTORY TO A.D. 100—*Continued*

525 ——————— 525

(521–486) DARIUS I

HAGGAI 520 **ZECHARIAH**
516 **Jerusalem TEMPLE** Restored

515 Greece Invaded
    by Darius I

Palestine

Governed

500 ——————— 500

by

Persian

Officials

Civil

(486–466) XERXES I

Persians Defeated by Greeks
(480) Salamis, (479) Plataea
(470) Driven from Europe

Affairs

in

Jerusalem

and

475 ——————— 475

(466–424) ARTAXERXES I

Environs
Administered

by the

HIGH PRIESTS

450 ——————— 450

640

425 ————

(425–424) XERXES II
(424–404) DARIUS II

Assuan Papyri
Destruction of Jewish Temple at Elephantine

MALACHI

(404–358) ARTAXERXES II

400 ————

398 **EZRA** the Scribe

385 **NEHEMIAH**
Governor of the
Restored Jewish Community

Jerusalem Rehabilitated

TORAH Canonized

375 ————

(358–338) ARTAXERXES III
(OCHUS)

A CHRONOLOGICAL CHART OF BIBLICAL HISTORY TO A.D. 100—*Continued*

350 — 325 — 300

331 Alexander Conquers Egypt
Alexandria Founded

Samaritan-Jewish Schism
Mt. Gerizim Temple Built

(338–335) ARSES
(335–331) DARIUS III
END OF PERSIAN EMPIRE
331 Alexander Conquers Persia

THE GREEK MASTERY OF PALESTINE

ALEXANDER THE GREAT
332 Conquers Palestine

323 Death of Alexander

North Syria Ruled by ANTIGONUS

(312–281) SELEUCUS I
(Nicator)

PTOLEMY I (323–285)
(Soter)

Palestine
Ravaged
by
Rival Contestants
(Antigonus, Ptolemy, Seleucus)

Palestine

Under

the

Ptolemies

(281–261) ANTIOCHUS I
(Soter)

PTOLEMY II (285–247)
(Philadelphus)

SEPTUAGINT
Begun

275 — 275

250 — 250

225 — 225

(261–246) ANTIOCHUS II (Theos)

264–248 Palestine Again Ravaged by Contest Between Ptolemy II and Antiochi I, II

(246–226) SELEUCUS II (Kallinikos)

(226–223) SELEUCUS III (Keraunos)

(223–187) ANTIOCHUS III (The Great)

Palestine Under the Ptolemies

PTOLEMY III (246–221) (Euergetes)

Palestine Again Ravaged by Contest Between Antiochus III and Ptolemies IV, V

PTOLEMY IV (221–205) (Philopator)

PTOLEMY V (205–181) (Epiphanes)

A CHRONOLOGICAL CHART OF BIBLICAL HISTORY TO A.D. 100—*Continued*

200 ——————————————————————————————————————— 200

198 Palestine Finally Taken by Antiochus III

The PROPHETS Canonized

Attempted Confiscation of Temple Treasure

(187–176) Seleucus IV
(Philopator)

(176–164) Antiochus IV
(Epiphanes)

175 ——————————————————————————————————————— 175

169 Jerusalem Ravaged and Temple Plundered
Jews Forced to Adopt **Hellenistic Religion**
168 **Temple Desecrated**

DANIEL
165 **Temple Rededicated, First Hanukkah Celebrated**
(166–161) Judas Maccabeus

THE MACCABEAN KINGDOM

(164–162) Antiochus V
(Eupator)
(162–150) Demetrius I
(Soter)

(161–143) Jonathan
Judea Politically Independent

The Maccabean Revolt

150 ——————————————————————————————————————— 150

(150–145) Alexander Balas
(145–138) Demetrius II
(Nicator)
[(145–142) Antiochus VI
[(142–138) Tryphon]
(138–129) Antiochus VII
(Sidetes)
(129–125) Demetrius II
(Nicator)

(143–135) Simon
First Hasmonean King

(135–105) John Hyrcanus

Samaria, Idumea, and Perea Annexed
Mt. Gerizim Temple Destroyed
Pharisees vs. Sadducees

644

125 ——————— 125

(125–96) ANTIOCHUS VIII
(Grypos)
[(115–95) ANTIOCHUS IX]

Sadducees Dominant

(105–104) ARISTOBULUS I
(104–78) ALEXANDER JANNAEUS

100 ——————— 100

(95–73) Contest for the
Seleucid Throne
by Rival Claimants

Sadducees Dominant

(78–69) QUEEN ALEXANDRA
Pharisees Dominant

75 ——————— 75

(73–74) ANTIOCHUS XIII
(Asiaticus)

64 *End of the Seleucid Kingdom*

THE ROMAN PERIOD

Rabbi Ben-Shetach Elementary Schools Established
Yearly Temple Tax Instituted
(67–63) ARISTOBULUS II
Civil War over Succession: Hyrcanus II vs.
Aristobulus II

63 PALESTINE ANNEXED BY ROME

ANTIPATER

(63–48) Palestine under Pompey
Temple Plundered by Crassus

TETRARCH

(48–44) Palestine under Julius Caesar
(44–42) Palestine under Cassius
(42–40) Palestine under Antony
ANTIGONUS Made King and High Priest by the Parthians
41 Parthians Capture Jerusalem

50 ——————— 50

(40–4) HEROD THE GREAT, King of the Jews

AUGUSTUS (27 B.C.—A.D. 14)

25 —————————————————————————————————————— 25

20–19 Jerusalem TEMPLE Reconstructed
Philo of Alexandria (*ca.* 20 B.C.—*ca.* A.D. 50)

Ca. 6 **Birth of JESUS CHRIST**

HEROD ANTIPAS	ARCHELAUS	PHILIP
(4 B.C.—A.D. 39)	(4 B.C.—A.D. 6)	(4 B.C.—A.D. 34)
Tetrarch of Galilee and Perea	Ethnarch of Judea	Tetrarch of Iturea

Judea under Roman Procurators
(7–9) Coponius
(9–12) M. Ambibulus

Ca. 1 **Birth of PAUL**

(12–15) Annius Rufus
(15–26) Valerius Gratus

TIBERIUS (14–37)

(26–36) Pontius Pilatus

A.D. ————————————————————————————————————— A.D.

Ca. 29 **Death of JESUS CHRIST**

25 —————————————————————————————————————— 25

CAIUS CALIGULA (37–41)

(36) Marcellus
(37–41) Marullus
(41–44) HEROD AGRIPPA I, King of the Jews
Judea Again under Roman Procurators
(44–48) Fadus
(48) Alexander
(48–52) Cumanus

CLAUDIUS (41–54)

PAUL'S

Missionary

646

50 — 50

Journeys

NERO (54–68)

(52–60) Felix

Persecution of Christians
Ca. 64 Death of PAUL and PETER

(60–62) Festus
(62–64) Albinus
(64–66) Florus

66 Outbreak of the Jewish War against Rome

GALBA, OTHO, VITELLIUS (68)
VESPASIAN (69–79)

H
E
R
O
D

A

G

70 DESTRUCTION OF JERUSALEM BY TITUS

FINAL DESTRUCTION OF THE TEMPLE

75 — 75

TITUS (79–81)
DOMITIAN (81–96)

Flavius Josephus
(37—ca. 100)

R
I
P
P
A

II

Jammia and Tiberias, chief centers of
Palestinian Judaism

Pella, chief center of Christianity in
Palestine.

Persecution of Christians

NERVA (96–98)
TRAJAN (98–117)

100 — 100

647

INDEX OF STARRED BIBLE PASSAGES

(Alphabetically listed)

ACTS

AMOS

COLOSSIANS

I CORINTHIANS

EZEKIEL

GALATIANS

GENESIS

HABAKKUK

HEBREWS

JAMES

544

JEREMIAH

JOB

JOEL

JOHN

II KINGS
(*Continued*)

LEVITICUS

LUKE

MARK

MATTHEW

GENERAL INDEX

Aaron, 99, 113, 119, 134, 182, 314, 381
Ab, 278
Abana River, 17
Abba, 526
Abd-Khiba, 28
Abel, 22
Abel-beth-maacha, 193
Abi, 204
Abiathar, 185, 194, 195, 213
Abib, 278
Abiezer, 144
Abijam (Abijah), 223
Abimelech (king of Gerar), 92, 108
— (son of Gideon), 122, 145, 157
Abinadab, 180
Abinoam, 167
Abomination of Desolation, 416
Abominations, 127, 333
Aboth; see Sayings of the Jewish Fathers
Abner, 188
Abraham (Abram), 30, 33, 34, 41, 47, 88, 89, 91 f., 93, 108, 109, 116, 120, 122, 129, 130, 139, 171, 279, 298, 377, 437, 463, 464
Absalom, 185, 192 f., 215
Abu Simbel, 63
Abyssinia, 7
Achish, 163, 188
Acre, Plain of, 13
Acrostics, 366, 401
Actium, 423, 546
Acts, 485, 519, 520, 537, 568–570, 573, 580 f., 582, 596, 597
Adad-nirari III, 242
Adah, 112
Adam, 22, 121, 406, 455, 456
Adar, 278, 408, 418
—, Second, 278
Aden, Gulf of, 4
Adonijah, 121, 124, 194, 195
Adonis, 564
Adoption, 89
Adoram, 218
Adullam, 164
Adversary; *see* Satan
Aegean, 19, 349
Aelia Capitolina, 549, 557
Africa, 8, 9, 24
Agade, 67
Agag, 211

Agape, 530, 615
Agricultural deities, 174
Agricultural festivals, 179
Agriculture, 33, 98, 151–154, 202, 271, 281 f., 358, 473
Agrippa, I, 546, 550 f., 570
—, II, 551 f., 578
Ahab, 74, 147, 160, 206, 226, 228, 230, 231–237, 241, 289, 311 f., 314, 317, 499
Ahaz, 146, 248 ff., 253, 260, 278, 295, 312, 322, 331, 372, 416
Ahaziah (of Israel), 235, 312
— (of Judah), 237 f.
Ahijah, 121, 171, 199 f., 207, 215, 218, 220, 222, 299
Ahimaaz, 185
Ahimelech, 213
Ahi-ya-mi, 171
Ahura Mazda, 393, 565
Ai, 140
Aijalon, 16, 48, 140
Ain el-Guderat, 17
Akabah, Gulf of, 8, 11, 13, 99, 101, 105, 195, 196, 197, 198
Akiba, 557
Akkad, 6, 67
Akkadian (Babylonian) language, 70
Akkadians, 67
Albania, 576
Albinus, 553
Albright, W. F., 55, 182
Aleph, 205
Alexander (the Great), 8, 78, 386 ff., 413, 427, 562
— (Jannaeus), 419, 424
— (son of Aristobulus II), 421
— (brother of Philo), 550
— (procurator), 552
Alexandra (queen), 420, 424
— (daughter of Hyrcanus II), 423, 424
Alexandria, 8, 388, 389, 413, 421, 430, 431, 435, 436, 438, 439, 452, 462, 473, 550, 557, 562, 580 ff., 590, 599, 600
Alexandrinus Codex, 610
Alfred (king), 605
Aliyn Baal; *see* Baal
Allegory, 368
Allen, Wm., 609

661

MAPS

INDEX TO MAPS *

Maps and Plans.

1. ANCIENT WORLD, showing the probable Distribution of the Nations after the Flood. *Inset*—Canaan in the Time of the Patriarchs.
2. EGYPT AND THE SINAI PENINSULA, with the Journeyings of the Israelites. *Inset*—Horeb and Sinai.
3. CANAAN as divided among the Twelve Tribes. *Inset*—The Dominions of David and Solomon.
4. ASSYRIA AND OTHER COUNTRIES ADJOINING CANAAN, illustrating the Captivity of the Jews. *Inset*—The Kingdoms of Judah and Israel.
5. PALESTINE. From the raised Map constructed from the Surveys of the Palestine Exploration Fund.
6. PALESTINE. Northern Division.
7. PALESTINE. Central Division.
8. PALESTINE. Southern Division.
9. PALESTINE, illustrating the New Testament. *Inset*—Palestine under the Maccabees.
10. ANCIENT JERUSALEM AND MODERN JERUSALEM.
11. ENVIRONS OF JERUSALEM.
12. SCENE OF PAUL'S JOURNEYS, AND OF THE EARLY CHURCHES.

List of Biblical Names,

WITH FIGURES AND LETTERS INDICATING THEIR SITUATION ON THE MAPS.

NOTE.—*Figures in bold type indicate the numbers of the Maps; the other figures and letters denote the squares of the Maps where the places are to be found:—thus, Antioch (in Syria)—4 - 2 A; 12 - 2 G— appears on Map 4 in the square 2 A, and on Map 12 in the square 2 G.*

The Publishers have to acknowledge the help given by Professor Sayce in preparing the Map of the Ancient World and the Map of Egypt and Sinai; Colonel Conder, R.E., who has edited the Maps of Palestine, Jerusalem, and Assyria; Sir Charles Wilson, who has prepared the Map illustrating the Travels of St. Paul; and George Armstrong, Esq., Secretary to the Palestine Exploration Fund, who has given the use of photographs of his raised Map of Palestine.

* These maps together with their index are from publications of Thomas Nelson and Sons and are used with their permission.

2

4

Lebahim . . . . 1 - 3 B
Lebanon, mount . . 1 - 2 H; 3 - 2 D; 3 - 6 E;
    4 - 2 A; 4 - 1 D; 6 - 1 B; 9 - 2 D
Lebanon, valley of . . . . . . 4 - 1 D
Leboda . . . . . . 6 - 1 D; 9 - 2 E
Lebonah . . . . 7 - 3 B
Lemnos . . . . 12 - 2 D
Leontes, river . . . 3 - 2 C; 6 - 1 A; 9 - 2 C
Leptis Magna . . . . 12 - 3 A
Leucas . . . . 12 - 2 C
Libya, or Africa 1, 12
Lod (=Lydda) . . . . 3 - 5 B; 7 - 3 A
Lud . . . . 1 - 3 C
Ludim . . . . 1 - 3 C
Luz (=Bethel) . . 1 - 3 H; 3 - 5 C; 7 - 3 B;
    9 - 5 C; 11 - 1 B
Luz (Judg. 1. 26) . . . . . 6 - 2 B
Lycaonia . . . . 12 - 2 F
Lycia . . . . 12 - 2 E
Lydda (=Lod) . . . . 7 - 3 A; 9 - 5 B
Lystra . . . . 12 - 2 F

Macedonia . . . . 1 - 3 C; 12 - 1 C
Machærus . . . . . 8 - 2 D; 9 - 5 D
Madai . . . . 1 - 3 E
Madmannah . . . . 8 - 2 B
Madurah, Jebel . . . . . . 2 - 2 G
Magdala . . . . . 6 - 3 B; 9 - 3 C
Mahanaim . 1 - 3 H; 3 - 4 D; 4 - 1 D; 7 - 3 D
Makkedah . . . . 8 - 1 B
Mamre . . . . 3 - 5 C
Mamre, plain of . . . . . . 8 - 2 B
Manahath . . . . 11 - 4 B
Manasseh . . . . 3 - 3 E
Manasseh, allotment of . . . . 3 - 4 C
Maon . . . . 3 - 6 C; 8 - 2 C; 9 - 6 C
Marah . . . . 2 - 3 D
Mareshah . . . 3 - 5 B; 8 - 2 B; 9 - 5 B
Masada . . . . . 8 - 2 C; 9 - 6 C
Masios, mount . . . . . . 4 - 1 B
Maskhuteh, Tell el (=Pithom) . . . 2 - 2 D
Mauritania . . . . 1 - 3 A
Mechash, W. . . . . . . 11 - 6 C
Medeba . . . 3 - 5 D; 8 - 1 D; 9 - 5 D
Media . . . . 4 - 2 D
Medinet el Faiyum (=Arsinoe) . . . 2 - 3 B
Megiddo . 3 - 3 C; 4 - 3 A; 7 - 1 B; 9 - 3 C
Me-jarkon . . . . 3 - 4 B
Melita . . . . 12 - 3 A
Melos . . . . 12 - 2 D
Memphis, or Noph . . . . . 2 - 3 C
Menzaleh, lake . . . . . . 2 - 1 D
Merom, waters of . 1 - 2 H; 3 - 2 D; 4 - 1 D;
    6 - 2 B; 9 - 2 D
Meronoth . . . . 11 - 6 A
Mesha . . . . 1 - 4 D
Meshech . . . . 1 - 3 D
Mesopotamia . . . . . . 4 - 2 B
Michmash . . . 3 - 5 C; 7 - 3 B; 8 - 1 C;
    9 - 5 C; 11 - 2 C
Midianites . . . . 2 - 4 F
Migdal-el . . . . 6 - 2 B
Migdol . . . . 2 - 2 D
Miletus . . . . 12 - 2 D
Millo (Jerusalem) . . . . . 10 - 3 E
Minni . . . . 1 - 3 E
Mitylene . . . . 12 - 2 D
Mizpeh . . . . 7 - 2 D
Mizraim (=Egypt) . . . 1 - 4 D; 2 - 3 C
Moab . . 2 - 1 G; 3 - 6 D; 4 - 3 A; 8 - 3 D
Moeris, lake . . . . . . 2 - 3 B
Moesia Superior . . . . . 12 - 1 C
Mohammedan Cemetery at Jerusalem . 10 - 2 B

6

Mohammedan Quarter (Jerusalem) . . 10 - 2 B
Moreh, hill of . . . 3 - 3 C; 7 - 1 B; 9 - 3 C
Moriah . . . . . 10 - 3 B; 10 - 3 E
Moses' Well . . . . . . 2 - 3 D
Mount Zagros . . . . . . 4 - 2 C
Mount Zion Street (Jerusalem) . . 10 - 3 B
Mozah . . . . 11 - 3 A
Musurr, W. . . . . . . 11 - 5 A
Myra . . . . 12 - 2 E
Mysia . . . . 12 - 2 D

Naamah . . . . . 7 - 3 A; 8 - 1 B
Naarath . . . . 7 - 3 C
Nahallal . . . . 6 - 3 B
Nain . . . . . . 7 - 1 B; 9 - 3 C
Nairi, lands of . . . . . . 4 - 1 B
Nakhl, castle . . . . . . 2 - 3 E
Naphtali, allotment of . . . . 3 - 3 C
Naphtuhim . . . . 1 - 4 C
Nasor, plain of . 3 - 2 D; 6 - 2 B; 9 - 2 D
Nazareth . . . . 6 - 3 A; 7 - 1 B; 9 - 3 C
Neapolis . . . . 12 - 1 D
Nebaioth . . . . 1 - 4 D
Neballat . . . . 7 - 3 A
Nebo . . . . 8 - 1 B
Nebo, mount . . . 2 - 1 G; 3 - 5 D; 4 - 2 D;
    8 - 1 D; 9 - 5 D
Neby Haroon, Jebel . . . . . 2 - 2 G
Negeb . . . . 3 - 6 B
Nephtoah . . . . 8 - 1 C; 11 - 5 A
Netophah . . . . 11 - 4 B
Neve . . . . 6 - 2 C
Nezib . . . . 8 - 2 B
Ngab Hawa . . . . 2 - 3 G
Nicopolis (=Emmaus) . . . 8 - 1 B; 9 - 5 B
Nile, river . . . . . 1 - 4 D; 2 - 3 C
Nimroud (Calah) . . . . . 4 - 2 B
Nineveh . . . . . 1 - 3 D; 4 - 1 B
Niphates, mount . . . . . 4 - 1 B
Noph, or Memphis . . . . . 2 - 3 C
Numidia . . . . 1 - 3 B

Offence, mount of . . . . . 10 - 4 C
Old Gate (Jerusalem) . . . . 10 - 2 D
Olives, mount of . . . 3 - 5 C; 8 - 1 C; 9 - 5 C;
    10 - 2 C; 10 - 2 F; 11 - 3 B
On . . . . 2 - 2 C
Ono . . . . 7 - 3 A
Ophel . . . . . 10 - 3 B; 10 - 3 E
Ophni . . . . . 7 - 3 B; 11 - 1 B
Ophrah (Ephraim) . 3 - 5 C; 7 - 3 B; 11 - 1 C
Ophrah, or Ophra . . . . . 7 - 2 B
Orfa, or Edessa . . . . . 4 - 1 B
Orontes, river . . . . . . 4 - 2 A

Padan-aram . . . . 1 - 3 D; 4 - 2 B
Palmyra (=Tadmor) . . . . 3 - 6 E
Pamphylia . . . . . . 12 - 2 E
Paneas (=Cæsarea Philippi) . . . 6 - 2 B
Panormus . . . . . . 12 - 2 A
Paphlagonia . . . . . . 12 - 1 F
Paphos . . . . 12 - 3 F
Parah . . . . 11 - 3 C
Paran, wilderness of . . 2 - 2 E; 3 - 7 E
Parthia . . . . 1 - 3 E
Patara . . . . 12 - 2 E
Pathrusim . . . . 1 - 4 D
Patmos . . . . 12 - 2 D
Pella . . . . . 7 - 1 C; 9 - 4 D
Pelusium . . . . 2 - 1 D; 12 - 4 F
Penuel . . 1 - 3 H; 3 - 4 D; 7 - 3 C; 9 - 4 D
Peræa . . . . . 9 - 4 D; 12 - 3 G
Perga . . . . 12 - 2 E

7

Suez Canal . . . . 2 - 2 D	Tyropeon Valley (Jerusalem) . 10 - 3 B ; 10 - 3 E
Suez, Gulf of . . . . 2 - 4 E	Tyrus . . . . 7 - 3 C
Surar, W. . . . . 11 - 4 A	Tyrus, Ladder of . . 3 - 2 C ; 6 - 2 A ; 9 - 2 C
Susiana . . . . 4 - 3 D	
Sychar . . . . 3 - 4 C ; 7 - 2 B ; 9 - 4 C	Ummah . . . . 6 - 2 A
Sychem, or Shechem . . . . 7 - 2 B	Umm Alawi, J. . . . . 2 - 4 J
Syracuse . . . . 12 - 2 B	Umm Loz, J. . . . . 2 - 3 J
Syria . . . . 3 - 6 E ; 9 - 6 E ; 12 - 3 G	Umm Shomer . . . . 2 - 4 E
Syria (=Aram) . . . 4 - 2 A ; 4 - 1 D	Ur of the Chaldees . . 1 - 3 E ; 4 - 3 C
Syrian Desert . . . . . . 4 - 2 B	Urartu . . . . 4 - 1 C
Syrtis Major (=The Quicksands) . . 12 - 4 B	Urumiyah, lake . . . . . . 4 - 1 C
	Uz . . . . 1 - 4 D
Taanach . . . 3 - 3 C ; 7 - 1 B ; 9 - 3 C	
Taanath-shiloh . . . . . . 7 - 2 B	Van, lake . . . . 4 - 1 B
Tabor, mount 1 - 3 H ; 3 - 3 C ; 4 - 1 D ; 6 - 3 B ;	Via Dolorosa . . . . . . 10 - 2 B
7 - 1 B ; 9 - 3 C	
Tabriz . . . . 4 - 1 C	Walls of Jerusalem 10
Tadmor (=Palmyra) . . . 3 - 6 E ; 4 - 2 A	Water Gate (Jerusalem) . . . . 10 - 3 E
Tahpanhes (=Daphnæ) . . . . 2 - 2 D	Well of Harod . . . . . 7 - 1 B
Tamireh, W. . . . . 11 - 5 C	Wilderness of Beth-aven . . . 11 - 1 C
Tanis, or Zoan . . . . . . 2 - 2 C	Wilderness of Jeruel . . . . 11 - 6 B
Taprobane (=Ophir) . . . . 1 - 5 G	Wilderness of Judah . . . . 3 - 5 C
Tarentum . . . . 12 - 1 B	Wilderness of Judea . . . . 9 - 5 C
Tarichææ . . . . 9 - 3 D	Wilderness of Paran . . . 2 - 2 E ; 3 - 9 E
Tarshish . . . . 1 - 3 A	Wilderness of Sin . . . . . 2 - 4 E
Tarsus (Cilicia) - . . 4 - 1 A ; 12 - 2 F	Wilderness of Sinai . . . . 2 - 4 E
Taura, Nahr, or Pharpar 3 - 1 E ; 6 - 1 D ; 9 - 1 E	Wilderness of Tekoa . . . . 11 - 6 C
Taurus, mount . . . 4 - 1 A ; 12 - 2 F	Wilderness of Zin . . . 2 - 2 F ; 3 - 7 C
Tekoa . . 3 - 5 C ; 8 - 1 C ; 9 - 5 C ; 11 - 6 B	
Tekoa, wilderness of . . . . 11 - 6 C	Yagur . . . . 8 - 1 A
Tema . . . . 1 - 4 D	Yam Suph . . . . 2 - 2 D
Temple at Jerusalem . . . . 10 - 3 E	Yarmuk, river . . . . 7 - 1 C ; 9 - 3 D
Temple Street (Jerusalem) . . . . 10 - 3 B	Yazur . . . . 7 - 3 A
Thapsacus (=Tiphsah) . . . . 3 - 6 E	
Thebez . . . 3 - 4 C ; 7 - 2 B ; 9 - 4 C	Zaanaim, plain of . . . . . 6 - 3 B
Thessalia . . . . 12 - 2 C	Zacynthus . . . . 12 - 2 C
Thessalonica . . . . 12 - 1 C	Zamzummim, or Zuzim . . . . 1 - 3 H
Thimnathah . . . . 7 - 3 B	Zanoah (Josh. 15. 34) . . . . 8 - 1 B
Thracia . . . . 12 - 1 D	Zanoah (Josh. 15. 56) . . . . 8 - 2 B
Thyatira . . . . 12 - 2 D	Zaphon Amatha . . . 6 - 3 B ; 7 - 1 C
Tiberias . . . . . 6 - 3 B ; 9 - 3 D	Zarephath . . . . 3 - 2 C
Tigris, river . . . 1 - 3 D ; 4 - 3 C	Zarthan . . . . 7 - 3 C
Timnath, or Timnah . . . 3 - 5 B ; 8 - 1 B	Zawatin, W. . . . . 2 - 4 H
Timnathah . . . . . . 9 - 4 C	Zebulun, allotment of . . . . 3 - 3 C
Timnath-serah . . . . 3 - 4 C ; 7 - 3 B	Zephath . . . . 3 - 7 C
Timsah, lake . . . . 2 - 2 D	Zered, brook . . . 2 - 1 G ; 3 - 6 D ; 9 - 6 D
Tiphsah (=Thapsacus) . 3 - 6 E ; 4 - 2 B ; 7 - 2 B	Zered, valley . . . . . . 8 - 3 D
Tiras . . . . 1 - 3 C	Zereda . . . . 11 - 1 B
Tirzah . . . 3 - 4 C ; 7 - 2 B ; 9 - 4 C	Zidon, see Sidon . . . 3 - 1 C ; 6 - 1 B
Tob . . . . . . 3 - 3 D ; 7 - 1 C	Ziklag . . . . 3 - 6 B ; 8 - 3 B ; 9 - 6 B
Tophel . . 2 - 2 G ; 3 - 7 D ; 3 - 7 E ; 9 - 7 D	Zin, wilderness of . . . 2 - 2 F ; 3 - 7 C
Tower that lieth out, the (Jerusalem) . 10 - 3 E	Zion . . . . . 10 - 3 A ; 10 - 3 B
Trachonitis (=El Leja) . . . 6 - 2 D ; 9 - 3 E	Zion Gate (Jerusalem) . . . . 10 - 3 B
Tripolis . . . . . 4 - 2 A ; 12 - 3 F	Ziph . . . . 3 - 6 C ; 8 - 2 C ; 9 - 6 C
Troas . . . . 12 - 2 D	Ziz, cliff of . . . . 8 - 2 C
Trogyllium . . . . 12 - 2 D	Zoan, or Tanis . . . . . . 2 - 2 C
Tubal . . . . 1 - 3 D	Zoar . . . . 3 - 5 D ; 8 - 1 D ; 9 - 5 D
Tuscum, Mare . . . . . . 12 - 2 A	Zoheleth . . . . 10 - 4 E
Tyre 1 - 2 H ; 3 - 2 C ; 3 - 6 E ; 4 - 2 A ; 4 - 1 D ;	Zorah . . . 3 - 5 B ; 8 - 1 B ; 9 - 5 B
6 - 1 A ; 9 - 2 C ; 12 - 3 F	Zorava . . . . . 6 - 3 D ; 9 - 3 E
	Zuzim, or Zamzummim . . . 1 - 3 H

REFERENCES TO PLAN OF MODERN JERUSALEM.

1. Grotto of Jeremiah.	10. Greek Convent.	19. Mosque El Aksa.
2. Church of the Tomb of the Virgin.	11. Pool of Hezekiah.	20. Solomon's Porch.
3. Pool of Bethesda.	12. Knights of St. John Hospital.	21. Tomb of Jehoshaphat.
4. St. Anne's Church.	13. Bazaars.	22. Tomb of Absalom.
5. Tower of Antonia.	14. Tower of David, Hippicus.	23. Tomb of St. James.
6. Austrian Hospice.	15. Barracks.	24. Tomb of Zechariah.
7. Latin Convent.	16. Armenian Convent.	25. Fountain of the Virgin.
8. Goliath's Castle.	17. Jewish Synagogue.	26. Lepers' Village.
9. Latin Patriarchate.	18. Jews' Wailing Place.	27. House of Caiaphas.

CANAAN
in the time
OF THE PATRIARCHS
Illustrating the Pentateuch

Scale of Miles
0 10 20 30 40

ANCIENT WORLD
Showing the probable
DISTRIBUTION OF NATIONS AFTER THE FLOOD

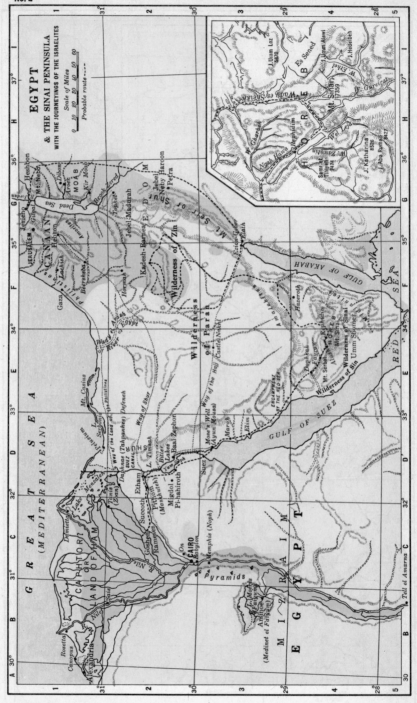

EGYPT
& THE SINAI PENINSULA
WITH THE JOURNEYINGS OF THE ISRAELITES

Scale of Miles
0 10 20 30 40 50 60
Probable route ----

CANAAN
as divided among
THE TWELVE TRIBES

Scale of Miles
0   10   20   30

Cities of Refuge are underlined

Zidon
Zarephath

Mount Lebanon
R. Leontes
Ijon
Dan or Laish
GESHUR
Mt. Tabor (Phazos)
N. el Barada
DAMASCUS
The Abana
Nahr el Awaj

TYRE
Abel-beth-maachah
Kanah
Horem
Kedesh Naphtali
Hammon
Ramah
Abdon Hebron
Achzib

Ladder of Tyrus

ASHER
ACCHO
Beth Dagon
Rimmon
Cabul
Hannathon
Hukkok
plain of Nasor
Hazor
Waters of Merom
GOLAN
Golan
Ashteroth Karnaim
BASHAN
Aere
ARGOB
MANASSEH

ZEBULON
Harosheth
Daberath
Chesulleth
Jokneam
Megiddo
Sea of Chinnereth
Aphek
HAURAN
HAVOTH JAIR
Edrei
R. Hieromax

NAPHTALI

The Great Plain of Esdraelon
Hill of Moreh
Endor
Adami
Shunem
Valley of Jezreel
LAND OF TOB
Tob
Ramath Mizpeh
Arbela
Bozrah

ISSACHAR
Taanach
Beth Shean
Mt. Gilboa
Engannim
Dothan
Abel Meholah
Jabesh Gilead
Thebez
Tirzah

MANASSEH
SAMARIA
Mt. Ebal
Shechem
Mt. Gerizim
Sychar
Gilgal
Gibeah
Phinehas
Adam
Kanah R.
GAD
Gerasa
Ramoth Gilead
Succoth
R. Jabbok
Mahanaim
Penuel
Jogbehah

Plain of Sharon

Rakkon
Me Jurkon
JOPPA or Japho
Bene Berak
Jehud
Timnath Serah
Mount Ephraim
Shiloh
EPHRAIM
Gilgal
Ophrah

DAN
Lod
Ekron
Beth Horon
Gezer
Ajalon
Zorah
Eshtaol
Sorek
Timnath
Beth Shemesh
Kirjath Jearim
Val. of Elah
Adullam
BETHEL
Rock Rimmon
Ai-Hai-Alath
Upper Gibeon
Michmash
Geba
Anathoth Gilgal
Mt. of Olives
BENJAMIN
JERICHO
JERUSALEM
BETHLEHEM
Tekoa
Gedor

Jabneel
Jamnia
Valley of Sorek

Ashdod
Ashkelon
GAZA
Gerar
Eglon
Mareshah
Adoraim
Lachish
Sharuhen
En Rimmon
JUDAH
HEBRON
Dumah
Dehir
Ziph
Carmel
Maon
Eshtemoa
Jattir
Arad
Adadah
En Gedi
City of Salt

BEERSHEBA
Aroer
Rehoboth
Bered?
Ziklag?
NEGEB
SIMEON
Zephath
Hezron

River Jordan
Beth Nimrah
AMMON
Rabbath Ammon

Zoar
Heshbon
Beth-Jesimoth
Mt. Piggah
Mt. Nebo
Elealeh
Medeba
Beth Peor
REUBEN
Ataroth
Kiriathaim
Beth Gamul
Bezer
Aroer
Dixon

THE SALT SEA

R. Arnon
Ar of Moab
Rabbath Moab
Kir of Moab

Brook Zered
Tophel
Bozrah
EDOM
MOAB
Arabah
Wilderness of Zin

A   30'   B   35° Longitude   C   East   of   30'   Greenwich   D

33°
32°
31°

THE DOMINIONS OF
DAVID & SOLOMON

Scale of Miles
0 20 40 60 80 100

GREAT SEA
Arvad
Gebal
Berothah
Sidon
Tyre
Mt. Carmel
Joppa
JERUSALEM
Gaza
JUDAH
ISRAEL
Dan
Mt. Hermon
Sea of Chinnereth
Kenath
Salcah
Rabbath Ammon
Heshbon
Rabbath Moab
Tophel
Elath
Hamath
Typhsah (Thapsacus)
ARAM OR SYRIA
Kedesh of the Hittites
Tadmor (Palmyra)
DAMASCUS
Great Desert
Desert of Paran

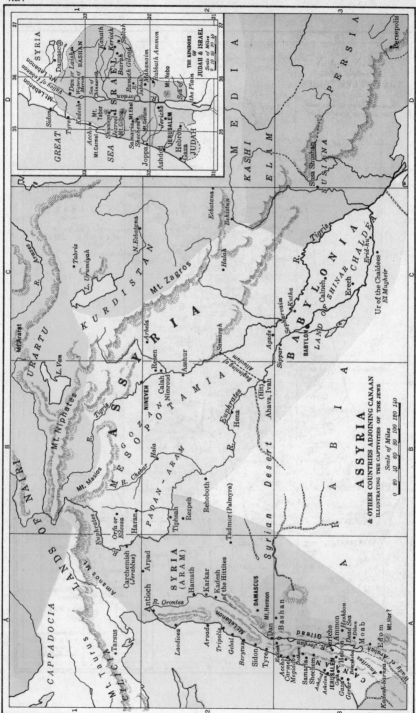

ASSYRIA
& OTHER COUNTRIES ADJOINING CANAAN
ILLUSTRATING THE CAPTIVITIES OF THE JEWS

Scale of Miles
0 20 40 60 80 100 120 140

THE KINGDOMS OF JUDAH & ISRAEL
Scale of Miles
10 20 30 40

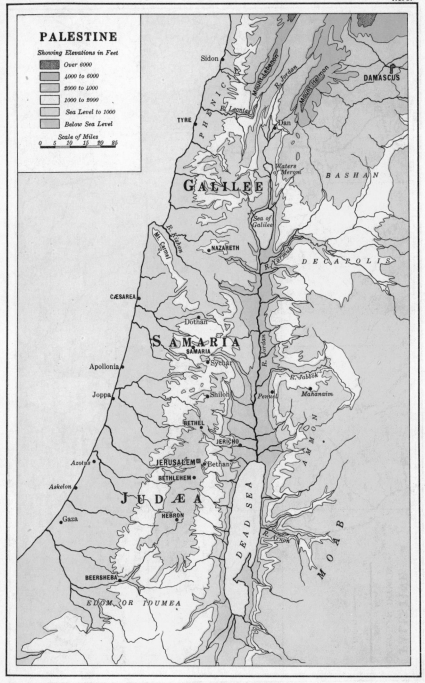

PALESTINE

Showing Elevations in Feet

Over 6000
4000 to 6000
2000 to 4000
1000 to 2000
Sea Level to 1000
Below Sea Level

Scale of Miles
0   5   10   15   20   25

Sidon

DAMASCUS

TYRE

R. Leontes

PHŒNICIA

Mount Lebanon

R. Jordan

Mount Hermon

Dan

Waters of Merom

BASHAN

GALILEE

Sea of Galilee

NAZARETH

Mt. Carmel

R. Kishon

R. Yarmuk

DECAPOLIS

CÆSAREA

Dothan

SAMARIA

SAMARIA

Sychar

R. Jordan

Apollonia

Shiloh

R. Jabbok

Penuel

Mahanaim

Joppa

BETHEL

AMMON

JERICHO

Azotus

JERUSALEM   Bethany

BETHLEHEM

Askelon

JUDÆA

HEBRON

DEAD SEA

Gaza

R. Arnon

MOAB

BEERSHEBA

EDOM OR IDUMEA

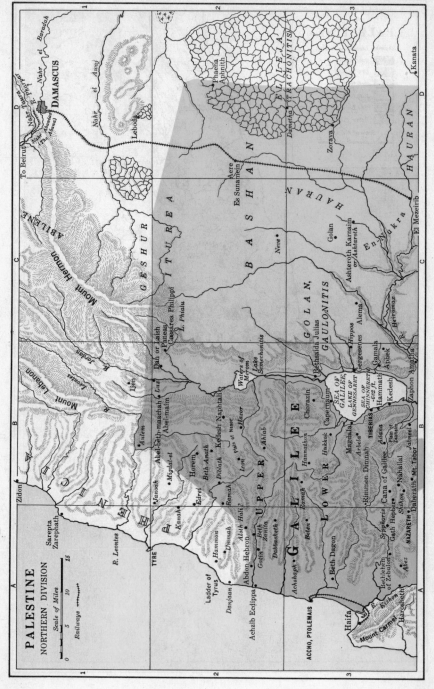

PALESTINE
NORTHERN DIVISION

Scale of Miles

Railways

ABILENE

Mount Hermon

Mount Lebanon

DAMASCUS

To Beirut

Lebodo

Nahr el Barada

Nahr el Awaj

Nahr el Awaj

GESHUR

ITURÆA

PHÆNA ITURÆA (TRACHONITIS)

Phaena Aphnith

Dametha

Kanata

HAURAN

HAURAN

BASHAN

Aere
Es Sunamein

Zoraya

El Mezeirib

En Nukra

Golan

Neve

Ashteroth Karnaim
or Ashtaroth

Alema

Berromax

GOLAN, GAULONITIS

Dan or Laish
Paneas
Cæsarea Philippi
L. Phiala

Hippos
Gergesenes

Gamala
Aphek

Bethsaida Julias

Waters of Merom

Lake Semechonitis

Abel-beth-maachah
Abel-maim

SEA OF GALILEE,
LAKE OF GENNESARET
—682 ft.
SEA OF
CHINNERETH

Zaphon

Janoah
Ijon

Luz
Hazor

Chorazin
Capernaum
Magdala
Arbela

Hammath
Kedesh

Jabneel

Megiddo-el

Kedesh Naphtali
Ahlab

TIBERIAS

Adaza

Plain of
Zaanim

Beth-Anath
Diblath

Plain of Naser
Iron

Hammon
Ramah

Hukkok

Hannathon

Rimmon

Dimnah

Ramah

Beten

Daberath

Mt. Tabor

Horem
Edrei

Kanah

UPPER GALILEE

LOWER GALILEE

Nahalal

Cana of Galilee
Sepphoris
Gath Hepher
Shihon
NAZARETH

Beth Zenita
Gath

Hammon
Alah Huli

Umnah

Dabbasheth

Jabneel

Achshaph

Beth Dagon

Bethlehem
of Zebulon

Aboz

TYRE

Ladder of Tyrus

Achzib Hebron
Abdon

Donjaan

Achzib Ecdippa

Haifa

ACCHO, PTOLEMAIS

Mount Carmel

R. Kishon

Harosheth

Zidon

Sarepta
Zarephath

R. Leontes

R. Leontes

R. Jordan

R. Leontes

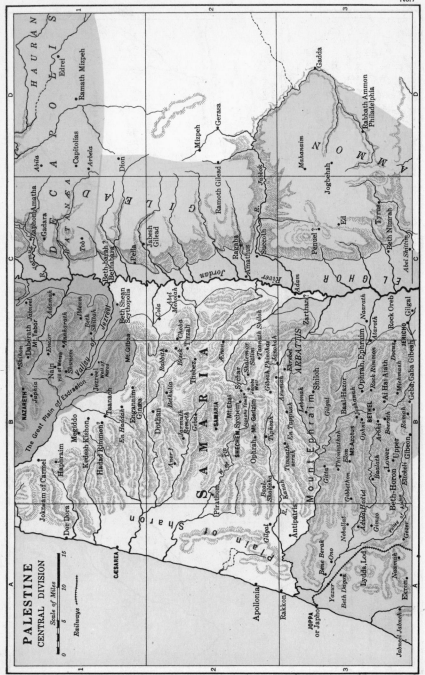

PALESTINE
CENTRAL DIVISION

Scale of Miles

0 5 10 15

Railways

PALESTINE
SOUTHERN DIVISION

Scale of Miles

0   5   10   15

Railways

DEAD SEA, THE SALT SEA
1292 Feet below Mediterranean

Shittim Valley

To Jaffa

Ashkelon, Askelon

Ashdod, Azotus

Jabneh, Jobneh
Jamnia

Ekron

Naamah
Makkedah

Gazer

Emmaus
Nicopolis

Gederah

Beth-Horon
Upper Ranges

Gibeon

Gath,

Shaphir

Eglon

Lachish
Tell el Hesy

GAZA

Gerar

Rehoboth

Beth-shemesh
Kiriath-Jearim

Michmash

Anathoth

Geba Gibeah

Alemeth, Almon

Mt. of Olives

Bethany

JERUSALEM

BETHLEHEM

Netophah

Beth Zacharias

Valley of Timnath

Timnath

Zorah

Socoh

Timnah

Elah

Adullam

Gedor

Nob

Beth Zur

Plain of
Mamre

HEBRON

Beth Tappuah

Keilah

Debir

Anab

En-Rimmon
Madmannah

BEERSHEBA

Bered?Khalasa

Ziklag

JERICHO

Gilgal

Beth-Hoglah

Adummim

Brook Kedron or Cedron

Shepherd's
Field

Tekoa

Choseba
Halhul
Beth Jamek

Jaisom?

Cain

Ziph

Carmel
Siphon

Juttah

Arab

Eshtemoa

Jattir

Jaluim

Anim

Zanoah?

Eshan

Ain

Sheba

Madaba

En
Gedi

Cliff
of Ziz

Masada

Arad

Adadah

Ascent of
Akrabbim

Aroer

J U D Æ A

J U D A H

I D U M Æ A

S H E P H E L A H

P H I L I S T I A

Jazer

Elealeh

Heshbon

Beth Haran

Beth-Jeshimoth
Jesimoth

Ashdoth Pisgah

Mt. Pisgah

Bamoth Baal

Medeba

Mt. Nebo

Beth Meon
Baal Meon

Ataroth

Kiriathaim

Bezer

Dibon

Aroer

Arnon

R. Arnon

Machaerus

Callirrhoe

Ar of Moab
Rabbath Moab

Kir of Moab

The Valley Zered

M O A B

M t s

P i s g a h

Abel
Shittim

Zoar

Beth Peor

PALESTINE
Illustrating
THE NEW TESTAMENT

Scale of Miles
0   10   20   30

PALESTINE
under
THE MACCABEES
Scale of Miles
0   20   40

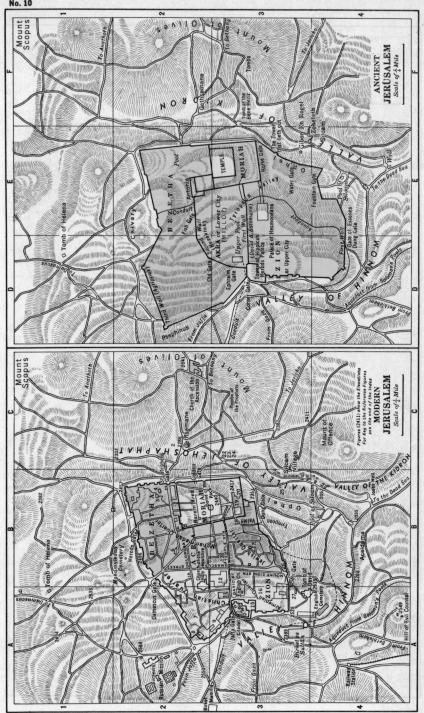

ANCIENT
JERUSALEM
Scale of 1/4 Mile

MODERN
JERUSALEM
Scale of 1/4 Mile

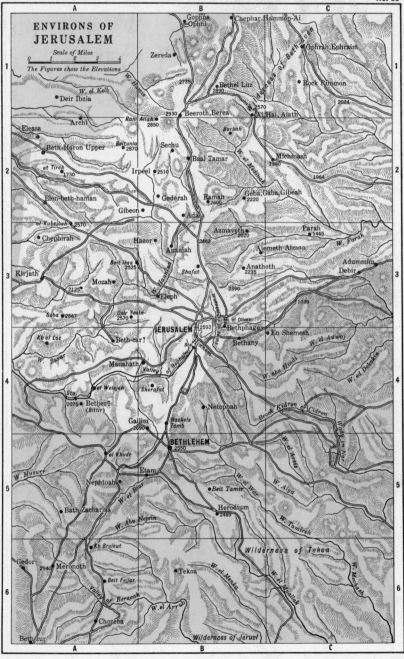

ENVIRONS OF JERUSALEM

Scale of Miles

0   1   2   3   4

The Figures show the Elevations

Gophna
Ophni
Chephar Hammon-Ai
Ophrah, Ephraim
Zereda
2735
Bethel Luz
2890
Wilderness of Bethaven
Rock Rimmon
2024
W. el Kelb
Deir Ibzia
Ram Allah
2850
2930
Beeroth, Berea
2570
Ai, Hai, Aiath
Archi
Burkah
Eleasa
Beth-Horon Upper
Beitunia
2870
Sechu
Baal Tamar
W. el Medineh
Michmash
1980
1964
et Tireh
1730
Irpeel
2510
Geba, Gaba, Gibeah
2220
Elon-beth-haman
Gederah
Ramah
2600
Gibeon
Adasa
Azmaveth
2020
Parah
1465
el Kubeibeh
2570
Hazor
2462
Alemeth Almon
W. Farah
Chephirah
Ananiah
Anathoth
2235
Adummim
Debir
Beit Iksa
2525
Shafat
Kirjath
W. Hanineh
2390
1030
Mozah
2125
Eleph
Soba
2567
Deir Yasin
2570
Mt. of Olives
JERUSALEM
2593
Bethphage
En Shemesh
Kh el Loz
Beth-car?
Sta
Bethany
W. el Aswaj
W. Suwar
Manahath
Valley
of Rephaim
W. abu Hindi
W. el Dabahna
Bet Weisjeh
Sherafat
Sta
2075
Bether?
(Bittir)
Netophah
Brook Kidron or Cidron
W. en Nar
Gallim
2690
Rachels
Tomb
el Khudr
BETHLEHEM
2550
W. el Areis
Etam
Nephtoah
Beit Tamir
W. el War
W. Alya
W. el Bier
Bath-Zacharias
Herodium
2489
W. Tamirek
W. Abu Nejein
Kh Breikut
Wilderness of Tekoa
Gedor
2940
Meronoth
Tekoa
W. el Menka
W. el Mijallah
W. Michash
Beit Fejjar
Valley of Beracah
Chozeba
W. el Arrub
Beth-zur
Wilderness of Jeruel

SCENE OF PAUL'S JOURNEYS
& OF THE EARLY CHURCHES

Scale of Miles

0 20 40 60 80 100

PONTUS EUXINUS

THRACIA

MOESIA SUPERIOR

DALMATIA

ILLYRICUM

MACEDONIA

THESSALIA

ACHAIA

ITALY

ROME

Appii Forum

Puteoli

Mare Tuscum

Panormus

SICILIA

Syracuse

Melita

Mare Hadriaticum

Dyrrachium

Brundisium

Tarentum

Rhegium

Mare Ionium

Corcyra

Cephallenia

Zacynthus

Leucas

Nicopolis

Actium

Beroea

Thessalonica

Amphipolis

Apollonia

Philippi

Neapolis

Samothrace

Lemnos

Euboea

ATHENS

Corinth

Cenchreae

Cythera

Melos

Mare Aegaeum

CRETE

Lasea

Phoenice

Fair Havens

Cauda

Pr. Salmone

BITHYNIA ET PONTUS

PAPHLAGONIA

PONTUS GALATICUS

Amastris

Sinope

Amasia

REGNUM POLEMONIS

ARMENIA MINOR

Caesarea

CAPPADOCIA

GALATIA

Ancyra

Pessinus

MYSIA

Byzantium

Propontis

Chalcedon

Cyzicus

Pergamum

Adramyttium

Troas

Assos

Mitylene

Lesbos

Chios

Smyrna

Sardis

Thyatira

Philadelphia

Laodicea

Colossae

Hierapolis

Ephesus

Tralles

Miletus

Samos

Coos

Cnidus

Rhodes

Patmos

ASIA

Mons Taurus

REGNUM ANTIOCHI

LYCAONIA

Iconium

Antioch

Lystra

Derbe

PISIDIA

PHRYGIA

CILICIA TRACHEA

Tarsus

PAMPHYLIA

Perga

Attalia

LYCIA

Myra

Patara

CYPRUS

Salamis

Paphos

SYRIA ET CILICIA

Antioch

Seleucia

Chalcis

ET PHOENICIA

Tripolis

Sidon

Tyre

Ptolemais

Caesarea

Samaria

Joppa

JERUSALEM

PERAEA

REGNUM HERODIS

JUDEA

IDUMAEA

ARABIA

Damascus

Petra

AEGYPTUS

DELTA

Heliopolis

Pelusium

Alexandria

MARE INTERNUM

ADRIA

Syrtis Major

CYRENAICA

Cyrene

Leptis Magna

AFRICA